Research Methods in
Social Network Analysis

Research Methods in Social Network Analysis

Edited by

Linton C. Freeman
Douglas R. White
A. Kimball Romney

Transaction Publishers
New Brunswick (U.S.A.) and London (U.K.)

Library of Congress Catalog Number: 91-23740
ISBN: 1-56000-569-6
Printed in the United States of America

Library of Congress Cataloging-in-Publication Data

Research methods in social network analysis/Linton C. Freeman, Douglas R. White, A. Kimball Romney, [editors].
    p.   cm.
    Based on a conference held in Laguna Beach, Calif., 1980. Sponsored by the University of California, Irvine, Research Program in Social Network Analysis.
    Reprint. Originally published: Fairfax, Va.: George Mason University, c1989.
ISBN: 1-56000-569-6 (pbk.)
1. Social networks–Methodology–Congresses. 2. Social sciences–Network analysis–Congresses. I. Freeman, Linton C. II. White, Douglas R. III. Romney, A. Kimball (Antone Kimball) IV. University of California, Irvine. Research Program in Social Network Analysis.
[HM131.R465   1991]
300–dc20   91-23740
                                                           CIP

TABLE OF CONTENTS

Introduction 1

I.   Network Representations

Chapter 1.   Social Networks and the Structure Experiment
             Linton C. Freeman 11

Chapter 2.   A Formal Unification of Anthropological Kinship and Social
             Network Methods
             Brian L. Foster and Steven B. Seidman 41

II.   Network Boundaries

Chapter 3.   The Boundary Specification Problem in Network Analysis
             *Edward O. Laumann, Peter V. Marsden,
             and David Prensky* 61

III.   The Structure of Relations

Chapter 4.   Inferring Meaningful Global Network Properties from
             Individual Actor's Measurement Scales
             William H. Batchelder 89

Chapter 5.   Stochastic Modeling and the Analysis of Structural Data
             David Strauss and Linton C. Freeman 135

Chapter 6.   Relational Contents in Multiple Network Systems
             Ronald S. Burt and Thomas Schøtt 185

Chapter 7.   Social Semigroups and Green Relations
             John P. Boyd 215

IV.   **Implications of Relational Structure**

Chapter 8. What Is a Homomorphism?
            Phillip Bonacich 255

Chapter 9. Models of Network Effects on Social Actors
            Patrick D. Doreian 295

V.   **Clustering and Positioning of Actors**

Chapter 10. Algorithms and Network Analysis: A Test of Some Analytical
            Procedures on Kapferer's Tailor Shop Material
            J. Clyde Mitchell 319

Chapter 11. Conceptions of Overlap in Social Structure
            Phipps Arabie and J. Douglas Carroll 367

Chapter 12. Empirical Blocking Methods
            Gregory H. Heil 393

Chapter 13. Rethinking the Role Concept: Homomorphisms on
            Social Networks
            Karl P. Reitz and Douglas R. White 429

Chapter 14. Methods for the Characterization of Role Structures in
            Network Analysis
            Peter V. Marsden 489

Participants in the Laguna Beach Conference
Spring, 1980

Phipps Arabie
Department of Psychology
University of Illinois

Linton C. Freeman
School of Social Sciences
University of California, Irvine

William H. Batchelder
School of Social Sciences
University of California, Irvine

Gregory Heil
Delta Graphics
Bolt, Beranek, and Newman

Steven Berkowitz
Department of Sociology
University of Vermont

E. O. Laumann
Department of Sociology
University of Chicago

Phillip Bonacich
Department of Sociology
University of California, Los Angeles

Peter Marsden
Department of Sociology
Harvard University

Scott A. Boorman
Department of Sociology
Yale University

J. Clyde Mitchell
Nuffield College
Oxford University

John P. Boyd
School of Social Sciences
University of California, Irvine

Ronald Rice
Annenburg School
University of Southern California

Ronald S. Burt
Department of Sociology
Columbia University

William Richards
Department of Communications
Simon Fraser University

Patrick D. Doreian
Department of Sociology
University of Pittsburgh

A. Kimball Romney
School of Social Sciences
University of California, Irvine

Brian L. Foster
Department of Anthropology
Arizona State University

Stephen Seidman
Department of Computer Science
George Mason University

John A. Sonquist
Department of Sociology
University of California, Santa Barbara

David Strauss
Department of Statistics
University of California, Riverside

Douglas R. White
School of Social Sciences
University of California, Irvine

INTRODUCTION

This volume grew out of a conference on methods of research in social networks. The conference was sponsored by the University of California, Irvine, Research Program in Social Network Analysis. It was held in Laguna Beach, California, in the spring of 1980.

Many of the scholars who were active in social networks research attended the Laguna Beach conference. They are listed on pages *viii* and *ix*.

Participants were broadly representative of a range of perspectives in networks research. No attempt was made to load the roster with proponents of one or any small set of viewpoints. Obviously, there is a bias towards participation by those working or—at that time—visiting on the West Coast. This bias was based on economic considerations; the budget was limited. But in any case, care was taken to assure a sampling of divergent views on current problems in network study.

Participants were asked to prepare drafts of papers on topics of general methodological interest to those working in the area of social networks research. The group met and explored alternative conceptions of key problems in this area of research. Finally, after two days of discussion, the broad outline for this volume emerged. It was conceived as a state of the art statement of research problems and methods from the varying perspectives of those assembled.

Individuals and pairs working in collaboration staked out areas for exploration and report. Drafts of chapters and revisions were prepared. Finally, the three editors undertook the task of tying it all together into what we hope is a reasonably coherent volume.

Although no one planned it that way in advance, this book has five sections. They arise from the major types of problems addressed in the book which can logically be ordered as stages or processes in social structural or network analysis.

I. Network Representations. What are the fundamental modes by which social structural phenomena are to be represented? What is the nature of the units of social structure? What are the basic types of relations between them? What are the processes that affect these units and their relations over time? The choice of a mode of representation thus implies a phenomeno-logical orientation, as well as a methodological strategy. The latter includes choice of representational models, measurement axioms, and the like.

II. Network Boundaries. How do we set the limits to a network or social structural problem, and how does the choice of boundaries limit the suitability of various models or methods? The problem might also include the question of the boundaries of the elementary units related in the network.

III. The Structure of Relations. How are the relations of a network defined and measured? What is their structure and content? These are central foundational problems distinctive to the networks approach. How is the type of measurement related to the detection of structure? What are the appropriate probabilistic or deterministic models for structural analysis?

IV. Implications of Relational Structure. A central feature of network analysis is the ability to represent the ways in which the relational structure of a network impacts on system actors. This may include impact on the environment of the actors, the positions of the actors, or the actors themselves (i.e., on their attributes or relations).

V. Clustering and Positioning of Actors. How are actors clustered in a social network into groups or cliques? Such clusters are formed on the basis of social relations within the group in contrast to those outside. How does this clustering idea differ from the idea of positions or roles in the social structure, based on patterns of relations with occupants of other roles? What are the preconditions and consequences of actors' occupancies of groups or cliques as opposed to roles?

I.   Network Representations

Network representations utilize elements and their relations. The elements are not all necessarily of the same type: they may be individuals, sets of individuals, groups, organizations, activities, or some combination thereof. The relations are not all necessarily of the same type: they may be reflexive (one element relations), dyadic (two element relations), or polyadic (multi-element relations) for elements of a single type. Relations among two or more different types of elements may also be examined. There are many different types of network representations in common use. In all of its varieties, the network approach is quite general. There are, however, common features and issues which run through these varieties.

Types of empirical, graphic, or mathematical representations of networks are often interchangeable. For example, isomorphic mappings can be defined among (1) concrete actors and their social relations, (2) points and edges in one or more graphs of the network, (3) matrices in which rows or columns are related by cell entries, and (4) various abstract algebraic structures.

Chapter 1 sets the groundwork for network analysis of systems of dyadic relations. Freeman reviews the intuitive antecedents for network study and systematically builds a formal representation for the study of social structure, including temporal processes. Isomorphisms between graph, matrix, and algebraic representations are explored as they relate to the phenomenology of systems of elements and dyadic relations. He defines this field as currently conceived and sets the range of tasks for developing a coherent perspective.

Chapter 2 presents a broad overview of a general structuralist perspective for the study of social networks, incorporating polyadic as well as dyadic relations. Foster and Seidman discuss polyadic relations as different types of subgraphs defined on subsets of actors or elements. Drawing on their own rich lines of anthropological and mathematical research, they go beyond problems of representation to present a unified set of concepts and tools for structural analysis. Their vocabulary is strongly graph-theoretic, but they also show some of the isomorphisms between the graph and algebraic representations.

The differences in the phenomenology and methods of Chapters 1 and 2 may be of considerable interest to those who adopt a structuralist perspective. Consider, for example, shared fields of interaction between multiple actors, such as co-participation in specified social contexts, groups, or roles. In the framework of Chapter 1, group memberships might, for example, be represented as attributes of actors. From the somewhat different perspective of Chapter 2, groups might be viewed as a second kind of node which interconnect subsets of actors, which might imply a phenomenological difference between group memberships and other attributes (e.g., age, sex) which merely categorize (but do not necessarily interconnect) subsets of actors. The frameworks of representation here are, in one sense, interchangeable, but one frame of reference might be more natural and more productive to work with substantively or analytically. Often, new and productive approaches are preceded by such shifts of perspective. In this case, Foster and Seidman are attempting to capture the richness of anthropological concepts of social structure. Out of their perspective has grown a number of new and fruitful mathematical concepts and procedures for structural analysis.

II. Network Boundaries

Chapter 3 examines problems of specifying units of analysis in the study of social networks. In particular, Laumann, Marsden, and Prensky fix our attention on questions concerning specifying boundaries of human collectivities. This is not a new problem in sociology, but it gains fresh insights when viewed from a structural perspective. They also lead us to consider problems of the suitability of various classes of structural models in the context of varying kinds of group boundary specifications.

III. The Structure of Relations

In Chapter 4, Batchelder explores some of the ramifications of measurement theory for the study of social relations and networks. The theory of measurement has developed for the most part in mathematical psychology. But it turns out to have considerable power when it is focused on networks problems. The most striking results, perhaps, are those that bear on the appropriateness of various classes of structural models in the context of varying measurement axioms.

Statements about network structure require invariance across transformations of the measurements which are compatible with the measurement scales. Batchelder's major contribution is to show the implications of different measurement scales for such invariant statements about transitivity, reciprocity, and cliqueing.

Chapter 5 by Strauss and Freeman gives a broad perspective derived from probability theory on the structure of relations in a network. Their treatment organizes and gives coherence to a wide range of older specific network models in the light of modern stochastic theory. Finally, they wind up with an examination of a set of quite general and powerful contemporary perspectives all derived from log-linear analysis.

In Chapter 6, Burt and Schøtt develop a model designed to begin to come to terms with a very difficult problem: the content of social relations. Most network researchers seek to uncover clusters of actors. They stress structural patterns and seemingly avoid any discussion of relational content at all. In this chapter an elaborate device for exploring clustering among relations is introduced.

Chapter 7 by Boyd provides empirical and algebraic methods for analysis of the structure of relations. Here the set of primary relations is expanded to include the semigroup of all compound relations. Results from the theory of semigroups are used to contribute to our understanding of network structures. Boyd solves the difficult problem of how to construct meaningful semigroups from empirical network data. He also shows how the semigroup can be homomorphically decomposed to show subsystems of relations in equilibrium.

Boyd, like Batchelder in Chapter 6, examines the problem of level of measurement of social relations. Here, however, he asks how different kinds of measurement—Boolean versus real valued relations—and different kinds of composition of relations, as in Boolean versus ordinary matrix products, affect the detection of different kinds of structural properties in semigroups of relations. He decides in favor of real valued measures and operations in order to reveal the kinds of equilibrium subsystems in which he is interested.

There is also a close connection between Chapters 6 and 7. Burt uses correlations between different primary relations to analyze questions of content. Boyd uses correlations between primary and compound relations in a semigroup to analyze questions of relational structure.

IV. Implications of Relational Structures

In Chapter 8, Bonacich questions how homomorphisms of a network semigroup—preserving properties of the structure of relations—can be interpreted in terms of graph homomorphisms which either collapse sets of relations or sets of actors in the orginal network. Four approaches are suggested, none of which provides a complete solution to the question. The approaches are shown to be appropriate to different kinds of structural representations, and each applies under different conditions. Many of these problems of the relation between semigroup and graph homomorphisms have not yet been solved mathematically.

Boyd, in the previous Chapter, also discusses how the structure of relations in a semigroup has important consequences for the types of positions occupied by actors.

Doreian's Chapter 9 uses the recently developed method of network autocorrelation to solve problems of estimating how the attributes of system actors may be affected not only by their other attributes (as in regression models), but by the attributes of other actors with whom they interact in a network.

Foster and Seidman, in Chapter 2, are also concerned with the question of how relational structures constrain or facilitate decisions taken by system actors. In their approach, however, they are able to define a great variety of intra-unit (i.e., subgraph level) and inter-unit relational structures.

V. Clustering and Position of Actors

The cliquing and clustering of subgroups of actors has a long history in social network analysis. Only in the last decade or so has the more general problem of the equivalence of positions of actors been addressed. Thus, in order of generality, we now have three concepts of positioning: (1) *cluster equivalent* sets of actors are those who have more relations within the cluster than with sets of actors in other clusters; (2) *structurally equivalent* sets of actors are those who have the same (or similar) relations with other actors, regardless of how they are internally related; (3) *regularly equivalent* sets of actors are those who have the same (or similar) relations with one or more equivalent actors.

A sociological clique is a kind of cluster where relations are within the cluster are dense. Cliques represent a special case of structural equivalence. Cliquing however, is a "group" concept based on internal connectedness, while structural equivalence is partly a "role" concept based on general patterns of external connectedness. Regular equivalence, on the other hand, is more purely a role concept. Regular equivalence implies nothing about closeness of connections among actors, while connecting paths between structurally equivalent actors are always of length no greater than two.

There is a fourth approach to the positioning of actors, where relationally equivalent sets of actors are those who have similar patterns of internal and external relations, without regard to whom the external relations are with. This represents a "local" rather than a "global" approach of regular equivalence to social roles. The chapters in this section deal with all four concepts of position.

Before discussing the chapters in this section, we might note that Foster and Seidman, in Chapter 2, provide a generalization of the ordinary concept of cliques and maximally complete subgraphs. They also provide a general discussion of the concept of position in a network, in graph-theoretic terms. A subgraph has an intrinsic structural feature as a function of its self-contained relations. It has a positional characteristic as a function both of internal relations and those with outside elements. A clique or cluster is thus defined positionally. Structural equivalence and regular equivalence, as role concepts, are also defined positionally.

In Chapter 10, Mitchell applies both cliquing and structural equivalence algorithms to Kapferer's Zambian data, before and after a labor dispute, on shop-floor networks. He examines the extent to which these analyses, as well as graph theoretic measures based in reachability and distance, support and refine Kapferer's hypotheses about the structure and shifts of patterns in the network.

In Chapter 11 a new algorithm (MAPCLUS) for finding overlapping subsets is applied to matrices of structural equivalence coefficients from two classic sociometric data sets: the Bank Wiring Group, and the Sampson Monastery. Arabie and Carroll's results are similar in spirit to the representations discussed in Chapter 2 for overlapping subsets and those of Chapter 10 on "islands." The algorithm could be applied to any of the three main types of positional problems above: (1) to find overlapping cliques, using as input the raw relations of a symmetric graph; (2) to find overlapping positions of structural equivalence, as exemplified here; or (3) to find overlapping roles, using as input the regular equivalence coefficients of Chapter 13.

Arabie and Carroll also note the difficulties of the classic clique-finding problem of finding maximally complete subgroups of a graph. The problem is NP-complete, and is thus likely to continue generating a plethora of competing algorithms. MAPCLUS, on the other hand, uses a computationally tractable procedure. It differs from other clustering techniques in allowing implicit overlap, and providing explicit tests of goodness-of-fit.

Chapter 12 examines the problem of finding non-overlapping clusters of structurally equivalent points in a network. In the resulting blockmodel of patterns of relatedness between sets of equivalent points, Heil shows how to measure goodness-of-fit as a departure—towards high or low density blocs—from expected density under the null hypothesis. Using the fit measure, he develops a procedure (COBLOC) for evaluating successive agglomerations of points, resulting in a family of blockmodels. He exemplifies the approach using the Bank Wiring Room data and shows improvements in the COBLOC approach as compared to earlier blockmodeling methods.

Chapter 13 takes the third approach to positions in a network, based on "global" role structures. Reitz and White generalize the blockmodeling approach to capture broader intuitions about the nature of such roles. They develop two new types of blockmodels based on positional equivalences that capture patterns of single-link and multiplex connectivities so that positions in the network correspond to actor/counterpart relations in a system of interconnected roles. Unlike the structural equivalence approach, they do not require that equivalent actors are identically related to other actors, but only that they have the same relations with some actors in counterpart equivalence sets.

Thus, Reitz and White extend the network representation developed in Chapter 1, but introduce a number of new structural concepts and definitions to represent the roles occupied by actors. They follow the strategy of Chapter 2, moreover, in drawing on anthropological research on role structures and attempting to formalize this richness in mathematical terms. They present a number of new theorems about the hierarchical ordering of positional equivalences (of types 2, 3, and 4 above), their uniqueness properties, and connectivity properties. They show the implications of each type of equivalence for inducing homomorphic images of the semigroup of relations on a graph. This part of the chapter is closely related to Chapters 7 and 8, dealing with relational semigroups. In connection with Bonacich's question, Reitz and White completely specify the conditions for graph homo - morphisms to induce semigroup homomorphisms or isomorphisms, and they provide tools for opening up new lines of research on graph and semigroup structure.

Reitz and White introduce measures of regular equivalence and an algorithm for finding regular blockmodels based on regular equivalence coefficients. Their example shows the difference between the abstract approach to role regularity and the approach based on structural equivalence.

Chapter 14 provides a probabilistic model for evaluating both local and global aspects of role structure. Marsden asks three types of questions about roles or subgroups: (1) what are the internal relations within the category; (2) what are the types of relations by which category members are connected to other members of the total network (e.g., isolate, receiver, transmitter, carrier); and (3) do relations in the network differ depending on the position occupied by an external transaction partner? Like Chapter 5, they provide an integrated set of log-linear statistical models for the evaluation of these questions in network data sets. The approach is exemplified using data on interorganizational relations in a midwestern community.

All of the papers in this last section build on solutions to problems in the previous sections: a representation must be chosen, boundaries to the problem must be set, and relations must be measured. Clustering of actors is often implied by certain aspects of relational structure. A symmetric and transitive relation, for example, will cluster actors into equivalence sets (cliques). Clustering and positional problems thus come late in our ordering of the logical priorities of network analysis.

CHAPTER 1

SOCIAL NETWORKS
AND THE STRUCTURE EXPERIMENT*

Linton C. Freeman

1. The Purpose of this Chapter

The aim of this chapter is to define a class of data that will be the focus of attention in the remainder of this book. In defining a class of data, the problem is essentially that of finding a formal way to characterize the observations of interest (Fararo, 1973, p. 7). This requires that we develop an exact formal *representation* that specifies—as Merton (1957, p. 89) suggests—"... the definitions (or prescriptions) of what is to be observed." Or, more precisely, as Homans (1961, p. 958) quoting Gibbs says, the representation dictates "... the form in which the results of experiment may be expressed." In this context the word "experiment" is used as it is in probability theory. It is not intended to imply systematic comparison of controlled "treatments" as it often does in biology or psychology; instead it

* The author is grateful to Douglas White and Peter Marsden for helpful comments on an earlier draft of this chapter.

suggests only that we must have a set of explicit guidelines for looking at the world—a plan for collecting data.

In this chapter—and in this book—we will be examining a kind of data that form the basis for studying *social structure*. These are the data of *social networks*. As it is used here "social structure" refers to a bundle of intuitive natural language ideas and concepts about the patterning in social relations among people. In contrast, "social networks" is used to refer to a collection of more or less precise analytic and methodological concepts and procedures that facilitate the collection of data and the systematic study of such patterning.

A minimal design for the collection of social networks data—*a structure experiment*—will be introduced. It will then be generalized to allow for enough complexity to permit the serious study of social structure.

The discussion will begin with a review of the intuitive ideas generated by a concern with social structure. It will be shown that these ideas can be embodied and explicated in terms of the formalisms of social networks.

2. Intuitive Background for the Representation of Social Structure

The use of social structure as a sensitizing concept dates back at least to the original publication of *Principles of Sociology* in 1875 by Herbert Spencer (1925). Spencer and subsequent writers in this tradition have produced a large collection of creative speculations, insights and intuitions about social life. Their work provides a rich storehouse of ideas that can be used as the raw materials for building an analytic structural theory of social behavior. However, writers in this tradition do not provide the sorts of formal definitions and propositions that are themselves the building blocks for such a theory.

In his lectures at the University of Chicago in 1937, Radcliffe-Brown (1957) began systematically to explore the intuitive foundations of social structure. He recognized that the use of the term *structure* implied a concern with the form of relations among the parts of some whole. Given this assumption, social structure had to be concerned with the forms taken by the relations among the parts of human society. For him the parts of society were persons and the relations were those occurring between persons.

Subsequent writers in this tradition have almost universally adopted Radcliffe-Brown's idea of patterned relationships among parts as the key to understanding social structure. Firth (1951, p. 30) said social structure is "the arrangement in which the elements of the social life are linked together." To Nadel (1957, p. 7), it is "an ordered arrangement of parts." To Fortes (1963, p. 56) it is "parts that have an ordered arrangement." And to Blau (1964, p. 3) social structures are emergent properties that "are essentially relationships between elements." Thus, as Nadel (1957, p. 4) suggested, there is no controversy about the broad intuitive conception of social structure. It is agreed that social structure is an ordered arrangement of parts.

There has, however, been a history of disagreement over what parts should be viewed as the appropriate components of social structure. Nadel (1957, p. 5) described a range of opinion on this question. Some writers have supported the position of Radcliffe-Brown that the basic parts out of which social structures are built are individual human beings. Others apparently were troubled by the fact that while individuals may come and go, the patterns of relationships among roles or groups or institutions remain pretty much the same. As Firth (1951, p. 30) put it, the idea of social structure as a network of relations among persons, "makes no distinction between ephemeral and the more enduring elements of social activity." Based on this sort of thinking, various writers have proposed that the units out of which social structure be built might be social positions, statuses, roles, groups or even institutions (Nadel, 1957, p. 5).

It is intuitively obvious that these higher order concepts, if used as the units for building structures, would show greater stability of patterned relationships than if persons were used. But the point that is missed by writers who argue this position is that the degree of stability at various levels of social structure might itself be a central topic for study. Fortes (1963, p. 56-57) has made this point,

> The real problem is that in social structure we are always faced with parts and relations of diverse nature and variability. There may be parts and relations which recur in all situations in which the organization or institution we are studying emerges, and others which seem to occur only by chance ... (a constant) may be what persists as opposed to what varies over time, so that 'constant' means the frame of continuity and 'variable' the process of growth or change ... Or again 'constant' may refer to what is considered essential or intrinsic, 'variable' to what is considered incidental.

One approach to this problem has been suggested by Blau (1964, p. 2): The problem is to derive the social processes that govern the complex structures of communities and societies from the simpler processes that pervade the daily intercourse among individuals and their interpersonal relations.

This is an essentially reductionist view in which the structural units at any particular level are composed of the interrelations among those at the next lower level. From this perspective, organizations, for example, would be conceived as made up of patterned interrelations of roles or positions. Positions, in turn, would be seen as embodying patterned interrelations among persons and so on. Emergent social units at each level are specified from patterned relations at the next lower level.

Regardless of the overall perspective taken on appropriate levels or units for the study of structural patterning, however, all conceptions of social structure seem always to involve the idea of patterning of the interrelations among social units. This whole intuitive outlook on social structure has been best expressed by Roger Brown (1965):

> Social structure becomes actually visible in an anthill; the movements and contacts one sees are not random but patterned. We should also be able to see structure in the life of an American community if we had a sufficiently remote vantage point, a point from which persons would appear to be small moving dots. We should see these dots mobile by day and immobile for much of the night. We should see that these dots do not randomly wander over the terrain but follow fixed paths and return regularly to what appear to be family territories. We should see that these dots do not randomly approach one another, that some are usually together, some meet often, some never. The determinants of perceptual structure called 'proximity' and 'common fate' would group the dots for us into cohering dyads, families, and strata. The determinant of perceptual structure called 'similarity' would cause us to notice that dots with trousers lift their hats to dots with skirts, that dots in blue uniforms stand in the street blowing whistles and waving their arms at dots in cars. If one could get far enough away from it human social life would become pure pattern.

Intuitively, then, social structure is not random but patterned. It is patterned behavior in which each social unit is seen as embedded in a network or web of other social units who respond to it and to whom it responds. At whatever level we choose to tap in to the study of social structure, our interest is always in patterning.

At the lowest level of analysis, the relevant social units are individual persons and the social behavior of interest is interpersonal. Obviously this includes a great many interesting forms of human activity. From one view, since nearly every act performed by any person has either direct or indirect effects on others, almost all behavior might be called interpersonal. But even if we take a narrower view, and accept only acts directed toward another person as interpersonal, a major proportion of human behavior is still included.

In any case, the behavior of interest in the present context must involve at least two persons and some sort of connection or *social relation* between them. Moreover, it is likely that some, but not all, relations between pairs of persons may productively be viewed as expressing social relations. Thus, the expression, "John lent money to Bill," probably describes or implies a social relation, while, "John is taller than Bill," probably does not. But even this latter case might indicate the existence of an important social relation if, for example, Bill were aware of and sensitive to John's greater height.

Some writers suggest that, to be considered social, relations must be characterized by awareness or mutual awareness between the persons involved (Weber, 1947, p. 88). Others insist that a relationship must embody consensual norms before it may be viewed as social (Parsons and Shils, 1951, p. 195). But regardless of the position held on the question of necessary conditions for calling a relation social, according to Wallace (1969, p. 5) all writers agree on the fundamental need for at least two persons and at least one connection of some special sort between them.

Since our concern here is with defining a kind of data—based on social relations—these restrictions need not trouble us. In specific research applications concerned with particular data sets, one or several qualifications on the kinds of social relations studied may be appropriate. But in the general case, an unrestricted conception provides maximum flexibility.

For our purposes, then, a social relation at the interpersonal level may be considered to be any binary (on-off) relation between a pair of persons. Such relations may be formal or informal, lasting or transitory, ascribed or achieved, symmetrical or non-symmetrical, deep or superficial, conscious or unconscious or whatever (which is very close to the conception of Simmel as translated in Blau, 1964, p. 12). Included are such relations as acquaintance, communication, friendship, fatherhood, conflict, exchange, influence, sexuality, enmity, dominance, marriage, or any of the thousands of other simple social connections that can be observed between pairs of human beings.

Obviously, these lists do not define interpersonal social relations—they provide only an intuitive "feel" of the concept as it is intended here. Fortunately, in developing this general scheme, the question of producing a rigorous universally acceptable definition of social relations is irrelevant. Here, the term will be taken as primitive. Particular studies may mobilize particular definitions and interpretations of social relations that are meaningful in their context. In this overall conception, however, such a primitive term need be defined only intuitively to give a "feel" for its use and implicity by its place in the structure of the reasoning.

The intuitive view presented here stresses that social structure is concerned, not simply with the study of social relations, but with patterns expressed in those relations. This patterning is, in part, interesting in and of itself. To the degree that patterns of social relations can be uncovered they stand in need of explanation. Wallace (1969, pp. 1-59) has outlined eleven perspectives in sociological theory that are designed to provide explanations of patterned social behavior on the basis of factors that are either part of or external to the social structure. The attempt to provide explanations of patterns of social relations is, in Wallace's view, the main preoccupation of sociological theorists.

Others, however, are interested in patterning to the degree that it may be used to make predictions about the behavior of individuals. Predictions of this sort are built upon the assumption that if different individuals are placed in the same group or in similar social situations—similar places in a pattern of social relations—they will act similarly. Thus, to the degree that a person's actions depend upon his social situation or place in a social pattern with respect to others, his behavior can be predicted from that situation. Stinchcombe (1968, p. 149) has put it in these terms:

> ... often a person's behavior cannot be predicted without predicting the actions of other people, whose actions in turn can be predicted only by predicting the actions of still others. *Structural phenomena* are phenomena which determine the form and substance of such systems of interaction."

In this context, structural concepts like status, role, social position, station, class, stratum, group and sub-group are used to summarize relevant social connections, situations or positions with an eye toward predicting the behavior of individuals. Often elaborate systems of speculations embodying the ideas of compliance, conformity, labelling, role socialization, and the like are developed to facilitate reasoning from structural patterns to predictions of behavior. So far no systematic theory has been produced in this area, but this probably cannot be done until a conceptual foundation is provided by further work in social structure theory. Since these concepts assume coherent patterning in social behavior, their development awaits the clarification resulting from rigorous theory about the kinds of patterns that exist.

The problem of determining the patterning of inter-unit relations is not restricted to the case where the units are individual persons. Inter-role relations, inter-group relations and inter-organizational relations are other obvious candidates for structural studies. And at all these levels the intuitive literature is rich with structural speculations. What is needed, then, is a set of *general* procedures for discovering patterns of inter-unit relations regardless of the levels at which units are specified.

The first problem in seeking to uncover patterning of social relations is to provide a representation broad enough to handle patterning of any sort that might arise in the study of any social relations whatever. It must permit the representation of large amounts of extremely complex data and afford a basis for examining structural patterns generally. Moreover it must provide guidelines for developing measures of particular patterns in the context of specific problems and at specific levels of analysis.

The notion of social networks is an obvious candidate for the job of providing a representation for social structure. As a matter of fact, Radcliffe-Brown (1940) wrote that,

> ... direct observation does reveal to us that these human beings are connected by a complex network of social relations. I use the term 'social structure' to denote this network ...

Such a conception is quite natural and probably very old. But it is essentially nothing more than a vague metaphor. Subsequent work, however, has refined and elaborated the network concept to the point where it can be used as an exact representation of at least some central elements of social structure. Here I shall attempt further refinements and elaborations and suggest that an extended network concept can be used to represent all the complexity of our structural intuitions.

3. Social Networks—An Exact Statement

The development of relatively formal structural concepts and procedures that I am calling social networks began with the work of Moreno (1934) who introduced the concepts and tools of sociometry in the early 1930s. In the 1940s Bavelas (1948) began his work on group structure and communications at the Group Networks Laboratory at M.I.T. and Levi-Strauss (1949) began the first explicitly algebraic study of the structure of kinship. Then in the 1950s Hägerstrand (1953) developed a computer simulation model for spatial ordering in the adoption of innovations based on patterns of human contact and Barnes (1954) mobilized the idea of social networks in a Norwegian community study.

The simplest kind of social network can be found in a descent list. Consider, for example, the list of male descendants of Noah from the Book of Genesis:

> Now these are the generations of the sons of Noah: Ham, Shem, Japbeth; and unto them were sons born after the flood.
> The sons of Japbeth: Gomer, and Magog, and Madai, and Javan, and Tubal, and Meshech, and Tiras. And the sons of Javan: Elishah, and Tarshish, Kittam, and ...

There are many ways of presenting the information contained in such a list. The traditional geneological chart shown in Figure 1 is a way that calls attention to the network of connections among the descendants of Noah. The chart of course communicates all the information about descent contained in the quotation. Each box represents a person and each line connects a pair of boxes and indicates a father-son relationship between the persons connected. Fathers are all above their sons and each horizontal level represents a single generation.

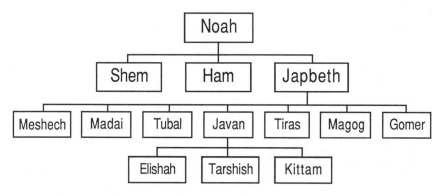

Figure 1. Geneological Chart of Some of the Male Descendents of Noah

The fact that Noah's descendants can be presented in a list like that in the book of Genesis or equally well in a chart like Figure 1 illustrates an important point about such data: the same information may be recorded in different ways. In fact such simple data of social relations may be expressed in literally hundreds of different forms. In every case, however, data of this sort must contain two kinds of information: (1) a set of social units (here, persons), and (2) a set of pairs of social units that exhibit some social relation of interest (in this case, fatherhood) between the first and the second member of each pair. Formally, such data specify a set

$$P = \{p_i \mid p_i \text{ is a social unit}\},$$

and a set

R = {⟨p$_i$, p$_j$⟩ | social unit p$_i$ has a relation to social unit p$_j$}.

Thus the form of such data may always be expressed as an ordered pair,

$$S = \langle P, R \rangle,$$

which may be defined as an algebraic structure. An algebraic structure, S, specifies the fundamental or *canonical* form of simple social relations data.

For the data from Genesis:

$$P = \{\text{Noah, Shem, Ham, Japbeth, ...}\}$$

and

$$R = \{\langle \text{Noah, Shem} \rangle, \langle \text{Noah, Ham} \rangle, \langle \text{Noah, Japbeth} \rangle,$$

$$\langle \text{Japbeth, Gomer} \rangle, \langle \text{Japbeth, Magog} \rangle, ...\}.$$

Of course such data can always be presented in some other form (such as the list in Genesis) but to be complete they must always contains enough information to permit their unambiguous conversion into this canonical form.

S, then, is a standard representation of the data of social relations. It specifies the form such data must take and thereby defines a simple social structure experiment.

There is another standard representation of social relations data that provides greater intuitive appeal in defining networks: the directed graph. The appropriate directed graph consists of a set of points representing the relevant social units and a set of directed lines representing the relevant social relation. Thus, the same information contained in the passage from Genesis and in the geneological chart is presented as a directed graph in Figure 2.

Formally, such a graph may be defined as an ordered pair,

$$S = \langle P, R \rangle,$$

where S is a graph, and the set

$$P = \{p_i \mid p_i \text{ is a point}\}$$

and the set

$$R = \{\langle p_i, p_j \rangle \mid \text{there is a directed line from } p_i \text{ to } p_j \}.$$

Thus S and S are formally identical and the directed graph constitutes a complete representation of the information from Genesis.

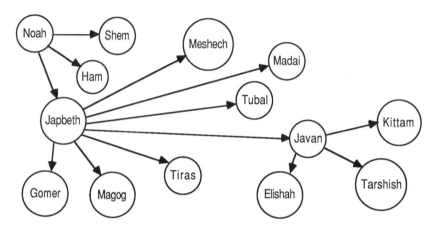

Figure 2. Linear Directed Graph of Some of the Male Descendents of Noah

Still another representation of data of this sort is well known. Consider the Cartesian product set, $P \times P$: the set of all possible ordered pairs of elements in P. In a simple network experiment, the fundamental question we always ask is whether $\langle p_i, p_j \rangle \in R$: whether a particular ordered pair is or is not present in the relation under study. If we repeat this question for all possible ordered pairs in $P \times P$, obviously the data are completely reproduced. It is natural therefore to define a characteristic function (or binary random variable as seen in Chapter 5), x_{ij}, corresponding to each of the questions asked. Thus, let

$$x_{ij} = \begin{cases} 1 \text{ if and only if } \langle p_i, p_j \rangle \in R \\ \\ 0 \text{ otherwise.} \end{cases}$$

This, of course, specifies a function from the Cartesian product, $P \times P$, to a binary subset of the real numbers:

$$\{\langle p_i, p_j \rangle \rightarrow x_{ij} \mid \langle p_i, p_j \rangle \in P \times P \text{ and } x_{ij} \text{ is } 0 \text{ or } 1\}.$$

The standard—and probably most convenient—way to represent data is in terms of values—0's or 1's—taken by each element in this set of random variables. This set of values may be recorded in the form of a matrix.

$$X = [x_{ij}].$$

If we let n = number of persons in P, we can specify an $n \times n$—person by person—matrix that shows all the n^2 values in $P \times P$. The Genesis data are displayed in matrix form in Figure 3 where a person listed in a row is the father of a person listed in a column if and only if the numeral 1 is located where the row intersects the column.

Obviously, the information contained in the matrix is exactly that contained in the graph. The matrix, however, contains an additional element: numerical expression of the binary relational data. Such numerical representation depends upon a mapping that specifies a set of functions—or random variables—from the set of ordered pairs to a binary subset of the real numbers. As we shall see in subsequent chapters this numerical representation turns out to be a useful form for the manipulation of social relations data.

We can now set down the general abstract properties of simple social relations data like those contained in Genesis. It will be convenient to define

$$N = \langle S, S, X \rangle$$

as a social network. Here,

1. S is an algebraic structure, $\langle P, R \rangle$,
2. S is a directed graph $\langle P, R \rangle$ and
3. X is an incidence matrix or a matrix of random variables mapping each element of $P \times P$ into a binary subset of the real numbers: 0 and 1.

In general, then, a social network consists of an algebraic structure, a directed graph and a matrix of random variables, all built from a social relation. Any data that can be expressed in the form N may be described as arising from a *simple structure experiment*.

Noah	0	1	1	1	0	0	0	0	0	0	0	0	0	0
Shem	0	0	0	0	0	0	0	0	0	0	0	0	0	0
Ham	0	0	0	0	0	0	0	0	0	0	0	0	0	0
Japbeth	0	0	0	0	1	1	1	1	1	1	1	0	0	0
Meshech	0	0	0	0	0	0	0	0	0	0	0	0	0	0
Madai	0	0	0	0	0	0	0	0	0	0	0	0	0	0
X = Tubal	0	0	0	0	0	0	0	0	0	0	0	0	0	0
Javan	0	0	0	0	0	0	0	0	0	0	0	1	1	1
Tiras	0	0	0	0	0	0	0	0	0	0	0	0	0	0
Magog	0	0	0	0	0	0	0	0	0	0	0	0	0	0
Gomer	0	0	0	0	0	0	0	0	0	0	0	0	0	0
Elishah	0	0	0	0	0	0	0	0	0	0	0	0	0	0
Tarshish	0	0	0	0	0	0	0	0	0	0	0	0	0	0
Kittam	0	0	0	0	0	0	0	0	0	0	0	0	0	0

Figure 3. Matrix of Binary Random Variables Representing Some of the Male Descendants of Noah

A great many standard kinds of social research data can be represented in this canonical form. Consider, for example, the classical sociometric experiment of Moreno (1934). A natural bounded social collectivity like a school class is studied. Each person is asked to list the names of others in the collectivity whom he or she likes or considers as friends. Sometimes each person's list is restricted—he or she is instructed to list only the two or three, say, he or she likes best—and sometimes list length is unrestricted. In any case, lists are prepared that permit the examination of patterns of verbal expression of interpersonal choice. On the basis of applications of this procedure Moreno and his followers have studied such phenomena as reciprocity of choice and the existence of cliques, isolates and sociometric "stars."

Although this sociometric experiment yields data that are quite different in content than those provided by the list of the descendants of Noah, these two sets of data turn out to be identical in form. The Moreno procedure can be used to produce a list of persons who are members of the collectivity studied and a list of ordered pairs of persons who claim the social relation of friendship.

Thus,

$$P = \{p_i \mid p_i \text{ is a person in the collectivity}\},$$

and.

$$R = \{ \langle p_i, p_j \rangle \mid p_i \text{ lists } p_j \text{ as a friend} \}.$$

And, of course, such data may be expressed as an ordered pair,

$$S = \langle P, R \rangle,$$

or as a directed graph,

$$S = \langle P, R \rangle,$$

or as a matrix

$$X = [x_{ij}],$$

by the same reasoning as that used above. Thus the network,

$$N = \langle S, S, X \rangle,$$

represents all information contained in the Moreno data and the data therefore result from a structure experiment.

In the general case, any experiment that yields a set of persons and a set or ordered pairs of those persons that are connected by a social relation may be recorded in the minimal canonical form,

$$N = \langle S, S, X \rangle,$$

and described as a simple social structure experiment.

This is about as far as the usual discussion of social networks is developed. It provides an explicit definition of network through the use of the algebraic structure. A broad intuitive "feel" for the concept is given by demonstrating its identity to the directed graph. And a convenient computational device is afforded by transforming the graph into an incidence matrix.

4. Social Networks—Generalization

Before the social networks idea can begin to deal with the intuitive ideas of social structure, it must be generalized. If we start from simple social relations, and our intent is to build up to the complexities usually faced in thinking about social structure, we need to develop a data form that will tolerate greater complexity. A great many experiments of interest in the study of social structure are quite a bit more complicated than the ones described above. Our minimal canonical definition needs to be extended so that it can cover these more complex cases.

There have, over the years, developed a number of different and more general procedures for collecting data on and related to social networks. These embody at least some of the complexities that seem to be important in thinking about social structure. Here, then, the formal representation of the structure experiment will be generalized to permit consideration of six of these more complicated kinds of networks data.

First, the definition of networks must be generalized to allow us to examine more than a single relation. This is demanded by a form of the structure experiment called here the *Moreno-Davis experiment*. Second, it should be possible to examine relations among two or more types or levels of social units as in the *Jeidels experiment*. Third, we need to be able to look at changes in network linkages as they unfold through time as in the *Bales experiment*. Fourth, the set of social units studied must be allowed to grow or shrink during the course of observation. This case is illustrated in the *Milgram experiment*. Fifth, we should be able to study the traits or attributes of our social units as they are relevant to the patterning of social relations. These attributes are not, themselves, network properties, but they may be important in the study of social networks. This problem is illustrated by the *Galton-Watson experiment*. And sixth, the traits or attributes may themselves change as they are conditioned by patterns of social structure. This last problem is embodied in the *Hägerstrand experiment*. All of these generalizations will be examined in the present section.

We can begin the process of generalization with another example from Moreno. Moreno (1934) typically used another form of his sociometric experiment: one in which he recorded not only friendship but enmity as well. Because of the recent interest of James A. Davis (1963, 1967, 1968, 1970) in the data generated by experiments of this sort, they will be called here Moreno-Davis experiments.

A Moreno-Davis experiment begins with a set of persons, P, exactly like the set specified in the Moreno experiment described above. Each person is asked to record the names of the persons in the set that he or she likes the most and the names of those he or she likes the least. The output, then, is not one, but two, sets of ordered pairs of persons: one connected by the relation, expressed liking; and one connected by the relation, expressed disliking. These can be designated R_1 and R_2 respectively, and our basic structure, S, generalized accordingly. Thus, the expression

$$S = \langle P, R_1, R_2 \rangle$$

defines an algebraic structure containing, not one, but two relations.

To illustrate this point let us assume that set P contains three persons, John, Bill and Peter, who respond to the Moreno-Davis task in the following way:

> John likes Bill,
> John dislikes Peter,
> Bill likes John,
> Bill dislikes Peter,
> Peter dislikes Bill, and
> Peter dislikes John.

We can draw a directed graph to express both of these relations simply by labeling each of the directed lines in such a way that each directed line tagged with a plus sign indicates the relation "likes," and each one with a minus sign shows the relation "dislikes." Both relations then may be represented in one graph called a dissected multigraph of strength 2 (expressing two relations); see Figure 4.

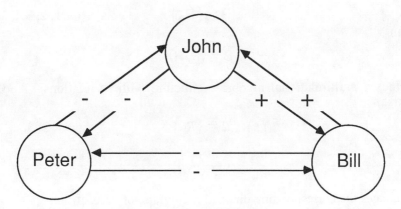

Figure 4. Directed Multigraph of Hypothetical Data from a Moreno-Davis Experiment

Similarly, to represent these data in matrix form, we need two sets of functions defining two sets of random variables and consequently two matrices. X_1 might designate a set of random variables for liking and X_2 a set of random variables for disliking. The matrices for these data are shown in Figure 5.

$$X_1 = \begin{array}{l} \text{John} \\ \text{Peter} \\ \text{Bill} \end{array} \begin{array}{ccc} 0 & 0 & 1 \\ 0 & 0 & 0 \\ 1 & 0 & 0 \end{array} \qquad X_2 = \begin{array}{l} \text{John} \\ \text{Peter} \\ \text{Bill} \end{array} \begin{array}{ccc} 0 & 1 & 0 \\ 1 & 0 & 1 \\ 0 & 1 & 0 \end{array}$$

Figure 5. Matrices of Hypothetical Data from a
Moreno-Davis Experiment

This solution, however, is obviously not general enough. A network experiment might be designed to record more than two relations over a set of people. Indeed, if we are to talk at all realistically about observed social structures we well might wish to record 20 or 200 or 2000 relations. What is needed is a general expression that will reflect any number of social relations in an algebraic structure, a directed multigraph and a family of matrices.

We can arbitrarily designate m different relations with integers 1, 2, 3, ..., m. Then we can generalize the definition of R to permit any number of relations to be examined:

$$R = \{R_g\} \qquad\qquad (g = 1, 2, 3, ..., m).$$

Then

$$S = \langle P, R \rangle$$

defines a multirelational algebraic structure with m relations. And, of course,

$$R = \{R_g\} \qquad\qquad (g = 1, 2, 3, ..., m).$$

so

$$S = \langle P, R \rangle$$

designates the corresponding directed multigraph of order m.

Correspondingly, we can redefine

$$X = \{X_g\} \qquad\qquad (g = 1, 2, 3, ..., m)$$

such that for each of the m relations

$$X_g = [x_{g \cdot ij}].$$

Thus X is a set of matrices and our network,

$$N = \langle S, S, X \rangle$$

is now m dimensional.

Given data of this sort, investigators frequently combine several binary relations into a single n-ary relation. Corresponding to such an n-ary relation is a valued graph where a number representing the degree of the relation is associated with each directed line in the graph. And, of course, the associated matrix also takes numeric values in its cells. In combining these relations, graphs and matrices we are constructing *measures*, and we are constrained to comply with measurement axioms. This sort of question is examined in detail in the Chapter by Batchelder (in this volume).

The second complication results when more than one class of social objects is defined. The problem is illustrated by an experiment by Jeidels (1905) in which he examined the patterning of interlocking corporate directorates. He started with the six biggest Berlin banks and uncovered 1350 interlocks involving German industrial firms. He reasoned that banks were in a special position to coordinate a community of interests among diverse and competing industries.

In any case, Jeidels data involved social units of two types: persons and corporations. Persons were linked to corporations by serving on their corporate boards. And corporations, in turn, could be viewed as linked to one another and coordinated by sharing board members.

For data resulting from this sort of experiment the set of social units is non-homogeneous; there are two (or more) different kinds of social units. Thus, the set of social units is composed of subsets,

$$P = \{P_d\} \qquad\qquad (d = 1, 2, ..., e),$$

and the set,

$$S = \langle P, R \rangle,$$

defines a non-homogeneous algebraic structure with e classes of *social* units.

Of course the graphic representation must be generalized correspondingly so that

$$P = \{P_d\} \qquad\qquad (d = 1, 2, ...,e)$$

and the points must be *labelled* to identify the class membership of each point. And the rows and columns of each matrix must also carry corresponding labels.

This labelling permits us to include social units of as many types as we like in our network. We can then use standard matrix analytic procedures (Harary, Norman and Cartwright, 1965) to extract the matrix of interlocks for any unit of interest. Thus, for the Jeidels data on interlocking directorates we may study the relations between persons and organizations or we can create a person by person matrix or a matrix of corporate interlocks.

The third complication may be illustrated by reference to an experiment by Bales (1950). A homogeneous set, P, of previously unacquainted persons is specified by random assignment. They are brought to a laboratory equipped with one-way glass so their behavior can be observed. Each person is given a five-page summary of the facts that describe an administrative problem, and is instructed to join a group discussion of the case for forty minutes and arrive at a recommendation for action.

Observers, behind the glass, keep a chronological record of who displays what kind of behavior directed toward whom. Behavior is classified according to a scheme involving twelve categories:

1. shows solidarity	7. asks for orientation
2. shows tension release	8. asks for opinion
3. agrees	9. asks for suggestion
4. gives suggestion	10. disagrees
5. gives opinion	11. shows tension
6. gives orientation	12. shows antagonism

The result, of course, is a record of 12 different relations between pairs of people *as they unfold through time.* Data rising during any small segment of time obviously give rise to a multirelational algebraic structure. But to represent data of this sort in terms of time sequences, we need some way to take time into account. Consequently, we must again generalize our algebraic structure. We can generalize

$$R = \{R_{gt}\} \qquad\qquad (g = 1, 2, 3, ..., m)(t = 0, 1, 2, ...)$$

such that it permits us to record the order of events in any discrete time process. Our conception of time may be continuous, but since our observations are always of discrete events, we suffer no loss of generality by adopting this rule.

Bales' data give rise to a directed multigraph of strength 12, but we must also develop a method for taking time into account in the graph theoretic representation. Thus we must define

$$R = \{R_{gt}\}$$

which permits us to specify S as a directed dynamic multigraph in which directed lines may appear and disappear as time passes.

The simple pictorial displays of Figures 2 and 4 above are not appropriate for dynamic graphs. Instead we should need a different picture for each time (or time-segment) or, ideally, a dynamic display device like a motion picture or television screen.

And of course we need an incidence matrix for each time as well as for each relation. Thus,

$$X = [x_{gt}]$$

where each

$$X_{gt} = [x_{g \cdot ij}(t)]$$

redefines the set of matrices to permit the representation of binary social relations data as they change through time.

The fourth important complication to be examined here may be illustrated by considering Milgram's (1967) Small World Experiment. This experiment was designed to determine the number of steps in an acquaintanceship linkage between a pair of individuals in a large society. A "target" person is designated, named and described. Then a sample of "starters" is selected and sent a packet outlining the task. Each starter is instructed to send the packet to some acquaintance who will, in his or her view, be able to move it along toward the target. Each person who receives the packet, then, is asked to comply with these same instructions. The main point of interest in this research is the number of intermediate steps required to move a packet from a starter to a target. Such information reveals something about the density and closeness of acquaintanceship linkage among members of a society.

Clearly, data provided by a Milgram experiment refer to a single relation: acquaintanceship. Like data from the Bales' experiment, however, these data do reflect a time dependent process since pairs are linked as the packet is moved from person to person as time goes on. But in addition the Milgram data introduce an entirely new kind of complexity with respect to defining the set, P, of relevant persons.

At the start of a Milgram experiment, the initial set P contains the target person and a list of starters. But as soon as a starter sends the packet to an acquaintance who is not the target person, an entirely new person is introduced. This schedule continues, of course, until the target is reached. Thus, the final set is potentially much larger than the set initially defined.

To handle data of the Milgram type, where the set of persons grows—or, alternatively, shrinks—during the progress of the experiment, we must extend our basic representation. The set of persons, P, may no longer be considered as constant; instead we will have a potentially different set,

$$P_t \qquad\qquad (t = 0, 1, 2, ...)$$

for each time segment in the experiment. Instead of defining P at the start of the experiment we can consider in the analysis the union of all of the persons introduced into and/or deleted from the experiment with the passage of time. Thus, the set of persons to be studied must be defined after the experiment rather than before. We can define

$$P = \{P_{dt}\}$$

to permit the inclusion of data representing not only different kinds of social units but different sets of units at different times. Thus we include any birth and death process.

These four extensions complete the necessary generalization of the structure experiment itself. The two remaining problems have to do, not with the problem of the structure of relations, but with the *attributes* of the social units under study.

Traditional non-structural mainstream social science usually focuses on an examination of attributes, traits or properties of organizations, groups or individuals. Data on, say, the size of a group or the education of a person are recorded. Then calculations are made of the relationships among sets of these attributes.

In the context of the present discussion concern with the analysis of attributes is not—in itself—a part of structural analysis. Yet there are a great many structural conceptions that involve attributes in one way or another. It may be suggested, for example, that certain kinds of relations between persons are conditioned by particular attributes of those persons. A rich person, say, may in certain circumstances be easier than a poor person for others to like. In other cases, the possession of an attribute may be viewed as resulting from a person's relations with others. A person's decision to become a migrant, for example, might be dependent upon his or her contacts with previous successful migrants.

In any case, if our formal representation is to capture the richness of ideas about social structure, we must develop a way to include attributes whenever appropriate. This fifth problem is illustrated by looking at an experiment on the distribution of family names defined by Galton and Watson (1875).

Galton and Watson were concerned with the changing distribution of various family names in a society where such names are acquired by offspring from their fathers. They reasoned that, since in any generation some males might not produce male offspring, changes in the initial relative frequencies of family names might be expected in succeeding generations of a given population. They showed, in fact, that given enough time, any starting name might be expected to "die out."

On the face of it, this data set seems to be similar in form to that generated by the Milgram experiment described above. Galton and Watson, however, because their concern with the distribution of family names, have added a new dimension to the problem. Their interest is in the relationship between a social relation (in this case, fatherhood) and an attribute of the persons involved in the relation (here the attribute is family name). Thus, in order to represent data of this kind we must permit the inclusion of relevant personal characteristics or attributes of the persons in P.

To handle this problem we may define a new *associated* algebraic structure, C, in the following way:

$$C = \langle P, L \rangle,$$

where P is the same set of persons considered above and the associated set is

$$L = \{L_h\} \qquad (h = 1, 2, 3, ..., r).$$

Each L_h is a partition of P into relevant subsets. Such partitioning permits the specification of peoples' attributes or characteristics to the degree that such characteristics are theoretically involved in the social relations under consideration.

In the Galton and Watson example one partition would be according to family name, where the subsets might be Smith, Jones, Brown, ..., and a second might be in terms of their number of male offspring (0, 1, 2, ...). Thus for a problem of this sort, we need to define r different partitions of the set of social units and each social unit must be assigned to its appropriate subset for each partition.

This same structure may be expressed in graph theoretic terms. We can let

$$C = \langle P, L \rangle,$$

where C is a structure associated with the graph, S , consisting of the set of points, P, and the set of partitions

$$L = \{L_h\} \qquad\qquad (h = 1, 2, 3, ..., r).$$

In this case, each point is labelled with r different names or numerals to record its subset memberships.

Each partition results in a set of labels and each point is associated with those labels that indicate its subset memberships. Thus each point in P is labelled with all the different names that record all of its relevant attributes.

The graph of a social structure experiment must, therefore, be multi-labelled. Our new general graph is defined as a directed multi-labelled dynamic multigraph.

To make this multi-labelling convenient for computation we can define a new class of random variables, one for each of the r partitions of P. For example, if we were concerned with family name we could define

$$v_i = \begin{cases} 1 \text{ if person i is a Smith,} \\ 2 \text{ if person i is a Jones and} \\ 3 \text{ if person i is a Brown} \end{cases}$$

Or, in general, for any partition, h,

$$v_{h \cdot i} = z$$

where z is:

1. a real number
2. assigned to a person in P
3. by a function from the subsets specified by partition h.

Thus, each person in P is assigned a numerical label that designates his or her subset membership for each partition.

Each person has r such labels, one for each partition. A natural way of organizing these labels is by defining a vector,

$$V_h = [v_{h \cdot i}]$$

for each partition. Each element in this vector is a real number designating the subset membership of a person i in a subset defined by partition h.

These real numbers can, of course, be assigned to reflect order or distance between subsets or more powerful measurement properties than mere subset membership. The problems of such assignment are perfectly standard and are covered in other works (e.g., Fararo, 1973). The minimal condition though is that they embody the equivalence relation defined by partitioning.

When we have more than one partition we can specify a collection of vectors,

$$V = [V_h],$$

such that we have a vector for each partition and the set as a whole permits representation by a standard person by attribute matrix, V. V will permit us to record data on the attributes of persons whenever they are considered to be relevant—either as antecedents or consequences—of social relations.

In order to take relevant personal attributes into account we have had to define three new structures: first

$$C = \langle P, L \rangle$$

where

$$L = \{L_h\},$$

the set of partitions of persons; second,

$$C = \langle P, R \rangle$$

where

$$L = \{L_h\},$$

the multilabelled graph; and third,

$$V = [V_h]$$

where

$$V_h = [v_{h \cdot i}].$$

Clearly it is the case that all of these structures are equivalent. This permits us to define a new object,

$$A = \langle C, C, V \rangle,$$

that is simply a social attribute space associated with a network,

$$N = \langle S, S, X \rangle,$$

Together, these two objects permit the study of the relationships between the social attributes of persons and their social relations.

A sixth and final complication must be considered with respect to the attributes of individuals as they relate to the structure of social relations. Consider the experiment of Hägerstrand (1953). Hägerstrand was concerned with the diffusion of an innovation through a population of persons located in a bounded geographic region. He conceived of the problem as involving a starter—a first transmitter who introduced a given innovation into the region. This starter contacts other persons until ultimately one is persuaded to accept the innovation.

Then, of course, both become transmitters and as they continue to contact others more and more people accept the innovation and help to transmit it. As time passes each person is changed from a non-acceptor to an acceptor and transmitter of the innovation.

The new factor here is that the attributes of individuals change through time as a consequence of their social relations. In this context we cannot therefore define a fixed set of individual attributes as we have so far. Instead we must permit attributes—like relations—to change as a function of time.

In the case of Hägerstrand's experiment the critical attribute is acceptance of the innovation. Individuals are expected to change from non-acceptance to acceptance during the course of the experiment. What we need, therefore, is a way to record changes in individual social attributes. Thus, we must redefine

$$L = \{L_{ht}\}$$

in order to take time into account. This specifies a partition for each time value and permits recording changes in social attributes during the course of an experiment.

Correspondingly, the labels on points in the graph must be allowed to change as time passes:

$$L = \{L_{ht}\}.$$

Our new graph, therefore, is a directed dynamically multilabelled dynamic multigraph.

Each vector must also be redefined to permit changes in individual value through time. Thus,

$$V_{ht} = [v_{h \cdot i}(t)]$$

for each partition at each time. And, of course

$$V = [V_{ht}]$$

to allow for the specification of a vector for each partition and at each time.

This completes the generalization of the structure experiment. We end up with a network

$$N = \langle S, S, X \rangle$$

and an associated social attribute structure

$$A = \langle C, C, V \rangle.$$

The network itself contains an algebraic structure,

$$S = \langle P, R \rangle,$$

where the set of social units,

$$P = \{P_{dt}\}$$

reflects different classes of social units and different sets of units at different times permitting the study of a birth and death process, and

$$R = \{R_{gt}\}$$

the examination of many social relations and their changes with the passage of time.

The network also contains an equivalent directed graph,

$$S = \langle P, R \rangle,$$

and an equivalent collection of matrices,

$$X = \{X_{gt}\},$$

of binary random variables,

$$X_{kt} = [x_{g \cdot ij}(t)].$$

The social attribute structure,

$$A = \langle C, C, V \rangle,$$

captures the relevant social characteristics of individuals in the network. It contains

$$C = \langle P, L \rangle,$$

an associated algebraic structure, where

$$L = L_{ht}$$

permits partitioning the persons on many personal attributes and recording changes in these partitions with the passage of time.

The social attribute structure also contains

$$C = \langle P, L \rangle,$$

the dynamic set of labels on the graph of the social network, and a person by attribute matrix that is a collection of vectors,

$$V = \{V_{ht}\},$$

each made up of a set of random variables,

$$V_{ht} = \{v_{h \cdot i}(t)\},$$

that reflect socially relevant personal attributes. Together these two objects define a *social structure space*:

$$Z = \langle N, A \rangle,$$

that specifies exactly the components of a *maximal social structure experiment*. Any data that can be represented by Z are social structure data.

In practice this general data representation will often be reducible to a simpler form. If we examine only one type of social unit and if individual social attributes are irrelevant,

$$L_{ht} = \varnothing$$

for all h and t, the result will be an *homogeneous* data form. If

$$P_t = P$$

for all t—if the persons in P do not change throughout the experiment, Z will be considered a *stable* form. If

$$m = 1,$$

only one relation is studied, Z becomes a *simple* form. And, of course, if only a single time slice is recorded Z will be a *static* form. The minimal data set for a social structure experiment is reflected in the data from Genesis and the first Moreno experiment described above: they refer to a single relation recorded at a single time over an undifferentiated and unchanging population. Such data are homogeneous, stable, simple and static. This is the *minimal* reduction. *In the absolute minimum case, to have a structure experiment, we must have a nonempty set of social objects and at least one relation over that set of objects.*

Through generalizing the social network notion a new data form has been defined. This definition provides the groundwork for specifying a system complex enough to allow us to begin to think about social structures.

5. *Summary and Conclusions*

Specifying the network idea in this way serves two purposes. First, it provides a firm foundation upon which theoretical and methodological efforts can be built. It can, as will be seen in subsequent chapters, facilitate the building of the critical link between very simple ideas about social relations and extremely complicated notions about social roles, social groups, and social structures. Second, the network idea is heuristic. It is like a histogram, for example, that helps us picture distributions of data but provides no analytic capacity in and of itself. Specifying the structure experiment in general terms calls attention to both the necessary and the possible components of data that are to be used in the study of social structure—it more or less maps the terrain. The idea of the structure experiment can be used as a guide to help us think about possibilities and limitations in both theoretical and analytic work.

This generalized conception of the structure experiment provides a broad representation of social structure data. It specifies both minimum and maximum conditions for defining social networks and it calls attention to the fact we cannot study social structure without reference to social relations.

We know that an experiment in the structure of social relations can be expressed in social network with, perhaps, an associated attribute structure. On the face of it, this seems simple enough. Traditional statistics and research methods as taught in social science are focused on problems of analysis of the person by attribute matrix. It turns out, however, that analytic problems in the person by person matrix are a good deal more complex as well as far less standardized.

In the intuitive definition above it was established that social structure obtains only in a *patterned* arrangement of social relations. The problem, then, is to define what a pattern is. It is this problem that is addressed by the subsequent chapters in this volume. They introduce a range of analytic strategies designed to uncover sociologically important kinds of patterning in the data produced by the structure experiment.

REFERENCES

Bales, R. F.
  1950 Interaction Process Analysis. Cambridge, Mass.: Addison-Wesley.
Barnes, J. A.
  1954 Class and committees in a Norwegian island parish. Human Relations 7:39-58.
  1972 Social Networks. Boston: Addison-Wesley Module No. 26.
Bavelas, A.
  1948 A mathematical model for group structure. Applied Anthropology 7:16-30.
Brown, R.
  1965 Social Psychology. New York: Free Press.
Davis, J. A.
  1963 Structural balance, mechanical solidarity and interpersonal relations. American Journal of Sociology 68:444-462.
  1967 Clustering and structural balance in graphs. Human Relations 20:181-187.
  1968 Social structures and cognitive structures. *In* R. P. Abelson, W. J. McGuire, T. M. Newcomb, M. J. Rosenberg and P. H. Tannenbaum, eds. Theories of Cognitive Consistency. Chicago: Rand McNally, 544-550.
Fararo, T. J.
  1973 Mathematical Sociology: An Introduction to Fundamentals. New York: Wiley.
Firth, R.
  1951 Elements of Social Organization. London: Watts.
Fortes, M., ed.
  1963 Social Structure: Studies presented to A. R. Radcliffe-Brown. New York: Russell and Russell.
Galton, F. and Watson, H. W.
  1875 On the probability of the extinction of families. Journal of the Anthropological Institute 4:138-144.
Hägerstrand, T.
  1953 Innovations forloppet ur Korologisk Synpunkt. Lund: Lund Universitet Geografiska Institutionen.
Harary, F., Norman, R. Z. and Cartwright, D.
  1965 Structural Models: An Introduction to the Theory of Directed Graphs. New York: Wiley.
Homans, G.
  1961 Social Behavior: Its Elementary Forms. New York: Harcourt, Brace, Jovanovich.

Jeidels, O.
    1905   Das Verharltnis der Deutschen Grossbanken zur Industrie mit
           besonderer Berucksichtigung der Eisenindustrie. Leipzig.
Levi-Strauss, C.
    1949   Les structures elementeries de la parente. Paris: Presses
           Universitaires de France.
Merton, R.
    1957   Social Theory and Social Structure. New York: Free Press.
Milgram, S.
    1967   The small world problem. Psychology Today 1:61-67.
Mitchell, J. C.
    1969   The concept and use of social networks. *In* J. C. Mitchell, ed.
           Social Networks in Urban Situations: Analyses of Personal
           Relationships in Central African Towns. Manchester: Manchester
           University Press.
Moreno, J. L.
    1934   Who Shall Survive? Washington, D. C.: Nervous and Mental
           Disease Monograph No. 58.
Nadel, S. F.
    1957   The Theory of Social Structure. London: Cohen and West.
Parsons, T. and Shils, E.
    1951   Toward a General Theory of Action. Cambridge, Mass.: Harvard
           University Press.
Radcliffe-Brown, A. R.
    1940   On social structure. Journal of the Royal Anthropological Institute
           of Great Britain and Ireland 70:1-12.
    1957   A Natural Science of Society. Glencoe, Ill.: Free Press.
Spencer, H.
    1925   Principles of Sociology. Vol. I, 3rd Edition. New York: D.
           Appleton.
Stinchcombe, A. L.
    1968   Constructing Social Theories. New York: Harcourt, Brace and
           World.
Wallace, W. L.
    1969   Overview of contemporary sociological theory. *In* W. L. Wallace,
           ed. Sociological Theory, An Introduction. Chicago: Aldine.
Weber, M.
    1947   The Theory of Social and Economic Organization. Tr. T.
           Parsons. New York: Free Press.

CHAPTER 2

A FORMAL UNIFICATION OF ANTHROPOLOGICAL KINSHIP AND SOCIAL NETWORK METHODS

Brian L. Foster and Stephen B. Seidman

About five years ago, we began to develop a mode of social network analysis that would build on the considerable success anthropologists had achieved using kinship-based methods but would be applicable in situations where kinship was not of overriding importance. We consciously intended that our methodology would arise from several features of anthropological theory. In a general sense, this objective is similar to that of earlier anthropological network researchers, although our program differed insofar as we sought to preserve a rather different mix of features of the older kinship-based studies and weighted them rather differently (see Foster, 1979). Like the earlier network researchers, we focus on individuals' behavior within the constraints imposed by their social networks, and we insist that our approach be useful crossculturally. Unlike them, however, we wished to work with models in which individuals and sets of individuals are the units of analysis in a very direct way; Levi-Strauss (1963), who calls such models "mechanical models," has argued that they are a fundamental characteristic of anthropological analysis. Moreover, we wished to formalize the individual behavior aspect of the analysis far more than had been done in the earlier network research and to do so in such a way that it could be fully integrated with the method of structural analysis. This formalization was to be achieved by incorporating some features of cognitive anthropological decision theory which, in addition, contributed to the cross-cultural applicability of the method. Although the point cannot be developed here, we wish to emphasize that each of these features is motivated by a large body of anthropological theory (see Foster, 1979; Foster and Seidman, 1981).

In general, then, our approach to social networks is built around two principles. On the one hand, it is an explicitly relational, structural approach, while on the other hand it takes explicit account of individual behavior. Work done in this mode has led us recently to incorporate a third major feature, which is an unusual way of handling structure induced by overlapping subsets of a population (Seidman, 1981). Each of these three aspects of our approach has affinities with a variety of different kinds of work both within and outside anthropology. Although we will occasionally allude to these affinities to clarify our exposition, this paper primarily concerns the articulation of these three aspects of our work as they combine to form a unified anthropological approach to social networks.

Before proceeding on to the main body of our discussion, it should be noted that an integrated system of software has been developed parallel with the theoretical and more general methodological work (Foster and Seidman, 1978; Seidman and Foster, 1978c, 1979). Although the software is not discussed in detail here, a brief outline of its capabilities will be useful later in the discussion. The SONET-I package consists of four parts, the first of which is a utility program which constructs and formats matrices in a form usable to the other programs. Part II consists of four data transformation programs which perform matrix operations on relations, subset populations and relations, and incorporate files of attribute data in the analysis. Part III performs structural analysis on the networks. Part IV contains facilities for characterizing and comparing structures. The programs are fully operational and can perform all of the basic operations in the structural analysis and individual behavior components of our method; SONET-I did not include procedures for working with overlapping subsets, but that capability has now been added by straightforward extensions of the existing procedures and is available from the authors.

1. Structural Analysis

One prominent feature of anthropologists' successful kinship-based methods is the identification of certain discrete groupings of kinsmen related by descent ties. These groupings, which are called lineages, are found in societies with unilineal descent—i.e., societies where descent relationships are reckoned either through the male line or the female line but not both. The concept of lineage was useless in systems of nonunilineal descent, and even worse, it gave no clue as to how it should be generalized to situations not defined in terms of descent. At a more abstract level, however, the lineage idea can be seen as identifying "significant" subsets of a population, raising the possibility that analogous units can also be identified in social systems not defined in terms of descent. This idea of significant subsets of a population was fundamental for the development of our theoretical framework. Of course, this concept was undefined computationally or mathematically in the older anthropological work, and no general means was suggested by which significant subsets (or types of significant subsets) could be defined or identified.

To qualify as "significant" in our analytical scheme, a subset must have two properties: it must be capable of being defined in a general fashion (not merely by an enumeration of its points) and it must have sociologically important properties. We call such a subset a *basic structural unit* (BSU). A lineage is a BSU in this sense, insofar as it is an important entity in a unilineal society, but also insofar as it can be defined either as a maximal tree or as a connected component in a graph defined by unilineal descent. We will return to the BSU concept in more detail below, but we want to emphasize here that there has been a significant transition between the concept of significant subset and that of BSU.

Having formally and generally defined the notion of significant subset, it was possible to ask *why* lineages as opposed to other types of kinship groupings had been a particularly productive kind of subset in anthropological analyses. It seemed clear that lineages had structural features that made them useful units of analysis. To make the idea of structural features more precise—i.e., to define and identify them—we turned to the mathematical formalism of graph theory. The mathematics permit the development of computational procedures to locate and carry out analyses using the actual BSU's.

Regarding the lineages as graphs, two of their mathematical properties seemed important; they were connected and they were trees (they had no cycles). Even more, they were disjoint, since they were defined as connected components of the descent graph. Both the fact that these sets were disjoint and that they had tree structures seemed to carry sociological significance, and we decided that properties of this general type were what we meant by "structural features." Actually, this idea is implicit in our definition of BSU, for when we said that a BSU "can be defined in a general fashion," we were thinking of statements like "... is a tree". A more detailed discussion of the implications for anthropological analysis of structural features of significant subsets of populations can be found in our other papers (Foster, 1979; Foster and Seidman, 1981).

There is a fundamental difference between the sociological motivations for the concept of BSU and the concept of "block" as used in blockmodeling. Most generally, the block concept arose from a concern with the sociological notion of "role", which is associated with structurally equivalent subsets of individuals. Although the "role" concept has taken many forms (Banton 1965, Goodenough 1965, Nadel 1957), blockmodeling was fashioned after the ideas developed in S. F. Nadel's *Theory of Social Structure* (1957). Many concepts of "role" and the closely allied notion of "status" are explicitly defined in terms of rights and duties. Nadel's "roles", however, are induced from observed relationships among individuals, who are grouped into structurally equivalent subsets. Theoretically, roles are associated with "blocks". Blocks are computed by various techniques which produce a partition of a population into sets of individuals who are asserted to be structurally equivalent. Pairs of individuals are equivalent if they have similar patterns of ties to other equivalent pairs.

The notions of role and structural equivalence play no part in the development of the BSU concept. To define structurally equivalent subsets, it is necessary to examine patterns in one individual's relationships with others and to compare these patterns with those of other individuals. Although BSU's may be constituted in this way, entirely different principles may be involved, as for example in the case of lineages. For units of the latter type, attention focuses not on individuals' relationships *per se*, but on emergent properties of relationships among individuals. This being so, two important differences between blocks and BSU's are immediately apparent. Most important, all members of a block are presumed to be structurally equivalent, but this is not necessarily the case for BSU's, whose internal structure may be of great importance. For example, if the BSU is a lineage we do not want to regard the lineage head as equivalent to a member of a minor segment. Second, blocks must be disjoint, while BSU's are not necessarily so.

The BSU concept itself is far too general to be of use in sociological analysis, and it was necessary to construct an inventory of different "types of BSU's". Since the term "type of BSU" was a bit awkward, we replaced it by the term *basic structure*. Thus a BSU is a basic structure with a sociological interpretation. It was relatively easy to make up a preliminary inventory (all one really needs to do is to skim any graph theory text), but of course the question remains as to which basic structures can be given reasonable sociological interpretations and thus be fruitfully converted into BSU's—a question which required us to return to the social science literature. The first basic structure that we seriously considered as a BSU candidate was the maximal complete subgraph, or clique, which had a long history in sociometry and sociology. Since it was easy to justify the significance of cliques in (say) friendship networks, we regarded cliques as BSU's and wrote a clique-finding computer program which articulated with our other software that transformed relational input data into a graph representation and performed other utility operations.

In carrying the work on cliques further, we immediately had to confront a problem with the clique approach—that most naturally occurring networks just didn't have many nontrivial cliques. Various solutions to this problem have been proposed by others. All of these proposals define subsets of a population, members of which are linked together in some sense less strongly than would be represented by a complete graph. One approach to the problem is to identify these subsets statistically, using factor analysis or various clustering techniques (see Lankford, 1974 for an overview). Another approach is to weaken some aspect of the complete graph structure in such a way as to retain some critical features of the complete graph while allowing more and larger "cliques" to be found in a given population. Luce and Perry (1949), Alba (1973), and Mokken (1979) have pursued this strategy, in each case preserving different clique features.

Our theoretical orientation led us to follow the second strategy, but the existing generalizations of the clique concept troubled us due to the vulnerability of the units to removal of even a single point. Once we understood the problem in these terms, we began trying to define a basic structure that would generalize the clique concept in a way that suited our needs. We did this by defining a *k-plex* to be a graph in which each point is adjacent to all but k-1 other points. Thus a clique is a 1-plex, and k-plexes provide a generalization of cliques. Actually, the useful basic structures are the maximal k-plexes, just as the cliques are the maximal complete subgraphs. The addition of maximal k-plexes to the inventory of basic structures led to important computational and mathematical developments. First, an algorithm to find maximal k-plexes had to be developed and coded.

Second, we were able to demonstrate that k-plexes had interesting mathematical properties. A full discussion of these properties can be found in our papers (Seidman and Foster, 1978a, 1978b), and we will restrict ourselves here to a brief mention of one example. If $k < (n + 2) / 2$, a k-plex with n points must have diameter at most 2. Thus if k is relatively small (by comparison with n), all points of the k-plex can reach all others in at most two steps. This observation seems to us to be of real sociological interest, since not only do we have a mathematical result, but we also now have a better idea as to what the theoretically interesting values of k and n are. It soon became clear, moreover, that these ideas allowed us to look more closely at the nature of "cliqueness" itself; we were now able to define precisely several independent aspects of "cliqueness," especially a reachability, a directness, and a robustness aspect. This led to an understanding of just how our generalization of the clique concept differed from those due to Luce and Perry (1949), Alba (1973), and Mokken (1979).

Although the reachability and directness aspects seem to be important, our own research focused more on the robustness. A BSU is robust insofar as many points can be removed from it without disconnecting it. This idea gave rise to two important developments. First, the redundancy of ties became a theoretical concern. Second, we realized that an entire body of mathematical results was relevant to redundancy questions in clique-like objects. The fundamental theorem is due to Menger (Harary, 1969) and (stated informally) says that the minimum number of people whose removal from a network makes it impossible for some two people to reach one another by a path is equal to the maximum number of disjoint paths joining the two people. Many extensions and generalizations of Menger's theorem have been discovered (Woodall, 1978), and they clearly suggest ways in which the idea of redundancy can be refined and further developed. The sociological importance of all these ideas is partly that they define an analytical relationship between the concepts of redundancy and robustness (Seidman and Foster, 1978a, 1978b; Foster, 1980). In addition, the definition of abstract network properties like this are grist for the individual behavior component of our approach. For instance, we can investigate which kinds of culturally conditioned individual behavior give rise to robust units only after we have a clear understanding of the abstract concept of robustness. We return to individual behavior later.

This line of thought concerning internal structure of k-plexes and other BSU's was paralleled by a line of inquiry concerning the ways in which the set of all cliques or other BSU's in a population can be made to capture the global structure of that population. In clique studies formal analysis often was regarded as complete once cliques were identified. The enumeration and verbal interpretation of a set of cliques seemed to be the objective. This contrasts strongly with the anthropological lineage studies, in which relationships among lineages or other groupings were essential, since these relationships were a major constituent of the social structure. The formal treatment of the relationships among subsets is in some ways analogous to the algebraic analysis of role structures in blockmodeling and to the somewhat less formal construction of clique structures by Laumann and Pappi (1976).

If the simple enumeration of BSU's will not exhaust the structure, we must be able to address the ways in which properties of the BSU's interact when the BSU's are combined and the ways in which the BSU's are situated in the entire population which contains them. We had two fundamental (and related) approaches to this problem. First, we observed that the significant structural features possessed by a BSU were of two distinct types—those that were defined only with reference to the members of the BSU itself, and those whose definition required reference to points outside the BSU. Once the theoretical distinction was precisely formulated in graph theoretic terms, it was easy to find examples. For instance, a clique has two defining properties: it is a *complete* subgraph and it is *maximal* as a complete subgraph. The completeness of a subgraph can be defined solely by reference to the subgraph itself, but the maximality can only be defined by looking at the entire graph. Properties of a basic structure that involve only points of that structure are called *intrinsic* properties, while properties that involve points outside the structure are called *positional* properties.

As with many other features of our approach, the usefulness of the distinction between intrinsic and positional properties can be exemplified by the kinds of analysis anthropologists have carried out on lineage structures. In classic segmentary lineage systems, leadership of the lineage is determined by the members' unilineal descent relationships, which are represented formally by the internal tree structure of the unit. These intrinsic properties of the lineages must be taken into account in discussing positional properties, since relationships *among* lineages are determined by the unilineal descent relationships among heads of lineages (e.g., see Evans-Pritchard, 1940). Simultaneous consideration of intrinsic and positional properties is particularly important in view of the fact that lineages segment at different points (i.e., at different generations), depending on the nature of the oppositions in, say, a particular dispute. Thus lineage A may segment into sublineages B and C under some conditions, in which case the relationships between leaders B and C are critical for defining the global structure (see Figure 1). If segmentation takes place such that B and C are unified as parts of A, then their relationship plays a much less important part in defining the global structure than, say, the relationship between A and M.

In Figure 1, then, the circles might be seen as representing heads of lineages, while lines represent unilineal descent relationships among the heads of lineages. Lineage A would segment if members of B and C were involved in a dispute, but B and C would combine under A if B were involved in a dispute with N.

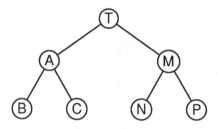

Figure 1. Schematic Representation of Segmentary Lineage System

Our second idea about sets of BSU's was to build upon the anthropological technique regarding lineages as constituent units of a larger descrete structure (i.e., the whole society). That seemed to suggest shrinking BSU's to points, which, together with some relation on the original set of points, are used formally to define a *reduced graph*. A mathematical definition can be found in our papers, and an algorithm to perform these reductions was incorporated into SONET (Foster and Seidman, 1978; 1983). After working for some time with the reduced graphs and with the distinction between intrinsic and positional properties, we realized that the reduced graph idea had important theoretical implications. For example, it leads to a new understanding of the logic of the anthropological structural analyses. If we shrink BSU's to points, all intrinsic properties of the BSU's disappear, placing total emphasis on their positional properties. Reduction can actually be seen as a process converting intrinsic properties to positional ones in order to characterize the global structure, which is composed of BSU's, in terms of the intrinsic properties of the reduced graph (Foster and Seidman, 1981).

A second theoretical line of thought developed as we perceived that the distinction between intrinsic and positional properties of BSU's was analogous to the rather loose distinction which is often made between local and global properties of social structures. The attempt to formalize analysis of the set of BSU's by looking at relations among them, along with the development of software which converted the BSU's to points, made us realize how much information is lost when local structure disappears as a consequence of the reduction process. We obtain crucial information about emergent properties of the reduced graph, and therefore, about properties of the global structure, but we do so at the cost of discarding information on local structure. We therefore sought a means of retaining both the local and the global structure—i.e., both the reduced graph and the internal structure of the BSU's themselves. To achieve this, we developed what we called a *total reduced graph*, in which the points are the points of the original graph along with a point representing each BSU. There are three types of edges—those of the original graph, those of the reduced graph, and those linking the point representing a BSU with each of its constituent elements. Definition of the total reduced graph raised a new computational problem. We soon found that the form of the algorithm that generated the reduced graph was such that the total reduced graph could easily be obtained. Thus it was a simple matter to complete the computational procedures for implementing the core of our approach to structural analysis.

Just as blocks and BSU's are very different kinds of objects, the ways in which they are incorporated into further structural analysis contrast sharply. Although the concept of structural equivalence arises from consideration of the pattern of individuals' relationships with other individuals, the result of blockmodeling is to collapse sets of structurally equivalent individuals to points, thus removing individuals from the analysis. In practice, this data reduction is so extreme that all significant structure disappears in the blockmodels themselves. But interesting structure is generated by using algebraic techniques.

Since one important dimension of our approach concerns individual behavior, the kind of data reduction that occurs in blockmodeling would preclude further analysis. In contrast to blockmodeling, although the reduced graphs also provide a form of data reduction, their inclusion in total reduced graphs preserves information on individuals' membership in BSU's as well as on the internal structure of these units. The object of analysis becomes reduced graphs, adjacency matrices and total reduced graphs.

This complex of ideas including BSU's, reduced graphs, redundancy and robustness, intrinsic and positional properties, and total reduced graphs constitutes the structural foundation of our approach to social networks. Although many details are yet to be worked out, the main features are well understood, and research on them is essentially completed in the sense that the major features of the anthropological structural method have been incorporated, formalized, generalized, and in some cases elaborated. Building on this foundation, we can now consider how the structural method articulates with our approach to individual behavior and to overlapping subsets.

2. Individual Decision Component

The articulation of the structural aspect of our approach with our interest in individual behavior was strongly colored by a rather different aspect of the anthropological tradition—i.e., the characteristic anthropological concern with cross-cultural variation. In particular, we focus on cross-cultural variation in the ways individuals process information about their social, cultural, and natural environment in making "social decisions." This kind of cognitive orientation has been the subject of a great deal of research in cognitive anthropology. It is wholly consistent with our structural approach insofar as the fundamental objects of study are relationships among individuals, and the cognitive perspective, therefore, underscores our commitment to discrete mathematical models. Our point here is to emphasize the fact that our relational orientation has conditioned our approach to individual behavior and, as we shall see shortly, to attributes of individuals. In fact, the mathematical formalism and the software developed for our structural approach led to a natural way of formalizing the cognitive anthropological approach to individual behavior.

It was quite clear to us from the beginning that individual attributes were important in the analysis of individual behavior. The most natural way to work with attributes is to introduce some kind of statistical analysis, but that aggregates the data in such a way as to make it difficult to articulate with the discrete structures, and compromises the usefulness of our underlying theoretical orientation. To represent attributes in a form consistent with the methodological developments that had already taken place, we conceived of them as giving rise to relations. For example, information on sex yields the relation "is the same sex as." Age yields "has age within five years of ...," and residence location can be used to generate propinquity relations. Once we had decided to represent attributes in this way, we developed software that allowed us to construct relationships from a file of attribute data for the members of the population.

Using attributes to generate relationships provides the computational basis for our anthropological decision-theory approach to individual behavior. Anthropologists have for many years been interested in unraveling the processes underlying individuals' decisions. Their models depart radically from the more common approaches to rational decision making based on, say, expected utilities or on game theoretic ideas, focusing more on information processing and on cognitive processes (Quinn, 1975; Geoghegan, 1971; Fjellman, 1976). Characteristically they concern such topics as peoples' choice of post-marital residence. They might also be used to investigate decision processes by which individuals choose their friends.

To address either of these problems, it is necessary to incorporate attribute data and relational data, along with information on more abstract structural features of the society. Age, sex, occupation, and residence location are clearly relevant attributes while, on the other hand, kinship relationships and, say, lineage structure or friendship relations are equally involved in the decision process. For example, if we want to regard a network of friendship relations as evolving over time, then network properties of the already existing friendship network become relevant (e.g., perhaps links are likely to be created to "complete" an already existing maximal k-plex).

One way of conceptualizing a decision which leads to a social relationship or relationships is to regard the "choice" made as a subset of ego's population. Accordingly our procedure for representing decision structures consists of a series of subsets of the population which are defined in terms of the individuals' attributes and their social relationships. The subsets may be defined taking each individual's attributes separately (e.g., male) or in pairs (e.g., same sex). Thus, we could "model" a friendship network in which individuals chose friends who were within five years in age, were of the same sex, had the same occupation, and were not primary kinsmen.

The modeling of decision processes requires that contingent transformation be performed on social relationships including those created from the attributes. For example, ethnographic research may have determined that a friendship choice be made from individual x to individual y if (say) y is no more than five years younger than x and no more than ten years older than x, unless y is in the same occupational category as x, in which case the age limits are ten and fifteen years. In addition, choice among individuals who are equivalent according to the above might be made within a clique-like object as if to "complete" the clique. The software, therefore, must be able to accomodate such transformations. In SONET we do this by establishing dominance relations among relationsips by which we can construct a new contingent relation as illustrated by the following example. Suppose we are modeling individuals' choices of persons from whom they could request aid during an emergency. The rule is, say, that an individual will choose his father if the father lives in the same village, otherwise he will choose his father-in-law who is in the same village. Basically the compu - tational procedure is to assume the father-in-law choice, which is overridden (i.e., dominated) by the father-in-the-same-village if one exists. Logically, x chooses y if y is x's father who lives in the same village; otherwise x chooses y if y is x's father-in-law who lives in the same village (for details see Foster and Seidman, 1978; Seidman and Foster, 1977). Procedures for performing such logical transformations are complemented by others which perform all standard operations on relations—i.e., composition and various Boolean operations. For example, compound relations such as "friend's brother" can be obtained, as can logical combinations such as "member of the same occupational category or neighbor". This is an important feature if cross-cultural variation is to be accomodated—for example, using kinship relations in different kinship terminology systems.

To summarize: the objective of this set of procedures is to create a new network which is the outcome of each individuals' "social decisions"—that is, the outcome of a set of "choices" by each individual in the population. The decisions are conceived as the end product of a procedure which processes information on the attributes of the individuals and on the structure of existing social networks. The procedures are adapted from a body of research in cognitive anthropology. Operational details of the individual behavior component of our network method are described in our other papers (Foster and Seidman, 1978; Foster, 1979; Seidman and Foster, 1977). The method can be used to examine many questions concerning the relationship of individual behavior and network structure. For example, the procedures allow us to investigate network implications of varying the rules which govern individual behavior. (We use the term "rules" here very broadly to include descriptive statements of empirical regularities, not just normative rules in the usual sense.) Similarly, we can examine effects of changing features of the input networks, of individuals' attributes, or even of fundamental cultural categories (e.g., definition of kinship categories). The procedures are fully integrated with the structural analysis procedures, both theoretically and computationally.

3. *Overlapping Subsets*

Once we had programmed the subsetting procedures, their use was, of course, in no way restricted to modeling decision processes. In particular, we soon saw that any attribute or collection of attributes can be used to induce a subset of a population. We recognized immediately that our clique detection routines could find these subsets and, moreover, that structures could be built of these subsets using our reduction procedure. This idea seemed interesting, but in all honesty we never knew quite what to do with it and, in fact, we never pursued this line of inquiry further until recently when Seidman's work on an entirely different problem led us back to the topic.

This most recent line of inquiry rests on the idea suggested by the works of Ronald Atkin concerning structures induced by overlap of subsets of a population. For example, attributes partition a population into subsets as discussed above, and the subsets arising from various attributes (e.g., occupational categories, ethnic categories) overlap in complex ways. It seems reasonable to believe that significant social structure can arise from the pattern of overlap among these subsets. From a different point of view, events also influence social structure insofar as subsets are defined by mutual attendance at crucial events, such as weddings, funerals, harvests, and scholarly conferences. These subsets also overlap in complex ways. Finally, emergent network structures (e.g., cliques, k-plexes) can also be seen to overlap in this way. To paraphrase Atkin (1974b), the attributes, events, and emergent structures induce a "backcloth" against which social action takes place. It is thus an important theoretical idea that significant social structure be sought in the pattern of overlap among subsets of a population.

As with the other two major components of our strategy, the overlapping subset idea is a prominent one in anthropological kinship literature. A lively topic in the 1950's and 1960's concerned groupings known as kindreds, which were often found in societies with bilateral or cognatic kinship, which lack lineages. Kindreds differ from lineages dramatically, since they are not discrete groupings, and accordingly anthropological studies necessarily took a new twist. Rather than combining kindreds to form global structures as had been done with lineages, the overlapping kindreds were used to define new structures within which social action occurred—an idea closely related to Atkin's notion of the backcloth.

Once this backcloth induced by overlapping subsets had been recognized, it had to be translated into methodology for it to be of practical use. Several such translations have been made. Breiger (1974) grasped the essential idea and applied it to one case, but he developed no general methodology. Atkin (1972, 1974a, 1974b, 1976) has consistently emphasized the fundamental importance of the pattern of overlap among subsets of populations, and he has developed a substantial body of methodology, both mathematical and computational, to enable populations to be studied from his point of view. A serious weakness of Atkin's approach, however, is that the mathematical ideas used in its formal conceptualization are based on ideas taken from algebraic topology. Atkin defines structures and concepts by analogy with the algebraic-topological concepts but spends little time justifying the sociological-theoretical relevance or significance of the concepts.

The foregoing discussion refers primarily to the concepts of "q-hole" and "q-object" found in Atkin's later work (Atkin, 1976). It is far less true in Atkin's earlier paper (Atkin, 1972) where the "q-component structure" of a population is described. The q-component ideas arise naturally and directly once it has been decided that the structure induced by overlapping subsets is worthy of study. Thus it is not at all surprising that the most interesting sociological analyses using Atkin's approach restrict themselves essentially to the analysis of q-compoents (Freeman, 1980; Doreian, 1980).

The most recent implementation of the overlapping subsets idea has been made by Seidman (1981). The mathematics is taken from the theory of hypergraphs, which along with the theory of graphs, is a branch of combinatorics. A hypergraph is a collection of subsets of some given set; thus hypergraphs are well suited for the analysis of structure induced by collections of overlapping sets. Since hypergraphs are generalizations of graphs (think of the subsets as being the pairs of adjacent points), they allow us to accomodate at the same time certain crucial features of sets, attributes, and relations, thus providing a kind of generality that has been a major objective of our research since its inception. Hypergraphs are also discrete structures, and their use conforms with our bias toward the use of discrete models in social network analysis. The hypergraph formulation produces the q-component structure in precisely the same way as does Atkin, but a crucial contrast arises from important differences between the kinds of questions asked by combinatorics and algebraic topology. With a combinatorial approach, theoretical considerations can more readily influence the direction of the mathematical reasoning; with an algebraic-topological approach, the direction of the mathematical reasoning is highly constrained by the geometric roots of the mathematics. Application of hypergraph models is still in an early stage (see Seidman, 1981; also see Foster and Seidman, 1982, 1984). The relevant software has only recently been developed, and it remains to be seen whether the hypergraph models will prove as fruitful as early applications suggest. We are particularly encouraged by three facts, the first being the cogency of the theoretical motivation of the ideas. Second, the q-components, which are basic to the hypergraph formulation, have proven useful in Freeman's and Doreian's work. Third, these new ideas provide a theoretical justification for a set of procedures we developed earlier but dropped when we were unable to formally incorporate them into our theoretical framework or even into our general method other than from a computational standpoint. The procedures for subsetting on the basis of attribute data and for creating reduced graphs out of the subsets clearly yield a primitive and highly restrictive example of hypergraphs.

While reduced graphs can often be viewed as hypergraphs, it would be misleading to think that the reduced graph concept alone would be sufficient to study collections of overlapping subsets. The hypergraph formalism is mathematically far richer and permits us to pose questions about emergent properties of such collections, in precisely the same way as the graph-theoretic formalism made it possible to investigate emergent properties of networks induced by relations. On the other hand, since hypergraphs generalize graphs, it may be possible to recast the graph-theoretic formalization in hypergraph terms. This would represent a formal integration of all three aspects of our network approach.

4. Conclusion

To summarize briefly, the structural analysis and individual behavior aspects of our work are completely integrated via a set of graph theoretic procedures which, taken together, allow us to examine individuals' behavior within constraints posed by their social networks. The procedures for working with overlapping subsets are less well developed in their own right and even less well integrated with the other two components into the overall approach, but the general nature of the articulation is well understood. Generalizing the entire method in terms of hypergraph theory, though clearly desirable and, in principle, feasible, will require a great deal of work. Similarly, the software for the structural analysis and individual behavior component is complete for all the essential operations; procedures for the basic hypergraph analysis have not been completed, but they can be developed as straight-forward extensions of the routines for constructing total reduced graphs.

Although we earlier stressed distinctions between our procedures and the more traditional forms of anthropological network analysis, it would be a mistake to draw this distinction too sharply. As we also mentioned, our general objectives are essentially the same; we are interested in individuals' social action within the constraints of their social networks, and we are interested in problems posed by cultural factors (cf. Kapferer, 1976). Moreover, our procedures are motivated by essentially the same theoretical concerns which have motivated the work of Barnes, Mitchell, Kapferer, Boissevain, Wolfe, Bernard, Douglas White, and others. The important distinctions—and they are important—are in the relative emphasis given to the different theoretical ideas lying behind the work. Most important, we have chosen to carefully preserve the "mechanical models" mode of analysis somewhat more directly than have most others. We work more directly with the graphic representation of networks, whereas most other investigators have concentrated more on various enumerative properties of graphs such as density, distance, and so on. Second, we have formalized the individual behavior component more thoroughly than other approaches and given it a prominent place in our overall formulation in such a way as to utilize the results of cognitive anthropological decision theory. In a word, we see ourselves directly in the line of anthropological network analysis and, equally, in the direct line of social anthropological structural studies and of cognitive anthropology, from which we draw out theoretical orientation.

REFERENCES

Alba, R. D.
   1973   A graph-theoretic definition of a sociometric clique. Journal of
          Mathematical Sociology, 3:113-126.
Atkin, R. H.
   1972   From cohomology in physics to q-connectivity in social science.
          International Journal of Man-Machine Studies 4:139-167.
   1974a Mathematical Structure in Human Affairs. New York: Crane,
          Russak.
   1974b An algebra for patterns on a complex, I. International Journal of
          Man-Machine Studies, 6:285-307.
   1976   An algebra for patterns on a complex, II. International Journal of
          Man-Machine Studies, 8:483-498.
Banton, M. R., ed.
   1965   The Relevance of Models for Social Anthropology. London:
          Tavistock.
Breiger, R. L.
   1974   The duality of persons and groups. Social Forces 53:181-190.
Doreian, P.
   1980   On the evolution of group and network structure. Social
          Networks, 2: 235-252.
Evans-Pritchard, E. E.
   1940   The Nuer. Oxford: Oxford University Press.
Fjellman, S.
   1976   Talking about talking about residence: An Akamba case.
          American Ethnologist, 3:671-683.
Foster, B. L.
   1979   Formal network studies and the anthropological perspective.
          Social Networks, 1:241-255.
   1980   Minority traders in Thai village social networks. Ethnic Groups,
          2:221-240.
Foster, B. L. and Seidman, S. B.
   1978   SONET-I: Social Network Analysis and Modeling System.
          Volume I, User's Manual. Binghamton, N.Y.: State University of
          New York at Binghamton, Center for Social Analysis.
   1979   Network structure and the kinship perspective. American
          Ethnologist, 8:329-355.
   1982   Urban structures derived from collections of overlapping subsets.
          Urban Anthropology, 11:177-192.
   1983   A strategy for the dissection and analysis of social structures.
          Journal of Social and Biological Structures, 6:49-64.

1984   Overlap structure of ceremonial events in two Thai villages. Thai Journal of Development Administration, 24:143-157.

Freeman, L.
1980   Q-analysis and the structure of friendship networks. International Journal of Man-Machine Studies, 12:367-378.

Geoghegan, W.
1971   Information processing systems in culture. *In* Explorations in Mathematical Anthropology, P. Kay, Ed. Cambridge: MIT Press. pp. 4-35.

Goodenough, W.
1965   Rethinking status and role. *In* The Relevance of Models for Social Anthropology, M. R. Banton, ed. London: Tavistock, pp. 1-24.

Harary, F.
1969   Graph Theory. Reading, Mass.: Addison-Wesley.

Kapferer, B.
1976   Introduction. *In* Transaction and Meaning, Directions in the Anthropology of Exchange and Symbolic Behavior. Philadelphia: Institute for the Study of Human Issues.

Lankford, P. M.
1974   Comparative analysis of clique identification methods. Sociometry, 37:287-305.

Laumann, E. O. and Pappi, F. U.
1976   Networks of Collective Action: A Perspective on Community Influence Systems. New York: Academic Press.

Levi-Strauss, C.
1963   Structural Anthropology. New York: Basic Books.

Luce, R. D. and Perry, A. D.
1949   A method of matrix analysis of group structure. Psychometrika, 14:95-116.

Mokken, R.J.
1979   Cliques, clubs and clans. Quality and Quantity, 13:161-173.

Nadel, S. F.
1957   The Theory of Social Structure. London: Cohen and West.

Quinn, N.
1975   Decision models of social structure. American Ethnologist, 2:19-46.

Seidman, S. B.
1981   Structures induced by collections of subsets: A Hypergraph approach. Mathematical Social Sciences, 1:381-396.

Seidman, S. B. and Foster, B. L.
1977   The use of attribute data in network modeling. Paper presented to Conference on Structural Analysis, University of Toronto.

1978a A graph theoretic generalization of the clique concept. Journal of Mathematical Sociology, 6:139-154.

1978b A note on the potential for genuine cross-fertilization between anthropology and mathematics. Social Networks, 1:65-72.

1978c SONET-I: Social Network Analysis and Modeling System. Volume 2, Program Listings and Technical Comments. Binghamton, N.Y.: State University of New York at Binghamton, Center for Social Analysis.

1979 SONET-I: Social network analysis and modeling system. Social Networks, 2:85-90.

Woodall, D. R.

1978 Minimax theorems in graph theory. *In* Selected Topics in Graph Theory. Lowell W. Beineke and Roben Wilson, Eds. London: Academic Press. pp. 237-269.

CHAPTER 3

THE BOUNDARY SPECIFICATION PROBLEM IN NETWORK ANALYSIS*

Edward O. Laumann, Peter V. Marsden, and
David Prensky

1. Introduction

The set of techniques and methods collectively known as "network analysis" has proliferated rapidly in recent years. There are several reasons for this development. Within sociology, network analysis provides the basis of a coherent, falsifiable methodology for the study of both small-and large-scale social systems composed of *interrelated* units of analysis (Laumann, 1973, 1979; Laumann and Pappi, 1976). That is, network analysis shows promise as a device with which sociologists can escape from the "aggregate psychology" characteristic of much survey analysis, and move toward the

* Writing of this paper was supported by National Science Foundation grant SOC 77-26038. For helpful comments and suggestions, we are indebted to Stephen Berkowitz, Ronald S. Burt, James S. Coleman, Jean Comaroff, Joseph Galaskiewicz, David Knoke, J. Clyde Mitchell, Franz U. Pappi, Barry Wellman, and Christopher Winship. Reprinted from Ronald S. Burt, Michael J. Minor and associates (1983) *Applied Network Analysis: A Methodological Introduction* , pp. 18-34, by permission of Sage Publications.

study of social relations and their consequences for individual and group behavior (Coleman, 1958).

A second basis for the increased appeal of network analytic methods derives from anthropology. Authors such as Barnes (1954), Bott (1957), Mitchell (1969), and Boissevain (1974) saw that the concept of network, together with analytic methods based on that concept, constitutes a potentially liberating alternative to the approach of structural-functionalists such as Radcliffe-Brown (1952; see also Forde and Radcliffe-Brown, 1952). In the view of Barnes and others, the merit of studying networks of actual social relations lies in the attention this draws to the frequency with which the idealized structural components stressed by the structural-functionalists— such as kinship, political, religious, and economic subgroups—are *ignored* in the daily interactions of people. Network analysis is thus to be seen as a solvent for the boundaries of these observer-defined and overly reified groups in nonliterate societies. The implication, of course, is that such unitary concepts are even less useful in the study of the more fluid social circumstances of economically advanced or urbanized societies (Mitchell, 1969).

Whether used as a basis for analyzing the structure of social systems or as a means of discovering the interaction-based group memberships of actors, the eventual intent of a network analysis "is to explain, at least in part, the behavior of network elements ... and of the system as a whole by appeal to specific features of the interconnections among the elements" (Laumann, 1979: p. 394; see also Mitchell, 1969: pp. 1-7). The approach thus appears ideally suited for integrating different levels of analysis (Coleman, 1975); features of a network can be used to show effects of membership in a collectivity on individual attitudes and behavior (e.g., Erbring and Young, 1979), or to show the consequences of individual level network processes at the level of the collectivity (e.g., Marsden, 1981).

In this paper we are concerned with a metatheoretical issue of central importance in the design of network studies: the problem of *specifying system boundaries*. Because individual behavior is viewed as at least partially contingent on the nature of an actor's social relationships to certain key others, or the outcomes of events are seen to be partially dependent on the presence of a specific network configuration, care must be given to specifying rules of inclusion. Such rules pertain both to the selection of actors or nodes for the network *and* to the choice of types of relationships among those actors to be studied. The latter issue is sometimes overlooked, but is of enormous importance, especially with the development of analytic methods designed for analysis of multiple relations (White, Boorman and Breiger, 1976; Burt, 1977).

In studies concerned with the explanation of particular events (e.g., Granovetter, 1973; Wheeldon, 1969), it is obviously of great consequence if a key intervening actor or "bridging" tie is omitted due to oversight or use of data that are merely convenient; such an error, because it distorts the overall configuration of actors in a system, may render an entire analysis meaningless. Carelessness in system specification is probably a more serious issue for network analysis than for much survey analysis. Survey analyses are concerned with individual level processes thought to be uniformly applicable to each unit of analysis in some population, and incorrect system specification may result in problems such as slightly biased estimates of population means, proportions, etc., or in inefficiency in statistical estimation. Misspecification will not, however, cause a fundamental misrepresentation of the process under study. The latter is precisely the outcome of errors in the definition of system boundaries in a network analysis.

In view of the potential consequences of an incorrect specification of system boundaries in network analysis, it is somewhat surprising that the published literature in anthropology, sociology, and social psychology reporting studies of social networks shows, with some notable exceptions (e.g., Burt, 1978a), little concern for the problem of specifying the inclusion rules used in defining the membership of actors in particular networks and in identifying the types of social relationships to be analyzed. Often times the sole justification for selecting a particular portion of the "total network" (Mitchell, 1969; Barnes, 1969) for the empirical focus of an investigation has been an apparent appeal to common sense; at other times the availability of data in some published form appears to be the only basis of an investigator's claim that a set of actors linked in some way possesses an apparent "entitativity" as a self-evident natural object (Campbell, 1958). Clearly, a given empirical analysis carries conviction only to the extent that such a claim can be accepted.

In this paper, we discuss the various criteria that have been explicitly or implicitly employed in defining boundaries of social networks. In the course of our discussion, we will attempt to trace the consequences of assuming different rules. We shall see, for instance, that the use of particular inclusion rules renders the results of certain analytic procedures artifactual (see also Barnes, 1979). We do not advocate any particular strategy among those we discuss; the appropriate choice of rules remains contingent on the object of explanation for a given study. We *do* suggest, however, that, irrespective of the solution chosen, the problem of boundary definition should be given conscious attention when studies using a network approach are designed.

As noted, network analysts have, to date, been relatively mute on the matter of boundary definition. For this reason, we have been forced to adopt an inductive approach in this review, deriving metatheoretical views on the question of network closure from an inspection of published studies of social networks. In the next section, we distinguish two major approaches to boundary definition, the *nominalist* and *realist* approaches. We later distinguish several definitional foci used in the boundary specification process, for delimiting the set of actors to be studied. We then illustrate a typology of approaches developed by reference to extant network studies. We later discuss issues concerning the choice of particular social relationships to generate networks linking actors. Throughout, we comment on the implications of the different approaches considered for the use of analytic techniques, as well as on some unresolved theoretical issues that must be confronted if network analysis is to achieve the goal of providing new insights into social phenomena. To make our task manageable, we have paid little attention to egocentric approaches to network analysis that have been ably reviewed and explicated by Mitchell (1969) and Barnes (1972),[1] focusing attention instead on sociocentric or structural approaches.

2. *Approaches to Boundary Definition*

As we shall see, the rules followed by investigators in establishing network closure or boundaries are quite varied; they range from highly diffuse and implicit notions to some quite self-conscious formalizations. It often appears that the matter of boundary definition is one of no particular import; the boundaries of a network are presented as so self-evident in a

---

[1] Because they anchor a network on a focal individual or set of individuals of interest to an investigator, egocentric approaches to network analysis avoid some of the problems of boundary delimitation we note below for sociocentric approaches. Even here, there are issues about the lengths to which an investigator must go in identifying relevant indirect ties that might affect the attitudes or behavior of the focal actor. The problems are pragmatic as well as theoretical: Boissevain (1974), for example, enumerated a set of over 1000 persons related in some fashion to an "ordinary" person in the island society of Malta. Mitchell (1969) and Barnes (1969) suggest that in practice it is rarely necessary to inquire into indirect ties involving more than one intermediary; in Barnes' terminology, inspection of the "primary" and "second-order" zones is usually sufficient. Thus a "stopping rule" used to establish network closure is obviously a necessity for egocentric as well as structural approaches; but we shall not consider such problems here.

social situation studied as to require no comment (cf. the classic description of the bank-wiring room in Roethlisberger and Dickson (1939), or Sampson's (1969) study of novitiates in a monastery). Other rules for establishing network limits appear to have solely an operational justification: limited resources constraining researchers to stop pursuing chains of contacts after a certain point (e.g., Travers and Milgram, 1969), or respondent recalcitrance preventing full disclosure of the actors in a network.

Nonetheless, our reading of the presently published studies suggests that researchers have generally bounded their studies in one of two basic ways. We distinguish between these two alternatives by referring to the time-honored controversy in the social sciences between *nominalist* and *realist* views of the ontological status of social phenomena (see, e.g., Lenski, 1952; Ossowski, 1963). Having made this distinction, we hasten to add that many network studies do not fall neatly into one category or the other, perhaps because researchers have not been sufficiently self-conscious about the matter.

In the *realist* approach, the investigator adopts the presumed vantage point of the actors themselves in defining the boundaries of social entities. That is, the network is treated as a social fact only in that it is consciously experienced as such by the actors composing it; Braithwaite (1959) refers to this as a phenomenalist conception of facts. For example, in Weber's (1947:p. 145) classic definition of a corporate group (*Verband*) as a "a social relationship which is either closed or limits the admissions of outsiders by rules," stress is placed on the subjective meaningfulness to participants of the bounded nature of group membership. Thus, the 800-plus students in the high school studied by Coleman (1961) clearly recognize their common membership status when contrasting themselves with students attending any other high school. The fact that any given member may not even know, let alone sustain social relationships with, all other members of the corporate group has no significance for the specification of a network inclusion rule in terms of group membership.

The realist strategy of setting network boundaries by definition assumes the proposition that a social entity exists as a collectively shared subjective awareness of all, or at least most, of the actors who are members. It does not often empirically examine this assumption.[2] This may not be especially problematic in the case of studies of formally constituted groups which have widely agreed-upon labels, like General Motors or the University

---

[2] For research strategies relevant to assessing this hypothesis, see Laumann and Senter (1976); Broom and Jones (1977); or Gurin, Miller, and Gurin (1980).

of Chicago. As one examines more informally and fluidly constituted groups, such as Whyte's (1955) street corner society, tribal societies lacking fully differentiated political and social institutions (cf. Cohen, 1969), or ethnic groupings (Barth, 1969; Cohen, 1974; Wellman, 1979), matters become more uncertain. Consider, for esample, the dormitory at the University of Michigan studied by Newcomb (1961). This had no officially constituted status, beyond that of being an experimental observation site in which some students had been given housing in exchange for their willingness to submit to certain testing procedures. It is difficult to be confident that the persons thus recruited had much of the "we-feeling" characteristic of a corporate group, or that the relations they maintained with others in the dormitory were imbued with much in the way of meaning or affect. As Mitchell (1969:p.13) points out in discussing sociometric studies of school classrooms, there can be danger in uncritically accepting the proposition that common sense groupings of actors possess subjective meaning to those in them: "the behavior of individuals ... may be affected by circumstances beyond the immediate context."

The second major approach used to define network closure is the *nominalist* perspective on social reality. Here, an analyst self-consciously imposes a conceptual framework constructed to serve his or her own analytic purposes. Delineation of network boundaries is analytically relative to the purposes of the investigator, and thus network closure has no ontologically independent status. There is no assumption that reality itself will naturally conform to the analyst's distinctions; the perception of reality is assumed to be mediated by the conceptual apparatus of the analyst, be he or she an active participant in the social scene under study or an outside observer.[3]

The theoretical treatment of the social system, and of social action more generally, by Parsons (1951, 1961) exemplifies the nominalist strategy. With such an approach, the match between the investigator's analytically drawn boundaries and the subjective awareness of these distinctions by participants becomes an empirical question rather than an assumption. Thus, with Marx's conception of social class (Bendix and Lipset, 1966), one begins with the nominalist concept of class-in-itself (*Klasse an sich*), and inquires into the conditions under which this will or will not be transformed into the

---

[3] What we have called here the nominalist approach to boundary definition appears to correspond to Braithwaite's (1959) realist view of social facts as things accessible to some falsefiable method of observation—irrespective of whether they are experienced as facts by participants. It also reflects Kaplan's (1964) instrumentalist view of the nature of theories and concepts, seeing these as the investigator's tools of inquiry rather than as necessarily accurate pictures or maps of the world.

realist grouping, a class-for-itself (*Klasse für sich*; see, e.g., Rosenberg, 1953; Broom and Jones, 1977).

In addition to utilizing a nominalist or realist metatheoretical approach, investigators also set boundaries on the inclusion of actors by focusing on particular components or "primitive elements" of a network. In the next section, we discuss the ways in which these definitional foci have been used in the specification of network boundaries.

3. Definitional Foci for the Inclusion of Actors

In the process of choosing a set of actors composing a network, analysts focus on one or more of three sets of components: actors, relations, or activities. In part inspired by the distinction between nodes and relations in graph theory (Harary, Norman, and Cartwright, 1965), a branch of mathematics often used in the representation of social networks (see, e.g., Freeman, this volume), studies of social networks have generally stressed the sharp analytic distinction between actors and social relationships. Somewhat less common, but important, is a third approach adopted explicitly or implicitly by other investigators, in which participation in some activity or event of relevance is the criterion of membership.

The choice of a definitional focus is of importance, in that it fixes certain features of a network while leaving the remaining features free to vary. It is important that an investigator's choice of definitional focus be made explicit, in order to avoid circular analytic procedures leading to tautological results referring to the features fixed by the inclusion rule. For instance, it is scarcely informative to learn that a network constructed by a snowball sampling procedure is well connected or "integrated."

The most commonly used definitional tactic is that of using a restriction based on some attribute or characteristic of the actors or nodes in the network. Actors may be persons, corporate actors, or other collective entities or groupings (e.g., social classes, ethnoreligious groups) that are to be treated as unique elements. Two well-worn approaches to the determination of boundaries on the inclusion of actors in this way are the *positional* approach and the *reputational* approach. In the positional approach, the membership test refers to the presence or absence of some attribute, most commonly the occupancy of a position in a formally constituted group. The reputational approach, on the other hand, utilizes the judgments of knowledgeable informants in delimiting participant actors.

The two approaches to constructing a nodal inclusion rule are, of course, sometimes combined (e.g., Laumann and Pappi, 1976).

With the adoption of some approach restricting the number of actors in a network on the basis of nodal characteristics, the nature of the interconnectedness among these actors, as well as the participation patterns of actors in events or activities, are empirically free to vary. It is, however, of little more than descriptive interest to learn about the distribution of actors on the nodal characteristics used for boundary delimitation.

A second definitional focus used to select actors in network studies is that of specifying the network such that it includes those actors participating in a social relationship of a specified type. For instance, Haas and Drabek (1973:p. 65) suggest that organizational boundaries be drawn on the basis of interaction frequency. The relational approach to boundary definition includes the procedure known as "snowball sampling" (Erickson, 1978). In this procedure, a study initially is concerned with a small set of individual actors; the networks or chains of contact of actors in this set with others are traced until some criterion of termination or network closure is satisfied.

Because the relational approach to boundary definition is used rather infrequently, there appear to be few routinized methods of applying it, comparable to the positional or reputational methods for delimiting a set of actors. Seiler and Summers (1974) propose a method of locating community boundaries on the basis of interaction frequency and other measures of the degree to which places are of common relevance to one another.

Use of a relational approach to boundary definition rules out certain questions about the morphology of a network, in that the design of the study fixes or constrains these relational features. On the other hand, issues referring to the composition of the interrelated actors in terms of individual attributes, or to the participation patterns of actors, are empirical ones in a network with a relationally defined boundary.

A final element sometimes used to set boundaries is that of a defining event or activity, participation in which serves to select individual actors and the social relationship among them into a network. Pfeffer and Salancik (1978:p. 32) perfer this as a solution to the vexing problem of defining membership in an organization:

> When it is recognized that it is behaviors, rather than individuals, that are included in structures of coordinated behavior, then it is possible to define the extent to which any given person is or is not a member of the organization ... the boundary is where the discretion of the organization

to control an activity is less than the discretion of another organization or individual to control that activity.

The classic formulation of an inclusion rule based on participation in some activity is, of course, Dahl's (1958) decisional method for determining membership in a community elite. Of course, use of this or a related approach means that both the composition (in terms of the attributes of actors) and the relational pattern of a network are empirically at issue, while participation in the event or events on which the network is focused is predetermined.

Some investigators have stipulated inclusion rules in terms of two or more of our three definitional foci. While this may lead to theoretically elegant definitions of membership, it also has a major weakness, in that it reduces the number of problematic features to be explained given knowledge of network structure.

By crosstabulating the distinction between nominalist and realist views on the ontological status of social phenomena with the distinction among definitional foci drawn in this secton, we arrive at an eightfold typology of boundary specification strageties. This typology is presented in Table 1. The cells of the typolgy are filled with references to empirical studies of social networks which utilize the different approaches to boundary definition. We review these in the next section of the paper.

4. *Illustrative Boundary Specification Strategies*

The eight boundary specification approaches located on the basis of our search of the literature have been assigned Roman numerals in Table 1. We shall review studies illustrative of these strategies in the order indicted.

Above we have mentioned the most frequently adopted realist tactic, strategy I. Here, actors are treated as nodes in a network because they are members of a group which is closed or bounded according to the Weberian (1947) definition of a corporate group. The inclusion rule for actors refers to socially defined and recognized group memberships: Examples include attendance at a particular high school (Coleman, 1961; Fararo and Sunshine, 1964), employment in a particular work group in a factory (Roethlisberger and Dickson, 1939; Kapferer, 1969), residence in a monastery (Sampson, 1969) or parish (Barnes, 1954), or assignment to a particular classroom within a school (e.g., Davis, 1970). These examples should serve to indicate that strategy I is typically applied to the study of small, tightly bounded groups.

Table 1. A typology of boundary specification strategies for delimiting actors within a network, with examples.

Definitional Focus for Delimitation

Meta-theoretical Perspective	Attributes of Nodes	Relation	Participation in event or activity	Multiple Foci
Realist	I corporate group (Weber, 1947) bank wiring room (Roethlisberger and Dickson, 1939) monastery (Sampson, 1969 high school (Coleman, 1961; Fararo and Sunshine, 1964) Norwegian Island Parish (Barnes, 1954) cell room of Electrozinc Plant (Kapferer, 1969) school classroom (e.g., Davis, 1970)	III primary group, clique (Cooley, 1909)	V participants in a community controversy (Dahl, 1961) participants in common social events (Homans, 1950) street corner society (Whyte, 1955)	VII *Klasse für sich* (Marx) ethnic community (Barth, 1975; Laumann, 1973; Yancey, Ericksen, and Juliani, 1976)
Nominalist	II *Klasse an sich* (Marx) doctors in small cities (Coleman, Katz, and Menzel, 1966) formal organizations in a small city (Galaskiewicz, 1979) community influentials (Laumann and Pappi, 1973, 1976)	IV small world problem (Travers and Milgram, 1969; Erickson, 1978)	VI Invisible College (Crane, 1972; Burt, 1978b; Breiger, 1976)	VIII Supporters of psychotherapy (Kadushin, 1966) National elite circles (Moore, 1979

In contrast to this, strategy II, in which a nominally defined group is delimited on the basis of nodal attributes, is more often applied to larger networks. These may include hundreds or even thousands of individual actors. The actors, furthermore, are sometimes corporate actors or organizations rather than individual persons. Useem's (1979: p. 558) definition of the American business elite provides a good illustration of strategy II. He utilized a positional approach, defining the elite to include "... those who were directors of the 797 largest U.S. corporations in 1969." This criterion yielded a set of 8,623 directors. The interrelations among these members, measured most notably by membership on two or more corporate boards, were then studied empirically.

Another illustration of strategy II is given by Galaskiewicz's (1979) study of organizations in the small city of Towertown. In this study, a territorial criterion is initially used to restrict membership within a geographical area: As a second step, a functional or industry criterion is applied:

> Our target population included all industries, banks, savings and loans, newspapers, radio stations, service clubs, fraternal organizations, business associations, unions, law firms, health agencies, high schools, welfare agencies, churches, professional associations, county offices, municipal offices, and political parties. Commercial establishments, transportation facilities, public utilities, real estate offices, block clubs, community organizations, and elementary schools were excluded due to time and budget constraints (Galaskiewicz, 1979: 1350).

The rationale for including some types of organizations at the expense of others is not made explicit, but it would appear to pertain at least in part to the size of organizations.

Few empirical studies have relied exclusively on the relational nexus for determining memberships of actors in a network. We thus consider strategies III and IV, which use the relation as a boundary specifier, primarily for reasons of analytic completeness.

Cooley's (1909) concept of the primary group has been a key term in small group research. The primary group is defined as a face-to-face interacting group with diffuse positive affect. This definition is essentially relational; it requires direct linkages of positive affect among all members of a group, and excludes the possibility of "isolates" claiming subjective membership in the group but lacking relations with other members. Despite its time-honored place in the sociological literature, the primary group concept has rarely, if ever, served as the basis for identifying network limits. This is perhaps because analysts with a realist viewpoint have assumed a perfect correspondence among various features of such groups: complete connectedness, subjective we-feeling, diffuse positive sentiments toward all members, and multiple shared activities and interests, and then focused on one of the latter three features at the expense of connectedness. In our view, however, complete connectedness remains the litmus test for a primary group.

Of course, the connectedness criterion is frequently applied in efforts to locate subgroups or "cliques" within larger networks delimited in some other manner (see, e.g., Alba, 1973; Burt, 1978a). Subgroupings identified in this way are often believed to have an ontological status distinguishing them in socially significant ways from other actors in the larger network to whom they are more loosely and indirectly connected. Here, then, we have a combination of strategies I and III, with the former being used to delineate the inclusive network and the latter to define cliques within it. Methods for locating subgroups on the criterion of structural equivalence (Lorrain and White, 1971; White *et al.*, 1976; Burt, 1978a) proceed in a similar manner.

Studies of the "small world" problem (e.g., Travers and Milgram, 1969), provide a good illustration of strategy IV. Here, arbitrarily selected "starters" serve as initiators of chains intended to reach arbitrarily selected "target" persons by way of preexisting personal relationships. The inclusion rule is thus specified in terms of an actor's presence in a chain of ties of unspecified type. Both the attributes of the individual persons in the chain and the content of the relations composing it are theoretically and empirically free to vary given this inclusion rule (see Lin, Dayton, and Greenwald, 1978), and empirical variation in nodal characteristics may be used in efforts to discriminate between chains which are successful in reaching the intended target and those which are unsuccessful.

Strategy V, in which an actor's inclusion in a network is defined in terms of participation or interest in one or more events, activities, or concerns, is the primary alternative to strategy I from the realist perspective. Homans (1950: pp. 82-86) provides a classic instance of this strategy, drawn from the field work of Davis, Gardner, and Gardner (1941:esp. pp. 147-156). A clique structure among 18 women is induced from information about their participation in 14 informal social gatherings taking place over the course of several months. Similarly, Dahl (1961), in a quite self-conscious application of strategy V, specifies three community controversies in the city of New Haven as a basis for locating community influentials. In a somewhat more implicit fashion, Whyte's (1955) description of street corner society in an Italian-American neighborhood of Boston uses the physical setting of a particular street corner as a focal observational scene or frame (cf. Goffman, 1974) for identifying nodal elements of the "society" (see also Liebow, 1967; Anderson, 1978).

Researchers adopting a nominalist perspective have been somewhat more reluctant to employ an event-focused approach to boundary delimitation than the realists. Most notable in illustrating strategy VI is work on "invisible colleges" of scientists (Crane, 1972; Burt, 1978b), in which network members are identified on the basis of their interest in a particular field of research, irrespective of their disciplinary label. The membership criterion in Breiger's (1976) study of biomedical researchers is publication of one or more articles in the research area on which the "invisible college" is focused.[4]

The three definitional foci for boundary delimitation can be and are combined in some cases (strategies VII and VIII). An example from the realist perspective is the Marxian concept of class for itself (*Klasse für sich*) which simultaneously requires occupancy of a common position relative to the means of production, relations of solidarity with those in the class, relations of antagonism to those in other classes, recognition of the attendant interests implied by objective position, and establishment of a self-conscious political organization in pursuit of those interests. Similarly, in delimiting an ethnic community, some investigators require both the nodal feature of a common heritage and the presence of a disproportionate level of interaction among members in terms of intimate social relations such as marriage or friendship (Laumann, 1973; Barth, 1975). Thus Yancey, Ericksen, and Juliani (1976:p. 399) assert that

> ... ethnicity defined in terms of frequent patterns of association and identification with common origins ... is generated and becomes crystallized under conditions of residential stability and segregation, common occupational positions and dependence on local institutions and services.

The discussion of social circles by Kadushin (1966, 1968) in some ways combines elements of the realist and nominalist perspectives, and is therefore intermediate between the application of strategies VII and VIII. Kadushin defines social circles analytically, in terms of the sharing of certain broadly conceived social or political interests together with the presence of indirect relational connectedness to other members. He asserts, however, that groups thus defined are real social entities; in describing a social circle called the Friends and Supporters of Psychotherapy, he writes that " like all circles, the Friends do not have a listing in the telephone book, but only in that sense

---

[4] The researchers actually studied by Breiger were sampled from a population delimited by the criterion given here.

are they a non-existent social unit" (Kadushin, 1966:p. 792). In his actual analysis of data, Kadushin attempts to locate social circles within a group delimited on the basis of a nodel attribute (having made an application to a psychiatric clinic) using latent structure analysis of items measuring participation in certain types of cultural events and information levels concerning psychotherapy. His purpose in doing this is to "... define circles empirically without necessarily having to engage in extensive and difficult sociometric analysis" (Kadushin, 1966:p. 792). This is obviously an important operational advantage if there is a sufficiently close correspondence between the participation and knowledge measures and the unmeasured connectedness criterion. The procedure may be problematic in the absence of a close correspondence, and others have chosen to operationally define circles otherwise (e.g., Alba and Moore, 1978).

Moore's (1979; see also Alba and Moore, 1978) study of the American political elite is more clearly representative of the application of strategy VIII. The study design for identifying this elite involved an initial selection of 545 incumbents of command positions in key institutional sectors of American society, supplemented by another 331 persons identified on the basis of a reputational survey of the initial positionally identified group, and a snowball sampling procedure (see Moore, 1979:pp. 675-676).

Laumann and Marsden (1979) utilize multiple foci for defining "collective actors" within oppositional structures in political systems, i.e., for defining subgroups within networks delimited on some other basis. They define a collective actor in terms of individual members who "... (1) share an outcome preference in some matter of common concern, and (2) are in an effective communication network with one another" (Laumann and Marsden, 1979:p. 717).

As mentioned above, the central difficulty with strategies VII and VIII is that in using two or more analytic features of networks to define membership of actors in the network, they consume many theoretical degrees of freedom. Great caution must be used in drawing substantive inferences here. For instance, Moore's (1979) study concludes that the structure of the American elite is that of a large, integrated collection of interrelated actors rather than a set of fragmented groups. Despite her explicit attention to the issues (Moore, 1979:p. 677), the reader is left with the suspicion that her conclusion is necessitated, or at least made likely, by the boundary specification rule employed: the selection of certain institutional sectors (e.g., mass media leaders) carries strong relational implications; the use of snowball sampling requires connectedness among at least some members of the network; and the granting of discretion to respondents to select national events as discussion topics, and to give an unlimited number of responses to sociometric questions, in all likelihood encouraged the recognition of diverse and ramifying communication ties.

This concludes our review of strategies for delimiting boundaries of a network as far as actors are concerned. This is, to our minds, the most central issue in boundary specification, and it is certainly the issue that has received the most concerted attention. It is also of importance, however, to consider rules of inclusion for the other two analytic foci we have mentioned: relations and events or activities. We comment on problems and issues in these areas below.

5. On Inclusion Rules for Relations

The identification of the social relationship as a definitional focus above, together with the development of analytic techniques permitting consideration of multiple types of relationships (White *et al.*, 1976; Burt, 1977) points to the need for developing rules of inclusion for relationships studied as well as actors. A major barrier in this enterprise is the current lack of any well-articulated typology of social relationships which could lead to the development of explicit selection strategies parallel to those reviewed above for actors. Probably the best guidance we have available in this regard is derived from Parsons' (1951) set of five pattern variables. Particular attention has been given to the distinction between instrumental and expressive social relations; somewhat more implicit is a focus on the diffuseness-specificity dimension.

Even with a suitable classification of relationships, however, an analyst is left with the problem of selecting types to be analyzed. Rather little self-conscious attention appears to have been given to this matter; implicit appeals to common sense justifications for the use of particular relations as generators of a social structure or analyses of any available relational data run rampant. Probably the most serious consequence of such neglect is what we shall term the *partial system fallacy*. This is present wherever a set of relationships connecting a subset of the actors to which the relations are relevant is analyzed without prior attention to the entire set of actors. The result of such a procedure may be a seriously misleading description of network structure.

To clarify this point we refer to an illustrative case with which we have some familiarity, pertaining to the social structure of a community defined in terms of interorgranizational relations (see Laumann, Galaskiewicz, and

Marsden, 1978). Consider two specific types of interorganization relations, transfer of money and transfer of information pertinent to local community affairs. If the boundary for inclusion of organizations has been drawn on the basis of geography, then the analysis of social structure in terms of intracommunity money flows may be uninformative. This is because many of the central organizations in the total network of money flows would be excluded from the network by virtue of the geographically based nodal inclusion rule; examples of the excluded organizations would be state and federal government agencies, extra-local banks, headquarters or subsidiary organizations located elsewhere, supplier and consumer organizations. For many, or even most, local organizations, these might be more important sources or destinations of money than other organizations in the locality. Their omission from the network of money flows makes the analysis of such flows subject to the partial system fallacy. We would be more comfortable with an analysis based on information flows pertinent to community affairs. Because these relationships are defined with explicit reference to a criterion of common relevance to the organizations delimited on the basis of the nodal inclusion rule, it is plausible to treat the patterns of information flow analytically as a closed system, while such a treatment is implausible for the money flows.

Two other issues raised when we consider inclusion rules for relations are of special concern to multiple network studies using structural equivalence as the central concept. The procedures outlined by White *et al.* (1976) are premised on the idea that social roles can be understood by simultaneously considering or "stacking" several different relations or generators. Block-models of roles and positions are either induced by clustering nodes on the basis of the profile similarities across the multiple relations (Breiger, Boorman, and Arabie, 1975), or deduced by searching for "empty places" in the network (Heil and White, 1976). This approach has led to some interesting analyses of social structure (e.g., Breiger, 1976; Snyder and Kick, 1979). The approach does, however, place an obligation on investigators to be explicit regarding the rationale for merging different generators in a single analysis—that is, to indicate why these particular relations ought to be seen as jointly definitive of social roles in a given population. In some applications it appears that the social positions induced by the procedures mentioned above have been arbitrarily determined by the happenstance availability of particular generators. This appearance is accentuated by the inability of some analysts to find a meaningful substantive interpretation of the partitions of actors identified.

In our view, some potential generators ought not to be used at all in the defintion of social positions or roles, because to use them is to commit the partial system fallacy discussed above. In other cases, it may be preferable to utilize multiple network strategies like those advocated by Burt (1977). In this approach, several different sets of social positions or roles are induced on the basis of social relationships considered separately; the intersections among the different partitionings of actors into positions are then analyzed empirically.

One final point pertaining to multiple network approaches to the setting of boundaries on the inclusion of relations is of particular importance to those approaches and techniques assigning special weight to the absence of social ties as a criterion for locating social structure in networks. When applied to small, closed groups, these methods have been quite successful. As increasingly large networks are analyzed, however, the fact that any given actor is capable of maintaining a limited number of ties, together with the well-known generalization that the total number of ties increases as the square of the number of actors, creates a fundamental ambiguity about the absence of relations. Absent ties may appear either because of active avoidance or because of limited opportunity for contact. The implication of this is that in efforts to apply techniques resting on the notion of structural equivalence to large networks, care should be taken to obtain multiple measures which permit the analyst to discriminate between avoidance and lack of contact (see, e.g., Breiger's 1976 study of awareness relations among biomedical scientists, or the analysis by White *et al.* 1976 of positive and negative relations of affect, influence, etc., in the monastery studied by Sampson 1969).

6. Boundary Specification for Activities

We shall comment briefly on the question of setting limits on the inclusion of events, activities, or interests in network studies. It is obvious that the network boundaries for the inclusion of actors obtained using strategies V and VI above are entirely dependent on the selection of particular events or activities as ones of focal interest. An analytic rationale for event selection is generally not given by those applying these strategies.[5] It is often assumed that the relevant events are self-evident to any well-informed observer. This gives an unfortunate impression of arbitrariness, which leaves the reader to inquire what shape the leadership and power structure of New Haven would have taken had Dahl (1961) and his associates

---

[5] Consider, for instance, the advice given to those wishing to apply a decisional method of locating leaders by Polsby (1960:p. 495) who suggests that issues "which are generally agreed to be significant" be studied.

chosen to study additional or other issues; or what the changes in the clique structure of women in Old City would have emerged if other social gatherings that doubtless occurred during the observation period of Davis *et al.* (1941) had been mentioned in the newspapers or noticed by the participant observers.

Part of the issue here is whether an analyst is intrinsically interested in the events under study, or whether their selection is an intermediate step in an effort to obtain a description of a regularized structure of social relations among actors. In the former case, the rationale for event selection is straightforward and obvious. We are more concerned with the latter case. When the goal is to obtain a description of a presumably enduring social structure using an event-based strategy for boundary delimitation, steps should be taken to carefully delineate the event space to be explored.

Unfortunately, this problem is more easily posed than solved. As in the case of boundary specification for relations, development of a workable typology of issues or activities that might be used for sampling or selection of focal events would be a useful first step toward a solution. Aside from refer - ring to our previously published commentary addressing this problem (Laumann, Marsden, and Galaskiewicz, 1977), and to some efforts in the literature to develop classification schemes for issues (Barth and Johnson, 1959; Freeman, 1968; Molotch, 1976), we have little guidance to offer on it. Laumann and Knoke (1987) do make extensive use of the strategy in their study of national policy domains, with a number of useful practical suggestions.

7. Conclusion

In this chapter we have reviewed approaches to the problem of setting network boundaries. While we obviously feel that network analysis has a great deal to offer social scientists seeking to study social systems, we think it important to emphasize the point that *there is no sense in which social networks must "naturally" correspond to social systems.* Freeman (this volume) gives elegant formal criteria, in terms of nodes, relations, and attributes, for defining social networks. Adopting a nominalist view, we define a social system as "a plurality of actors interacting on the basis of a shared symbol system" (Parsons, 1951:p. 19). The problem of boundary specification in efforts to adapt network analysis to the study of social systems is essentially that of specifying the standard of common relevance (Newcomb, 1961:pp. 12-23)—that is, the basis of mutual orientation for actors—which circumscribes membership in the system. Given a suitable definition of this standard, the network boundaries for actors, relations, and activities or events may be specified such that they can be plausibly equated to those of the social system under study. Boundary specification also lays a basis for the identification of sets of social roles in that system, with respect to both its internal organization and its environment.

The question of boundary specification has received comparatively little attention in the past decade during which network analysis has largely come into its own, partly because of the preoccupation of the field with the development of novel strategies for analysis of relational data. It is a much less tractable sort of problem than those addressed by some of the papers concerned with analytic methods included elsewhere in this volume, and one on which there are few objective criteria which may be used to resolve conflicting positions. We have argued here, however, that networks can be meaningfully understood only in terms of the elements of focal interest used to define membership, whether that usage is explicit or is inadvertent. We feel that more explicit attention to boundary specification will contribute to the success of network methods in the study of social structures and systems as new studies are designed and new data collected.

REFERENCES

Alba, R. D.
  1973 A graph-theoretic definition of a sociometric clique. Journal of Mathematical Sociology.
Alba, R. D. and Moore, G.
  1978 Elite social circles. Sociological Methods and Research 7:167-188.
Anderson, Elijah
  1978 A Place on the Corner. Chicago: University of Chicago Press.
Barnes, J. A.
  1954 Class and committees in a Norwegian island parish. Human Relations 7:39-58.
  1969 Networks and political process. *In* J. Clyde Mitchell (Ed.) Social Networks in Urban Situations, pp. 51-66. Manchester, U.K.: Manchester University Press.
  1972 Social Networks. Module in Anthropology 26. Reading, MA: Addison-Wesley.
  1979 Network analysis: orienting notion, rigorous technique or substantive field of study? *In* Paul W. Holland and Samuel Leinhardt (Eds.) Perspectives on Social Network Research. New York: Academic Press.
Barth, E. A.T. and Johnson. S. D.
  1959 Community power and a typology of social issues. Social Forces 38:29-32.
Barth, F. (Editor)
  1969 Ethnic Groups and Boundaries. London: Allen and Unwin.
Barth, F.
  1975 Ritual and Knowledge among the Baktaman of New Guinea. New Haven: Yale University Press.
Bendix, R. and Lipset, S. M.
  1966 Karl Marx's theory of social classes. *In* Reinhard Bendix and Seymour M. Lipset (Eds.) Class, Status, and Power, pp. 6-11. Second edition. New York: Free Press.
Boissevain, J.
  1974 Friends of Friends: Networks, Manipulators and Coalitions. New york: St. Martin's.
Bott, E.
  1957 Family and Social Network. New York: Free Press.
Braithwaite, R.
  1959 Scientific Explanation: A Study of the Function of Theory, Probability, and Law In Science. Cambridge, U.K.: Cambridge University Press.

Breiger, R.
   1976   Career attributes and network structure: a blockmodel study of a
          biomedical research specialty. American Sociological Review
          41:117-135.
Breiger, R. L., Boorman, S.A., and Arabie, P.
   1975   An algorithm for clustering relational data, with application to
          social network analysis and comparison with multidimensional
          scaling. Journal of Mathematical Psychology 12:328-383.
Broom, L. and Jones, F. L.
   1977   Problematics in stratum consistency and stratum formation: an
          Australian example. American Journal of Sociology 82:808-825.
Burt, R.S.
   1977   Positions in multiple network systems, part one: a general
          conception of stratification and prestige in a system of actors cast
          as a social topology. Social Forces 56:106-131.
   1978a Cohesion versus structural equivalence as a basis for network
          subgroups. Sociological Methods and Research 7:189-212.
   1978b Stratification and prestige among elite experts in methodological
          and mathematical sociology circa 1975. Social Networks
          1:105-158.
Campbell, D. T.
   1958   Common date, similarity, and other indices of the status of
          aggregates of persons as social aggregates. Behavioral Science
          3:14-25.
Cohen, A.
   1969   Custom and Politics in Urban Africa: A Study of Hausa Migrants
          in Yoruba Towns. London: Routledge and Kegan Paul.
Cohen, A. (Editor)
   1974   Urban Ethnicity. London: Tavistock Publication.
Coleman, J. S.
   1958   Relational analysis: the study of social organization with survey
          methods. Human Organization 16:28-36.
   1969   The Adolescent Society. New York: Free Press.
   1975   Social structure and a theory of action. In Peter M. Blau (Ed.)
          Approaches to the Study of Social Structure, pp. 76-93. New
          York: Free Press.
Coleman, J. S., Katz, E., and Menzel, H.
   1966   Medical Innovation: A Diffusion Study. Indianapolis: Bobbs-
          Merrill.
Cooley, C. H.
   1909   Social Organization. New York: Schocken.
Crane, D.
   1972   Invisible Colleges. Chicago: University of Chicago Press.

Dahl, R.
  1958 A critique of the ruling elite model. American Political Science
       Review 52:463-469.
  1961 Who Governs? New Haven: Yale University Press.
Davis, J. A.
  1970 Clustering and hierarchy in interpersonal relations: Testing two
       graph theoretical models on 742 sociograms. American
       Sociological Review 33:843-852.
Davis, A., Gardner. B. B. and Gardner, M. R.
  1941 Deep South. Chicago: University of Chicago Press.
Erbring, L. and Young, A.
  1979 Individuals and social structure: contextual effects as endogenous
       feedback. Sociological Methods and Research 7:396-430.
Erickson, B. H.
  1978 Some problems of inference from chain data. *In* Karl F.
       Schuessler (Ed.) Sociological Methodology 1979, pp. 276-302.
       San Francisco: Jossey-Bass.
Fararo, T. J. and Sunshine, M. H.
  1964 A Study of a Biased Friendship Net. Syracuse University: Youth
       Development Center.
Forde, D. and Radcliffe-Brown, A.R. (Editors)
  1952 African Systems of Kinship and Marriage. London: Oxford
       University Press.
Freeman, L.
  1968 Social Networks and the Structure Experiment. Presented at a
       Conference on Methods in Social Network Analysis, Laguna
       Beach, CA., April.
Galaskiewicz, J.
  1979 The structure of community interorganizational networks. Social
       Forces 57:1346-1364.
Goffman, E.
  1974 Frame Analysis: An Essay on the Organization of Experience.
       Cambridge: Harvard University Press.
Granovetter, M.
  1973 The strength of weak ties. American Journal of Sociology
       78:1360-1380.
Gurin, P., Miller, A. H. and Gurin, G.
  1980 Stratum identification and consciousness. Social Psychology
       Quarterly 43:30-47.
Haas, J. E. and Drabek, Thomas E.
  1973 Complex Organizations: A Sociological Perspective. New York:
       MacMillan.

Harary, F., Norman, R. Z. and Cartwright, D.
  1965   Structural Models: An Introduction to the Theory of Directed
         Graphs. New York: Wiley.
Heil, G. H. and White, H. C.
  1976   An algorithm for finding simultaneous homomorphic
         correspondences between graphs and their image graphs.
         Behavioral Science 21:26-35.
Homans, G. C.
  1950   The Human Group. New York: Harcourt, Brace, and World
Kadushin, C.
  1966   The friends and supporters of psychotherapy: On social circles in
         urban life. American Sociological Review 31:786-802.
  1968   Power, influence, and social circles: A new methodology for
         studying opinion makers. American Sociological Review
         33:685-698.
Kapferer, B.
  1969   Norms and the manipulation of relationships in a work context. In
         J. Clyde Mitchell (Ed.) Social Networks in Urban Situations,
         pp. 181-244. Manchester, U.K.: Manchester University Press.
Kaplan, A.
  1964   The Conduct of Inquiry: Methodology for Behavioral Science.
         San Francisco: Chandler.
Laumann, E. O.
  1973   Bonds of Pluralism: The Form and Substance of Urban Social
         Networks. New York: Wiley Interscience.
  1979   Network analysis in large social systems: Some theoretical and
         methodological problems. In Paul W. Holland and Samuel
         Leinhardt (Eds.) Perspectives on Social Network Analysis,
         pp. 379-402. New York: Academic Press.
Laumann, E. O., Galaskiewicz, J., and Marsden, Peter V.
  1978   Community structure as interorganizational linkages. Annual
         Review of Sociology 4:455-484.
Laumann, E. O. and Knoke, D.
  1987   The Organizational State: Social Choice in National Policy
         Domains. Madison, WI: University of Wisconsin Press.
Laumann, E. O. and Marsden, P. V.
  1979   The analysis of oppositional structures in political elites:
         Identifying collective actors. American Sociological Review
         44:713-732.
Laumann, E. O., Marsden, P. V., and Galaskiewicz, J.
  1977   Community-elite influence structures: extension of a network
         approach. American Journal of Sociology 83:594-631.

Laumann, E. O. and Pappi, F. U.
  1973 New directions in the study of community elites. American
        Sociological Review 38:212-230.
  1976 Networks of Collective Action: A Perspective on Community
        Influence Systems. New York: Academic Press.
Laumann, E. O. and Senter, Richard
  1976 Subjective social distance, occupational stratification, and forms of
        status and class consciousness: A cross-national replication and
        extension. American Journal of Sociology 81:1304-1338.
Lenski, G. E.
  1952 American social classes: Statistical strata or social groups?
        American Journal of Sociology, 58:139-144.
Liebow, E.
  1967 Tally's Corner: A Study of Negro Streetcorner Men. Boston:
        Little, Brown, and Company.
Lin, N., Dayton, P. W., and Greenwald, P.
  1978 Analyzing the instrumental use of relations in the context of social
        structure. Sociological Methods and Research 7:149-166.
Lorrain, F. and White, H. C.
  1971 Structural equivalence of individuals in social networks. Journal
        of Mathematical Sociology 1:49-80.
Marsden, P. V.
  1981 Introducing influence processes into a system of collective
        decisions. American Journal of Sociology 86:1203-1235.
Mitchell, J. C.
  1969 The concept and use of social networks. In J. Clyde Mitchell (Ed.)
        Social Networks in Urban Sitations, pp. 1-50. Manchester, U.K.:
        Manchester University Press.
Molotch, H.
  1976 The city as growth machine: Toward a political economy of place.
        American Journal of Sociology 82:309-332.
Moore, G.
  1979 The structure of a national elite network. American Sociological
        Review 44:673-692.
Newcomb, T.
  1961 The Acquaintance Process. New York: Holt, Rinehart, and
        Winston.
Ossowski, S.
  1963 Class Structure in the Social Consciousness. London: Routledge
        and Kegan Paul.
Parsons, T.
  1951 The Social System. Glencoe, IL: Free Press.

1961   An outline of the social system. *In* Talcott Parsons, Edward Shils,
       Kaspar D. Naegele and Jesse C. Pitts (Eds.) Theories of Society,
       pp. 30-79. New York: Free Press.
Pfeffer, J. and Salancik, G. R.
1978   The External Control of Organizations: A Resource Dependence
       Perspective. New York: Harper and Row.
Polsby, N.
1960   How to study community power: The pluralist alternative. Journal
       of Politics 22:474-484.
Radcliffe-Brown, A. R.
1952   Structure and Function in Primitive Society. London: Cohen and
       West.
Roethlisberger, F. J. and Dickson, W. J.
1939   Management and the Worker. Cambridge, MA: Harvard
       University Press.
Rosenberg, M.
1953   Perceptual obstacles to class consciousness. Social Forces
       32:22-27.
Sampson, S. F.
1969   Crisis in a Cloister. Ph.D. dissertation, Department of Sociology,
       Cornell University.
Seiler, L. H. and Summers, G. F.
1974   Locating community boundaries: An integration of theory and
       empirical techniques. Sociological Methods and Research
       2:259-280.
Snyder, D. and Kick, E. L.
1979   Structural position in the world system and economic growth,
       1955-1970: A multiple-network analysis of transnational
       interactions. American Journal of Sociology 84:1096-1126.
Travers, J. and Milgram, S.
1969   An experimental study of the small world problem. Sociometry
       32:425-443.
Useem, M.
1979   The social organization of the American business elite. American
       Sociological Review 44:553-572.
Weber, M.
1947   The Theory of Social and Economic Organization. New York:
       Free Press.
Wellman, B.
1978   The community question: The intimate networks of East Yorkers.
       American Journal of Sociology 84:1201-1231.

Wheeldon, P. D.
1969 The operation of voluntary associations and personal networks in the political processes of an inter-ethnic community. *In* J. Clyde Mitchell (Ed.) Social Networks in Urban Situations, pp. 128-180. Manchester, U.K.: Manchester University Press.
White, H. C., Boorman, S. A., and Breiger, R. L.
1976 Social structure from multiple networks, I. blockmodels of roles and positions. American Journal of Sociology 81:730-780.
Whyte, William F.
1955 Street Corner Society. Chicago: University of Chicago Press.
Yancey, W. L., Erickson, E. P., and Juliani, R. N.
1976 Emergent ethnicity: A review and reformulation. American Sociological Review 41:391-403.

CHAPTER 4

INFERRING MEANINGFUL GLOBAL NETWORK PROPERTIES FROM INDIVIDUAL ACTOR'S MEASUREMENT SCALES[*]

William H. Batchelder

Many of the data sets that are analyzed by social network methods are obtained by having actors make judgments or sociometric choices about their fellow actors in a network. In such cases, each actor is instructed to provide data on how they regard each of the other actors on some relevant quality such as friendship, respecting, regarding as knowledgeable, etc. Usually such data are dichotomized in such a way as to reveal a directed graph where a directed link from actor p_i to actor p_j is formed in case actor p_i's data indicate that he or she is tied to p_j on the relevant quality. There are a number of network methods available for processing such network data, and many chapters in this book, such as those by Heil and Marsden, discuss a variety of such methods. These methods are designed mostly to analyze

[*] I am grateful to Phipps Arabie, John Boyd, Richard Degerman, Linton Freeman, R. Duncan Luce, Louis Narens, A. Kimball Romney, David Strauss, Peter Woodruff, and Ryozo Yoshino for discussions or written comments on earlier drafts of this paper. It is not the case, however, that all of these colleagues necessarily agree with all of the positions taken in the paper.

network data and discover interesting global (sociological) properties that are perhaps hidden in the raw data themselves.

As a newcomer to the social network area, I have been struck by the apparent lack of serious concerns with the measurement-theoretic underpinnings of various network methods. Burt (1980, p. 85) comments on the concerns of Lindzey and Byrne (1968) that the ratings of inter-personal attraction have been typically ad hoc in nature as follows, "however, there are still no systematic studies of differences in basic network findings across different measures of relational form." The goal of this chapter will be to attempt to provide one systematic approach to the problem that Burt and others have noted.

Most of the tools and ideas that will be employed in this chapter will come from work on scaling and foundations of measurement done mostly by psychologists and philosophers with strong formal backgrounds. The initial focus will be on the individual subject scaling data concerning the quality being used to create ties between actors in the network. An individual actor's data, under certain conditions, can be merged into an individual actor measurement scale, and interesting global properties in a network then arise because of interrelations between how different actors scale each other on the quality under investigation.

A great deal is known about individual subject scaling, and the area has been an active one in psychology since Gustav Fechner's pioneering treatise, *Elemente der Psychophysik*, published in 1860. Fechner defined the notions of outer and inner psychophysics. Outer psychophysics concerns how one scales a subject's sensations of subjective qualities such as loudness, brightness, and heaviness where there are corresponding physical qualities with known measurement properties. Inner psychophysics, on the other hand, concerns the scaling of such subjective qualities as beauty, value, and preference, where there are no known corresponding physical qualities.

One of our theses in this chapter is that the scaling of affective qualities leading to sociometric judgments such as friendship can be treated in the same way as other subjective qualities without corresponding physical counterparts. As such, there are measurement assumptions which, if satisfied, yield intra-actor measurement scales of various types, and in Section 2 we will survey network data from the point of view of the scale-type of the individual actor scales.

From our individual actor perspective, what is fascinating about global network properties is that they depend on inter-actor comparisons among scale values. Given individual actor scales of a given scale-type, how can we meaningfully compare the scale values between actors? For example, consider the property that friendship is reciprocated among a set of social actors who judge their degree of friendship toward each other. Since most scale-types have a certain amount of arbitrariness in them, such things as unit size, origin, etc., it is not at all obvious how to decide in a meaningful way if, say, actor p_i's scale value of friendship for actor p_j is "reciprocated" in p_j's scale value for p_i. One of the goals in this chapter will be to formulate criteria for revealing meaningful global structure contained in inter-scale comparisons as a function of the underlying scale-type. Most of the problems in inter-scale comparisons disappear when one individual (or objective measure) external to the system makes judgments about all pairs of actors in the system. Hence, our discussion will concern only the sociometric case where actors judge each other. In this case, one cannot avoid the fact that global network properties, if they exist, derive from comparing scales between actors.

We will not solve all the problems we raise in this chapter, and many of the "solutions" we do provide will be immediately recognized as corresponding to some standard practice in social network methodology. However, what we do hope to accomplish is a careful, if not painstaking, development of criteria for detecting meaningful global properties in network data that is grounded directly in measurement theory.

The first section of the chapter provides a definition of the situation that will be considered in the remainder of the chapter. For simplicity, all our analyses will concern the case of the quality of perceived friendship. Elements of basic measurement theory will be briefly reviewed, and the particular global network properties that will be tracked throughout the different scales of measurement will be described. The second section is divided into subsections according to the type of measurement assumed—dichotomous, ordinal, interval, ratio, absolute. In each case, the effort will be made to specify adequate criteria for meaningfully detecting our global properties. The third section will consider a possible prior, global hypothesis about how different actor's "cognitive structures" of friendship are interrelated. In this case, it will be possible to develop sharper criteria that bear on the global properties. Rather than detecting global properties directly from interscale comparisons, the separate scales can be used to test the adequacy of the global hypothesis itself, and, if satisfied, the underlying structure will reveal the global properties indirectly.

1. Preliminaries

In the next few sections, it will be assumed that each of n people in a set of actors P evaluate each of the other $n - 1$ actors on the degree to which they feel friendship toward them. Each person $p_i \in P$ will be assumed to have some cognitive structure[1] of friendship C_i, and this structure, as well as the group experimental instructions, are assumed to determine a unidimensional quantity m_{ij}, for all $1 \leq i \neq j \leq n$, where m_{ij} is a measurement, or scale value, of i's friendship directed toward j. Throughout, we assume that the m_{ij} values are arranged in the matrix $\mathbf{M} = (m_{ij})_{n \times n}$, where the diagonal cells m_{ii} are not of interest and are usually set at the arbitrary value zero. Quite frequently the person indices i, j, k, etc. will crop up without quantification, and, unless otherwise mentioned, they are assumed to be *distinct* and selected from the first n integers. Our working hypothesis is that friendship provides a prototype of a variety of affective qualities and that our results will apply to sociometric data on a variety of other network qualities.

For each level of measurement underlying $\mathbf{M}$, we will concern our-selves with three properties of friendship each of which is global in that it relates to transpersonal properties of friendship, and hence represents a group-level or sociological property, as opposed to an individual or psycho-logical property. The first global property of friendship, T_1, concerns the degree to which friendship is propagated in the group. Intuitively the idea of propagation is represented in the statement "a friend of a friend is a friend," i.e., if p_j is a friend of p_i and p_k is a friend of p_j, then p_k should be a friend of p_i. This property will be called chaining.

The second property, T_2, concerns the degree to which friendship is reciprocated in the group. Intuitively the idea of reciprocation is that p_j is a friend of p_i if and only if p_i is a friend of p_j.

The third global property of friendship that we will consider, T_3, concerns the detection of friendship cliques within the group. Intuitively a

---

[1] Throughout the paper I refer to an individual's "cognitive structure" of friendship. This is a convenient term to imply that a person's judgments of their friendship towards others depend on processes within their own head. However, I am not advocating any particular cognitive model nor do I mean to imply that an understanding of friendship judgments must necessarily be based on a cognitive model.

clique is a subset A of P such that every pair of people in A are friends with each other and that A is maximal with respect to this property.

The properties of chaining (T_1), reciprocation (T_2), and clique detection (T_3) are typical of the global properties investigated by network methodologists and several formal definitions for them already exist in the network literature. Our focus here is on individual actor scaling of friendship and, from this perspective, we attempt to develop reasonable formal criteria for T_1, T_2, and T_3. The issue is not to provide alternative network definitions of these properties, but rather, to relate the formal requirements of a global property such as T_1, T_2, and T_3 to the underlying individual actor scales.

In the next few sections, a variety of measurement scales will be discussed. Our view of a measurement scale is similar to that originally espoused by Stevens (1946) and considerably refined in the literature on foundations of measurement (see Suppes and Zinnes, 1963; Krantz, Luce, Suppes, and Tversky, 1971; Roberts, 1979; or for an introduction, Coombs, Dawes, and Tversky, 1970, Ch. 2; or Roberts, 1976, Ch. 8). The basic idea is that each type of measurement scale can be characterized by the class of transformations of scale values that preserve the meaningful structure in the scale values as invariants. For example, if one has an ordinal scale, then any monotonically increasing transformation of the scale values is valid because it preserves the ordering of objects on the scale, which is all the meaningful information that is provided in the first place.

The main contribution of the foundations of measurement literature is to provide a number of qualitative axiom schemes, each of which has the following two properties. First, a *representation theorem* is proved, that is, the sorts of quantitative numerical structures that are isomorphic (or homomorphic) to the particular empirical system under investigation are specified. Second, given two isomorphic numerical structures for any given empirical structure, a *uniqueness theorem* is proved which states the necessary quantitative relationship between the two representing numerical structures. These necessary relationships between alternative numerical systems provide the scale-type of the underlying scale of measurement axiomatized in the qualitative structure. The axiomatic approach is particularly suited for scaling affective qualities like friendship, because the axioms can be tested with data and if the tests prove positive, one can rest confidently in the knowledge that their scale really is of the type specified in the appropriate uniqueness theorem.

One of the central concerns in foundations of measurement is to provide the conditions under which a proposition concerning numerical scales is "meaningful." The main criterion for such a proposition to be meaningful is that its truth or falsity remains unchanged if every scale involved is replaced by another (equally) permissible scale[2] (see Luce, 1978, Roberts, 1976, pp. 489-502 or Suppes and Zinnes, 1963, pp. 64-74). To illustrate, suppose we regard temperature as on an interval scale. This means, for example, that if a set of n systems, S_1, S_2, ..., S_n, receives temperature measurements t_1, t_2, ..., t_n, respectively, on a valid scale of temperature, and t'_1, t'_2, ..., t'_n, respectively, constitute another valid scaling of the same n systems, then there must be constants a > 0 and b such that $t'_i = at_i + b$, for $1 \leq i \leq n$. Suppose we consider the proposition that system S_1 has twice the temperature of system S_2. It is easy to show that this statement is *not* meaningful. For example, pick a = 1 and b = 1 so that $t'_1 = t_1 + 1$ and $t'_2 = t_2 + 1$, then if $2t_1 = t_2$, we have $2t'_1 = 2(t_1 + 1) = t_2 + 2 \neq t'_2$, as required for meaningfulness.

For another example (due to Roberts, 1979, p. 82), suppose each of n raters give a ratio scale measurement of the "beauty" of each of two paintings, a and b . Let r_{ia} and r_{ib} be the ratings of the ith rater. Consider the proposition that the arithmetic mean of the ratings of painting a is greater than the arithmetic mean of the ratings of painting b. This proposition can be represented by the equation

$$\frac{1}{n}\sum_{i=1}^{n} r_{ia} > \frac{1}{n}\sum_{i=1}^{n} r_{ib}.$$

This proposition is not meaningful. For example, suppose n = 2 and $r_{1a} = 3$, $r_{2a} = 1$, $r_{1b} = 1$, and $r_{2b} = 2$. Then, the proposition is true since the average of the ratings for a is 2, and this number exceeds the average of the ratings to b,

---

[2] The rationale for the importance of formulating meaningful propositions about data has its roots in the philosophy of science. It can be argued that one of the aims of a science is to formulate truths about the empirical world that are general and not based on "accidental" or "occasional" aspects of empirical data. If a set of data has several equally permissible numerical representations, one seeks to avoid formulating truths that depend on any particular (arbitrary) representation of the data. It should be mentioned that the proper definition of meaningfulness for measurement is, itself, currently being debated. The one offered in this chapter may not be the most suitable; however, it is adequate for our purposes.

namely, 1.5. Now, suppose rater 2 changes his unit by a factor of 3 so that $r'_{2a} = 3$ and $r'_{2b} = 6$. Assume that rater 1's unit remains fixed, then the average of the ratings to a is now 3 and the average for b becomes 3.5; hence the proposition is now false.

A meaningful proposition in the preceeding case is that the geometric mean of the ratings to painting a is greater than the geometric mean for painting b. Stated mathematically, this proposition becomes

$$\sqrt[n]{\prod_{i=1}^{n} r_{ia}} > \sqrt[n]{\prod_{i=1}^{n} r_{ib}}\,.$$

To see that the above inequality is preserved under valid scale transformations, suppose that rater i's scale is changed by a similarity transformation $\alpha_i > 0$ so that the new scale is $r'_{ix} = \alpha_i r_{ix}$, where $i = 1, 2, \ldots, n$ and x is either a or b. Then

$$\sqrt[n]{\prod_{i=1}^{n} r'_{ia}} = \sqrt[n]{\prod_{i=1}^{n} \alpha_i} \sqrt[n]{\prod_{i=1}^{n} r_{ia}} > \sqrt[n]{\prod_{i=1}^{n} \alpha_i} \sqrt[n]{\prod_{i=1}^{n} r_{ib}} = \sqrt[n]{\prod_{i=1}^{n} r'_{ib}}\,,$$

hence the proposition is meaningful.

To adapt these concepts to our problem, assume that, for every $p_i \in P$, there is a set Φ_i of functions from the reals to the reals so that if $\langle m_{ij} \rangle_{j=1}^{n}$ is a permissible scale of p_i's friendship structure and if $\phi_i \in \Phi_i$, then $\langle \phi_i(m_{ij}) \rangle_{j=1}^{n}$ is also a permissible scale. In most of the work to follow, Φ_i will correspond to one of the usual scale-types, ordinal, ratio, etc. Global propositions about friendship may depend on all of the m_{ij}, $i \neq j$, in **M**, and in order for such a proposition to be meaningful, its truth (or falsity) must remain invariant under permissible rescalings of **M**. Since this notion is central to this chapter, we capture it in the next definition.

Definition 1. Suppose $\mathbf{M} = (m_{ij})_{n \times n}$ represents a scaling of friendship in P, where for all $p_i, p_j \in P$, m_{ij} is actor p_i's scale value of friendship toward actor p_j, and let Φ_i represent the permissible rescalings of p_i's friendship scale. Let S be a proposition whose truth (or falsity) depends, possibly, on all of the m_{ij}, with $i \neq j$. Then, S is said to be *meaningful* if for any set $\phi_i \in \Phi_i$, $1 \leq i \leq n$, its truth (or falsity) remains unchanged when each m_{ij} is replaced by $\phi_i(m_{ij})$.

In Sections 2 and 3, we will seek propositions corresponding to our global properties of chaining, reciprocation, and clique detection whose truth value is invariant under permissible changes of each actor's scale of friendship. Definition 1 is a strong criterion, so intuitively we expect it to place considerable restrictions on the sorts of meaningful interscale propositions that relate to our global properties.

For the scale-types discussed here, one can differentiate between nonprobabilistic[3] and probabilistic versions. The probabilistic versions assume that the underlying scale is of a fixed type but that object scale values themselves may change randomly from one scaling to the next. In the probabilistic case, meaningfulness does not require that the truth of a statement remains invariant between alternative sets of scale values obtained at different time points. In this case, the randomness of the scale values may render a statement true at one time and false at another. Rather, the invariance required for meaningfulness must hold for rescalings of a particular, fixed sample of scale values, i.e., a permissible change in the measurement scale itself. However, if the friendship structure is assumed to be unchanged over a period of time, it will be natural to suppose that we have several independent scalings and use these samples to estimate underlying, fixed parameters of the probabilistic process. This chapter will not concern itself in detail with particular probabilistic laws; however, it will be shown how one often can treat the probabilistic case as a special case of a nonprobabilistic case—usually with a stronger level of measurement. Thus,

---

[3] It is sometimes argued that work in the foundations of measurement overemphasizes algebraic or deterministic assumptions; whereas, real data, at least in the social sciences, has a random component and hence is fallible. Consequently, so the argument goes, foundational work based on error-free data assumptions has little or no practical value for social science. I think this argument is shortsighted. The rationale for considering error-free data follows a tradition in philosophical analysis designed to establish how to think correctly about ideal cases first. The hope is that if one can think clearly in the error-free cases, then the approach to handling fallible data will be on better grounding. One can think of most of the situations analyzed in this paper as ideal ones, that is, ones that would occur if nature were kind enough to supply us with errorless data. Whether or not the exercise of considering meaningfulness in such ideal cases will aid in the development of better grounded network methods in the future remains to be seen. Suffice it to say, such an approach has registered successes in a number of other sciences such as economics, physics, and psychology.

the main emphasis of the paper is on ideal, error-free data, and most of the results are contained in the sections that avoid probabilistic considerations.

2.1. Dichotomous Scales

Perhaps the simplest underlying cognitive structure of friendship perception is the case where each actor $p_i \in P$ has an unordered, fixed subset, $F_i \subseteq P - \{p_i\}$, of members of P that actor p_i feels friendship towards. In this case, if data permit the determination of the F_i, it is easy to characterize the **M** matrix, namely

$$m_{ij} = \begin{cases} 1 \text{ if } p_j \in F_i \\ 0 \text{ otherwise.} \end{cases}$$

Property T_1 (chaining) can be characterized by the condition that $m_{ij} = 1$ and $m_{jk} = 1$ implies $m_{ik} = 1$ (transitivity). Property T_2 (recipro - cation) is characterized by the condition that $m_{ij} = 1$ if and only if $m_{ji} = 1$ (symmetry). Property T_3 (clique detection) is accomplished in a strong form by a search for maximal subsets $A \subseteq P$ satisfying the property that, for all $p_i, p_j \in A$, $m_{ij} = 1$. In such a case, A is a maximal, completely connected subgraph of the graph corresponding to **M**.

It should be noted that all three conditions in the preceding paragraph are of a standard graph-theoretic character, and that other, weaker graph-theoretic conditions for the properties have been formulated in the literature. From the measurement-theoretic perspective developed in this chapter, the optimal approach to data collection in the case of a nonprobabilistic dichotomy would be one that maximizes the likelihood that each actor p would produce his or her entire list F_i. In this case, the data will provide two ordered indicators of friendship, and all the meaningful information in the scaling is retained in the 1-0 matrix **M**. Since permissible rescalings leave the derived **M** invariant, it follows immediately that the global properties of the preceding paragraph are meaningful from the point of view of Definition 1.

If the data provide only subsets of F_i, then it is necessary to propose a model for how the obtained m_{ij} values derive from F_i. In this case the graph-theoretic definitions, at least the strong ones, would not suffice for manifest data, and some model of how actors' pick reported subsets of their friends would be necessary to formulate before meaningful conditions for representing properties T_1, T_2, and T_3 could be developed. In the case where actors are only allowed to report their top k-friends, Holland and Leinhardt (1973) have provided such criteria based on tabulations of various triad frequencies. However, in Holland and Leinhart's work, the dichotomous data produced by a subject is based on a probabilistic sampling model and therefore is relevant to the next section.

2.2. Probabilistic Dichotomous Scales

In this case, we suppose that at any instant each actor p_i has a subset of perceived friends $F_i \subseteq P - \{p_i\}$; however, this set is assumed to vary probabilistically from time to time. The **M** matrix can be characterized as having elements m_{ij}, where m_{ij} is one if person p_i includes p_j in set F_i at a given random time point, otherwise $m_{ij} = 0$.

If one only had dichotomous data at one time point, one could mean - ingfully use the graph-theoretic definitions of the previous subsection to formulate properties T_1, T_2, T_3. However, because of the underlying probabilistic process and the strictness of the previous algebraic conditions, one would expect such properties as transitivity and symmetry of **M** to be rare occurrences.

Assuming no systematic variations in underlying tendencies over time, as well as independence from sample to sample, there is an underlying matrix of probabilities, $Q = (q_{ij})_{n \times n}$, where $q_{ij} = \Pr(M_{ij} = 1)$. By repeated sampling, one could collect empirical estimates of these probabilities q_{ij} by observing the proportion of times actor p_i included actor p_j in his or her list of friends. These empirical proportions can be arrayed in a new matrix **M'**, which is a better data structure to analyze than the initial one with just dichotomous scales, at least for our present purposes. In the general case, the m_{ij}'s are constrained only by rule $0 \leq m_{ij} \leq 1$ (with $m_{ii} = 0$ by convention); although additional assumptions relating interactor scales (see Section 3) may place greater restrictions on the m_{ij} values. In any case, the m_{ij} probabilistic values constitute an absolute scale of friendship. Such scales are taken up in Section 2.7. In this section, only conditions that relate to the probabilistic interpretation of the scale values will be offered.

Property T_1 (chaining) presents us with several natural conditions all capturing the notion that if m_{ij} and m_{jk} are sufficiently large then so too is m_{ik}. Coombs (1964, p. 106) lists three precise versions of the preceding idea that go by the name of stochastic transitivity conditions and are popular throughout the probabilistic choice literature (see Luce and Suppes, 1965). The next definition adapts these definitions to our situation.

Definition 2. Let the $n \times n$ matrix M have terms m_{ij} equal to the proportion of times that person p_i indicates friendship toward person p_j. Then for all distinct indices $1 \le i, j, k \le n$, M is said to satisfy:

(1) *Weak stochastic transitivity* in case $m_{ij} \ge .5$ and $m_{jk} \ge .5$ implies $m_{ik} \ge .5$;

(2) *Moderate stochastic transitivity* in case $m_{ij} \ge .5$ and $m_{jk} \ge .5$ implies $m_{ik} \ge \min(m_{ij}, m_{jk})$;

(3) *Strong stochastic transitivity* in case $m_{ij} \ge .5$ and $m_{jk} \ge .5$ implies $m_{ik} \ge \max(m_{ij}, m_{jk})$.

Clearly (3) implies (2) and (2) implies (1) in the preceding definition. The choice about which condition to adopt would depend on the assumed underlying structure of friendship judgments as well as the probabilistic sampling model.

In the current case, property T_2 (reciprocation) and property T_3 (clique detection) can be formalized in a strong way; however, these definitions are developed in Section 2.5. Because of the probabilistic interpretation of the m_{ij} values, it would make sense to use a .5 threshold in the Section 2.5 conditions.

From the perspective being developed in this chapter, when dealing with a probabilistic dichotomy, effort should be made to collect network data from several different time periods in order to obtain estimates of the m_{ij}'s. Once these estimates are obtained, they can be treated as estimates of values on an absolute scale. In the case of an absolute scale, Section 2.7 discusses criteria for the global properties. The statistical interpretation of the m_{ij} values in this case may motivate other, more testable, criteria for the properties; however, such developments do not fall within the coverage of this chapter.

2.3   Ordinal Scales

In the simplest version, we suppose that each actor p_i's friendship judgments result in an ordering of values (no ties) of the other $n - 1$ actors. The **M** matrix can be meaningfully transformed to ranks and characterized by the condition that m_{ij} is person p_j's rank on p_i's order-1 for top friend, 2 for next best, etc. (set $m_{ii} = 0$ by convention).   Statements involving interscale comparisons are meaningful by our criterion only if they are meaningful on the rank data.   In other words, the truth (or falsity) of a proposition that mentions only the rank numbers is invariant under permissible ordinal scale transformations.

Consider property T_1 (chaining). It holds to the degree that if p_j is low on p_i's list (gets a low number indicating a high degree of friendship) and p_k is low on p_j's list, then p_k should be low on p_i's list. In terms of the matrix **M**, if m_{ij} is small and m_{jk} is small, then m_{ik} is small.

One idea that needs sharpening is the criterion for being low. If we pick an arbitrary criterion c, $1 \leq c \leq n - 1$, then we might meaningfully say that **M** satisfies property T_1 with criterion c in case $m_{ij} \leq c$ and $m_{jk} \leq c$ implies that $m_{ik} \leq c$. To illustrate this concept, suppose that there are $n = 4$ actors with matrix **M** given by

$$\mathbf{M} = \begin{array}{c} \\ p_1 \\ p_2 \\ p_3 \\ p_4 \end{array} \begin{array}{cccc} p_1 & p_2 & p_3 & p_4 \\ \left[\begin{array}{cccc} 0 & 1 & 2 & 3 \\ 1 & 0 & 2 & 3 \\ 2 & 3 & 0 & 1 \\ 3 & 2 & 1 & 0 \end{array}\right] \end{array},$$

then it is easy to verify that property T_1 holds for criteria $c = 1$ and $c = 3$; however, it fails for $c = 2$ because $m_{43} \leq 2$ and $m_{31} \leq 2$ yet $m_{41} = 3$.

Since the value of c seems arbitrary, it is natural to investigate a stronger condition; namely, M is said to be *0-transitive* in case, for all $1 \leq c \leq n - 1$, $m_{ij} \leq c$ and $m_{jk} \leq c$ implies $m_{ik} \leq c$. The rationale for calling this property 0-transitivity will follow shortly. For now, however, the next theorem shows that for $n \geq 3$, 0-transitivity *cannot* hold. This somewhat surprising result frustrates our efforts to capture property T_1 in a straightforward way.

Theorem 1. For all $n \geq 3$, any matrix M of friendship rankings for n actors violates 0-transitivity.

Proof: Assume $n = 3$ and consider the matrix $M = (m_{ij})_{3 \times 3}$. Without loss of generality we can assume $m_{12} = 1$ and, of course, $m_{13} = 2$. For 0-transitivity to hold, we must have $m_{23} = 2$, since otherwise we could pick $c = 1$ and $m_{12} \leq 1$ and $m_{23} \leq 1$ but $m_{13} = 2$ violating 0-transitivity. Since $m_{23} = 2$ we have $m_{21} = 1$. Now either $m_{31} = 1$ and $m_{32} = 2$ or $m_{31} = 2$ and $m_{32} = 1$. If $m_{31} = 1$, since $m_{12} = 1$ we must have $m_{32} = 1$ which contradicts $m_{32} = 2$. If $m_{31} = 2$, since $m_{32} = 1$ and $m_{21} = 1$ we must have $m_{31} = 1$ which is a contradiction. Thus if $n = 3$, 0-transitivity cannot hold.

Suppose $n > 3$ and without loss of generality $m_{12} = 1$, $m_{13} = 2$, and $m_{1i} > 2$, for $i > 3$. Now $m_{2i} > 2$ (and $m_{3i} > 2$) or else $m_{2i} \leq 2$ and $m_{12} \leq 2$ would compel $m_{1i} \leq 2$ by 0-transitivity. Thus $m_{21}, m_{23}, m_{31}, m_{32} \leq 2$. As shown above, no assignments of these four values is possible. ♦

Rephrasing theorem 1, given a matrix M based on more than two actors, there is always at least one criterion $1 \leq c \leq n - 1$ that violates 0-transitivity. For property T_1 to hold for all criteria c, it would be necessary that, for all distinct indices i, j, k, $m_{ik} \leq \max\{m_{ij}, m_{jk}\}$, which is a form of the ultrametric inequality (Johnson, 1967). This inequality is well known to require lots of tied m-values; however, the requirement of a strict ordering on each actor's scale means that no ties within any row of M are allowed, and this restriction on ties is enough to reject the inequality needed for 0-transitivity.

It is possible to weaken 0-transitivity in a productive way as is done in the next definition.

Definition 3. Let n actors each rank the other $n - 1$ actors in order of their friendship—1 for best friend, 2 for next best, etc. For all distinct indices $1 \leq i, j, k \leq n$, let the orders be represented in the $n \times n$ matrix $M = (m_{ij})_{n \times n}$, where m_{ij} is p_j's order in p_i's list ($m_{ii} = 0$). Then M is said to manifest d-transitivity, for $0 \leq d \leq n$, in case for all $1 \leq c \leq n$, $m_{ij} \leq c$ and $m_{jk} \leq c$ implies $m_{ik} \leq c + d$.

Theorem 2. For all $n \geq 3$, there exists a matrix M which satisfies 1-transitivity.

Proof: Suppose that the actors are linearly ordered in "absolute attractiveness" in such a way that for each person i and indices $j \neq i$ and $k \neq i$, $m_{ij} < m_{ik}$ if and only if $j < k$. We need to show that for all $1 \leq c < n$, $m_{ij} \leq c$ and $m_{jk} \leq c$ implies $m_{ik} \leq c + 1$. By construction, for all distinct indices $1 \leq s, t \leq n$,

$$m_{st} = \begin{cases} t - 1 & \text{if } s < t, \\ t & \text{if } t < s. \end{cases}$$

From the preceding fact, it follows that $m_{ik} \leq m_{jk} + 1$ so if $m_{ij} \leq c$ and $m_{jk} \leq c$, we have $m_{ik} \leq c + 1$ as required.   ♦

The preceding definition and two theorems suggest that if we had the matrix M, a test of the property T_1 could proceed in a natural way. First one could obtain for M the smallest d for which d-transitivity holds. Since $(n - 1)$-transitivity must hold, such a smallest d must exist. One measure of the degree to which the property holds would be to refer the observed d_{min} to a distribution of d_{min} obtained by considering all possible M matrices of order n. While we will not develop the distribution of d_{min} for various n in this chapter, the route to obtaining them by Monte Carlo or possibly combi - natorial methods, though possibly tedious, should be straightforward.

The alternative to testing our property more in tune with contemporary network methodology would be to impose some task instruction on the set of people leading to dichotomous choices and try to see if the resulting directed graph of the friendship relation could be analyzed structurally for some version of property T_1. However, it should be clear that a lot of information about each subject's rank order is lost in obtaining the dichotomous network data. Particularly unfortunate would be the case where the instruction resulted in different people selecting different criteria to include friends (see Section 3.1). In such a case 1-transitivity might hold at the ordinal level but transitivity, itself, might be strikingly absent in the directed graph.

What is being suggested from this example is that if the property under consideration is considered of primary importance and if one believes that the underlying judgmental process fits the current (ordinal) case, then more work in data collection designed to reveal each subject's friendship ordering would be more worthwhile than the development and implementation of high powered network methods that apply to the impoverished network data themselves.

Next consider property T_2 that friendship is reciprocated. Reciprocity is easy to define in the case of our ordinal scale; namely, $m_{ij} = m_{ji}$, i.e., p_j's rank on p_i's list is the same as p_i's rank on p_j's list. However surprisingly, strict reciprocity can *not* hold when there are an odd number of actors in the set P. To see this, suppose that there are $2n + 1$ actors for some positive integer n. Consider only the top choices of each actor. If these are reciprocated, there must be n pairs of mutual top choices; however, in such a case someone must be left over whose top choice is not reciprocated.

Complete reciprocity is possible for some sets P as the following **M** based on $n = 6$ illustrates:

$$
\mathbf{M} = \begin{array}{c} \\ p_1 \\ p_2 \\ p_3 \\ p_4 \\ p_5 \\ p_6 \end{array}
\begin{array}{c} \begin{array}{cccccc} p_1 & p_2 & p_3 & p_4 & p_5 & p_6 \end{array} \\
\left[\begin{array}{cccccc}
0 & 1 & 2 & 3 & 4 & 5 \\
1 & 0 & 4 & 5 & 3 & 2 \\
2 & 4 & 0 & 1 & 5 & 3 \\
3 & 5 & 1 & 0 & 2 & 4 \\
4 & 3 & 5 & 2 & 0 & 1 \\
5 & 2 & 3 & 4 & 1 & 0
\end{array} \right] \end{array}.
$$

To properly motivate a weakened condition for property T_2 in the spirit of Definition 3 would require some work on the combinatorial possibilities of nearly reciprocal **M** matrices for arbitrary n. In particular, strict reciprocity appears in many cases to be incompatible with d-transitivity for small d. For example, in the matrix above, $m_{12} = 1$ and $m_{26} = 2$; however, $m_{16} = 5$. In fact, in the linear ordering case, discussed earlier, where 1-transitivity holds in **M**, reciprocity is strikingly absent. Considerable empirical work with $n = 4$ and $n = 6$ has led me to conclude that this example is no accident and that strict reciprocity places some constraints on **M** that considerably constrain the possibilities for d-transitivity for reasonably small d. Further analysis of the apparent chaining reciprocity trade-off seems quite interesting, but will have to await another time.

Property T_3 (clique detection) appears easy enough to state informally in the current case. Essentially, one seeks maximal subsets $A \subseteq P$ where, for all p_i, $p_j \in A$, m_{ij} is small. However, formalizing this condition in a productive way proves to be a difficult one in the case of ordinal data for reasons of the sort indicated in the last paragraph. It is possible to make progress in defining conditions for global properties with ordinal data if additional assumptions are made relating the various actor's cognitive structures (see Section 3). However, in the absence of such assumptions, the problem of developing both useful and meaningful conditions for properties T_1, T_2, and T_3 for individual subject ordinal data seems quite complex.

It might reasonably be argued that the difficulties in this case are arising because ties in the ordering are not permitted. In the case where the friendship scale is ordinal with only several possible values, perhaps the formulations of conditions would be facilitated. Winship (1977) presents one possible model of the friendship situation which combines ordinal assumptions on a small set of possible friendship evaluations with a non-additive, binary combining operation on that set. Based on his structure, reasonable definitions corresponding to properties T_1, T_2, and T_3 are provided. Winship's structure may provide an interesting new scale-type for measurement theory; however, it has yet to be investigated as an individual subject scaling tool.

As a possible subject for future work, it should be noted that there are several other algebraic ordinal scaling models that permit ties that are discussed in the foundation of measurement literature. These are the *quasi-series* and the *semiorder* (see Suppes and Zinnes, 1963). The quasi-series is an ordinal scale where there can be an equivalence class of mutually tied objects at any point on the scale. The axioms for a quasi-series adapted to our case are presented in the next definition.

Definition 4. Let P be a set of n actors and, for each $p_i \in$ P, let I_i and R_i be binary relations on the set $P - \{p_i\}$. Then the relational systems $a_i = \langle P - \{p_i\}; I_i, R_i \rangle$ form quasi-series in case, for all distinct j, $k \neq i$, the following three axioms hold:

1) I_i is an equivalence relation.
2) R_i is a transitive relation.
3)   Exactly one of the following holds: $p_j R_i p_k$, $p_k R_i p_j$, $p_j I_i p_k$.

If Definition 4 holds for a set of actors, then it is easy to construct (see Suppes and Zinnes, 1963, pp. 23-29), for all $p_i \in$ P, individual subject ordinal scales

$$f_i: P - \{p_i\} \to \text{reals}$$

such that, for all j, $k \neq i$, $p_j R_i p_k$ if and only if $f_i(p_j) < f_i(p_k)$ and $p_j I_i p_k$ if and only if $f_i(p_j) = f_i(p_k)$.

If the axioms for a quasi-series were jointly met by all actors in P, then the resulting ordinal scales could be transformed to rank numbers allowing ties. It is a reasonable project for future analysis to see if such a scheme would support more natural conditions for defining global properties than afforded by our initial model with no ties.

A second, somewhat more psychologically motivated ordinal model for dealing with ties is the semiorder. It has received much attention in the foundations of measurement literature (Luce, 1956; Suppes and Zinnes, 1963; Coombs, Dawes, and Tversky, 1970). The idea behind a semiorder is that a given subject will not show a preference for one object over another unless the difference is sufficiently perceivable. The idea is adapted to our friendship example in the following definition.

Definition 5. Let P be a set of n actors and, for each $p_i \in$ P, let R_i be a binary relation on $P - \{p_i\}$. Then the structures $a_i = \langle P - \{p_i\}, R_i \rangle$ form friendship semiorders in case the following three axioms hold for all p_j, p_k, p_ℓ, $p_m \in P - \{p_i\}$:

1)   Not $p_j R_i p_j$.
2)   If $p_j R_i p_k$ and $p_\ell R_i p_m$, then either $p_j R_i p_m$ or $p_\ell R_i p_k$.
3)   If $p_j R_i p_k$ and $p_k R_i p_\ell$ then either $p_j R_i p_m$ or $p_m R_i p_\ell$.

The intended interpretation of the relation R_i is that $p_j R_i p_k$ in case p_i judges his or her degree of friendship to p_j strictly greater than his or her degree toward p_k. The axiom system is powerful enough to lead to an interesting representation theorem as follows.

Theorem 3. Let P be a set of n actors and for $p_i \in P$ suppose $a_i = \langle P - \{p_i\}, R_i \rangle$ satisfies the semiorder axioms of Definition 5. Then there exists positive constants d_i and functions f_i from $P - \{p_i\}$ into the positive real numbers so that for all $p_j, p_k \in P - \{p_i\}$,

$$p_j R_i p_k \text{ if and only if } f_i(p_j) < f_i(p_k) + d_i.$$

The force of Theorem 3 is that a given actor p_i may not be able to directly distinguish between a pair of people on friendship even though it is possible that a complete listing of R_i supports differentiating the pair on scale value. To use the semiorder idea of scaling, it would be necessary to conduct a complete paired-comparison experiment (allowing ties) with each actor in P; however, if the three axioms of Definition 5 hold for any given actor, Suppes and Zinnes (1963, pp. 29-34) provide constructive methods for obtaining the measurement scales promised in Theorem 3. We will not develop conditions on the various actors' semiorders corresponding to properties T_1, T_2, T_3 in this paper. However, the discursion into semiorder theory reveals another facet of our measurement-theoretic perspective for network data, namely, to construct appropriate scalings of a given actor's sociometric judgmental processes on some affective quality may require data collection procedures other than simple listing or ranking typically employed in network research. In this case an ordinal-like scale is developed from the interplay of paired-comparison data and algebraic axioms.

Overall, the analysis of the individual subject ordinal scale data reveals that the problem of producing meaningful conditions for global network properties is not at all straightforward. Some of the reasons for these difficulties will become apparent in Section 3; however, the topic, itself, seems interesting enough to motivate further investigation.

2.4. *Probabilistic Ordinal Scales*

There are a number of probabilistic models in the literature that imply that paired-comparison or complete rank data on objects is probabilistic.

One of the earliest ideas was Thurstone's (1927) law of comparative judgment. Thurstone's idea was that each object to be scaled is characterized by a normally distributed random variable whose value, at any instant, represents the momentary value of the object on the scale (actually an interval scale). A choice among two objects is determined by which object receives the higher momentary value, and entire ranks are similarly determined. A related model, known as the Bradley-Terry-Luce system (see Coombs, Dawes, and Tversky, 1970 for an introduction), has been developed both for psychophysical scaling as well as preference scaling by Luce (1959, 1977) and others.

The general area of paired-comparison scaling is reviewed in Davidson and Farquhar (1976), and this approach to judgmental and preference situations involving human subjects is frequently employed in psychological literature to construct subjective scales. In this light, it seems somewhat surprising that such methods have not been used extensively in the social network area to provide data preliminary to actual network construction and analysis.

Most of the probabilistic models for paired-comparison and rank data have underlying, fixed parameters in them that correspond to each object. Such parameters can be estimated from that data and they generally are unique up to at least a linear transformation, that is, the underlying parameters constitute at least nonprobabilistic, interval-level measurement of the objects to be scaled. For this reason, the parameter estimates can be entered in the M matrix and the problem of formulating criteria for our global properties can proceed by methods to be discussed in Section 2.5. As with other probabilistic measurement situations that we describe, the particular underlying probability model may suggest sharper and more easily tested criteria for our properties than these that we provide in the relevant nonprobabilistic measurement cases.

2.5. Ratio and Interval Scales

There are a number of individual subject scaling methods that give rise to object scale values that have either ratio or interval scale properties. Some of these methods are discussed in Coombs (1964) and Torgerson (1958) and others are found throughout the literature on foundations of measurement. These methods can be divided into the so-called direct methods and the indirect methods. The direct methods, popularized by Stevens (1961), require the subjects to generate positive numbers to the stimulus objects according to some stated restrictions. One such restriction is provided by giving the subject a particular stimulus and an assigned number and then require that the other numbers be given by the subject so that ratios of these numbers with the provided number match subjective stimulus ratios on the dimension being measured. Studies have shown that in some situations subjects can reply to such instruction by producing a pattern of numbers that (approximately) preserves ratios under changes in the initial object and its assigned number. Such scaling leads to ratio level measurement.

There is also a large variety of indirect methods each of which is based on a designed choice task for each subject. For example, in Thurstone's paired-comparison scaling procedure, mentioned in Section 2.4, a subject makes repeated paired-comparison choices among the $\binom{n}{2}$ distinct pairs from n-objects leading to proportion measurements P_{ij} of the underlying proba - bility that object i is preferred to object j. These estimates are processed to yield scale values of each object on an interval scale (see Torgerson, 1958). Other methods exist that require subjects to do such things as to select which of three objects is least like the other two (one version of the method of triads), sorting objects into piles of equal intervals, and ranking pairs of pairs of objects for relative closeness, etc. Most of these indirect methods have some internal validation properties, and they provide ways to convert choice data into scale values having interval or ratio properties.

For our purposes, we suppose that some direct method of data collection has been used and that each actor in the set P provides data on the other $n - 1$ actors sufficient to construct interval or ratio scale values m_{ij} arrayed in the matrix $\mathbf{M} = (m_{ij})_{n \times n}$, where $m_{ii} = 0$. For the moment, suppose that each subject's ratings are on a ratio scale characterized by a common zero point (say for neutrality); however, we do not know each actor's unit a_i. All that can be asserted is that if the system was rescaled with possibly different units, producing a new matrix $\mathbf{M}'$, then there must exist positive constants c_i so that

$$\mathbf{M}' = \begin{bmatrix} c_1 & & & & 0 \\ & c_2 & & & \\ & & \cdot & & \\ & & & \cdot & \\ 0 & & & & c_n \end{bmatrix} \mathbf{M},$$

that is $m'_{ij} = c_i m_{ij}$.

Several actors may regard the same fixed actor as having a different value on their subjective scale (even if all actors happened to have the same unit), i.e., there is no guarantee that any two actors perceive another actor at the same subjective degree of friendship. Thus it appears that there is no natural way to compare scale values between actors. Without such interactor comparisons, it does not seem to be straightforward to formulate meaningful criteria for our global properties on the data in **M** that satisfy Definition 1 (however, see Section 2.9).

To facilitate the analysis, consider an analogy from physics. Suppose there are n laboratories, each of which has measured the mass of ℓ objects on a ratio scale and has reported scale values without reporting units. Further, suppose there is no guarantee that any pair of laboratories have scaled a common object. Obviously in such a case as this, it would not be possible to figure out any given laboratory's unit nor could we compare the different scale values between laboratories in a meaningful way.

We could make one conclusion involving the laboratories, however. Suppose each lab indexes its ℓ objects arbitrarily, and the data are provided in a matrix $\mathbf{W} = (w_{ij})_{n \times \ell}$, where w_{ij} is laboratory i's scale value for its jth object. Since each laboratory's unit is arbitrary, we could conclude that $\mathbf{W}'$ represents a valid rescaling of mass if and only if

$$\mathbf{W}' = \mathbf{CW},$$

where **C** has the form

$$
\mathbf{C} = \begin{bmatrix} c_1 & & & & 0 \\ & c_2 & & & \\ & & \cdot & & \\ & & & \cdot & \\ & & & & \cdot \\ 0 & & & & c_n \end{bmatrix},
$$

and $c_i > 0$ for all $1 \le i \le n$. Unfortunately for our analogy to friendship scaling, nothing further could be said about laboratory measurements unless the labs have measured common objects.

Accordingly, suppose each lab measured exactly one common object, say the one indexed by $j = 1$. Assuming accuracy of measurement, then we could convert all the measurements to a common scale (having the same unit) by the rescaling given by

$$W' = DW,$$

where

$$D = \begin{bmatrix} \dfrac{1}{w_{11}} & & & & 0 \\ & \dfrac{1}{w_{21}} & & & \\ & & \cdot & & \\ & & & \cdot & \\ 0 & & & & \dfrac{1}{w_{n1}} \end{bmatrix}.$$

Such a rescaling would enable us to formulate meaningful statements concerning the degree to which each of the other $\ell - 1$ objects measured in the different labs were, say, identical in mass.

Let us follow this analogy for friendship scaling. Suppose that the experimenter provided a description or story involving two hypothetical actors, say John and Jim. If the story is clear and commonly perceived by all actors in P (a rather strong assumption), then the experimenter could request a direct estimate of the value of John's friendship toward Jim on each person (p_i's) friendship scale, say the values are b_i, for $1 \leq i \leq n$. Under our assumptions, such values would permit the experimenter to rescale the original friendship matrix M to a common unit by the formula

$$M' = BM,$$

where

$$B = \begin{bmatrix} \dfrac{1}{b_1} & & & & 0 \\ & \dfrac{1}{b_2} & & & \\ & & \cdot & & \\ & & & \cdot & \\ 0 & & & & \dfrac{1}{b_n} \end{bmatrix}.$$

In this new form, we can begin to formulate meaningful conditions for assessing our global properties T_1, T_2, and T_3.

Property T_1 (chaining) means that if m_{ij} and m_{jk} are "suitably high" then also m_{ik} should be "suitably high." Since the criterion for suitably high is arbitrary, we could pick any value $c > 0$ and demand that if $m_{ij} \geq c$ and $m_{jk} \geq c$ then m_{ik} must be sufficiently large, say, $m_{ik} \geq f(c)$, where $f(c)$ provides the chaining threshold. However, it is not clear what the function $f(c)$ should be.

Many network methods require that the input data be dichotomized. This is easily accomplished by defining a network matrix

$$\mathbf{X}(c) = (x_{ij})_{n \times n},$$

where

$$x_{ij} = \begin{cases} 1 \text{ if } m_{ij} \geq c \\ 0 \text{ otherwise.} \end{cases}$$

In the graph underlying $\mathbf{X}(c)$, chaining would correspond to transitivity, i.e., if $x_{ij} = 1$ and $x_{jk} = 1$ then $x_{ik} = 1$, and this condition translates to the requirement that if $m_{ij} \geq c$ and $m_{jk} \geq c$ then $m_{ik} \geq c$. By a simple argument presented in Section 2.3, if $\mathbf{X}(c)$ is to be transitive for all values of $c \geq 0$, we must have the ultrametric inequality, namely, for all distinct indices i, j, and k, $m_{ik} \geq \min(m_{ij}, m_{jk})$ (note in this section large values of m_{ij} correspond to high degrees of friendship so the ultrametric inequality has changed from its form in Section 2.3). This condition leads naturally to the requirement that $f(c) = c$.

Unfortunately, as we have remarked earlier for the ultrametric inequality, for a matrix $\mathbf{M}'$ to satisfy our chaining condition with $f(c) = c$, there must be a large number of tied values in $\mathbf{M}'$. Since there seems no reason why different actors would yield ratio estimates of friendship which are equal to each other, the criterion on chaining given by $f(c) = c$ seems too strong. The next definition weakens the criterion.

Definition 6. Suppose each of n actors provides ratio scale values of their friendship toward the other n − 1 actors and these quantities are arrayed in the matrix $\mathbf{M} = (m_{ij})_{n \times n}$ (with $m_{ii} = 0$ set arbitrarily). Suppose the scale values are transformed to a scale with a common unit and arrayed in the matrix $\mathbf{M}' = (m'_{ij})_{n \times n}$. Then $\mathbf{M}'$ is said to manifest d-transitivity for nonnegative d in case, for all $c \geq 0$ and all distinct indices $1 \leq i, j, k \leq n$, $m'_{ij} \geq c$ and $m'_{jk} \geq c$ implies $m'_{ik} \geq c - d$.

Definition 6 corresponds to picking the criterion function $f(c) = c - d$. While there is no natural choice for d, it is possible to measure the degree of chaining in $\mathbf{M}$ by the quantity d_{min} which is the smallest d such that $\mathbf{M}'$ satisfies d-transitivity. A referent distribution for d_{min} could be obtained by calculating d_{min} for all combinations of permutations of the scale values in each of the rows in $\mathbf{M}'$. In Section 3, we will assume something about the underlying common structure of friendship, and these assumptions will permit a sharper criterion for chaining.

Property T_2 (reciprocity) is easy to handle in the current case; namely, we can say that $\mathbf{M}'$ manifests reciprocity at threshold $c > 0$ in case $m'_{ij} \geq c$ if and only if $m'_{ji} \geq c$. For this condition to hold for all $c > 0$, it would be necessary that $m'_{ij} = m'_{ji}$ which seems to be a very strong demand in the case of interval or ratio measurement. A more relaxed criterion is provided in the next definition.

    Definition 7. Under the conditions of Definition 5, $\mathbf{M}'$ is said to manifest d-symmetry, for nonnegative d, in case for all $1 \leq i, j \leq n$, $|m'_{ij} - m'_{ji}| \leq d$.

While there is no natural value to set equal to d, we can make the same move as we did for property T_1, that is, given $\mathbf{M}'$ we could compute the smallest value of d, namely d_{min}, for which $\mathbf{M}'$ manifests d-symmetry. A referent distribution for d_{min} can be provided in the same way as was suggested for the case of d-transitivity.

Property T_3 (clique detection) is accomplished in the next definition.

Definition 8. Under the conditions of Definition 5, a set $A \subseteq P$ is a c-clique in case it is maximal with respect to the property that for all distinct $p_i, p_j \in A, m'_{ij} \geq c$.

The approach to clique detection in Definition 8 is rather usual and has the wise property that if **M'** is dichotomized by threshold c, then its c-cliques correspond to those that graph-theory specifies, namely, maximal completely connected subgraphs of actors. Standard ways to weaken Definition 8 are easily produced to correspond to standard network concepts leading to weaker criteria for defining cliques and clusters in a directed graph.

Thus far, we have been dealing with ratio scaling. In the case of interval scaling, it would be necessary to transform the original **M** matrix so that each actor's scale had both a common origin and a common unit. One way to seek an additional constraint might be to read a story about several hypothetical actors where two of them, say, Frank and George were never implicated, directly or indirectly, in a friendship context. Each actor p_i could be asked to rate Frank's friendship for George on the same scale as they rated the other actors providing the value e_i. These e_i values could be combined with the previously obtained b_i values, and the transformed matrix **M'** can be obtained by the formula

$$
\mathbf{M'} = \begin{bmatrix} \frac{1}{b_1} & & & 0 \\ & \frac{1}{b_2} & & \\ & & \ddots & \\ 0 & & & \frac{1}{b_n} \end{bmatrix} \bullet \mathbf{M} - \begin{bmatrix} e_1 \\ e_2 \\ \vdots \\ e_n \end{bmatrix} \bullet \mathbf{U}
$$

to yield a common scaling for all subjects, where **U** is an n-dimensional row vector of ones. Then the same criteria for properties T_1, T_2, and T_3 as developed for ratio scaling could be applied to the transformed matrix **M'**.

In conclusion, ratio or interval scaling of individual actor's sociometric friendship choices do not provide raw data in **M** from which conditions of inter-actor friendship properties can be meaningfully formulated. Some technique for constraining the actors' data to a common scale seems required. The suggestion of providing stories about hypothetical people seems one way to provide data that can be used to transform **M** to a common scale. The suggestion is in the spirit of Steven's direct scaling techniques. Another possibility for analyzing the data is provided in Section 2.9; however, our point here is that it doesn't make sense to transform **M** directly to a directed graph without serious concern with the possibility that different actors have used different units and/or origins for their scale. "Successful" network analyses for this case that have not dealt with these constraints have probably used data that were collected in such a way that the actors implicitly selected common units and origins for their scale. Another, less satisfactory, possibility is that they have "discovered" substantively meaningless global structure in their network data.

2.6. *Probabilistic Ratio and Interval Scales*

It is possible to imagine that each actor's scale is ratio or interval in character with the property that the actual scale values vary from time to time according to some probabilistic law. One way to realize this would be to develop a probabilistic process for selection of the zero point and unit value on the scale. However, I do not know of any applications of this idea in the scaling literature.

A more natural way that the probabilistic case could be realized would be if the scale itself were, say, interval but the particular values of a given object could vary from time to time. For example, suppose friendship were an interval scale but the particular value of p_j on p_i's scale might vary depending on recent events concerning their social interaction. To realize such a situation formally one would have to specify a class of probability models that governs such random variation in scale values. In most cases that I can imagine, the underlying model would have object parameter values that are fixed in value and could be regarded as at least having interval scale properties. Consequently, if the **M** matrix were composed of estimates of these parameter values, the various nonprobabilistic subsections of Section 2.5 would cover these cases. Of course, the probability models themselves might provide a tight structure within which better motivated criteria for properties T_1, T_2, and T_3 could be developed. However, it is not the subject of this chapter to consider any of these in detail.

2.7. *Absolute Scales*

Absolute scales are ones where there are not valid rescalings except the identity transformation. If meaningful, they are usually defined by some sort of counting operation. There are probably a number of examples of absolute scales in the network literature such as those based on the number of times actor p_i engages in some well-defined activity with actor p_j. However, when actors make their own judgments about other actors (the case we are investigating), it does not seem very plausible that an absolute scale of friendship would characterize the level of measurement underlying each actor's judgments. The case of a probabilistic dichotomy (see Section 2.2) does provide scale values that can be interpreted as being on an absolute scale.

If the **M** matrix can be regarded as comprised of individual subject absolute scales, it is straightforward to formulate criteria for properties T_1, T_2, and T_3. In fact, in Section 2.5, transformations of the **M** matrix were suggested which were designed to produce a matrix **M'** where each actor's data were transformed so that there were common units and origins. The criteria developed there to assess properties T_1, T_2, and T_3 seem equally well suited to deal with the case of absolute scales so we will not present additional details here.

2.8. Probabilistic Absolute Scales

In an absolute scale, there are no valid transformations of scale values other than the identity transformation, so it might seem that there would be no realization of scales in this subsection. However, what is meant by probabilistic here is not the values on the scale, which are fixed, but rather the possibility that a particular object may vary on the scale from time to time. Suppose, for example, that the scale-value of an object is determined by counting the occurrence of some event—an absolute scale—but the number of occurrences of the event in a random time interval for any given object might be governed by a stochastic counting process, say, a Poisson process. This situation is studied in the chapter by Strauss and Freeman in this book.

In such cases, the rate parameters (or other parameters of the counting process) could be regarded as on an absolute scale. In our case, where actors judge their fellow actors, the counting process would be postulated as a psychological model of an individual subject's judgmental processes. In any event, estimates of these parameters could be entered in the **M** matrix and conditions for properties T_1, T_2, and T_3 would be covered in Section 2.7 concerning nonprobabilistic absolute scales. As before, it should be stressed that the particular underlying stochastic processes may motivate better criteria for properties T_1, T_2, and T_3 than those presented in this chapter.

2.9. Interactor Similarity Measures

A number of network methods work with "similarity coefficients" between all pairs of actors. These coefficients are obtained by analyzing $\mathbf{M}$, and constructing a matrix $\mathbf{S} = (s_{ij})_{n \times n}$, where s_{ij} is some derived index of the similarity between p_i and p_j in the network. Then $\mathbf{S}$ is submitted to some multidimensional scaling algorithm (see Section 3 for a further discussion of this strategy), and the resulting structure locates actors in a metric space in locations that best reproduce at least the order of the values in the original matrix $\mathbf{S}$. Since propositions about the actor locations in the resulting metric space bear on our global properties T_1, T_2, and T_3,[4] it is desirable to consider whether or not such indirectly defined global propositions are meaningful in the sense of Definition 1.

For example, blockmodeling (Arabie, Boorman, and Levitt, 1978) often proceeds by correlating the scale values associated with each pair of actors p_i and p_j. There are two ways to obtain such correlations depending on whether one looks at how p_i and p_j scaled the other $n - 2$ actors or whether one looks at how the other $n - 2$ actors scaled p_i and p_j. In the first case, one computes row by row correlations from $\mathbf{M}$ for every pair of actors on the other $n - 2$ actors, and in the second case one computes column by column correlations. In some applications, it is desirable to consider both types of correlation at the same time.

To illustrate, suppose the individual actor scales are interval scales and that the matrix $\mathbf{M}$ is obtained. Then, the row by row similarity of actors p_i and p_j can be defined by the Pearson product moment correlation coefficient given by

$$r_{ij} = \sum_{\substack{k = 1 \\ k \neq i,j}}^{n} \frac{(m_{ik} - \overline{m}_{i.}) \, (m_{jk} - \overline{m}_{j.})}{(n - 2) \, S_{i.} S_{j.}},$$

where, for example,

---

[4] For example, if actors were in a metric space with d_{ij}, the distance between actors p_i and p_j, one could select a threshold t and define a (nondirected) graph by the property that a tie holds between p_i and p_j if and only if $d_{ij} \leq t$. Reciprocity necessarily holds in the graph, and chaining and clique detection could be defined in the usual graph-theoretic ways (See Section 2.1).

$$\overline{m}_{i.} = \frac{1}{n-2} \sum_{\substack{k=1 \\ k \neq i,j}}^{n} m_{ik},$$

and $S_{i.}$ are the sample mean and sample standard deviation corresponding to p_i's relevant scale values. It is well known that the correlation between two random variables $\mathbf{X}$ and $\mathbf{Y}$ is invariant under separate linear transformations in the variables, $a\mathbf{X} + b$ and $c\mathbf{Y} + d$, where a, $c > 0$. Using this fact, we see that the row by row intercorrelation matrix $\mathbf{R} = (r_{ij})_{n \times n}$ is invariant under permissible interval scale transformations on each actor's scale. Because of this fact, propositions about $\mathbf{M}$ that depend only on the values in $\mathbf{R}$ are meaningful, that is, they satisfy our Definition 1.

However, some of the network methods use column by column correlations (Arabie, Boorman, and Levitt, 1978, p. 36), and these values are *not* invariant under all permissible interval transformations of the individual actor scales. To see this, define the column similarity between p_i and p_j to be

$$c_{ij} = \sum_{\substack{\ell=1 \\ \ell \neq i,j}}^{n} \frac{(m_{\ell i} - \overline{m}_{.i})(m_{\ell j} - \overline{m}_{.j})}{(n-2)\, S_{.i} S_{.j}},$$

where $\overline{m}_{.i}$, $\overline{m}_{.j}$, $S_{.i}$, and $S_{.j}$ are the appropriate column means and standard deviations, respectively. Now suppose a proposition depends on the values in the column by column intercorrelation matrix $\mathbf{C} = (c_{ij})_{n \times n}$. Suppose each actors p_i's scale is transformed to the values $m'_{ij} = a_i m_{ij} + b_i$, where $a_i > 0$. Then, the corresponding value of c'_{ij} is given by

$$c'_{ij} = \sum_{\substack{\ell=1 \\ \ell \neq i,j}}^{n} \frac{(a_\ell m_{\ell i} + b_\ell - \overline{m}'_{.i})(a_\ell m_{\ell j} + b_\ell - \overline{m}'_{.j})}{(n-2)\, S'_{.i} S'_{.j}},$$

where, for example,

$$\overline{m}'_{\cdot i} = \frac{1}{n-2} \sum_{\substack{\ell = 1 \\ \ell \neq i,j}}^{n} (a_\ell m_{\ell i} + b_\ell).$$

To see that permissible rescalings may change C, consider the following M matrix for four actors:

$$M = \begin{array}{c} \\ p_1 \\ p_2 \\ p_3 \\ p_4 \end{array} \begin{array}{cccc} p_1 & p_2 & p_3 & p_4 \\ \left[\begin{array}{cccc} 0 & 7 & 2 & 1 \\ 2 & 0 & 6 & 3 \\ 2 & 4 & 0 & 5 \\ 1 & 1 & 3 & 0 \end{array}\right] \end{array}.$$

To generate a permissible rescaling, set $a_1 = a_2 = a_3 = 1$, $a_4 = 3$, $b_1 = b_2 = b_3 = b_4 = 0$. Then

$$M' = \left[\begin{array}{cccc} 0 & 7 & 2 & 1 \\ 2 & 0 & 6 & 3 \\ 2 & 4 & 0 & 5 \\ 3 & 3 & 9 & 0 \end{array}\right].$$

It is easy to compute that $c_{12} = 1$ (remember we ignore the first two rows in computing the column correlation between p_1 and p_2); however, $c'_{12} = -1$. Since permissible rescalings of M do not leave C invariant, propositions based on C may not be meaningful in the sense of Definition 1.

More generally, each class of measurement scales for individual actors has one (or more) standard row by row correlation index whose values are invariant under permissible rescalings. Propositions based on these values are, in general, meaningful. On the other hand, several of the measurement models relevant to sociometric choice data do *not* have natural column by column correlation indices that are invariant under permissible changes in individual actors' scales. Global propositions about the network based directly or indirectly on such indices may not be meaningful.

3. Implications of an Unfolding Model

In this section we impose additional theoretical structure on the system of actors. The extra assumptions form a theory about how the actors' cognitive structures are interrelated and how sociometric friendship judgments are made for each actor. The assumptions are testable from the data in **M**, and if they prove viable, the hypothesized structure, itself, will motivate the criteria for the global properties under consideration. Further, the data in **M** can be used to estimate the location parameters for each actor in the system.

Coombs (1964) describes a number of measurement models for the case where various subjects provide data on a common set of stimuli. He makes the point that if any sense is to be made from comparing different subjects, they must have some common perceptions of the stimuli. In cases of preference judgments in psychology, it has become usual in the psychological scaling area to suppose that the stimuli lie in a common perceptual space equipped with a distance function. Then individual differences in preferences arise from differences in valuation of the commonly perceived stimuli. The idea developed extensively in Coombs (1964) is to suppose that the subjects, themselves, occupy ideal points in the same space as the stimuli and that a subject tends to prefer stimuli that occupy positions in the space which are close to his or her ideal point.

The earliest and simplest version of this idea is one-dimensional unfolding theory (see Coombs, 1964). Suppose, say, that five stimuli A, B, C, D, E are located in one dimension at, say, the values 1, 5, 6, 7, 10, respectively. Then, if a subject's ideal point is, say, at $x = 4.5$, his ordering of the stimuli from most to least preferred will be BCDAE. Other orderings are possible for different x values; however, all orderings are not possible, for example, BCAED cannot occur. The reason for calling this model an "unfolding theory" is the geometric idea of imagining that the stimulus scale is, say, a string with labeled knots where the stimuli are. Then, if the string is picked up at any point x, assuming that gravity is operating, the ordering of stimuli corresponding to x can be read from top to bottom along the folded-over string.

Coombs (1964) also discusses a multidimensional version of unfolding theory. In this theory each stimulus corresponds to a point in some r-dimensional Euclidean space and subjects' ideal points are also located in the same space. Then, a subject with ideal point $x = (x_1, ..., x_r)$ will prefer stimulus S to stimulus T, at points $s = (s_1, ..., s_r)$ and $t = (t_1, ..., t_r)$, respectively, only if the Euclidean distance between x and s is less than the distance between x and t, i.e.,

$$\sqrt{\sum_{\ell=1}^{r} (x_\ell - s_\ell)^2} < \sqrt{\sum_{\ell=1}^{r} (x_\ell - t_\ell)^2} \, .$$

By now a great deal is known about how to test the assumptions of the unfolding models with data, as well as how to use them to locate both subjects and objects in a common Euclidean space from subjects' ordinal judgment data.

Taking the lead from Coombs (1964, p. 425), we will adapt the model to network data by assuming that the actors each occupy points in an r-dimensional Euclidean space and that their sociometric judgments of friendship are a function of the Euclidean distances between actors in that space. More formally we assume that there is a dimension number r such that each actor $p_i \in P$ corresponds to the point $x_i = (x_{i1}, ..., x_{ir})$ in Euclidean r-space. Then, the true distance between actors p_i and p_j is given by

$$d_{ij} = \sqrt{\sum_{\ell=1}^{r} (x_{i\ell} - x_{j\ell})^2} \, ,$$

and these distances can be arrayed in the matrix $D = (d_{ij})_{n \times n}$. The judgmental model will depend on the particular kind of judgments requested of the actors, but, in general, the model will require that if actor p_i "indicates" a higher amount of friendship toward p_j than toward p_k, then $d_{ij} < d_{ik}$, i.e., we will consider only nonprobabilistic versions of the model here.

The model we are assuming directly builds in strong chaining and reci - procity properties. For example, $d_{ij} \leq a$ and $d_{jk} \leq b$ requires that $d_{ik} \leq a + b$—the triangle inequality. The impact of this requirement on actual judgment data would depend both on the judgment task and the location of other actors in the space; however, the theoretical structure, itself, satisfies a form of the idea behind chaining. Reciprocity is represented in the model by the requirement that $d_{ij} = d_{ji}$, for all $1 \leq i, j \leq n$. If we had the actual distances, following Johnson's (1967) "diameter method," clique detection might be accomplished by finding maximal sets A where, for all p_i, $p_j \in A$, $d_{ij} \leq a$ for some suitable threshold a. Of course there are many alternative cliquing and clustering definitions in the literature relevant to the current situation. Putting things differently, if the judgment data **M** fit the model well and also provide estimates of **D**, it would be superfluous to provide additional conditions for our global properties.

Previous tests and applications of the unfolding model have usually (but not always, see Carroll and Arabie, 1980, pp. 625-627) required that each subject strictly ranks all the stimulus objects by order of preference; however, from the point of view of the model itself, there is no necessity to restrict the data to strict rank orders. In the remaining subsections we will consider, respectively, dichotomous (3.1), ordinal (3.2), and ratio (3.3) level judgment data from each actor on the other $n - 1$ actors. We will assume, for the sake of argument, that the data are error-free. Thus, the point of view will not be to focus on estimation and goodness of fit criteria for the model at each level of measurement. Instead, we will focus mostly on the data implications of the model, itself, relevant to the global network properties investigated in the previous section. In many cases, the model will motivate sharper, meaningful criteria for T_1, T_2, and T_3 than offered for corre - sponding levels of measurement in the previous section. Thus our approach will be to use the model as a hypothetical device to restrict further the measurement theory underlying the data obtained in **M** in order to see the consequences at the data level itself. Of course, in the case of non-ordinal measurement, it will be necessary to augment the judgmental assumptions of the model and this will be done, hopefully, in a natural way.

As with any strong theoretical assumption, objections and alternative assumptions can always be raised. For example, Coombs (1964, p. 426) suggests that in sociometric judgment tasks each actor's self-perception might be at a different location in the space than the location corresponding to how others regard him or her. Coombs (1964) also provides alternative models with a common subject space, and more recently, Carroll (1980) and his colleagues have developed an impressive set of techniques for combining similarity and preference data in multi-dimensional spaces.

A number of multidimensional scaling algorithms not based on the unfolding idea exist where stimuli lie in a common space but there may be individual differences in how particular subjects view them, for example,

INDSCAL (Carroll and Chang, 1970). Finally, numerous multidimensional non-Euclidean spaces as well as tree metrics and other exotic metric spaces have been developed in the measurement and scaling area (see review by Carroll and Arabie, 1980) that might provide interesting alternative spaces within which to represent actors. The main thesis developed in this chapter will be served best by picking one hypothetical structure to analyze from a measurement-theoretic perspective, and therefore, we will discuss only the multidimensional unfolding model, though occasionally we may focus on the one-dimensional case.

Coombs (1964) observes that the multidimensional unfolding model can perfectly accommodate strict order data from n stimuli in an $(n - 1)$-dimensional Euclidean space. By this statement, he means that in the accommodating $(n - 1)$-dimensional model there are ideal points corre - sponding to every possible subject ranking of the n stimuli. In our case, however, the data provide only n rankings corresponding to ideal points located at the stimulus points, themselves. There are n! possible rankings, and the data provide a subset of n of these rankings. It is not the case that all of the $\binom{n!}{n}$ subsets of n rankings are possible to accommodate in some Euclidean space (for example, see Theorem 6), so the model, even for arbitrarily large r, is not universally applicable to any set of sociometric ranking data.

3.1. Dichotomous Scale

Suppose each actor $p_i \in P$ is asked to list a set of friends, F_i. As in Section 2.1, let $\mathbf{M} = (m_{ij})_{n \times n}$, where

$$m_{ij} = \begin{cases} 1 \text{ if } p_j \in F_i \\ 0 \text{ otherwise.} \end{cases}$$

To analyze actors' sociometric choices in the context of the unfolding model, suppose that corresponding to each actor p_i is a positive number t_i that determines the set F_i by the rule

$$F_i = \{p_j \mid p_j \in P - \{p_i\} \text{ and } d_{ij} < t_i\}.$$

The judgmental assumption amounts to the condition that each actor de - termines his or her own friendship threshold t_i, and he or she includes as friends all actors within a neighborhood about themselves of threshold radius t_i.

Despite the arbitrariness of each actor's threshold, the underlying model makes inferences about our properties of chaining and reciprocity. Consider property T_1 (chaining). It is clear that transitivity in the directed graph corresponding to **M** (viewed as an incidence matrix) need not hold. In particular, the conditions $m_{ij} = 1$ and $m_{jk} = 1$ imply only that the underlying distances and thresholds are such that $d_{ij} < t_i$ and $d_{jk} < t_j$. The triangle inequality assures that $d_{ik} \leq d_{ij} + d_{jk}$, so we can conclude only that $d_{ik} < t_i + t_j$, and there is no guarantee that $d_{ik} < t_i$, which would imply that $m_{ik} = 1$, which is needed for transitivity.

Somewhat more surprising than the failure of transitivity in the directed graph to be a meaningful property of dichotomous data is the fact that *atransitivity* in the graph is compatible with the model, i.e., $m_{ij} = 1$ and $m_{jk} = 1$ imply $m_{ik} = 0$ for all distinct i, j, k. To see this, imagine that each actor p_i is located at point $x_i = i$ on a line and that $t = 3/2$. Then $m_{ij} = 1$ and $m_{jk} = 1$ occur only when either $j = i + 1$ and $k = i + 2$ or that $j = i - 1$ and $k = i - 2$; however, in neither case do we have $m_{ik} = 1$.

It is possible to establish a property of **M** which is related to chaining, and it is stated in the next Theorem.

Theorem 4. Suppose the unfolding model of Section 3 and that each actor $p_i \in P$ chooses a threshold t_i and determines m_{ij} by the rule

$$m_{ij} = \begin{cases} 1 \text{ if } d_{ij} < t_i \text{ and } i \neq j \\ 0 \text{ otherwise.} \end{cases}$$

Then, for all distinct indices i, j, and k, $m_{ij} = 1$, $m_{jk} = 1$, $m_{ik} = 0$, $m_{ji} = 0$ jointly imply $m_{kj} \geq m_{ki}$.

Proof: The four conditions are easily seen to require $d_{ij} < d_{ik}$ and $d_{jk} < d_{ji}$. Since distances are symmetric in the model, $d_{jk} > d_{ij}$. By transitivity (of numbers) we have $d_{jk} < d_{ik}$, and by symmetry of distances this requires $d_{kj} < d_{ki}$. This last condition implies that, for all thresholds t_k, $d_{ki} < t_k$ implies $d_{kj} < t_k$, which, in turn, implies $m_{kj} \geq m_{ki}$.   ◆

The condition developed in Theorem 4 is a long way from the manifest transitivity in the directed graph, however, it is derived from the symmetry and transitivity of the underlying distances, themselves, and so it can be regarded, in the context of the model, as a meaningful chaining condition concerning interscale comparisons.

Property T_2 (reciprocity) is built into the model by the requirement that $d_{ij} = d_{ji}$; however, it is easy to see that in the case where different actors have different thresholds, this property need not be revealed as a symmetry condition in **M**, that is, it need not be the case that $m_{ij} = 1$ implies that $m_{ji} = 1$. However, in cases where $m_{ij} = 1$ and $m_{ji} = 0$, we can conclude that $t_i > t_j$.

Despite a high density of ties, it is possible for the manifest data (or the corresponding directed graph) to satisfy *asymmetry* for the model, that is, $m_{ij} = 1$ implies $m_{ij} = 0$. To see this suppose that n actors are arrayed on a line with actor p_i at point $x_i = 1 - 2^{-(i-1)}$ and threshold $t_i = 1 - 2^{-(n-i+1)}$. In this case, the ties occur for 50% of the opportunities; however, $m_{ij} = 1$ implies $m_{ji} = 0$. For example, suppose that n = 5, then the positions and thresholds of the actors are given by the following table:

actors	position (x_i)	threshold (t_i)
p_1	0	31/32
p_2	1/2	15/32
p_3	3/4	7/32
p_4	7/8	3/32
p_5	15/16	1/32 ,

and the interpoint distances are given by

$$
\mathbf{D} = \begin{array}{c} \\ 1 \\ 2 \\ 3 \\ 4 \\ 5 \end{array} \begin{array}{ccccc} 1 & 2 & 3 & 4 & 5 \\ \left[\begin{array}{ccccc} 0 & \dfrac{16}{32} & \dfrac{24}{32} & \dfrac{28}{32} & \dfrac{30}{32} \\[2ex] \dfrac{16}{32} & 0 & \dfrac{8}{32} & \dfrac{12}{32} & \dfrac{14}{32} \\[2ex] \dfrac{24}{32} & \dfrac{8}{32} & 0 & \dfrac{4}{32} & \dfrac{6}{32} \\[2ex] \dfrac{28}{32} & \dfrac{12}{32} & \dfrac{4}{32} & 0 & \dfrac{2}{32} \\[2ex] \dfrac{30}{32} & \dfrac{14}{32} & \dfrac{6}{32} & \dfrac{2}{32} & 0 \end{array} \right] \end{array},
$$

and finally the resulting sociometric choice matrix is

$$
\mathbf{M} = \begin{array}{c} \\ 1 \\ 2 \\ 3 \\ 4 \\ 5 \end{array} \begin{array}{ccccc} 1 & 2 & 3 & 4 & 5 \\ \left[\begin{array}{ccccc} 0 & 1 & 1 & 1 & 1 \\ 0 & 0 & 1 & 1 & 1 \\ 0 & 0 & 0 & 1 & 1 \\ 0 & 0 & 0 & 0 & 1 \\ 0 & 0 & 0 & 0 & 0 \end{array} \right] \end{array}.
$$

It is easy to see that in $\mathbf{M}$, the density of ties is 50% (excluding the main diagonal) and that the directed graph corresponding to $\mathbf{M}$ has the property of asymmetry.

It is possible to state a condition on $\mathbf{M}$ for the model which relates to reciprocity and which is meaningful, and this condition is stated in the next corollary to Theorem 4.

Corollary 4.1. Suppose the unfolding model with threshold as stated in Theorem 4. Then, for all distinct i, j, k, $m_{ij} = 1$, $m_{ji} = 0$, $m_{jk} = 1$, $m_{kj} = 0$ jointly imply that $m_{ik} \geq m_{ki}$.

Proof: It is easily seen that the first two conditions require $t_i > t_j$, and the second two conditions require $t_j > t_k$. Consequently $t_i > t_k$, and if $m_{ki} = 1$, this means that $d_{ki} = d_{ik} < t_k < t_i$ so $m_{ik} = 1$. Alternatively, one could add the condition that $m_{ki} = 1$, and then a simple application of Theorem 4 shows that $m_{ik} = 1$.   ◆

The consequence of Corollary 4.1 is that while the directed graph corresponding to **M** need not satisfy symmetry (the graph-theoretic definition of reciprocity), there are, nevertheless, conditions on other points that can guarantee that a particular tie in the graph will be reciprocated regardless of the choice of underlying subject threshold values.

Theorem 4 and Corollary 4.1 state meaningful global properties of M under the measurement assumptions of this section (multidimensional unfolding, arbitrary thresholds that determine interactor dichotomous scales). The interesting thing about them is that they are a good bit weaker than the graph-theoretic properties of transitivity and symmetry usually investigated. Even with the strong unfolding assumptions, these graph-theoretic properties are not meaningful in the arbitrary threshold case.

It is possible to add an additional strengthening of the measurement assumptions in this section and derive stronger, meaningful properties of **M** as is illustrated in the next theorem.

Theorem 5. Suppose a *one-dimensional* unfolding model holds under the remaining conditions of Theorem 4. Then, there exists an ordering $\langle p_i \rangle_{i=1}^n$ of the n members of P so that for each $p_i \in P$, there are integers $0 \le K_i \le i$ and $0 \le K'_i \le n - i$ so that $p_j \in F_i$ if and only if either $i - K_i < j < i$ or $i < j < n + 1 - K'_i$.

Proof: The proof is tedious but elementary. First, one serially orders the members of P by their assumed one-dimensional location parameters. Then one notes that F_i forms a possible null, but connected segment about p_i, bordering p_i, but excluding p_i.   ◆

Theorem 5 provides an elementary seriation property of the sort studied by graph theorists. Such work usually develops conditions under which a graph or a directed graph can be represented as an "interval graph" (see Roberts, 1976, pp. 122-129). In our case, one might seek necessary and sufficient conditions under which each $p_i \in P$ could be mapped into an open interval (a_i, b_i) so that $m_{ij} = 1$ if and only if ($a_j + b_j$) / 2 $\in$ (a_i, b_i), that is the interval corresponding to p_i includes the midpoint of the interval corre - sponding to j. In such a case, the set of actors could be located in a one-dimensional Euclidean space at the midpoints of their corresponding intervals.

For our purpose, Theorem 5 has a different thrust; namely, it says that if the conditions of Theorem 5 hold, the conclusion is invariant under permissible rescalings (changes in thresholds t_i) of the system. Hence, the conclusion of Theorem 5 is a meaningful global property of **M** under current assumptions. Even in this case, however, graph transitivity and graph symmetry are not meaningful properties of **M**.

We will not consider clique detection (T_3) in any detail here. As with T_1 and T_2, the usual graph-theoretic definitions are not meaningful in the context of the conditions of this subsection. From a measurement-theoretic viewpoint, a reasonable approach to clique detection would be to develop necessary (and hopefully sufficient) conditions on dichotomous data in the matrix **M** for representing the actors in an r-dimensional Euclidean space for either aribtrary or fixed r. Hopefully the proof of these conditions would be constructive in that it would provide a constructive method for obtaining a possible **D** matrix (interactor distances). Additional work would be designed to study the uniqueness of the underlying **D** matrix, and, only then, could adequate criteria for the meaningful detection of cliques be formulated. The implementation of this program as well as the search for additional meaningful global properties of **M** implied by the current measurement assumptions seem to be interesting projects, but they will have to await another time.

3.2. Ordinal Scale

In this case, the data from each actor lead meaningfully to ranks of the other n − 1 actors in terms of friendship—one for best friend, 2 for next, etc. As we have seen from Section 2.3, **M** can be characterized by the rule that m_{ij} is p_j's rank on p_i's order. Under the assumptions of the unfolding model, **M** can be viewed as a conditional proximity rank matrix. The model permits the inference that if $m_{ij} < m_{ik}$, then $d_{ij} < d_{ik}$. Because of this relationship between model and data, **M** must satisfy a transitivity condition that relates to our chaining property, which is stated in the next theorem adapted from Coombs (1964, Ch. 19).

Theorem 6. Suppose the unfolding model holds exactly and yields the conditional proximity rank matrix $\mathbf{M} = (m_{ij})_{n \times n}$, where m_{ij} is p_j's rank on p_i's order. Then, for all distinct triples of indices i, j, and k, $m_{ij} < m_{ik}$ and $m_{jk} < m_{ji}$ imply $m_{kj} < m_{ki}$.

Proof: The two conditions imply, respectively, $d_{ij} < d_{ik}$ and $d_{jk} < d_{ji}$. By symmetry of distances and transitivity of numbers we can conclude that $d_{kj} < d_{ki}$, which, in turn, implies that $m_{kj} < m_{ki}$.   ♦

There are no simple reciprocity conditions for the unfolding model because the tendency to reciprocate low ranks between a pair of actors p_i and p_j is entirely a property of the locations of other actors in the space. If the dimensionality of the space is restricted relative to $\mathbf{M}$, it is possible to state conditions that relate to reciprocity; however, this possibility will not be pursued here.

Another possible approach to reciprocity conditions is to make distributional assumptions about the location of actors in the space, and derive estimates of statistics related to reciprocity from these distributional assumptions. For example, Schwarz and Tversky (1980) study conditional proximity distance orders under the assumption that the points are a random sample from some "smooth" distribution in r-dimensional Euclidean space. To state one of their results, Schwarz and Tversky show that for their Euclidean model, the expectation is that over 50% of the first choices (rank 1) are reciprocated; whereas in some other spatial models, and, of course, for arbitrary conditional proximity matrices, the reciprocation indices can be quite a bit lower. Overall, the Schwarz and Tversky approach seems like a promising one for motivating indices of global properties like chaining and reciprocity when the conditional proximity matrices come from ordinal sociometric choice data.

3.3. Ratio Scale

Suppose each actor p_i provides data on a ratio scale of his or her degree of "lack of" friendship for p_j. Analyzing "lack of friendship" rather than "friendship" in this subsection is convenient because increasing distance between actors leads to less perception of friendship in the unfolding model. Such estimates could be obtained in practice by the variety of direct magnitude estimation scaling methods developed by Stevens as discussed in

Section 2.5. For now, we assume the data are error-free and derive directly from the distances between actors in the underlying spatial model. Of course, subject p_i's unit $b_i > 0$ is arbitrary, so the **M** matrix is related to the underlying distance matrix **D** by the formula

$$
\mathbf{M} =
\begin{bmatrix}
b_1 & & & & 0 \\
& b_2 & & & \\
& & \cdot & & \\
& & & \cdot & \\
0 & & & & b_n
\end{bmatrix}
\mathbf{D},
$$

assuming that b_i is p_i's unit of lack of friendship relative to the scale that characterizes **D**.

Because of the symmetry of distance, there are a number of meaningful consequences of the unfolding model at the data level that relate to our properties of chaining and reciprocity. One example is that it is easy to show that, for all distinct $1 \le i, j, k \le n$,

$$
\frac{m_{ij} m_{jk} m_{ki}}{m_{ji} m_{kj} m_{ik}} = 1
$$

by noting that $m_{ij} = b_i d_{ij}$ and $d_{ij} = d_{ji}$. In fact, the previous matrix equation requires that there exists a vector $\mathbf{b} = (b_1, b_2, ..., b_n)$ such that the derived matrix $\mathbf{P} = (m_{ij} / m_{ji})_{n \times n}$ is reproducible by the equation

$$
\mathbf{P} =
\begin{bmatrix}
b_1 \\
b_2 \\
\cdot \\
\cdot \\
\cdot \\
b_n
\end{bmatrix}
\begin{bmatrix}
b_1^{-1} & b_2^{-1} & \cdot & \cdot & \cdot & b_n^{-1}
\end{bmatrix}.
$$

Both of the preceding properties are meaningful because their truth is invariant under permissible rescalings.

The overall conclusion is that the unfolding model under the current interpretation has a number of strong, meaningful, and easily tested properties at the ratio level of measurement. In case some external knowledge determines the scaling units b_i, it is possible to recover the distance matrix, itself, from M by the equation

$$
D = \begin{bmatrix} b_1^{-1} & & & & & 0 \\ & b_2^{-1} & & & & \\ & & \cdot & & & \\ & & & \cdot & & \\ & & & & \cdot & \\ 0 & & & & & b_n^{-1} \end{bmatrix} M,
$$

and, in this case, the unfolding model can be characterized by the Young-Householder conditions (see Torgerson, 1958) on D that are necessary and sufficient for embedding the n points in a multidimensional Euclidean space of dimensionality $1 \le r < n$. These conditions include $d_{ij} = d_{ji}$ and $d_{ik} \le d_{ij} + d_{jk}$, which are the ways T_1 and T_2 are represented in the unfolding model. If the conditions are satisfied, metric multidimensional scaling provides a constructive way to find the minimum dimensionality r and obtain coordinate locations on all actors that are unique up to Euclidean transformations.

4. Conclusions

This chapter has discussed the logic of inferring global or socio - logically interesting properties that are meaningful from individual subject sociometric judgment data. Careful attention has been paid to the scale-type of the judgmental data. The analysis we present has been designed to fill a perceived void in the social network theory area; however, for the most part, the chapter does not develop clear-cut criteria that can be adopted as rational substitutes for previous practices. Instead, our goal in this chapter has been to increase the awareness of networkers for the measurement-theoretic character of their work. If we have been successful in this goal, then the direction should be clear for future productive work designed to ground social network theory in the overall conception of the foundations of measurement area.

We close with a quote from Coombs' *Theory of Data* (1964). Coombs has a brief section on sociometric choice behavior in the context of his elaborate measurement-theoretic work on psychological scaling, and he comments as follows:

> "... The important lesson in all of this, it seems to me, is that the models for inferential classification designed for quite different contexts, in these examples sociometric choice and scaling theory, are seen to deal with identical relations. The problems and techniques in each content area are, at least in principle, transferable from one to the other. Surely workers in either content area would gain new tools and insights by recognizing the correspondences and reinterpreting the work in one context in terms of the other context." (Coombs, 1964, p. 425)

REFERENCES

Arabie, P., Boorman, S. A., and Levitt, P. R.
  1978 Constructing blockmodels: How and why. Journal of
      Mathematical Psychology 12, 21-63.
Burt, R. S.
  1980 Models of network structure. Annual Review of Sociology 6,
      79-141.
Carroll, J. D.
  1980 Models and methods for multidimensional analysis of preference
      choice (or other dominance) data. *In* E. D. Lantermann and H.
      Feger, eds. Similarity and Choice. Bern: Hans Huber.
Carroll, J. D. and P. Arabie.
  1980 Multidimensional scaling. Annual Review of Psychology 31,
      607-649.
Carroll, J. D. and J. J. Chang.
  1970 Analysis of individual differences in multidimensional scaling via
      an N-way generalization of Eckart-Young decomposition.
      Psychometrika 35, 283-319.
Coombs, C. H.
  1964 A Theory of Data. New York: Wiley.
Coombs, C. H., Dawes, R. M., and Tversky, A.
  1970 Mathematical Psychology, Englewood Cliffs, N.J.: Prentice Hall.
Davidson, R. R. and Farquhar, P. H.
  1976 A bibliography on the method of paired-comparisons.
      Econometrica 32, 241-252.
Holland, P. W. and Leinhardt, S.
  1973 The structural implications of measurement error in sociometry.
      Journal of Mathematical Sociology 3, 85-111.
Johnson, S. C.
  1967 Hierarchical clustering schemes. Psychometrika 32, 241-254.
Krantz, D. H., Luce, R. D., Suppes, P., and Tversky, A.
  1971 Foundations of Measurement, vol. 1. New York: Academic Press.
Lindzey, G. and Byrne, D.
  1968 Measurement of social choice and interpersonal attractiveness. *In*
      G. Lindzey and E. Aronson, eds. Handbook of Social Psychology,
      vol. 2. Reading, Mass.: Addison-Wesley.
Luce, R. D.
  1956 Semiorders and a theory of utility discrimination. Econometrica
      24, 178-191.
  1959 Individual Choice Behavior. New York: Wiley.

1977   The choice axiom after twenty years. Journal of Mathematical
        Psychology 15, 215-233.
1978   Dimensionally invariant numerical laws correspond to meaningful
        qualitative relations. Philosophy of Science 45, 1-16.
Luce, R. D. and Suppes, P.
1965   Preference, utility, and subjective probability. *In* R. D. Luce, R.
        R. Bush, and E. Galanter, eds., Handbook of Mathematical
        Psychology, vol. III. New York: Wiley.
Roberts, F. S.
1976   Discrete Mathematical Models. Englewood Cliffs, N.J.: Prentice
        Hall.
1979   Measurement theory: With applications to decision-making,
        utility, and the social sciences. Encyclopedia of Mathematics and
        Its Applications, Reading, Mass.: Addison-Wesley.
Schwarz, G. and Tversky, A.
1980   On the reciprocity relation. Journal of Mathematical Psychology
        22, 157-175.
Stevens, S. S.
1946   On the theory of scales of measurement. Science 103, 677-680.
1961   The quantification of sensation. *In* D. Lerner, ed. Quantity and
        Quality. New York: Glencoe.
Suppes, P. and Zinnes, J. L.
1963   Basic measurement theory. *In* R. D. Luce, R. R. Bush, and E.
        Galanter, eds. Handbook of Mathematical Psychology, vol. I. New
        York: Wiley.
Thurstone, L. L.
1927   A law of comparative judgment. Psychological Review 34,
        273-286.
Torgerson, W. S.
1958   Theory and Methods of Scaling. New York: Wiley.
Winship, C.
1977   A distance model for sociometric structure. Journal of
        Mathematical Sociology 5, 21-39.

CHAPTER 5

STOCHASTIC MODELING AND THE ANALYSIS OF STRUCTURAL DATA

David Strauss and Linton C. Freeman

1. The Components of a Stochastic Structural Model

There is a more or less standard problem that arises in the use of formal models in the study of social phenomena. Massarik and Ratoosh (1965, p. 17) have called it the "seductiveness of mathematics" and described it in these terms:

> There are some reasonable and appropriate assumptions about human behavior that at the outset guide the development of a given mathematical model. The basic propositions are stated abstractly, and from them a number of consequences quickly follow. These, too, are amenable to succinct and precise notation. Soon a network of rigorous propositions is derived and mathematically manipulated. However, as the tower of derived propositions is built higher and higher, the danger increases that knowledge (or assumptions empirically based) about human behavior is left further and further behind. The model itself becomes a soul-satisfying, plausible, and conceptually elegant end product. It may prove *logically* sound—or it may be attacked on *logical* grounds. But the temperament of the model builder may be such that he is more comfortable with the abstraction than with the hard, somewhat "dirty" data, especially whole-system, gestaltist data, naturalistically derived. The model itself has become an "autonomous

motive"; and now its empirical test appears less urgent, a digression from the exciting schematic "mainstream."

In this chapter a way around the problem will be suggested. A paradigm for a class of stochastic models will be introduced that *requires* a continual interplay between model and data. Use of this paradigm leads to the development of models that are specifically designed to guide the analysis of structural data. Because data are an integral part of model building in this case, the models are always tied directly to behavioral observations. Thus, what will be suggested is a procedure that draws upon the power of formal methods and, at the same time, requires that any formalisms developed are constantly kept in direct touch with their empirical roots.

What is being proposed in this chapter, then, is a very general probabilistic approach to the study of social structure—one is tempted to say a mathematical *theory* of social structure. What follows is a mathematical theory in the sense Grenander (1978, p. 2) used the term when he suggested that it "... is really a collection of special cases treated from a unifying perspective." In effect, we are suggesting that models of social structure may be viewed as a special class of models of probability theory. As such, they all share certain defining characteristics. In this sense, a stochastic model of social structure must include the specification of three properties:

     A. A *structure experiment.*
     B. One or more *measures.*
     C. A *biased stochastic process.*

These three components of a stochastic structural model will be examined in the remainder of the first part of this chapter. We shall then proceed in the second part to review a number of older existing models. We hope thereby to reveal a unity between models which at first sight appear to have little in common, and provide a schema which may facilitate the development of further models for social networks. Finally, we will wind up in the last part of the chapter by examining some newer models that have been explicitly introduced in the context of a perspective like that expressed here.

   A. *The Structure Experiment.* The notion of the generalized structure experiment was set down in Chapter 1 above. It was indicated there that the study of social structure necessarily involves a look at at least one social relation among members of a set of social units. This results in the creation of a family of matrices, X, where each matrix is composed of binary random variables,

$$X_{kt} = \left[x_{k \cdot j}(t) \right].$$

Consider the object formed by assigning a value (0 or 1) for each random variable. Since from this collection of 0's and 1's we could work back to a graph of observed social relations, any particular matrix constitutes a *realization* of a social network. Now if we let

c_{kt} = the number of cells in a matrix, X_{kt},

m = the number of different matrices of relations, and

p = the number of different times of observation,

then

c = $c_{kt}mp$

= the total number of cells in the family, X.

Since each cell can be filled two ways—with either a 0 or a 1,

2^c = the number of possible realizations of the social network.

In the most general case, we could define some process that resulted in entering a 0 or a 1 in each cell in each matrix. Thus, each of the 2^c possible realizations of X would be equally likely. In real data sets, however, such an unrestricted realization set would seldom be of interest. Any actual structure experiment is apt to be subject to *constraints* of one sort or another.

As an example of a constraint, let us consider the simplest network embodying one relation recorded at one time over a stable set of persons. Let

n = a number of persons.

Then

$c = n^2$ = the number of pairs of persons or the number of cells in the matrix.

And, since each cell can be filled two ways—with either 0 or 1,

2^c = the number of possible realizations of the network.

If n = 5,

2^c = 33,554,432.

Thus, a single matrix expressing one relation at one time among five persons has over thirty-three million possible realizations.

If n = 6, there would be over ten billion realizations and if n were greater than 18, there would be more realizations than Eddington's estimate of the number of particles in the universe!

Without constraints, then, it is clear that the realization set grows extremely rapidly with n. When constraints are imposed—as they almost always are—the realization set is much more manageable. Suppose, for example, we were considering a relation like interpersonal acquaintanceship (Poole and Kochen, 1978). By definition, acquaintanceship is symmetrical (and, for convenience, can be taken to be irreflexive). These constraints profoundly reduce the size of the set of matrices we might possibly observe. In the present case c, the number of cells to be specified is reduced from n^2 to $\binom{n}{2}$. Thus with n = 5, for instance, the number of realizations is reduced from 2^{25} to 2^{10}.

Such constraints will be used in almost any structural study. Frequently, for example, the total number of pairs in the relation will be constrained. Or restrictions will be imposed in the distributions of the row and/or column totals in each matrix. Controls may be imposed in terms of reflexivity, symmetry or transitivity as in the example above. But, in any case, most actual structure experiments will involve constraints of one or more sorts. Such constraints are important; they must be specified and taken into account in calculating expectations based on the stochastic processes to be described below.

B. *Constructing Measures.* Once we have defined a structure experiment with its associated constraints, we can make observations and generate a family of structure matrices. Our actual recorded data, then, consist of some particular family of matrices with its unique pattern of 0's and 1's. We shall wish to determine whether the observed realization of 0's and 1's reflects an unobserved but underlying biased stochastic process. At this point, however, such a determination is impossible. Since all of the possible realizations are equally likely under the assumption of an unbiased process, *any* particular realization is simply an event with a very small probability of occurring; no basis for decision-making exists.

The answer to this problem lies in reducing the complexity of our realization set still further, in a fashion dictated by our particular theoretical concerns. We achieve this by switching attention from the realization to some appropriate *measures* calculated from that realization (Grenander, 1976, p. 63). The measures chosen contain all the information about the values of the parameters in the underlying stochastic model, and thus two realizations are equivalent if they give rise to the same values of the measures. Like the poker player who doesn't care whether his three aces are in hearts, clubs and diamonds, or in spades, hearts and clubs, the social theorist will typically be interested in some—but not all—of the details of experimental observations. Thus, the set of all possible realizations of a family of matrices will be reduced by partitioning it into a smaller number of equivalence sets. Insofar as a particular theory is concerned, only realizations that fall in different classes according to the partition will be viewed as showing theoretically interesting differences. Different realizations that fall into a single class will be viewed as equivalent—they are, in the context of the problem addressed, indistinguishable.

Another example may help to clarify this point. In a model of voting behavior by Kreweras (1966), concern is with voting for, say, officers in an organization. Imagine an organization with five members. On the basis of the reasoning presented above, in the most general case, the number of possible realizations, r, in an organization with $n = 5$ members has been established to be 33,554,432. This calculation ignores the fact that, here, we are dealing with the relation of voting. Most voting involves the one-man-one-vote rule, so let us assume it as a constraint of the sort described above. This restricts the set of possible realizations to those in which there is only one entry of 1 in each row of the matrix. In this case, since each row can have n different realizations and since there are n rows, the total number of realizations is now only

$$n^n = 5^5 = 3,125.$$

But here a new sort of simplifying rule—this time based on theoretical interests—is relevant. In most balloting situations we are not interested in the full "nominative" state of opinion where information on *who* voted for *whom* is recorded. Instead we are concerned with a numerical state: specifically in the number of votes received by each candidate. This is, as a matter of fact, precisely the principle underlying the secret ballot. Thus our measures here are the numbers of votes for the various candidates.

In this context, a record of numerical states permits the organization of data in the form prescribed by Kreweras' theoretical concerns. His model is designed to explore the bias introduced by a "bandwagon effect" on successive ballots. In the model, therefore, voters are seen as responding to the previous ballot in their voting at a given time. The one aspect of the previous ballot to which they are thought to respond is its numerical state or distribution.

It would be natural, then, to sum the columns of our voting matrix and define a vector, V, of measures with the following entries:

v_1 = the number of votes received by member 1 as a candidate

v_2 = the number of votes received by member 2 as a candidate

.

.

.

Thus, in this case, we are not interested in whether member 1 got his or her two votes from members 2 and 3 or 4 and 5; we are interested only in the fact of his or her getting two votes. All the ways in which a candidate gets two votes are grouped together into a single equivalence class, thereby defining a measure of the property of the relation in which we are interested.

It should be noted here that this process of partitioning into equivalence classes further reduces the realization set. In the present illustration, the number of realizations is[1]

$$\binom{2n-1}{n}$$

and since $n = 5$, the number of possible outcomes is 126.

Again, this reduction is critical in actually working out the distributions under an assumed underlying stochastic process. The important thing to note, however, is that it is simply impossible to determine expectations at all unless one or more measures are specified by partitioning the realization set into equivalence classes. That is a necessary step in the construction of any stochastic social structural model.

---

[1] The derivation of this formula is instructive. Represent the n available votes as n stars arranged on a line. Each assignation to the candidates corresponds to a partition by n-1 bars. For example, **|*||** is the pattern for which the first candidate gets 2 votes, the second gets 1 vote, the third gets no votes, the fourth gets 2 votes, and the fifth gets none. The number of distinct patterns is clearly

$$\binom{n+n-1}{n}$$

C. *Biased Stochastic Processes.* We have seen that in order to model social structure we must specify a structure experiment and construct one or more measures of relevant properties of the structure matrices. The final step requires that we specify an explicit stochastic process that conditions those relevant structural properties. We must, in effect, construct a story about how our expected structural properties might be generated. Moreover, the process itself must be non-random; it must be *biased* in some systematic way.

The intuitive discussion in Chapter 1, above, stressed the fact that social structure is always a *patterned* arrangement of relations among social units. In the present context we can define patterning as any arrangement of links that did not arise at random. Thus, in order to be consistent with these ideas, a useful model must first of all specify a process leading to a realization of a structure experiment. Second, the process specified must be stochastic. And third, it must be biased. Only by compliance with all three of these conditions can a model begin to provide an appropriate basis for the study of social structure as it is defined here.

A very simple illustration will make these ideas clear. Let us suppose that we have a simple structure experiment involving observations of two persons over one relation at one time. We shall assume further that the relation is constrained to be irreflexive. This means that of the

$$2^{\left(2^2\right)} = 16$$

possible realizations only the four that are irreflexive can occur. They are shown in Table 1.

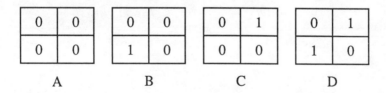

0	0
0	0

A

0	0
1	0

B

0	1
0	0

C

0	1
1	0

D

Table 1. The four possible irreflexive realizations
of a one-time one-relation structure experiment
involving two social objects

Now let us suppose that our measure of interest is simply in the number of ordered pairs in the relation under examination. Thus, we define as equivalent all realizations that generate the same number of ones. In Table 1, B and C each sum to one. They are, therefore, equivalent, and in all the four realizations yield three distinguishable outcomes.

An unbiased stochastic process would assign equal probabilities to the four realizations and yield the distribution shown in Table 2.

Sum	Probability
0	.25
1	.50
2	.25

Table 2. Distribution under the assumption of
equiprobability for the results of Table 1

This is exactly equivalent to the assumption that each social object generates directed lines with probability $p = .5$. Since there are two potential lines the expected number of lines in such a case is $2 \times 1/2 = 1$.

Suppose, however, we have reason to believe that the social objects here are biased towards generating lines. Assume that, given an opportunity, the probability of generating no line is .25. The the distribution is that shown in Table 3 and the expected number of lines is now $2 \times 3/4 = 1.5$.

Sum	Probability
0	.0625
1	.375
2	.5625

Table 3. Distribution outcome under the
assumption of $p = .75$ for the results of Table 1

In this case, we have a biased stochastic process and a model of social structure. The distribution could be compared with observed results and a decision concerning the relevance of the model could be made.

In general, then, these are the steps in building a social structure model:

1. *Specify a structure experiment* generating one or more matrices and usually involving structural constraints.

2. *Define one or more partitions of the realization set according to measures of theoretically relevant properties* of the structural phenomena under study. The measures are the *sufficient statistics* for the underlying parameters of a model. It will then be simple to formulate a natural *null*, or *randomness* model.

3. *Define a biased stochastic process* that results in the unequal assignment of probabilities to the simple events of the outcome set. The measures contain all the information about the process parameters.

To these we should add a fourth step which is a vital one if we are to avoid the "seductiveness of mathematics":

4. *Evaluate the fit of the model.* According to circumstances, this may involve our comparing the observed data with the best fit under the model, testing our measures against their distribution according to the model, etc.

A considerable number of stochastic models that are implicitly of this sort have already been proposed. Next, we shall review some existing models in order to illustrate some of the range and power of this approach.

2. *Traditional Models*

A. *Rapoport and Horvath's Random and Biased Nets.* In one of the first major contributions to social network theory, Rapoport and Horvath (1961) adapted an earlier model from neural anatomy to the study of data generated by a Moreno experiment (see Chapter 1). They assume that they have data on sociometric friendship choices for a defined set of N persons. They begin by defining a strictly random choice process and later add biases. We shall follow their approach here and first review their random model.

Rapoport and Horvath assume a discrete pseudo-time-dependent process. They randomly select a small set of n(t = 0) persons to be "starters" at the beginning of the process at time t = 0. They are assumed to make all of their friendship choices at time t = 0; this ends the first step of the process and a new "generation" is constructed at t = 1. This new generation consists of all the newly chosen persons introduced at that stage of the process and they, in turn, set about the task of making their choices. "Time" continues to pass in discrete steps (t = 1, 2, 3, ...) until the process finally ends when at some step no new contacts are introduced.

Rapoport and Horvath define a whole series of measures and parameters for the structural properties that were important to their analysis:

$n(t) =$ the number of newly chosen persons at time = t.

$p(t) = \dfrac{n(t)}{N}$,   the proportion of newly chosen persons at time = t.

$x(t) = \sum\limits_{j=0}^{t} p(j)$,   the cumulative proportion of persons chosen by time = t.

All of these quantities are random variables, since their values will vary from realization to realization. Expectations of variables are denoted by a circumflex.

Let a be the contact density, or average number of directed lines generated per person. This may be a constant throughout the process, or a variable; in the latter case a will be the expected number of lines generated per person. The number of starters, n(0), is small compared to the total number eventually contacted. In the random net each point chooses targets equiprobably from the $N - 1$ remaining. Under these conditions, Rapoport gives an interesting and useful approximate recurrence relationship for the expected values:

$$\hat{p}(t + 1) = \left[1 - x(t)\right]\left[1 - e^{-a\hat{p}(t)}\right] \qquad (1)$$

Let us examine this relationship. To begin with, it is based on a simplifying assumption: at time t the variables are equal to their expected values. Such an assumption seems indispensable for tractability, since otherwise having obtained the expectation p(t + 1) conditional on p(t), one would have to compound it with respect to the (unknown) distribution of p(t). Rapoport and Horvath do not investigate the magnitude of the error induced by this simplification.

Suppose, then, that at time t there are exactly n(t) = Np(t) persons newly contacted and ready to make choices. Each generates an expectation of a directed lines, so we expect

$$N\hat{p}(t)a$$

lines to be generated at t. Some will, of course, target on points already in at time t, and some on new points. According to the simplifying assumptions, the probability that a randomly selected target has already been contacted by t is exactly $\hat{x}(t)$. Thus

$$\hat{x}(t)N\hat{p}(t)a$$

lines should target on points already in by t. Therefore,

$$\left[1 - \hat{x}(t)N\hat{p}(t)a\right]$$

is the number of lines expected to target on newly contacted points at t + 1.

Now we consider that set of previously uncontacted points. Each has the same probability of being the target of a line that is directed to some previously uncontacted point. The proportion uncontacted so far is

$$1 - \hat{x}(t),$$

and therefore the number uncontacted is

$$N\left[1 - \hat{x}(t)\right].$$

The probability that a particular one of these points is the target of an arbitrary line directed to a previously uncontacted point is

$$\frac{1}{N\left[1 - \hat{x}(t)\right]},$$

and the probability that such a point is *not* the target of any line whatsoever at time t is

$$\left(1 - \frac{1}{N\left[1 - \hat{x}(t)\right]}\right)^{\left[1 - \hat{x}(t)\right]N\hat{p}(t)a},$$

where the exponent is the number of lines going to previously uncontacted points.

We can simplify by letting

$$k = N\left[1 - \hat{x}(t)\right],$$

then

$$1 - \left(1 - \frac{1}{k}\right)^{k\hat{p}(t)a},$$

is the probability that a particular new point is contacted at $t + 1$ by at least one of the lines generated at t.

At this point Rapaport and Horvath introduce an approximation. From elementary calculus we know that as y grows,

$$\left(1 - \frac{1}{y}\right)^{y} \to e^{-1},$$

so we can approximate this probability as

$$1 - e^{-\hat{p}(t)a}.$$

Now recall that the probability of a point not being contacted by t is

$$1 - \hat{x}(t),$$

so the expected proportion of new contacts at $t + 1$ is

$$\hat{p}(t + 1) = \left[1 - \hat{x}(t)\right]\left[1 - e^{-a\hat{p}(t)}\right],$$

which is formula (1).

With the aid of this result, Rapoport and Horvath are able iteratively to compute the expected cumulative fraction x̂(t) reached by the tth step. This can be compared with the observed data, as in Figure 1 below. Here Rapoport and Horvath begin with initial samples of nine (= n(0)), and trace, for each person, the choices as best friend and second best friend (a = 2). The solid line, corresponding to random net theory, gives Nx̂(t) from (1), starting with Nx̂(0) = 9. The dots denote the average, over a number of replications, of actual tracings through the data: starting with a random sample of nine, the choices as first and second best friend are noted, together with the actual number of new people contacted at each step, until no new people are being contacted. It is clear from the figure that the actual tracings are incompatible with random net theory; it seems quite clear, for instance, that a reciprocity or "cliquishness" effect causes fewer new people to be contacted at each step than would be expected under randomness.

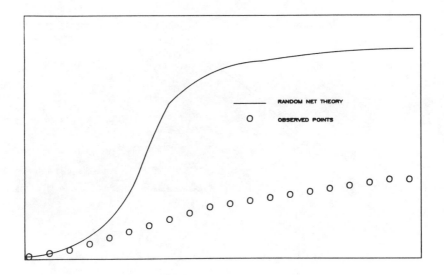

Figure 1. Comparison of tracings with random net theory
(from Rapoport and Horvath, 1961, Figure 2)

Since randomness must be rejected, attempts have been made to introduce biases into the models (see in particular Foster, Rapoport and Orwant, 1963). Remarkably, even with biases it still proves possible to give approximate results of the form (1), with slight modifications. For instance, a parameter θ may be introduced which measures the "tightness" of the friendship relation, including the tendency to be symmetric and transitive. θ = 0 corresponds to the randomness model. It is shown that if we replace the contact density a by

$$1 - e^{a\theta} + (1 - \theta)a \qquad\qquad (2)$$

then (1) still holds, under the same assumptions. The introduction of a single parameter θ here results in a drastic improvement of the fit to the data. Figure 2 shows the same observed data as Figure 1, but the expected values calculated from (1) are based on a contact density which corresponds to θ = 0.8 in (2). Although Figure 2 still reveals some systematic discrepancy between theory and data, the fit is clearly much better.

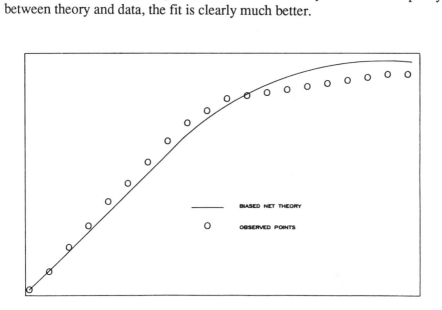

Figure 2. Comparison of tracings with biased net theory
(from Rapoport and Horvath, 1961, Figure 3)

Other bias parameters which have been introduced include

(i) A "parent bias", or symmetry parameter, π , being the probability that a person chooses the person who chose him. Under the randomness model this probability would be negligibly small, since $a \ll N(t)$, $t \rightarrow \infty$.

(ii) A "sibling bias" σ, being the probability that i chooses j, given that there is a k who chose both i and j so that i, j are siblings. Again, under randomness σ would be negligible.

For further discussion of these topics, see Rapoport (1957), Fararo and Sunshine (1964), and Rapoport (1979), in addition to the primary references already cited. We note that the estimation of the parameters only makes sense if the rather restrictive assumptions of the model do in fact hold. In more general models, such as that of Holland and Leinhardt to be discussed later, it is possible to estimate parameters under various assumptions; naturally we could then have several different estimates of the same parameter, each with its own interpretation.

We conclude this discussion of the Rapoport-Horvath model with a formal statement of the model in terms of our schema.

1. Structure experiment: a *Moreno* experiment, the relationship being friendship. On occasion the data are taken as having been derived from a *Milgram* experiment, which gives rise to the tracings through the graph as we have seen.

2. Theoretically relevant measures and randomness model (we refer here to the tracings data): the measures are the numbers $n(t)$ giving the number of new persons contacted at each step. The natural randomness model assumes that all choices, or directed lines, are independent and equiprobable.

3. Biased probability model: several have been developed, incorporating such bias parameters as the parent bias π, the sibling bias σ, the "tightness of friendship" parameter θ, etc.

4. Evaluating the fit of the model (again, with reference to the tracing data): for the most part, efforts have been confined to graphical comparison such as those shown in Figs. 1 and 2.

We have dealt with this model at some length partly for its intrinsic interest, but also to indicate the wealth of material in an apparently simple model. We shall deal with the other models more briefly, leaving the interested reader to flesh out our outlines for himself.

B. *The "Popularity" Model of Rapoport and Horvath (1961)*. We have been concerned with the tracing model of Rapoport and Horvath for the multiple friendship network. It operated as if the data embodied a time-dependent process. Their data, however, did not reflect such a process. They were generated by asking each of a group of schoolchildren to name his or her best friend from the group, together with his or her second best friend and so on, to the eighth best friend. Thus we really have eight binary matrices.

In their pioneering paper they offer a model for this synchronic friendship data. They concentrate on the indegrees, giving the number of times each person *was chosen* as first friend, second friend, etc. The outdegrees, being the number of *choices* by each person, were fixed by the experimenters. Thus the *structure experiment* is a $n \times n \times 8$ binary array $X_{k \cdot ij}$, where $X_{k \cdot ij} = 1$ means that i chose j as k^{th} best friend. The *measures* chosen are the joint indegrees $X_{k \cdot +j}$, where, as usual, a + sign indicates summation over the missing subscript. The *equivalence classes* of the n n 8 arrays are defined by the set $\{X_{k \cdot +j}\}$.

The naturally induced *randomness model* is

(i)   The $(n-1)$ possible choices as k^{th} best friend are equally likely.

(ii) For each child, the k choices are independent.

(iii) The n vectors of eight choices for the n children are independent.

If (i)-(iii) hold then the number of times one is chosen as k^{th} best friend has a Poisson distribution with mean 1; these Poisson variates are independent across k and across children.

In the *stochastic model of bias*, (iii) is still assumed. The primary bias model, however, replaces (i) and (ii) by

(i)   "Popularity" (expected indegree) for each person is a random realization from a gamma distribution 2 with shape parameter α and scale parameter γ.[2]

---

[2] The gamma family is chosen for technical convenience; the restriction is generally not serious because the gammas include a rich variety of distributional shapes.

(ii) Conditional on the popularity μ_i for the ith person, his indegrees as first, ..., eighth friends are independent Poisson variables, with common mean μ_i.[3]

According to the randomness model, in which popularities are constant, we would have $\alpha = \gamma = 1$. Rapoport and Horvath found that the best fitting values were typically in the range 2-4. The popularity bias afforded a much better fit to the data than the pure randomness (Poisson) model; see for example, Table 4 below, for the case of second friend.

Number of votes	Observed Frequency	Fitted Poisson	With Popularity Bias
0	399	356	399
1	257	314	267
2	145	138	122
3	33	40.5	46.6
4	19	8.9	16.2
5	3	1.54	5.3
6	1	.23	1.6
7	1	.029	.49
8	1	.003	.15
	859	859.2	858.3

Table 4. Observed and fitted values for second best friend (from Rapoport and Horvath, 1962)

Having demonstrated that their popularity bias gives a satisfactory fit to the distribution of number of times chosen as k^{th} best friend, Rapoport and Horvath proceed to consider the joint distribution for k ranging from 1 to 8. Here a "null" model would be that the number of votes as first, second, ... friend are independent, the marginal frequencies being taken as the observed data. An alternative model, more in keeping with popularity bias would be that, in effect,

(i) A child's popularity parameter is chosen from the gamma distribution as before.

---

[3] If there are no unused ballots, then the mean of the indegrees must be 1. So, apart from sampling variation, the parent distribution of the i, which is the gamma distribution, must have mean 1. Since the mean of a gamma distribution is $\alpha \mid \gamma$, we must have $\alpha = \gamma$.

(ii) Conditional on his popularity being equal to μ, the frequencies of choice as first, ..., eighth friend are independent Poisson variates, each with mean μ.

Rapoport and Horvath show from the data that this second model affords a better fit than the null model.

C. *Kreweras' (1966) "bandwagon" model.* Entitled "a model for opinion change during repeated balloting", Kreweras' article models the bandwagon effect which can eventually transform a well matched contest into a clear majority for one party. Although Kreweras did not cast the model in social network terms, it fits easily into our schema.

The structure experiment: we have a collection of n voters. Of these, a subset D is "decided", and the remainder "undecided", on how they will vote. In the original formulation the voting options are arbitrary, but with a slight modification we may take the options to be a subset S of the n voters themselves. Ballots take place at discrete times indexed by t. Thus we have a *Bales experiment* (see Chapter 1), consisting of matrices $X_{ij}(t)$; for a given t, $X_{ij}(t) = 1$ if $j \in S$ and i votes for j, and is 0 otherwise. With a one-man-one-vote rule we have that the outdegree $X_{i+}(t) = 1$ for all i and t.

The objective is to model a bandwagon effect, whereby a large vote for j at time t tends to induce a still larger one for j at $(t + 1)$.

The theoretically relevant *measures* here are the indegrees $X_{+j}(t)$, for $j = 1$ to n and $t = 1, 2, \ldots$, since we are concerned with the number of votes for each candidate but not with the origin of these votes. As usual, then, we would say that two realizations $X_{ij}(t)$, $X_{ij}*(t)$ are equivalent if they have the same vectors of indegrees.

A natural *model for randomness* is that the binary variables $X_{ij}(t)$ for $i \in \bar{D}, j \in S$, and all t, are independent and identically distributed. Of course for $i \in D$ the $X_{ij}(t) = 0$ or 1 deterministically, and do not change with t, since the voters in D are decided. Thus for $i \in \bar{D}, j \in S$, we have

$$E(X_{ij}(t)) = P(X_{ij}(t) = 1) = \frac{1}{|S|}.$$

Alternatively, one might take as a baseline model for randomness that the $\{X_{ij}(t)\}$ are independent, together with

$$P\left(X_{ij}(t) = 1\right) = \pi_j$$

where π_j depends on j but not on the voter i or on t.

The *biased stochastic process* proposed by Kreweras modifies the randomness model by letting the distribution of $X_{ij}(t)$ depend on j and on **X** at time $t - 1$. Specifically,

$$E\left\{ X_{ij}(t) \mid \mathbf{X}(s), s = 1, 2, ..., t - 1 \right\} = \frac{1}{n} X_{+j}(t - 1).$$

That is, for an undecided voter i the chance of voting for j at time t is proportional to the number of votes cast for j at the previous ballot. The process is clearly a Markov chain, a property exploited by Kreweras in investigating its behavior.

D. *A Model for Dominance.* Bartos (1967) describes a model for dominance in a society, based on earlier work by Landau (1951a, b; 1953). At each step of the process a randomly chosen pair of individuals "fight", the success probabilities for each outcome depending on the previous success of the two individuals. Thus a tendency for success to lead to further success may be modelled. It then becomes possible to investigate such questions as whether the process leads eventually to equality or to a hierarchy.

The *structure experiment* is a "Bales experiment", as is the Kreweras model. The *dominance matrix* is an n × n binary array $X_{ij}(t)$, for $t = 0, 1, ...$. Here $X_{ij}(t) = 1$ means that i dominates j at time t. In addition

(i) $X_{ii}(t) = 0$ (No-one dominates himself)

(ii) $X_{ij}(t) + X_{ji}(t) = 1$ for all i, j and for all t, since for any pair one must dominate the other in this model.

At each step t, a single pair "fights", and may or may not change their dominance relationship; that is, which of X_{ij} and X_{ji} is 0 and which is 1. Thus two sets of parameters are involved:

(i) $e_{ij}\left(\mathbf{X}(t), t\right)$ giving the chance that at time t and state $\mathbf{X}(t)$ it is pair (i, j) that "fight".

(ii) p_{ij} ($X(t)$), the chance that, given i and j fight at time t, i will win. These probabilities for winning are taken to be some monotonic function of the difference in the two "dominance indices", $v_i(t)$ and $v_j(t)$. The indices, however, are taken to be simply the outdegrees $X_{i+}(t)$, the number of individuals that i dominates, and thus are already determined by $X(t)$.

The theoretically relevant *measures* are the outdegree vectors $X_{i+}(t)$, giving the number of people dominated by i at time t. This induces equivalence classes on the $\{X(t)\}$ as usual. For some purposes the labelling of individuals is irrelevant, in which case the criterion for equivalence is that the outdegree vector of one array is at least a permutation of the vector for the other.

In one version of *randomness* we would have

(i) The encounter probabilities e_{ij} are all equal to

$$\frac{2}{n(n-1)}$$

(ii) $p_{ij} = 1/2$, independently of t and of $X(t)$.

This corresponds to a freely mixing and non hierarchic society. In the *biased stochastic model*

(i) the encounter probabilities e_{ij} are still equal;

(ii) p_{ij} is still to be independent of t, but dependent on $X_{i+}(t)$, $X_{j+}(t)$ by the relation

$$p_{ij} = \frac{1}{2}\left\{ 1 + w(X_{i+}(t) - X_{+j}(t)) \right\}, \qquad (3)$$

where w is a "dominance" parameter. The use of this linear function, as opposed to the more usual choices such as sigmoid or logistic, is perhaps reasonable here, where the difference between the dominance indices must be an integer between n − 1 and − (n − 1). One feature of the way the model is set up as a Markov chain is that only the latest encounter between two individuals counts. Thus, for example, whether A won the last 1 or the last 10 fights against B is irrelevant, and if B eventually wins a fight A's earlier wins are forgotten. It would be easy to define a model, still generating a Markov chain, where the chance that A beat B depended on, say, the *proportion* of previous encounters won by A.

Landau discusses the equilibrium distribution of the process. For the case of the 3 man group (n = 3), he is able to show that the equilibrium probability of a hierarchy in the group is

$$\frac{3}{4 - 2w},$$

where w is the dominance parameter in (3). Thus when w = 0 the probability is 3/4, while at w's maximum of 1/2 the probability of a hierarchy is 1. When the group is at all large, however, there is high probability that the group will be rather egalitarian.[4]

E. *Anatol Rapoport's "Outline of a probabilistic approach to animal sociology": I, II and III.* (1949a; 1949b; 1950). These articles mark one of the first attempts at modeling simple social structures. Their common concern is with the possible dominance patterns in a society. The ideas are clearly related to those of Landau that we have just discussed, although Rapoport's treatment goes considerably further in several ways.

The *structure experiment* is focussed on a binary asymmetric relation on the set of n individuals. Thus we have an n × n binary array $\{X_{ij}\}$ where for every pair (i, j), i ≠ j, $X_{ij} = 1 - X_{ji}$. We can interpret $X_{ij} = 1$ to mean "i dominates j" Given any such matrix **X**, we can define the dominance structure, by which is meant the unordered set of outdegrees $\{X_{i+}\}$. These are the relevant measures here. In Rapoport's papers interest focuses on the structure rather than on the array **X**, so that two dominance matrices are equivalent iff they have equivalent outdegrees (i.e. the same except for a permutation).

In I, Rapoport assumes in effect that the X_{ij} are independent and identically distributed, each with $P(X_{ij} = 1) = 1/2$. This may certainly be considered a model of randomness. Rapoport proceeds to discuss the probabilities of the various structures, such as chain, cycle, etc.

---

[4] At least, according to the "hierarchy index" h proposed by Landau. This is defined as the variance of the ranks X_{i+}, scaled so as to attain a maximum of 1 for a perfect hierarchy.

In II, $\{X_{ij}\}$ becomes a discrete time stationary Markov chain $\{X_{ij}(t)\}$. The states are still the structures. The defining parameters of the system are the transition probabilities a_{rs} for passing from structure r at time $t-1$ to s at time t. Rapoport shows that, under mild assumptions, the process is ergodic. The equilibrium probabilities of the structures, p_r, satisfy $p = ap$.

In III, he takes up the question of *random* and *biased models* for the process studied in II. Let

$$a_{rs} = \sum_{i,\,j} e_{ij} p_{ij},$$

the sum being over those pairs (i, j) such that if i were to beat j the result would be a change from structure r to structure s. Here e_{ij} is the chance that i, j are the next pair to "fight", and p_{ij} is the chance that i does in fact beat j. We can see here the similarity with the Landau/Bartos model. As we discussed in connection with the latter, *randomness* might be interpreted as

(i) the e_{ij} are equal,

(ii) Each p_{ij} is 1/2.

If (i) and (ii) hold then the probability distribution of dominance structures does not depend on t, and we have the situation of paper I.

Rapoport discusses three possible *biased processes*.

(a) A bias against reversal of dominance order. Here, if individual i dominates j at time t, then at their next encounter $p_{ij} > 1/2$. The Landau/Bartos model deals with just such a bias.

(b) A bias in favor of certain encounters; for example the encounter probability for i, j might be monotonic in the rank difference $(X_{i+}(t) - X_{j+}(t))$.

(c) An "inherent skill" bias, making the p_{ij} unequal from the outset. Rapoport discusses one such model, namely

$$p_{ij} = f(x_i - x_j)$$

for some monotonic f, where x_i, x_j are the skill parameters.

F. *Participation in small groups*. Several attempts have been made explicitly to model a *Bales experiment*. In a Bales experiment, a small group of subjects is assigned a task, such as designing a crossword puzzle. The proceedings are recorded by observers outside the room, perhaps on film and with a microphone in the room. The task is to model, and if possible to explain, the pattern of interactions of the group members as they unfold through time.

Naturally, the information latent in a film of a group in operation is exceedingly rich—perhaps too rich for quantitative analysis, since even if we disregard non-verbal behavior, we could attend to who is talking to whom at a given moment, what kind of interaction it is (interrogatory, imperative, encouraging, discouraging, etc.) how long it lasted and what else was going on at the time. At any rate, much of the considerable body of research on this topic cited in Gray and von Broembson, 1976, and Doreian, 1979) has confined itself to consider

(a) The number of times each member makes a verbal contribution.

(b) The number of times each is addressed by another group member.

(c) The nature of the interaction.

These restrictions simplify the task, but at a price. Thus, for example, we cannot study changes over time in group behavior, even though it seems likely that group relations will take time to become established. Nor can we consider questions such as whether the frequency of $i \rightarrow j$ interactions is explained solely by i's overall propensity to talk and j's to listen. Further, we lose information on the temporal sequence; we would expect, for instance that an $i \rightarrow j$ interaction would be followed relatively often by a $j \rightarrow i$ interaction, but the data on this is lost. We shall return to some of these points shortly.

With these restrictions, the *structure experiment* is now a directed graph with multiple links; each link from i to j represents an occasion when i addresses j. Note that some contributions will be to the whole group; these could be ignored, treated separately, or taken as links to each of the other members. The *measures* customarily made are, as we have seen, merely the indegrees and outdegrees of the graph. These define equivalence classes as usual. Correspondingly, the appropriate parameters for our models are the proportions p_i, of participations by (or, alternatively, to) the ith member. It is convenient to label the n members so that the $p_1 > p_2 > \ldots > p_n$.

One simple *model for randomness* is that the probabilities of participation are all equal. This does not imply that the expected values of the p_i are equal, however, since the p_i are put into rank order. In fact the expected p_i's under randomness are difficult to calculate and depend on strong assumptions. If, for instance we were willing to assume successive contributions to be independent and identically distributed then the joint distribution of the *unordered* p_i would be multinomial with a common mean.

A number of *biased models* have been suggested. Bales *et al.* (1951) discussed the fitting of a harmonic series to the p_i, but concluded that the fit was unsatisfactory. Stephan and Mishler (1952), however, argue that an excellent fit is obtained with an exponential series

$$p_i = ar^{i-1} \tag{3}$$

for some $r \in (0, 1)$ and appropriate normalizing constant a. This well known result appears to hold up under a wide range of conditions, and has, for example, been selected by Coleman (1964) as a prime example of a sociological law. Unfortunately no very convincing mechanism has been proposed to explain the exponential series. Stephan and Misher point out that it could result if a hierarchy is established in the group such that the top man speaks with probability r; if he does not then the next man speaks with probability r, etc. If nobody chooses to speak (an event of probability $(1 - r)^n$) then the opportunity reverts to the top man, and so on.

Validation of the model rests on a number of tables showing that the exponential series, with parameters a and r in (3) estimated by a modified least squares method, fits the observed series p_i to a good approximation. (Naturally, the parameters vary across experiments.) Significance tests are not carried out by Stephan and Mishler. Two possible reasons are:

(a)   The assumptions needed for the usual χ^2 test—the participations being independent and identically distributed—are hard to justify.

(b)   In practice the number of contributions by or to the ith most prolific participant is obtained separately for several different independent experiments and aggregated. In a genuinely probabilistic model this procedure will cause problems, since the ordering of the p_i in each sub-experiment is itself stochastic.

For example, there will be a tendency to overestimate p_1 because the procedure can capitalize on change fluctuation.

It seems very natural to try to model the relationship between in-and out degrees jointly. The only model of this sort that we are aware of is the so-called "social law of effect", discussed by Gray and Von Broembson (1976) and by Doreian (1979). This is

$$\ln \frac{p_i}{1 - p_i} = a + b \ln \frac{q_i}{1 - q_i} \qquad (4)$$

where a, b are constants and q_i is the proportion of participations to the ith member. Equation (4) reduces to a null model $p_i \equiv q_i$ when $a = 0, b = 1$. No convincing mechanism to produce (4) has been suggested, and indeed the log-odds form

$$\ln \left\{ \frac{p_i}{1 - p_i} \right\}$$

seems somewhat *ad hoc*.

Other models that seem worth investigating are

(a) *A model for the interaction frequencies* rather than just the marginal totals. The simplest model in the spirit of the exponential would be

$$p_{ij} = ar^{i-1}s^{j-1} \qquad (5)$$

where p_{ij} is the proportion of (i, j) interactions, r is the indegree parameter as before, and s is the outdegree parameter. Such a model corresponds to independence of participant and his target, conditional on their respective rank order.

(b) *A Markov chain model for the time sequence* of interactions. The parameters here might be

$$p_{ij,rs}$$

giving the probability that the next participation will be from r
to s, conditional on the current one being from i to j. Here a null
model might be

$$\ln p_{ij,rs} = a + b_r + c_s,$$

a log linear model in which the present "state" i,j has no
influence on the next state, and for which the conditional
independence form (5) holds. It is then easy to add biases. For
instance, one could add a constant for the case $i = r$, $j = s$, since
an interaction from i to j tends to be reciprocated. We are
currently working along these lines.

G. *Local Rationality Model.* Christie, Luce and Macy (1952) report
on the extensive work done at MIT in the early 1950's in the Group Networks
Laboratory. A typical experiment would involve a group of five subjects
attempting to solve a problem. For instance, each subject might be given a
bowl of colored marbles; the bowls would have only one color in common,
and the task was to find what that color was in the minimum number of steps.
An imporant feature of the experiments was that some, but not all, of the
possible lines of communication were open. One structure studied is shown
in Figure 3(a); it is characterized by each subject's having access to two of the
others and the remaining two subjects having access to him. Christie *et al.*
call this the pinwheel. Experimental conditions were controlled so that at
discrete times $t = 1, 2, \ldots$ each of the five subjects simultaneously sent a
message to one of his two possible choices.

One aspect of the study was the time sequence in the choices. It was
supposed that the probability of a subject's alternating from his previous
choice might depend only on the number of messages which reached him on
the previous step. The three topologically distinct cases for the previous step
are shown in Figure 3(b); the number of messages reaching the subject are
shown below each pattern.

The *structure experiment* here is a Bales experiment. We may define a
stochastic process on the graph in terms of the matrix **X**, where

$$m_{ij}(t) = \begin{cases} 1 \text{ if i contacts j at time t} \\ 0 \text{ otherwise.} \end{cases}$$

Some of the contacts are forbidden throughout. We write A for the set of ordered pairs (i, j) for which i may contact j. The main *measure* considered by Christie *et al.* is the distribution of the number of acts of communication required to solve the problem. This is influenced by the distribution of $X(t)$. If, for example, subjects do not alternate their choice even when they received 0 messages on the previous trial, so that they are conveying no new information, the number of acts until solution is likely to be large. A natural *null model* of *randomness* here would be that the choice of each subject is made at each trial by tossing a fair coin. That is, for (i, j) ∈ A the random variables $X_{ij}(t)$ are all independent Bernoulli variables with expectation 1/2.

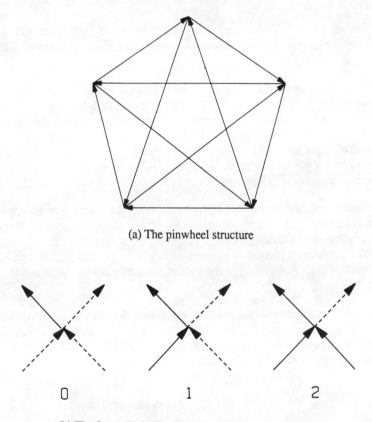

(a) The pinwheel structure

(b) The 3 topologically distinct patterns for the previous message; solid arrows indicate messages, dotted arrows indicate unused channels of communication.

Figure 3. (from Christie, Macy and Luce, 1956)

Christie *et al.* introduce a *bias* which they call "local rationality." According to this, a subject who received no new information at time t − 1 is sure to alternate his choice at the present time. A subject who received one or two messages at time t − 1 should have a probability of at least 1/2 of alternating, since he has at least as much information for the alternative contactee as he had for his previous contactee. This defines a Markov chain process for **X**. For $(i, j) \in A$ we have

$$E\left\{X_{ij}(t) \mid X_{+i}(t-1)\right\} = \left\{1 - X_{ij}(t-1)\right\} \text{ if } X_{+i}(t-1) = 0$$
$$= p\left\{1 - X_{ij}(t-1)\right\} \text{ if } X_{ij}(t-1) = 1 \text{ or } 2$$

Christie *et al.* show that this forecasts their experimental results reasonably well, particularly after the group has had experience with the task.

H. *A Markov Model for the Small World Experiment: Hunter and Shotland (1974).* Milgram's Small World technique begins by issuing a booklet to a starter person, together with instructions to move the booklet to a person designated as a target. If the starter does not know the target, he is instructed to pass the booklet to a person he does know, who has a better chance of knowing the target. The process is repeated until the booklet reaches the target, or it is lost in some way.

Hunter and Shotland offer a stochastic model for this process, based on a classification of the participants according to their personal characteristics—which might be age, gender or occupation, etc. If on the tth pass of the booklet, it passes to someone in class v, we say that the process is in state v at time t. According to the model the process is a stationary Markov chain.

Here the *structure experiment* is a combination of the *Milgram* and the *Galton-Watson* experiment. The set of persons in the experiment consists of all the persons to whom the booklet might be passed. We index persons by i and j, as usual, and write

$$X_{ij}(t) = \begin{cases} 1 \text{ if the i}^{th} \text{ pass is from i to j,} \\ 0 \text{ otherwise.} \end{cases}$$

As in a Galton-Watson experiment, each individual has an *attribute* indicating, say, his occupation. The occupation of person i is denoted by v_i. The state space S consists of these v_i's augmented by two absorbing states corresponding to "booklet has reached its target" and "booklet is lost."

The measures relevant to Hunter and Shotland's model are the number of times the process passes from state u at some time t to state w at $t + 1$, for all pairs of states $\{\langle u, w \rangle: u, w \in S\}$. The expectation of these counts are proportional to the transition probabilities of the Markov chain, and the measures are sufficient statistics for these probabilities.

Naturally the matrix of transition probabilities depends on the state of the target individual; if the target is in state w, then, for instance, the booklet is relatively more likely to be passed to someone in w. Therefore Hunter and Shotland condition the process on the state of the target.

The natural null model for the process is that all persons are equally likely to be the next recipient of the booklet. In particular, the chance that person j is the next recipient is independent of v_j. In this case the transition probabilities $p(u, w)$ are independent of u, being merely proportional to the number of persons in state w. In the Hunter and Shotland biased model we have a stationary Markov chain on S, governed by the transition probabilities $p(u, w)$, but any set of p's defining a valid transition matrix is permitted. In practice $p(u, w)$ is estimated from the measures as the fraction of times a booklet currently in state u is next passed to someone in state w. Given knowledge of the relative sizes of the groups we could then equivalently define a Markov chain on the set of individuals in our universe. Thus the time sequence of j's such that $X_{ij}(t) = 1$ is itself a Markov chain.

Hunter and Shotland show that the kind of biases one would expect are indeed present. Thus, for example, we generally find that $p(u, w) < p(w, w)$ for $u \neq w$; that is, there is a bias against passing across attribute classes. Further, the classes vary considerably in their propensity to lose the booklet. Amongst students, for instance, their data showed that freshman and graduate students are both about twice as likely to lose the booklet as sophomores, juniors and seniors.

Validation of the model: Hunter and Shotland usefully note that formal statistical testing of such models is not appropriate, since we know in advance that the model cannot provide a perfect description of the process, and we would really be testing whether we had sufficient data to establish a significant departure from the model. We know that the model will be falsified if we look for appropriately subtle effects. In a study at a university where the target was an administrator, for instance, it was found that the transition probability from the category "full professor" to "administrator" was relatively much larger if the full professor was reached late in the chain. This is not surprising, since if the professor is reached after many passes of the booklet it is likely that he was selected as someone acquainted with the target, or perhaps with administrators in general. Instead, Hunter and Shotland consider various statistics derived from the data, and compare them with the predictions from the model. The statistics considered are

(a) The k-step transition rates $p_k(u, w)$ giving, for k = 2, 3, or 4, the conditional probability of being in a state w given that k steps earlier the process was in a state u. The model-predicted k step transition rates were derived from raising the one step probability matrix to the kth power, as is standard for Markov chains. The agreement between model and data here seemed satisfactory in the experiment reported.

(b) The average length of the chain from starter to target, or from starter to the loss of the booklet. Here the model fitted the experimental data well.

(c) The variance of the chain length. The model tended to overestimate the variance of chain length. As Hunter and Shotland note, such discrepancies are themselves helpful to our understanding of the process. They suggest that in practice if there have already been many passes then people are likely to be invoking relevant non-attribute material information ("Oh, that's my girl-friend's roommate") to shorten the chain.

I. *Rainio's Model of Social Interaction.* In a series of articles, Rainio (1961, 1965, 1966) proposes a very complex model of social interaction as a stochastic learning process. He is primarily concerned, however, with two special cases: a theory of social contacts and a theory of group problem solving. Here we shall describe a somewhat simplified version of the social contact theory.

Rainio conducted experiments of the following kind. He installed each of a group of six subjects in a separate box, so that information could be conveyed only through a special message apparatus. Subjects would be given a statement, such as "The population of Stockholm is larger than that of Mexico City." They were then asked to indicate whether they thought it was true or false and how strongly they held this opinion. Next, each subject was allowed to choose just one of the other five with whom to exchange opinions about the statement. After this they were asked again to express the strength of their opinions. This was repeated with 20 or more different statements. The key feature of the experiment was that subjects displayed an increasing tendency to contact individuals who shared their opinions, and to strengthen or weaken their beliefs according to whether their chosen colleague agreed or disagreed with them. The biases in Rainio's model are designed to capture these tendencies.

In our terms the *structure experiment* is a *Hägerstrand experiment*. We have a matrix $X_{ij}(t)$, where $t = 1, 2, \ldots$ indexes the number of the statement and thus corresponds to discrete time, and

$$X_{ij}(t) = \begin{cases} 1 \text{ if subject i chooses to exchange} \\ \quad \text{opinions with j at time t,} \\ 0 \text{ otherwise.} \end{cases}$$

Thus $X_{ii}(t) = 0$ and $X_{i+}(t) = 1$ for all i and t. The *associated attribute,* which in Hägerstrand's work is the binary attribute adopter/non adopter at time t, is here i's opinion on the statement at time t, together with his strength of belief, before and after exchanging opinions. We write

$a_i(t) = 1$ if subject i agrees with statement t, before exchanging opinions,

$a_i(t) = 0$ if he disagrees with it,

$v_i(t) =$ i's strength of belief in the statement t before exchanging opinions.

We donote the corresponding quantities *after* exchanging opinions by $a_i'(t)$ and $v_i'(t)$. Thus our attribute set consists of ordered pairs

$$\langle (a_i(t), v_i(t)), \ (a_i'(t), v_i'(t)) \rangle$$

ranging over subjects i and statements t.

Given that i contacted j at time t, it is convenient to denote by $A_{ij}(t) = 1$ the event that $a_i(t) = a_j(t)$, so that i and j agreed at time t. We write $A_{ij}(t) = 0$ if $a_i(t) \neq a_j(t)$.

The *theoretically relevant measures* correspond to the two tendencies we have noted: to associate with subjects who have previously been in agreement, and to change one's belief according to the opinion of the currently contacted subject. Thus the measures are

(i) For each i, the time sequence of values of j for which $X_{ij}(t) = 1$, together with the associated values $A_{ij}(t)$.

(ii) Separately and independently for each subject i and statement t combination, the $\langle v_i(t), v_i'(t) \rangle$ pairs as a function of $A_{ij}(t)$.

These two sets of measures correspond to the two simultaneous stochastic processes inherent in the model, one for the choices of contacted subjects for $t = 1, 2, \ldots$, and the other for the changes from $a_i(t), v_i(t)$ to $a_i'(t), v_i'(t)$ due to the exchange of opinion at each value of t.

According to the *null model*

(i) For each i, the distribution of the vector $\langle X_{i1}(t), \ldots, X_{in}(t) \rangle$ is independent of t. In particular, this says that the chance that i contacts j is not modified by the outcome of previous contacts.

(ii) The distribution of $(a_i'(t), v_i'(t))$, given $(a_k(t), v_k(t))$, $k = 1, 2, \ldots, n$, depends only on $(a_i(t), v_i(t))$. That is, the opinions of others about statement t do not affect one's revised opinion.

Rainio's *biased stochastic process* is based on the well known Bush-Mosteller *two-operator learning model*. Suppose a subject repeatedly chooses between two alternatives in a series of trials. After each choice, the subject is either rewarded or punished. If p_n is the subject's probability of choosing a certain alternative on trial n then, according to the model,

$$p_{n+1} = \begin{cases} p_n + \alpha(1 - p_n) & \text{if the behavior at n was rewarded,} \\ p_n - \beta p_n & \text{if the behavior at n was punished.} \end{cases}$$

Here α and β are parameters governing the "learning rate" $(0 \le \alpha, \beta \le 1)$.

In Rainio's model,

(i) The probability $p_{ij}(t + 1)$ that i contacts j at time t + 1, given that i contacted j at time t, depends on $p_{ij}(t)$ according to the learning model. Here $A_{ij} = 1$ (denoting concurrence of opinion) corresponds to a reward and $A_{ij} = 0$ to a punishment, applying to both i and j.

(ii) The strength of i's belief in statement t, which we denoted by $v_i(t)$, also increases or decreases after the opinion sharing according to the learning model. Again reward and punishment correspond to $A_{ij} = 1$ and 0 respectively, but the parameters α and β in the model need not be the same as in (i).

Thus the setting of the parameters α and β to 0 leads us back to a null model.

Rainio has conducted extensive efforts at *model validation*. His laboratory data seem to be compatible with the learning model, although the fitted parameters vary across individuals. He has also programmed the stochastic process so as to generate Monte Carlo simulations for comparison with actual data. The reader is referred to Rainio's articles for the details.

J. *Hägerstrand's Spatial Model for Diffusion.* In a series of articles, Hägerstrand (1965a; 1965b) has developed a simulation model for the spatial diffusion of an innovation. He works with recent phenomena for which detailed information is available, such as the spread of Rotary Clubs, public swimming, baths, or government inspection of forms for a cattle disease. In all these cases geographic propinquity is a major factor in determining where the innovation will next be passed. Figure 4 (from Hägerstrand, 1965a), showing a typical series of diffusion maps, illustrates the propinquity effect. At first sight this work may seem quite unrelated to social network models, but we shall see that this is not so.

If we label the potential adopters—which may be individuals, farms, households, cities, etc.—of the innovation in some arbitrary fashion, we can immediately speak of a structure experiment and a null model in network terms. The potential adopters are the nodes of a graph, and the relevant attribute is the labelling of the nodes as currently adopters or non-adopters. If we take a snapshot at each time the innovation is passed to a new adopter from one who possessed it already then we have a stochastic process defined on the graph. This structure was described formally in Chapter 1, where it was termed a *Hägerstrand experiment*. The obvious *null model* is that all the current non-adopters are equally likely to be the next convert. Here the null hypothesis is that geographic location plays no part, and the model is rather similar to the null tracing model of Rapoport and Horvath (1961); see A above.

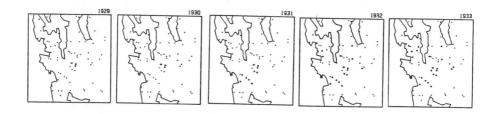

Figure 4. Spread of subsidy for improved pasture on small farms. Small points: potential adopters. Black dots: adopters. (From Hägerstrand, 1965a, Figure Ia)

Naturally, such a null model in this context serves only as an aid to thought; the interesting question is how we can sensibly model a bias. Hägerstrand works with several models, of varying degrees of sophistication, but all based on the following ingenious idea. Given the location of the adopter who is going to pass on the innovation at the next step of the simulation, we note his distances from all the current non-adopters. Then their probabilities of being the next adopters are a function of their distance. The function has to be determined empirically from exogenous data. Hägerstrand's approach here is use a floating 5 × 5 grid of squares with an associated set of adoption probabilities $\{p_{ij}\}$, for $i, j = -2, -1, 0, 1, 2$. The individual about to spread the innovation is at the center of the grid and the chance that a potential adopter in square (i,j) will be the chosen one is weighted by p_{ij}. Outside the grid the chance of being chosen are taken to be zero.

How are the p_{ij}'s determined numerically? Hägerstrand takes existing data on frequency of telephone calls, marriages or migrations as a function of distance, noting the decay as distance increases, and uses the observed relative frequencies for the p_{ij}'s. Refinements are added to the model; for example a long narrow lake reduces the interaction between households on opposite sides, as reflected by the data on telephone calls, marriages, etc. In his simulations, Hägerstrand represents such a barrier by halving, or eliminating altogether, the chance of a non-adopter located across the barrier. Clearly biased models of this kind can be made increasingly realistic—and complex—in many ways, and later workers in geographic diffusion have refined the approach considerably (see, for example, Morrill and Pitts, 1967).

The *evaluation* of such biased models is not altogether straight - forward. Because of the dependence of the process on the initial locations of potential adopters, one cannot hope for some routine χ^2 type test to compare an "observed" map with some expectation. Hägerstrand tries several kinds of informal evaluation. Two examples

(i) He takes "snapshots" of a simulation at various stages of growth, repeats this for several other simulations, and compared the maps with the actual process, taken at the same "time periods". Visually, the actual process seems quite compatible with the simulations.

(ii) Dividing the region into squares, he takes a given snapshot and graphs the number of squares where more than x% of the units are adopters, for various values of x. This gives a kind of cumulative frequency curve, which is repeated for other snapshots of the same simulation. The set of these curves, arising from a simulation, are again compared to the others and to those arising from the actual data. Again, the agreement seems reasonable in Hägerstrand's example.

In general, to evaluate these simulations one must decide on some *measures*, or statistics, of the process. It seems to us that the measure inherent in Hägerstrand's models is the *probability density function of the distance* from the initial innovator. A discretized version of this function is defined by the 5×5 grid of squares discussed above. One can thus test the agreement between a theoretical and an empirical data-based density function of distance with a statistical significance test, such as the Kolmogorov-Smirnov.

3. Some recent models

The remaining models we shall discuss, which are of very recent vintage, are explicitly designed according to our paradigm; each offers a broad class of biased probabilistic processes, with the null case arising when parameters are set to zero.

   K. *Wasserman's Continuous Time Model.* We begin with some recent models for networks evolving in *continuous* time, the main reference here being Wasserman (1980). The structure experiment is a set of binary matrices $X(t) = \{X_{ij}(t)\}$, where the time parameter t is continuous. As usual, $X_{ij}(t) = 1$ denotes a link from i to j; by convention $X_{ii}(t) = 0$ for all i and t. In a time interval (t, t + dt), a state X_{ij} may or may not change (to $1 - X_{ij}$); in general the transition probability may depend on the whole array $X(t)$, or even the set of all previous states $\{X(s): s \leq t\}$; clearly some restrictions are necessary if any progress is to be made. The two following assumptions, due originally to Holland and Leinhardt (1977), are made throughout this work.

1. X(t) is a Markov chain.

2. For small intervals of time dt, changes in the links are independent. More formally, if x, y denote states of X, and $P_{xy}(s, t)$ denotes the chance of being in state y at t given state x at s, then

$$P_{xy}(t, t + dt) = \prod_{i, j} P\{X_{ij}(t + dt) = y_{ij} \mid X(t) = x\} + 0(dt)$$

where $\dfrac{0(dt)}{dt} \to 0$ as dt $\to 0$.

   This second assumption prevents links from changing in collusion; the chance of two or more simultaneous changes is zero. Together, the two assumptions greatly simplify the problem, as the parameters of the system are now the *instantaneous transition rates* λ defined by

$$\lambda_{ijk}(x, t) = \lim_{dt \to 0} \left[\frac{1}{dt} P\{X_{ij}(t + dt) = k \mid X(t) = x, X_{ij}(t) = 1 - k\} \right]$$

for k = 0, 1.

The λ's, which may vary with **x** and t, measure the relative likelihood of an instantaneous change in $X_{ij}(t)$. By taking simple special forms for the λ's, we arrive at some tractable models.

Wasserman (1980) describes two such simple models. The first is his *reciprocity model,* for which

$$\lambda_{ij0}(\mathbf{x},t) = \lambda_0 + \mu_0 x_{ji}$$

$$\lambda_{ij1}(\mathbf{x},t) = \lambda_1 + \mu_1 x_{ji}.$$

That is, the chance of a link from i to j being created or withdrawn during a short time period depends only on the presence or absence of the reciprocated choice from j to i. In addition, the transition rates are time homogeneous, giving us a stationary process. Our *null,* or *randomness, model* would set the μ_k's to zero (and perhaps the λ_k's also), giving us a system where the $n(n-1)$ potential links flash on and off randomly and independently.

According to the reciprocity model, the $1/2\, n(n-1)$ *dyads*

$$D_{ij}(t) = \left\{ X_{ij}(t), X_{ji}(t) \right\}$$

are all mutually independent. Thus the study of the system reduces to that of the D_{ij}'s, which have but three distinguishable states: (0, 0), (0, 1) or (1, 0), and (1, 1). Plainly, such a model has limited practical applicability, since in general one would expect a change in a link (i, j) to have effects throughout the system, and not just on (j, i). However, as Wasserman points out, such simple models may be viewed as benchmark null models.

The *measures* for the reciprocity model are the sufficient statistics for its parameters. These are

$$M(t) = \sum_{i>j} x_{ij} x_{ji},$$

the number of mutual links,

$$A(t) = \sum_{i>j} \left[(1 - x_{ij}) x_{ji} + x_{ij} (1 - x_{ji}) \right],$$

the number of asymmetric links, and

$$N(t) = \sum_{i,j} (1 - x_{ij})(1 - x_{ji}),$$

the number of unlinked pairs. Since these measures sum to $1/2\, n(n-1)$, we have only two pieces of information, and thus can estimate only two functions of the parameters $\lambda_0, \lambda_1, \mu_0, \mu_1$. Wasserman discusses the interpretation of these functions, as well as the (rather involved) estimation procedures.

In the second, "popularity", model examined by Wasserman the transition rates are given by

$$\lambda_{ij0}(\mathbf{x},t) = \lambda_0 + \pi_0 x_{+j},$$

$$\lambda_{ij1}(\mathbf{x},t) = \lambda_1 + \pi_1 x_{+j},$$

where x_{+j} is the indegree

$$\sum_i x_{ij},$$

the number of links directed to j, which may be interpreted as j's popularity. The parameters π_0 and π_1, measure the importance of popularity. Instead of $1/2\, n(n-1)$ independent and identically distributed dyads, we have n i.i.d. vector processes

$$\{X_{ij}(t), ..., X_{nj}(t)\} \text{ for } j = 1, ..., n.$$

Again, see Wasserman for the estimation procedures, together with numerical illustrations.

Evaluation of the models, as opposed to estimation of their parameters, appears difficult, and little progress has been made. The question is the validity of assumptions, such as the Markov property, the time homogeneity and the i.i.d. condition for the dyads of the reciprocity model. Ideally, a number of different statistical tests need to be applied for each fitting of a model. These continuous time stochastic processes pose many technical problems, many of which remain to be solved, but it seems to us that a promising beginning has been made.

L. *The Holland-Leinhardt Model.* A common feature of the models in part III is the parametric form of their biases—an *exponential* family. As we see, for such a parametric family the statistical tasks of fitting and testing the models becomes straightforward, at least in principle. We now turn to the Holland-Leinhardt (1980) model; its exponential form in some respects parallels the Rapoport Horvath approach, but has some striking advantages.

The *structure experiment* is the basic digraph represented by an $n \times n$ binary matrix $\mathbf{X}$, although the generalization to multi-relational Moreno-Davis type experiments would not be difficult. The experiment is synchronic, with no time parameter. The choice of theoretically relevant measures is extremely flexible; one can at will add or delete terms for indegrees, outdegrees, various triad counts, etc. In the "p_1 model" we have

$$M = \Sigma \, X_{ij}X_{ji}, \text{ the number of symmetric edges,}$$

$$\{X_{i+}\}, \text{ the vector of outdegrees,}$$

$$\{X_{+j}\}, \text{ the vector of indegrees.}$$

If $\mathbf{x}$ is a generic $n \times n$ binary matrix for which $M = m$, $X_{i+} = x_{i+}$, etc., then

$$P(\mathbf{X} = \mathbf{x}) = \exp\{\rho m + \theta x_{++} + \Sigma \alpha_i x_i +$$

$$\Sigma \beta_j x_{+j}\} \, K(\rho, \theta, \{\alpha_i\}, \{\beta_j\}) \qquad (6)$$

where $\rho, \theta, \{\alpha_i\}, \{\beta_j\}$ are the bias parameters, $\Sigma \alpha_i = \Sigma \beta_j = 0$ and K is a normalizing constant.

The equation (6) defines an *exponential family* of probability distributions, with the statistics x_{i+}, x_{+j}, x_{++} and m being *sufficient* for the bias parameters. The following derivation of (6) aids in the interpretation of the parameters.

(i) Assume that the dyads $D_{ij} = (X_{ij}, X_{ji})$, for $i < j$, are independent. This means that tendencies towards transitivity, cliquing etc. cannot be expressed. We need now only specify the distribution of the D_{ij}'s.

(ii) Let ρ, assumed to be independent of i and j in (6), be (the log odds on $X_{ij} = 1 \mid X_{ji} = 1$) − (the log odds on $X_{ij} = 1 \mid X_{ji} = 0$). Thus ρ measures the strength of the reciprocation effect.

(iii) Let θ_{ij} be the log odds on $X_{ij} = 1$ given $X_{ji} = 0$. Suppose that θ_{ij} can be decomposed, as in the log-linear model, thus:

$$\theta_{ij} = \theta + \alpha_i + \beta_j,$$

with

$$\Sigma\, \alpha_i = \Sigma\, \beta_j = 0.$$

Then α_i governs the outdegree tendency for person i, β_j governs the indegrees, and θ controls the overall tendency for X_{ij} to be 1 rather than 0.

Holland and Leinhardt show that under these assumptions the density of X is given by (6). They describe (6) as a "null" model, since it assumes dyad independence, but by earlier standards it is a very sophisticated one. The most extreme interpretation of *randomness*, that all arrays **X** are equally likely, is achieved by setting all parameters in (6) to zero. If, for example, we set all parameters to zero except θ and the $\{\alpha_i\}$ we arrive at a null model discussed by Moreno (1934). It says that, conditional on the observed outdegrees $\{X_{i+}\}$, all matrices are equally likely.

A most attractive feature of the Holland-Leinhardt approach is that one can immediately build desired additional biases into the model. For example the statistic

$$T = \sum_{i \neq j \neq k} X_{ij} X_{ik} X_{jk}$$

may be taken as a possible measure of *transitivity;* unlike other measures so far discussed, it is a function of triads rather than dyads. To modify (6) to include the effect measured by T, one need only add a term τ to the exponent. The null hypothesis of no transitivity effect would then be that $\tau = 0$. It will be noted that the model forces us to clarify exactly what we mean by terms such as reciprocity and transitivity. Thus, for instance, we might want to test for a reciprocity bias. That is, we ask whether the parameter ρ in (6) differs from zero. The point is that the question is not well posed until we specify which other parameters are to be set to zero and which are to be estimated. The presence or absence of in or outdegree biases, or triad-type effects will affect the reciprocity parameter. Failure to recognize the interrelation between the various effects has lead to controversy in the past over the "right" interpretation of reciprocity, etc. (See, for instance, Holland and Leinhardt, 1971). It seems to us that this automatic clarification of the bias structure represents an important advance over the earlier Rapoport-type models.[5]

Parameter estimation and significance testing for the models are performed in the standard way for the exponential family. The equations for the maximum likelihood estimaters of the parameters are all of the form "expected values of the measures are set equal to their observed values"; significance tests are the customary χ^2 tests based on the log likelihood ratio.

We conclude with an extract from a numerical example analyzed by Holland and Leinhardt. The data, from the oft-quoted monastery friendship data of Sampson (1969), is shown in Figure 4. There is essentially no variation in the outdegrees because only the top three choices (with ties allowed) were taken. The variation in indegrees is consistent with chance: the variance of the indegrees is 2.99, compared to a theoretical chance variance of 2.54. There is, however, clear evidence of reciprocity; there are 15 cases of reciprocal pairs, compared to 5.12 expected by chance given the outdegrees. There are also significantly more *transitive triads* than expected by chance; this, together with the reciprocity, suggests a tendency to cliquing.

---

[5] It will be recalled that Rapoport and his collaborators discuss various biases, such as

(a) A reciprocity bias, π, increasing the chance that $X_{ij} = 1$ given that $X_{ji} = 1$.

(b) A sibling bias, σ, increasing the chance that $X_{ij} = 1$ given that the is a k such that $X_{ki}X_{kj} = 1$.

When these biases operate, the induced probability distribution on the space on binary matrices is certainly not a "random" or "uniform" one, but it does imply that the marginal distributions of the indegrees is uniform, and similarly for that of the outdegrees. When, as in practice will generally be the case, the nodes are clearly heterogenous with respect to in or outdegree, the parametric structure will be distorted in a way that the model does not take care of. For example, if some of the nodes have very high in and outdegree, the reciprocity tendency will be high independently of an explicit bias built in through the parameter π. In this situation there is clearly ambiguity in the meaning of reciprocity.

The model (6) fitted to the data gives a matrix of probabilities. It is frequently interesting to examine the residuals, or differences between data and expectations. Figure 6 shows one such residual plot. Here a + denotes a residual of +0.7 or more, corresponding to link unanticipated by the model. A − sign (there are none here) would indicate residuals less than −0.7, while intermediate residuals are left blank. Because there are more zeroes than ones in the data, the majority of residuals are negative. More interestingly, it can be seen that the majority of +'s in Figure 6 occur within the blocks, which are the subgroups identified by White, Boorman and Brieger (1976). This supports the contention that these blocks tend to cliquishness.

	1	2	3	4	5	6	7	8	9	10	11	12	13	14	15	16	17	18	SUM
1	0	1	1	0	1	0	0	0	0	0	0	0	0	0	0	1	0	0	4
2	0	0	1	0	1	1	0	0	0	0	0	0	0	0	0	0	0	0	3
3	0	1	0	0	0	0	1	1	0	0	0	0	0	0	0	0	0	0	3
4	0	1	1	0	1	0	0	0	0	0	0	0	0	0	0	0	0	0	3
5	0	1	0	1	0	1	0	0	0	0	0	0	0	0	0	0	0	0	3
6	0	1	0	0	0	0	1	0	0	0	1	0	0	0	0	0	0	0	3
7	0	0	1	1	1	0	0	0	0	0	0	0	0	0	0	0	0	0	3
8	0	0	0	0	0	0	0	1	1	0	0	1	0	0	0	0	0	0	3
9	0	0	0	0	0	0	0	1	0	0	1	0	0	0	0	1	0	0	3
10	0	0	0	0	0	0	0	1	1	0	0	0	1	0	0	0	0	0	3
11	0	0	0	0	0	0	0	1	1	0	0	1	0	0	0	0	0	0	3
12	0	0	0	0	0	0	0	1	0	1	0	0	1	0	0	0	0	0	3
13	0	0	0	0	0	0	0	1	0	1	0	0	0	1	0	0	0	0	3
14	0	0	0	0	0	0	0	0	0	1	0	1	1	0	0	0	0	0	3
15	0	1	0	0	0	0	0	0	0	0	0	0	1	0	0	0	0	1	3
16	0	0	0	0	0	0	0	0	1	0	0	0	0	0	1	0	1	1	4
17	0	0	0	0	0	0	0	0	0	1	0	0	0	0	0	1	0	1	3
18	0	0	0	0	0	0	0	0	0	1	0	0	0	0	0	1	1	0	3
SUM	0	6	4	2	4	2	2	6	4	6	2	2	5	1	2	3	2	3	56

Figure 5. Adjacency matrix (from Sampson, 1969)

The estimate of the reciprocity parameter ρ is $3.1 = \log_e 22.2$, so that

$$P(X_{ij} = 1 \mid X_{ji} = 1) = 22.2 \times P(X_{ij} = 1 \mid X_{ji} = 0).$$

This estimate for ρ assumes that $\{\alpha_i\}$ and $\{\beta_j\}$ are in the model; setting the α's and β's to zero gives a different estimate, and its interpretation would also differ. The estimate of θ, the log odds on an arbitrary X_{ij}'s being 1, is −2.5, indicating the preponderance of zeroes. The estimates of the α_i and β_j are given in Table 5.

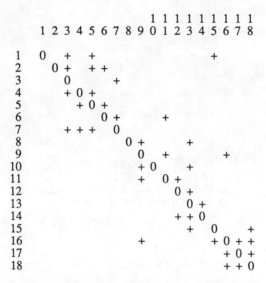

Figure 6. Residual plot (from Holland and Leinhardt, 1980)

It can be seen that the relationship between the β_j's and the indegrees $X_{.j}$ is nearly monotonic. The estimate $-\infty$ for β_1 is necessary because we must have

$$\sum_i p_{i1} = X_{+1} = 0.$$

The other β's are normed so their sum is zero. If, in (6), we set the reciprocity parameter ρ to zero then equal $X_{.j}$'s would give rise to equal estimates for β_j's. This, however, is not the case here, where we have $\hat{\rho} \neq 0$. We note that the α's vary considerably, despite the near equality of the X_{i+}'s. This, too, is a consequence of the reciprocity.

i, j	α_i	β_j
1	1.15	1.25
2	-.73	.49
3	-.30	-.62
4	.22	.49
5	-.30	-.62
6	.22	-.62
7	.22	1.25
8	-.73	.49
9	-.30	1.25
10	-.73	-.62
11	.22	-.62
12	.22	.89
13	-.53	-1.53
14	.49	-.62
15	.22	-.25
16	.48	-.25
17	.22	-.62
18	-.0	0.00

Table 5. Estimates for α_i and β_j

As an example of a likelihood ratio test for significance, consider the null hypothesis

$$H_0: \rho = 0; \theta, \{\alpha_i\}, \{\beta_j\} \text{ unconstrained,}$$

versus

$$H_1: \rho, \theta, \{\alpha_i\}, \{\beta_j\} \text{ all unconstrained.}[6]$$

There is one degree of freedom because H_1 has one more parameter than H_0. The log likelihood-ratio, with appropriate parameter estimates substituted into (6), is 30.41. If H_0 is true, twice this quantity is an observation from a χ^2 distribution with one degree of freedom. Thus we can reject H_0 and conclude that there is a reciprocity effect.

M. *Log-linear Modeling for Role Structure (Marsden).* Peter Marsden (in this volume) develops an exponential-type model for choices amongst groups. We give here a very brief synopsis to put the model in the perspective of this chapter, referring the reader to Marsden for a full account.

---

[6] This, of course, is different from a simple test for reciprocity in the absence of row and column effects α_i and β_j, and seems to us a more appropriate test. Such distinctions would not be easy to make with earlier models.

We have groups of organizations, there being g_i members in the ith group. For a given pair (i, j), there are thus $g_i g_j$ potential ties. Let x_{ij2} be the actual number of links from group i to j, and x_{ij1} be the $g_i g_j - x_{ij2}$, the number of potential links which did not materialize. Let m_{ijk} be the expectation of x_{ijk}, according to some model.

The saturated log-linear model (see, e.g., Bishop, Feinberg and Holland, 1975) for the situation may be written as

$$\log m_{ij1} = \lambda_{ij}$$

$$\log m_{ij2} = \lambda_{ij} + \theta + \alpha_i + \beta_j + \gamma_{ij} \qquad (7)$$

This defines an exponential family for the m's akin to the Holland-Leinhardt model just described. The parameters λ_{ij} merely reflect the group sizes g_i and g_j. The other parameters have more interesting interpretations: θ indicates the overall volume of relations in the network; α_i measures the outflow tendency for group i, β_j the inflow for group j, and γ_{ij} is the "interaction" between i and j unaccountable by the other terms. The groups can be classified according to their α and β values: a group high on both is a "carrier", one low on both is an "isolate", and so on.

A null model can be defined from (7) by setting the γ_{ij}'s to zero, giving us independence conditional on the in and outdegrees. One might instead also set the α's and β's to zero, when the expected numbers m_{ijk} are computed as in an ordinary χ^2 test for independence. Naturally, some kind of bias, as represented by the γ_{ij}'s, is likely to be needed in practice. The interesting question is the structural form of the γ's, since unrestricted γ's give us the fully saturated case. Marsden considers the case where the γ_{ii}'s are free and the γ_{ij}'s for $i \neq j$ determined from them. The γ_{ii}'s measure the amount of participation between organizations in the same group. Following Burt (1980), Marsden as able to give appealing descriptions in terms of the parameter values. Among those with positive α_i and negative β_i, for instance, a group with positive γ_{ii} is a "low status clique," while one with a negative γ_{ii} is a "sycophant".

REFERENCES

Bales, R.F., Strodbeck, F.L., Mills, T.M., Roseborough, M.E.
    1951   Channels of communication in small groups. American
           Sociological Review, 16, 461-468.
Bartos, O.J.
    1967   Simple Models of Group Behavior. Columbia University Press.
Bishop, Y.M., Feinberg S.E. and Holland, P.W.
    1975   Discrete Multivariate Analysis. Cambridge: MIT Press.
Burt, R.S.
    1981   Models of network structure. Annual Review of Sociology, 6,
           79-141.
Christie, L. L., Luce, R. D. and Macy, J.
    1952   Communication and Learning in Task-Oriented Groups.
           Cambridge: Research Laboratory of Electronics, M.I.T.
Coleman, J.S.
    1964   Introduction to Mathematical Sociology. New York: Free Press of
           Glencoe.
Doreian, P.
    1979   On the "Social Law of Effect" for task oriented groups. Social
           Psychology Quarterly, 42, 222-31.
Fararo, T.J. and Sunshine, M.H.
    1964   A study of a biased friendship net. New York: Syracuse
           University Youth Development Center.
Foster, C.C., Rapoport, A., and Orwant, C.J.
    1963   A study of a large sociogram. II. Elimination of free parameters.
           Behavioral Science, 8, 56-65.
Gray, L.N. and von Broembson, M. H.
    1976   On the generalizability of the law of effect. Sociometry, 39,
           175-183.
Grenander, U.
    1976   Pattern Synthesis: Lectures in Pattern Theory, Vol. I. New York:
           Springer Verlag.
    1978   Pattern Analysis: Lectures in Pattern Theory, Vol. II. New York:
           Springer Verlag.
Hägerstrand, T.
    1965a A Monte Carlo approach to diffusion. European Journal of
           Sociology, 6, 43-67.
    1965b Aspects of the spatial structure of social communication and the
           diffusion of information. Regional Science Association: Papers,
           XVI, Cracow Congress.

1965   Quantitative techniques for analysis of the spread of information and technology. *In* C.A. Anderson and M.J. Bowman, eds., Education and Economic Development. Chicago: Aldine.

1966   Aspects of the spatial structure of social communication and the diffusion of information. Regional Science Association Papers, 16, 27-42.

Holland, P.W. and Leinhardt, S.

1971   Transitivity in structural models of small groups. Comparative Group Studies, 2, 107-124.

1977   A dynamic model for social networks. Journal of Mathematical Sociology, 5, 5-20.

1980   An exponential family of probability distributions for directed graphs. Journal of the American Statistical Association.

Hunter, J.E. and Shotland, R.L.

1974   Treating data collected by the "small world" method as a Markov process. Social Forces, 52, 321-332.

Kreweras, G.

1966   A model for opinion change during repeated balloting. *In* P.F. Lazarsfeld and N.W. Henry, eds., Readings in Mathematical Social Science. Chicago: Science Research Associates, Inc.

Landau, H.G.

1951a On dominance relations and the structure of animal societies. I. Effects of inherent characteristics. Bulletin of Mathematical Biophysics, 13, 1-19.

1951b On dominance relations and the structure of animal societies: II. Some effects of possible social factors. Bulletin of Mathematical Biophysics, 13, 245-262.

1951   On dominance relations and the structure of animal societies: III. The condition for a score structure. Bulletin of Mathematical Biophysics, 15, 143-148.

Massarik, F. and Ratoosh, P.

1965   Mathematical Explorations in Behavioral Science. Homewood, Ill.: R. D. Irwin and Dorsey Press.

Moreno, J.L.

1934   Who shall survive? Beacon, New York: Beacon House, Inc.

Pool, I.S. and Kochen, M.

1978   Contacts and Influence. Social Networks, 1, 5-51.

Rainio, K.

1961   Stochastic process of social contacts. Scandinavian Journal of Psychology, 2, 113-128.

1965   Social interaction as a stochastic learning process. Archives of European Sociology, VI, 68-88.

1966   A study of sociometric group structure. *In* J. Berger, M. Felditch and B. Anderson, eds., Sociological Theories in Process. Vol. 1, Boston: Houghton-Mifflin.

Rapoport, A.

1949   Outline of a probabilistic approach to animal sociology. I. Bulletin of Mathematical Biophysics, 11, 183-196.

1949   Outline of a probabilistic approach to animal sociology. II. Bulletin of Mathematical Biophysics, 2, 273-81.

1950   Outline of a probabilistic approach to animal sociology. III. Bulletin of Mathematical Biophysics, 12, 7-17.

1957   Contribution to theory of random and biased nets. Bulletin of Mathematical Biophysics, 19, 257-277.

1979   A probabilistic approach to networks. Social Networks, 2, 1-18.

Rapoport, A. and Horvath, W.J.

1961   A study of a large sociogram I. Behavioral Science, 6, 279-91.

Sampson, S.F.

1969   Crisis in a Cloister. Ann Arbor, Michigan: University microfilms No. 69-5775.

Stephan, F.F., and Mishler, E.G.

1952   The distribution of participation in small groups: An Exponential approximation. American Journal of Sociology, 17, 598-608.

Wasserman, S.

1980   Analyzing social networks as a stochastic process. Journal of the American Statistical Association, 75, 280-294.

White, H.C., Boorman, S.A., and Brieger, R.L.

1976   Social structure from multiple networks. I. Blockmodels of roles and positions. American Journal of Sociology, 81, 730-80.

CHAPTER 6

RELATIONAL CONTENTS IN MULTIPLE NETWORK SYSTEMS*

Ronald S. Burt and Thomas Schøtt

This chapter is about ways in which models of relational form can be used to describe the substantive contents of personal relationships. Kinds of interaction are viewed as components in the sentences that people use to describe their relationships with one another. These components are distinguished and interpreted with respect to semantic criteria derived from the structure of the circumstances in which interaction occurs.

* This chapter is a by-product of support from the National Science Foundation (SOC79-25728, SES82-08203) and has received direct support from the Pacific Institute for Research and Evaluation under a grant from the National Institute on Drug Abuse (DA02566). Mr. Schøtt was supported by research grants from the Danish Natural Science Research Council and the Danish Social Science Reseach Council and a Lazarsfeld Fellowship from Columbia University. An initial draft of this chapter was written by Mr. Burt during a brief leave of absence spent in the School of Social Sciences, University of California at Irvine. Greatly appreciated were the facilities provided there by Linton C. Freeman and the many helpful comments provided by the Irvine faculty during a colloquium presentation of the nascent ideas from which this chapter developed.

More specifically, we elaborate three ideas: (a) the semantic context in which kinds of interaction occur is defined by a network of confusion relations, each relation measuring th tendency for one kind of interaction to be confused for another in described relationships. (b) The concept of structural equivalence is used to define content domains as kinds of interaction that are substitutable for one another in described relationships. (c) The concept of network prominence is used to define the ambiguity with which kinds of interaction appear in described relationships.

This chapter is little more than a rough sketch of how these ideas could guide an analysis of relational content. Readers interested in more applied discussion are referred to an analysis of substitutability and ambiguity in relationships among several hundred Northern Californians during the late 1970s (Burt and Minor, 1983: Chp. 2). What we do here is elaborate some ideas indicating the significant, unexplored, potential that formal network models hold out as guides for analyzing relational content. Not only does this imply that relational form and content can be analyzed simultaneously in terms of the same concepts, it means that network models other than the few explicitly discussed here might offer new insights into the meaning of personal relationships.

1. The Problem of Relational Content

Relational content is a problem for network analysis. The problem is nicely illustrated in the distinction between naturally occurring relations and analytical relations—the first being the relations in which people are actually involved, the second being the recreation of relations for a network analysis. For example, when you go to a colleague for advice, that interaction occurs in the context of other activities for which you have sought her out; lunch, cocktails, dinner, committee work, colloquia, leads to new acquaintances, and so on. Your naturally occurring relation to this person, your relation to her as it exists in fact, is a bundle of different kinds of interaction. Similarly, your naturally occurring relations to other people are bundles of specific interaction activities, some consisting of many activities, others containing very few.

With the notable exception of ethnographers, network analysts rarely capture the complexity of naturally occurring relations. Their concern is less the complexity of the typical relationship between a pair of individuals than it is the complexity of the structure of relations among many individuals as a system. The relations described are analytical constructs—a relation's form being its intensity or strength as a tendency to occur and its content being its substance as a reason for occurring. The form of a friendship relation, for example, would refer to the intensity or strength of the relation while its content, its substantive meaning, would be friendship. Network models of social structure typically describe the form of relations while taking the content of those relations as a given, an item exogenous to the model. The most general of these models purport to describe formal structure in multiple networks among individuals in a system where each network consists of relations having the same content. The questions of why certain networks are to be distinguished in a system, how individuals within the system interpret their interaction activities, and how they distinguish different kinds of interaction are assumed to be resolved *a priori*.

Unhappily, these unasked questions are quite unresolved; not only in general, but in the particular. When someone poses a sociometric question to you asking for the names of people to whom you go for such-and-such, you must disentangle the welter of interactions in your naturally occurring relations and classify some as such-and-such before you can answer the question. If you are asked to name your best friends, for example, you must decide which of your interaction activities indicate friendship. If you are asked to name the people with whom you engage in leisure activities, you must decide which of your activities indicate leisure. If you are asked to name the people who most influence your thinking with their personal comments, you must decide which of your activities indicate influence. Obviously, people can differ in their interpretation of specific interaction activities as manifestations of more general types of interaction; some viewing as intimate, for example, what others view as no more than friendly. More obviously, people in diferent social situations or from different subcultures will differ in their interpretation of specific interaction activities as indicators of more general relational content.

The distinctions between relational contents needed to formulate sociometric questions before collecting network data are thus unsettlingly *ad hoc*. The sociometric questions finally selected can be no moe than a compromise between the theoretical extreme of initial hunches regarding significant dimensions of interaction—this determining a minimum number of different contents—and the empirical impossibility of gathering data on all kinds of interacton in which respondents might be involved—this defining a maximum number of contents limited by the number of different sociometric questions that respondents will tolerate.

This problem in data definition creates problems for data analysis. *Ad hoc* definitions of relational contents increase the likelihood of misinterpreted relations. The kind of interaction solicited in a sociometric question might be understood by a social scientist in a way distinct from its understanding in a study population.   There is the related problem of erroneous inferences from comparative research.   Even if identical sociometric questions are posed to individuals in two study populations, there is no guarantee that the question has the same interpretation in the two populations. More generally, *ad hoc* distinctions between relational contents make it difficult to analyze the coordination of different types of interaction. But such analysis is integral, almost by definition, to a description of social structure in a multiple network system.   Consider the concept of multiplexity. A relationship is multiplex to the extent that multiple contents occur together in the relationship. For example, you have a multiplex relation to your colleague as described above. You have social, economic, and collegial kinds of interaction with the person. The relationship would be uniplex if you had only one kind of interaction.

Who is to say when one kind of interaction stops and another begins? When does a colleague relation become a friendship relation? One observer might decide that each of the above kinds of interaction constitutes a different relational content—social, economic, and collegial—whereupon the relationship would be multiplex. Another observer might only distinguish two kinds of interaction, kinship and nonkinship, whereupon the described relationship would be uniplex—it consists of multiple examples of nonkinship interaction activities. Without empirical guidance regarding relational contents, these alternative distinctions between contents are *ad hoc*, raising an important analytical question: When is a uniplex relationship mistakenly treated as if it were a multiplex relationship merely because a network analyst has considered various aspects of a single relational content to be different contents? Consequential as a clear understaning of relational content is for describing social structure with network models ranging in sophistication from ego-network multiplexity to multiple network role structures, very little is known about it.   Research inferences are correspondingly equivocal.   Fortunately, available network models of relational form can be used to great advantage in studying relational content. We begin with an idea for describing the semantic context in which interaction occurs.

2. Confusion Relations

One key to the meaning of relations lies in the variable tendencies for different kinds of interaction to be perceived in the same naturally occurring relations. Confronted with a sociometric question, a respondent must sort through his relationships and identify those containing one or more of the specific kinds of interaction solicited by the question. By confronting the person with repeated questions asking him to identify specific kinds of interaction in his relationships, we can see variable tendencies for the same relationships to be identified in response to different questions. In other words, we can see variable tendencies for analytically distinct kinds of interaction to be confused for one another in naturally occurring relations.

More specifically, suppose that K different questions are put to a respondent each asking him to identify a kind of interaction in his relationships. Who are your best friends? With whom do you discuss your important personal decisions? And so on for K questions. For the moment, let each question define a kind of interaction as a relational content. Responses to the K questions define a (K, K) symmetric matrix of frequency data where variable n_{ij} is the number of relationships in which the respondent identified both content i and content j. For example, if i refers to question asking the respondent to name his best friends and j refers to a question asking him to identify people from whom he has borrowed a large sum of money, then n_{ij} would be the number of his friends perceived to have loaned him a large sum of money, n_{ii} would be the number of people he considers to be his best friends, and n_{jj} would be the number of people from whom he has borrowed a large sum of money.

Such data are available in diverse research designs. The respondent could be an actor in the closed system typically described by network models or a respondent in a random sample of survey interviews. Data on relations to the respondent from others are not necessary here; only the respondent's perception of his relationships is needed. Moreover, the respondent could be evaluating his personal relationships, relationships in which a corporation is involved, or relationships in which some informal social group is involved.

These frequency data define two types of informative variables that we shall discuss as confusion relations.

Let c_{ii} be the probability that the respondent perceives the ith kind of interacton in any one of his naturally occurring relations. For the purposes here, c_{ii} can be computed as the following ratio of frequencies:[1]

$$c_{ii} = \frac{n_{ii}}{N},$$
(1)

where N is the number of different people a respondent names in answering all K sociometric questions and n_{ii} is the number of those relationships reported to contain the ith kind of interaction. The n_{ii} relationships form a subset of all N relationships in which the respondent is involved so c_{ii} will vary from a minimum of 0 (no relationship contains content i) up to a maximum of 1 (each relationship contains content i). When content i refers to a question asking the respondent to name his friends, for example, c_{ii} equal to .67 would indicate that two out of every three people named by the respondent for any of K contents is perceived to be a friend.

Let c_{ij} be the conditional probability that the respondent perceives the jth kind of interaction in any one of his naturally occurring relations known to contain content i. In other words, c_{ij} is the probability of content j being perceived in a relationship given content i. For the purposes here, c_{ij} can be computed as the following ratio of frequencies.

$$c_{ij} = \frac{n_{ij}}{n_{ii}},$$
(2)

---

[1] There are two special cases that deserve mention here. First, we assume that data on several relationships have been obtained. The smaller that N is, the less variable confusion relations can be. For an N of 2, confusion relations have three possible values (.0, .5, 1.0). For an N of 1, confusion relations have two possible values (.0 and 1.0). For the respondent acknowledging no relationships, N = 0, confusion relations could be set equal to 0 by definition. There is little knowledge to be gained from such computation, but isolates can occur in a large sample of respondents so there is value in anticipating case in which N = 0. The second special case to be acknowledged is missing data. Suppose that N people were named by a respondent, but only N^*_i of those people have nonmissing data on sociometric question i. In other words, N^*_i, not N, is the upper limit for n_{ii}. In keeping with the probability interpretation of c_{ii}, the following ratio of frequencies with missing data gives the number of times that content i was prceived in any relationship in which it could have been perceived; $c_{ii} = n_{ii}/(N^*_i + a)$, where a is the constant in footnote 2 (included in Case $N^*_i = 0$).

ignoring the easily resolved problem of n_{ii} equal to zero[2] and the less easily resolved problem of missing data.[3] The n_{ij} relationships perceived to simultaneously contain contents i and j form a subset of all n_{ii} relationships containing content i so c_{ij} will vary from a minimum of 0 (no relationships contain both contents) up to a maximum of 1 (content j is perceived in every relationship containing content i). Note that n_{ii} need not equal n_{jj}, so c_{ij} need not equal c_{ji} even though n_{ij} equals n_{ji}.

The confusion relation c_{ij} is bettern known to network analysts in a regression equation. Let each of the N persons named by a respondent be a unit of analysis. In other words, let each observed naturally occurring relation be a unit of analysis. Let X_{jn} be a binary variable equal to 1 if the jth kind of interaction appears in the nth relationship and let it equal 0 if such interaction does not appear in the relationship. Let x_{in} be a similarly defined variable for the ith kind of interaction. Ordinary least squares estimates of parameters in the following equation could be computed:

$$X_{jn} = b + b_{ji}X_{in} + E_n,$$

where b, b_{ji}, and E_n respectively are regression intercept, coefficient, and residual in predicting the appearance of content j from the appearance of content i in relationship n. The intercept b is the probability that content j appears in a relationship in which content i is absent. The coefficient b_{ji} is the change in that probability associated with the appeaance of content i in the relationship. The sum of these two parameters is the conditional probability

---

[2] It is quite possible for one or more contents not to occur in a particular respondent's relationships. In other words, values of n_{ii} equal to 0 are to be expected. In computer programs generating confusion relations, the following is a useful version of Eq. (2); $c_{ij} = n_{ij}/(n_{ii} + a)$, where a is a constant equal to $1/10^r$ where the exponent r is an integer equal to one greater than the number of digits to which confusion relations will be rounded. If confusion relations are to be rounded to two decimal places, then a = .001 (r = 3). If they are to be rounded to three decimal places, then a = .0001 (r = 4), and so on. This constant is only needed to avoid the definitional awkwardness of dividing by zero when n_{ii} equals 0.

[3] Of alternative, reasonable, computations allowing for missing data, we have yet to see the following produce odd results (e.g., probabilities greater than one) in our research; $c_{ij} = n_{ij}/(N^*_{ij} + a)$, where a is the constant in footnote 2 (included in case $N^*_{ij} = 0$) and N^*_{ij} is the number of relationships containing content i and nonmissing data on content j. In other words, N^*_{ij} is the upper limit for N_{ij} so the ratio of n_{ij} to $(N^*_{ij} + a)$ is the number of times that content j was perceived in a relationship containing content i over the number of times that content j could have been perceived in such a relationship.

of content j appearing in a relationship given content i and equals the confusion relation c_{ij} (i.e., $c_{ij} = b + b_{ji}$).[4] In other words, the regression

---

[4] This statement merits a brief explanation. The regression coefficient b_{ji} is defined as follows:

$$b_{ji} = \frac{\sum_n (X_{jn} - \overline{X}_j)(X_{in} - \overline{X}_i)}{\sum_n (X_{in} - \overline{X}_i)^2},$$

where summation is across the N relationships, X_{jn} and X_{in} are the binary variables indicating the jth and i^{th} kinds of interaction in relationship n, $\overline{X}_j$ is the mean of X_{jn} across all N relationships, and $\overline{X}_i$ is similarly the mean of X_{in}. Expanding the number of relationships, N, would not change the following. If means are deleted from this definition by the imposition of a zero intercept, the definition of b_{ji} simplies to:

$$\frac{\sum_n (X_{jn})(X_{in})}{\sum_n (X_{in})^2},$$

which equals n_j/n_{ii}—since $n_{ij} = \Sigma_n X_{jn} X_{in}$ and $n_{ii} = \Sigma_n X_{in}^2$—and so equals the confusion relation c_{ij} defined in Eq. (2). This equality is not true if means are retained in the definition of b_{ji}. Rewriting the definition in terms of sociometric citation data yields the following:

$$b_{ji} = \frac{\sum_n (X_{jn} X_{ij} - X_{jn} \overline{X}_i - \overline{X}_j X_{in} + \overline{X}_j \overline{X}_i)}{\sum_n (X_{in}^2 - 2\overline{X}_i X_{in} + \overline{X}_i^2)},$$

$$= \frac{n_{ij} - \dfrac{n_{ii}n_{jj}}{N} - \dfrac{n_{ii}n_{jj}}{N} + \dfrac{n_{ii}n_{jj}}{N}}{n_{ii} - \dfrac{2n_{ii}^2}{N} + \dfrac{n_{ii}^2}{N}} = \frac{n_{ij} - \dfrac{n_{ii}n_{jj}}{N}}{n_{ii} - \dfrac{n_{ii}^2}{N}},$$

where $\overline{X}_i = n_{ii}/N$ and $\overline{X}_j = n_{jj}/N$. This can be rewritten to express the difference between the regression coefficient and the confusion relation:

$$b_{ji} = \frac{n_{ij}}{n_{ii}} - \left(\frac{n_{jj}}{N} - \frac{b_{ji}n_{ii}}{N} \right) = c_{ij} - (\overline{X}_j - b_{ji}\overline{X}_i) = c_{ij} - b,$$

where b is the intercept in the regression equation containing b_{ji}. Thus, c_{ij} equals $b + b_{ji}$ as discussed in the text.

coefficient b_{ji} is the conditional probability of j given i—minus the probability of j occurring in the absence of i. Equivalently, the confusion relation c_{ij} is the zero-order regression coefficient predicting the appearance of j from the occurrence of i—plus the mean tendency for j to appear in the absence of i.

The elements c_{ii} and c_{ij} form an asymmetric (K, K) matrix C that describes the semantic context in which the respondent perceives specific kinds of interaction. The diagonal element c_{ii} measures the extent to which the respondent perceives content i in all relationships. *Ceteris paribus*, the more often that he perceives a content in his interactions with different persons (i.e., the higher than c_{ii} is), the less clearly defined the ith content is in terms of specific activities with specific people. The off-diagonal element c_{ij} measures the extent to which the repondent always perceives content j in any relation containing content i. *Ceteris paribus*, the more often that he cannot identify a relationship containing content i without content j being present (i.e., the higher than c_{ij} is), the less likely he will be to think about content i as something distinct from content j—the more likely he will be to confuse content i for content j. What we are proposing is that the respondent makes distinctions among relational contents insofar as he is able to refer to different people with the contents. Distinct relationships are suggested to underly cognitive distinctions between relational contents. Confusion relations are thus semantic data in the sense that they define the variable extent to which any one kind of interaction, any one content, can be distinguished in descriptions of actual relationships from any other kind of interaction. More to the point, network models can be used to derive insights about relational content when the models are used to describe the structure of confusion relations.

3. Content Domains

For example, it is possible to identify general domains of relational content underlying respondent perceptions of specific kinds of interaction. The semantic position of the ith kind of interaction in a respondent's description of relationshis is described by elements in the ith row and column of the matrix C. Off-diagonal elements in row i define tendencies for the ith kind of interaction to be confused for each other content k (the c_{ik}). Off-diagonal elements in column i define tendencies for each content k to be confused for the ith kind of interaction (the c_{ki}). When two kinds of interaction i and j have identical patterns of confusion relations, they occupy identical semantic positions in respondent descriptions of relationships. Kinds of interaction such as these are substitutable indicators of a more general content domain. They are semantically interchangeable examples of the same general content in naturally occurring relations.

Detecting Content Domains

More specifically, two kinds of interaction i and j are substitutable in this semantic sense to the extent that; (a) they have equal tendencies to be perceived in relationships (i.e., $c_{ii} = c_{jj}$), (b) they have equal tendencies to be confused for one another (i.e., $c_{ij} = c_{ji}$), and (c) they tend to be confused identically with each other type of interaction (i.e., $c_{ik} = c_{jk}$ and $c_{ki} = c_{kj}$ for all kinds of interaction k, $i \neq k \neq j$). The first two conditions are determined by the extent to which the two kinds of interaction occur with equal frequency.[5] The third condition is determined, in part, by the extent to which

---

5 The diagonal elements c_{ii} and c_{jj} equal n_{ii}/N and n_{jj}/N respectively and so are equal—ignoring the possibility of missing data—when i and j occur with equal frequency; $n_{ii} = n_{jj}$. The off-diagonal elements c_{ij} and c_{ji} equal n_{ij}/n_{ii} and n_{ji}/n_{jj} respectively and so are equal—again ignoring the possibility of missing data—when i and j occur with equal frequency since n_{ij} by definition equals n_{ji}.

This second criterion merits a brief note. It might seem reasonable to require substitutable contents to be completely confused for one another in the sense that c_{ji} and c_{ij} both equal their maximum value, 1. Not only does this trivialize the idea of content substitutability (cf. footnote 7), it is very sensitive to questionnaire design. For example, a respondent could seek advice from superiors and subordinates where he works. This interaction would give his work relations an advice-seeking content. But suppose that two sociometric questions were used to solicit advice-seeking relations from the respondent; question i asking about superiors and question j asking about subordinates. A single person could not be named on both questions so c_{ij} and c_{ji} would equal zero, implying that advice-seeking from superiors means in no way the same thing as advice-seeking from subordinates. Such may be the case, but here it is defined to be true by question wording. The same problem would arise if interaction with living ancestors was solicited by a question separate from the question soliciting interaction with living descendants. More generally, the problem arises when sociometric questions solicit kinds of interaction with people who have particular attributes (e.g., superiors, subordintes, older than repondent, younger than respondent, etc.) or interaction in particular contexts (e.g., at home, at work, etc.). We are grateful to William Batchelder for calling attention to this issue during a colloquium discussion of content substitutability.

which the two kinds of interaction occur with equal frequency in any relationship containing any other kind of interaction.[6]

It is convenient to adopt a spatial representation of substututability. To the extent that the ith and j^{th} kinds of interaction meet the above three conditions for substitutability, the following Euclidean distance will equal zero:

$$d_{ij} = \sqrt{(c_{ii} - c_{jj})^2 + (c_{ij} - c_{ji})^2 + \sum_k \left[(c_{ik} - c_{jk})^2 + (c_{ki} - c_{kj})^2 \right]}, \quad (3)$$

where summation is across all K kinds of interaction excluding the two being assessed for their substitutability ($i \neq k \neq j$). This equation defines the distance between each pair i and j, of K contents within a $2 + 2 (K - 2)$ dimensional semantic space.

Two kinds of interaction occupying the same point in this space are substitutable in repondent descriptions of his relationships. The three substitutability conditions correspond respectively to the three summed terms in Eq. (3): (a) When contents i and j have the same probability of appearing in one of the respondent's relationships, c_{ii} equals c_{jj} so the first squared term in Eq. (3) equals zero. (b) When the contents are equivalently confused for one another, c_{ij} equals c_{ji} so the second squared term in Eq. (3) equals zero. (c) When the contents are equivalently confused with ever other kind of interaction under consideration, the bracketed term in Eq. (3) equals zero; c_{ik} equals c_{ki} equals c_{kj} for every other content k.

Thus we can say that the ith and j^{th} kinds of interaction are completely substituable when d_{ij} equals 0. They fall within the same domain of relational content in the sense that, for the responent under consideration at least, they are used in a semantically identical way to describe relationships. When the

---

[6] This statement refers to the two squared terms bracketed in Eq. (3). The second of those terms, the difference between c_{ki} and c_{kj}, is zero when i and j occur with equal frequency in any relationship containing some other kind of interaction k. Since c_{ki} and c_{kj} equal n_{ki}/n_{kk} and n_{kj}/n_{kk} respectively, they will be equal when n_{ki} equals n_{kj}. The first of the bracketed squared terms, the difference bewteen c_{ik} and c_{jk}, does not reduce to a direct equivalence of requencies. Since c_{ik} and c_{jk} equal n_{ik}/n_{ii} and n_{jk}/n_{jj} respectively, they are only equal when the frequency with which i and k occur together—relative to the overall frequency of i—equals the frequency with which j and k occur together—relative to the overall frequency of j.

i^{th} or the jth kind of interaction occurs in a relationship, the respondent imputes the same meaning, the same relational content, to the relationship. This is not to say that other meanings are excluded from the relationship. Discussing personal problems and having dinner together are two kinds of interaction that could indicate friendship content in a relationship. If the two diners are also related by blood, then their relationship would contain both friendship and kinship content.

More generally, the content domain containing the ith and j^{th} kinds of interacion consists of contents i and j plus all other contents substitutable for i and j. So defined, a content domain is a maximal complete set of substitutable kinds of interaction—it contains all and only those kinds of interaction that are substitutable for one another. One content domain is distinct from another in the sense that each has a nonsubstitutable semantic meaning, a distinct semantic position, in the respondent's descriptions of his relationships. Underlying the K kinds of interaction arbitrarily distinguished by sociometric questions are one or more domains of relational content, each domain containing one or more substitutable kinds of interaction.

In order to detect these content domains we could compute a (K, K) matrix of the distances defined in Eq. (3) and look for values of d_{ij} equal to 0. Each set of interaction activities (i, j, ..., k) separated by zero distance $(d_{ij} = ... = d_{ik} = d_{jk} = 0)$ would constitute a content domain.

In practice, however, this is an inappropriate criterion. Diverse research errors such as poorly constructed questionnaires, respondent fatigue, coding errors, and so on are likely to distort the estimation of confusion relations. Moreover, people do not maintain computer consistency in their descriptions of relationships. Words used to describe a domain of content in today's relationships are likely to be replaced with other words at other times—not to mention actual changes in the bundle of interactions comprising a relationship—so that a degree of inaccuracy, of ambiguity, is expected in descriptions of relationships. For reasons of research errors, living language variations in the use of words, or the shifting coincidence of interactions in relationships, nonzero distances between substitutable kinds of interaction are to be expected.

Instead of restricting content domains to be points in a semantic space defined by the distances in Eq. (3) therefore, domains should be defined as discernable areas, fields, in the space. So defined, a content domain consists of all kinds of interaction i and j that are separated by negligible distance:

$$d_{ij} \leq \delta, \qquad\qquad (4)$$

where δ is a criterion of negligible distance. If δ equals 0, then the content domain consists of completely substitutable kinds of interaction. The higher δ is, the more equivocally content domains are defined in terms of specific kinds of interaction. With respect to a semantic space, high values of δ allow content domains to include areas and so, *ceteris paribus*, large numbers of specific kinds of interaction distributed in the space.

Content domains of substitutable kinds of interaction can be detected now in the same ways used to detect stautses of structurally equivalent actors. We have used the formal concept of structural equivalence to define substitutable kinds of interaction. Contents i and j are substitutable to the extent that they are structurally equivalent in a network of confusion relations. That is, substitutable kinds of interaction occupy structurally equivalent semantic positions in respondent descriptions of relationships. In Eq. (4), $\delta = 0$ corresponds to a strong criterion of structural equivalence and $\delta > 0$ corresponds to a weak criterion. The cluster analysis and factor analysis operations used to locate actors structurally equivalent in social networks would be applied in the same ways to locate substitutable contents in a network of confusion relations (e.g., see Burt, 1982:Chps. 2,3; Burt and Minor, 1983:Chps. 13, 14 for review and numerical illustration.)[7]

---

[7] Of the two concepts used to define network subgroups, cohesion and structural equivalence, there are several reasons for preferring structural equivalence. The cohesion versus structural equivalence distinction is elaborated at length in Burt and Minor (1983:Chp. 13). This general preference is particularly sharp with respect to content substitutability. Structural equivalence groups together individuals who have similar patterns of relations with all other individuals in a network. Cohesion groups together individuals who have strong relations with one another. With respect to a network of confusion relations, two kinds of ineraction, i and j, would be grouped together as cohesive to the extent that they were complete confused for one another ($c_{ij} = c_{ji} = 1$). This criterion is only met when the two kinds of interaction always occur with one another in the same relationships. Such a criterion would define a trivial form of content substitutability. It is more an indicator of poor questionnaire construction. The ith and j^{th} sociometric questions refer to identical relationships and so neither offers a gain in information over the other (cf. footnote 5). The structural equivalence criterion of substitutability is more suited to the purpose of studying relational content, with respect to confusion relations at least. Two kinds of interaction, i and j, need never appear in the same relationships in order to be structurally equivalent (i.e., c_{ij} and c_{ji} could equal 0). In order to be structurally equivalent, however, they would have to appear to the same extent with every other kind of interaction. In short, structural equivalence captures a semantic sense of content substitutability while cohesion would merely capture redundancy.

Confusion Relations among Content Domains

Let κ equal the number of different content domains detected in a respondent's description of his relationships. Where c_{ij} is a confusion relation between the ith and j^{th} kinds of interaction, let c_{IJ} be a confusion relation between the Ith and J^{th} domains of relational content. If each kind of interaction on which data are obtained is discovered to be nonsubstitutable for every other, then each would define its own content domain. In other words, K would equal κ and each c_{ij} would correspond to a c_{IJ}. But if two or more of the K initial contents are substitutable, i.e., if $K > \kappa$, then confusion relations between some content domains I and J would be a reduction of multiple confusion relations between specific kinds of interaction observed within each domain. The reduction of c_{ij} to c_{IJ} is straightforward and should be completed before formal network models are used to interpret contents.[8]

Where c_{ii} is the probability with which the ith kinds of interaction occurs in a respondent's relationships, c_{II} is the probability with which interactions indicating the Ith domain of content occur in his relationships. The following ratio of frequencies defines the latter probability:[9]

$$c_{II} = \frac{N_{II}}{N},$$

(5)

where N is the number of different relationships named by the respondent (cf. Eq. 1), and N_{II} is the number of those relationships that contain any one of the substitutable interactions within content domain I. If data are obtained on two kinds of interaction (i and j) within content domain I, then N_{II} equals $n_{ii} + n_{jj} - n_{ij}$, where n_{ii}, n_{jj}, and n_{ij} respectively are the number of respondent's relationships that contain the ith, the jth, and both, kinds of interaction. If data are obtained on three kinds of interaction (i, j and k) within content domain I, then N_{II} equals $n_{ii} + n_{jj} + {}_{kk} - n_{ij} - n_{ik} - n_{jk} + n_{ijk}$, where n_{ijk} is the number of the respondent's relationships that contain all three kinds of interaction, i, j and k. For example, if data are obtained on two

---

[8] The application of formal network models to the C matrix can be distorted by the pesence of substitutable contents in the matrix (e.g., see footnote 15).

[9] The issues raised in footnote 1 with respect to computing c_{ii}, low N and missing data, apply in the same way to Eq. (5).

kinds of interaction—discussing personal problems and socializing—within the content domain of friendship, domain I, then the probability of friendship being a content in a respondent's relationships (c_{II}) equals the number of the people named by the respondent as individuals with whom he socializes or discusses personal problems (N_{II}) divided by the total number of people he named (N). In short, c_{II} is defined by the union of kinds of interaction within content domain I.[10] Of course, if data were obtained on only one kind of interaction i within content domain I, then N_{II} would equal n_{ii}, so c_{II} would equal c_{ii} in Eq. (1).

Inter-domain confusion relations are also defined by the union of specific kinds of interaction. Corresponding to c_{ij} in Eq. (2), let c_{IJ} be the

---

[10] Continuing tne analogy with structural equivalence models, it might seem reasonable to compute the density of confusion relations among substitutable kinds of interaction. This is the usual procedure by which group relations are obtained from relations among structurally equivalent actors. Densities, or weighted averages, are not appropriate to the probabilistic meaning of c_{II} in Eq. (5). Routinely computed, an intra-domain confusion relation would be the average c_{ij} between all kinds of interaction i and j substitutable within domain I; $\Sigma_i \Sigma_j c_{ij}/I^2$, where I equals the number of contents i and j within content domain I. As an average of probabilities (diagonal elements of C) and conditional probabilities (off-diagonal elements of C), this is a nonsensical computation (excluding the trivial case of a domain based on a single sociometric question, whereupon the average would equal c_{ii} in Eq. 5). If only the off-diagonal elements only were summed; $\Sigma_i \Sigma_j c_{ij}/I$ (I − 1), i ≠ j, it would not capture the probability of interactions with domain content I occurring in the respondent's relationships. It would instead measure their tendency to occur together. Nor would an average of diagonal elements; $\Sigma_i c_{ii}/I$, capture the probability of interactions with domain content I. It would instead measure the average probability of each kind of substitutable interaction occurring in the respondent's relationships:

$$\sum_i \frac{c_{ii}}{I} = \frac{\sum_i \left(\frac{n_{ii}}{I}\right)}{N} = \frac{\bar{n}_{II}}{N},$$

where $\bar{n}_{II}$ is the average number of different relationships elicited form the respondent in regard to any one kind of interaction within content domain I. For example, an $\bar{n}_{II}$ of 2 would mean that the respondent named two people on average in answering each of the sociometric questions indicating domain I content. This average is replaced in Eq. (5) with N_{II}—the number of different people with whom the respondent has domain I content relationships—in order to preserve the probabilistic meaning of c_{II}. As illustration, suppose that discussing personal problems and socializing were substitutable friendship contents for a respondent and four of his ten relationships contains friendship content; two people were named as individuals with whom he socialized and two others were named as individuals with whom he discussed personal problems. The average number of people named on friendship contents is 2, so the average diagonal confusion element is .2 for the domain ($\bar{n}_{II}/N = 2/10 = .2$). But this is not the probability of friendship content interactions. Four of the respondent's ten relationships contain friendship content interactions. Friendship content therefore has a .4 probability of occurring in a relationship and c_{II} in Eq. (5) would equal .4 for this respondent.

conditional probability of an ineraction with domain J content occurring in a relationship containing an interaction of domain I content. The following ratio of frequencies defines the inter-domain confusion relation:[11]

$$c_{IJ} = \frac{N_{IJ}}{N_{II}},\tag{6}$$

where N_{II} is given in Eq. (5) and N_{IJ} is the number of relationships in which any content domain I interactions occur with any content domain J interactions. For example, suppose that data are obtained on two kinds of interaction—discussing personal problems and socializing—within the content domain of friendship, domain I, and data are obtained on two kinds of interaction—job related advice-seeking and supervision—within the content domain of work, domain J. The denominator in Eq. (6), N_{II}, equals the number of different people named by the respondent as individuals with whom he discusses personal problems or socializes. The numerator in Eq. (6), N_{IJ}, is the number of people with whom he has any of four combinations of interacion; discussing personal problems and work supervision, socializing and seeking advice about his job, or socializing and work supervision. The ratio of N_{IJ} to N_{II}—that is to say, c_{IJ} in Eq. (6)—is then the probability of a work content appearing a relationship containing a

---

[11] We are here ignoring problems created by missing data and N_{IJ} of zero. These problems can be handled in Eq. (6) in the same ways that they were handled with respect to Eq. (2). See footnote 2 regarding zero N_{IJ} and footnote 3 on missing data.

friendship content.[12] Naturally, if data were only obtained on a single kind of interaction i within content domain I and a single kind of interaction j in content domain J, N_{IJ} would equal n_{ij}, so c_{IJ} would equal c_{ij} in Eq. (2).

Subculture Content Domain

The ideas proposed for studying the way in which an individual describes his relationships can be used to study the ways in which members of different subcultures describe their relationships. Chicano relationships can be compared to those of Blacks. The content of a failure's relationships can be compared to the content of a successful person's relationships. The

---

[12] This probability is not captured by the density of confusion relations between kinds of interaction within each domain for the same reasons that the density of diagonal confusion matrix elements is an inappropriate measure of c_{II} (cf. footnote 10). The point is worth demonstrating because densities are so often used to represent relations among structurally equivalent actors. The density of confusion relations from content domain I to J is the average relation from any kind of interacton in domain I to any kind of interaction in domain J; $\Sigma_i\Sigma_j c_{ij}/IJ$, where i is one of the I kinds of substitutable interactions with domain content I and j is one of the J kinds of substitutable interactions with domain content J. Rewritten in terms of sociometric citations, this density is given as:

$$\frac{\sum_i\left(\sum_j \frac{n_{ij}}{n_{ii}}\right)}{IJ} = \frac{\sum_i\left(\frac{\sum_j \frac{n_{ij}}{J}}{n_{ii}}\right)}{I} = \frac{\sum_i \frac{\bar{n}_{iJ}}{n_{ii}}}{I},$$

where $\bar{n}_{iJ}$ is the mean number of persons cited by the respondent as the object of interaction i and any one of the J kinds of interaction in content domain J. For example, if the respondent named five persons as the object of interaction i, and each was named as the object of a different one of the five kinds of substitutable interactions in content domain J, then n_{ii} equals 5 and $\bar{n}_{iJ}$ equals 1 (an average of one person was named as the object of interaction i and any one of the contents in domain J; $1 = 5/5 = \Sigma_j n_{ij}/J = \bar{n}_{iJ}$). The simplest case is sufficient to illustrate our point here. Suppose that content domain I consists of only interaction i. The confusion relation from i to each of the j kinds of interaction is 1/5 so the density of confusion relations from domain I to J is .2 (also given by $\bar{n}_{iJ}/n_{ii} = 1/5 = .2$). This is not the probability of a content J interaction appearing in a relationship containing a content I interaction. Each of the five relationships containing content I interaction contains one of the j kinds of interaction with content J. Content J interaction therefore has a 1.0 probability of occurring in a relationship containing content I interaction and 1.0 is the value for this respondent of c_{IJ} in Eq. (6).

Catholic's view of relationships can be compared to the Protestant's. In fact, relational contents can be a guide to detecting subcultures—two subcultures are distinct to the extent that the semantic meanings of interaction in the two subcultures are distinct. These ideas are illustrated in a data analysis elsewhere (Burt and Minor, 1983:49-66).

The semantic meanings of interaction within a subculture are inferred from the structure of confusion relations typical of individuals within the subculture. Data on respondent m, one of M persons sampled from a subculture study population, will be indexed by a subscript m. Respondent m's tendency to perceive the jth kind of interaction in a relationship containing the ith kind of interaction, $c_{ij(m)}$, is defined in Eq. (2). The subcultural tendency to see interaction j in a relationship containing interaction i, c_{ij}, is then the expected value of these respondent specific tendencies:

$$c_{ij} = \frac{\sum_m c_{ij(m)}}{M}. \tag{7}$$

At a higher level of abstraction, respondent m's tendency to perceive the Jth domain of content in a relationship containing the Ith, $c_{IJ}(m)$, is defined in Eq. (6). The subcultural tendency for interactions of content J to be perceived in relationships containing interactions of content I is then the expected value of these respondent specific tendencies:

$$c_{IJ} = \frac{\sum_m c_{IJ(m)}}{M}. \tag{8}$$

where content domains I and J are defined across individual respondents within the subculture.

The distance data needed to detect substitutable kinds of interaction within subculture content domains can be obtained in several ways. Two are illustrative. The simpler is to compute distances from average confusion relations. Subculture distances between kinds of interaction can be computed from Eq. (3) using the average confusion relations defined in Eq. (7). Alternatively, subculture distances can be computed directly from each respondent's confusion relations. The distance between the ith and j^{th} kinds of interaction within the semantic space created by resondent m's description of his relationships, $d_{ij(m)}$, is defined in Eq. (3). The square root of the sum across respondents of these distances squared is the Euclidean distance between the ith and j^{th} kinds of interaction across all respondents sampled from the subculture:

$$d_{ij} = \sqrt{\sum_m (d_{ij(m)})^2}. \qquad (9)$$

This equation defines the distance between each pair, i and j, of K kinds of interaction within an M $[2 + 2 (K - 2)]$ dimensional semantic space. Distances computed from the mean confusion relations for a subculture define the distance between each pair, i and j, of K kinds of interaction within a $2 + 2 (K - 2)$ dimensional semantic space. The greater dimensionality of the semantic space in Eq. (9) references differences in the way that individual members of a subculture describe their relationships. These differences can be striking and are ignored by distances based on confusion relations averaged across individuals.[13] The distance in Eq. (9) is better definition of content substitutability whenever individuals within a subculture are noted to differ in their descriptions of relationships.

---

[13] This point is easily illustrated. Consider three contents and a subculture from which two respondents have been sampled. Suppose that contents i and j have equal probability of appearing in either respondent's relationships ($c_{ii} = c_{jj}$ and $c_{ji} = c_{ij}$). Hence, these elements have no effect on d_{ij}. Suppose further that the first respondent has values of .00 and 1.00 for two confusion relations; c_{ik} and c_{jk}. In other words, he never perceives contents i and k in a relationship together but content k appears in every one of his relationships containing content j. Finally, suppose that the opposite is true of the second respondent; content k is perceived in every one of his relationships containing content i ($c_{ik} = 1.00$) while contents j and k never appear in the same relationships ($c_{ik} = .00$). With respect to their tendencies to be confused for content k, contents i and j are clearly not substitutable in either respondent's described relationships. The nonzero distance in Eq. (9) would indicate that fact. With respect to c_{ik} and c_{jk}, d_{jk} in Eq. (9) equals the square root of two;

$$d_{ij} = \sqrt{(.00 - 1.00)^2 + (1.00 - .00)^2}$$

which is the square root of 2. In contrast, a distance based on mean confusion relations would indicate complete substitutability. The mean value of c_{ik} is one half, $(1.00 + .00)/2$. The distance computed from these mean relations would then be zero; d_{ij} in Eq. (3) equals $[(.5 - .5)^2]^{1/2}$. Across the many confusion relations compared when computing distance, in short, subculture mean relations can obscure striking nonsubstitutabilities in the way individuals describe their relationships.

Once defined, distances between contents within a subculture would be analyzed to detect substitutable kinds of interaction within subculture cntent domains in the same way that respondent specific distances were analyzed to detect respondent specific content domains. Kinds of interaction within each subculture content domain define a distinct network among people within the subculture; the total number of distinct networks in the subculture equalling the number of content domains its members distinguish.[14]

4. Content Ambiguity

Having detected the semantic positions of content domains, consider the form of the confusion relations defining those positions. This is an analytical shift from describing semantic distinctions between contents to describing the semantic meaning of contents. Content ambiguity is one such meaning.

With the concept of content ambiguity we refer to the diversity of semantic meanings that a content appears to have. This diversity in meanings is evident from confusion relations indicating the diversity of empirical circumstances in which a relational content appears. The more relationships in which a content appears, and the more ambiguous the content of other kinds of interaction in those relationships, then the more difficult it would be to assign a single concrete meaning to the content—and so the more ambiguous any meaning ascribed to the content. In a sentence, a domain of relational content is ambiguous to the extent that it appears in relationships containing ambiguous contents. This ostensibly circular idea is greatly clarified with a little algebra.

---

[14] This has an interesting implication; individuals within a subculture should have a content label for each of these networks. If a set of interaction activities seem to reflect a single content domain, then respondents in the subcuilture containing that domain should have some term they use to identify that content. For example, if shared leisure activities, intimacy, and economic exchanges are found to be substitutable kinds of interaction, then people in the subculture for which such interactions are substitutable should have a word, a role label, for relationships consisting of leisure-intimacy-economic interactions. This provides an interesting strategy for checking on proposed content domain models as well as a strategy for interpreting role relations unique to specific subcultures. We are grateful to Linton Freeman for calling attention to this issue during a colloquium discussion of content domains.

The Form of Ambiguity

Ambiguity has absolute and relativistic qualities. Let u denote the ambiguity of the most ambiguous of κ content domains. We shall refer to this maximally ambiguous content as numeraire content, the ambiguity of which is the criterion against which other contents are evaluated. Let g_I be the ratio of content domain I ambiguity to numeraire ambiguity. Content I is less ambiguous than the numeraire by definition, so g_I is a fraction. Specifically, it is the fraction by which numeraire ambiguity would be multiplied in order to express the ambiguity of interactions with domain I content. In other words, the absolute ambiguity of content I is the following product:

$$ug_I, \tag{10}$$

and the relative ambiguity of content I is the ratio of this absolute over numeraire ambiguity:

$$g_I = \frac{ug_I}{u}. \tag{11}$$

Content ambiguity is generated by the ambiguity of the contents with which it appears in relationships. The conditional probability of interactions with domain I content appearing in a relationship containing content J is defined in Eq. (6) as c_{JI}. Content I is therefore ambiguous to the extent that high values of c_{JI} occur with high values of g_J. Summing the product of these terms across all κ content domains J yields a fractional measure of content I ambiguity:

$$\sum_J c_{JI} g_J. \tag{12}$$

Equations (10) and (12) both define measures of content I ambiguity, Eq. (10) with respect to the ambiguity of other contents and Eq. (12) with respect to the circumstances generating ambiguity. Bringing the two measures together yields the following equation:

$$ug_I = \sum_J c_{JI} g_J. \tag{13}$$

Thus the form of content ambiguity. Numeraire ambiguity is defined in Eq. (13) as follows (recalling that the relative ambiguity of the numeraire, Eq. 11, equals 1); $u = c + \Sigma_J c_{JI}$, where the summation across all κ contents J excludes the numeraire. In other words, numeraire ambiguity is high ($u \gg 0$) to the extent that numeraire content interactions appear in many relationships (i.e., the numeraire's diagonal confusion element, c is much greater than 0) and appear in relationships containing other interactions of especially ambiguous content (i.e., c_J, the confusion relation from content domain J to the numeraire domain, is much greater than 0 at the same time that domain J ambiguity, g_J, is much greater than 0). More generally, the ambiguity of content domain I is defined as follows:

$$g_I = \frac{c_{II}g_I + \sum_J c_{JI}g_J}{u},$$

where the summation is across all κ domain contents J except I. In other words, the ambiguity of interactions with domain I content will be low (i.e., g_I close to 0) to the extent that they very rarely appear (i.e., c_{II} close to 0) and rarely appear in relationships containing contents of high ambiguity relative to the numeraire content (i.e., c_{JI} close to 0 for all contents J for which g_J / u is nonzero).[15] In sum, Eq. (13) is the mathematical expression of an earlier

---

[15] Note that content ambiguity can be distorted by misspecified content domains. Suppose that the substitutable kinds of interaction within some content domain occur with one another in the same relationships. Confusion relations among them are therefore high. Suppose further that each kind of interaction occurs with low probability and rarely occurs with other domain contents. The domain level confusion relations for this content domain are therefore low; low c_{II} because its constituent kinds of interaction occur rarely and low c_{JI} because its constituent kinds of interaction occur rarely and low c_{JI} because they rarely occur in conjunction with other contents. Given these low confusion relations, domain ambiguity is low. But its ambiguity would be inflated by including each of its constituent kinds of interaction in the C matrix from which ambiguity is derived. In such a misspecified matrix of domain level confusion relations, there would be high off-diagonal elements among the constituent kinds of interaction. While the true c_{JI} in Eq. (13) are low for this content domain, in other words, inclusion of substitutable kinds of interaction would introduce high confusion relations. This in turn would increase the ambiguity with which the content seemed to be used in describing relationships and would inflate nummeraire ambiguity. The moral is that ambiguity should be derived from confusion relations among nonsubstitutable contents, especially when substitutable contents are connected to one another by high confusion relations.

verbal statement: A content is ambiguous to the extent that it appears in diverse relationships containing ambiguous contents.

Content ambiguity can be obtained in the sam ways that prestige and centrality scores are obtained to measure actor prominence in a network (e.g., see Burt, 1982) 35-37; Burt and Minor, 1983:Chp. 10, for review and illustration). In the same sense that a central, prestigious, person is prominent in a network of relations among other individuals, an ambiguous content is prominent in a network of confusion relations among other contents. That is to say, a content is ambiguous to the extent that it occupies a prominent semantic position in respondent descriptions of relationships. More generally, there are a great variety of network models like the model used here in the sense that they describe observed forms of relations in terms of their similarity to theoretically significant idealized forms. Examples are multiplexity, range, structural autonomy, and so on; not to mention the diversity of alternative centrality and prestige models. Each of these formal models could be used to glean insights concerning the semantic meaning of a content from the form of the content's confusion relations. More specifically, however, ambiguity has been defined here as an eigenvector model of prestige/centrality and, while the model is elegant, obtaining scores from it requires some caution.

Obtaining Ambiguity Scores

Matrix notation is convenient here. The κ equations represented by Eq. (13), one for each content domain I, can be expressed as the following matrix equation:

$$uG = GC,$$

where C is the (κ, κ) matrix of confusion relations and G is a row vector containing the κ content ambiguities defined in Eq. (11), i.e.,

$$G = (g_1, g_2, ..., g_\kappa).$$

This equation can be rewritten to:

$$0 = GC - uG,$$
$$= G(C - uI), \qquad (14)$$

which is the characteristic equation for the matrix C where I is a (κ, κ) identity matrix, u is the maximum eigenvalue for C, and G is its corresponding left-hand eigenvector. The maximum eigenvalue is appropriate here because it equals numeraire ambiguity, the maximum possible. Note that domain-level confusion relations can be defined for individuals (Eqs. 5, 6) or subcultures (Eq. 8), so content ambiguity can be analyzed as an individual or subcultural phenomenon.

Equation (14) provides an unequivocal definition of content ambiguity as long as a satisfactory, unique, solution exists.[16]

If the confusion relations *cannot*, by some reordering of rows and columns in C, be reduced to the form:

$$C = \begin{bmatrix} A & 0 \\ 0 & B \end{bmatrix},$$

with A and B square, then Eq. (14) has a dominant, positive eigenvalue u, $u > |v|$ for any other eigenvalue v for the matrix C, and a unique corresponding left-hand eigenvector G composed of positive elements (e.g., see Gantmacher, 1954:65). This eigenvector is a satisfactory solution yielding positive content ambiguities unique to a factor, here chosen to be the eigenvalue u denoting numeraire ambiguity.

If the confusion relations *can* be reduced to the above form of two (or more) square matrices A and B, then there are two (or more) independent subsystems of domain contents in the described relationships. These subsystems should be analyzed separately. For contents in subsystem A, ambiguities can be obtained from the characteristic equation;

$$0 = G_A(A - U_A I),$$

and ambiguities for the contents in subsystem B can be obtained from the characteristic equation;

$$0 = G_B(B - U_B I).$$

---

[16] In the trivial case of some content domain never appearing, we assign it zero ambiguity. This will be consistent with the following where we, for the sake of simplifying the discussion, only consider contents I for which c_{II} is nonzero.

Ambiguities within each subsystem would be obtained from Eq. (11) using the appropriate maximum subsystem eigenvalue, U_A or U_B. The relative magnitudes of U_A and U_B would indicate the relative ambiguity of contents on average in the two subsystems, the larger indicating the more ambiguous.

Separating the content subsystems preserves a complete description of content ambiguities. Simultaneous anaysis of all k contents in a reducible C matrix would result in all contents in the less ambiguous subsystem receiving ambiguity scores of zero. If U_A were greater than U_B, for example, the ambiguities in Eq. (14) for subsystem **B** contents would be 0. Clearly, this is less informative than the proposed procedure.

REFERENCES

Burt, R. S.
   1982   Toward a Structural Theory of Action: Network Models of Stratification, Perception and Action. New York: Academic Press.
Burt, R. S. and Minor, M. J., eds.
   1983   Applied Network Analysis: A Methodological Introduction. Beverly Hills: Sage Publications.
Gantmacher, F. P.
   1954   Applications of the Theory of Matrices, trans. and revised in 1959 by J. L. Brenner, D. W. Bushaw and S. Evanusa. New York: Interscience Publishers.

CHAPTER 7

SOCIAL SEMIGROUPS AND GREEN RELATIONS

J. P. Boyd

1. Introduction: Semigroups and Social Relations

A *semigroup* is a set S together with an associative binary operation. In the context of social relations, the set S is generally taken to be a set of binary social relations on an underlying set E of people or sets of people, and the associative operation is taken to be the composition of relations. While the theory of semigroups is full of rich ideas and results that may have intriguing and useful applications in social networks, there are a number of common pitfalls along the way. I have used four guidelines to try to avoid these pitfalls.

First, a social science modeler must be somewhat familiar with the basic mathematical theory. I have drawn on Clifford and Preston (1961, 1967), Howie (1976) and Lallement (1979) all of whom are indispensable for the understanding of semigroup theory. Second, I have tried to curb the natural tendency of any modeler to create a menagerie of new definitions. While a crucial definition or two may be essential, there is an obvious cost to overusing this uniquely human characteristic of defining new terms. The existing definitions have stood the test of time and should be carefully considered before overloading the reader with a lot of new ones. Next, there is the difficult problem of creating a palpable semigroup that is plausibly related to some data. I have tried to stay close to a data set. Finally, the problem of having too many subdirect representations of a semigroup is overcome for a special class of semigroups (those with nontrivial kernels), which are argued to be important on substantive grounds. This method uses the Schützenberger representations, and is the principal contribution of this paper.

The most obvious way to come up with a semigroup is to gather a few sociograms of several different relations and then multiply them together using Boolean matrix multiplication as the semigroup operation. That is, if A and B are two square Boolean matrices representing social relations corresponding to the descriptive labels, a and b, then the matrix A ∘ B is defined by

$$(A \circ B)_{ij} = \sum_k (A)_{ik} \cdot (B)_{kj}$$

where "·" is Boolean "and," and the "+" implied by the summation is Boolean "inclusive or." That is, the Cayley table for the + operation is given below:

+	0	1
0	0	1
1	1	1

There are two critical difficulties with this approach. First, if the average number of ones per row is less than one, there may be a "word" (i.e., "string") of basic relations, $s_1 s_2 ... s_n$, whose corresponding matrix product $S_1 \cdot S_2 \cdot ... \cdot S_n$ equals the empty relation $\emptyset_n$, consisting of a matrix of all zeros. This leads to serious technical difficulties in applying semigroup theory because one has an infinite set of strings that are equated only because they are empty. Thus, the set of homomorphic images may be severely limited. This difficulty may be overcome by considering the "universal semigroup" that allows strings whose products are empty to remain as separate elements in the semigroup (Boyd, 1980). Unfortunately, this case arises very seldom in practice. The more usual case is where the average number of 1's per row is greater than one. In this case, the Boolean product

$S_1 \circ S_2 \circ \ldots \circ S_n$ has the unfortunate property of having the total number of 1's increasing monotonically with the length n. This means that eventually one may get the universal relation ω_n consisting of the matrix of all 1's. To see why this is undesirable requires some basic semigroup theory.

2. Definitions from Semigroup Theory

A *binary operation* on a set S is a function $\bullet : S \times S \to S$, where the value of $\bullet$ at the pair (s,t) is denoted by $s \bullet t$, or sometimes, just by the juxtaposition, st. A set S together with a binary operation $\bullet$ is a *semigroup* iff the *associative* law holds:

$$(s \bullet t) \bullet u = s \bullet (t \bullet u).$$

If the associative law holds, then parentheses are unnecessary since all possible arrangements of parentheses give the same answer. A binary operation on S may be extended to subsets of S by the following natural definition: if $U, V \subseteq S$, then

$$U \bullet V = \{u \bullet v \mid u \in U \text{ and } v \in V\}.$$

A subset T of a semigroup S is a *subsemigroup* of S iff $TT \subseteq T$. That is, a subsemigroup of a semigroup S is a subset T of S such that the product of any two elements in T is again in T. A sub-semigroup is a semigroup since the associative law is "inherited" by subsets. Much of semigroup theory is concerned with finding subsemigroups that are "groups."

Being a subsemigroup is a property of *subsets* of the semigroup. Individual elements of a semigroup also may possess special properties. For example, an *identity* element of a semigroup S is an element 1 such that for every s in S, $1s = s1 = s$. For any semigroup S, the notation S^1 is defined to be S itself if S already has an identity, or, if S has no identity, $S^1 = S \cup \{1\}$, where 1 is an element not in S and where $s1 = 1s = s$ for all s in S^1. S^1 is called "the semigroup obtained from S by adding an identity if necessary."

Similarly, a *zero* element 0 satisfies the equation $0s = s0 = 0$ for all s in S. Also, S^0 denotes the semigroup obtained from S by adding a zero if necessary. It is easy to show that a semigroup may contain at most one identity and at most one zero. However, a semigroup may contain more than one *right zero* z defined by the equation $sz = z$ for all s in S. (A *left zero* z is defined "dually" by $zs = z$ for all s.) In fact, for each natural number n we may define the *right zero semigroup,* R_n, consisting of n right zeros. A right zero semigroup satisfies the "last letter law" of Lorrain (1975): if $s_1, \ldots, s_k$ is any sequence of social relations considered as semigroup elements, then $s_1 \bullet s_2 \bullet \ldots \bullet s_k = s_k$. We shall find evidence for the last letter law (i.e., a right zero homomorphic image) but not for the dual concept, the first letter law.

Another special element is defined relative to other elements. If S is a semigroup with an identity element 1, then the *right inverse* of an element s is an element s^{-1} such that $ss^{-1} = 1$. A *group* can then be defined as a semigroup with an identity such that every element has a right inverse. Every group also has *left* inverses since

$$s^{-1}s = s^{-1}s1 = s^{-1}ss^{-1}(s^{-1})^{-1} = s^{-1}(s^{-1})^{-1} = 1.$$

It is also easy to show that in any group, inverses commute and are unique. A *subgroup* of a semigroup is a subsemigroup which is a group.

Perhaps the most important special element in a semigroup is an *idempotent,* an element e such that $e \bullet e = e$. Let eSe denote those elements of S of the form ese, for s in S, where e is an idempotent. Then let H_e be the set of all u in eSe such that there is a u' in eSe such that $uu' = u'u = e$. The reader can verify that H_e is a group with e as its identity element. In fact, H_e is the maximal subgroup of S having e as its identity element. These maximal subgroups are disjoint, for if s were an element in two subgroups, H_e and H_f, where the inverse of s in H_f is a, and the inverse of s in H_f is b, then

$$e = as = asf = ef = esb = sb = f.$$

Since these maximal subgroups H_e are disjoint, Clifford and Preston (1961) suggest we visualize them as "islands in a sea."

Finally, the concepts of "homomorphism," "congruence relation" and "free semigroup" have to be defined in order to talk about semigroups of relations. A *homomorphism* φ from a semigroup $(S,*)$ to a semigroup $(T,\cdot)$ is a function[1] $\varphi:S \rightarrow T$ such that $(s * s')\varphi = (s\varphi) \cdot (s'\varphi)$ for all s,s' in S. A *congruence* on a semigroup S is an equivalence relation $\equiv$ on S such that $s \equiv s'$ implies that

$$us \equiv us' \text{ and } su \equiv s'u$$

(left and right compatible) for all u,s, and s' in S. It is easy to show that the set of all congruences on a semigroup S forms a complete sublattice of the

---

[1] Note that we are following the common practice in abstract algebra of writing the function φ after its argument. That is, we will write $a\varphi$ instead of φa or $\varphi(a)$.

lattice of all equivalences on S (see e.g., Clifford and Preston, 1961). If ρ is any relation on S, then the intersection of all congruences containing ρ is the minimal congruence ρ^* *generated* by ρ, and ρ is called a *generating relation*. The relation ρ is also referred to as a set of *generating equations* because ρ^* is always symmetric. If $\equiv$ is a congruence on S, then the *quotient* semigroup S/$\equiv$ is defined on the equivalence classes of S by the formula [s] • [t] = [st], where [s] denotes the equivalence class of s with respect to $\equiv$. The compatibility conditions defining a congruence relation are exactly what is needed in order to make the multiplication in the quotient semigroup "well-defined." That is, the definition is independent of the choice of representatives for the congruence classes. The function η:S $\rightarrow$ S/$\equiv$, defined by sη = [s], can be shown to be a homomorphism onto S/$\equiv$, again because of the compatibility conditions. Conversely, if φ:S $\rightarrow$ T is a homomorphism, then the relation $\equiv\varphi$ on S, defined by s $\equiv\varphi$ s' iff sφ = s'φ, is a congruence on S. The "first isomorphism theorem" states that if φ:S $\rightarrow$ T is a homomorphism onto T, then S/$\equiv\varphi$ is isomorphic to T under the mapping that sends [s] to sφ. Thus to study all homomorphic images of a semigroup S, it suffices to study the lattice of all congruences on S. For finite semigroups, then, the concept of congruence reduces an infinite task, the study of all homomorphic images, to the consideration of a finite lattice.

3. Construction of Social Semigroups

In order to use semigroups for the study of social relations, one must make the distinction between the "name" of a social relation and the actual set of ordered pairs of people who may engage in that relation. This is useful substantially as well as mathematically. Surely it is reasonable to distinguish, for example, the name "friendship" from the set of ordered pairs of "friends" in some particular group. One could then discuss the cultural norms or ideals attached to the relation. However, the only property that we will use in this paper is that there is a set of Σ of names for relations. That is, Σ is a nominal scale. Every set Σ generates a unique "free" semigroup which can be informally described as the semigroup generated by Σ with no constraints placed on multiplication, except, of course, for associativity.

More formally, the *free semigroup generated* by the *alphabet* Σ (where Σ is thought of as a set of "names" for social relations) is defined as the set Σ^+ of all *words* (i.e., finite sequences) over Σ, where the multiplication is just concatenation. For example, if Σ = {a,b}, then aab and bab are two typical words, whose concatenation is (aab)(bab) = aabbab, which may be abbreviated by a^2b^2ab. Σ may be considered as a subset of Σ^+ by identifying each x in Σ with the one letter word x in Σ^+. This identification function $\Sigma \rightarrow \Sigma^+$ is denoted by η_Σ. The free semigroup Σ^+ is characterized by the fact that, corresponding to every semigroup S and every function $f: \Sigma \rightarrow S$, there is a unique homomorphism $\varphi: \Sigma^+ \rightarrow S$ such that $f = \eta_\Sigma \varphi$. That is, the following diagram "commutes":

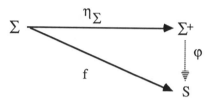

It is obvious that the image Σf generates S iff φ is onto S.

For any free semigroup Σ^+, we can define the concept of the *length* of each word over Σ. The inductive definition of length is that the *length* of each element in $\Sigma \eta_\Sigma$ is 1, and that the *length* of xy is the sum of lengths of x and y.

Since we want to preserve generators as in White *et al.* (1976), we need only consider congruences on the free semigroup Σ^+, where Σ is a set of names for generator relations. For example, if $\Sigma = \{a,b\}$, then suppose that two $n \times n$ matrices, af = A and bf = B, are assigned to a and b, respectively, and that a particular matrix multiplication operation $\cdot$ is chosen such that the set S of all $n \times n$ matrices (over some suitable semiring) is a semigroup with respect to the operation $\cdot$. Since Σ^+ is free, the function $f: \Sigma \rightarrow S$ can be uniquely extended to a homomorphism $\varphi: \Sigma^+ \rightarrow S$ such that $\eta_\Sigma \varphi = f$. In fact, φ is given for each x in Σ^+, where $x = a_1 a_2,...,a_k$ for a_i in Σ, by the expression,

$$x\varphi = (A_1) \cdot (A_2) \cdot \,_{...} \cdot (A_k),$$

where $a_i \varphi = A_i$. We can define a congruence relation $\equiv \varphi$ on Σ^+ by the condition

$$x \equiv \varphi \; y \; (\text{in } \Sigma^+) \; \text{iff} \; x\varphi = y\varphi \; (\text{in } S).$$

The quotient semigroup $\Sigma^+/\equiv\varphi$ is isomorphic to the subsemigroup of S generated by af and bf.

Returning to the difficulty with Boolean matrix multiplication, we see that if the number of ones in the matrix increases (as is true statistically if the number of ones per row is greater than one in the set of generator relations) then the only idempotent is the universal relation U. Therefore, there is only one subgroup, H_U. Furthermore, H_U is the trivial one element semigroup since $U = U \cdot r\varphi \cdot U$ for any nonempty relation r. Since a semigroup with only trivial subgroups can be pretty uninteresting from the point of view of both semigroup theory and sociological interpretation, it looks like Boolean matrix multiplication should be abandoned.

Fortunately, there is a better way to multiply matrices together: just consider the Boolean matrices as real matrices and use ordinary matrix multiplication. Once one gets over his sentimental attachment to discrete structures, the advantages that can be achieved by this method are numerous. First, the real matrix product AB of two relational matrices, A and B, of 1's and 0's has the added richness of interpretation as a labelled multigraph, where $(AB)_{ij}$ is the number of two step paths from i to j where the first arc is an A-arc and the second, a B-arc. This will enable the investigator to distinguish different degrees of relations. Secondly, many sociograms start out with some intensity information, which now need not be thrown away in order to obtain a Boolean matrix. Third, the similarity of matrices, X and Y, which represent social relations, may now be assessed by an appropriate measure of similarity, $r_0(X,Y)$, where X and Y are in $\Sigma^+\varphi$, the subsemigroup of the matrix semigroup S generated by the homomorphism φ. We now turn our attention to developing the measure r_0.

The minimum requirement that r_0 must satisfy is that, in the limit, the equivalence induced by r_0 must be a congruence. That is, if $r_0(X,Y) = 1$ (representing a "perfect" relationship for the matrices X and Y), then for any other matrix U, we should have $r_0(UX,UY) = r_0(XU,YU) = 1$. The obvious first candidate for r_0 is the Pearson product moment correlation r, where the matrices X and Y are each considered as uniformly distributed random variables on the set of all pairs of individuals. This does not work, however, since $r(X,Y) = 1$ is neither right nor left compatible. For example, let

$$X = \begin{bmatrix} 1 & 0 \\ 1 & 1 \end{bmatrix}, \ Y = \begin{bmatrix} 2 & 1 \\ 2 & 2 \end{bmatrix}, \text{ and } U = \begin{bmatrix} 1 & 1 \\ 0 & 1 \end{bmatrix}.$$

Here $r(X,Y) = 1$, but the matrices

$$UX = \begin{bmatrix} 2 & 1 \\ 1 & 1 \end{bmatrix} \text{ and } UY = \begin{bmatrix} 4 & 3 \\ 2 & 2 \end{bmatrix}$$

have a correlation of only .87. This loss of equality is distressing since it shows that the relation ρ_1, defined by

$$X\rho_1Y \text{ iff } r(X,Y) = 1,$$

is not left compatible, and hence is not a congruence relation. More generally, if $c \leq 1$ is a real number, then the relation ρ_c is defined on the semigroup $\Sigma^+\varphi$ by the condition,

$$X\rho_cY \text{ iff } r_0(X,Y) \leq c.$$

Naturally, if $c < 1$, then the relation ρ_c need not be a congruence relation. When $c = 1$, however, ρ_c should be a congruence if possible. This is achieved by a modification of the Pearson correlation coefficient r.

The cause of this difficulty with correlation is that $r(X,Y) = 1$ means that there are real numbers α,β such that $Y = \beta X + \alpha C$, where C is the constant matrix of all 1's. Then $UYV = \beta UXV + \alpha UCV$, but the matrix UCV is not, in general, a constant matrix. This suggests forcing α to be zero, but otherwise imitating the derivation of r. That is, find the β such that the line βx best approximates y, where x is an entry in X; and y, in Y. Then measure the proportional reduction of error (PRE) to find r_0^2. The first part of this plan is easy: to minimize the squared error, given by

$$\sum_{j=1}^{n}\sum_{i=1}^{n} (y_{ij} - \beta x_{ij})^2 = \sum (y - \beta x)^2,$$

where n is the number of individuals and the right hand side is an abbreviated form equivalent to the left hand side, one differentiates with respect to β and equates the result to zero to obtain

$$-2\Sigma x(y - \beta x) = 0.$$

Solving for β, the slope is

$$\beta_Y = \frac{\Sigma xy}{\Sigma x^2},$$

where the subscript Y indicates that this slope minimizes the squared deviations along the Y-axis. The proportional reduction of error for the Y-model is

$$\text{PRE}_Y = 1 - \frac{\sum (y - \bar{y})^2 - \sum (y - \beta x)^2}{\sum (y - \bar{y})^2} = \frac{\dfrac{\left(\sum xy\right)^2}{\sum x^2} - \dfrac{\left(\sum y\right)^2}{N}}{\sum y^2 - \dfrac{\left(\sum y\right)^2}{N}},$$

where N in this case is n^2. Interchanging the roles of x and y, we get another slope β_X (but with the same sign) and a PRE_X. Unlike the case for r^2, $\text{PRE}_Y \neq \text{PRE}_X$, and they each have a lower bound of $-\infty$ instead of 0. This is because if the y-values are a nonzero constant, then the constant model y fits perfectly, and the best line through the origin can only introduce error, not "reduce" it. For example, if the (x,y) pairs are (0,1) and (1,1), then $\beta_Y = 1$ but $\beta_X = 1/2$, and $\text{PRE}_Y = -\infty$ but $\text{PRE}_X = 1/4$. Since the larger measure seems intuitively to give a better fit, we will define

$$\text{PRE} = \max(\text{PRE}_X, \text{PRE}_Y).$$

We're not out of trouble yet since we have to take a square root and decide on a sign to make it analogous to r. It seems reasonable to make the sign negative if PRE is negative or if the slopes β_X and β_Y are negative, remembering that the β's have the same sign as $\sum xy$. The ALGOL expression for the final coefficient is

$$r_0 = (\text{IF pre} < 0 \text{ THEN} -\text{SQRT}(-\text{pre}) \text{ ELSE}$$

$$(\text{IF xy} < 0 \text{ THEN} -\text{SQRT(pre) ELSE SQRT(pre)}));$$

the coefficient r_0 will be called the *0-correlation*. By construction, $r_0{}^2 \leq r^2$, and $r_0 = r$ if the y-intercept is zero in the linear regression model. That is, if the best fitting line would have passed through the origin anyway, the 0-correlation number r_0 agrees with the usual Pearson product moment correlation r. See Figure 1 for examples of how r_0 is computed and compares with r. Actually, it will turn out that with the Sampson

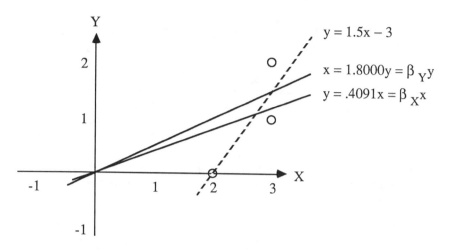

Figure 1. An Example of the 0-correlation
measure r_0 for N = 3. The two solid lines represent
the best-fitting lines through the origin (the dotted
line is the standard regression line for
comparison.) Here PRE_Y = .3409 but
PRE_X = −7.7000. Since β_Y gives a better PRE,
r_0 = SQRT(PRE_Y) = .5839

data it makes no difference which coefficient is used. The only advantage of
r_0 is that it overcomes the theoretic difficulty of perfect similarity not being a
congruence relation. To see this, suppose that X and Y are two matrices such
that $r_0(X,Y) = 1$. This means that there is a real number β such that Y = βX,
with no constant term. Then if Z is any other matrix, we have

$$ZY = Z\beta X = \beta ZX,$$

so that equivalence modulo $r_0 = 1$ is left compatible. By a similar argument,
r_0 with a cutoff of 1 induces a right compatible equivalence. Therefore,
equivalence modulo $r_0 = 1$ is a congruence relation.

4. Generating Relations: The Word Problem

Of course, the equivalence relation generated by any cutoff other than
1 will not, in general, be a congruence relation. Furthermore, not every

matrix induced in theory can be examined in practice since there are generally an infinite number of distinct matrices in the image $\Sigma^+\varphi$. A solution to both these problems is to consider the relation $\rho_{c,m}$ on words in the free semigroup $\{a,b\}^+$, defined for each real number c, the *cutoff*, and for each natural number m, the *maximal word length*. This relation is defined for each pair of words, s,t in $\{a,b\}^+$ by the condition

$$s\rho_{c,m}t \text{ iff}$$

(i) $r_0(s\varphi,t\varphi) \geq c$ and

(ii) s and t are each of length less than or equal to m.

Conceptually, it is easy to convert $\rho_{c,m}$ into a congruence $\rho^*_{c,m}$ by taking the intersection of all congruences containing the "generating relation," $\rho_{c,m}$. Practically, of course, it is impossible to construct a general algorithm for computing $\rho^*_{c,m}$. That is, the "word problem" for semigroups is recursively unsolvable (Davis, 1958). This means that, given a relation ρ on Σ^+, there is no general algorithm for deciding whether or not two words over Σ are equivalent modulo the congruence ρ^* determined by ρ. To see intuitively why the word problem is unsolvable, let us describe more carefully when two words in Σ^+, x and y, are equivalent modulo ρ. First, an *elementary* ρ-*transition* is a relation ~ on Σ^+ defined by

$$w \sim w' \text{ iff } w = usv \text{ and } w' = us'v,$$

where s,s',u, and v are in Σ^{+1} and where $s\rho s'$ or $s'\rho s$ holds. If we are given the generating relation ρ and an elementary ρ-transition, x ~ x', then right and left compatibility forces x and y to be equivalent modulo the congruence ρ^*. However, the relation ~ need not be transitive. Therefore, define $x \equiv y \pmod{\rho^*}$ iff there is a sequence $w_1 \sim w_2 \sim \ldots \sim w_n$ of elementary ρ-transitions such that $w_1 = x$ and $w_n = y$. If such a sequence is found, then we know that x and y are congruent, but if no sequence is found, it may be that we didn't look hard enough. In fact, the word problem for semigroups is unsolvable in exactly the same sense that Gödels' incompleteness theory shows that there are true, but unprovable, statements in arithmetic.

The practical implications of the recursive insolvability of the word problem is that a computer program cannot be written to construct the semigroup obtained from $\rho_{c,m}$. Despite this unsolvability in general, we can sometimes decipher the semigroup in particular cases. For example, if there is only one generator, then the word problem is solvable. It is known, however (Davis, 1958), that the word problem for two-generator semigroups is unsolvable.

Things are not as gloomy as might be inferred from the unsolvability of the word problem because there are a number of heuristic procedures for solving the word problem that seem to work in a great many cases. One method is to try to find a set of "canonical forms" for each congruence class. These canonical forms can then be used to represent, in a concrete way, each congruence class. More precisely, a set of *canonical forms* for the congruence ≡ on Σ^+ is a subset Y of Σ^+ such that each congruence class x meets Y at exactly one element. Moreover, the function $\Sigma^+ \to Y$, defined by $\{\bar{x}\} = Y(x\equiv)$, is called a ≡-*canonical projection.* Croisot (1954) has shown that if is a binary relation on Σ^+, then a function $x \to \bar{x}$ for x in Σ^+ is a ρ^*-canonical projection iff

   (i) $x\rho^*\bar{x}$ holds

   (ii) $x\rho y$ implies $\bar{x} = \bar{y}$

   (iii) $\overline{\bar{x}\,\bar{y}} = \overline{xy}.$

In words, (i) says that each word is congruent to its projections (canonical form); (ii) says that the two sides of a generating equation have the same projection, and (iii) states that the projection of a product is equal to the projection of the product of the projections. Let ≡ be the equivalence relation on Σ^+ defined by $x \equiv y$ if $x = y$. Then (i) implies that the equivalence relation ≡ is contained in ρ^*; (ii) means that ρ is contained in ≡; and (iii) means that ≡ is compatible (and hence is a congruence).

In practical terms, the search for the semigroup generated by a set $\rho\Sigma^+ \subseteq x\Sigma^+$ of generating equations is carried out by finding a set Y of canonical forms and a projection operation $\Sigma^+ \to Y$ that satisfies (i) through (iii) above. For example, if $\Sigma = \{a,b\}$ and $\rho = \{(ab,ba)\}$ (i.e., the single equation $ab = ba$ is imposed), then a set of canonical forms is given by

$$Y = \{a^m b^n: m,n \geq 0, m+n > 0\},$$

where $a^m b^0$ is interpreted as a^m; and $a^0 b^n$, as b^n. The projection operation sends each x in Σ^+ onto the word $a^m b^n$, where m is the number of a's in x; and n, the number of b's. The solution to the word problem in this case is that two words are equivalent iff they have the same number of a's and b's. This choice of canonical forms is not unique: the set

$$Y' = \{b^n a^m : m,n \geq 0, m + n > 0\}$$

is another set of canonical forms.

A second example is given by the equation $ba = a$ imposed on Σ^+. Here the last Y is again a set of canonical forms, but Y' is not. The projection operation is different, however, sending each x in Σ^+ onto $a^m b^n$, where m is the number of a's in x, but where n is the number of consecutive b's at the end of x. This is because any b's preceding a's get "erased" by the generating equation. Other canonical forms could have been used, but none so "natural" as Y since the canonical form for each congruence class is the shortest word in its class.

5. The Sampson Semigroup

The detailed account by Sampson (1969) of social relations is well-known not only for its own sake, but also because it has been analyzed by several others (White *et al.*, 1976; Lorrain, 1975). Sampson defined eight types of relations: Like, Esteem, Influence, and Praise; plus their negative counterparts. Each of 18 novices in a monastery were asked to name the "best" three novices (in order) on the four positive relations and the "worst" three on each of the four negative relations. The raw data, then, consists of eight 18 by 18 matrices with entries from the set $\{0,1,2,3\}$, whose meaning ranges in the obvious way from no relation to the strongest tie of that kind. Although it would be possible to examine a semigroup with eight generators, the complexity involved would be too great since the number of words of length n would be 8^n. Besides, the "positive" relations are pretty highly correlated. The "negative" relations are also highly correlated (though less so than the positives), and the "positives" and "negatives" are negatively correlated, as can be seen from Table 1. Using Fisher's z-transformation,

$$z = \frac{1}{2} \ln \frac{1 + r}{1 - r},$$

it can be shown that all of the correlations are different from 0 at the 5% confidence level except for the $-.05$ between Liking and negative Praise, and for the $-.10$ between negative Liking and Influence. For example, the 5% confidence interval around the $-.10$ correlation is given by the pair $(-.207, +.009)$. This test is valid in that r can be shown to be asymtotically normally distributed even without assuming the underlying variables to be normal (van der Waerden, 1969, p. 310).

	Like (+)	Like (−)	Esteem (+)	Esteem (−)	Influence (+)	Influence (−)	Praise (+)
Like (−)	−16						
Esteem (+)	66	−13					
Esteem (−)	−16	69	−17				
Influence (+)	65	−10	80	−13			
Influence (−)	−15	53	−16	67	−16		
Praise (+)	56	−13	63	−14	64	−13	
Praise (−)	−5	34	−13	43	−14	32	−12

Table 1. Correlations (× 100) between the
Sampson relations coded 0,1,2,3

More generally, the overall pattern of positive and negative correlations would seem to justify combining the relations into two relations. This was done by adding (as integers) the entries from the four positive relations to obtain a matrix A of "amicable" ties. Similarly, the four negative relations were added to obtain a "bad" relation matrix B. Both A and B are 18 by 18 matrices with integer entries from 0 through 12.

Next, let $\Sigma = \{a,b\}$ and let $af = A$ and $bf = B$. That is, a and b are the "labels" for the matrices A and B. We will construct the congruence $\rho^*_{.8,4}$ determined by considering all words over Σ up to length 4 and with a cutoff of .8 with respect to the 0-correlation matrix in Table 2. If the cutoff was properly chosen, then the semigroup will be finite and will contain some

	A	B	AA	AB	BA	BB	
B	-46	B					
AA	22	-47	AA				
AB	-45	48	-64	AB			
BA	-43	12	-61	-20	BA		
BB	28	-40	21	-41	-56	BB	
AAA	67	-44	67	-60	-58	36	AAA
AAB	-40	69	-61	73	-20	-23	AAB
ABA	-37	-5	-52	-8	60	-4	ABA
ABB	34	-19	-9	-37	-59	76	ABB
BAA	-38	43	-51	19	64	-47	BAA
BAB	23	-22	-30	-11	-59	78	BAB
BBA	43	-41	59	-54	-49	32	BBA
BBB	-35	70	-55	68	9	20	BBB
AAAA	48	-43	87	-55	-48	38	AAAA
AAAB	-37	59	-58	85	-20	26	AAAB
AABA	-25	10	-31	13	74	-37	AABA
AABB	22	22	-21	29	-54	83	AABB
ABAA	-25	15	-40	44	53	-32	ABAA
ABAB	18	28	-28	28	-50	67	ABAB
ABBA	33	-35	64	-50	-23	9	ABBA
ABBB	-27	52	-48	79	-27	49	ABBB
BAAA	-29	28	-34	9	77	-37	BAAA
BAAB	18	22	-28	31	-53	81	BAAB
BABA	33	-29	57	-42	-27	34	BABA
BABB	-32	55	-52	64	-26	50	BABB
BBAA	40	-36	65	-48	-45	51	BBAA
BBAB	-30	53	-50	67	14	35	BBAB
BBBA	-22	-14	-19	-27	79	-36	BBBA
BBBB	16	29	-29	34	-52	88	BBBB

Table 2(a).

Social Semigroups and Green Relations

	AAA	AAB	ABA	ABB	BAA	BAB	BBA	BBB	
AAB	-73								
ABA	-55	-39							
ABB	30	25	-57						
BAA	-55	-8	54	-47					
BAB	-36	31	-59	71	-60				
BBA	68	-69	-41	-22	-55	-16			
BBB	-55	81	-31	42	44	34	-55		
AAAA	87	-69	-56	34	-53	-32	72	-48	AAAA
AAAB	-68	91	-43	35	-33	49	-65	79	AAAB
AABA	-27	-18	79	-38	63	-46	16	16	AABA
AABB	-13	39	-56	89	-48	72	-29	57	AABB
ABAA	-32	-13	71	-42	76	-48	-31	32	ABAA
ABAB	-38	58	-70	81	-64	85	-46	57	ABAB
ABBA	70	-61	-33	15	-40	-40	79	-47	ABBA
ABBB	-53	79	-35	55	-18	54	-57	84	ABBB
BAAA	-28	-30	63	-39	86	-56	-18	42	BAAA
BAAB	-39	47	-81	73	-59	92	-34	54	BAAB
BABA	62	-51	-14	10	-38	30	86	-35	BABA
BABB	-52	72	-39	62	30	46	-51	91	BABB
BBAA	74	-61	-50	34	-40	29	81	-39	BBAA
BBAB	-61	80	-40	42	-3	55	-64	87	BBAB
BBBA	-12	-43	72	-43	72	-52	33	18	BBBA
BBBB	-24	47	-52	83	-42	85	-1	62	BBBB

Table 2(b).

	AAAA	AAAB	AABA	AABB	ABAA	ABAB	ABBA	ABBB	
AAAB	-71								AAAB
AABA	2	-24							AABA
AABB	18	54	-44						AABB
ABAA	-27	16	61	-33					ABAA
ABAB	-48	62	-53	78	-60				ABAB
ABBA	77	-65	40	-27	-44	-49			ABBA
ABBB	-51	87	-19	73	41	64	-55		ABBB
BAAA	-14	-40	78	-38	77	-65	29	-9	BAAA
BAAB	-41	59	-47	77	-48	86	-46	61	BAAB
BABA	68	-52	46	-18	-28	-39	74	-40	BABA
BABB	-46	73	-25	76	25	62	-42	84	BABB
BBAA	79	-61	-35	30	-18	-42	65	-42	BBAA
BBAB	-58	84	13	48	-7	67	-58	78	BBAB
BBBA	23	-48	85	-46	60	-63	46	-39	BBBA
BBBB	-9	58	-38	91	-29	79	-29	72	BBBB

Table 2(c).

	BAAA	BAAB	BABA	BABB	BBAA	BBAB	BBBA	
BAAB	-56							BAAB
BABA	31	20						BABA
BABB	36	62	-38					BABB
BBAA	7	13	76	-33				BBAA
BBAB	-13	66	-39	78	-50			BBAB
BBBA	88	-53	46	-15	-18	-16		BBBA
BBBB	-30	88	30	76	44	60	-39	BBBB

Table 2(d).

Tables 2(a)–2(d). 0-correlations of products of the combined "positive" relation A and the "negative" relation B

nontrivial subgroups. It would also be nice if every congruence class has a representative of length less than or equal to 4. The easiest way to proceed is to first find the equivalence relation generated by the pairs that meet the cutoff criterion. This can be done by observing the connected components of the graph of $\rho_{.8,4}$ in Figure 2. The dotted lines indicate congruence ties

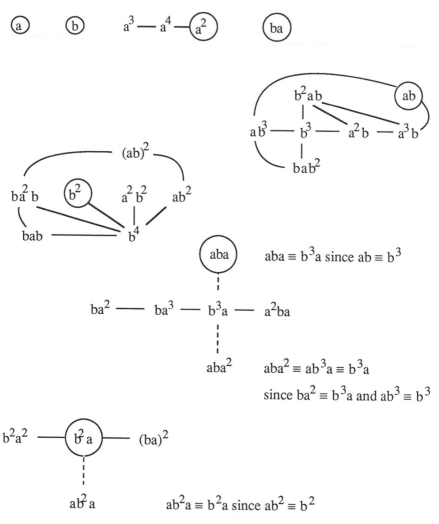

Figure 2. Graph of the relation $\rho_{.8,4}$ formed by
equating words of length ≤ 4 whose
0-correlation is $\geq .8$. The circled words are
canonical forms; the dotted words, derived
equivalences

derived by an elementary ρ-transition. For example, the dotted line between
aba and b^3a is derived by noting that $ab \equiv b^3$ because of transitivity, and then

both sides of this equation are multiplied on the right by a. The circles indicate the canonical form for each congruence class. The canonical forms were chosen to be of minimal length, and in case of ties for minimal length, the word which came first alphabetically was chosen. Transitivity implies that a word is congruent to any word connected to it. The reader must avoid the temptation to cancel or commute letters: e.g., $ab = b^3$ does not imply that $a = b^2$, nor does the equation $ab = ba$ hold.

Now we must verify that a canonical projection can be defined that sends each word w in Σ^+ onto a canonical form $\overline{w}$ in such a way that (i), (ii) and (iii) are satisfied. The canonical projection is defined by breaking the problem into cases, and into steps within cases.

Case 1: length of $w \leq 2$. Then $\overline{w} = w$.

Case 2: length of $w > 2$. There are a number of subcases.

   Case 2a: $w = a^n$ for $n > 2$. Then $\overline{w} = a^2$ by repeated applications of the relation $a^3 \equiv a^2$.

Case 2b: w contains at least one b.

   Case 2b (b-end): $w = a^{m_1}b^{n_1}a^{m_2}b^{n_2}...a^{m_k}b^{n_k}$ where $k \geq 1$ and all exponents are ≥ 1, except $m_1 \geq 0$. Then

   $w \rightarrow a^p b^{n_1}ab^{n_2}...ab^{n_k}$, where $p = 0$ or 1, by $a^2b \equiv ab$,

   $\rightarrow a^p b^n$, where $n = \Sigma n_i$, by $bab = b^2$.

   (The arrow is read "reduces to." We have not yet finished computing $\overline{w}$ for this case.)

Case 2b (b-end) even: If n is even, then

   $a^p b^n \rightarrow a^{p+n/2}b^2$, by $b^3 \equiv ab$,

   $\rightarrow b^2$, by $a^2b^2 \equiv b^2$. So $\overline{w} = b^2$ in this case.

Case 2b (b-end) odd: If n is odd, then

   $a^p b^n \rightarrow a^{p+(n-1)/2}b$, by $b^3 \equiv ab$,

   $\rightarrow ab$, by $a^2b \equiv ab$. So $\overline{w} = ab$ in this case.

Case 2b (a-end): $w = xba^n$, where $n > 1$ and x may be empty unless $n = 1$. If $n = 1$ and $x = a$ or b, then $\overline{w} = w$. Otherwise, $xba^n \rightarrow xa^{n-1}ba$, by $ba^2 \equiv aba$. Then apply Case 2b (b-end) to the word $xa^{n-1}b$, so that $\overline{w} = b^2a$ if the number of b's is even, and $\overline{w} = aba$ if odd.

The reader may verify that properties (i)-(iii) are satisfied. The quotient semigroup $R^+/\equiv$ is presented in Table 3 as a Cayley multiplication table,

	a	b	ba	a^2	b^2	ab	b^2a	aba
a	a^2	ab	aba	a^2	b^2	ab	b^2a	aba
b	ba	b^2	b^2a	aba	ab	b^2	aba	b^2a
ba	aba	b^2	b^2a	aba	ab	b^2	aba	b^2a
a^2	a^2	ab	aba	a^2	b^2	ab	b^2a	aba
b^2	b^2a	ab	aba	b^2a	b^2	ab	b^2a	aba
ab	aba	b^2	b^2a	aba	ab	b^2	aba	b^2a
b^2a	b^2a	ab	aba	b^2a	b^2	ab	b^2a	aba
aba	aba	b^2	b^2a	aba	ab	b^2	aba	b^2a

Table 3. The Sampson Semigroup S. This is the semigroup generated by two relations, a positive relation *a*, and a negative relation *b*. The cuttoff for the 0-correlation measure was .8 and all strings up to length of four were considered

where the entry represents the row label times the column label (in that order). In terms of the projection operator x y = xy. The only generating equations that were used in defining the projection operation were

(1) $a^3 \equiv a^2$

(2) $a^2b \equiv ab$

(3) $bab \equiv b^2$

(4) $b^3 \equiv ab$

(5) $ab^2 \equiv b^2$

(6) $ba^2 \equiv aba,$

so that these six equations represent a smaller, but equivalent, set of generating equations as compared to the original 29 pairs. Finally, the projection operation solves the word problem for this particular semigroup: since S is finite, just compare w_1 and w_2 to see if they have the same projection. That is,

$$w_1 \equiv w_2 \text{ iff } \overline{w}_1 = \overline{w}_2.$$

Note that for a fixed string length in the string length

$$C_m = \{\rho_{c,m} : 0 \le c \le 1\}$$

is a finite chain (linear order) of congruences on the free semigroup Σ^+. Furthermore, if $\rho_{c,m}$ is a fixed congruence in C_m, then not every congruence ρ, such that $\rho \supseteq \rho_{c,m}$, is of the form $\rho_{a,m}$, where $0 \le a \le c$. Therefore, C_m cannot be detected on purely algebraic properties alone, but is intrinsically a function of the similarity coefficients. This has the advantage that not every congruence on Σ^+, or even on $\Sigma^+/\rho_{c,m}$, need be considered.

A sensitivity analysis was performed on the following apparently crucial assumptions of this method: the 0-correlation r_0 and the 3,2,1-coding of the relational data. First, the same analysis was carried through using the Pearson product moment correlation r. The correlation between the matrix of r_0's and the matrix of r's was found to be .9453. The agreement was especially close on the high positive correlations. In fact, with the identical cutoff of .80, the very same semigroup was generated There were a few links in the graph analogous to Figure 2 which were different. However, the new r-links which were introduced were already implied by the old r_0-links; and the r_0-links which were missing in the r-graph were implied by transitivity or an elementary transition. Thus, there was more robustness to this technique than one might imagine.

Second, the weights were changed from the 3,2,1-coding to 1,1,1 and 9,4,1. An argument for the 1,1,1-coding might be that since we don't know exactly what the relative weights ought to be, we could finesse the problem by assigning equal weights. In any event, the correlation between the two

30 by 30 correlation matrices (i.e., using r and r_0) was .9770 and resulted in the same semigroup S. Similarly, the 9,4,1-coding was formed by squaring the 3,2,1, and seemed just as reasonable. The correlation between the 3,2,1-correlation matrix and the 9,4,1-matrix was even higher than the others, .9900. However, with a cutoff of .80 the 9,4,1-graph is a proper subgraph of the 3,2,1-correlation graph. All the same congruence classes result with the exception that the a^2-class breaks up into two classes, a^2 and $\{a^3, a^4, \ldots\}$. Algebraically, however, the resulting congruence $\equiv'$ is very close to the one obtained by the previous methods: $\equiv'$ is a refinement of $\equiv$, and hence $R^+/\equiv$ is a homomorphic image of $R^+/\equiv'$. Furthermore, the congruence classes are all the same, except for the a^2-class being split in two. The reader may wonder why the threshhold was not lowered to .79, say, in order to gain a few links. When that is done, however (and this is true of all the matrices), the two subgroups $H_{b^2} = \{b^2, ab\}$ and $H_{b^2a} = \{b^2a, aba\}$ are destroyed. Since one is bound to lose all the nontrivial subgroups if the cutoff is low enough, it seems like a good idea to set the cutoff just above the point where there are still some left.

The insistence of the author on the importance of subgroups is based on more than algebraic convenience. In the context of social relations, a subgroup H represents a steady-state aspect of the social system. That is, after a few compositions of the generating equations, one may reach a subgroup H which has the stable property that all of its relations are reversible (i.e., have inverses). In general, semigroups represent irreversible systems, which of course is necessary, but it is also important to note the reversible aspects of its subsystems. For example, the subgroups, H_{b^2} and H_{b^2a}, can be interpreted in this light as representing "unfriendly balance" and "friendly balance," respectively. That is, in $H_{b^2a} = \{b^2a, aba\}$, the identity element b^2a represents a stable structure of friendship, reinforced by a bond of a common enemy (the b^2 factor). The relation aba is a hostile relation modified by a friendly aspect (the trailing a). It is reversible because each relation is its own inverse. That is

$$(aba)^2 = (b^2a)^2 = b^2a.$$

Thus, even though aba is hostile, the friendship structure b^2a, can be completely recovered by squaring it. Similarly, the subgroup H_{b^2} has a stable structure of cooperation, represented by the idempotent b^2, but it is based purely on opposition to the enemy. The fact that ab occurs rather than b alone indicates that the loyal hatred of a friend's enemy is more stable than one's own personal set of enemies.

These interpretations are expanded and connected up with the "last letter law" in later sections. The justification for considering b^2a as a variant of the "friendly" relation a is justified by the fact that they have a common image in the Schützenberger representation to be discussed two sections from now.

6. Green Relations

Now that the Sampson semigroup S is finally in hand, we can proceed with the algebraic analysis of S. The most basic analysis would be to look at the lattice of congruence relations on S and the lattice of subsemigroups of S.

The problem with this approach is that in most naturally occurring semigroups, only a few have direct product representations. On the other hand, a typical semigroup has so many subdirect product representations that it becomes a problem of finding a principle which picks out one rather than another. The principal contribution of this paper is to suggest a way of choosing a unique subdirect product representation. This method always works, so long as the semigroup has a nontrivial subgroup. It is based on the Schützenberger representations to be discussed in the next section. The present section presents the material on Green relations and ideals necessary for the method. The idea is to look for direct product or subdirect product representations of a semigroup S. This approach works for any algebraic system (Birkhoff, 1967). First, we need to introduce a few new semigroup concepts. Let S and T be two semigroups. Then the *direct product* $S \times T$ is the semigroup defined on the Cartesian product $S \times T$ by

$$(s,t)(s',t') = (ss',tt').$$

A semigroup is said to be a *subdirect product* of S and T if it is isomorphic to a subsemigroup of the direct product $S \times T$. Two congruences ρ_1, ρ_2 on S detect a *direct product* by the conditions:

$$\rho_1 \cap \rho_2 = \iota_S, \text{ and}$$

$$\rho_1 \cdot \rho_2 = \rho_2 \cdot \rho_1 = \omega_S$$

where ι_S is the identity congruence; and ω, the universal congruence (i.e. is $S \times S$) on S, and where $\cdot$ is composition of relations. Next, congruences ρ_1, ρ_2 detect a *subdirect product* by the conditions

$$\rho_1 \cap \rho_2 = \iota_S, \text{ and}$$

$$\rho_1 \vee \rho_2 = \omega_S$$

In fact, these necessary and sufficient conditions could be taken for definitions. The point is that in a direct product, S is isomorphic to $(S/\rho_1) \times (S/\rho_2)$. In a subdirect product, S is isomorphic to a subsemigroup of $(S/\rho_1) \times (S/\rho_2)$. If the latter condition (that the join equal ω_S) is dropped, then S can be homomorphically mapped into the direct product. This is called a *subdirect product representation* (Birkhoff, 1967, p. 140).

A nonempty subset T of a semigroup S is a *left ideal* if $ST \subseteq T$. Comparing this with the definition of a subsemigroup (i.e., that $TT \subseteq T$), it is clear that every left ideal is also a subsemigroup. There is, of course, a concept of a *right ideal*, a nonempty subset T of S such that $TS \subseteq T$. Finally, T is a *(two-sided) ideal* if it is both a right and a left ideal. Referring to Table 3 for S, we see that $H_b{}^2 = \{b^2, ab\}$ and $H_b{}^2{}_a = \{b^2a, aba\}$ are both left ideals. The visual implication of the definition of a left ideal is that T is a left ideal iff for each t in T the column in the multiplication table for S under t contains only elements from T. For example, the columns under b^2 and ab contain only b^2's and ab's. Note that $H_b{}^2$ and $H_b{}^2{}_a$ are not only left ideals, but they also are subgroups, with identities b^2 and b^2a, respectively. On the other hand, neither subgroup is a right ideal: $(b^2)a = b^2a \notin H_b{}^2$ shows that $H_b{}^2$ is not a right ideal, for example.

The smallest left ideal containing an element x of a semigroup is S^1x, and is called the *principal left ideal generated by* x. The principal *right* ideal generated by x is, of course, xS^1. The reason for writing S^1 instead of S in these definitions is to insure that each x is an element of the ideal it generates. The principal left ideal S^1x is easily read off from the Cayley table: S^1x is simply the set of entries in the x-column (including x). Similarly, the principal right ideals correspond to the set of entries in a given row (including the row-label). In the Sampson semigroup, for example, the principal right ideal generated by a is

$$aS^1 = \{a, a^2, ab, aba, b^2, b^2a\}.$$

The principal two-sided ideal generated by x is S^1xS^1. For example, $b^2S^1 = \{b^2, ab, aba, b^2a\} = K$ is the smallest right ideal containing b^2 in the Sampson semigroup. K is also a two-sided ideal. In fact, K is the intersection of all ideals in S: that is, K is the minimal ideal, called the *kernel*. It is easy to show (Clifford and Preston, 1961, p. 67) that every finite semigroup has a kernel; for infinite semigroups, the intersection of all ideals might be empty.

Note that in the special case of the Sampson semigroup, the kernel is the union of two subgroups $H_b{}^2$ and $H_b{}^2{}_a$.

Green's relations (Green, 1951) are a series of equivalence relations on semigroups that equate elements if they generate the same right, left, or two-sided ideals. More specifically, for any elements x,y in a semigroup S, the equivalence relations L, R, J, H, D are defined by

$$xLy \text{ iff } S^1x = S^1y \text{ (same columns)}$$

$$xRy \text{ iff } xS^1 = yS^1 \text{ (same rows)}$$

$$xJy \text{ iff } S^1xS^1 = S^1yS^1$$

$$H = L \cap R$$

$$D = L \cdot R = R \cdot L.$$

The J-relations is the coarsest of the five Green relations, and H is the finest. The diagram below summarizes the inclusion relations among the Green relations:

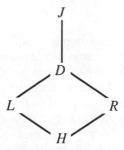

The following useful facts are true for Green relations (Eilenberg, 1976; and Clifford and Preston, 1961).

1. If an H-class H contains an idempotent e, then $H = H_e$, the maximal subgroup containing e. Since H is a partition, this gives another proof that distinct maximal subgroups are disjoint, like "islands in a sea." E.g., in the Sampson semigroup, the maximal subgroups are $H_a{}^2 = \{a^2\}$, $H_b{}^2 = \{b^2, ab\}$, and $H_b{}^2{}_a = \{b^2a, aba\}$.

2. All H-classes within a given D-class are isomorphic as sets and, if they are subgroups, as groups. This gives the "eggbox" picture for a typical D-class.

L-classes ⟶

	L_1	L_2	L_3	L_4	L_5	L_6
R_1	H_{11}	H_{12}	...			
R_2	H_{21}	...				

R-classes

and also explains why $L \circ R = R \circ L$. For the Sampson semigroup, the only nontrivial D-class is the kernel K:

	L_1	L_2
R_1	b^2, ab	b^2a, aba

,

consisting of two H-classes H_{b^2} and H_{b^2a}.

3. If S is a *finite* semigroup, then $D = J$. An example of an infinite semigroup where $D = J$ is given by Clifford and Preston (1961, p. 51). In their example, each D-class is a single element, but J has only one equivalence class, equating everything.

4. An element s in a semigroup S is called *regular* if there is some x in S such that s = sxs. It can be shown that if even one element of a D-class is regular, then all elements of that class are regular. A D-class is said to be *regular* if one (and hence all) of its elements are regular. A D-class D is regular iff it contains an idempotent. (Proof: If D is regular, then it contains elements s and x such that s = sxs, but then sx = sxsx is an idempotent. Conversely, if D contains an idempotent, then that idempotent, and hence D, is regular.) The importance of regularity is due to the fact that regular D-classes contain all the idempotents and hence all the subgroups in the semigroup. Note, however, that an element might be regular and yet not a member of any subgroup. In fact, Clifford and Preston (1961, p. 60) show that for the class of "inverse semigroups" each D-class is regular but contains the minimum possible number of subgroups, namely, only one per R-class and one per L-class in the egg-box picture.

5. The J-classes may be partially ordered by the rule that $J_x \leq J_y$ if $S^1xS^1 \leq S^1yS^1$. If S is finite, then S contains a minimum J-class with respect to this ordering. This minimum J-class is the kernel K. This ordering on the Sampson J-classes is given below

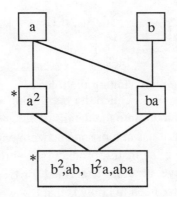

where * indicates regular $D(=J)$ classes.

6. Although none of the Green relations are in general congruences, L and R can be shown to be right and left congruences, respectively. That is, xLy implies xs$L$ys, and the dual laws holds for R. Notice that although there may be many difference congruence relations on a semigroup, there is only one of each of the Green relations.

For example, in English kinship "mother" and "father" are R-equivalent (modulo some "step"-complications) since "father" = "mother's husband" and "mother" = "father's wife."

7. Simplified Schützenberger Representations

Schützenberger (1957) gives a representation of S (i.e., a homomorphism from S) for any D-class of a semigroup. The construction is somewhat simplified if we only consider regular D-classes and finite semigroups. Let D be a regular D-class of a finite semigroup S, and let R_i:i = 1,...,m and $\{L_\lambda : \lambda = 1,...,n\}$ be the R- and L-classes, respectively, of S contained in D. The H-classes of S contained in D are the intersections $H_{i\lambda} = R_i \cap L_\lambda$. Since D is regular, we may assume the classes are numbered so that H_{11} is a group. For each λ, pick an h_λ in $H_{1\lambda}$. Since $h_\lambda R h_1$, there exist elements q_λ and q_λ' in S^1 such that $h_\lambda = h_1 q_\lambda$ and $h_1 = h_\lambda q_\lambda'$. Assume that a fixed choice has been made for the h_λ, q_λ, and q'_λ where $\lambda = 1,...,n$. Corresponding to each element s in S, we define an n by n matrix sM_D over H^0_{11} as follows:

$$\left(sM_D \right)_{\lambda\mu} = \begin{cases} q_\lambda s q'_\mu \text{ if } H_{1\lambda}s = H_{1\mu} \\ 0 \text{ if not.} \end{cases}$$

A similar construction, interchanging the roles of R- and L-classes, produces another homomorphism M_D^*, called the *dual* Schützenberger representation of S. We will not need to go into the details of M^*, however. Note that sM_D is *row-monomial* in that it has at most one nonzero entry in each row. If sM_D were not monomial, then the matrix product $(sM_D)(tM_D)$ would not be well-defined since no additive structure is defined for H_{11}. With row monomial matrices, however, all we need to know is that $0 + x = x + 0 = x$. It is easy to show that $(sM_D)(tM_D) = (st)M_D$, i.e., that M_D is a representation of S. Despite the apparent dependence on a number of arbitrary choices, this representation is essentially unique. To be precise, different choices of the group H_{11} and elements q, q' give a matrix for each s that differs from sM_D only in that the group entries may be replaced by elements from an isomorphic group. The pattern of zeros, however, remains the same (Clifford and Preston, 1961, p. 115).

For example, let us find the Schützenberger representation for $D = K$, the kernel of the Sampson semigroup. There is only one R-class in K, so $R = K$. There are two L-classes, $L_1 = H_b{}^2$ and $L_2 = H_b{}^2{}_a$. Choose $h_1 = b^2$ and $h_2 = b^2a$. Then $q_1 = 1$ and $q_2 = b^2a$ are solutions of $h_\lambda = h_1 q_\lambda$, and $q'_1 = 1$ and $q'_2 = b^2$ are solutions of $h_1 = h_\lambda q'_\lambda$, for $\lambda = 1,2$. Then M_k sends

$$a, a^2, b^2a \text{ onto } \begin{bmatrix} 0 & b^2 \\ 0 & b^2 \end{bmatrix},$$

$$b^2 \text{ onto } \begin{bmatrix} b^2 & 0 \\ b^2 & 0 \end{bmatrix},$$

$$ba \text{ and } aba \text{ onto } \begin{bmatrix} 0 & ab \\ 0 & ab \end{bmatrix}, \text{ and }$$

$$b \text{ and } ab \text{ onto } \begin{bmatrix} ab & 0 \\ ab & 0 \end{bmatrix}.$$

For example, to show that $(aM_K)_{12} = b^2$, note that

$$H_{11}a = \{b^2, ab\}a = \{b^2a, aba\} = H_b{}^2{}_a = H_{12}$$

so that $(aM_K)_{12} = 1 \cdot a \cdot b^2$.

The reader can verify that these four matrices are isomorphic to the kernel K. The significance of this is that each element in S may be analyzed into a kernel and nonkernel aspect. The *Rees factor semigroup* S/I is defined for every ideal I of a semigroup S as follows: the elements of S/I are the set $(S - I) \cup \{0\}$, where 0 is a symbol not in S and where multiplication is defined by

$$st = \begin{cases} 0, & \text{if s or t} = 0, \text{ or st} \in I \\ st, & \text{otherwise.} \end{cases}$$

The homomorphism $\rho: S \rightarrow S/I$ is defined by

$$s\rho = s \text{ if } s \in S - I \text{ and } s\rho = 0 \text{ if } s \in I.$$

With these definitions in mind we have the following easy theorem.

Theorem 1. If I is an ideal of a semigroup S and $\varphi: S \rightarrow T$ is a homomorphism such that φ is one-to-one on I, then S is a subdirect product of S/I and Sφ.

Proof: Consider the function $\sigma: S \rightarrow (S/I) \times S\varphi$ defined by $s\sigma = (s\rho, s\varphi)$. Clearly, σ is one-to-one, for if $s\sigma = t\sigma$, then s and t must either both be in $S - I$ or both in I, else their ρ-images would differ on their first coordinates. If they are both in $S - I$, then $s = s\rho = t\rho = t$; if they are both in I, then, since φ is one-to-one on I, $s = t$ again. It is also clear that σ is a homomorphism since

$$(st)\sigma = ((st)\rho, (st)\varphi) = ((s\rho)(t\rho), (s\varphi)(t\varphi))$$

$$= (s\rho, s\varphi)(t\rho, t\varphi) = (s\sigma)(t\sigma).$$

This theorem applied to the kernel of the Sampson semigroup gives the subdirect product representation in Table 4. Here the kernel K is the ideal I of the theorem, the Schützenberger representation M_K is the homomorphism φ, and the image $S\varphi = SM_K$ is isomorphic to K itself. Notice that only 8 out of a possible 20 elements in $(S/K) \times K$ were used. In general, there will be a

S	a	b	ba	a^2	b^2	ab	b^2a	aba
Sσ	(a,b^2a)	(b,ab)	(ba,aba)	(a^2,b^2a)	$(0,b^2)$	$(0,ab)$	$(0,b^2a)$	$(0,aba)$

Table 4. The Sampson Semigroup as a Subdirect
Product of S/K and K, Given by σ:S → (S/K) × K

fair amount of redundancy using the representation σ: if S has n elements; and K has k elements, then S will have n elements, compared with $(n - k + 1)k$ elements in the direct product, (S/K) × K. Note that the Schützenberger representation of the kernel K does not always result in a subdirect product of (S/K) × K. The trouble is that SM_K may not be isomorphic to K: i.e., there may be an element s not in K such that its image sM_K is a matrix different from any matrix corresponding to elements in the kernel. For example, if we adjoin the identity element to the Sampson semigroup, then the monomial matrix corresponding to the identity element is

$$\begin{bmatrix} b^2 & 0 \\ 0 & b^2 \end{bmatrix}$$

which does not match any of the four kernel matrices. Therefore S^1 is not the subdirect product of the Rees factor semigroup S^1/K and the kernel K. This example shows why Theorem 1 expresses S as a subdirect product of (S/I) × Sφ instead of the more tempting direct product, (S/I) × I. So in the Sampson case we were just lucky to find that S was a subdirect product of (S/K) × K since in general the best that can be expected is that K is isomorphic to a *subsemigroup* of KM_K.

The next theorem shows that such a homomorphism φ:S → T exists for every regular ideal of S, where an ideal I is said to be *regular* if every element in I is regular. The homomorphism φ is the *direct sum* of all the Schützenberger representations M_D (and their duals M_D*) for each *D*-class D ⊆ I. The *direct sum* of representations, $φ_i$:S → T_i:i = 1,...,n, is the homomorphism φ:S → T_1 × ... × T_n given by sφ = $(sφ_1,...,sφ_n)$. The direct sum φ is generally denoted by $φ_1 ⊕ ... ⊕ φ_n$.

In the case of the Schützenberger representations, we can think of the direct sum of several such representatives as assigning to each s in S a giant matrix with the matrices sM_D and sM_D* appearing as blocks along the main diagonal, and with zeros elsewhere. For example, there is the Schützenberger representation corresponding to the only other regular D-class in the Sampson semigroup, and that is the singleton, $\{a^2\}$. Here the "matrices" sM_{a^2} are of dimension 1 by 1:

$$sM_{a^2} = \begin{cases} a^2 \text{ if } s = a \text{ or } a^2 \\ 0, \text{ otherwise.} \end{cases}$$

This representation can be thought of as classifying social relations into "pure" (all "amicable" a's) and "impure" (at least one "bad" b). The direct sum $M_K \oplus M_{a^2}$ sends

$$a \text{ and } a^2 \text{ onto } \begin{bmatrix} a^2 & 0 & 0 \\ 0 & 0 & b^2 \\ 0 & 0 & b^2 \end{bmatrix},$$

$$b^2a \text{ onto } \begin{bmatrix} 0 & 0 & 0 \\ 0 & 0 & b^2 \\ 0 & 0 & b^2 \end{bmatrix},$$

and the rest of the elements s of S onto the matrix with the smaller matrix sM_K as a block in the last two rows and columns, and with all zeros in the first row and column. Thus, the only new distinction offered by adding M_{a^2} to M_K is to separate b^2a from a and a^2. Note that $K \cup a^2$ is a regular ideal of the Sampson semigroup.

Theorem 2. Let I be a regular ideal of a finite semigroup S. Then S is the subdirect product of S/I and the image of S under the direct sum $M_{D1} \oplus M_{D1}* \oplus \ldots \oplus M_{Dn} \oplus M_{Dn}*$ of all the Schützenberger and dual Schützenberger representations for each D-class D_i in I.

The proof requires several results from the semigroup literature. One must carefully note that a D-class of an ideal I may not be a D-class of S itself. When there is danger of ambiguity, we will write D^I, or D^S, to distinguish the D-relation relative to I, or relative to S. Similar use of superscripts will indicate the relevant semigroup for the other Green relations. Tilson (1976, p. 291), however, has shown the following.

Lemma 1. Let I be an ideal of a finite semigroup S. Then the following are equivalent:

    (i) D is a regular D^I-class

    (ii) D is a regular D^S-class and $D \subseteq I$

    (iii) D is a regular D^S-class and $D \cap I \neq \emptyset$.

Of course, Lemma 1 does not directly deal with the L- and R-classes, which are used in the Schützenberger representations. For these, the following lemma from T. E. Hall (1972) is needed.

Lemma 2. If T is a regular subsemigroup of S, then each of the "fine" Green relations (L, R, and H) is found in T by restriction:

$$L^T = L^S \cap (T \times T), \ \ R^T = R^S \cap (T \times T), \ \ H^T = H^S \cap (T \times T).$$

Proof: See Howie (1976, p. 50).

The next lemma combines these two results in a form which can be used directly in the proof of the theorem.

Lemma 3. Let I be a regular ideal of a finite semigroup S, and let G be any one of the "fine" Green relations L, R, or H. Then the following are equivalent.

    (i) G is a G^I-class

    (ii) G is a regular G^S-class and $G \subseteq I$

    (iii) G is a regular G^S-class and $G \cap I \neq \emptyset$.

Proof: As noted before, every ideal is also a subsemigroup, so Lemma 2 applies. Also, we shall use the fact that if one element of a D-class is regular, then every element is regular. We will only prove (i) $\Rightarrow$ (ii) since this is the only implication we will really use and since the proofs of the other implications are similar.

Let R^I be an R^I-class, where I is a regular ideal of a semigroup S. By Lemma 2, there is an R^S-class R^S such that $R^I = R^S \cap I$. Since $R^I \subseteq R^S$ and R^I is regular, so is R^S. Let D^S be the regular D^S-class containing R^S. By Lemma 1, $D^S = D^I \subseteq I$, where D^I is the regular D^I-class containing R^I. Therefore R^S is also contained in I, so that $R^I = R^S \cap I = R^S$. A dual argument shows that if L is a regular L^I-class, then it is also a regular R^S-class. Finally, if H is a regular H^I-class, then it is the intersection of an R^I-class, R^I, and an L^I-class, L^I. Since R^I and L^I are regular, the previous results imply that they are also R^S- and L^S-classes, respectively. H, therefore, is also an H^S-class.

The next lemma is found in Clifford and Preston (1961, p. 119).

Lemma 4. Let S be a regular semigroup, and let M be the direct sum of all the Schützenberger representations and their duals. Then M is one-to-one.

We are now ready to prove the theorem.

Proof of Theorem 2: Let I be a regular ideal of a finite semigroup S, and let D be a D^I-class, which must then be regular. By Lemma 1, D is a regular D^S-class also. By Lemma 3, the L^I-, R^I-, and H^I-classes contained in D are also L^S-, R^S-, and H^S-classes, respectively. Therefore, if H_{11} is a group and a choice for the Schützenberger representation $M_D{}^I$ (relative to I) is made of elements $h_\lambda \in H_{1\lambda}$, q_λ, $q'_\lambda \in I$, then this same choice of elements also determines the Schützenberger representation $M^S D_I$, which agrees with $M_D{}^I$ on I. If M^I is the direct sum over all D^I-classes D of the Schützenberger representations, $M^I{}_D$ and $M^{I*}{}_D$, then by Lemma 4 M^I is one-to-one. Since M^S, the direct sum of all the corresponding extensions, $M_D{}^S$ and $M_D{}^{S*}$, agrees with M^I on I, then M^S is a homomorphism that is one-to-one on I. Finally, by Theorem 1, S is the subdirect product of S/I and SM^S. ◆

Given a finite semigroup S and regular ideal I, Theorem 2 gives a canonical decomposition of S into the subdirect product of S/I and the image of S under the Schützenberger representation M. The usefulness of Theorem 2 is enhanced by the next theorem, which shows that there is a unique maximal regular ideal I.

Theorem 3. Any finite semigroup S has a unique maximal regular ideal I_0.

Proof: Let I be the collection of all regular ideals in S. I is nonempty since the kernel is regular (Tilson, 1976, p. 293) and since every finite semigroup has a kernel. Finally, $I_0 = \cup I$ is a regular ideal since the union of regular ideals is a regular ideal (unlike the case for subsemigroups). Furthermore, I_0 is the unique maximal regular ideal since it contains every member of I.   ◆

Although these theorems are easy consequences of existing theorems, they are believed to be new results and, more importantly, they do give practical guidance in the application of semigroup theory to the study of social relations. Since the maximal regular ideal I_0 is likely to contain all the groups in S, the factorization given by Theorem 2 may separate S into a group and a group-free part. In the Sampson semigroup, for example, the maximal regular ideal $I_0 = \{a^2\} \cup K$. Semigroups where S/I_0 contain nontrivial subgroups are of a higher "complexity" (Tilson, 1976) than those where S/I_0 is group-free.

Of course, one could discover any decomposition of S as a subdirect product by finding congruences ρ_1, ρ_2 such that $\rho_1 \cap \rho_2$ is the identity relation on S (Birkhoff, 1967, p. 140). For example, the congruences corresponding to Theorem 3 in the Sampson semigroup are

$$\rho_1 = \{\{a,a^2\}, \{b^2a\}, \{b^2\}, \{ba,aba\}, \{b,ab\}\} \text{ and}$$

$$\rho_2 = \{\{a\}, \{b\}, \{ba\}, \{a^2,b^2,ab,b^2a,aba\}\},$$

where S/ρ_1 corresponds to the image of S under the Schützenberger representation; and S/ρ_2, to the Rees factor semigroup modulo the maximal regular ideal. The problem, as emphasized before, is that there may be so many such decompositions that it is difficult to choose one over another. Also, the search for all such congruences may be computationally unfeasible. For an ideal I of S, however, this method may be possible because the congruence lattice for I may be much smaller than the lattice for S. For example, the kernel K of the Sampson semigroup has only the following two nontrivial congruences:

$$\beta = \{\{b^2,b^2a\}, \{ab,aba\}\}$$

$$\lambda = \{\{b^2,ab\}, \{b^2a,aba\}\}.$$

Note that $\beta \cap \lambda$ is the identity relation on K, so that K is the subdirect product of K/β and K/λ. In fact, we are lucky to find in this case that K is the direct product of these two factors. The quotient semigroup K/λ is a "last letter law" for K (and hence for all of S via the homomorphism $M_K:S \rightarrow K$) in that it is the right zero semigroup of order 2. Similarly, K/β is isomorphic to the cyclic group of order two, corresponding to a generalized kind of structural balance. More generally, each *D*-class may be represented and decomposed by "Rees sandwich matrices" (Clifford and Preston, 1961; Rees, 1940), but this is beyond the scope of this paper.

Summary and Discussion

The strategy followed in this paper was to generate a relatively large semigroup of relations and then to decompose this semigroup by algebraic techniques. In order to give the semigroup a chance to have nontrivial subgroups, it was necessary to replace Boolean multiplication of matrices by the matrix product over the real numbers. The correlation coefficient as a measure of similarity between matrices was found to be theoretically inadequate in that perfect positive correlation is not preserved under multiplication by another matrix. When a theoretically acceptable measure was found, however, it generated the same semigroup as when the correlation coefficient was used. Furthermore, rather different codings of the rank order data gave essentially the same semigroup. Thus a surprising amount of robustness was found in the usually tricky process of going from messy data to a structural model.

The unsolvability of the word problem for semigroups did not present a practical obstacle for this paper. Although it is true in general that the generating equations ρ (here determined by the similarity measure r_0, the maximal word length of 4, and a cutoff value of 0.8) do not enable one to tell if two words are equivalent modulo the congruence ρ*, or even to tell if the quotient semigroup Σ^+/ρ^* is finite or infinite, we can recognize a correct answer when given a semigroup in the form of a Cayley table. That is, if we are given a finite semigroup S over the alphabet Σ, then it is easy to compute the associated congruence such that $S = \Sigma^+/\sigma$. Then we have to check the following two points.

(i) Does S satisfy all the ρ-equations? If so, then $\rho^* \subseteq \sigma$.

(ii) Is each of the entries in the Cayley table justified by a sequence of elementary ρ-transitions? If so, then $\sigma \subseteq \rho^*$.

The verification of (i) is automatic, and it shows that the semigroup is not too large. However, since the one element semigroup satisfies all relations, it may be too small. The second condition (ii) is more difficult since we can not prove that no such sequences exist. We can, however, verify them when they are present, and the conclusion when such a series of ρ-transitions has been exhibited is that the quotient semigroup S is not too small. However, since the free semigroup Σ^+ has no relations to satisfy, it is consistent with (ii), so that S might be too big. The two conditions together, however, mean that we have exactly the right semigroup.

The Sampson semigroup that was finally obtained had three idempotents, a^2, b^2, and b^2a. An idempotent is interesting for two reasons. First, the maximal subgroups of the semigroups are found as H-classes containing those idempotents. In the case of the idempotent a^2, the corresponding subgroup H_a^2 was a trivial one-element group, but in the other two cases, H_b^2 and $H_b^2{}_a$, the subgroups were isomorphic to the cyclic group of order two. These subgroups were vital in using the Schützenberger representations. The second reason that idempotents are important is that the equation $e^2 = e$ represents a projection (in the linear algebra sense) onto a subspace of the underlying set of individuals. This second property of idempotents was not developed in this paper, but it represents the next logical step in the analysis of social relations under non-Boolean matrix multiplication. Without additional work along these lines one might well criticize this approach as merely dealing with semigroups of relations and having nothing to say about how individuals relate to this structure. Thus, I foresee a continuous model of structural similarity being developed which will complement the discrete approach of White *et al.* (1976) and Sailer (1978).

The Schützenberger representation M and the three theorems associated with it showed how to decompose (uniquely) the Sampson semigroup as a subdirect product of a Rees factor semigroup S/I and the image of I under M, where I is a maximal regular ideal of S. In the special case of the Sampson semigroup, the image of S under M_K, where K is the kernel, was isomorphic to K itself.

The structure of the kernel K was particularly illuminating for the Sampson semigroup. It was shown to be isomorphic to the direct product of the cyclic group of order two and the right zero semigroup of order two. The cyclic groups of order two represented a kind of generalized structural balance, where the identity elements, corresponding to b^2 and b^2a, respectively, are the "positive" relation, and where the group generators, corresponding to ab and aba, are the "negative" relation. Thus, although a and b do not directly satisfy the assumptions of structural balance, the semigroup that they generate can be homomorphically mapped onto such a structure.

The right zero semigroup K/λ of order two is a generalized version of the "last letter law." Some caution must be exercised in explaining why the last letter law holds, while the first letter law does not. At least the following points must be taken into consideration. First, it is not known how statistically significant is the difference between the two laws. A glance at Table 2, however, seems to indicate that the difference is a strong one: the 0-correlation between ABA and AAB is −.39, whereas the relationship between BAA and the pair AAB and ABA is −.08 and +.54. This triple holds the structural balance variable constant (the number of B's) while showing that the only positive relation is the last letter law. A similar result holds for BBA, BAB, and ABB. Secondly, the last letter law may be partly an artifact of the way the data was collected. That is, the column variance could be very large since a person may be chosen by nobody or everybody, whereas the row variance would have been zero if everyone had followed directions. It is not true that this completely accounts for the last letter law; it is merely suggested that some left-right asymmetry may have been introduced in this way. Thirdly, however, there is an interesting sociological interpretation of the last letter law which ties into results in psychology: the reason that words ending in the same letter are similar is that there may be a generalized dimension of popularity that is agreed upon by everyone in the group. For example, the relational words xa and ya ending in a "positive" relation "a" are similar in that people recognize that there must be something "popular" about person k whom person j regards as a "positive" person, regardless of what relation ("x" or "y") these people have with the intermediary person j who likes (has relation "a" with) person k. E.g., an "enemy's friend" and a "friend's friend" may both be "popular."

The difference between the approach taken in this paper and the blockmodelling ideas is that the structure comes out of the semigroup rather than being assumed or postulated, either as an *a priori* "image" or as the result of an iterative procedure such as CONCOR. The only arbitrary decision in the process is the cutoff for the generating equations and the maximum word length to be examined. In both cases, however, we were guided by the principle of obtaining nontrivial subgroups.

Previous applications by the author of algebraic theory were confined mainly to kinship studies where the semigroups were obtained from the idealized data of kinship diagrams representing the anthropologist's model of how the system works (Boyd, 1969; Boyd, Haehl, and Sailer, 1972). It has taken the author ten years to figure out how to get a semigroup out of data that is noisy both inherently and as a result of measurement problems. Now that we can get semigroups, the huge literature on the decomposition and representation of these structures may be applied in a way that will enrich both network theory and algebra.

REFERENCES

Birkhoff, G.
  1967 Lattice Theory, 3rd ed. Providence, R.I.: American Mathematical
        Society.
Boyd, J. P.
  1969 The Algebra of Group Kinship. Journal of Mathematical
        Psychology 6:139-167.
  1980 The Universal Semigroup of Relations. Social Networks 2:1-27.
Boyd, J. P., J. Haehl, and L. Sailer
  1972 Kinship Systems and Inverse Semigroups. Journal of
        Mathematical Sociology 2:37-61.
Clifford, A., and G. Preston
  1961 The Algebraic Theory of Semigroups, Vol. I. Providence, R.I.:
        American Mathematical Society.
  1967 The Algebraic Theory of Semigroups, Vol. II. Providence, R.I.:
        American Mathematical Society.
Croisot, R.
  1954 Automorphismes Interieures d'un Semi-groupe. Bulletin de la
        Société Mathématique de France 82:161-194.
Davis, M.
  1958 Computability and Unsolvability. New York: McGraw-Hill.
Eilenberg, S.
  1979 Automata, Languages, and Machines, Vol. B. New York:
        Academic Press.
Green, J.
  1951 On the Structure of Semigroups. Annals of Mathematics
        54:163-172.
Hall, T.
  1972 Congruences and Green's Relations on Regular Semigroups.
        Glasgow Mathematical Journal 13:167-175.
Howie, J.
  1976 An Introduction to Semigroup Theory. New York: Academic
        Press.
Lallement, G.
  1979 Semigroups and Combinatorial Applications. New York: Wiley.
Lorrain, F.
  1975 Reseaux Sociaux et Classifications Sociales. Paris: Herman.
Rees, D.
  1940 On Semi-groups. Proceedings of the Cambridge Philosophical
        Society 36:387-400.

254   *Social Semigroups and Green Relations*

Sailer, L.
    1978 Structural Equivalence: Meaning and Definition, Computation and
          Application. Social Networks 1:73-90.
Sampson, S.
    1969 Crisis in a Cloister. Ph.D. Dissertation, Cornell University.
Schützenberger, M.
    1957 D̄ Representation des Demi-groupes. Comptes Rendus des
          l'Academie des Sciences 244:1994-1996.
Tilson, B.
    1976 Depth Decomposition Theorem, and Complexity of Semigroups
          and Morphisms. *In* Eilenberg (1976:287-384).
van der Waerden, B. L.
    1969 Mathematical Statistics. New York: Springer-Verlag.
White, H., S. Boorman, and R. Breiger
    1976 Social Structure from Multiple Networks. I. Blockmodels of
          Roles and Positions. American Journal of Sociology 81:730-780.

CHAPTER 8

WHAT IS A HOMOMORPHISM?

Phillip Bonacich

1. Introduction

A homomorphism is an algebraic transformation that plays a large role in blockmodeling. However, it is unclear what homomorphisms are in terms of transformations of the data. What is the relation between the homomorphic image of a semigroup and the matrices that generated the semigroup? Homomorphisms are algebraic simplifications, but do they imply a corresponding simplification of the data? This is the basic issue of this chapter.

This problem does not yet have a perfect solution. All the approaches described in this chapter are more or less inadequate. My expectation is that organizing this material will help either myself or someone else find better solutions to this important problem.

2. *Semigroups of Relational Matrices*

A semigroup is any set of objects with an associative binary operation ∘; for any a, b, and c in the semigroup S, (a ∘ b) ∘ c = a ∘ (b ∘ c) (Howie, 1976:1). Let S be a set of binary valued matrices describing different kinds of relations between a set of people and all the Boolean products of these matrices. This set forms a semigroup under the operation of Boolean matrix multiplication. Each matrix describes a direct or indirect relation between people. For any matrix A ∈ S, $A_{ij} = 1$ if person i and person j have relationship A, and $A_{ij} = 0$ otherwise.

For example, consider the following matrices:

$$P = \begin{bmatrix} 1 & 1 & 1 & 0 \\ 1 & 1 & 1 & 0 \\ 0 & 1 & 1 & 0 \\ 0 & 0 & 1 & 1 \end{bmatrix} \qquad N = \begin{bmatrix} 1 & 1 & 1 & 1 \\ 1 & 0 & 1 & 1 \\ 1 & 0 & 0 & 1 \\ 1 & 1 & 0 & 0 \end{bmatrix}$$

These two matrices generate the following additional matrices:

$$PN = \begin{bmatrix} 1 & 1 & 1 & 1 \\ 1 & 1 & 1 & 1 \\ 1 & 0 & 1 & 1 \\ 1 & 1 & 0 & 1 \end{bmatrix} \qquad NP = \begin{bmatrix} 1 & 1 & 1 & 1 \\ 1 & 1 & 1 & 1 \\ 1 & 1 & 1 & 1 \\ 1 & 1 & 1 & 0 \end{bmatrix}$$

$$N^2 = \begin{bmatrix} 1 & 1 & 1 & 1 \\ 1 & 1 & 1 & 1 \\ 1 & 1 & 1 & 1 \\ 1 & 1 & 1 & 1 \end{bmatrix} \qquad P^2 = \begin{bmatrix} 1 & 1 & 1 & 0 \\ 1 & 1 & 1 & 0 \\ 1 & 1 & 1 & 0 \\ 0 & 1 & 1 & 1 \end{bmatrix}$$

$$P^3 = \begin{bmatrix} 1 & 1 & 1 & 0 \\ 1 & 1 & 1 & 0 \\ 1 & 1 & 1 & 0 \\ 1 & 1 & 1 & 1 \end{bmatrix}$$

Table 1 gives the multiplication table for this semigroup, which we will call S_1.

Table 1. Multiplication Table for Semigroup S_1

	P	N	P2	NP	PN	N2	P3
P	P2	PN	P3	N2	N2	N2	P3
N	NP	N2	NP	N2	N2	N2	NP
P2	P3	N2	P3	N2	N2	N2	P3
NP	NP	N2	NP	N2	N2	N2	P3
PN	N2	N2	N2	N2	N2	N2	N2
N2	N2	N2	N2	N2	N2	N2	N2
P3	P3	N2	P3	N2	N2	N2	P3

As a second example, to be used throughout the paper, consider the semigroup generated by the following pair of matrices.

$$P = \begin{bmatrix} 1 & 1 & 0 \\ 0 & 1 & 0 \\ 0 & 0 & 1 \end{bmatrix} \qquad N = \begin{bmatrix} 0 & 0 & 1 \\ 1 & 0 & 1 \\ 1 & 1 & 1 \end{bmatrix}$$

These two matrices generate the following additional matrices.

$$PN = \begin{bmatrix} 1 & 0 & 1 \\ 1 & 0 & 1 \\ 1 & 1 & 1 \end{bmatrix} \qquad NP = \begin{bmatrix} 0 & 0 & 1 \\ 1 & 1 & 1 \\ 1 & 1 & 1 \end{bmatrix} \qquad N^2 = \begin{bmatrix} 1 & 1 & 1 \\ 1 & 1 & 1 \\ 1 & 1 & 1 \end{bmatrix}$$

The multiplication table for this second illustrative semigroup is given in Table 2.

Table 2. Multiplication Table for Semigroup S_2

	P	N	PN	NP	N^2
P	P	PN	PN	N^2	N^2
N	NP	N^2	N^2	N^2	N^2
PN	N^2	N^2	N^2	N^2	N^2
NP	NP	N^2	N^2	N^2	N^2
N^2	N^2	N^2	N^2	N^2	N^2

3. Homomorphisms

A homomorphism between two semigroups S_1 and S_2 is a mapping h from S_1 to S_2 such that for every pair a and b in S_1, abh = (ah)(bh). If ch = dh, c and d are said to be congruent or in the same congruence class, and this can be written as $c \equiv d$. If $a \equiv b$ and $c \equiv d$, it can be shown that $ac \equiv bd$.

For example, consider the semigroup S_1 of Table 1. One set of congruence classes is: P / N,P^2 / NP,PN,N^2,P^3. Slashes are used to separate the congruence classes. This congruence relation can be produced by this mapping h: Ph = P, Nh = P^2h = N, NPh = PNh = N^2h = P^3h = N^2. Table 3 is the multiplication table for the image semigroup.

Table 3. Image Semigroup for S_1

	P	N	N^2
P	N	N^2	N^2
N	N^2	N^2	N^2
N^2	N^2	N^2	N^2

Another partition of the same semigroup into a different set of congruence classes is: Ph = P^2h = P^3h = P, Nh = N, NPh = NP, and

$PNh = N^2h = N^2$. Table 4 gives the multiplication table for this homomorphism.

Table 4. Another Image Semigroup for S_1

	P	N	NP	N^2
P	P	N^2	N^2	N^2
N	NP	N^2	N^2	N^2
NP	NP	N^2	N^2	N^2
N^2	N^2	N^2	N^2	N^2

4. The Uses of Homomorphisms in Blockmodeling

The use of homomorphisms pervades blockmodeling. They are useful because they cluster relations into sets, thus simplifying, yet they preserve algebraic structure.

1. Boorman and White (1976) use homomorphisms in two ways. First, the "joint reduction semigroup," which is designed to locate the common patterns present in a set of semigroups, is a homomorphic image of every one of the semigroups. Second, Boorman and White use the fact that a theory-based semigroup is a homomorphic image of a more complex data-based semigroup as evidence for the theory.

2. Bonacich (1980) uses the "common structure semigroup" to isolate the patterns common to two or more semigroups. All these semigroups are homomorphic images of the common structure semigroup.

3. Pattison (1977) suggests that semigroups can be "factored" into simpler constituent patterns. The factors of a semigroup are a particular set of homomorphic images of that semigroup.

5. The Problem

Let I be a set of people or blocks of people, and let R be a set of relationships, both direct and compound, among these people. Two relationships are equal if their graphs (or matrices) are equal. Let S be the abstract semigroup describing the Boolean multiplicative relations among these relationships R. Let h: S → Sh be a homomorphism sending semigroup S into a homomorphic image semigroup Sh.

Sh is a more elementary semigroup than S in that it clusters the elements of S into a smaller number of congruence classes that are "equal" under h. The basic question is: does Sh describe the "data," the relationships R between the individuals I? Are there a set of relationships Rm between the individuals I whose relations are described by Sh? The relationships Rm would each be amalgams of the relationships in a congruence class. Or, are there blocks of individuals Ip, combinations of or selections from the individuals in I, whose relationships are described by Sh? If Rm and Ip do not exist, then in what sense does Sh provide a simplified but meaningful description of the data?

Table 5 diagrams the problem. The question marks are the mappings we are looking for. The three objects in the "Data" column of Table 5 are related to each other; S describes the relations among the relationships R between the people I. We want to find an Rm and Ip that bear the same relation to Sh.

Table 5. A Diagram of the Problem

	Data	Mapping	Image
Semigroup	S	h	Sh
Relations	R	m(?)	Rm
Units	I	p(?)	Ip

None of the techniques we will examine is perfect, so we will need some way of comparing their adequacy. Boorman and White suggest a dissimilarity measure between semigroups with the same generators (1976:

1422-23).[1] We will use it to compare Sh with the semigroups implied by the various techniques. The measure equals zero when two semigroups are the same (then the representation of Sh in terms of Ip and/or Rm is perfect) and has a maximum value of two when there is maximum dissimilarity between the semigroups.

Here it should be stressed that the Lorrain-White and Wu approaches were named by the author of this chapter. Lorrain, White, and Wu were not trying to solve the problem analyzed in this paper and bear no responsibility for the failures of these approaches.

6. The Lorrain-White Approach

Lorrain and White (1971) use the algebra of categories rather than semigroups, and their goal is to propose a definition of structural equivalence between individuals. This section is not intended to be a description of their approach; instead it describes a solution to the problem of understanding homomorphisms (not a problem to Lorrain and White because they do not use homomorphisms) inspired by their approach.

The Lorrain-White inspired approach is to create a set of relationships, one for each congruence class of a homomorphism, such that the new relationships both reflect the relationships in their congruence classes *and* generate the semigroup Sh. In terms of Table 5, this strategy

---

[1] Boorman and White (1976:1422-1423) describe the following measure of dissimilarity between two semigroups with the same generators. Let $P = (c_1, c_2, ..., c_m)$ be a partition of a finite semigroup S into congruence classes, $|c_i|$ = size of c_i, and N = size of S. The "coarseness" h(P) of the partition P is defined as:

$$h(p) = \frac{\sum_{i=1}^{m} \binom{|c_i|}{2}}{\binom{N}{2}}.$$

h(P) = 0 when each element is its own congruence class and equals one when all elements are in the same congruence class. The joint reduction of two semigroups S_1 and S_2 implies a partition P_1 and P_2 of each of them. The measure of dissimilarity δ between the two semigroups is:

$$\delta(S_1, S_2) = h(P_1) + h(P_2)$$

involves defining a mapping m from the set of relational matrices R to a smaller set Rm. Let the relationship corresponding to each congruence class simply be the union of the relationships in each class (its matrix is the Boolean sum of the matrices of the relations in each class). For example, in the homomorphism of Table 4, $Ph = P^2h = P^3h$, so two people are connected by the relation Pm if they are connected by P, P^2, or P^3, but since N is the only member of its congruence class, $Nm = N$.

$$Pm = P + P^2 + P^3 = \begin{bmatrix} 1 & 1 & 1 & 0 \\ 1 & 1 & 1 & 0 \\ 1 & 1 & 1 & 0 \\ 1 & 1 & 1 & 1 \end{bmatrix}$$

$$Nm = N = \begin{bmatrix} 1 & 1 & 1 & 1 \\ 1 & 0 & 1 & 1 \\ 1 & 0 & 0 & 1 \\ 1 & 1 & 0 & 0 \end{bmatrix}$$

Pm and Nm succeed in generating the image semigroup of Table 4. If the Lorrain-White approach always succeeded in producing matrices that generated the image semigroup it would be a perfect solution to the problem diagramed in Table 5. However, it doesn't. Consider, for example, the homomorphism in Table 3. For this homomorphism:

$$Pm = P = \begin{bmatrix} 1 & 1 & 1 & 0 \\ 1 & 1 & 1 & 0 \\ 0 & 1 & 1 & 0 \\ 0 & 0 & 1 & 1 \end{bmatrix}$$

$$Nm = N + P^2 = \begin{bmatrix} 1 & 1 & 1 & 1 \\ 1 & 1 & 1 & 1 \\ 1 & 1 & 1 & 1 \\ 1 & 1 & 1 & 1 \end{bmatrix}$$

These two matrices generate the following semigroup.

Table 6. Semigroup Generated by Pm and Nm

	Pm	Pm^2	Nm	Pm^3
Pm	Pm^2	Pm^3	Nm	Pm^3
Pm^2	Pm^3	Nm	Nm	Nm
Nm	Nm	Nm	Nm	Nm
Pm^3	Pm^3	Pm^3	Nm	Pm^3

This is not the semigroup of Table 3, the homomorphic image semigroup. In this instance, Pm and Nm do not adequately capture the homomorphism.

Table 7 gives the results of applying the Lorrain-White approach to all the congruence relations of S_1 and S_2. The first column lists all congruence relations. The second column gives the semigroups generated by Pm and Nm for each congruence. All these semigroups were isomorphic to a homomorphic image semigroup, but this need not always by the case. The last column gives the Boorman-White dissimilarity measure δ between the congruence relations and the semigroups generated by Pm and Nm. As was stated before, $\delta = 0$ when two semigroups are equal and δ has a maximum value of 2.00.

Table 7. Lorrain-White Representations for S_1

	Congruence	L-W Representation	δ
7a.	$P/P^2/P^3/NP/PN/N/N^2$	7a	.00
6a.	$P/P^2,P^3/N/NP/PN/N^2$	7a	.05
6b.	$P/P^2/P^3/PN/N/NP,N^2$	7a	.05
6c.	$P/P^2/P^3/NP/N/PN,N^2$	7a	.05
5a.	$P/P^2/P^3/N,NP/PN,N^2$	5a	.00
5b.	$P/P^2/P^3/N/NP,PN,N^2$	7a	.29
5c.	$P/P^2/N/PN/P^3,N^2,NP$	7a	.29
5d.	$P/P^2,P^3/NP,N^2/N/NP$	7a	.10
5e.	$P/P^2,P^3/PN,N^2/N/NP$	7a	.10
4a.	$P,P^2,P^3/N/NP/PN,N^2$	4a	.00
4b.	$P/P^2/P^3/N,PN,NP,N^2$	4b	.00
4c.	$P/N/PN/P^2,NP,P^3,N^2$	7a	.29
4d.	$P/N/P^2,PN/P^3,N^2,NP$	7a	.19
4e.	$P/P^2/N/PN,NP,P^3,N^2$	7a	.29
4f.	$P/P^2,P^3/N,NP/PN,N^2$	5a	.10
4g.	$P/P^2,P^3/N/NP,PN,N^2$	7a	.19
3a.	$P/N,P^2/NP,P^3,PN,N^2$	4b	.83
3b.	$P/P^2/N,P^3,PN,N^2,NP$	4b	.83
3c.	$P/P^2,P^3/N,NP,PN,N^2$	4b	.83
3d.	$P/N/P^2,N^2,P^3,PN,NP$	7a	.46
3e.	$P,P^2,P^3/PN,N/NP,N^2$	3e	.00
3f.	$P,P^2,P^3/PN,N/NP,N^2$	3f	.00
2a.	$P,N/P^2,NP,P^3,PN,N^2$	2a	.00
2b.	$N/P,P^2,PN,P^3,PN,N^2$	2b	.00
2c.	$P/P^2,NP,PN,N^2,P^3,N$	2d	.00
1a.	P,P^2,P^3,N,N^2,PN,NP	1a	.00

Table 7 (continued)

Lorrain-White Representations for S_2

	Congruence	L-W Representation	δ
5a.	P/N/NP/PN/N^2	5a	.00
4a.	P/N/NP/PN,N^2	5a	.10
4b.	P/N/PN/NP,N^2	5a	.10
3a.	P/N/PN,NP,N^2	5a	.30
3b.	P/N,NP/PN,N^2	3b	.00
3c.	P/N,PN/NP,N^2	3c	.00
2a.	N/P,NP,PN,N^2	2a	.00
2b.	P/N,PN,NP,N^2	2b	.00
1a.	P,N,NP,PN,N^2	1a	.00

This approach succeeds in producing Pm and Nm matrices that generate the homomorphic image semigroups in only eleven out of twenty-seven homomorphisms for S_1 and in six out of nine homomorphisms for S_2. For twelve homomorphisms of S_1 and for three of S_2 Pm = P and Nm = N, so the semigroup generated by the image matrices is just the original S. For these cases the technique gets no purchase on the homomorphism at all. Later in the paper we will use the δ column of dissimilarity measures to compare the different techniques.

7. Pattison's Approach

Pattison's approach (1977) is to choose graph homomorphic images of the matrices of a semigroup to represent the homomorphic image semigroup Sh. In terms of Table 5, her approach is to find a mapping p of the units I so that the relations Rm between the blocked units Ip produce a semigroup identical to or at least close to the semigroup Sh.

Do not confuse graph homomorphisms and semigroup homomorphisms. The latter is a structure-preserving mapping from one semigroup to another. The former is a mapping from one set of graphs or matrices to another in which vertices (individuals or blocks of individuals) are combined, and the aggregated vertices are connected in the image graphs only if at least one pair of their constituent vertices are connected in the first set of graphs.

Let T be a matrix in which $T_{ij} = 1$ if block i is a member of aggregated block j for graph homomorphism m and $T_{ij} = 0$ otherwise. Let A be the matrix of any element in the semigroup S. Then, the graph homomorphism m can be represented as a mapping m: A → Am where

$$Am = T^tAT$$

in Boolean matrix multiplication, where T^t is the transpose of T. For example, consider a relation A on X = {1,2,3}, where A connects point 1 to 3. Let m: ⟨X,A⟩ → ⟨Xm,Am⟩ be a graph homomorphism mapping points {1,2} in X onto {x} in Xm, and point {3} in X onto {y} in Xm, as represented by

$$T = \begin{bmatrix} 1 & 0 \\ 1 & 0 \\ 0 & 1 \end{bmatrix}.$$

Then

$$Am = \begin{bmatrix} 1 & 1 & 0 \\ 0 & 0 & 1 \end{bmatrix} \begin{bmatrix} 0 & 0 & 1 \\ 0 & 0 & 0 \\ 0 & 0 & 0 \end{bmatrix} \begin{bmatrix} 1 & 0 \\ 1 & 0 \\ 0 & 1 \end{bmatrix} = \begin{bmatrix} 0 & 1 \\ 0 & 0 \end{bmatrix}$$

so that the connection from point 1 to 3 is reflected in the image as a connection from x to y.

Every partition π on X is associated with a matrix T_π which defines a graph homomorphism m. Let S be the semigroup generated from a set of matrices G = {$R_1, R_2, ..., R_n$} under Boolean multiplication. Let

$$G/\pi = Gm = \{R' \mid R' = R_im \text{ for some } i = 1,n\}$$

be the set of graph homomorphic images of the generating matrices. Let S/π be the semigroup generated by these matrices.* Unfortunately, S/π is not necessarily a semigroup homomorphic reduction of S. For example, let T combine the second and third positions of the two matrices producing S_1. It

---

* Editor's note: In terms of White and Reitz' definitions, G/π is a full graph homomorphism, but not necessarily S/π .

can be shown that $P^2m = T'P^2T \neq T'PTT'PT = (Pm)(Pm)$. Therefore, the graph homomorphism is not an algebraic homomorphism.

Neither can all semigroup homomorphisms S/α of a semigroup S be represented by some graph homomorphism S/α for a partition π. To find a one-to-one correspondence between semigroup and graph homomorphisms it is necessary to choose a "best" graph homomorphism for each semigroup homomorphism.

Pattison's procedure involves "associating" a set of homomorphic images with all possible partitions of the objects or blocks of the original matrices. To do this, let ρ_π be a partition of *all* the matrices of S where two matrices are in the same class if their graph homomorphic images are equal. ρ_π may not be an algebraic congruence relation; $\rho_{\pi*}$ is the "finest" congruence relation containing ρ_π, and $S/\rho_{\pi*}$ is the semigroup for the congruence relation $\rho_{\pi*}$.[2]

S/π and $S/\rho_{\pi*}$ are both semigroups with the same abstract generators as S. They are both faithful to S and to π but in different ways. S/π is entirely a function of what π does to the generators, whereas S/ρ_π and $S/\rho_{\pi*}$ are functions also of what π does to all the elements of S.

The common abstract generators of S/π and S/ρ_π generate a free semigroup. S/π and S/ρ_π are both homomorphic reductions of this free semigroup and both can be thought of as congruences on this free semigroup. As congruences on the same semigroup their join can be determined, $S/\pi \vee S/\rho_\pi$ (Boorman and White, 1976: 1421; Bonacich and McConaghy, 1980: 521-24).[3] The joint reduction of semigroups S/π and $S/\rho_{\pi*}$ is a simplification of both of them; it equates elements of the free semigroup that are equated by either S/π or by $S/\rho_{\pi*}$.

---

[2] Congruence relations are a special type of equivalence relation. One equivalence relation E_1 on a set S is said to contain another equivalence relation E_2, written as "$E_1 \geq E_2$," if $xE_2y \Rightarrow xE_1y$ for x and y in S.

[3] The join $E_1 \vee E_2$ of any two equivalence relations E_1 and E_2 is defined as the least upper bound of all equivalence relations containing both E_1 and E_2. It can be shown (Howie, 1976:27-28) that the join of any two congruence relations of the free semigroup with a certain set of generators is also a congruence relation. Thus, if S/π and $S/\rho_{\pi*}$ are used to refer both to the semigroups and to the associated congruence relations of the free semigroup that they imply, $S/\pi \vee S/\rho_{\pi*}$ is also a congruence relation and we will refer to its semigroup also as $S/\pi \vee S/\rho_{\pi*}$.

Let α be any congruence relation among the elements of S and let S/α be the implied homomorphic image semigroup. S/α is said to be "associated with" the partition π if S/α is a homomorphic reduction of Sπ/ $\vee$ S/$\rho_{\pi*}$.[4] If S/α is associated with π, the congruence α equates all pairs of relations that are implied to be equal by π, either through S/π or through S/$\rho_{\pi*}$. In a sense, α is a cruder simplification of the relations between relations implied by π.

Figure 1 is a diagram of the relations among the various semigroups or congruences. In the diagram one semigroup is above another if the former is a homomorphic reduction of the latter, or, equivalently, one congruence relation is above another if the latter is a refinement of the former.

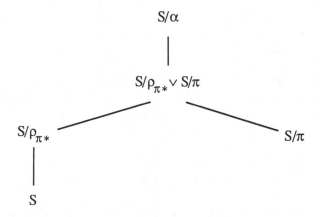

Figure 1. Lattice Relations Among Semigroups

We have associated with each partition π a set of homomorphic images S/α, but the relation "associated with" is symmetric, so we have also associated with each homomorphic image a set of partitions. All these partitions have in common the property that the semigroups they generate (through S/π and S/$\rho_{\pi*}$) all have S/α as their homomorphic simplification.

The set of partitions associated with a given S/α may contain a least upper bound partition in the lattice of all partitions of the objects X. This partition, if it exists, will be the most aggregated blocking of the original matrices that remains consistent with S/α.

---

[4] If α and β are two congruence relations on a free semigroup such that $\alpha \geq \beta$, then S/α is a homomorphic reduction of S/β.

We will use S_1 and S_2 as examples. Figure 2 shows the lattices of all congruence relations for semigroups S_1 and S_2 using the numbering system employed in Tables 7 and 8; these show the S/α of Pattison's model. Figure 3 shows the lattices of all partitions of four and of three objects; these show the π of the model.

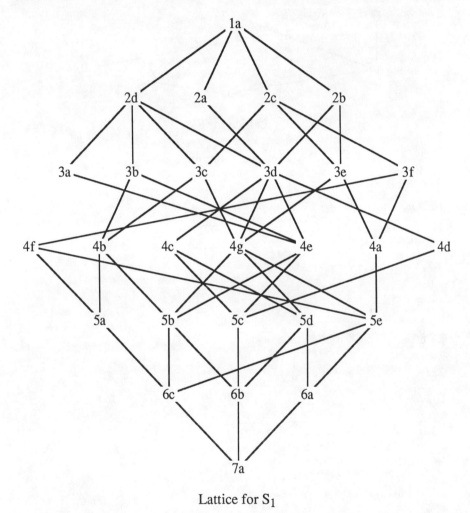

Lattice for S_1

Figure 2. Lattices of Congruence Relations

What is a Homomorphism?

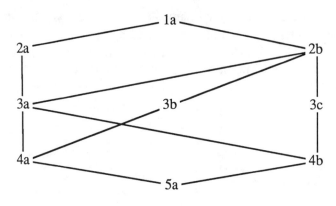

Lattice for S_2

Figure 2 (continued)

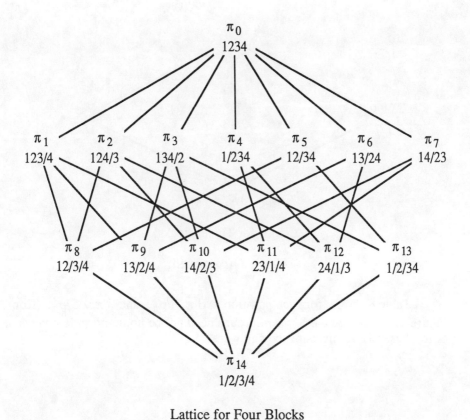

Lattice for Four Blocks

Figure 3. Lattices of Partitions of Four and Three Blocks

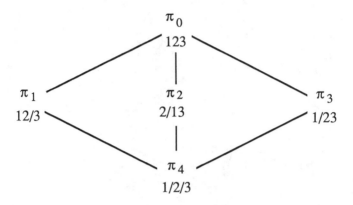

Lattice for Three Blocks

Figure 3 (continued)

Table 8 shows, for each partition π, S/π, $S/\rho_{\pi*}$, and $S/\pi \vee S/\rho_{\pi*}$ (from Figure 2). Although the S/π semigroups need not be homomorphic images of S, for these two semigroups they all were.

Table 8. Homomorphisms Associated with Each Partition for S_1 and S_2

Associated Homomorphisms for S_1

π	S/π	$S/\rho_{\pi*}$	$S/\pi \vee S/\rho_{\pi*}$	Associated Homomorphisms
$\pi_0 = 1234$	1a	1a	1a	1a
$\pi_1 = 123/4$	3f	3f	3f	3f,2c,1a
$\pi_2 = 124/3$	2b	2b	2b	2b,1a
$\pi_3 = 134/2$	2b	2b	2b	2b,1a
$\pi_4 = 1/234$	1a	1a	1a	1a
$\pi_5 = 12/34$	1a	1a	1a	1a
$\pi_6 = 13/24$	1a	1a	1a	1a
$\pi_7 = 14/23$	1a	1a	1a	1a
$\pi_8 = 12/3/4$	6c	6c	6c	6c,5a,5b,5e,4f,4b,4g,4e,4a, 3a,3b,3c,3d,3e,3f,2a,2d,2c, 2b,1a
$\pi_9 = 13/2/4$	5e	5e	5e	5e,4a,4f,4g,3c,3d,3f,3e,2a, 2b,2c,2d,1a
$\pi_{10} = 14/2/3$	4c	4c	4c	4c,3d,2a,2d,2b,1a
$\pi_{11} = 23/1/4$	4f	3f	3f	3f,2c,1a
$\pi_{12} = 24/1/2$	3d	3d	3d	3d,2a,2d,2b,1a
$\pi_{13} = 1/2/34$	3d	3d	3d	3d,2a,2d,2b,1a
$\pi_{14} = 1/2/3/4$	7a	7a	7a	all

Associated Homomorphisms for S_2

π	S/π	$S/\rho_{\pi*}$	$S/\pi \vee S/\rho_{\pi*}$	Associated Homomorphisms
π_0	1a	1a	1a	1a
π_1	2b	2b	2b	1a,2b
π_2	3c	3c	3c	1a,2b,3c
π_3	3b	3b	3b	1a,2b,3b
π_4	5a	5a	5a	all

Each congruence relation is associated with all the partitions whose joint reductions $S/\pi \vee S/\rho_{\pi*}$ (from Table 8) lie below it (in Figure 2). The last column of Table 7 gives all the homomorphisms associated with each partition π. Table 9 is, in a sense, the opposite of Table 8. It gives for each homomorphism the associated partitions (the second column of Table 9). The other columns of Table 9 give the least upper bound partitions of these sets of associated partitions (when the set contains its own least upper bound) from Figure 3, the semigroup $S/\pi \vee S/\rho_{\pi*}$ of the least upper bound partition associated with each homomorphism (from Table 8), and the Boorman-White measure of dissimilarity between the homomorphic image semigroup of column 1 and the semigroup produced by the least upper bound partition (from column 4). For those homomorphic images where the set of associated partitions does not contain its own least upper bound partition (so that the join of the associated partitions is not itself associated with the homomorphism), there are question marks in columns three, four, and five of Table 9. For these homomorphisms we chose from the set of associated partitions the one producing a semigroup most like (using the Boorman-White measure) the homomorphic image semigroup. These partitions, their semigroups, and the dissimilarity scores are in parentheses in Table 9.

Table 9. Results for and Success of Pattison Technique

Semigroup S_1

Homomorphic Image	Associated Partitions (From Table 8)	Least Upper Bound Partition (From Figure 3)	Semigroup for LUB Partition (From Table 3)	δ
7a	π_{14}	π_{14}	7a	.00
6a	π_{14}	π_{14}	7a	.05
6b	π_{14}	π_{14}	7a	.05
6c	π_{14},π_8	π_8	6c	.00
5a	π_{14},π_8	π_8	6c	.07
5b	π_{14},π_8	π_8	6c	.07
5c	π_{14}	π_8	7a	.14
5d	π_{14}	π_{14}	7a	.10
5e	π_{14},π_8,π_9	? (π_9)	? (5e)	? (.00)
4a	π_{14},π_8,π_9	? (π_9)	? (5e)	? (.10)
4b	π_{14},π_8	π_{14}	7a	.19
4c	π_{14},π_{10}	π_{10}	4c	.00
4d	π_{14}	π_{14}	7a	.19
4e	π_{14},π_8	π_8	6c	.20
4f	π_{14},π_8,π_9	? (π_9)	? (5e)	? (.10)
4g	π_{14},π_8,π_9	? (π_9)	? (5e)	? (.10)
3a	π_{14},π_8	π_8	6c	.27
3b	π_8,π_{14}	π_8	6c	.40
3c	π_{14},π_8,π_9	? (π_9)	? (5e)	.30
3d	$\pi_{14},\pi_8,\pi_9,\pi_{10},\pi_{12},\pi_{13}$	? (π_{12},π_{13})	? (3d)	? (.00)
3e	π_{14},π_8,π_9	? (π_9)	? (5e)	? (.20)
3f	$\pi_{14},\pi_8,\pi_9,\pi_1,\pi_{11}$	π_1	3f	.00
2a	$\pi_{14},\pi_8,\pi_9,\pi_{10},\pi_{12},\pi_{13}$	? (π_{12},π_{13})	? (3d)	? (.33)
2b	$\pi_{14},\pi_8,\pi_9,\pi_{10},\pi_{12},\pi_{13},\pi_2,\pi_3$	? (π_2,π_3)	? (2b)	? (.00)
2c	$\pi_{14},\pi_8,\pi_9,\pi_1,\pi_{11}$	π_1	3f	.33
2d	$\pi_{14},\pi_9,\pi_{10},\pi_{12},\pi_{13}$	? (π_{12},π_{13})	? (3d)	? (.33)
1a	All	π_0	1a	.00

Table 9 (continued)

Semigroup S_2

Homomorphic Image	Associated Partitions (From Table 8)	Least Upper Bound Partition (From Figure 8)	Semigroup for LUB Partition (From Table 3)	δ
5a	π_4	π_4	5a	.00
4a	π_4	π_4	5a	.10
4b	π_4	π_4	5a	.10
3a	π_4	π_4	5a	.30
3b	π_4,π_3	π_3	3b	.00
3c	π_4,π_2	π_2	3c	.00
2a	π_4	π_4	5a	.60
2b	π_4,π_3,π_2,π_1	π_1	2b	.00
1a	$\pi_4,\pi_3,\pi_2,\pi_1,\pi_0$	π_0	1a	.00

There are 34 congruences in Table 9 (excluding the two isomorphisms 7a for S_1 and 5a for S_2). Table 9 shows that Pattison's is not a perfect solution:

1. For ten of the congruences the sets of partitions with which they are associated do not contain their own least upper bounds. Pattison's technique does not prescribe what to do in this case.

2. For nine of the homomorphisms the only associated partition is the trivial one with one block in each class (1/2/3/4 for S_1 and 1/2/3 for S_2). In these instances, Pattison's technique does not give us any new matrices representing the homomorphisms.

3. For only ten of the 34 homomorphisms does the technique give a set of matrices that produce the homomorphic image semigroup exactly.

We will save a detailed comparison between the techniques using the Boorman-White dissimilarity measure for later in the chapter.

8. *Local Structures: Wu Approach*

Mandel (1978) defined "local" structural equivalence between pairs of individuals in terms of the types of relationships received and sent by each person. In Mandel's approach, people are clustered into structurally equivalent sets on the basis of the similarity of their rows and columns in the relational matrices. Two individuals are locally structurally equivalent if the structure looks the "same" from their local perspectives in the sense that both receive and send the same combinations of relations.

Inspired by this idea, Wu (1980) has developed a way of classifying not individuals but semigroup matrices into congruence classes based on whether they (the semigroup matrices) appear identical from the limited perspective of some person or set of people. We will show how this type of congruence, based on the relational patterns of subsets of people, can be used to interpret homomorphic images.

Using Wu's symbols, let $i*A$ be the ith row of matrix A, $(i,j)*A$ is the ith and jth rows of matrix A, $j\circ A$ is the jth column of matrix A, and so forth. Define a set of equivalence relations among the elements A and B of a matrix semigroup in the following way.

$$A E*_i B \Leftrightarrow \quad i*A = i*B$$
$$A E\circ_i B \Leftrightarrow \quad i\circ A = i\circ B$$
$$A E*_{ij} B \Leftrightarrow (i,j)*A = (i,j)*B$$

and so forth.

Any equivalence relation E on a semigroup S is a right congruence if $A E B \Rightarrow AX E BX$ for any $X \in S$. Similarly, E is a left congruence if

$$A E B \Rightarrow XA E XB$$

for any $X \in S$. It can easily be shown that all $E*$ relations are right congruences and all $E\circ$ relations are left congruences (Wu, 1980:17).

Let R and L be the sets of all right and left congruences of a semigroup S. Let $R*$ and $L\circ$ be the right and left congruences produced by equating matrices which are equal in subsets of the rows and columns respectively. The following can easily be shown to be true.

1. L and R are both sublattices of the lattice of all equivalence relations of S, i.e., if l_1 and l_2 are two left congruences, then $l_1 \vee l_2$ are also left congruences, and similarly for the right congruences.

2.   There may be right congruences not in $R*$ and left congruences not in $L\circ$.

3. $L\circ$ and $R*$ are both subsemilattices of the sublattices of L and R; $L\circ$ and $R*$ are both closed under the meet operation but not under the join. In fact (Wu, 1980:19), if t and w are two subsets of the people of blocks whose relations generated the semigroup, then

$$E\circ_t \wedge E\circ_w = E\circ_{t \cup w}$$

and

$$E*_t \wedge E*_w = E*_{t \cup w}.$$

Each congruence is both a left and a right congruence. Ideally, every congruence would be equal to the left and right congruence produced by some set; for any congruence C there would be some subset $w \subseteq X$ such that

$$C = E*_w = E\circ_w.$$

Then we could identify every congruence with a subset of the people whose view of the structure that congruence represented, but unfortunately this is not the case. For example, in S_2 there are four right congruences in $R*$ and four left congruences in $L\circ$, but only two congruences that appear in both sets: $E*_{12} = E\circ_{12} = 5a$ and $E*_3 = E\circ_3 = 3b$. Therefore, congruence 5a is the structure from the point of view of individuals 1 and 2, and congruence 3a is the structure from the point of view of person 3, but seven of the nine congruences have no such representations.

We will loosen the criterion by picking the right or left congruence in $R*$ *or* $L\circ$ that is *closest* to a given congruence we want to interpret, rather than trying to find a congruence in $R* \wedge L\circ$ that is exactly equal to it. Thus, if a congruence is equal or close to (as measured by the Boorman-White index δ) $E*_y$, then that congruence is the structure that set y see when they send ties, and if it is close to $E\circ_y$, then it is the structure that set y receive from others.

Let us again consider the two illustrative semigroups S_1 and S_2. Table 10 shows all the members of $R*$ and $L\circ$ for S_1 and S_2.

Table 10. R∗ and L∘ Congruences

R∗ Congruences for S_1

$E*_{1234} = E*_{124} = E*_{134} = E*_{24} = E*_{34} = E*_{14} = P/P^2/P^3/N/PN/NP/N^2$
$E*_4 = P/N/PN/NP/P^2/N^2,P^3$
$E*_3 = E*_{13} = E*_{23} = E*_{123} = P/P^2,P^3/N/PN/NP,N^2$
$E*_2 = E*_{12} = P,P^2,P^3/N/PN,NP,N^2$
$E*_1 = P,P^2,P^3/N,PN,NP,N^2$

L∘ Congruences for S_1

$E\circ_{1234} = E\circ_{124} = E\circ_{134} = P/N/PN/NP/N^2/P^2/P^3$
$E\circ_{234} = P/N/PN/NP/N2/P2,P^3$
$E\circ_{12} = E\circ_{13} = E\circ_{123} = P/P^2/N/PN/NP,N^2,P^3$
$E\circ_{14} = P/P^2/P^3/N/NP/N^2$
$E\circ_{24} = P/P^2,P^3/N/NP/PN/N^2/NP$
$E\circ_{34} = P,P^2,P^3/N/NP/PN/N^2$
$E\circ_{23} = E\circ_2 = P/N/PN/NP,P^2,P^3$
$E\circ_1 = P/P^2/N,PN,NP,N^2,P^3$
$E\circ_3 = P,NP,N^2,P^3,P^2/N/PN$
$E\circ_4 = P/P^2,P^3/N,NP/PN,N^2$

R∗ Congruences for S_2

$E*_{12} = E*_{123} = P/N/PN/NP/N^2$
$E*_{13} = E*_1 = P/N,NP/PN/N^2$
$E*_{23} = E*_2 = P/N,NP/PN/N^2$
$E*_3 = P/N,PN,NP,N^2$

L∘ Congruences for S_2

$E\circ_{12} = E\circ_{123} = P/N/NP/PN,N^2$
$E\circ_1 = E\circ_{12} = P/N,NP/Pn,N^2$
$E\circ_2 = E\circ_{23} = P/N,PN/NP/N^2$
$E\circ/_3 = P/N,PN,NP,N^2$

For each congruence the Boorman-White dissimilarity between it and its best-fitting left or right congruence in L° or $R*$ was computed. If a set defining a congruence was contained in another set defining the same congruence, only the smaller set is listed (e.g., if $E*_{123} = E*_{12}$, only the latter is listed). The results are in Table 11.

Table 11. Best-fitting Member of R∗ or L∘

For S_1

Congruence	Best Fit in R∗ or L∘	δ
7a	$E*_{24} = E*_{34} = E*_{14}$	.00
6a	$E°_{234}$	.00
6b	$E*_{24} = E*_{34} = E*_{14}$	.05
6c	$E*_{24} = E*_{34} = E*_{14}$	.05
5a	$E°_{14}$	.00
5b	$E*_{24} = E*_{34} = E*_{14}$	.14
5c	$E°_{12} = E°_{13}$	.00
5d	$E*_3$	.00
5e	$E°_{234}$	.07
4a	$E°_{34}$	.10
4b	$E°_{14}$	.10
4c	$E°_2$	.00
4d	$E°_{12} = E°_{13}$	.10
4e	$E°_{12} = E°_{13}$	.10
4f	$E°_{14}$	.10
4g	$E*_{13}$	.10
3a	$E°_{12} = E°_{13}$	.10
3b	$E°_1$	.00
3c	$E°_{14}$	.20
3d	$E°_2$	.17
3e	$E°_4$	.00
3f	$E*_3$	.20
2a	$E°_2$	.33
2b	$E*_3$	.33
2c	$E*_1$	.00
2d	$E°_1$	.33
1a	any	1.00

Table 11 (continued)

For S_2

Congruence	Best Fit in R* or L∘	δ
5a	$E*_{12} = E∘_{12}$	.00
4a	$E*_{12} = E∘_{12}$	.10
4b	$E*_{12} = E∘_{12}$	.10
3a	$E*_{12} = E∘_{12}$	.33
3b	$E∘_1$	.00
3c	$E*_2$	.00
2a	$E*_{12} = E∘_{12}$	.60
2b	$E*_3 = E∘_3$	.00
1a	any	1.00

9. Modified Wu Approach

Let A by any n by n relational matrix defined on n people or blocks of people in a semigroup S, and let T be any binary-valued matrix with n columns. Let Am = TA define a mapping m. The mapping m can be used to define a right congruence; $A \equiv B$ if TA = TB. It is a right congruence because if TA = TB, then TAC = TBC for any C in S. Thus, $AC \equiv BC$.

All congruences in R* can be expressed in terms of pre-multiplication of the matrices in S by some matrix T. For example, when n = 4, $E*_1$ can be found with the matrix [1 0 0 0], which isolates the first row of matrices; $AE*_1 B$ if [1 0 0 0]A = [1 0 0 0]B. Similarly, $E*_{12}$ can be found with the matrix

$$\begin{bmatrix} 1 & 0 & 0 & 0 \\ 0 & 1 & 0 & 0 \end{bmatrix}$$

through post-multiplication by a matrix T.

However, right or left congruences other than those in R* and L∘ can be expressed through pre- and post-multiplication. For example, when n = 4, pre-multiplication by T = [1 1 0 0] equates two matrices if the sums of their first and second rows are equal and their equation is a right congruence.

$$T = \begin{bmatrix} 1 & 0 & 0 & 0 \\ 0 & 1 & 1 & 0 \end{bmatrix}$$

would equate matrices on the basis of the first row and the sum of the second and third rows, and so forth.

Let R^T and L^T be the sets of right and left congruences generated in this manner. These sets contain $R*$ and $L\circ$ respectively. There are potentially as many members of R^T and L^T as there are different matrices T. Considering R^T, any row of T can have $2^n - 1$ different patterns, excluding the row of all zeros that selects none of the rows of the matrices of S. No two rows of T should be equal because equal rows equate the same sums of rows. Also, the order of the rows is irrelevant. Therefore, there are

$$2^{2^{n-1}} - 1$$

ways of selecting one or more of the 2^{n-1} row patterns to create a T matrix. Not all the congruences will be unequal.

In labelling the new congruences, $E*_{(12)}$ will mean that the sending patterns of the first and second individuals are combined and that two relations are right congruent if their combined first two rows are equal; in other words, pre-multiplication by $T = [1\ 1\ 0\ 0\ ...]$. $E*_{(12)3}$ would mean that two relations were right congruent if the sums of their first two rows were equal *and* their third rows were equal;

$$T = \begin{bmatrix} 1 & 1 & 0 & 0 & ... \\ 0 & 0 & 1 & 0 & ... \end{bmatrix}.$$

Table 12 gives the new congruences in $R^T - R*$ and in $L^T - L\circ$ for S_1 and S_2.

Table 12. Additional congruences for S_1

Type of congruence	T or T transpose	Congruent elements
$E*_{(14)}$ or $E*_{(24)}$	$[1\,0\,0\,1]$ or $[0\,1\,0\,1]$	P,N,P^2,P^3,PN,NP,N^2
$E*_{(34)}$	$[0\,0\,1\,1]$	P/N/PN,NP,N^2,P^2,P^3
$E*_{2(34)}$ or $E*_{1(34)}$	$\begin{bmatrix}0&1&0&0\\0&0&1&1\end{bmatrix}$ or $\begin{bmatrix}1&0&0&0\\0&0&1&1\end{bmatrix}$	P/N/P^2,P^3/PN,NP,N^2
$E°_{(23)}$ or $E°_{(34)}$	$[0\,1\,1\,0]$ or $[0\,0\,1\,1]$	N/P,NP,PN,N^2,P^2,P^3
$E°_{(12)(34)}$	$\begin{bmatrix}1&1&0&0\\0&0&1&1\end{bmatrix}$	P/N/NP,PN,N^2,P^3
$E°_{14(23)}$	$\begin{bmatrix}1&0&0&0\\0&0&0&1\\0&1&1&0\end{bmatrix}$	P/P^2/N/PN,NP,N^2,P^3
$E°_{(12)4(34)}$	$\begin{bmatrix}0&0&0&1\\1&1&0&0\\0&0&1&1\end{bmatrix}$	P/N/NP/P^2,P^3/PN,N^2
$E°_{1(23)}$	$\begin{bmatrix}1&0&0&0\\0&1&1&0\end{bmatrix}$	P/P^2/N/PN,NP,N^2,P^3

Additional congruences for S_2

Type of congruence	T or T transpose	Congruent elements
$E*_{(13)}$ or $E°_{(13)}$	$[1\,0\,1]$	P,N,PN,NP,N^2

10. Comparison of the Lorrain-White, Pattison, Wu, and Modified Wu Approaches

    Table 13 shows the mean dissimilarity scores between congruences and their representations for all four approaches for semigroups S_1 and S_2.

Table 13. Mean Dissimilarities

	S_1	S_2
Lorrain-White	.19	.06
Pattison	.13	.14
Wu	.13	.24
Modified Wu	.05	.12

There is not a lot of consistency in these results. The Lorrain-White approach is the worst for S_1 and the best for S_2. The modified Wu approach, which is the best for S_1, is in the middle for S_2.

One way of accounting for these results is that for the Pattison approach and for both Wu approaches the number of possible representations from which to choose increases as the number of blocks increases, but this selection process does not exist for the Lorrain-White approach, and thus it should do relatively less well for S_1, with four blocks, than for S_2, with three blocks. For the Pattison approach the number of possible representations is equal to the number of partitions of the blocks (five partitions when there are three blocks and fifteen when there are four blocks). For the Wu approach the number of possible representations is $2^{n+1} - 2$ with n blocks (fourteen when there are three blocks and 30 when there are four blocks). For the modified Wu approach there are

$$2^{2^{n-1}+1} - 2$$

possible left and right congruences (thirty when there are three blocks and 510 for four blocks). Therefore, we would expect these approaches to work better for S_1 than for S_2.

11. Meanings of the Approaches

All the approaches have as a goal the interpretation of homomorphic images in terms of some aspect of the data. They differ in their foci. In the Lorrain-White oapproach congruent relations are equivalent or substitutable for each other in the sense that the representative relation for each congruence class is the Boolean union of the relations. The researcher might use this technique if he felt that relations within a class were merely different expressions of some underlying basic relation. The researcher might say something like: "In this congruence relations R_1, R_2, and R_3 are all different measures of dominance. Relations R_4 and R_5 are two alternative signs of attraction" and so forth.

In the Pattison approach the emphasis is on sets of individuals who are equivalent. One might use the pattison approach when one knew more about about the individuals than about the relations. In this approach one would interpret a homomorphism in the following way: "This homomorphism distinguishes the upper status individuals P_1, P_2, and P_3 from the lower status individuals P_4, P_5, and P_6. On the other hand, this other homomorphism distinguishes the male group members P_2, P_4, and P_6 from the female group members P_1, P_3, and P_5."

The Wu approach selects subsets of individuals to interpret the homomorphism. It would be most appropriate, perhaps, if one believed there were a small number of elite individuals whose positions, in some sense, determined the structure. For example, if one were studying relations between large, powerful firms in an economy, one might say: "This homomorphism reflects the structure as perceived by the Bank of America, the largest bank, and General Motors, the largest industrial firm."

These different approaches can be classified in a two-dimensional typology which in turn suggests another as yet undeveloped approach. The two dimensions are, first, whether the approach focuses on individuals or on relations, and second, whether the approach focuses on representative elements from sets or on the unions of elements in sets.

Table 14. A Typology of Approaches

	Individuals	Relations
Single Representative Elements	Wu	?
Unions	Pattison	Lorrain-White

The "missing" approach would be to select one element from each congruence class and to look at the subsemigroup generated by this subset of relations. If this subsemigroup were isomorphic to the homomorphism, then this technique would give a perfect representation of the homomorphism in terms of a subset of the relations. One might use this approach if one believed that there was a hierarchy among the elements in a congruence class so that some relations were more central than others. For example, one might say: "This homomorphism reflects the pattern generated by the relation 'friend of subordinate' and 'enemy of subordinate.'" A preliminary examination shows that this approach is not more successful than the others, so we will not work out its implications for all the homomorphisms of the two illustrative semigroups.

12. A Fifth Approach: Bonacich

The final approach, less well worked out than the others, is based on the idea that every finite semigroup can be represented by a set of matrices with a standard form. This type of matrix representation has the desirable feature that any algebraic homomorphism corresponds to a graph homomorphism of these matrices. Finally, we will try to relate these matrices to the data matrices.

Let S be a finite semigroup with elements A_1, A_2, ..., A_m and let S^1 be the same semigroup with an identity "1" appended as the m+1 element if the semigroup lacks an identity. For any $A_i \in S$, let $A_i\alpha$ be a matrix in which $(A_i\alpha)_{jk} = 1$ if $A_jA_i = A_k$ and $(A_i\alpha)_{jk} = 0$ otherwise. We will call these the "canonical" matrix representations of the elements of S. This set of canonical matrices, S, is itself a semigroup under Boolean matrix multiplication, and the mapping α from S to Sα is an isomorphism (Howie, 1976:6).

For example, the canonical matrices generating S2 are:

$$P\alpha = \begin{bmatrix} 1 & 0 & 0 & 0 & 0 & 0 \\ 0 & 0 & 0 & 1 & 0 & 0 \\ 0 & 0 & 0 & 0 & 1 & 0 \\ 0 & 0 & 0 & 1 & 0 & 0 \\ 0 & 0 & 0 & 0 & 1 & 0 \\ 1 & 0 & 0 & 0 & 0 & 0 \end{bmatrix} \quad N\alpha = \begin{bmatrix} 0 & 0 & 1 & 0 & 0 & 0 \\ 0 & 0 & 0 & 0 & 1 & 0 \\ 0 & 0 & 0 & 0 & 1 & 0 \\ 0 & 0 & 0 & 0 & 1 & 0 \\ 0 & 0 & 0 & 0 & 1 & 0 \\ 0 & 1 & 0 & 0 & 0 & 0 \end{bmatrix}$$

In each of these matrices, the last row and column are for the identity element. The other rows and columns are in the same order as in Table 1: P, N, PN, NP, N2. $(P\alpha)_{35} = 1$ because $(PN)(P) = N^2$, and $(N\alpha)_{62} = 1$ because

$1N = N$. The reader should be able to verify that these matrices produce S_2 and that for any pair of elements A_i and A_j, $A_iA_j\alpha = (A_i\alpha)(A_j\alpha)$.

These canonical matrices $A_i\alpha$ have the very desirable feature that homomorphic image semigroups can always be produced by graph homomorphic images of the matrices $A_i\alpha$. As we saw in examining Pattison's approach, not every set of matrices have this property. If one's data have this form, a homomorphism simply corresponds to a cruder blocking of the data. Later we examine the relation between these canonical matrices and any set of data matrices producing the semigroup; in other words, we will examine the degree to which the canonical matrices are in fact "canonical."

Figure 4 diagrams these relations. S is an abstract semigroup. α is the isomorphism between semigroup S and its canonical matrix representation $S\alpha$. One could also think of $S\alpha$ as the data and S as the abstract semigroup generated by that data, if one's data happened to have the right form. The mapping h is any homomorphism on S and Sh is the abstract homomorphic image semigroup. $Sh\alpha'$ is the semigroup of canonical matrices for Sh, and Sh and $Sh\alpha'$ are isomorphic just as S and $S\alpha$ are isomorphic. $S\alpha h'$ is a graph homomorphism h' (of a particular type to be described later) of the matrices of $S\alpha$. The important facts are that $S\alpha h' = Sh\alpha'$, so that the graph homomorphism h' is actually a semigroup homomorphism as well that mirrors perfectly the effects of h. For every homomorphism h there is a graph homomorphism h' having the same effect, so that the matrices of $S\alpha h'$ produce the abstract semigroup Sh.

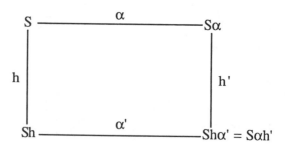

Figure 4. Relations Between Algebraic and
Graph Homomorphisms for Canonical Matrices

What we need to show is that for any h there exists a graph homomorphism h' such that for any $A_i \in S$, $A_ih\alpha' = A_i\alpha h'$, so that h' mirrors, between $S\alpha$ and $S\alpha h'$, the mapping h between S and Sh.

Let S have m elements and Sh n elements. Let X be an m+1 by n matrix in which $X_{ij} = 1$ if an $A_i \in S^1$ is in congruence class j and $X_{ij} = 0$ otherwise. Now we can define h':

$$A_i\alpha h' = X^t A_i\alpha X.$$

Thus, h' has the form of a graph homomorphism. What needs to be shown is that $A_ih\alpha' = A_i\alpha h'$, or, equivalently, $A_ih\alpha' = X^t A_i\alpha X$.

$$(X^t A_i\alpha X)_{jk} = 1 \quad \Leftrightarrow \quad \sum_l \sum_p X_{lj} A_i\alpha_{lp} X_{pk} = 1$$

$\Leftrightarrow$ $\exists\ A_1$ such that A_1h is the jth element of Sh and A_1A_ih is the kth element of Sh.

$\Leftrightarrow$ A_ih is the jth element of Sh and $(A_1h)(A_ih)$ is the kth element of Sh, because h is a homomorphism.

$\Leftrightarrow$ $(A_ih\alpha')_{jk} = 1$, by the definition of α'.

Therefore, if the data happen to have this "canonical" form, then semigroup homomorphisms can be understood as graph homomorphisms of the matrices generating the semigroup. However, data will hardly ever have this form. For example, in the canonical matrices there is exactly one "1" in any row.

However, there is a relationship between the data matrices and the canonical matrices. Let's examine the following semigroup.

	P	N
P	P	N
N	N	N

The canonical matrices have the following form. There are only two rows and columns because the semigroup already has an identity, P.

$$P\alpha = \begin{bmatrix} 1 & 0 \\ 0 & 1 \end{bmatrix} \qquad N\alpha = \begin{bmatrix} 0 & 1 \\ 0 & 1 \end{bmatrix}$$

Are there sets that can be defined whose relationships are described by the above matrices? Yes! Let x be any individual or block of individuals among those whose relationships are described by the above semigroup. Let xP be the set of people (or blocks) to whom x is connected by relation P (i.e., $y \in xP \Leftrightarrow xPy$). Similarly, let xN be the set of people to whom x has a negative connection. The question is, do the canonical matrices describe the relations between these blocks?

$(P\alpha)_{11} = 1$. This should correspond to some relation among those in xP. Because $P^2 = P$, everyone in xP must be the object of a P relation from someone in xP. So, $(P\alpha)_{11} = 1$ corresponds to the necessity of there being some P relations among those in xP.

$(N\alpha)_{12} = 1$. Because PN = N, every person in xN is the object of an N tie from someone in xP, and all N ties from someone in xP terminate with someone in xN. So, $(N\alpha)_{12} = 1$ corresponds to a necessary set of negative relations between those in xP and those in xN.

$(P\alpha)_{21} = 0$. Unfortunately, the zeros mean a lot less than the ones in these matrices. $(P\alpha)_{21} = 0$ merely means that NP = P cannot be universally true. The instances in which it fails need not involve person x at all. Therefore, it is possible that all relations between xN and xP are of type P, even though $(P\alpha)_{21} = 0$.

More generally, $(A_i\alpha)_{jk} = 1$ corresponds to the fact that $A_jA_i = A_k$. Therefore, everyone in xA_k is the object of an A_i tie from at least one person in xA_j, and all A_i relations emanating from those in xA_j terminate with someone in xA_k. However, $(A_i\alpha)_{jk} = 0$ means little, merely that $A_jA_i = A_k$ cannot hold for all triads. Person x need not even be a member of one of the triads for which $A_jA_i = A_k$ is not true.

Because of the weak relation between the matrices in Sα and the data matrices producing S, this approach does not yet lead to a set of matrices that both produce the homomorphic image semigroup and are related to the data. I do have some ideas about directions that might lead to a more useful technique.

1.   xA was the set of people to whom person x had relation A. The canonical forms corresponded only very roughly to the relations between these sets. Let Bx be the set of people who have relation B to person x. There is a very strong inference that can be made about the relations between people in set Bx and those in set xA; *all* pairs *must* have the relation BA. The problem is how to put these necessary relations in a matrix form whose multiplication will produce S.

2.   The person chosen as x is arbitrary and the choice will affect the participation of the rest of the system into sets xA. Perhaps in some formulation all x's could be treated simultaneously, or perhaps an imaginary x^i could be created who divides individuals into especially useful sets x^iA.

3.   Let G_1 and G_2 be any two sets of matrices, perhaps from different studies, with the same generators. Let $G_1 \geq G_2$ mean that G_1 is a graph homomorphic reduction of G_2 and let $G_1 = G_2$ mean that G_1 and G_2 are isomorphic (permutations of the rows and columns of either set will produce identical sets of matrices). The relation "$\geq$" is a partial order among sets of isomorphic graphs; the relation "$\geq$" is transitive, reflexive, and anti-symmetric.

It would be nice if this partial order induced a semilattice relation among sets of matrices with the same generators. For any pair of sets of matrices G_1 and G_2 one could speak of unique "join" $G_1 \vee G_2$ which would be a least upper bound for all sets of matrices that were homomorphic images of G_1 and G_2. $G_1 \vee G_2$ would be what the two sets of matrices had "in common," just like the Boorman-White "joint reduction" (1976) is what two semigroups have in common. $G_1 \vee G_2$ would imply partitions of the vertices of G_1 and of G_2 such that, under graph homomorphisms, the two sets of matrices were equal, and they would be the finest pair of partitions with this property.

Now, let G be the generating matrices of a semigroup S and let $S\alpha$ be the canonical representations of the generators. $G \vee S\alpha$ would be a way of combining G, the data, with S, the set of matrices with the desirable property that graph homomorphisms and algebraic homomorphisms coincided.

Let h be any homomorphism of S. Using the symbols of Figure 4, $S\alpha h'$ will be a graph homomorphism of $S\alpha$ that produces Sh. The change from the partition of people implied by $S\alpha \vee G$ to the partition implied by

Sαh' ∨ G would reflect h; it would be a further agglomeration of the people associated with the homomorphism h.

Unfortunately, the partial order ≥ does not induce a semilattice. For pairs of sets of matrices there may be no single least upper bound; the set of common homomorphic images may have more than one lower bound. However, there may be some way of ordering or selecting from these lower bounds so that the join can be defined and this approach is usable.

REFERENCES

Bonacich, P.
1980 The 'common structure semigroup': an alternative to the Boorman and White 'joint reduction.' American Journal of Sociology: (in press).

Bonacich, P. and McConaghy, M.
1980 The algebra of blockmodeling. *In* K.F. Schlessler (ed.) Sociological Methodology, pp. 489-532. San Francisco: Jossey-Bass.

Boorman, S.A. and White, H.C.
1976 Social structure from multiple networks. II. American Journal of Sociology, 81:1384-1446.

Howie, J.M.
1976 An Introduction to Semigroup Theory. London: Academic Press.

Lorrain, F.P., and White, D.C.
1971 Structural equivalence of individuals in social networks. Journal of Mathematical Sociology, 1:49-80.

Mandel, M.J.
1978 Roles and networks. B.A. thesis, Harvard University.

Pattison, P.
1977 On analyzing a blockmodel. unpublished manuscript.

Wu, L.
1980 Role structures in networks of trade and economic interdependence: a local blockmodel algebraic analysis. B.A. thesis, Harvard University.

CHAPTER 9

MODELS OF NETWORK EFFECTS ON SOCIAL ACTORS

Patrick Doreian

1. Introduction

This chapter is concerned with an old and deeply sociological problem: what is the impact of a social structure on the behavior and (certain) social characteristics of the social actors comprising the social structure? The imagery used to pose and address this question is that of social networks, as detailed in earlier chapters, but it carries no commitment concerning the level of analysis.[1] The use of a network approach shows the above (traditional) question to be, in fact, illposed and allows it to be posed in a more adequate fashion.

Consider a social network of N social actors. Two sets of characteristics can be defined, operationalized, and measured for the network. Given the N members of a network we have, ideally, (i) a representation of some social relation(s) defined over the N members, and

---

[1] The network approach described here, in common with most network procedures, can accommodate either macro or micro level phenomena.

(ii) measurements of attributes or characteristics of the N members. In graph theoretic terms, we have data on the form and content of the social relations (Simmel, 1917; Burt, 1981) represented as arcs or edges of the graph and we have data characterizing the nodes. The central problem can now be stated in the following form: How can we account for the distribution of some characteristic, or behavior, over a collection of social actors that form a social network?

When social actors are located within a network, they are interdependent, and this interdependency is of prime theoretical interest here. Consider alternative strategies for dealing with the data described above. One strategy allows us to detail the nature of the interdependency by describing or characterizing the structure of the social network. Indeed, many of the procedures outlined in later chapters of this volume are designed to do this.

Another strategy, indeed the most common strategy in sociological research, is to use some of the characteristics of the social actors to account for the distribution of some other characteristic across those social actors. Both are legitimate and fruitful strategies. However, they each have severe shortcomings in the light of the central problem posed earlier. The characterization of the structure of the social network does not deal with any of the attributes of the nodes and dealing only with the attributes of the nodes ignores the structure of the network. By simultaneously exploiting the two sets of characterizations (of the network structure and nodal attributes) considerable progress can be made in detailing how social structure affects the behavior of social actors. Notice that, in this reformulation, "social structure" is not a causal variable in any obvious sense. Rather, particular patterns of social relationships operate so as to determine the behavior exhibited (at the nodes) in the network. The social structure mediates processes that are operative on the nodes.[2] Social actors are affected by interactional processes mediated by the social structure or by processes that operate in certain fashions at specific points of the social structure.

The models presented in this chapter, together with their associated maximum likelihood estimation strategies provide ways (but certainly not the only ways) of achieving progress in representing how the social structure of a network operates so as to affect the behavior of the social actors of the network.

---

[2]   This does not rule out the possibility that behavior exhibited at the nodes, in turn, affects the form (and possibly the content) of the social relationships. However, in this discussion the network properties (social structure) will be taken as given.

The remaining sections of this chapter are structured as follows: a section on representing the relevant structure of the network; a section on modeling the network effects on social actors given this representation; a section on the estimation of these models, and, finally, a section discussing future avenues of research.

2. On Social Structure

In reviewing models of network structure, Burt (1980b) (see also Burt, 1978 and Burt (this volume)), makes a fundamental distinction between relational and positional approaches to representing network structure. In the relational approach, network models are concerned to describe the nature of the relations between specific actors in the network. Within the positional approach, network models are concerned to detail the position of a social actor which is defined in terms of that actor's relationship(s) to all other members of the network. Within either of these approaches considerable effort has been devoted to constructing indices of structure, partitions of networks into subnetworks, and measures describing the location of specific nodes (see Burt, 1980b). The models described in this chapter build on this work.

Among other things, network analysis provides a description of the social structure within which social actors are located and, moreover, provides suggestions concerning paths over which social effects pass. An early study by Festinger and his colleagues (Festinger *et al.,* 1950) demonstrated that individuals connected by friendship relations tended to have similar attitudes toward a student cooperative organization to which they belonged. Festinger, *et al.* distinguished two characteristics of a general phenomenon that are of interest here. First, strong relations between members of a group, or of a network, are channels through which members of the group (or network) can communicate information. If these relations can be charted, then we have a representation of the social structure that mediates an influence process of network members on each other. These communication and influence processes together constitute a socialization process that is mediated by the network. Second, group, or network, consensus concerning some item of interest to the group is re-inforced by the group members through the network structure. Again, there is a network process which, it is suggested, leads to a distribution of a social characteristic, in this case an attitude, according to the structure of the network. In other words, social homophily is conditioned on the social structure of the network.

Festinger and his colleagues pointed out a third characteristic of this phenomenon that is also of interest here. The enforcement, or reinforcement, of a group consensus is a likely process to the extent that the perceptions of group members have an ambiguous basis in reality. If something can be checked by individual members of the group, there is little scope for the network process to be operative. On the other hand, if the object of interest cannot be checked against an objective criterion, then reality is grounded in the intersubjective perceptions of social actors and there is full scope for the network process. Most situations will contain a composite of the two where the distribution of a social characteristic is partially grounded in an external reality and partially on the social contexts of the actors.

The discussion of Festinger's study fits naturally into the relational perspective. So, too, does the study by Coleman, Katz and Menzel (1966) where they show that the time at which a physician begins to prescribe a new antibiotic is contingent upon the time at which specific other physicians also begin prescribing the new drug. The specific other physicians are those to whom sociometric citations are made. Again, it appears there is an influence process over a network where behavior at the nodes, prescribing a drug, is contingent upon the structure of the network connecting the nodes.

The models discussed in the following sections hinge upon representing this network structure in matrix form. A matrix, called a structure matrix and denoted by W will be used generically to denote this. For relational models, W can be constructed in a variety of fashions and the particular matrix used will depend upon the substantive context.[3] For example, for $Z = [z_{ij}]$ where $z_{ij} = 1$ if there is a relation from social actor I to social actor J and $z_{ij} = 0$ otherwise,[4] W can be constructed as follows. Let $z_{i.}$ denote the ith row sum of Z. Then define $W = [w_{ij}]$ where $w_{ij} = z_{ij}/z_{i.}$. Such a matrix preserves particular properties of Z as the absence of a relation ($z_{ij} = 0$) is preserved by $w_{ij} = 0$ and the presence of a relation is indicated by a non-zero w_{ij}. If the set of social actors for which there is a relation from I to

---

[3]   The class of models considered here have their origins in models of spatially distributed phenomena, especially in the work of Ord (1975). There the matrix W represents the spatial structure defined over a set of areas that define a region. There is some controversy over the definition of W and some authors, for example Arora and Brown (1977), have argued against using any W. Such a conclusion is premature (see Doreian, 1981) insofar as the real issue is the adequate specification of an appropriate W.

[4]   By convention, $z_{ii} = 0$ for social actors, I, in the network.

those actors is construed as a reference group then a non-zero w_{ij} is simply the reciprocal of the size of the reference group. An alternative set of W matrices can be defined that allow different social actors to be differentially influential on a specific social actor. Such a matrix is that operationalized by Burt (1976; Appendix A) as the tendency to initiate interaction.[5]

The "structure" of a social network within the positional approach can also be represented by a matrix, W, but the underlying conceptualization is fundamentally different (Burt, 1980b). It stems from a consideration of structural equivalence (Lorrain and White, 1971; Burt, 1977; Sailer, 1978). In Burt's formulation, the network position of a social actor is defined by all the relations of that actor to the N actors of the network. Operationally, for a single network, the position of an actor, I, is the $(2N \times 1)$ vector constructed from the ith row and the ith column of a network operationalized as a matrix Z.[6] From this Burt obtains the jointly occupied network position as a set of structurally equivalent actors. Social actors are structurally equivalent (under a strong criterion) if they have identical relations with all other actors in a network. They are structurally equivalent (under a weak criterion) if they have sufficiently similar relations to the other actors of the network. Having defined positions as vectors then it is straightforward to obtain the Euclidean distance between all pairs of them. This defines an $(N \times N)$ matrix D of Euclidean distances that is used to obtain the jointly occupied network position as a maximal set of structurally equivalent actors.[7] However, the interest of this chapter is not in partitioning the social actors into structurally non-equivalent positions rather it is the use of D to construct matrices, W, that reflect positional properties of a social network. This extends also to regular equivalence (c.f. White and Reitz, 1983).

The relational approach argues that social homophily is conditioned on the relations between social actors in a network. The positional approach argues that social homophily is conditioned on positional equivalence. That is, social actors occupying similar positions will share certain social

---

[5] Strictly, Burt constructs a matrix where the elements represent the probability of not initiating interaction. However, the probabilities of initiating interaction can be readily obtained from such a matrix.

[6] This definition extends readily to deal with multiple networks defined over the N actors. If K such networks are defined, then a social actor's position is given by a $(2NK \times 1)$ vector where the ith row and the ith column are taken from each of the K network matrices. See Burt (1977) for details.

[7] If $D = [d_{ij}]$, then the strong criterion of structural equivalence is that actors i and j are structurally equivalent if $d_{ij} = 0$. The weak criterion of structural equivalence of $d_{ij} < \alpha$ for some (arbitrarily chosen) small value of α.

characteristics by virtue of their positional location regardless of whether they are directly connected or not. Positional equivalence effects are both more and less restrictive than relational effects (Burt and Doreian, 1982). Positional equivalence is more restrictive insofar as it excludes similarities between nodes connected by a relation but are neither structurally nor regularly equivalent. It is less restrictive insofar as it includes similarities between nodes having no relation between them.

As was the case for representing relational effects, so there are choices over W for representing positional effects. For illustrative purposes, consider the following for a network made up of individuals. The matrix D is meaningful only for the network for which it is defined and can be normalized without loss of generality. One such normalization can be constructed as follows. Let

$$z_{ij} = \frac{\max(d_j) - d_{ij}}{\sum\limits_{j=1}^{N} \max(d_j) - d_{ij}},$$

where $\max(d_j)$ is the largest distance separating actor J from any other actor in the system. Then define

$$w_{ij} = \begin{cases} \dfrac{z_{ij}}{1 - z_{ii}} & \text{for } i \neq j \\[2mm] 0 & \text{for } i = j. \end{cases}$$

Burt (1980a) has argued that the perception of distance as the basis of social similarity is itself subjective and if subjective perceptions of distance given objective distance stimuli satisfy Steven's (1957) power function, then I's perception of lack of distance from I is given by $\mu[\max(d_j) - d_{ji}]^\nu$ where μ and ν are constants to be determined empirically. Then w_{ij} is given by

$$w_{ij} = \frac{\ell_{ij}}{1 - \ell_{ii}}$$

where

$$\ell_{ij} = \frac{[\max(d_{ij}) - d_{ji}]^{\nu}}{\sum\limits_{j=1}^{N} [\max(d_{ij}) - d_{ji}]^{\nu}}.$$

These are but two of the possibilities for constructing a positional structure matrix.

In summary, within either the relational approach or the positional approach it is possible to construct an (N × N) structure matrix W that represents a structural property of interest to an investigator.[8] The precise rationale for constructing this matrix is made clearer in the following section.

3. *Models of Network Effects*

The attributes characterizing the social actors can be partitioned into an endogenous variable and a set of exogenous variables. Let X denote a vector of values for the exogenous variables (including a column of 1s corresponding to the intercept term). A simple non-network model is

$$Y = X\beta + \varepsilon, \tag{1}$$

with $\varepsilon \sim IN(0,\sigma^2 I)$ where the vector of parameters, β, and $\omega = \sigma^2$ are to be estimated. Given this specification, OLS is an appropriate estimation procedure. However, the model totally ignores the network structure and is devoid of network effects. A reformulation is required in which the value of Y for actor I, say y_i, is contingent not only on attributes of I but also the values y_j for other actors, J, in the network.

---

[8]   These structural characteristics can be obtained from many sources. For example they could be obtained directly from sociometric citations as discussed earlier; they could be obtained, in studies of the sociology of science for example, from the written record of citations; they could be obtained from direct observation of participants of a Bales' (1950) experiment and so on. They could be obtained from joint occurrence in archival data (Burt and Lin, 1977) or the sharing of corporate directors (Levine, 1972). Alternatively, the measures of structural characteristics may be obtained after considerable data manipulation of structural data: the examples of tendencies to not initiate interaction (Burt, 1976; Appendix A) and measures of positional and structural equivalence (Burt, 1977) discussed earlier exhibit this. Measures of q-connectivity between actors (Doreian, 1980a), or of centrality (Freeman, 1977) may also serve as bases for the construction of W. In order to construct W, a specific network process has to be specified.

One modeling response to this general problem is given by Duncan, Haller and Portes (1971) where for each individual there is a peer whose aspirations may affect the aspirations of the individual. A non-recursive linear structural equation model is specified where the endogenous variables of aspirations and peer's aspirations can simultaneously affect each other when certain background variables serve as instruments for estimating peer effects. However, the Duncan *et al.* model is not a general model for assessing network effects on individual actors (nor was it intended as such). Moreover, it does not extend readily to deal with more than one cited peer. The following models do overcome this limitation.

Consider a matrix W as defined in the previous section. One way of capturing network effects is to consider Y as being dependent upon WY. WY is a vector whose elements are weighted combinations of values of Y. For actor I, the element of this vector is

$$\sum_{j=1}^{N} w_{ij} Y_j.$$

In the relational perspective this is a weighted combination of the values of Y for only those actors who are related to I in the network. In general, those actors that are relationally the most important to I contribute most to the particular sum defined for I. Within the positional perspective the vector WY is again a weighted sum of the Ys where those actors that are more positionally similar to I contribute most to the weighted sum corresponding to I. A model[9] that naturally incorporates network effects, either relational or positional, is

$$Y = \rho WY + X\beta + \varepsilon, \qquad (2)$$

where ρ is a network effects parameter. As before, ε is a vector of parameters and $\varepsilon \sim IN(0,\sigma^2 I)$. According to Ord (1975) it is useful to have the row sums of W equal to 1. As Erbring and Young (1979) point out, this means that WY has the same metric as Y and permits a simple interpretation of ρ. The network effects parameter, viewed as an endogenous feedback

---

[9] Strictly speaking, the presence of "network autocorrelation" which is formally identical to spatial autocorrelation should be dealt with here. See Cliff and Ord (1973) for an extensive discussion of spatial autocorrelation, its detection and its treatment. As my main purpose here is to discuss a certain class of models, I shall eschew any extended discussion of network autocorrelation in this context. In addition, the statistical assessment of $\hat{\rho}$ in any of the models discussed here is useful in its own right.

parameter, can be interpreted as the share of the individual I's characteristic, Y_i, that is determined by the network process rather than by individual mechanisms.

Notice that if there were no exogenous variables of interest, then a pure network effects model could be written as

$$Y = \alpha + \rho WY + \varepsilon, \tag{3}$$

where, as before, ρ is a network parameter and ε is multivariate normal. The parameter, α, must be specified, otherwise, estimates of ρ are likely to be spuriously inflated or deflated.[10] The need to specify α can also be given a substantive rationale. In discussing the Festinger *et al.* study the point was made that the endogenous variable can be grounded partially in a reality external to the network and partially due to a network process. The parameter α can be interpreted in terms of the value of Y determined externally to the network. In the subsequent discussion it is not necessary to deal specifically with the estimation of (3) as it is a special case of (2).

An alternative method of dealing with the interdependence among social actors in a social network is a network (autocorrelation) disturbances model (Dow *et al.*, 1979). Here no direct effect is posited to exist among network members, rather there is network autocorrelation of the disturbance term:

$$Y = X\beta + \varepsilon \tag{4a}$$

$$\varepsilon = \rho W\varepsilon + v \tag{4b}$$

where v is independent multivariate normal.

Given these two alternatives, a third naturally suggests itself: a model where there is both a network effect and a network autocorrelation of the disturbance term. Before considering this model in detail one minor generalization can be made. Let W_1 denote the matrix of weights for the network effects and let W_2 denote the matrix of weights for the network autocorrelation of the disturbance term. The network effect-network disturbance model can be written as

---

[10] The situation is somewhat akin to a bivariate regression being forced through the origin when otherwise there would be a non-zero intercept.

$$Y = \rho_1 W_1 Y + X\beta + \varepsilon \qquad (5)$$

$$\varepsilon = \rho_2 W_2 \varepsilon + \nu, \qquad (6)$$

with ν being independent multivariate normal. Here ρ_1 is the network effects parameter and ρ_2 is the network disturbances parameter. For all three network models the objective is to estimate the parameters specified in each model (including the variance of the disturbance term).

4. The Estimation of Models of Network Effects

The network models of the previous section are formally identical to models used to analyze linear models using spatially distributed data (Ord, 1975; Doreian, 1980b, 1981, 1982). This section provides the estimation details without derivations as these derivations are available elsewhere. The estimation procedure for the network effects model (in its original spatial context) can be found in Ord (1975) with a derivation provided in Doreian (1981). The estimation procedure for the network disturbance model can also be found in Ord (1975) with a derivation provided by Doreian (1980b) and the estimation details for the mixed network effect-network autocorrelation model can be found in Doreian (1982).

4.1. A Network Effects Model. Consider the network effects model. Given the specification of ε, the likelihood function is

$$L(\varepsilon) = \left(\frac{1}{2\pi\sigma^2} \right)^{\frac{N}{2}} \exp\left(-\frac{\varepsilon'\varepsilon}{2\sigma^2} \right), \qquad (7)$$

where part of the specification of ε is $E\varepsilon\varepsilon' = \sigma^2 I$ with I being the identity matrix[11] and E the expectation operator. Writing $A = I - \rho W$, then $|A|$ is the Jacobian of the transformation from the ε to the observed Y (where the observed Y will be denoted by y). The log-likelihood function (given $Y = y$) to be maximized is (with $\omega = \sigma^2$ to simplify notation).

---

[11] Henceforth, I will denote the $N \times N$ identity matrix and will not refer to the individual I in the network.

$\ell(y) =$

$$\text{const} - \left(\frac{N}{2}\right) \ln \omega - \frac{1}{2\omega}\left[y'A'Ay - 2\beta'X'Ay + \beta'X'X\beta\right] + \ln |A|. \tag{8}$$

The maximization is done with respect to ρ, $\omega = \sigma^2$ and β.

Minimizing $\ell(y)$ with respect to β and ω gives

$$\hat{\beta} = (X'X)^{-1}X'Ay \tag{9}$$

and

$$\hat{\omega} = \left(\frac{1}{N}\right)\left(y'A\,Ay - 2\beta'X'Ay + \beta'X'X\beta\right) \tag{10}$$

as the estimating equations for β and ω, respectively. With these "estimates"[12] substituted back into (8) we have

$$\ell(y: \rho, \hat{\omega}, \hat{\beta}) = \text{const} - \left(\frac{N}{2}\right)\ln \hat{\omega} + \ln |A|. \tag{11}$$

It is straightforward (Doreian, 1981) to show that $\hat{\rho}$ is the value of ρ that minimizes

$$-\left(\frac{2}{N}\right)\sum_i \ln (1 - \rho\lambda_i) + \ln (y'My - 2\rho y'MWy + \rho^2(Wy)'MWy) \tag{12}$$

where $M = I - X(X'X)^{-1}X'$ is an idempotent and symmetric matrix. The key observation on which the minimization hinges is that if $\{\lambda_i\}$ are the eigenvalues of W, then

$$|A| = \prod_{i=1}^{N}(1 - \rho\lambda_i)$$

(Ord, 1975:121). The minimization of (12) is done by a direct search on ρ or iteratively. With $\hat{\rho}$ found by either search procedure, then equations (9)

---

12 The quotation marks are used because both of the estimating equations for β and ω contain ρ which, as yet, remains unknown.

and (10) can be used to obtain the estimators of β and ω. With these estimators found, empirical estimates of the variance-covariance matrix for these estimators is given by

$$V(\hat{\omega},\hat{\rho},\hat{\beta}) =$$

$$\omega^2 \begin{bmatrix} \dfrac{N}{2} & \omega\text{tr}(B) & 0 \\[2ex] \omega\text{tr}(B) & \omega^2\{\text{tr}(B'B) - \alpha\} + \omega\beta'X'B'BX\beta & \omega X'BX\beta \\[2ex] 0 & \omega(X'BX\beta)' & \omega X'X \end{bmatrix}^{-1} \qquad (13)$$

where 0 is a null column vector of zeroes, $B = WA^{-1}$ and

$$\alpha = -\sum_i \frac{\lambda_i^2}{(1 - \rho\lambda_i)^2}.$$

Examples of the use of this estimation procedure are found in Doreian (1981) for spatial models and Burt and Doreian (1982) for network models.

4.2. A Network Disturbances Model. The discussion of the network disturbances model starts with the likelihood function

$$L(v) = \left(\frac{1}{2\pi\omega}\right)^{\frac{N}{2}}\exp\left(-\frac{v'v}{2\omega}\right). \qquad (14)$$

The log-likelihood function for the Y (given Y = y) is obtained through two transformations; (i) from v to ε where the Jacobian is $|A|$ and (ii) from the ε to the observed y where the Jacobian is I. We get

$$\mathfrak{L}(y) = \text{const} - \left(\frac{N}{2}\right) \ln \omega$$

$$\text{(15)}$$

$$- \frac{1}{2\omega}\left[y'A'Ay - 2\beta'X'A'Ay + \beta'X'A'AX\beta\right] + \ln |A|.$$

Minimization of (15) with respect to $\hat{\beta}$ and $\hat{\omega}$ yields

$$\hat{\beta} = (X'A'AX)^{-1}X'A'Ay \qquad \text{(16)}$$

and

$$\omega = \frac{1}{N}\left[\varepsilon'A'A\varepsilon\right]. \qquad \text{(17)}$$

Notice that with ρ known (16) is a Generalized Least Squares estimator with $A'A = \Omega^{-1}$ with Ω being standard notation in the econometric literature[13]. Notice also that as $\varepsilon = Y - X\beta$ equation (17) is equivalent to

$$\hat{\omega} = \frac{1}{N}\left[y'A'Ay - 2\beta'X'A'Ay + \beta'X'A'AX\beta\right]. \qquad \text{(17a)}$$

Substitution of (16) and (17a) into (15) and tidying the algebra reveals $\hat{\rho}$ to be the value of ρ that maximizes

$$\ln (y'A'PAy) - \left(\frac{2}{N}\right)\sum_i \ln (1 - \rho\lambda_i). \qquad \text{(18)}$$

where P is the matrix $I - (AX)((AX)\ AX)^{-1}(AX)'$. (See Doreian, 1980b.) Again with $\hat{\rho}$ found from a direct search procedure equations (16) and (17a) can be used to provide estimates of β and ω. With the same definitions of α and B as used for the network effects model the variance-covariance matrix of these estimators is

---

[13] Given the specification of the network disturbances model in (4a) and (4b),

$$\varepsilon = (I - \rho W)^{-1}v = A^{-1}v; E\varepsilon\varepsilon' = A^{-1}Evv'A^{-1} = \sigma^2 A^{-1}A^{-1\prime} = \sigma^2\Omega.$$

$$V(\hat{\omega},\hat{\rho},\hat{\beta}) = \omega^2 \begin{bmatrix} \dfrac{N}{2} & \omega tr(B) & 0' \\ \omega tr(B) & \omega^2\{tr(B'B) - \alpha\} & 0' \\ 0 & 0 & \omega X'A'AX \end{bmatrix}^{-1} \qquad (19)$$

Notice that if either (i) $\rho = 0$ or (ii) W is the null matrix, then $A = I$ and the specialized non-network regression outcomes are reached. In this sense, the network disturbances model is a proper generalization of the conventional regression model of equation (1). Estimated examples of this procedure are found in Doreian (1980b).

4.3.   A Mixed Network Effects and Network Disturbances Model. The model incorporating both a direct network effect and a network autocorrelated disturbance term is considerably more complex. Using the definitions of W_1 and W_2, two further notational definitions are useful: $A_1 = I - \rho_1 W_1$ and $A_2 = I - \rho_2 W_2$. The estimation procedure for this model also starts with the likelihood function given in equation (14). To reach the log-likelihood function for the Y, given $Y = y$, there are again two transformations: (i) from v to ε where the Jacobian of the transformation is $|A_2|$ and (ii) from the ε to the y where the Jacobian of this transformation is $|A_1|$. The log-likelihood function to be maximized is

$$\ell(y) = const - \left(\frac{N}{2}\right) \ln \omega$$

$$- \frac{1}{2\omega}\left[y'A_1'A_2'A_2A_1y - 2\beta'X'A_2'A_2A_1y + \beta'X'A_2'X\beta\right] \qquad (20)$$

$$+ \ln |A_1| + \ln |A_2|.$$

Minimizing (20) with respect to $\hat{\beta}$ and setting the result to zero yields

$$\hat{\beta} = (X'A_2'A_2X)^{-1}X'A_2'A_2A_1y. \qquad (21)$$

If ρ_1 and ρ_2 were known then equation (21) with $A_2'A_2 = \Omega^{-1}$ and $A_1y = y_1$ can be written $\hat{\beta} = (X'\Omega^{-1}X)^{-1}X'\Omega^{-1}y_1$ showing it, too, is a Generalized

Least Squares estimator. Minimizing (20) with respect to $\hat{\omega}$ and setting the result to zero gives

$$\hat{\omega} = \frac{1}{N}\left[y'A_1'A_2'A_2A_1y - 2\beta'X'A_2'A_2A_1y + \beta'X'A_2'A_2X\beta\right]. \quad (22)$$

While equations (21) and (22) do provide estimating equations for $\hat{\beta}$ and $\hat{\omega}$ respectively they each contain ρ_1 and ρ_2 which remain unknown. The log-likelihood function (20) can be rewritten as

$$\mathfrak{L}(y, \rho_1, \rho_2; \hat{\omega}, \hat{\beta}) = \text{const} - \left(\frac{N}{2}\right)\ln \hat{\omega} + \ln |A_1| + \ln |A_2|$$

and the estimation task is now to find the combination of ρ_1 and ρ_2 that maximizes this expression or, equivalently, minimizes

$$\left(\frac{N}{2}\right)\ln \hat{\omega} - \ln |A_1| - \ln |A_2|. \quad (23)$$

Using the insight of Ord for A in the previous cases we have

$$|A_1| = \prod_{i=1}^{N}(1 - \rho_1\lambda_i)$$

and

$$|A_2| = \prod_{i=1}^{N}(1 - \rho_2\mu_i)$$

where $\{\lambda_i\}$ and $\{\mu_i\}$ are the eigenvalues of W_1 and W_2 respectively. It can be shown (Doreian, 1982) that $(\hat{\rho}_1, \hat{\rho}_2)$ is the combination of values of ρ_1 and ρ_2 that minimize

$$\ln (y'A_1'A_2'M_2A_2A_1y)$$

$$-\left(\frac{2}{N}\right)\sum_i \ln (1 - \rho_1\lambda_i) - \left(\frac{2}{N}\right)\sum_i \ln (1 - \rho_2\mu_i) \quad (24)$$

where $M_2 = I - A_2X\{(A_2X)'(A_2X)\}^{-1}(A_2X)'$, which, again, is done by a direct search procedure. With $\hat{\rho}_1$ and $\hat{\rho}_2$ found, then equations (21) and (22) can be used to provide final estimates of β and ω respectively. The variance-covariance matrix for these estimators is more complex than the previous two cases and requires some additional notation:

$$B_1 = A_2W_1A_1^{-1}A_2^{-1}$$

$$B = WA^{-1}$$

$$C = A_1^{-1}W_1'A_2'A_2W_1A_1^{-1}$$

$$V_2 = W_2' + W_2 - 2\rho_2W_2'W_2$$

$$D = A_2'^{-1}A_1'^{-1}W_1V_2A_2^{-1}$$

$$\alpha_1 = -\sum_i \frac{\lambda_i^2}{(1-\rho_1\lambda_i)^2}$$

$$\alpha_2 = -\sum_i \frac{\mu_i^2}{(1-\rho_2\mu_i)^2} .$$

With this notation, the variance-covariance matrix for the estimators is given by

$$V(\hat{\omega}, \hat{\rho}_1, \hat{\rho}_2, \hat{\beta}) = \tag{25}$$

$$\omega^2 \begin{bmatrix} \dfrac{N}{2} & \omega \text{tr}B_1 & \omega \text{tr}B_2 & 0' \\[2ex] \omega \text{tr}B_1 & \omega^2\{\text{tr}(B_1'B_1) - \alpha_1\} + \omega\beta'X'CX\beta & \omega^2\text{tr}D & \omega(X'A_2'A_2W_1A_1^{-1}X\beta)' \\[2ex] \omega \text{tr}B_2 & \omega^2\text{tr}D & \omega^2\{\text{tr}(B_2'B_2) - \alpha_2\} & 0' \\[2ex] 0 & \omega X'A_2'A_2W_1A_1^{-1}X\beta & 0 & \omega X'A_2'A_2X \end{bmatrix}^{-1}$$

This model is a generalization of both the network effects model and the network disturbances model which can be readily checked. If $\rho_1 = 0$ and if the second row and column of the matrix of equation (25) are deleted then (25) reduces to equation (19) which is the equation established for the network disturbances model. Similarly, if $\rho_2 = 0$ and if the third row and column of the matrix in (25) are deleted then (25) reduces to (13) which is the equation established for the network effects model. Further, when either $\rho_1 = 0$ or $\rho_2 = 0$, the estimation equations reduce to those established for the earlier models. Examples of the use of this procedure can be found in Doreian (1982).

5. *Discussion*

In this chapter I have outlined three models that may be used to capture network effects on individual actors. Each of these models (the network effects model, the network disturbances model, and the network effects-network disturbances model) incorporates both the relevant characteristic in order to account for the distribution of some attribute or characteristic across the social actors embedded in the social network. A maximum likelihood estimation procedure was provided for each model. As such, these models have considerable utility not only in dealing with but actually exploiting the interdependence among social actors in a social network and getting at social structural explanations of the behavior of individual actors.

However, there are limitations that need to be addressed in order to extent this approach further. First, and perhaps foremost, there is the need to deal with multiple network effects. That is, there may be more than one network effect operating simultaneously on the individuals in a social network and, if so, it would be desirable to model these jointly.[14] More specifically, if W_1 is a relational structure matrix and W_2 a positional structure matrix defined for the same network, we may want to comparatively evaluate the relative strengths of the two effects. Thus, a model like

$$Y = \rho_1 W_1 Y + \rho_2 W_2 Y + X\beta + \varepsilon \qquad (26)$$

---

[14] This is quite different to using multiple networks to define, say, a position and positional equivalence or to define the probability of initiating interaction across multiple networks. The discussion here is focused on effects as defined in the previous sections.

with $\varepsilon \sim \text{IN}(0, \omega I)$ can be specified and estimated. The maximum likelihood estimator for this has been derived (Doreian, 1986). In the context of considering spatial autocorrelation of a disturbance term, Brandsma and Ketellapper (1979) provide a maximum likelihood approach for dealing with two regimes of spatial autocorrelation. Specifically, they specify

$$Y = X\beta + \varepsilon \qquad (27)$$

$$\varepsilon = \rho_1 W_1 \varepsilon + \rho_2 W_2 \varepsilon + v \qquad (28)$$

with $v \sim \text{IN}(0, \omega I)$ and provide a maximum likelihood estimation procedure together with likelihood ratio tests for hypothesis testing. These models together with their estimation strategies need to be considered further.

A second avenue for further research stems from the observation of Coelen (1975) that a single ρ implies a process that is uniform over a region in a spatial context or over an entire network in a network context. It may be the case that network effects do not operate uniformly throughout an entire network. For empirical situations where this is the case, it would seem fruitful to develop procedures to (i) detect this and (ii) adapt our modeling procedures to incorporate such non-uniformity across a social network.

A third avenue of research is that of dynamic network effects. Combining the discussion of Doreian and Hummon (1976:Ch. 6, 7) with the previous discussion of network effects may provide a starting point. Consider $Y* = \rho Wy$ as discussed earlier. For each member of the network, I, the value Y_i* can be regarded as a target value towards which the characteristic of that social actor is moving. At any given point in time, let $Y*(t)$ and $Y(t)$ be the vectors of control values and observed values respectively. Let Δt be an increment of time and let $\Delta Y(t)$ be an increment of change in Y in Δt. Then, adopting the perspective of structural control, we can specify

$$\Delta Y(t) = \gamma(Y*(t) - Y(t)) \Delta t \qquad (29)$$

where γ is a sensitivity parameter. Rearranging (29) and taking the limit gives

$$\frac{dY(t)}{dt} = \gamma (Y*(t) - Y(t)) \qquad (30)$$

the solution of which is

$$Y(t) = \exp\left[-\gamma (I - \rho WY)t\right] Y(0). \qquad (31)$$

Given the panel or time series data such a model can be estimated although it would appear that the procedure will be complex. The exogenous variables and a disturbance term can be included by speciying

$$Y*(t) = \rho WY(t) + X(t)\beta + \epsilon(t), \tag{32}$$

which, when included in the structural control equation, leads to

$$\frac{dY(t)}{dt} = -\gamma (I - \rho W)Y(t) + \gamma X(t)\beta + \gamma\epsilon(t) \tag{33}$$

Denoting $\Phi(t) = \exp [-\gamma(I - \rho W)t]$, the solution of (33) can be written

$$Y(t) = \Phi(t)Y(0) + \int_0^t \Phi^{-1}(t - \tau)\left[X(t)\beta + \epsilon(t)\right] d\tau. \tag{34}$$

This equation can form the basis of an estimation procedure for obtaining the parameters of the model. Notice that if equilibrium is assumed in (33), with the left hand set to zero, we get

$$Y = \rho WY + X\beta + \epsilon \tag{35}$$

which is the network effects model discussed above. Thus, from a dynamic perspective, the network models considered earlier have an implicit assumption of equilibrium. Formulating and estimating dynamic models of network effects would appear to be another fruitful direction of research.

REFERENCES

Arora, S. S. and M. Brown
    Alternative approaches to spatial auto-correlation: an
    improvement over current practice. International Regional
    Science Review, Vol. 2, 1 (Fall), 197:67-78.

Bales, R. F.
    1950   Interaction Process Analysis: A Method for the Study of Small
           Groups. Cambridge, Mass.: Addison-Wesley.

Brandsma, A. S. and R. H. Ketellapper
    1979   A biparametric approach to spatial autocorrelation. Environment
           and Planning, Vol. 11, 51-58.

Burt, R. S.
    1976   Positions in networks. Social Forces, Vol. 55, 93-122.
    1977   Positions in multiple network systems, part I: a general conception
           of stratification and prestige in a system of actors cast as a social
           topology. Social Forces, 56, 106-131.
    1978   Cohesion versus structural equivalence as a basis for network
           subgroups. Sociological Methods and Research, Vol. 7, 189-212.
    1980   Actor interests in a social topology: foundation for a structural
           theory of action. Social Inquiry, Vol. 49, 107-132.
    1980   Models of network structure. Annual Review of Sociology,
           Vol. 6, 79-141.

Burt, R. S. and P. Doreian
    1982   Testing a structural model of perception: conformity and deviance
           with respect to journal norms in elite sociological methodology.
           Quality and Quantity, Vol. 16, 109-150.

Burt, R. S. and N. Lin
    1977   Network time series from archival records. *In* D. Heise (ed.),
           Sociological Methodology 1977, 224-254, San Francisco:
           Jossey-Bass.

Cliff, A. D. and J. K. Ord
    1973   Spatial Autocorrelation. London: Pion.

Coelen, S. P.
    1976   Book review: spatial autocorrelation by Cliff and Ord. Journal of
           Economic Literature (Sept.), 924-925.

Coleman, J. S., E. Katz and H. Menzel
    1966   Medical Innovation. New York: Bobbs-Merrill.

Doriean, P.
    1980   On the evolution of group and network structure. Social
           Networks, 2, 235-252.

1980 Linear models with spatially distributed data: spatial disturbances or spatial effects? Sociological Methods and Research, Vol. 9, No. 1 (August), 29-60.
1981 On the estimation of linear models with spatially distributed data. *In* S. Leinhardt (ed.), Sociological Methodology 1981, 359-388, San Francisco: Jossey-Bass.
1982 Maximum likelihood methods for linear models: spatial effect and spatial disturbance terms. Sociological Methods and Research , Vol. 10, 3, 243-269.
1986 Two regimes of network autocorrelation effects. *In* M. Kochen (ed.), Towards a Socio Dynamics Model of Social Behavior (forthcoming).
Doreian, P. and N. P. Hummon
1976 Modeling Social Processes. New York: Elsevier.
Dow, M. E., D. R. White and D. E. Hansen
1979 Regression Analysis and Network Autocorrelation. University of California, Irvine (mimeo).
Duncan, O. D., A. O. Haller and A. Portes
1968 Peer influences on aspirations: a reinterpretation. American Journal of Sociology, Vol. 74, 119-137 (reprinted with corrections *in* H. M. Blalock (ed.), Causal Models in the Social Sciences, Chicago: Aldine, 1971).
Erbring, L. and A. A. Young
1979 Individuals and social structure: contextual effects as endogenous feedback. Sociological Methods and Research, Vol. 7 (May 4), 396-430.
Festinger, L., S. Schachter and K. Back
1950 Social Pressures in Informal Groups, Stanford: Stanford University Press.
Freeman, L. S.
1977 A set of measures of centrality based on betweenness. Sociometry, Vol. 40, 35-41.
Levine, J. H.
1972 The sphere of influence. American Sociological Review, Vol. 37, 14-27.
Lorrain, F. P. and H. C. White
1971 Structural equivalence of individuals in social networks. Journal of Mathematical Sociology, 1, 49-80.
Ord, J. K.
1975 Estimation methods for models of spatial interaction. Journal of the American Statistical Association, Vol. 70 (March), 120-126.

Sailer, L. D.
1978 Structural equivalence: meaning and definition computation and application. Social Networks, 1, 73-90.
Simmel, G.
1950 Individual and society (1917). *In* The Sociology of Georg Simmel (trans. K. H. Wolf), pp. 3-84, New York: Free Press.
Stevens, S. S.
1957 On the psychophysical law. Psychological Review, Vol. 64, 153-181.
White, D. R. and K. P. Reitz
1983 Graph and semigroup homomorphisms on networks of relations. Social Networks, 5, 193-234.

CHAPTER 10

ALGORITHMS AND NETWORK ANALYSIS: A TEST OF SOME ANALYTICAL PROCEDURES ON KAPFERER'S TAILOR SHOP MATERIAL

J. Clyde Mitchell

1. Introduction

One of the striking characteristics of the decade 1970-1980 from the point of view of social network data, has been the verdant proliferation of procedures for their formal analysis. Until 1970 the emphasis in the analysis of network data was almost entirely on clique detection based mainly, though not entirely, on notions derived from graph theory.

In the 1970's however, several different approaches emerged and these have led to alternative modes of analysis. It is not my intention to provide a history of the development of network approaches but merely to establish, as a launching pad for what follows, that there are at present a large number of analytical procedures representing variations on three or four major themes.

The set of procedures with the longest history in network analysis is that based on basic graph theoretical notions. By the late 1960's the procedures depending on strict definition of a clique as a maximally dense subgraph was proving to be too limited to capture the regularities in less than perfect real data. Procedures thus emerged in which the notion of a cluster rather than a strict clique became the main operative idea, e.g., Hubbell (1965), MacRae (1960). Modern developments in these directions have led to consideration of points at more than one step from some specified anchor point (Alba, 1973), and for the relaxation of the requirement of strict maximal density in the specification of a missing member of a putatively complete clique (Seidman and Foster, 1978).

The utility of measures based upon simple graph theoretical notions as basic descriptive devices should not be overlooked. I hope to illustrate some of these (and some extensions) below:

A second major theme has been the development and extension of ideas based on the original notions of structural balance. This has led to a set of procedures premised essentially on the enumeration of different kinds of triads encountered in a set of empirical data (Davis, 1967; Holland and Leinhardt, 1970). The intention of these analyses is to draw sociological inferences from the distribution of different types of triads in the data.

A third theme and one which at present seems to be capturing a great deal of attention is based on the notion of structural equivalence (Lorrain and White, 1971; Boorman and Breiger, 1976; Boorman and White, 1976). There are several specific advantages of methods using this approach over competitors in the field. The first is that they draw upon the flexible yet vigorous postulates of semi-groups in mathematical analysis (Boyd, 1979, 1980). Secondly, they can be related directly to basic sociological theoretical notions. Thirdly, they are capable of handling multiple relationships and networks, and fourthly they can be converted into practical procedures of analysis. Developments are due to D. R. White (this volume), Sailer (1978), and Everett and Niemenin (1980).

A fourth approach which has only recently begun to be used in the analyses of empirical data, is based on algebraic topology and has come to be known as Q-analysis. The application of these procedures to social network data was first suggested by Abell (1969) but has recently been used in analyses by Gould and Gatrell (1980), Freeman (1980) and Doreian (1980).

The rapid development of analytical procedures in the decade 1970-1980 has certainly been due to the extension and wide-spread use of large capacity computers. But equally the use of these procedures in run-of-the-mill analysis has been impeded, I would argue, by two different but related circumstances. The first is that at the current stage of development the field is dominated by opposed and even sectarian camps in which particular kinds of analysis are being advocated. The literature is represented by descriptions of formal procedures of analysis, in which data sets, usually displaying clear-cut characteristics, are analysed and re-analysed, with the intention of illustrating the mode of analysis rather than contributing to our stock of substantive knowledge about the nature of network processes in general. The diffusion of analytical procedures is partly hampered by the difficulty of using programs developed in the context of some particular machine on some other machine, even when the programs are written in such allegedly 'universal' languages as FORTRAN.

But even more important is the fact that there seems to be a gap between those of our profession who are active in developing general analytical procedures as against those who are prepared to take the validity of the procedures incorporated in programs for granted and to seek instead some elucidation of these empirical data using these procedures. In the best of all worlds, no doubt, all kings would be philosophers, or all field-workers programmers, but with increasing sophistication and specialisation in the subject we will need to accept that some—and indeed probably most—users of network analysis programs in the future will be relatively naive users who will need to know whether their data meet the requirements of the system they intend to use and to be able to interpret the output from the program sufficiently accurately to be able to draw reasonably valid inferences regarding their data.

At the time of writing there are very few accounts available in the general sociological literature in which users have been able to use some analytical procedure *as a tool* to reveal the patterns in some body of network analysis. Instances of where a user has applied several *different* procedures to the same body of data with substantive analysis in view are even rarer.[1]

My intention here, as one interested primarily in substantive issues but yet not insensitive to matters of analytical procedure, is to attempt a preliminary step in this direction. The procedure that I intend to adopt is once more to take a body of existing material amenable to network analysis and bearing in mind the original problem in terms of which the data were collected, to subject the data to those analytical procedures as are available to me and then to interpret the results in terms of the substantive issues involved.

---

[1] Exceptions are Moore (1979), Alba and Moore (1978), Laumann, E. (1973).

2. The Body of Data

Several considerations led me to choose Bruce Kapferer's study of the development of a strike in a clothing factory in Zambia in 1965, as the basic body of data for re-analysis (Kapferer, 1972).[2] The data were collected by continuous direct observation between June 1965, and February 1966. Kapferer records that from his location of observation in the factory he was able to see most of the interactions going on. He recorded these in field notes. The categories of the contents of interaction used in his analysis were established after the data were collected. The interactions were restricted to those which he judged to be "regular" and occurred relatively frequently.

1. The first consideration was that Kapferer has presented his data in a form which enables formal methods of analysis to be used. I mean by this that he published what are in effect four adjacency matrices relating to the different kinds of relationships among the protagonists in the action and two different times in the events.

2. The second is that the relationships can be construed as multiplex (manifold). Kapferer distinguished between what he called sociational and instrumental transactions. Sociational transactions are essentially convivial interactions, which Kapferer instances as general conversation, the sharing of gossip or the enjoyment of a drink together (1972:164). These transactions, which may mirror the bonding together of particular actors, are inherently symmetric. Kapferer contrasts sociational with what he calls instrumental transactions such as the lending or giving of money, assistance at times of personal crisis, or help at work (1972:164). Instrumental transactions are, as Kapferer puts it, means to an end, rather than ends in themselves as sociational transactions are. Instrumental transactions are inherently asymmetric therefore, since they inevitably lead to a debt of obligation between actors and thus index differences in power, and hence prestige and status among the workers. It is of course, possible for the

---

2   At my suggestion several colleagues have submitted these data to analysis by existing procedures each of them based on somewhat different operational assumptions. I had originally hoped to include some of the results in this chapter but this would have complicated it so much that I have had to postpone consideration of these more complex analyses for a later date. In the mean time I would like to thank Professor Ron Burt of U.C. Berkeley for an analysis using his social topological approach; Dr. Martin Everett of Thames Polytechnic for an analysis using his cycle tracing blocking procedures; Professors William Richards of Simon Fraser University and Ron Rice of Stanford University for an analogy using NEGCOPY procedures; and Professor John Sonquist and his colleagues from U.C. Santa Barbara for an analysis using Alba's COMPLT and SOCK procedures.

balance of instrumental transactions between any two actors to be equal in which case the debt of obligation between them would be relatively balanced. When instrumental transactions took place reciprocally between two actors, Kapferer determined the direction of the balance by his judgment of the dominant element, according to his general knowledge of the nature of the relationships between the individuals engaged in the interaction (1972:164).

3. A third feature which makes these data attractive for re-analysis is that at the time when Kapferer was preparing these data for analysis he had very limited facilities for formal analyses. Several of the more powerful procedures currently in use now had at that time not yet been developed. Kapferer in fact used a version of the procedures advocated by Beum and Brundage (1950), to make the patterns in his data apparent.

4. The data are embedded in a detailed account of the general political and cultural context in which the action is played out and are supplemented with very detailed ethnograhpic accounts of a number of events from which the disposition of the actors towards one another may be assessed. In addition, although these data are not made extensive use of here, Kapferer provides systematic details on the background social attributes of the actors. This means that there is the possibility, though not the certainty of course, that supporting elaborations of the analysis might be sought in the descriptive material.

5. The network data are complex and large and the patterns in them are not immediately apparent or obvious. Even so, for the purposes of this analysis the material has been simplified. At time 1, Kapferer recorded the sociational and instrumental transactions of 43 persons. At time 2, some four of these persons had left employment and another 15 had been taken on. Since the basic proposition Kapferer is working on is that both sociational and instrumental transactions increase between time 1 and time 2 and in particular that the transactions increased between the upper status workers—the supervisors and line 1 tailors and the lower status workers—the line 3 tailors, ironers and cotton boys, it seemed reasonable to exclude all those who were not present at both time 1 and time 2 of the analysis. My own attention therefore has been linked to the transactions taking place among the 39 actors who had been involved in sufficient interaction to have been included by Kapferer at both time 1 and time 2.

The analyses that follow therefore relate to the interactions or transactions among 39 workers in the clothing factory involved in symmetric sociational transactions and in asymmetric instrumental transactions at both time points, i.e. four 39 × 39 adjacency matrices. In general the ranking of prestige of the various occupations in the factor were that the supervisor, cutters and head tailor were most prestigious followed by line 1 tailors, line 2 tailors, line 3 tailors, button machiners, ironers and last of all cotton boys. Of the 39 actors, 23 were in the same occupation at time 1 as at time 2, 13 had moved to more responsible and higher paid occupations and 3 had dropped slightly.

In the re-analysis of a data set such as is being attempted here, there are several approaches that could be adopted. These could range from simply working within the framework of the original analyst's framework to test and check the original findings, through variations of the basic hypothesis set up by the original analyst to the setting up of an entirely different hypothesis based on different assumptions which might possibly be tested using the data on hand. My own preference at this stage is work within Kapferer's original formulation which he succinctly states as "the support by all the factory employees of strike action at the late time period, in contrast to only limited support for similar industrial action at the close of the time period preceding it, is related to an extension of interactional relationships cross-cutting and modifying major divisions of interests" (1972:163).

3. Measures Based on Reachability and Graph Theoretical Distance

The use of graph theory and measures and indices derived from it have formed an important part of the analysis of network data from the earlier work of the sociometrists. Several measures of this have formed an important part of the analysis of network data from the earlier work of the sociometrists. Several measures of this kind may be used to reflect the tendencies Kapferer postulates in the two time periods under discussion. The simplest of these is density, i.e., the proportion of potential links (or transactional relationships in this instance) that in fact exist. At time 1, only 0.2132 of the potential $39 \times 38 = 1482$ sociational links in fact existed. At time 2, the proportion had risen to 0.3009. Insofar as instrumental relations are concerned, the density rose from 0.0735 at time 1 to 0.0992 at time 2. Thus among the same set of actors there had been a proportional increase of 41 percent in sociational and of 35 percent in instrumental relationships.

4. Graph Centrality

A change in the density, however, does not necessarily reflect an improvement in reachability. Reachability relates to the extent to which any actor is in contact with actors either directly or through intermediaries. Reachability, therefore, turns on the distance along paths in a network. There are several measures of overall reachability in graphs. The first thing to note is that the maximum number of finite steps for sociational relationships at time 1 is 4, but at time 2 it had fallen to 3, indicating the probably increased reachability at time 2. Similarly the maximum finite steps for instrumental relationships fell from 8 at time 1 to 7 at time 2. But the maximum number of finite steps does not *necessarily* reflect a change in reachability. To reflect this I have used a measure which depends on the number of steps each actor takes to reach as many as possible of other actors in the set. The greatest overall reachability would exist where every actor can reach every other actor in just one step. The minimum reachability would be reached where no actor can reach any other actor at all. For purposes of calculation unreachable distances may be given a value equal to the size of the network and on this basis an index of compactness (or graph centrality) may be computed which would be between 0 when no actor is reachable from any other actor and 1.0 when each actor can contact every other actor in just one step. An index of this sort computed for sociational relationships at time 1 has a value of 0.9725 whereas at time 2 it has a value of 0.9797. For instrumental relations the index in fact falls very slightly from 0.6519 to 0.6429. This is because at time 2 although the number of connections has increased there are nevertheless no less than five who are virtually unreachable by all of the rest of the 39 and there are an additional four who can themselves only reach others who cannot reach others or who have no instrumental transactions at all.[3]

5. First order Star Size

A more detailed analysis would need to reveal the way in which the links of those actors who played significant roles in the set of events

---

3 Given that unreachable cells from any element are given the value N of the size of the network (which is one larger than the longest possible geodesic path) then the index is

$$\frac{N^2(N-1) - \sum d_{ij}}{N(N-1)^2}$$

where $\sum d_{ij}$ is the sum of distances of each element from every other element in the set.

described had changed between times 1 and times 2. One of the simplest indicators of the changes going on in the tailor shop between time 1 and time 2 is the number of co-workers on the shop floor with whom each member had direct instrumental or sociational transactions at the two times provided. Table 1 sets out the relevant details classified in terms of the occupations of the actors at time 2.

It is clear that the number of both direct sociational links and instrumental links that members of the tailor shop had with one another increased between times 1 and 2, the former increasing by 41 percent and the latter by 35 percent. The number of instrumental links each member had on the average was only one quarter of the number of sociational links. Kapferer, it will be recalled, put much greater store on instrumental links as reflecting the disposition of power and influence in the tailor shop, so that the relative infrequency of instrumental ties belies their significance for the course of events in the Tailor shop.

	Sociational				Instrumental				N
	Time 1		Time 2		Time 1		Time 2		
	Obs.	Obs.	Exp.	Δ	Obs.	Obs.	Exp.	Δ	
Supervisors	17.00	21.67	18.24	3.42	9.00	7.33	9.23	−1.90	3
Line 1 Tailors	7.33	11.67	10.84	0.83	3.33	6.67	4.24	1.93	12
Line 2 Tailors	7.43	10.00	10.92	0.92	1.29	2.57	2.44	0.13	7
Line 3 Tailors	6.71	9.29	10.37	1.08	2.57	1.86	3.57	−1.71	7
Button Machiners	3.00	5.66	7.53	6.47	1.00	3.00	2.19	0.81	2
Ironers	9.80	10.80	12.74	1.94	1.60	2.20	2.72	−0.52	5
Cotton Boys	7.67	8.00	11.10	3.10	1.67	1.00	2.78	−1.78	3
Overall	8.10	11.43	11.43	0.00	2.79	3.77	3.77	0.00	39

Table 1. Observed and expected mean star size
for sociational and instrumental links at time 1
and time 2 by occupational categories

In examining the changes for occupational categories in both sociational and instrumental transactions from time 1 to time 2 we must take account of the overall changes in transactions of both types at both time periods. The simplest way of doing this is to calculate the expected number of links at time 2 for any given actor given the overall change from time 1 to time 2. This was done by a simple linear regression. The correlation between the size of the first order star for sociational relations at time 1 and time 2 was 0.6713 and that between the size of first order stars for instrumental relations was 0.6856.

Table 1 also shows the mean star size for both sociational and instrumental links for time 1 and time 2 together with the expected mean star size given the overall change between the two periods. The differences between the observed and the expected values are also shown.

There are interesting differences in the trends in instrumental as against sociational ties between the two time points. Line 3 Tailors, Ironers and Cotton Boys all in the lower reaches of the occupational table tend on the whole to establish and expand their sociational and instrumental links to a lesser degree than their co-workers. Line 1 Tailors consistently increase both sociational and instrumental ties more than the average, especially for the socially significant instrumental ties, a point which is significant in terms of Kapferer's analysis which emphasises the way in which Line 1 Tailors expand their links after the unsuccessful walk-out at time 1. Line 2 Tailors do not expand their sociational ties as much as their co-workers but they increase slightly their instrumental ties. The Supervisors and Head Tailors expand their convivial relationships to a greater extent than the average but significantly fail to expand their instrumental relationships. The Button Machiners present an anomaly. There are only two of them but unlike their co-workers at roughly equivalent social status, they increase both their sociational and instrumental links between the two time points. This change is due to the crucial role that one of the Button Machiners, 25 Meshak, played in the events in the Tailor Shop.[4]

These changes are in accord with Kapferer's postulate that between the time of the walkout of line 1 Tailors in July 1965 and the joint withdrawal of labor of all occupational groups in February 1966, the Line 1 Tailors had extended their ties to other members of the factory—particularly their instrumental links which, in Kapferer's view established obligations between Line 1 Tailors and those lower in the occupational ladder. The Supervisors and Head Tailors on the other hand in whom the factory owner had vested formal authority, had reduced their sociational links, and had significantly reduced their instrumental ties as compared with the general trend in the factory. Line 3 Tailors and Cotton Boys, both

---

[4] 25 Meshak who had worked at the factory for eleven years, together with a line 1 tailor 5 Chipata, were treated as 'supervisors' by the owner of the factory when it became clear that the formal supervisors and head tailor had lost credence with the workers. The numbers preceeding the names of actors are their identification numbers and included for ease of finding them in the matrices published in Figures 1 and 2.

of whom are towards the lower end of the occupational ladder also had developed fewer instrumental ties than the others on the shop floor.

6.   Point Centrality

The size of the protagonist's first order star, however, is an inadequate indicator of the extent to which the various actors are able to mobilise support and to instigate action. A member of the tailor shop may be able to mobilise a number of his co-workers because he is in direct sociational or instrumental relationships with them. But at the same time these workers, if successfully mobilised, may persuade those who are in direct contact with them to participate in the action. The point may well be illustrated by the different positions of 37 Angel, a cotton boy, and 29 John, a line 3 tailor, in respect of instrumental relations at time 1. Both have a first order star size of 3, but 37 Angel has a reciprocal instrumental link with 19 Mukubwa, who is a supervisor and has extensive instrumental links in the factory. The consequence is that Angel is in contact with seventeen of the 32 workers who are reachable through instrumental links in two steps and with all 32 in three steps. 29 John, however, because of his links with actors with less extensive links, would need to push his links to five steps to reach seventeen other workmen and to seven steps to reach all 32. We need a measure, therefore, of the extent to which a specified member of the tailor shop is sufficiently placed centrally in the network so as to be able to mobilise maximum support for any action he becomes involved in.

A classical measure of this kind is that of point centrality of which there are several versions. The particular measure I have used here is a modification of Bavelas' measure. Bavelas' original measure was the ratio of the sum of distances from actor i to all other actors to the aggregate of distances from all actors to all actors. I have normed this index to have a value of 1.0 when the actor can reach all other actors in one step only and zero when he can reach no other actor at all. For calculation purposes unreachable points are given an arbitrary distance of the size of the network. The normed Bavelas index on this basis for 37 Angel is 0.2038 and that for 29 John with the same star size is 0.0887.

Table 2 sets out the normalized Bavelas index for occupational categories for sociational and instrumental links at times 1 and 2. For comparison the expected value in mean index given the change between time 1 and time 2 shown together with the difference between the observed and expected value.

| | Time 1 | Time 2 | | |
		Expected	Observed	Δ
Supervisors	0.5270	0.5279	0.6017	0.0738
Line 1 Tailors	0.3649	0.4221	0.4353	0.0132
Line 2 Tailors	0.3825	0.4336	0.4083	−0.0253
Line 3 Tailors	0.3275	0.3977	0.3929	−0.0048
Button Machiners	0.3199	0.3927	0.4686	0.0759
Ironers	0.4026	0.4467	0.4214	−0.0253
Cotton Boys	0.3812	0.4327	0.3692	−0.0635
Total	0.3776	0.4304	0.4304	0.0000

(a). Sociational ties

| | Time 1 | Time 2 | | |
		Expected	Observed	Δ
Supervisors	0.2404	0.2509	0.2572	0.0063
Line 1 Tailors	0.1664	0.1908	0.2361	0.0453
Line 2 Tailors	0.0691	0.1118	0.1614	0.0496
Line 3 Tailors	0.1097	0.1448	0.1001	−0.0446
Button Machiners	0.1007	0.1374	0.1081	−0.0293
Ironers	0.0761	0.1174	0.0523	−0.0651
Cotton Boys	0.1344	0.1648	0.0910	−0.0708
Total	0.1270	0.1588	0.1588	0.0000

(b). Instrumental ties

Table 2. Normed Bavelas index for occupational categories for sociational and instrumental ties at times 1 and 2*

---

* The expected values at time 2 are derived from the linear equation of time 2 and time 1 values, which is why the total expected exactly equals the total observed. The correla-

The measures of point centrality with minor variations confirm the pattern based on first order star size. The focal position of the supervisors and head tailors in the factory is well reflected. Although the normed Bavelas index is lower in general for instrumental than for sociational relations the supervisors and head tailors nevertheless on the average have a higher index than for the other members of the work force.

The overall pattern of changes in the normed Bavelas index from time 1 to time 2 is that only the line 1 tailors increase both their sociational and instrumental links more than average between the two time periods. Line 3 tailors, the ironers and cotton boys, all of whom are relatively low in occupational status diminish both the sociational and instrumental links between the time periods. The supervisors and button machiners tend to increase proportionately, their instrumental relationships between the two time periods, while line 2 tailors tend on the whole to diminish their sociational relationships while increasing their instrumental linkages.

7.   *'Betweenness' Measures*

An alternative index of point centrality has been proposed by Freeman (1977). This measure avoids the difficulty inherent in most other indices when non-reachable elements exist in a network. The rationale behind this type of measure is that an element may be thought of as maximally 'central' in a network if it is located on every path of shortest distance linking all other elements in a set to every other element in that set. Freeman is careful to point out that the use of this measure 'is appropriate only in networks where betweenness may be viewed as important in its potential for impact on the process being examined' (1977:40). In terms of the basic hypothesis underlying Kapferer's analysis it would seem that 'betweenness' measures may indeed be construed to be relevent. The period between the initial unsuccessful walk-out of the line 1 tailors and strike some six months later was marked by a build-up of interaction, particularly of instrumental interaction, especially between line 1 tailors and the other workers in the factory. The interactions Kapferer observed were essentially dyadic in the sense that he noted that individual I was in conversation with J in sociational interaction or that I gave J a cigarette in instrumental interaction. There would be no meaning in imputing transitivity to the mainfest content of these interactions: it is not clear what the relationship of I is to K when I talks to J and J talks to K but I does not talk direct-

---

tion between sociational indices at times 1 and 2 is 0.6658 and between instrumental indices 0.6069.

ly with K. It is only to the imputed bonding of the actors to one another as indexed by their manifest exchanges that the transitivity may be attributed. On these grounds we may hypothesize that as the interaction increased with time after the initial walk-out then we might expect the 'betweenness' to increase.

'Betweenness' measures were computed for both sociational and instrumental ties at both times 1 and 2.[5] There was considerable variability in the betweenness measures ranging from 155.89 for 16 Chisokone to zero for six of the actors for sociational links at time 1. The range for sociational links at time 2 was from 75.28 for 19 Mukubwa to zero for only one actor 20 Sign. A check on the mean betweenness measure for sociational links at both times 1 and 2 showed that this had dropped from 19.8 at time 1 to 14.4 at time 2. The range for betweenness measures for instrumental links at time 1 was from 142.51 for 19 Mukubwa to zero for 11 actors and from 163.0 for ll Lyashi to zero for nine actors at time 2. The mean betweenness index had fallen from 30.17 at time 1 to 22.0 at time 2. We have already seen that the overall density for sociational ties had increased from 0.2132 to 0.3009 and for instrumental ties from 0.0735 to 0.0992: in fact both betweenness measures decrease almost exactly in inverse proportion to the increase in density. This suggests that the fall is a mechanical effect due simply to the increase in number of links between the two time periods.

But the changes in the index for the different occupational groups are instructive. Table 3 sets out the mean betweenness indices for occupational categories at times 1 and 2. In general the betweenness indices for all except the button machiners and the cotton boys decrease between time 1 and 2. The largest declines are for line 3 tailors and ironers, both of which groups fall at the lower end of the prestige scale. But it is interesting in terms of Kapferer's hypothesis that the index declines also for line 1 tailors as a whole and for the supervisors both of whom occupied positions of relative authority at time 1. The betweenness indices for button machiners and cotton boys, contrary to expectations, *increased* rather than decreased. The increase of the betweenness index for cotton boys was due to that of 35 Christian who at time 2 had developed a sociational

---

5   This was achieved using a FORTRAN IV version of a program written by Linton Freeman which I have adapted for use on the Oxford University ICL 2980. Although Freeman discussed 'betweenness' in his original paper in terms of undirected graphs, he has assured me that it may be used on directed graphs, but the measures then may not be considered as normed, as they are for undirected graphs. This means that we can consider sociational interactions at times 1 and 2 and instrumental interactions at times 1 and 2, but it would not be correct to compare sociational (reciprocal) interaction with instrumental (directed) interaction.

relationship with 16 Chisokone, the supervisor who still had extensive links. The increase in the betweenness index for the button machiners was due to the increase of the index from 1.17 at time 1 to 27.82 at time 2 for 25 Meshak, who was thrust into a quasi-supervisory role by the factory owner at time 2.

	Time 1		Time 2		N
	Soc.	Inst.	Soc.	Inst.	
Supervisors	79.87	83.86	55.98	32.42	3
Line 1 Tailors	14.29	25.56	8.56	56.79	12
Line 2 Tailors	19.38	16.51	17.46	22.69	7
Line 3 Tailors	16.02	38.73	8.19	18.23	7
Button Machiners	0.59	0.06	16.40	7.16	2
Ironers	19.95	17.61	9.94	13.40	5
Cotton Boys	4.38	48.61	10.05	7.03	3
Total	19.82	30.17	14.44	21.99	39

Table 3. Mean betweenness index for sociational
and instrumental ties at times 1 and 2 by
occupation

Of much greater interest, however, are the changes in the betweenness indices relating to instrumental links. A comparitively clear pattern emerges. The betweenness of the supervisors drops by 159 percent; that of line 1 tailors rises by 122 percent. The betweenness of line 2 tailors rises only 37 percent. The betweenness of all those in occupations of lower prestige (except the button machiners) falls: for the lowest prestige category, the cotton boys, it falls dramatically by 591 percent. The rise of the betweenness of the button machiners is entirely due to the position of 25 Meshak, whose elevation to a quasi-supervisory status led to a rise of his index from zero to 14.32. The index of 26 Adrian remained at zero at both time periods.

The indices of some of the protagonist actors in the saga reflect reasonably well the changes in their relationships in the workplace between the two time periods. The instrumental betweenness index of 16 Chisokone drops from 107.38 at time 1 to 83.84 at time 2; that for 19 Mukubwa from 142.51 at time 1 to only 11.44 at time 2. The indices for 13 Hastings, the supervisor from Malawi, remained marginal at 0.20 and 2.05 respectively, but the index for 11 Lyashi, who led the opposition to management, increased from 88.90 to 163.00. The instrumental betweenness for 5 Chipata who, like 25 Meshak, was elevated to quasi-supervisory status towards the end of time 2, rose from zero at time 1 to 60.44 at time 2.

In summary we can say that the betweenness measures as a whole, reflecting as they do a component of the social action different from that in the point centrality measures, captures a good deal of the flavour of the basic postulate that Kapferer had advanced in his analysis. A more detailed analysis of the role of some of the lesser actors such as 32 Henry, whose index of instrumental betweenness fell from 116.77 at time 1 to 20.46 at time 2 might enable us further to elucidate the substantive meaning of this measure in this analysis by reference to the ethnographic details.

8. Span

The size of the first order star and measures of point centrality enable us to appreciate the extent to which individual actors are able to contact either immediately or indirectly varying proportions of others in the network. Kapferer, however, has argued that we need to appreciate not only the number of individuals any actor can contact directly or indirectly but also the extent to which those individuals form a relatively dense cluster or not. He has proposed a measure, *span*, to reflect this. Kapferer defines span as 'the number of relationships out of the total viable interactional relationships operating between actors in the factory captured by Ego as a result of including specific individuals within his direct or first order zone of relationships' (1972, 170-171). His justification for using this measure is that, as he explains, it focusses on the number of links involved in a network rather than the number of individuals, thus laying emphasis on the 'differential quality' of ego-centered networks. The implication is that of an individual who has access to a tightly knit group is likely for that reason to command more support in a dispute than an individual in contact with sparsely linked individuals. The rationale behind the notion of span presumably draws from the well known proposition in network thinking which links normative control and pressure towards conformity of action to the members of densely connected network segments.

Numerically span expressed as the percentage that the number of links in Ego's first order zone is of the total number of links in the whole network.

Span may also be expressed as the product of the ratios of Ego's first order zone density to overall density and the total possible links in Ego's first order zone to the total number of possible links in the network as a whole. That is

$$\text{Span} = \frac{ZD}{D} \times \frac{S(S+1)}{N(N-1)}$$

where ZD is first order zone density, D is overall density, S is first order star size and N is size of the network.

As with first order star size and the index of point centrality the span of the different workers differs both according to their occupational role to the type of relationship (sociational or instrumental) and whether we are concerned with time 1 or time 2.

Table 4 reflects the average spans for occupational categories at times 1 and 2 for both sociational and instrumental relations as compared with the expected span for the occupational category given the overall change in span from time 1 to time 2.

The changes reflected in this table corroborate those which have manifested themselves in the changes in first order star size and point centrality set out in Tables 2 and 3. On the whole line 3 tailors. Ironers and Cotton Boys expand the span of their linkages more than the average. The supervisors and head tailors and the button machiners expand their sociational links while contracting their instrumental links. Insofar as instrumental links are concerned the details of the analysis summarized in Table 4 shows that those whose span contracted most in relation to the general trend were 19 Mukubwa and 16 Chisokone the head tailor and supervisor respectively who had become discredited by the time the strike took place at time 2. On the other hand those whose span expanded most were 11 Lyashi who had taken the initiative leading to the strike and 5 Chipata who had been ascribed supervisory roles by the owner after 16 Chisokone and 19 Mukubwa had become discredited. 34 Mubanga who had been involved in an incident flouting the authority of both the shop owner and the supervisor proportionately increases his instrumental span at time 2 as against his fellow ironers. It is interesting though that 25 Meshak who was also ascribed quasi-supervisory roles in the period leading up to the strike while he increased his sociational span displayed very little increase in instrumental span. Anomalies which emerge from this analysis are 12 Zulu, a line 1 tailor, who does not expand his instrumental span as much as the average. While line 2 tailor and operator of an overlock machine, 24 Ibrahim, gains instrumental span, his colleague 21 Kalamba in the same occupational category loses instrumental span.

	Sociational				Instrumental			
	Time 1	Time 2			Time 1	Time 2		
	Obs.	Obs.	Exp.	Δ	Obs.	Obs.	Exp.	Δ
Supervisors	38.18	49.18	39.08	10.10	24.16	15.87	23.82	-7.94
Line 1 Tailors	13.71	23.24	19.74	3.50	8.65	15.70	10.20	5.50
Line 2 Tailors	11.30	16.40	17.83	-1.43	1.96	5.05	4.34	0.71
Line 3 Tailors	11.30	14.67	17.83	-3.16	5.24	3.11	7.21	-4.10
Button Machiners	3.17	27.14	11.40	15.74	0.92	3.06	3.42	-0.36
Ironers	18.48	15.61	23.50	-7.89	3.12	4.49	5.35	-0.86
Cotton Boys	15.19	10.17	20.91	-10.74	3.67	1.36	5.83	-4.47
Overall	14.91	20.69	20.69	0.00	6.54	8.35	8.35	0.00

Table 4. Observed and expected spans for
sociational and instrumental links at times 1 and 2
by occupational categories[*]

The strategic importance of the changes in instrumental as against sociational span is brought out in the following Table 5.

In terms of Kapferer's argument an increase in sociational span has less consequence for social action than instrumental. We note that two of the three supervisors and head tailors suffer a decrease in instrumental span, but that after this 'reversal' of order the proportion suffering a relative decrease in instrumental span in general increases down the occupational ladder (line 1 = 3 of 12, line 2 = 2 of 7, line 3 = 7 of 7, button machiners 1 of 2, ironers 2 of 5 and cotton boys 3 of 3). The cases thrown up as anomalies here are the line 2 and line 3 tailors who suffer relative loss in sociational span but relative gain in instrumental span, the line 2 tailors (4 Seams, 8 Mateo, 18 Paulos, 28 Mpundu, and the ironers, 31 William, 33 Chobe and 34 Mubanga). At present I have no interpretation of this interesting juxtaposition of characters.

---

[*] Expected values estimated from the linear regression of time 2 on time 1. The correlation between time 1 and time 2 sociational spans is 0.6390 and that between instrumental spans 0.7044.

	Change				
	++	+−	−+	−−	Total
Supervisors	1	1	0	1	3
Line 1 Tailors	9	1	0	2	12
Line 2 Tailors	1	1	4	1	7
Line 3 Tailors	0	3	0	4	7
Button Machiners	1	1	0	0	2
Ironers	0	0	3	2	5
Cotton boys	0	0	0	3	3
	12	7	7	13	39

Table 5. Changes from time 1 to time 2 in sociational as compared with instrumental span*

In this section I have done no more than refine and confirm the earlier analysis that Kapferer had conducted on the tailor shop material. In his analysis he included all actors at time 2. In my analysis I have considered only those who were present for any time at both times.

In this sort of analysis the focus of attention is on the individuals concerned and the network characteristics considered are those centered on individuals as first order stars, point centrality and span are, and as such they shed a good deal of light on the course of events in the factory. The morphological characteristics of the network as a whole are not captured by these measures. For these we must turn to other procedures.

9. *Clustering*

One of the standard ways of approaching the analysis of the structure of relationships in social networks is through identifying relatively dense segments in the network as a whole on the postulate that these dense segments would then reflect significant collocations of actors in the network. The earliest procedures along this direction were directed towards the identification of cliques or maximally dense subgraphs, but it soon became

* ++ = increase in both sociational and instrumental span above median values;
 +− = increase in sociational but decrease in instrumental span above and below median;
 −+ = decrease in sociational and increase in instrumental span below and above median;
 −− = decrease in both sociational and instrumental spans.

apparent that the strict condition of 100 per cent density needed to define a clique in a strict sense was too vigorous a criterion for most empirical analyses. The procedure Kapferer used in his analysis was one proposed by Beum and Brundage (1950) which rearranged the adjacency matrix so as to cluster the entries as close as possible to the leading diagonal. This method had the advantage that it did not insist upon fully dense segments but sometimes was subject to cycling in the sense that several alternative solutions were sometimes possible.[6] Since the days of Beum and Brundage there have been many developments in clustering.[7] In general, there has been a move away from simple clique detection towards the determination of clusters sometimes within an hierarchical framework.

In the analysis which follows I have used a variation of an earlier clique detection procedure (Hubbell, 1965). The rationale behind this procedure seems appropriate for the sort of consideration Kapferer had in mind. Basically the Hubbell procedure traces the 'influence' or 'contact' of each actor with all other actors along all paths on the assumption that the influence will diminish with each additional link in the path. The rate of attenuation of the influence must be set by the user and this constitutes an arbitrary element in the use of the procedure. In the analyses presented here an attenuation value of 0.5 per step has been used so that after the 8th step for example the strength of the influence at that point would only be $0.5^8 = 0.0039$ of the value at the start.

Hubbell originally used this procedure to detect cliques by selecting an arbitrary cut-off point and treating all parts with influence values larger than the cut-off as 'linked.' I have modified this procedure by incorporating an hierarchical linkage procedure. The elements of the matrix are then aggregated into larger and larger clusters of decreasing density until all the elements are included in the final overarching cluster.

For the analysis here I have considered only the crudest of clusters by choosing clusters at the point where the maximum size clusters have been reached before large clusters are amalgamated. All elements not as yet in one of the larger clusters at this point are treated as a residual group (unclustered). Figure 1 represents this broad cluster structure of the sociational and instrumental relationships at times 1 and 2. The clusters marked D* and E* are the unclustered residues after the major clusters have been extracted. The somewhat higher densities (and therefore greater

---

6   See Lankford (1974) for a comparison of a number of different clique detection procedures.
7   See for example Peay (1974), Alba (1973), Seidman and Foster (1978).

```
TIME 1.INSTRUMENTAL. RENUMBERED

               1| 333133333|12      1 111|22322|122 112223
               44|042975839|5361259372163|91684|7078082561
               ::|:::::::::|:::::::::::::|:::::|:::::::::::

    4  SEAMS    D* | *        |    1        |     |
   14  LWANGA   D  | 1*       |    1        |   1 |1          1

   30  JOSEPH      | *11 1    |             |     |
   34  MUBANGA     | 1*1   1  |             |     |  1
   32  HENRY       | 11* 1 1 1|             |     |
   19  MUKUBWA  C 1|   *1   1 |11      1111 |  11 |           1
   37  ANGEL       | 1 11*    |             |     |
   35  CHRISTIAN   |  1    *  |             |     |
   38  CHILUEYA    |   1     *|             |     |
   33  CHOBE       |       *1 |             |     |
   39  MABANGE     |  1     1*|             |     |

   15  NYIRENDA    |          |*1        1  |  1  |
   23  BEN         |          |1*           |     |
    6  DONALD      |          |  *    1     |     |
    1  KAMWEFU     |          |  *        1 |     |
    2  NKUMBULA    |          |   *     1   |     |
    5  CHIPATA     |          |    *    1   |     |
    9  CHILWA   A  |          |     *   1 1 |     |
   13  HASTINGS    |          |      1*    11|    |
    7  NKOLOYA     |          |1      * 11  |1    |
   12  ZULU       1|          |    1 1  *111|1    |
   11  LYASHI     1|      1   |       111 11*11|   |
   16  CHISOKONE  1|1 1 1     |       11111* | 1 1|1
    3  ABRAHAM     |          |1 11  11 111*|     |

   29  JOHN        |        1 |             |*11  |
   21  KALAMBA     |          |             |1* 1 |
   36  KALONGA  B  |          |             |1 *  |
   28  MPUNDU      |          |             |   *1|
   24  IBRAHIM     |        1 |    1        |1 1* |

   12  ENOCH       |          |             |     |*
   20  SIGN        |          |             |     | *1
   27  KALUNDWE    |          |             |     | 1*
    8  MATEO       |          |             |     |   *
   10  CHIPALO     |          |             |     |    *
   18  PAULOS   D* |          |             |     |     *
   22  ZAKEYO      |        1 |             |     |1     *
   25  MESHAK      |        1 |    1        |     |       *
   26  ADRIAN      |          |             |     |        *
   31  WILLIAM     |          |             |     |         *

               ::|:::::::::|:::::::::::::|:::::|:::::::::::
```

Figure 1(a). Clustering of Sociational and Instrumental
Relations Time 1 by Hubbell Procedures

TIME 1.SOCIATIONAL. RENUMBERED

```
                    212|1 22|1 1    1   |233233333333|21212211|1
                    276|8807|13224631759|939551427680|44358169|0
                    :::|::::|::::::::::::|::::::::::::::|::::::::|:
22  ZAKEYO    E*    *  |    |            |            | 1      |
17  ENOCH           *  |    |            |            |1    1  |
26  ADRIAN          *  |    |            |      1     |     1  |
                    ---+----+------------+------------+--------+--
18  PAULOS    C        |*1 1| 1          |           1|11     1|
 8  MATEO              |1*  | 1          |            |       1|
20  SIGN              | *1 |            |            |        |
27  KALUNDWE         |1 1*|            |      1     |  1 1   |
                    ---+----+------------+------------+--------+--
11  LYASHI    A        |    |*1111111111 |     1      |      11|
 3  ABRAHAM           | 1  |1*1111111 1 |            | 1    11|
12  ZULU              | 1  |11*1111  1  |    1    1  |     111|1
 2  NKUHBULA          |    |111*1       |            |       1|
 4  SEAMS             |    |1111* 1     |            |1     11|
 6  DONALD            |    |111 *1      |            |      11|
13  HASTINGS          |    |111 11*  1  |1   1  1    |       1|
 1  KAMWEFU           |    |11 1 *   1  |            |        |
 7  NKOLOYA           |    |11     *11  |      1     |       1|
 5  CHIPATA           |    |1 1  1 1*1  |            |        |
 9  CHILWA            |    |11    111*  |1           |1     11|
                    ---+----+------------+------------+--------+--
29  JOHN              |    |          1 |*111     11 |     111|
33  CHOBE             |    |          1 |1*11111  1  |    1  1|
39  MABANGE           |    |            |11*    11  1|        |
25  MESHAK            | 1  |            |11 *        |      1 |
35  CHRISTIAN         |    |          1 |1  *111 11  |     1  |
31  WILLIAM           |    |    1       |1  1*1  1 1 |11 1 1  |
34  MUBANGA   D      | 1  |1           |11 11*11111 |1     11|
32  HENRY       1    |    |        1 1 |1 1 1*1111  |1   111 |
37  ANGEL             |    |            |     11*111 |        |
36  KALONGA           |    |    1       |11 11111*11 |        |
38  CHILUFYA          |    |            |11    1111*1|    1 1 |
30  JOSEPH           | 1  |            |1  111111*  |      11|
                    ---+----+------------+------------+--------+--
24  IBRAHIM     1   | 1  |            |       111  |*11 1111|
14  LWANGA            |    |1  1    1   |      1     |1*   1 1|
23  BEN         1   |  1 |            |            |1 *111 1|
15  NYIRENDA  B      |    |1           |            | 1*1 11 |
28  MPUNDU            |  1 |            |1   11    1 |1111*   |
21  KALAMBA           |    |    1     1 |       11   |1 1  *11|
16  CHISOKONE   11  | 1  |1111111 1 1 |1  1 1111 11|1  1 1*1|
19  MUKUBWA           | 1  |111 11      |11    11   1|1111 11*|
                    ---+----+------------+------------+--------+--
10  CHIPALO   E*       |    | 1          |            |        |*
                    :::|::::|::::::::::::|::::::::::::::|::::::::|:
```

Figure 1(b). Clustering of Sociational and Instrumental
Relations Time 1 by Hubbell Procedures

```
                    TIME 2.INSTRUMENTAL.  RENUMBERED

                  │1111   21 1  2│22112│323333│ 112 │3 3332223
                  │31932754410925│93561│704025│88784│369162678
                  │::::::::::::::│:::::│::::::│:::::│:::::::::
    3  ABRAHAM    │*1 1 11 11 1  │   11│      │  1  │
   11  LYASHI     │1*1111111111  │1    │11111 │  1  │  11   1
   19  MUKUBWA    │11*1 2 1      │1    │      │  1  │
   13  HASTINGS   │111*    1     │     │1     │     │
   12  ZULU       │ 1  *111    1 │     │      │     │
    7  NKOLOYA    │11  1*1 1 1   │     │   1  │     │
    5  CHIPATA    │11  11*     1 │1  1 │1     │  1  │
   24  IBRAHIM  A │ 1    *1      │   1 │ 111  │     │
   14  LWANGA     │11  1 1*    1 │     │      │     │
    1  KAMWEFU    │11    1  *  1 │  1  │      │     │
   10  CHIPALO    │ 1  1    *    │     │      │     │
    9  CHILWA     │11       *    │     │      │     │
    2  NKUMBULA   │     1    *1  │     │   1  │  1  │
   25  MESHAK     │ 1         *  │1    │1   1 │     │  11
                  ├──────────────┼─────┼──────┼─────┼─────────
   29  JOHN       │              │* 1 1│      │     │
   23  BEN      C │              │ *1  │      │     │       1
   15  NYIRENDA   │              │11*  │      │     │
   16  CHISOKONE  │1      11   11│1  *1│1  1  │  1  │
   21  KALAMBA    │              │1  1*│      │     │
                  ├──────────────┼─────┼──────┼─────┼─────────
   37  ANGEL      │              │     │*1  1 │     │
   20  SIGN       │              │     │1*    │     │
   34  MUBANGA  D │1      1 1    │     │  *111│     │
   30  JOSEPH     │              │     │  1*1 │     │
   32  HENRY      │         1    │     │1 11* │     │
   35  CHRISTIAN  │              │     │  1  *│     │
                  ├──────────────┼─────┼──────┼─────┼─────────
    8  MATEO      │       1      │     │      │*111 │
   18  PAULOS     │              │     │      │1*1  │
   17  ENOCH    B │       1      │     │      │11*  │
   28  MPUNDU     │1             │     │      │  *1 │
    4  SEAMS      │              │     │      │1  1*│
                  ├──────────────┼─────┼──────┼─────┼─────────
   33  CHOBE      │              │     │      │     │*11
    6  DONALD     │              │     │      │     │1*
   39  MABANGE    │              │     │      │     │1 *
   31  WILLIAM  E*│              │     │      │     │   *1
   36  KALONGA    │              │     │      │     │   1*
   22  ZAKEYO     │              │     │      │     │     *
   26  ADRIAN     │              │     │      │     │      *
   27  KALUNDWE   │              │     │      │     │       *
   38  CHILUFYA   │              │     │      │     │        *
                  ├──────────────┼─────┼──────┼─────┼─────────
                  │::::::::::::::│:::::│::::::│:::::│:::::::::
```

Figure 1(c). Clustering of Sociational and Instrumental
Relations Time 2 by Hubbell Procedures

TIME 2.SOCIATIONAL. RENUMBERED

```
               121 1122    1   1 2 3333333333 12221 11  2 2 2
               94631351 2149572 6 8527043169 53290 78487 860
               :::::::: :::::::  : :::::::::: ::::: :::::  :::
19 MUKUBWA     *1111111 111  11 1  1 111  1          1  11 1
24 IBRAHIM     1*111111 1111  1    1 1111             11 1      1
16 CHISOKONE   11*1 111 11 1 11      1111 111     1   1 11
3  ABRAHAM     111*1111 1111111 1     1             1
11 LYASHI  A   11 1*1 1 1111111 1     1  1      1  1  1        1
13 HASTINGS    11111*11 11  11 1        1 1      1111
25 MESHAK      1111 1*1 1 1 11 1     1 11   1 1  1    1
21 KALAMBA     1111111*    1  1        1 1  1  1 1    1  1

2  NKUMBULA    1 11111  *11 1 1        1  1
1  KAMWEFU     111111   1*111 1                        1
14 LWANGA      11 11 1  11*  1          1  1            1      1
9  CHILWA  B    1111  1  1 *111
5  CHIPATA     1 1111   11 1*11         11           1 1
7  NKOLOYA     1 11111     111*1 1      1            1        1
12 ZULU        11111  1  11 111*         1            1      1

26 ADRIAN E*   1  1111        1  *   1  11       1

38 CHILUFYA    1                *11111  1        1
35 CHRISTIAN   1                1*  11 111                    11
32 HENRY       111    11     1  1 *111  1        1
37 ANGEL       11                 1 1*11
30 JOSEPH      111 1111    1 11  1111*1 1
34 MUBANGA D   11 1  1  1   1  1 11111*111       1
33 CHOBE       1 1  1               1*111 1  1
31 WILLIAM      1 1  1             1  111*1       1            1
36 KALONGA      1           1 1   111  11 *1 1
39 MABANGE     1    1              1     1 1*       1

15 NYIRENDA    1    11               1 1 *111
23 BEN             11                    1*111                 1
22 ZAKEYO  C   1    1          1         11*1                  1
29 JOHN        1 1  1 1               1 1 111 1 111*
10 CHIPALO        1111       11                1   *

17 ENOCH       111         1 1                     *1 1  1
18 PAULOS E*   1 1 11  1    1                      1* 11
4  SEAMS       1                                    *1    1
8  MATEO       111                                  111*
27 KALUNDWE    1       1                            1   *  1

28 MPUNDU      1         1 11      1       1    11  1 1 1 *
6  DONALD         1                 1                       *
20 SIGN        1                    1                       *
               :::::::: :::::::  : :::::::::: ::::: :::::  :::
```

Figure 1(d). Clustering of Sociational and Instrumental
Relations Time 2 by Hubbell Procedures

reachability) in time 2 are reflected in the somewhat higher 'influence' values at which the clusters link as compared with time 1.

The letters identifying the clusters in the diagram have no significance as between diagrams. (The actual composition of the clusters is set out in Table 6.) Nevertheless there is some tendency for the same actors to

Sociational Time 1   Total

Cluster A	1 Kamwefu, 2 Nkumbula, 3 Abraham, 4 Seams, 5 Chipata, 6 Donald, 7 Nkoloya, 9 Chilwa, 11 Lyashi, 12 Zulu, 13 Hastings	11
Cluster B	14 Lwanga, 15 Nyerenda, 16 Chisokone, 19 Mukubwa, 21 Kalamba, 23 Ben, 24 Ibrahim, 28 Mpundu	8
Cluster C	8 Mateo, 18 Paulos, 20 Sign, 27 Kalundwe	4
Cluster D	25 Meshak, 29 John, 30 Joseph, 31 William, 32 Henry, 33 Cholu, 34 Mubanga, 35 Christian, 36 Kalonga, 37 Angel, 38 Chilufya, 39 Mabange	12
Unclustered Residue E*	10 Chipalo, 17 Enoch, 22 Zakeyo, 26 Adrian	4

Instrumental Time 1

Cluster A	1 Kamwefu, 2 Nkumbula, 3 Abraham, 5 Chipata, 6 Donald, 7 Nkoloya, 9 Chilwa, 11 Lyashi, 12 Zulu, 13 Hastings, 15 Nyerenda, 16 Chisokone, 23 Ben	13
Cluster B	21 Kalamba, 24 Ibrahim, 28 Mpundu, 29 John, 36 Kalonga	5
Cluster C	19 Mukubwa, 30 Joseph, 32 Henry, 33 Choke, 34 Mubanga, 35 Christian, 37 Angel, 38 Chilufya, 39 Mabange	9
Unclustered Residue D*	4 Seams, 8 Mateo, 10 Chipalo, 14 Lwanga, 17 Enoch, 18 Paulos, 20 Sign, 22 Zakeyo, 25 Meshak, 26 Adrian, 27 Kalundwe, 31 William	12

(a). Time 1

Sociational Time 2

Cluster A	3 Abraham, 11 Lyashi, 13 Hastings, 16 Chisokone, 19 Mukubwa, 21 Kalamba, 24 Ibrahim, 25 Meshak	8
Cluster B	1 Kamwefu, 2 Nkumbula, 5 Chipata, 7 Nkoloya, 9 Chilwa, 12 Zulu, 14 Lwanga	7
Cluster C	10 Chipalo, 15 Nyerenda, 22 Zakeyo, 23 Ben, 29 John	5
Cluster D	30 Joseph, 31 William, 32 Henry, 33 Chobe, 34 Mubanga, 35 Christian, 36 Kalonga, 37 Angel, 38 Chilufya, 39 Mabange	10
Unclustered Residue E*	4 Seams, 6 Donald, 8 Mateo, 17 Enoch, 18 Paulos, 20 Sign, 26 Adrian, 27 Kalundwe, 28 Mpundu	9

Instrumental Time 2

Cluster A	1 Kamwefu, 2 Nkumbula, 3 Abraham, 5 Chipata, 7 Nkoloya, 9 Chilwa, 10 Chipalo, 11 Lyashi, 12 Zulu, 13 Hastings, 14 Lwanga, 19 Mukubwa, 24 Ibrahim, 25 Meshak	14
Cluster B	4 Seams, 8 Mateo, 17 Ench, 18 Paulos, 28 Mpundu	5
Cluster C	15 Nyerenda, 16 Chisokone, 21 Kalamba, 23 Ben, 29 John	5
Cluster D	20 Sign, 30 Joseph, 32 Henry, 34 Mubanga, 35 Christian, 37 Angel	6
Unclustered Residue E*	6 Donald, 22 Zakeyo, 26 Adrian, 27 Kalundwe, 31 William, 33 Chobe, 36 Kalonga, 38 Chilufya, 39 Mabange	9

(b). Time 2

Table 6. Composition of clusters derived by
Hubbell procedures at time 1 and time 2

cluster together in terms of different kinds of relationships at both time periods. If the membership to clusters in respect of one type of relationship or at one point of time is classified against the membership to clusters in respect of a different relationship or time period, we are able to compute a simple measure of the extent to which there is some coincidence given the different sizes of clusters.[8]

Table 7 sets out the tau-b's derived from comparing the clustering of the data indexed by columns with the data indexed by row.

| | | Time 1 | | Time 2 | |
		Soc.	Inst.	Soc.	Inst.
Time 1	Sociational	*	0.5287	0.4388	0.2971
	Instrumental		*	0.3080	0.2183
Time 2	Sociational		0	*	0.4641
	Instrumental				*

Table 7. Association between membership of
clusters for different data sets. Goodman and
Kruskal's tau-b's

It is interesting that the clustering for instrumental relationships at time 2 shows most departure from that at time 1 with only 29.7 and 21.8 point reduction in error respectively, given knowledge of the cluster membership at time 1. Much of the discrepancy between the clustering in terms of instrumental relationships at time 1 as against time 2 arises because of the rather large unclustered residue at time 1 (twelve members) of whom only 4 (22 Zakeyo; 26 Adrian; 27 Kalindwe and 31 William) remained unclustered at time 2. The closest similarities pertain between sociational and instrumental ties at the same point of time with a 52.9 and 46.4 percent reduction in error in the clustering of instrumental links as related to the clustering of sociational links at the same time period. The highest association between the two time periods is that between sociational ties at time 1 and time 2 (0.4388).

These findings may be interpreted as supporting Kapferer's general analysis in the sense that Kapferer had postulated that the clique structure particularly in relation to instrumental links had broken down at time 2, thus allowing more cross-cutting ties between occupational status groups to

8   The measure used is Goodman and Kruskal's tau-b which is a 'proportional reduction in error' type of measure. It provides a measure of the extent to which we are able to predict the membership to a cluster in the second set given the knowledge of the cluster membership in the first set. It will vary between zero when the prior distribution provides no lead to the subsequent distribution and 1.0 when it predicts the membership perfectly.

develop as a necessary precursor to the strike at time 2. But the basis of the clustering at both time periods and for both kinds of relationship seems nevertheless to have been occupational status. Table 8 sets out the occupational composition of clusters for both relationships at both times.

Time 1	Sociational					Instrumental				Totals
	A	B	C	D	E*	A	B	C	D*	
1 Supervisors	1	2	0	0	0	2	0	1	0	3
2 Line 1 Tailors	8	0	0	0	0	8	0	0	0	8
3 Line 2 Tailors	2	3	1	0	2	1	2	0	5	8
4 Line 3 Tailors	0	3	3	0	1	2	1	0	4	7
5 Button Machiners	0	0	0	1	1	0	0	0	2	2
6 Ironers	0	0	0	3	0	0	1	2	0	3
7 Cotton Boys	0	0	0	8	0	0	1	6	1	8
Totals	11	8	4	12	4	13	5	9	12	39

Tau-b = 0.5841   Tau-b = 0.4986

Time 2	Sociational					Instrumental					Totals
	A	B	C	D	E*	A	B	C	D	E*	
1 Supervisors	3	0	0	0	0	2	0	1	0	0	3
2 Line 1 Tailors	2	7	1	0	2	10	1	0	0	1	12
3 Line 2 Tailors	2	0	0	0	5	1	4	1	0	1	7
4 Line 3 Tailors	0	0	4	2	1	0	0	3	3	1	7
5 Button Machiners	1	0	0	0	1	1	0	0	0	1	2
6 Ironers	0	0	0	5	0	0	0	0	1	4	5
7 Cotton Boys	0	0	0	3	0	0	0	0	2	1	3
Totals	8	7	5	10	9	14	5	5	6	9	39

Tau-b = 0.5126   Tau-b = 0.4161

Table 8. Occupational composition of clusters for
sociational and instrumental relationships at
time 1 and time 2

The extent to which clusters derived by the Hubbell procedures predominantly incorporate members from the same part of the occupational prestige scale is patent. The tendency is clearer for sociational relationship where the tau-b value for time 1 is 0.5841 and for time 2, 0.5126. Nevertheless even for instrumental relationships to which Kapferer attributed significance as reflecting the power relationships in the factory, a knowledge of the distribution in occupational categories enables us to reduce the errors in allocation to clusters by 50 per cent at time 1 and by 42 per cent at time 2.

On the surface Table 8 appears to support Kapferer's main postulate in that at time 2 the clustering that emerges from tracing the paths of influence reflects the occupational structure less clearly than at time 1 suggesting an increase in cross-cluster links.

Some of the appearance of members of the tailor shop as unclustered may be explained by special circumstances. The unclusterability of 6 Donald at time 2 (both instrumental and sociational) arises because he was in fact present into the period covered by time 2 for only a few days and was not there long enough to build up sufficient ties to link him into one of the other clusters. In fact 26 Adrian is unclustered on all four occasions, 17 Enoch, 22 Zakeyo and 27 Kalundwe in three of the four occasions, these four providing in all 13 of the 34 occasions when workers were unclustered.[9]

If the unclustered elements are omitted from the calculations of tau-b's between cluster membership and occupational categories the numerical values of the associations rise appreciably.

> From 0.5433 for sociational time 1 to 0.6818
>
> From 0.4662 for instrumental time 1 to 0.5809
>
> From 0.5127 for sociational time 2 to 0.6706.
>
> From 0.4161 for instrumental time 2 to 0.6334.

This shows that the presence of unclustered elements—which tend to be distributed widely in occupational categories—depresses the association between occupational category and cluster membership considerably. With the revised figures we see that clusters generated from sociational links seem to be related to a greater extent to occupational categories at time 1 but that clusters derived from instrumental links are linked almost as much with occupational categories at time 2 but that there was, if anything, a slight increase in the relationship between time 1 and time 2.

---

[9] They are all low interactors, but I would need to go back to the ethnographic account to discover whether there were special reasons why the linkages of these four were so unusual. I have not as yet done this.

The test of Kapferer's basic postulates about the organisation of social action between times 1 and 2 using clustering procedures, therefore, provides only very limited corroboration.

10. *Structural Equivalence*

The weakness of clustering procedures such as those using Hubbell procedures is that the basis of the clustering is confined to the one type of relationship at a time.

One of the great strengths of the notion of structural equivalence as developed by Harrison White and his colleagues (Lorrain and White, 1971; White, Boorman and Breiger, 1976; Boorman and White, 1976; Arabie, Boorman and Levitt, 1978; see also Light and Mullins, 1979) is that the analysis accepts that 'structural' equivalence may be assessed—perhaps ought to be assessed—from an actor's relationships with others in *several* different social contexts. With this tool in our hands we are able to examine the extent to which the actors in the tailor shop shared similar patterns of relationships at both times 1 and 2 for both sociational and instrumental relations.

The basic thinking behind structural equivalence makes it particularly appropriate for testing Kapferer's postulates that more links would have developed in off-diagonal blocks reflecting the cross-cutting ties which Kapferer maintains had developed in the period after time 1 leading up to the strike at time 2.

We are able, using the procedures available, to aggregate the members of the tailor shop into 'blocks' who have basically similar patterns of links with others in the tailor shop. If the pattern of relationships of line 1 tailors in general is similar to one another but different from that of line 2 or other workers then we would expect the line 1 tailors to emerge as a single block.

There are several ways in which this way of thinking could be used to analyse Kapferer's material. Since in this paper I am particularly interested in the changes in sociational and instrumental relations between time 1 and time 2 I have adopted the strategy of determining the blocks of workers who had similar patterns of relationships in sociational and instrumental relationships over both time 1 and time 2 simultaneously. This provides us, as it were, with a basic blocking applicable to any of the types of relationships at either time. From this vantage point we are able to trace differences either in sociational as against instrumental relations, or changes from time 1 to time 2.[10]

Figure 2 sets out the matrices for sociational and instrumental relations at times 1 and 2 rearranged in terms of the application of CONCOR procedures. In these matrices five sets of actors leading to 25 blocks in each matrix have been arbitrarily decided upon.[11] The blocks were all larger or equal to five but were large enough to derive some overall view of the structure of relationships.

The blocks isolated in this way relate to different degrees to the attributes of their members. The following list shows the proportional reduction in error measure (tau-b) for block membership given the distribution in different categories of attributes.

Occupation at time 1	0.6311
Occupation at time 2	0.5657
Age group	0.2478
Broad ethnic group	0.1421
Place of Origin	0.1809
Urban or rural birthplace	0.0064
Township of residence	0.1254
Conjugal status	0.1344
Religion	0.2480
Educational level	0.1511
Length of service in factory	0.1784

It is quite clear from this that the occupation of the worker provides the best basis of the variables considered for allocating a member to a particular block.

---

[10] The analyses were effected on a FORTRAN IV program embodying CONCOR procedures which I have implemented on the Oxford University ICL 2980.

[11] Not much attention has been given to indices for reflecting points of optimal blocking, i.e., the maximum dispersion of densities between blocks with the smallest number of blocks. But see Carrington, Heil and Berkowitz (1979/80).

```
REARRANGED MATRIX NUMBER 1: KAPFERER TAILOR SHOP.
STAYERS.TIME 1.INSTRUMENTAL. RENUMBERED

                      1   1 11| 1122|  11122|12222|233333233333
                    1922531646|70356|4878914|52378|002478939156
                    ::::::::::|:::::|:::::::|:::::|::::::::::::
   1  KAMWEFU       *    1     |     |       |     |
   9  CHILWA        *    11    |     |       |     |
  12  ZULU          1*1 11   1 |     |1      |     |   1
   2  NKUMBULA        *  1     |     |       |     |
   5  CHIPATA          * 1     |     |       |     |
   3  ABRAHAM   A   111  *11 1 |  1  |       | 1   |
  11  LYASHI        11111*   1 |1    |1   1  |     |
   6  DONALD           1 *     |     |       |     |
  14  LWANGA        1        * |     |1      | 1 1 |1           1
  16  CHISOKONE     11    1 1* |1 1  | 1   1 |     |  11          1

   7  NKOLOYA            11 1  |*    |       |     |        1
  10  CHIPALO                  | *   |       |     |
  13  HASTINGS  B   1    1   1 |  *  |       |     |
  25  MESHAK            1      |   * |       |     |     1
  26  ADRIAN                   |    *|       |     |

   4  SEAMS         1         |     |*      |     |
   8  MATEO                   |     | *     |     |
  17  ENOCH                   |     |  *  1 |     |
  18  PAULOS    C             |     |   *   |     |
  19  MUKURWA       1    11 11 |     |    * 1|1 1 1|    1   1 1
  21  KALAMBA                 |     |     *1|     |        1
  24  IBRAHIM                 |     |    1* | 1 1 |   1

  15  NYERENDA      1         |     |       |* 1 1|
  22  ZAKEYO                  |     |       | * 1 |             1
  23  BEN       D             |     |       |1 *  |
  27  KALUNDWE               |     |       |   * |1
  28  MPUNDU                  |     |    1  |    *|

  20  SIGN                    |     |       |     |*
  30  JOSEPH                  |     |       |     |*111
  32  HENRY                   |     |       |     |1*111 1
  34  MUBANGA                 |     |       |     |11*        1
  37  ANGEL                   |     |  1    |     |11 *
  38  CHILUFYA  E             |     |       |     | 1  *
  29  JOHN                    |     |  1    |     |     *   11
  33  CHOBE                   |     |       |     |      *1
  39  MABANGE                 |     |       |     |1    1*
  31  WILLIAM                 |     |       |     |       *
  35  CHRISTIAN               |     |       |     |  1     *
  36  KALONGA                 |     |       |     |      1   *
                    ::::::::::|:::::|:::::::|:::::|::::::::::::
```

Figure 2(a). Blocking of Sociational and Instrumental
Relations Time 1 by CONCOR Procedures

```
       REARRANGED MATRIX NUMBER 2: KAPFERER TAILOR SHOP.
            STAYERS.TIME 1.SOCIATIONAL. RENUMBERED

                       ..1    1 11| 1122|  11122|12222|233333233333
                       1922531646|70356|4878914|52378|002478939156
                       ::::::::::|:::::|:::::::|:::::|::::::::::::
   1   KAMWEFU         *1    11   |     |1      |     |
   9   CHILWA          1*   111 11|1    |      1|     |      1
  12   ZULU             *11111  1 | 11  |1  111 |     |         1 1
   2   NKUMBULA        1*  11   1 |     |1      |     |
   5   CHIPATA   A     11 *  1    |1 1  |       |     |
   3   ABRAHAM         1111 *11 1 |1 1  |11   1 |1    |
  11   LYASHI          111111*111 |1 11 |1    1 |     |   1
   6   DONALD          1   11*  1 |1    |     1 |     |
  14   LWANGA          1    1  *  |     |1  11 1|1    |          1
  16   CHISOKONE       111  111  *|1 111|111 111|1    |   111111  1

   7   NKOLOYA         1   111  1 |*    |       |     |   1
  10   CHIPALO         1          |  *  |       |     |
  13   HASTINGS  B     1  1111 1  |   * |       |     |   1    1   1
  25   MESHAK              1  1   |   * |       |     |        11
  26   ADRIAN              1      |    *|       |     |   1

   4   SEAMS          1 11 11 11  |  1  |*    1 |     |
   8   MATEO               1   1  |     | * 1   |     |
  17   ENOCH               1      |     |  *  1 |     |
  18   PAULOS    C     1    1      |     |1 *1 1 |1    |1
  19   MUKURWA        1   11111    |     |1  1*11|1 1  |111   11
  21   KALAMBA        11     1     |     |   1*1 |1    |1    1
  24   IBRAHIM               11    |     |1111*  |1 1  |11        1

  15   NYERENDA        1    1      |     |    1  |* 1 1|
  22   ZAKEYO                      |     |       |*1   |
  23   BEN       D                 |     |  111  |11*11|
  27   KALUNDWE                    |     |  1    | 1*1 |1   1
  28   MPUNDU              1       |     |      1|1 11*|     1 1 11

  20   SIGN                        |     |       |1    |*
  30   JOSEPH               1      |     |11     |     |*1111    11 1
  32   HENRY                1      |1 1 1|111    |     |1*111    1 11
  34   MUBANGA         1    1      |     |  1 1. |1    |11*11 11111
  37   ANGEL                1      |     |       |     |111*1
  38   CHILUFYA  E          1      |     |       |1    |1111*1    11
  29   JOHN                 1      |11   |11     |     |   1*11  1
  33   CHOBE          1            | 1   |1      |1    |   1 1*1111
  39   MABANGE                     |     |       |     |111  11*
  31   WILLIAM        1    11      |     |      1|1    |1 1  1  *11
  35   CHRISTIAN                   |  1  |       |1    |  11 1 1 1*1
  36   KALONGA        1            |     |       |     |1111111 11*
                       ::::::::::|:::::|:::::::|:::::|::::::::::::
```

Figure 2(b). Blocking of Sociational and Instrumental
Relations Time 1 by CONCOR Procedures

```
REARRANGED MATRIX NUMBER 3:KAPFERER TAILOR SHOP.
STAYERS.TIME 2.INSTRUMENTAL. RENUMBERED

                  1   1 11  1122   11122  12222 233333233333
                  1922531646 70356 4878914 52378 002478939156
                  :::::::::: ::::: ::::::: ::::: ::::::::::::
    1  KAMWEFU    *  1111            1
    9  CHILWA     *    11
   12  ZULU       *11 1    1            1
    2  NKUMBULA   *1          1              1   1
    5  CHIPATA  A 11*11  1 1        1         1    1.
    3  ABRAHAM    11  1*1 11 1 1        1      1
   11  LYASHI     111 11* 1  111          1 1 1    1 1111111
    6  DONALD          *                               1
   14  LWANGA         11 *  1 1          1
   16  CHISOKONE  1 111    *        1 11         1  1 1

    7  NKOLOYA    1 111 1  *1                  1
   10  CHIPALO       1     1*
   13  HASTINGS B   11 1    *      1            1
   25  MESHAK            *      1             1 1   111
   26  ADRIAN              *

    4  SEAMS             *1              1
    8  MATEO            1*11  1
   17  ENOCH      1      1*1
   18  PAULOS   C        11*  1
   19  MUKURWA       11 1 1    *         1          1
   21  KALAMBA          1       *                    1
   24  IBRAHIM       1 11       *              111

   15  NYERENDA                         * 1          1
   22  ZAKEYO                             *
   23  BEN      D                       11*
   27  KALUNDWE                           *
   28  MPUNDU        1                     *

   20  SIGN                                     *  1
   30  JOSEPH                                   *11
   32  HENRY                    1                1*11
   34  MUBANGA       1          1                11*      1
   37  ANGEL    E                                 1 *
   38  CHILUFYA                                      *
   29  JOHN                            1 1            *
   33  CHOBE        1                                  *1
   39  MABANGE                                         1*
   31  WILLIAM                                          * 1
   35  CHRISTIAN                                     1    *
   36  KALONGA                                          1 *
                  :::::::::: ::::: ::::::: ::::: ::::::::::::
```

Figure 2(c). Blocking of Sociational and Instrumental
Relations Time 2 by CONCOR Procedures

REARRANGED MATRIX NUMBER 4: KAPFERER TAILOR SHOP.
STAYERS.TIME 2.SOCIATIONAL. RENUMBERED

```
                        1   1 11| 1122| 11122|12222|233333233333
                     1922531646|70356|4878914|52378|002478939156
                     ::::::::::|:::::|:::::::|:::::|::::::::::::
 1  KAMWEFU          *111111 11|  1  |  11 1 |     |
 9  CHILWA           1*1 111  1|1    |    11 |     |
12  ZULU             11*1111  1|1    |  1111 |  1  |           1
 2  NKUMBULA         1 1*111 11|  11 |   1   |     |   1        1
 5  CHIPATA   A      1111*11   |1111 | 1   1 |     | 1 1
 3  ABRAHAM          11111*1 11|11111|  111  |     |   1
11  LYASHI           111111*11 |111 1|  1111 |  1  | 1          1
 6  DONALD                 1*  |     |       |     |           1
14  LWANGA           1  1 11  *|1  1 | 1 1 1 |  1  | 1          1
16  CHISOKONE        1111 1   *|1 11 |111 111|     |   11 1 11 111

 7  NKOLOYA          11 111 11 |*1111|   1   |   1 |1
10  CHIPALO             111    |1*11 |       |  1  |
13  HASTINGS  B      1  1111   |11*11|  111  | 11  |1        11
25  MESHAK             111   11|111*1| 1111  |1    |111      1
26  ADRIAN              11     |1 11*|   1   | 1   |11     1

 4  SEAMS                    1 |*1   |       |  1  |
 8  MATEO                    1 |1*111 1|     |     |
17  ENOCH               1    11|1*11 1|     |  1  |
18  PAULOS    C      1 1    1  |     |11* 11 |  1  |
19  MUKURWA          1 11 11 11|1 111|11 *11 |11 11|111    111
21  KALAMBA          11  11  1 |  11 |  11*1 | 1  1|11     1 1
24  IBRAHIM          111 111 11|  11 |11111* |     |111111

15  NYERENDA                  1|     |  11   |*11  |       11
22  ZAKEYO                    1| 1 1 |   1   |1*1 1|      1
23  BEN       D          1     | 11  |       |11*  1|     1
27  KALUNDWE                   |     | 111   |  *1 |
28  MPUNDU           1        1|1    | 1 1 1 |111* |             11

20  SIGN                       |     |   1   |     |*      1
30  JOSEPH              1 1 11 |1 11 | 111   |     |*1111     11
32  HENRY                    1 |  11 | 111   |     |1*1111      1
34  MUBANGA            111     |  11 | 1 1   |     |11*1111 111
37  ANGEL                    1 |     |   1   |     |111*1
38  CHILUFYA  E              1 |     |   1   |     |11111*1    11
29  JOHN                     1 | 1   |  11   | 111 |  11 1*111
33  CHOBE                    1 | 1 1 |   1   | 1   |   1  1*11 1
39  MABANGE                  1 |     |   1   |     |     11*  11
31  WILLIAM             1 1    |     |   1   |    1| 1 1   11 *11
35  CHRISTIAN             1 1  |     |       |    1| 1 1 1   11*1
36  KALONGA          11     11 |     |       |  1  |  11 1 1111*
                     ::::::::::|:::::|:::::::|:::::|::::::::::::
```

Figure 2(d). Blocking of Sociational and Instrumental
Relations Time 2 by CONCOR Procedures

Table 9 sets out the block densities and Z values for each block. The Z values are the one tailed probabilities of a difference occurring as large as or larger than that between the density of block and the density of the matrix as a whole. It is by no means certain that the Z values could be given a statistical interpretation since the basic sampling conditions are not fulfilled and I use the values merely as a convenient way of providing cutting points for deciding whether the blocks are to be treated as 1 or as zero, for the purpose of producing block images (see Table 11).

A chi-square value for each matrix suggests that the blocking achieved in each of the networks is unlikely to have arisen in a random distribution of links in blocks.[12] It is interesting that the blocking at time 2 for sociational links seems less distinct than that at time 1 but that for instrumental relationships stays the same. The rank order of the 'degree of blocking', as measured by three different indices[13] was the same: highest for Instrumental time 1, next Instrumental time 2, next Sociational time 1 and lowest for Sociational time 2.

These findings bear directly on Kapferer's postulates. Firstly, instrumental links tend to have higher indices than sociational. Secondly the indices of blocking at time 2 are lower than at time 1. My interpretation of these findings is firstly that linkages were becoming more diffuse at time 2, that is, clear blocking of the actors in terms of the structural similarity over both types of relationships and at both times was less evident at time 2. Secondly, the instrumental relationships on the whole index the basis of the structural similarity more clearly than the sociational. Both of these interpretations would be consistent with Kapferer's analysis of the course of events.

---

12 The maximum likelihood chi-squares were as follows:
    Sociational time 1   205.64   d.f. 24
    Instrumental time 1   116.93   d.f. 24
    Sociational time 2   170.42   d.f. 24
    Instrumental time 2   111.00   d.f. 24

13 These were the Carrington-Heil-Berkowitz 'B' (see Carrington, Heil, Berkowitz, 1979/80); the proportion of all links which fall into dense blocks (this will only be 1.00 if all sparse blocks are empty); and a modification of Tsuprow's T. The latter two indices are of my own devising and have not as yet been validated.

```
 1   2   3   5   6   9  11  12  13  16
 7  10  13  25  26
 4   8  17  18  19  21  24
15  22  23  27  28
20  29  30  31  32  33  34  35  36  37  38  39
```

(a). Partitioning of rows and columns simultaneously at step 4

1	0.5556	0.3000	0.3286	0.0600	0.1000
	7.9291	1.4981	2.3562	−2.6453	−3.0282
2	0.3000	0.0000	0.0280	0.0000	0.1167
	1.4981	−2.3281	−2.6672	−2.6029	−1.8261
3	0.3286	0.0286	0.3810	0.1714	0.1310
	2.3562	−2.6672	2.6539	−0.6037	−1.8410
4	0.0600	0.0000	0.1714	0.6000	0.1000
	2.6453	−2.6029	−0.6037	4.2231	−2.1413
5	0.1000	0.1167	0.1310	0.1000	0.5303
	−3.0282	−1.8261	−1.8410	−2.1413	8.8942

(b). Densities and Z values of blocks in matrix 1 at sociational time 1. Concentration of links in dense blocks = 0.6537. ML χ^2 = 205.64 with 24 degrees of freedom. TSTAR = 0.3645

1	0.3111	0.0800	0.0857	0.0400	0.0583
	8.6337	0.1747	0.3899	−0.9088	−0.6385
2	0.1400	0.0000	0.0000	0.0000	0.0333
	1.8000	−1.2601	−1.669	−1.4088	−1.1934
3	0.0857	0.0000	0.0952	0.1429	0.0595
	0.3899	−1.6669	0.5385	1.5708	−0.4924
4	0.0200	0.0000	0.0286	0.2000	0.0333
	−1.4506	−1.4088	−1.0194	2.1664	−1.1934
5	0.0000	0.0000	0.0238	0.0333	0.1591
	−3.0865	−2.1825	−1.7464	−1.1934	3.7650

(c). Densities and Z values of blocks in matrix 2 at instrumental time 1. Concentration of links in dense blocks = 0.6537. ML χ^2 = 205.64 with 24 degrees of freedom. TSTAR = 0.4680

1	0.6667	0.4600	0.4000	0.0600	0.1583
	7.5644	2.4521	1.8069	-3.7145	-3.4060
2	0.4600	0.9000	0.2571	0.2400	0.1833
	2.4521	5.8409	-0.5650	-0.6644	-1.9862
3	0.4000	0.2571	0.6190	0.2571	0.1905
	1.8069	-0.5650	4.4946	-0.5650	-2.2074
4	0.0600	0.2400	0.2571	0.6000	0.1167
	-3.7145	-0.6644	-0.5650	2.9159	-3.1121
5	0.1583	0.1833	0.1905	0.1167	0.5152
	-3.4060	-1.9862	-2.2074	-3.1121	5.3656

(d). Densities and Z values of blocks in matrix 3 at sociational time 2. Concentration of links in dense blocks = 0.5470. ML χ^2 = 170.42 with 24 degrees of freedom. TSTAR = 0.2793

1	0.3667	0.2000	0.1429	0.0800	0.1250
	8.4890	2.3847	1.2222	-0.4540	0.9459
2	0.1800	0.1000	0.0571	0.0000	0.1167
	1.9116	0.0121	-0.8322	-1.6592	0.4529
3	0.1000	0.0571	0.2381	0.0571	0.0595
	0.0227	-0.8322	3.0116	-0.8322	-1.2162
4	0.0200	0.0000	0.0286	0.1500	0.0167
	-1.8733	-1.6592	-1.3977	0.7602	-2.1385
5	0.0167	0.0167	0.0357	0.0167	0.1212
	-3.0243	-2.1385	-1.9462	-2.1385	0.8464

(e). Densities and Z values of blocks in matrix 4 at instrumental time 2. Concentration of links in dense blocks = 0.5470. ML χ^2 = 170.42 with 24 degrees of freedom. TSTAR = 0.3926.

Table 9. Block densities and Z values for difference between block densities and overall densities. Global concentration of links in dense blocks = 0.6330. Global ML χ^2 = 604.00 with 96 degrees of freedom. Global TSTAR = 0.2461

The composition of the blocks according to occupational classification at both times 1 and 2 is set out in Table 10.

	A	B	C	D	E	Totals
Supervisors	1	1	1			3
Line 1 Tailors	7	1				8
Line 2 Tailors	2	1	5			8
Line 3 Tailors			1	5	1	7
Button Machiners			2			2
Ironers					3	3
Cotton Boys					8	8
Totals	10	5	7	5	12	39

(a). Time 1, tau-b = 0.6311

	A	B	C	D	E	Totals
Supervisors	1	1	1			3
Line 1 Tailors	9	2	1			12
Line 2 Tailors			5	2		7
Line 3 Tailors				3	4	7
Button Machiners			2			2
Ironers					5	5
Cotton Boys					3	3
Totals	10	5	7	5	12	39

(b). Time 2, tau-b = 0.5656

Table 10. Occupational composition of blocks at
time 1 and time 2

The blocks emerge roughly in order of occupational prestige. Block A is composed at both times 1 and 2 largely of the prestigious line 1 tailors. Block B is more varied, containing a supervisor, line 1 and line 2 tailors and the two button machiners. Block C is largely composed of line 2 tailors, Block D of line 3 and Block E of line 3 the ironers and the cotton boys.

Time 1 Sociational

	A	B	C	D	E
A	1	?1	1	0	0
B	?1	0	0	0	?0
C	1	0	1	?	?0
D	0	0	?	1	0
E	0	?0	?0	0	1

Time 2 Sociational

	A	B	C	D	E
A	1	1	?1	0	0
B	1	1	?	?	0
C	?1	?	1	?	0
D	0	?	?	1	0
E	0	0	0	0	1

Time 1 Instrumental

	A	B	C	D	E
A	1	?	?	?0	?
B	?1	?0	?0	?0	?0
C	?	?0	?	?1	?
D	?0	?0	?0	1	?0
E	0	0	?0	?0	1

Time 2 Instrumental

	A	B	C	D	E
A	1	1	?1	?	?1
B	?1	?	?0	?0	?
C	?	?0	1	?0	?0
D	?0	?0	?0	?	0
E	0	0	?0	0	?1

Note: The interpretation of the symbols is as follows

$1.96 \leq z$		Symbol 1: Substantially blocked
$0.67 \leq z \leq 1.96$		Symbol ?1: Tending towards blocking
$-0.67 \leq z \leq 0.67$		Symbol ?: Indeterminate
$-1.96 \leq z < -0.67$		Symbol ?0: Tending towards zero block
$z < -1.96$		Symbol 0: Substantially zero blocked

Table 11. Block images for tailor shop material.
All matrices analysed simultaneously

Turning to Table 11 we see that the block image of sociational relationships at time 1 reflects reasonably well the position that Kapferer describes. The more prestigious members of Block A had more links than the average with themselves and with the slightly less prestigious members of Blocks B and C, but less than the average with the less prestigious D and E. Members of the latter two blocks had more than expected links only within their own blocks. Block C composed mainly of line 2 tailors had more links than the average with the prestigious Block A members, but none with the slightly more prestigious Block B. In fact the procedure seems to have separated out into Block B a set of actors who had very few definitive links with other actors.

Insofar as instrumental links at time 1 are concerned, the pattern of linkages is similar to that for sociational relationships at the same time except that there appears to be much less 'structure'. The only clear blocking seems to be the positive linkages within Block A at the top of the prestige ladder and within D and E at the bottom of the ladder. Significant also is the lack of instrumental ties of the lower prestige workers in Blocks D and E with the upper prestige workers in A and B.

At time 2 some interesting differences manifest themselves. Insofar as sociational links are concerned, there has been an increase of ties between members of Blocks A and B so that they form a solidly blocked upper segment of the matrix. The ties of Block C members with Block A seem to have weakened while the isolation from Block E has increased.

The concentration of links within blocks remains a strong characteristic of the pattern of sociational relationships at time 2.

At time 2 the sociational links of Blocks E members with those in other blocks seem to have increased marginally less than the average increase. The marginally zero links with Blocks B and C have now become more distinct. The main change seems to have been the expansion of links of the members of Block B to all blocks except the lowest in prestige.

The changes in instrumental relationships at time 2 as compared with time 1 reflect the process Kapferer has described. The line 1 tailors in Block A have increased their instrumental ties proportionately with members of Blocks C, D and E (especially with E). This was the process Kapferer described in which line 1 tailors build up obligations for support from the less powerful members of the work group by providing services of different kinds for them. The isolation of the members of Blocks D and E has been reduced by a marginal decrease in intra-block links.

The block image diagrams do not however reveal the size of the changes: they are not designed to do so. Table 12 is designed to reflect the size of changes in sociational and instrumental links between time 1 and time 2.

The procedure employed in Table 12 is the same as used earlier, i.e. the observed value at time 2 is compared with the value expected on the basis of the density in a block at time 1 and the overall change in all 25 block densities between time 1 and time 2.

Insofar as sociational relationships are concerned (Table 12a), the general pattern is that Blocks A and B seem on the whole to have increased their links with each other and internally more than the overall trend. Blocks D and E composed of lower prestige workers on the other hand, have decreased sociational links internally and with one another in com-

parison with the general trend. Block C seems to reflect changes characteristic of both of these opposites. Block C increased links internally with
itself (and with Block D) but like Block D, E loses links with Blocks A, D
and E.

	Blocks				
	A	B	C	D	E
A	0.0944	0.0654	-0.0145	-0.1698	-0.0973
B	0.0654	0.7139	0.0511	0.0539	-0.0839
C	-0.0145	0.0511	0.1680	-0.0481	-0.0867
D	-0.1698	0.0539	-0.0481	-0.0032	-0.1394
E	-0.0973	-0.0839	-0.0867	-0.1394	-0.0395

(a). Sociational relations, r = 0.5827

	Blocks				
	A	B	C	D	E
A	0.0705	0.1037	0.0416	0.0183	0.0474
B	0.0318	0.0728	0.0299	-0.0272	0.0607
C	-0.0013	0.0299	-0.0857	-0.0936	-0.0191
D	-0.0245	-0.0272	-0.0233	-0.0501	-0.0393
E	0.0105	0.0105	-0.0120	-0.0393	-0.0435

(b). Instrumental relations, r = 0.7999

Table 12. Changes in block densities in
sociational and instrumental relationships between
time 1 and time 2*

There seems to be no obvious characteristics of these particular
members of the tailor shop who were selected by the procedures
underlying CONCOR techniques to be classified as members of Block B
and Block C. 7 Nkoloya, 13 Hastings and 25 Meshak from Block B all
played significant roles in the events which led up to the February strike.
These links were not always 'positive' since we know that 7 Nkoloya was
very critical of 25 Meshak who had had authority thrust upon him by the
owner of the factory.

---

* Differences between values expected on the bases of linear trend and observed value.

In relation to Block C 19 Mukubwa played an important role in the events leading up to the strike. 24 Ibrahim also plays a substantive part but for the rest in the block they seem less obvious roles. I cannot as yet provide an explanation why these particular actors were classified as 'structurally equivalent' other than on the pattern of their linkages. Yet the evidence in the pattern of connections is clear enough—the members of Blocks B and C behave in a way which marks them off from the rest of the workers.

The evidence from the instrumental networks is in line with that from the sociational network, but is perhaps clearer. Both Blocks A and B increase the numbers of instrumental relationships they are involved in more than the average tailor shop worker. At the same time the members of Blocks C, D and E tend on the whole to expand their instrumental links less than the overall trend. This is of particular significance from the point of view of the interpretation Kapferer has put forward to explain the course of events in the tailor shop between times 1 and 2. The members of Blocks A and B are, as we have seen, the more prestigious and more powerful elements in the tailor shop. Members of Blocks C, D and E on the other hand are the less prestigious and less powerful. The members of A and B build up their expectations for support from the members of Blocks C, D and E, but the members of these blocks, on the whole, generate fewer support indebtednesses than the group does on the average. The increase of overall density of observed instrumental ties of members of Block A over that expected from the overall trend was 0.2815, the increase for members of Block B was 0.1680, the decrease of observed overall density from that expected on the basis of general trends for Blocks C, D and E were –0.1698, –0.1644 and –0.1248 respectively. In other words the closer these low prestige groups are in prestige terms to the top prestige groups, the more likely they are to fall short of the expected increase of instrumental links between times 1 and 2.

11. Conclusions

The general conclusion of this analysis must be that the reanalysis of Kapferer's material by and large has supported the analysis he originally put forward. With the development of computers and more sophisticated ways of analysing network data it has been possible to test his analyses in several different ways.

Kapferer's analysis was based on exchange theory and as would be consonant with an approach of that sort he made extensive use of such ego-centered network characteristics of the members of the tailor shop as star size, span and zone density. A reanalysis of the material along these lines but organised as to reflect the changes in star size, point centrality betweeness and span (which Kapferer did not use) between time 1 and time 2 in general supported Kapferer's findings. This is hardly surprising since much of Kapferer's interpretation in the first instance was based on his analysis of commensurate measurements.

Kapferer's exploration of the structural or morphological characteristics of the tailor shop networks was based on the matrix arrangement arrived at using Beum and Brundage procedures. On the basis of this Kapferer establishes three general clusters (and a small non-clustered residue) at both time periods. The basis upon which Kapferer established the cutting points between clusters is by no means clear: it seems essentially to have been a matter of personal judgment. The classification of clusters using Hubbell procedures which seemed to be appropriate for the sort of problem Kapferer was concerned with, revealed slightly different clusters from those that Kapferer had isolated. These clusters were arrived at by aggregating elements hierarchically into larger and larger and hence looser and looser clusters. The particular level of clustering selected for analysis also involved an arbitrary component for there could be no hard and fast rule to determine the most 'effective' clustering for purposes of analysis.

The coincidence of the clustering derived from Hubbell procedures and those Kapferer derived using Beum and Brundage procedures is not very great, the estimate of proportional reduction of error predicting Hubbell clusters given Kapferer's clusters being

> 0.4862 for sociational time 1,
>
> 0.2995 for instrumental time 1,
>
> 0.2562 for sociational time 2,
>
> 0.2383 for instrumental time 2.

Nevertheless, given that the boundaries of the clusters that Kapferer determined were not decided partly on occupational status—and we do not know why Kapferer chose those particular cutting points—the occupational composition accords better with his three broad clusters than it does with Hubbell clusters (tau-b's of 0.6262 at time 1 and 0.6877 at time 2 as against values ranging from 0.5433 to 0.4161 for Hubbell clusters).

The Hubbell clusters are of course of finer grain—there are five of them as against Kapferer's four at time 1 or three at time 2.

The conclusion must be that the alternative clustering procedure, apart from providing a sounder basis for choosing the clusters, does not seem to have added much to the analysis.

Structural equivalence procedures, of course, have come into being since Kapferer published his book and have only recently become widely available as computer programs. But the basic argument underlying these procedures when interpreted in terms appropriate for the type of analysis Kapferer was conducting proves to be promising.

The blocks derived from applying CONCOR procedures aligned better with occupational categories than Hubbell clusters (with tau-b's of 0.5944 and 0.5656) but not as well as Kapferer's original clusters. But the block images and block densities, premised as they are in isolating 'zero' blocks as well as dense blocks, raise questions about the structure of relationships in the tailor shop which the other forms of analysis had not. In particular the dramatic change in links of Block B (see Tables 8, 9, 11 and 12) between time 1 and time 2 calls for some explanation. At the same time the continued isolation of the members of Blocks D and E composed of lower prestige workers seems to be a factor which Kapferer may have underplayed in his analysis.

Further testing of the efficacy of the procedures used to reveal the patterns in the data will turn on a more intensive examination of the finer details of the analysis against the ethnographic facts.

REFERENCES

Abell, P.
  1969   Measurement in sociology: measurement structure and
           sociological theory. Sociology, 3:397-411.
Alba, R. D.
  1973   A graph-theoretic definition of a sociometric clique. Journal
           of Mathematical Sociology, 13:113-126.
Alba, R. and Moore, G.
  1978   Elite social circles. Sociological Methods and Research,
           7:167-188.
Arabie, Phipps, Boorman, S. A., and Levitt, P. R.
  1978   Constructing blockmodels: how and why. Journal of
           Mathematical Psychology, 17:21-63.
Beum, C. O. and Brundage, E. G.
  1950   A method for analysing the sociomatrix. Sociometry,
           13:141-145.
Boorman, S. A. and White, H. C.
  1976   Social structure from social networks II: role structures.
           American Journal of Sociology, 81:1384-1446.
Boyd, J. P.
  1979/80 The universal semigroup of relations. Social Networks,
           2:91-117.
Carrington, P. J., Heil, G. H., and Berkowitz, S. D.
  1979/80 A goodness-of-fit index for blockmodels. Social Networks,
           2:219-234.
Davis, J. A.
  1967   Clustering and structural balance in graphs. Human Relations,
           20:181-187.
Doreian, P.
  1980   On the delineation of small group structure. In Hudson, H. C.,
           ed. Classifying Social Data. San Francisco: Jossey-Bass.
Doreian, P.
  1981   Polyhedral dynamics and conflict mobilization in social
           networks. Social Networks, 3:107-116.
Everett, M. and Niemenin, J.
  1980   Partitions and homomorphisms in directed and undirected
           graphs. Journal of Mathematical Sociology, 7:91-111.
Freeman, L. C.
  1977   A set of measures of centrality based on betweenness.
           Sociometry, 40:35-41.

Freeman, L. C.
  1980   Q-analysis and the structure of friendship networks.
           International Journal of Man-Machine Studies, 12.
Gould, P. and Gatrell, A.
  1980   The Liverpool-Manchester cup final: a structural analysis of a
           game. Social Networks, 2:253-273.
Holland, P. W. and Leinhardt, S.
  1970   A method for detecting structure in sociometric data.
           American Journal of Sociology, 26: 492-513.
Hubbell, C. H.
  1965   An input-output approach to clique identification. Sociometry,
           28:377-399.
Kapferer, B.
  1972   Strategy and Transaction in an African Factory: African
           Workers and Indian Management in a Zambian Town.
           Manchester: Manchester University Press.
Lankford, P. M.
  1974   Comparative analysis of clique identification methods.
           Sociometry, 378:2 287-305.
Laumann, E. O.
  1973   The bonds of pluralism: the form and substance of urban
           social networks. London: John Wiley and Sons.
Light, J. M. and Mullins, N. G.
  1979   A primer on blockmodeling procedure. *In* Holland, P. W.
           and Leinhardt, S., eds. Perspectives on Social Networks
           Research. New York: Academic Press (85-118).
Lorrain, F., and White, H. C.
  1971   Structural equivalence of individuals in social networks.
           Journal of Math. Sociology, 1:49-80.
MacRae, D. J.
  1960   Direct factor analysis of sociometric data. Sociometry,
           23:360-371.
Moore, G.
  1979   The Structure of a National Elite Network. American
           Sociological Review, 44:673-691.
Peay, E. R.
  1974   Hierarchical clique structures. Sociometry, 37(1):54-65.
Sailer, L. D.
  1978   Structural equivalence: meaning and definition, computation
           and application. Social Networks, 1:73-90.
Seidman, S. B. and Foster, B. L.
  1978   A graph-theoretic generalization of the clique concept.
           Journal of Math. Sociology, 6:139-154.

White, H. C., Boorman, S. A., and Breiger, R. L.
1976   Social structure from multiple networks I—Blockmodels of roles and positions. American Journal of Sociology, 81:730-780.

CHAPTER 11

CONCEPTIONS OF OVERLAP IN SOCIAL STRUCTURE*

Phipps Arabie
J. Douglas Carroll

1. Introduction

In an early paper, Arabie (1977) made a distinction between explicit and implicit overlap in sociological data. The former approach can be further subdivided into research (a) that welcomes (and even seeks out) overlap versus (b) that which seeks to eliminate or diminish its presence. Perhaps the best known example of the "welcome" attitude toward overlap is in the study of corporate interlock (e.g., Levine, 1972; Subcommittee on Reports, Accounting and Management of the Committee on Government Affairs, United States Senate, 1978), where it is the actors who overlap on the boards of different corporations who are the focus of the data analyses. This substantive problem is subsumed in the more general framework for

* For helpful discussions of this work, we are indebted to S. A. Boorman, L. J. Hubert, R. N. Shepard, and A. Tellegen. We are also grateful to Dan C. Knutson and Tom Sharpe for assistance. This research was supported in part by LEAA Grant 78-NI-AX-0142 and NSF Grant SES 80 04815.

studying formal patterns of overlap in interorganizational networks of shared resources (Galaskiewicz and Marsden, 1978; Laumann, Galaskiewicz, and Marsden, 1978; Galaskiewicz and Wasserman, 1981; Knoke and Wood, 1981). Concern for overlap has also emerged sporadically in discussions of such other social processes as diffusion (Dodd and Winthrop, 1953, p. 191).

Perhaps the earliest example of the tradition to minimize the consequences of overlap where explicitly present is given by Winer (1955). His objective was to devise a measure of the relatedness of overlapping social or organizational groups, such that the measure would be relatively insensitive to the magnitude of the marginals in the 2×2 tables that can be constructed in the conventional manner for each pair of (potentially) overlapping groups. Since Winer's (1955) measure can be interpreted as a product-moment correlation coefficient between all pairs of social groups, a matrix of such coefficients, computed on all pairs of groups, is suitable as input to factor analysis and related techniques of data reduction. In such a factor analytic representation, "... the orthogonal reference vectors, or factors, represent the location of *ideal, non-overlapping* groups ..." (Winer, 1955, p. 67, italics added). Thus, the overlap that was explicit in the raw data is extirpated in the final representation. Much the same research problem was investigated by Bonacich (1972), apparently unaware of Winer's earlier work. Bonacich provided a brute-force approach to deriving a measure of overlap and obtained results not as elegant as those of Winer (1955).

2. *Implicit Overlap*

Reviews of the applications of various methods of overlapping clustering to data from the behavioral sciences have been given in Arabie (1977) and Shepard and Arabie (1979). With respect to sociometry, two approaches merit attention. The B_k method of overlapping clustering devised by Jardine and Sibson (1968) represents a generalization of single-link (hierarchical) clustering, so as to allow a maximum of $k - 1$ actors to overlap for any pair of clusters. Subsequent improvements in implementation of this method (Cole and Wishart, 1970; Rohlf, 1975) over the cumbersome algorithm given by Jardine and Sibson (1968) have still not fostered any subsequent published use of B_k in sociometry. (An unpublished paper by Elliott and Hallinan [1975] offered no substantive interpretation of the B_k solution those authors obtained.)

2.1 Maximal Complete Subgraphs. The alternatives to the B_k approach to overlapping clustering have generally been based upon the graph-theoretic concept of the maximal complete subgraph. We begin with a set A of N actors and an $N \times N$ sociomatrix S whose entries s_{ij} code some measure of relatedness (e.g., connectivity, or any of the traditional types of sociometric ties such as like, dislike, etc.). Such a matrix is typically binary or integer-valued (e.g., when respondents are asked to list their c best friends, those resulting entries may be coded as $c, c - 1$, etc.). Unfortunately, S is often nonsymmetric; that is, for one or more entries, $s_{ij} \neq s_{ji}$ for $i \neq j$. The concept of a maximal complete subgraph (defined below) assumes the link from actor i to distinct actor j is of the same strength as the link from j to i (symmetry). Thus, if we are to derive graph-theoretic representations of structure (such as maximal complete subgraphs) from the information in S, we often must first transform S to be a symmetric $N \times N$ matrix, T. One class of strategies calls for considering the *rows* of choices or ties the actors i and j send, s_i and s_j, as vectors (where $s_i = \{s_{iv}, v = 1, ..., N\}$ and similarly for s_j) and then computing a symmetric measure of relatedness between these two vectors. Alternatively, we could (with more substantive justification; see Arabie and Boorman, 1982) compute the measure between the *column* vectors s_p and s_r of choices received where

$$s_p = \{s_{vp}, v = 1, ..., N\}$$

and similarly for s_r), or over *both* choices sent and received. (Further details are given in Arabie and Boorman, 1982.) The measure of "profile similarity" computed between the vectors for each distinct pair of actors i and j (or p and r) could be Pearson correlations (suggested by Katz, 1947; also used in blockmodeling: Breiger, Boorman, and Arabie, 1975; Arabie, Boorman, and Levitt, 1978), Euclidean distance squared (Carroll, 1968) or other measures (Cronbach and Gleser, 1953). Alternatively, one can make the arguable assumption (cf. Laumann and Pappi, 1976, p. 137) that overt sociometric ties should be reciprocated, *viz.*, that $t_{ij} = t_{ji} = \max(s_{ij}, s_{ji})$, $i \neq j$, for binary data; or more generally that $t_{ij} = t_{ji} = f(s_{ij}, s_{ji})$, $i \neq j$, where f could be any statistic of central tendency. Without loss of generality, assume T is a measure of "similarity" between actors i and j. (If this assumption is false, transform T to be $t'_{ij} = K - t_{ij}$, thus "flipping around" the values T, where K is a large constant $\geq \max_{i \neq j} (t_{ij})$.) Given T, we can view it as inducing a graph G, having N nodes (actors) and $M = \dfrac{N(N-1)}{2}$

edges, connecting all pairs of nodes i, j, whose weights or strengths are defined by the values of t_{ij}. (Self-loops are not permitted in the graph, so that values of t_{ii} are irrelevant.) A subgraph G' ($G' \subseteq G$) having as nodes the set of n_u actors A' ($A' \subseteq A$) is a complete subgraph of G if for all distinct actors in A', $t_{ij} \geq \gamma$, where $i,j \, \varepsilon \, A'$.

That is, all the $\dfrac{n_u(n_u - 1)}{2}$ edges or links in the subgraph G' have a strength greater than or equal to a threshold γ. (Some authors also require $n_u > 2$.) The subgraph of G' is maximal if the addition of any of the remaining $(N - n_u)$ actors from the set $\{A - A'\}$ would incorporate a new edge in the augmented G' such that $t_{ix} < \gamma$, where $i \, \varepsilon \, A'$ and $x \, \varepsilon \, \{A - A'\}$. That is, the incorporation of new members in G' would no longer leave all edges with a strength $t_{ix} \geq \gamma$. (Note that the preceding definition relies only on ordinal properties of **T**—which may or may not be ordinally related to **S**.) Thus, for a given value of γ, the "coherence" of G' (as measured by the weakest or least-valued edge) is at least as great as threshold γ.

In spite of the problems posed by the lack of symmetry in most sociometric data, the concept of a maximal complete subgraph has long held substantive appeal as a model of "cliques" in social structure (e.g., see reviews by Hubert, 1974; Burt, 1980), even though the mandate "Let there be Cliques" has generally not given rise to any underlying model against which goodness-of-fit can be gauged. Moreover, in the graph-theoretic literature, maximal complete subgraphs are often referred to as "cliques," and as the advent of "catastrophe theory" has shown, the very name given to a mathematical concept or theory can heavily influence the substantive reception accorded the concept.

In spite of Doreian's view that "... the concept of the clique [maximal complete subgraph] is of limited theoretical value ..." (1974, p. 246), an energetic tradition of seeking maximal complete subgraphs as bases of social structure continues: Harary and Ross (1957), Doreian (1969), Alba (1973), Peay (1970a, 1970b, 1974, 1975), Alt and Schofield (1975, 1978), Seidman and Foster (1978), Alba and Moore (1978); still other references are given in reviews by Arabie (1977) and by Burt (1980, pp. 97-100).

In recent years, such publications have generally devoted at least as much attention to having the most efficient algorithm for finding maximal complete subgraphs as to obtaining a plausible interpretation of the representation (e.g., Alba, 1974; Alba and Moore, 1978). Since the problem of extracting all maximal complete subgraphs implied by a matrix has recently been shown to be NP-complete (see Karp, 1972, 1976; Weide, 1977; Hansen and Delattre, 1978), it is likely that the computer science literature will continue to provide new algorithms and thus the potential for new disputes as to which is the best algorithm for finding maximal complete subgraphs for sociometric data.

In contrast, relatively little attention has been paid to the fact that such data analyses generaly yield far too many maximal complete subgraphs to be interpreted as "cliques" or any other type of social unit. For example, Alba and Moore, who are much more forthright about this drawback than are many other researchers, note that for the 941 actors in those authors' analysis, there were 442 maximal complete subgraphs, based on a "low density" binary matrix. Alba and Moore (1978) then used some *ad hoc* rules to merge subsets or clusters of actors (corresponding to the nodes of the subgraphs) so that there were 46 aggregated subgraphs left to interpret. It is of interest to note that in surveys of algorithms for grouping machine components in production research, King and Nakornchai (1982, p. 118) faulted clique-based techniques because of the excessive number of such structures resulting from high density matrices.

Moon and Moser (1965) provided some ominous results concerning how many maximal complete subgraphs one can find in a (binary) matrix. For N actors, the upper bound, $B(N)$ is given by:

$$\text{If } N \geq 2, \text{ then } B(N) = \begin{cases} 3^{\frac{N}{3}}, & \text{if } N \equiv 0 \pmod 3; \\ 4 \times 3^{\left[\frac{N}{3}\right]-1}, & \text{if } N \equiv 1 \pmod 3; \\ 2 \times 3^{\left[\frac{N}{3}\right]}, & \text{if } N \equiv 2 \pmod 3, \end{cases} \quad (1)$$

(where [X] denotes the largest integer $\leq$ X). For instance, when $N = 30$, $B(N) = 59{,}049$, which would hardly provide a parsimonious representation of social structure for 30 actors. (Note that the lower bound will be 1, corresponding to a matrix **T** of all unities, in which case all N actors are lumped together in the same maximal complete subgraph.) Of course, not all sociometric data are binary; Doreian (1969) referred to the graphs from such integer-valued sociomatrices as "valued graphs." In the case of such data, the threshold in equation (1) would generally assume in decreasing sequence (for similarities data) each distinct value of the entries in **T**. Thus, the estimate in equation (2) must be multiplied by the number of distinct nonzero values in a non-binary matrix **T**, thus increasing the already potentially overwhelming number of maximal complete subgraphs.

3. A Model for Overlapping Clustering

Shepard and Arabie (1979; also see earlier presentations by the same authors, cited in the 1979 paper) and Arabie (1977) presented a model, ADCLUS (for ADditive CLUStering), of nonhierarchical overlapping clustering that has been applied to sociometric data (Breiger *et al.*, 1975; Arabie, 1977; Shepard and Arabie, 1979). That model states that

$$\hat{s}_{ij} = \sum_{k=1}^{m} w_k p_{ik} p_{jk} \,, \tag{2}$$

where $\hat{s}_{ij}$ is the theoretically reconstructed similarity (or relatedness) between actors i and j, where w_k is a nonnegative weight representing the psychological salience of subset k, and where

$$p_{ik} = \begin{cases} 1, & \text{if actor } i \text{ is in subset } k, \\ 0, & \text{otherwise.} \end{cases}$$

Equation 2 can be reformulated in matrix notation as

$$\hat{\mathbf{S}} = \mathbf{PWP'}, \tag{3}$$

where $\hat{\mathbf{S}}$ is an $N \times N$ symmetric matrix of reconstructed similarities $\hat{s}_{ij}$, **W** is an $m \times m$ diagonal matrix with nonnegative weights $w_k(k = 1, ..., m)$ in the principal diagonal (and zeros elsewhere), and **P** is the $N \times m$ rectangular matrix of binary values p_{ik}. Here **P'** is the $m \times N$ matrix transpose of the matrix **P**.

For sociometric data that are not symmetric, $\hat{\mathbf{S}}$ in equation (3) should, strictly speaking, be $\hat{\mathbf{T}}$, the symmetrized input data matrix, to be consistent with notation used earlier in this chapter. However, the distinction seems sufficiently apparent that confusion should not result from using **S** to denote the sociometric input data.)

As a measure of goodness-of-fit, there is the variance accounted for

$$\text{VAF} = 1.0 - \frac{\displaystyle\sum_{i}^{N} \sum_{j<i}^{N-1}(s_{ij} - \hat{s}_{ij})^2}{\displaystyle\sum_{i}^{N} \sum_{j<i}^{N-1}(s_{ij} - \bar{s})^2} \qquad (4)$$

The first algorithm, devised by Shepard and Arabie, for fitting the ADCLUS model was outlined in Arabie (1977) as well as in other papers cited in Shepard and Arabie (1979). The algorithm, tersely summarized, began with sorting the entries s_{ij} in order of decreasing similarity. Then, the largest of the s_{ij} served as the threshold γ, and all maximal complete subgraphs were extracted for that threshold. That is, although not implied by equation (3), only maximal complete subgraphs were deemed admissible clusters. Then γ was set equal to the next largest s_{ij}, etc., until all maximal complete subgraphs, implied by all the distinct entries of **S** as thresholds, had been extracted. Each such maximal complete subgraph was coded as a column in the binary matrix **P** in equation (3), with the unities in the columns defining the constituent actors of the corresponding maximal complete subgraph. In the second stage of the algorithm, a modified gradient procedure was used simultaneously (a) to estimate the positive weights for the diagonal matrix **W** (one such weight for each subset or cluster), and (b) to reduce the number of clusters (*viz.*, maximal complete subgraphs) to a manageable size while still approximately maximizing variance accounted for.

Although this algorithm sometimes succeeded in finding acceptable solutions (for examples, see Shepard and Arabie, 1979), it proved not to be generally usable. The difficulty was simply that the first stage was running headlong into the result of Moon and Moser (1965): there were too many maximal complete subgraphs. The data analyst had no direct control over the number of resulting clusters in the final solution, and simply hoped that sufficient compression would occur in the second stage of the algorithm.

(Note that the measure of goodness-of-fit, the variance accounted for expressed in equation (4), gives no explicit indication of the "appropriate" number of clusters.)

Fortunately, a completely different approach (Arabie and Carroll, 1980a, 1980b) has provided a generally usable algorithm for fitting the Shepard-Arabie ADCLUS model. This algorithm, which simultaneously fits the **P** and **W** matrices in (4), is called MAPCLUS (for MAthematical Programming CLUStering) and has been described at length in Arabie and Carroll (1980a), to which the reader is referred for computational details. With respect to the focus of this chapter, two features of MAPCLUS should be noted: (a) the user of the program explicitly declares the number of subsets for the (final) solution at the beginning of the analysis, and (b) the subsets are not required to correspond to maximal complete subgraphs (even though the clusters often do). We now turn to illustrative applications of MAPCLUS.

4. MAPCLUS Analysis

4.1. The Bank Wiring Group of Roethlisberger and Dickson (1939). These data were collected by an observer who recorded the social interactions among fourteen industrial workers in the Western Electric Company's Hawthorne Works in Chicago between March 1931 and May 1932, as part of the famous Hawthorne study of industrial productivity (Roethlisberger and Dickson, 1939). The data have been used extensively in blockmodeling (Breiger *et al.*, 1975; Boorman and White, 1976; White, Boorman, and Breiger, 1976; Noma and Smith, 1985; Wasserman and Anderson, 1987), which yields, among other things, a partition of the group of workers. Since extensive descriptions of these workers and their data have been given in Roethlisberger and Dickson (1939) and in Homans' (1950) review, as well as in the papers just cited, only a sketch is provided here.

The fourteen workers, classified as inspectors (I1, I3), wiremen (W1, W2, ..., W9) and soldermen (S1, S2, S4), were constructing banks of telephone switching apparatus in a specially designed room where an observer external to the group recorded instances of "liking," "playing games together," "antagonism," "helping on the job," and "disagreements over opening windows." For each of these five types of sociometric ties, a 14×14 sociomatrix was constructed. These matrices were in turn "stacked" to form a 70×14 matrix, and product-moment correlations were computed between all pairs of columns. The resulting 14×14 correlation matrix thus becomes S for the ADCLUS model of equation (3).

Before discussing the MAPCLUS solution for these data, we note that Roethlisberger and Dickson (1939) chronicled their perceptions of the social structure of these fourteen workers, largely on the basis of the ties of "helping on the job" and "playing games together." Two non-antagonistic groups A and B emerged, along with three social isolates. Table 1 summarizes the information provided by Roethlisberger and Dickson (1939). Although those authors labeled Groups A and B as "cliques," the term was clearly not intended to denote maximal complete subgraphs.

Earlier efforts to fit the ADCLUS model to these data, using the Shepard-Arabie algorithm that began with extracting all maximal complete subgraphs, obtained 91.2% variance accounted for with nineteen subsets (Breiger *et al.*, 1975), and 89.0% with ten subsets (Shepard and Arabie, 1979). The present MAPCLUS solution given in Table 2 uses six clusters to obtain a variance accounted for of 78.8%. (For similar analyses of the same data and conducted after the present description was written, see Mirkin, 1987, pp. 26-29.)

In Figure 1, the same solution is embedded in a two-dimensional nonmetric multidimensional scaling solution (Shepard, 1962a, 1962b; Kruskal, 1964a, 1964b) taken from Breiger *et al.* (1975) with the six clusters of workers enclosed by contours. In this figure, subscripts of A, B, and I denote, respectively, Group A, Group B, and Isolates, as given by Roethlisberger and Dickson (1939) in the present Table 1. A circle around the A for W2 and around the B for W6 indicates marginal membership within the corresponding group.

Considering the clusters in Table 1, which are rank-ordered by the magnitude of their associated weights, Cluster 1 consists of Roethlisberger and Dickson's Group B. Cluster 2 comprises the five solidly established members of Group A in Table 1. The third cluster consists of two Isolates (W5 and I3) and the marginal member of Group A (W2) not included in the preceding cluster. Cluster 4 joins two of the Isolates to three members of Group A, including the leader of that group, W3. In Cluster 5, another Isolate, S2, joins some members of Group A and B that are proximal in the scaling solution of Figure 2. Cluster 6, having the lowest weight, includes all the Isolates, the marginal members of Groups A and B (W2 and W6, respectively), and a member of Group A (W4) noted for his hostility to the

Actor's Identification	Roethlisberger and Dickson's Group assignment	Salient aspect of actor
W1	A	close friend of W3 (p. 460)
W3	A	most well-liked of group; leader (pp. 464-465)
W4	A	antagonistic to wiremen in Group B (p. 465)
S1	A	generally well-liked (p. 480)
I1	A	socially adroit, popular (pp. 484-486)
W2	-[a]	unsociable "rate-buster" (p. 463)
W7	B	slow worker
W8	B	slow worker
W9	B	slow worker
S4	B	socially regarded as inferior (p. 483)
W6	-[b]	unsuccessful aspirant to leadership and popularity (p. 471)
W5	isolate[c]	"without doubt the most disliked wireman in the group" (p. 468)
S2	isolate[c]	socially impeded by a speech difficulty (p. 482)
I3	isolate[c]	extremely unpopular and eventually had to be transferred from the room (p. 487)

Note: Page numbers refer to Roethlisberger and Dickson (1939).

[a] Actor W2 was affiliated with Group A, but was not a stable member of it (p. 510).

b "That he (W6) was not entirely accepted in clique [Group] B was shown in many ways, chief of which was the way in which clique [Group] B co-operated in resisting his attempts to dominate anyone in their group. Yet he participated in clique [Group] B much more than W2 did in Group A. It may be concluded that although W6 tended to participate in clique [Group] B, he was still in many ways an outsider" (p. 509).

c Three individuals, I3, W5, and S2, were clearly outside either Group A or B (p. 510).

Table 1. Social Categorization in the Bank
Wiring Observation Room of Roethlisberger and
Dickson (1939)

wiremen in Group B. Since two of the types of sociometric ties on which the data were based are representative of strife ("antagonism" and "fights over opening windows"), this cluster is perhaps not too surprising. However, when one looks at social structure expecting only to find nonoverlapping groups based largely on positive affect internal to the group (as in Table 1, extracted from Roethlisberger and Dickson, 1939), that bias will exclude patterns of overlap, as shown in Cluster 6, in spite of their plausibility.

Subset	Weight	Workers in the Subset
(1)	.523	W6 (B), W7 B, W8 B, W9 B, S4 B
(2)	.460	W1 A, W3 A, S1 A, W4 A, I1 A
(3)	.318	W2 (A), W5 I, I3 I
(4)	.238	W1 A, W2 (A), W3 A, W5 I, I1 A
(5)	.204	S1 A, W4 A, S2 I, W7 B, W8 B, W9 B
(6)	.158	W2 (A), S1 A, W4 A, W5 I, W6 (B), S2 I, I3 I

Note: A, B, and I denote membership, respectively, in Group A, Group B, or Isolates, according to Roethlisberger and Dickson (1939); see Table 1. Interpretations of the clusters are given in the text. With these six clusters and an additive constant of .20, the variance accounted for was 78.8%.

Table 2. MAPCLUS Solution for Bank Wiring
Room Data of Roethlisberger and Dickson (1939)

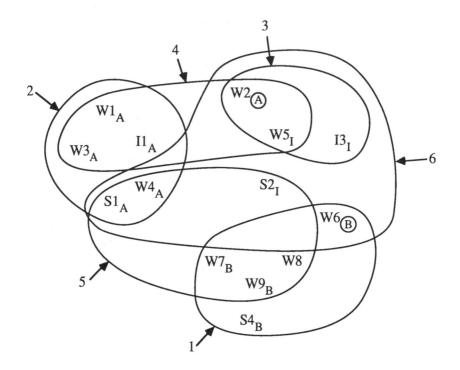

Figure 1. MAPCLUS representation for the data
from Roethlisberger and Dickson's (1939) bank
wiring observation room (superimposed on a two-
dimensional nonmetric scaling solution). 78.8%
variance accounted for by 6 subsets. Numbers
with arrows indicate the rank of the clusters
according to their numerical weights. Subscripts
attached to the workers' labels denote assignment
by Roethlisberger and Dickson to Groups A, B,
or Isolates. A circle around the subscript
indicates marginal status in that group.

(The additive constant in Table 1 corresponds to the "weight" for an
implicit additional cluster comprising the complete set of actors. This
constant is required for the measure of goodness-of-fit in equation (4) to be
a measure of variance accounted for. If the constant of .203 had been

added to each s_{ij} prior to the analysis, then the weight for this implicit cluster would have been 0.0.)

Arabie and Carroll (1980, pp. 226-227) noted the existence of nonunique (approximately) best solutions, having similar values of goodness-of-fit, and suggested the problem was pervasive for discrete models (cf. a parallel argument by Rotondo and Pankey, 1981, for the latent class model of Lazarsfeld, 1950). For the data on these fourteen workers, such a competing solution, having six clusters and accounting for 80.3% of the variance, was found. This alternative solution differed from that in Table 1 insofar as Cluster 3 consisted of W1, W2, and W3, and Cluster 4 consisted of W2, W5, I1 and I3. The remaining four clusters were common to both solutions, and the respective weights shifted only slightly (and maintained the same rank order) across the two solutions. (Still other six-cluster solutions, having very similar goodness-of-fit but far less interpretability, were also found using different initial configurations; see Arabie and Carroll, 1980b, as well as Mirkin, 1987.) We suggest that as discrete models and combinatorial data analysis become more widely used, then this problem of nonuniqueness will receive increasing attention.

Returning to an earlier theme of this chapter, there is the question of how many clusters to allow in a MAPCLUS solution. We noted above that the decision is made by the investigator at the start of the analysis. As in the traditional strategy in selecting the dimensionality for a factor analytic or multidimensional scaling representation, one typically decides upon a range of the acceptable number of clusters, and obtains a solution for different values within that range. Then, from these solutions, varying according to goodness-of-fit and interpretability, one seeks the solution having the best tradeoff between these two typically conflicting considerations. As in factor analysis and multidimensional scaling, much of the decision is based on subjective criteria. In the analyses of the Roethlisberger and Dickson (1939) data, the following solutions may give some idea of the tradeoff between number of clusters and goodness-of-fit: (8, 91.1%), (7, 83.1%), (6, 80.3% and 78.8%, as shown in Table 2 and Figure 1), (5, 75.6%) and (4, 65.8%). Cluster 1 from Table 2 is common to all these solutions; Cluster 2 appears in all but the eight-cluster solution; and Cluster 3 appears in most of them, but subsets with lesser weights tend to vary across the different solutions. The representation of the Roethlisberger and Dickson (1939) data given in Table 2 and Figure 1 seemed to us to offer the best tradeoff between interpretabilty and goodness-of-fit.

4.2. Sampson's (1968) Monastery. Frank Sampson's (1968) dissertation portrays in detail the social structure of a geographically isolated monastery in the Northeast during the mid-1960's. During this period, the monastery was attempting to adjust to the ecumenicism of Vatican II, and the strife between the traditional versus contemporary approaches to Catholic religious services emerged regularly within the monastery. The raw sociometric data used in this analysis were based on the novices' recall for a period prior to the effective breakup of the monastery. These raw data for eighteen members of the monastery during the fourth time period (T4) of Sampson's study are given in White *et al.* (1976, p. 705), and the 18×18 correlation matrix, S, used for the present analysis is given in Breiger *et al.* (1975, p. 351); also see Fienberg, Meyer, and Wasserman (1985).

Our description of the eighteen actors comes from Sampson (1968), who labeled the novices who had arrived in an earlier cohort as the "Loyal Opposition," generally opposed by the newer arrivals, the "Young Turks." In addition, there were three "Outcasts," whose sympathies lay with the Young Turks (Sampson, 1968, p. 372). There is some ambiguity in this classification since Novice 13 seemed to float between membership in the Loyal Opposition and the Outcasts. In addition, a differentiation of "Leaders" and "Followers" within the Young Turks and within the Loyal Opposition is made by Sampson. For two of the novices, this classification is subject to sufficient variability that we have designated Novice 12 as a Leader of the Young Turks and 8 as a Leader of the Loyal Opposition, following the blockmodel analyses cited earlier, rather than Sampson's (1968) prose description.

Table 3 lists an eight-cluster MAPCLUS solution, in which the ADCLUS model accounts for 62.4% of the variance. In Figure 2, these subsets are represented as closed contours embedded in a nonmetric multidimensional scaling solution taken from Breiger *et al.* (1975). Clusters 1, 2, and 5 comprise, respectively, the Loyal Opposition, the Outcasts (including Novice 13), and the Young Turks (not including 13). Nested within Cluster 1 of the Loyal Opposition are two overlapping dyads, Clusters 3 and 4, having the foremost leader of the Loyal Opposition (Novice 4) as their intersection. Note that this type of detail, partial overlap within a more inclusive structure, is precisely the type of social structure that a partition or hierarchical clustering *cannot* represent.

The sixth most heavily weighted cluster links Novices 1 and 2, the foremost leaders of the Young Turks (Sampson, 1968, p. 354) and one of their followers (14) with the three novices designated unambiguously as Outcasts by Sampson. Cluster 6 may underlie the observation cited above concerning the Outcasts' sympathies lying with the Young Turks.

Subset	Weight	Workers in the Subset
(1)	.298	4 LOL, 6 LOL, 8 LOL, 5 LOF, 9 LOF, 10 LOF, 11 LOL
(2)	.272	3 O, 17 O, 18 O, 13 LOF;O
(3)	.271	4 LOL, 11 LOL
(4)	.261	4 LOL, 9 LOL
(5)	.256	1 YTL, 2 YTL, 7 YTF, 12 YTL, 14 YTF, 15 YTF, 16 YTF
(6)	.146	1 YTL, 2 YTL, 14 YTF, 3 O, 17 O, 18 O
(7)	.134	5 LOF, 10 LOF, 13 LOF;O, 17 O, 18 O, 16 YTF
(8)	.114	2 YTL, 12 YTL, 15 YTF, 6 LOL, 8 LOL

Note: Abbreviations used above: LO - member of Loyal Opposition; YT - member of Young Turks; O - Outcast. Suffix of L denotes Leader; F denotes Follower. Novice 13 was variously regarded as a Follower in the Loyal Opposition and as an Outcast. With these eight clusters and an additive constant of .338, the variance accounted for was 62.4%.

Table 3. MAPCLUS Solution for Data from
Period T4 of Sampson's (1968) Monastery

As mentioned earlier, one of the intriguing aspects of Sampson's data is that they portray a strife-ridden social structure just prior to dissolving. Specifically, Outcasts 3, 17, and 18 were asked to leave the monastery, as was the leader of the Young Turks (2) for being "Not in conformity with the spirit of the Order" (Sampson, 1968, p. 373). In the ensuing weeks, the remaining Outcast (13), all but one of the Young Turks (12), but only two (8,10) of the Loyal Opposition left, all voluntarily. Now a partition-based model of the social structure would suggest that *all* the Young Turks should have left and *all* the Loyal Opposition should have remained. However, the pattern of overlap present in Table 3 and Figure 2 suggests which members of these two groups are likely to deviate from their affiliations' norms. Concretely, note that the two least heavily weighted Clusters, 7 and 8, are the ones portraying overlap between the opposing factions. Loyal

Opposition members 6 and 8 are in bi-partisan Cluster 8, and 5 and 10 are in bi-partisan Cluster 7. Recall that Novices 8 and 10 are the only members of the Loyal Opposition to exit in the style becoming a Young Turk. Similarly, of the four Young Turks included in the two bi-partisan clusters, Novice 12 was the only such Young Turk who stayed on with the Loyal Opposition at the monastery. Thus, the pattern of overlap between the two conflicting groups does give some suggestion of wavering and disloyalty in this struggle between the two antagonistic factions.

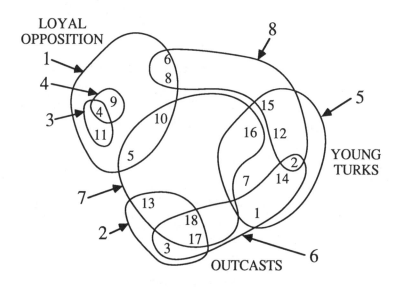

Figure 2. MAPCLUS solution for Sampson's (1968) monastery data (superimposed on a two-dimensional nonmetric scaling solution). 62.4% variance accounted for by 8 subsets. Numbers with arrows indicate the rank of the clusters according to their numerical weights.

Although we believe that the preceding interpretation of the MAPCLUS solution is reasonable, we expect some readers may be uneasy concerning the 62.4% variance accounted for. First, as mentioned earlier, these data were based on respondents' recall after the exodus of most of the novices, and are thus subject to the distortions of memory and accelerated antagonism. Second, we note that, as in the case of the widely used

INDSCAL model for individual differences scaling (Carroll and Chang, 1970), as well as many other approaches to multidimensional scaling and factor analysis, there is no well-structured distribution theory that can be invoked to suggest what constitutes an acceptable degree of variance accounted for. However, this situation compares favorably with some approaches to social structure for which not even an explicit algorithm is provided. For example, Bonacich (1977) offered only trial-and-error results with no stated algorithm for implementing his approach, even though an algorithm could be readily devised for the problem he considered.

ADCLUS/MAPCLUS provides a discrete portrayal of social structure, allowing for continuous variation through the weights corresponding to the (discrete) clusters. Since these weights are intimately associated with the variance accounted for, there is thus the opportunity to modify, delete, or add clusters and then to observe the ensuing change in goodness-of-fit. Contrast this situation to hierarchical clustering, where the user typically ignores various levels of embedding in the profusion of nesting found in the dendrogram (cf. Gordon, 1987), or in the exhaustive (and exhausting) list of maximal complete subgraphs (see references above), where the investigator typically must ignore some of the clusters or otherwise use *ad hoc* rules to aggregate those having highly similar membership. With ADCLUS/MAPCLUS, the effects of such modifications in a potential solution can be gauged through the variance accounted for. Going a step further, a user can even hypothesize a clustering of the actors (*viz.*, a user-"constrained" solution) and compute the variance accounted for according to the ADCLUS model. (See Shepard and Arabie, 1979, pp. 109-111 for an example using non-sociomentric data, and Arabie and Carroll, 1980a, 1980b for computational details.)

5. INDCLUS as the Three-Way Generalization

In each of the two applications given above, we noted that the raw data consisted of several sociomatrices based on different types of reported ties. Nonetheless, pre-processing was used to obtain a single $N \times N$ matrix as input for MAPCLUS. The same or similar pre-processing is also required for the approaches listed earlier that extract a list of all maximal complete subgraphs implied by sociometric data.

This reduction of several sociomatrices to a single input matrix raises several potential problems, both methodological and substantive. In the former category, there is, for example, the problem of weighting, resulting from differentially dense sociomatrices in the set of data. A substantive objection (also having implications for weighting) is that if there are r sociomatrices in the data set, they may not necessarily correspond to r substantively distinct types of sociometric ties. For example, in Roethlisberger and Dickson's (1939) data, one might ask how different is "liking" from "helping on the job"? Thus, we are faced with the problem of determining the relationships (a) among types of social ties as well as (b) among the actors engaging in those types of ties. Like many other current problems in sociometric data analysis, this problem was commented on in the 1950's (e.g., Massarik, Tannenbaum, Kahane, and Weschler, 1953, p. 312) and is now resurfacing as a topic of growing concern (e.g., Knoke, 1983, p. 1071).

Approaches to the problem of three-way data (in this case, types of ties × actors × actors) in multidimensional scaling (Carroll and Wish, 1974; Wish and Carroll, 1974; Carroll and Arabie, 1980; Arabie, Carroll, and DeSarbo, 1987) have often assumed a dimensional structure that is common in some sense across all sources of data (*viz.*, types of ties), but for which differential weighting (specific to a given type of tie) modifies the structure separately for each source of data. The comparable generalization of the ADCLUS model, to allow for fitting three-way data, has been given by Carroll and Arabie (1979, 1983a, 1983b). Concretely, the ADCLUS model of equation (2) is generalized to the form

$$\hat{s}_{ij}^h = \sum_{k=1}^{m-1} w_{hk} p_{ik} p_{jk} + c_h; \tag{5}$$

that is, we now have an index h for types of ties; for example, in the Roethlisberger and Dickson data, h would vary from 1 to 5, corresponding to the sociomatrices for "liking," ..., "fighting over opening windows." The weights w_{hk} now vary as a function of subset, k, as in the ADCLUS model, *and* type of tie, h. Note that the p_{ik}, p_{jk} do not vary over types of ties; the cluster structure is the same over all types of ties. However, the salience or importance of a cluster (w_{hk}) does vary. Thus, a subset of actors assumed to be heavily based on a given type of tie should have a relatively large weight for that type of tie, whereas on a type of tie irrelevant to the same group, the weight should be zero or very small.

(In equation (2) it was assumed that the mth subset was the complete set; i.e., $p_{im} = 1$, where $i = 1 ..., N$, so that w_m becomes the additive constant mentioned earlier. In equation (5), that constant may vary for each type of tie, and for convenience is separated from the summation over the $m - 1$ subsets.)

It is our hope that the INDCLUS model (for INdividual Differences CLUStering) may faithfully portray structure in sociometric data based on multiple types of ties. Successful applications to non-sociometric data are given in Carroll and Arabie (1983a).

REFERENCES

Alba, R. D.
1973   A graphic-theoretic definition of a sociometric clique. Journal
       of Mathematical Sociology, 3:113-126.
1975   Comment on mathematical models in sociometry. Sociological
       Methods and Research, 3:489.
Alba, R. D., and G. Moore
1978   Elite social circles. Sociological Methods and Research,
       7:167-188.
Alt, J. E., and N. Schofield
1975   Clique: A Suite of programs for extracting cliques from a
       symmetric graph. Behavioral Science, 20:134-135.
1978   Clique analysis of a tolerance relation. Journal of Mathematical
       Sociology, 6:155-162.
Arabie, P.
1977   Clustering representations of group overlap. Journal of
       Mathematical Sociology, 5:113-128.
Arabie, P., and S. A. Boorman
1982   Blockmodels: Developments and prospects. *In* H. Hudson (Ed.),
       Classifying social data: New Applications Of Analytic Methods
       For Social Science Research. San Francisco: Jossey-Bass.
Arabie, P., S. A. Boorman, and P. R. Levitt
1978   Constructing blockmodels: How and why. Journal of
       Mathematical Psychology, 17:21-63.
Arabie, P., and J. D. Carroll
1980a MAPCLUS: A Mathematical programming approach to fitting
       the ADCLUS model. Psychometrika, 45:211-235.
1980b How to use MAPCLUS, a computer program for fitting the
       ADCLUS model. Murray Hill, NJ: AT&T Bell Laboratories
       (Room 2F-128A).
Arabie, P., J. D. Carroll, and W. S. DeSarbo
1987   Three-way scaling and clustering. Newbury Park, CA: Sage.
Bonacich, P.
1972   Technique for analyzing overlapping memberships. *In* H. L.
       Costner (Ed.) Sociological methodology. San Francisco:
       Jossey-Bass, pp. 176-185.
1977   Using Boolean algebra to analyze overlapping memberships. *In*
       K. F. Schuessler (Ed.). Sociological methodology 1978.
       San Francisco: Jossey-Bass, pp. 101-115.

Boorman, S. A., and H. C. White
    1976   Social structure from multiple networks. II. Role structures.
            American Journal of Sociology, 81:1384-1446.
Breiger, R. L., S. A. Boorman, and P. Arabie
    1975   An algorithm for clustering relational data, with applications to
            social network analysis and comparison with multidimensional
            scaling. Journal of Mathematical Psychology, 12:328-383.
Burt, R. S.
    1980   Models of network structure. Annual Review of Sociology,
            6:79-141.
Carroll, J. D.
    1968   A Justification of D-Squared As a Second-Order Proximity
            Measure. Unpublished manuscript, AT&T Bell Laboratories,
            Murray Hill, NJ.
Carroll, J. D., and P. Arabie
    1979   INDCLUS: A Three-way approach to clustering. Paper
            presented at Meeting of the Psychometric Society, Monterey,
            CA, June.
    1980   Multidimensional scaling. In M. R. Rosenzweig and L. W.
            Porter (Eds.), Annual Review Of Psychology. Palo Alto, CA:
            Annual Reviews.
    1983a   INDCLUS: An individual differences generalization of the
            ADCLUS model and the MAPCLUS algorithm. Psychometrika,
            48:157-169.
    1983b   How to use INDCLUS, a computer program for fitting the
            individual differences generalization of the ADCLUS model.
            Murray Hill, NJ: AT&T Bell Laboratories (Room 2F-128A).
Carroll, J. D., and J. J. Chang
    1970   Analysis of individual differences in multidimensional scaling
            via an N-way generalization of "Eckart-Young" decomposition.
            Psychometrika, 35:283-319.
Carroll, J. D., and M. Wish
    1974   Models and methods for three-way multidimensional scaling. In
            D. H. Krantz, R. C. Atkinson, R. D. Luce, and P. Suppes (Eds.),
            Contemporary Developments In Mathematical Psychology,
            Vol. II. San Francisco: Freeman, pp. 391-447.
Cole, A. J., and D. Wishart
    1970   An improved algorithm for the Jardine-Sibson method of
            generating overlapping clusters. Computer Journal, 13:156-
            163.

Cronbach, L. J., and G. C. Gleser
  1953   Assessing similarity between profiles. Psychological Bulletin, 50:456-473.
Dodd, S. C., and H. Winthrop
  1953   A dimensional theory of social diffusion. Sociometry, 16:180-202.
Doreian, P.
  1969   A note on the detection of cliques in valued graphs. Sociometry, 32:237-242.
  1974   On the connectivity of social networks. Journal of Mathematical Sociology, 3:245-258.
Elliott, G., and M. Hallinan
  1975   An Analysis Of Group Structure By Sociometric And Multidimensional Scaling Techniques. Unpublished manuscript, University of Wisconsin-Madison.
Fienberg, S. E., M. M. Meyer, and S. Wasserman
  1985   Statistical analysis of multiple sociometric relations. Journal of the American Statistical Association, 80:51-67.
Galaskiewicz, J., and P. V. Marsden
  1978   Interorganizational resource networks: Formal patterns of overlap. Social Science Research, 7:89-107.
Galaskiewicz, J., and S. Wasserman
  1981   A dynamic study of change in a regional corporate network. American Sociological Review, 46:475-484.
Gordon, A. D.
  1987   Parsimonious trees. Journal of Classification, 4:85-101.
Hansen, P., and M. Delattre
  1978   Complete-link cluster analysis by graph coloring. Journal of the American Statistical Association, 73:397-403.
Harary, F., and Ross, I. C.
  1957   A procedure for clique detection using the group matrix. Sociometry, 20:205-215.
Homans, G. C.
  1950   The Human Group. New York: Harcourt-Brace.
Hubert, L. J.
  1974   Some applications of graph theory to clustering. Psychometrika, 39:283-309.
Jardine, N., and R. Sibson
  1968   The construction of hierarchic and non-hierarchic classifications. Computer Journal, 11:177-184.

Karp, R.M.
  1972   Reducibility among combinatorial problems. *In* R.E. Miller and
         J.W. Thatcher (Eds.), Complexity of computer computations.
         New York: Plenum.
  1976   On the probabilistic analysis of some combinatorial search
         algorithms. *In* J.F. Traub (Ed.), Algorithms and complexity.
         New York: Academic Press.
Katz, L.
  1947   On the matric analysis of sociometric data. Sociometry,
         10:233-241.
King, J. R., and V. Nakornchai
  1982   Machine-component group formation in group technology:
         Review and extension. International Journal of Production
         Research, 20:117-133.
Knoke, D.
  1983   Organizational sponsorship and influence reputation of social
         influence associations. Social Forces, 61, 1065-1087.
Knoke, D., and J. R. Wood
  1981   Organized For Action: Commitment In Voluntary Associations.
         New Brunswick, N.J.: Rutgers University Press.
Kruskal, J. B.
  1964a Multidimensional scaling by optimizing goodness of fit to a
         nonmetric hypothesis. Psychometrika, 29:1-27.
  1964b Nonmetric multidimensonal scaling: A numerical method.
         Psychometrika, 29:115-129.
Laumann, E. O., J. Galaskiewicz, and P. V. Marsden
  1978   Community structure as interorganizational linkages. Annual
         Review of Sociology, 4:455-484.
Laumann, E.O., and F.U. Pappi
  1976   Networks of collective action. New York: Academic Press.
Lazarsfeld, P. F.
  1950   The logical and mathematical foundation of latent structure
         analysis. *In* S. A. Stouffer, L. Guttman, E. A. Suchman, P. F.
         Lazarsfeld, S. A. Star, and J. A. Clausen (Eds.). Measurement
         and Prediction: Studies In Social Psychology in World War II,
         4. Princeton, NJ: Princeton University Press.
Levine, J. H.
  1972   The sphere of influence. American Sociological Review,
         37:14-27.
Massarik, F., R. Tannenbaum, M. Kahane, and I. Weschler
  1953   Sociometric choice and organizational effectiveness: A multi-
         relational approach. Sociometry, 16:211-238.

Mirkin, B. G.
  1987   Additive clustering and qualitative factor analysis methods for
          similarity matrices. Journal of Classification, 4:7-31.
Moon, J. W., and L. Moser
  1965   On cliques in graphs. Israel Journal of Mathematics, 3:23-28.
Noma, E., and D. R. Smith
  1985   Benchmark for the blocking of sociometric data. Psychological
          Bulletin, 97:583-591.
Peay, E. R.
  1970a   An interactive clique detection procedure. Michigan
          Mathematical Psychology Program, 70-74, Ann Arbor,
          Michigan.
  1970b   Nonmetric grouping: Clusters and cliques. Michigan
          Mathematical Psychology Program, 70-75, Ann Arbor,
          Michigan.
  1974   Hierarchical clique structures. Sociometry, 37:54-65.
  1975   Nonmetric grouping: Clusters and cliques. Psychometrika,
          40:297-313.
Roethlisberger, F. J., and W. J.Dickson
  1939   Management and the worker. Cambridge, MA: Harvard
          University Press.
Rohlf, F. J.
  1975   A new approach to the computation of the Jardine-Sibson B_k
          clusters. Computer Journal, 18:164-168.
Rotondo, J. A., and W. B. Pankey
  1981   Some problems in the logical and statistical foundations of latent
          class analysis. Paper presented at the Mathematical Psychology
          Meetings, Santa Barbara, CA, August.
Sampson, S. F.
  1968   A novitiate in a period of change: An experimental and case
          study of social relationships. Doctoral dissertation, Cornell
          University. (University Microfilms No. 69-5775).
Seidman, S. B., and B. L. Foster
  1978   A graph-theoretic generalization of the clique concept. Journal
          of Mathematical Sociology, 6:139-154.
  1962   Analysis of proximities: Multidimensional scaling with an
          unknown distance function. I. Psychometrika, 27:125-140.(a)
Shepard, R. N.
  1962   Analysis of proximities: Multidimensional scaling with an
          unknown distance function. II. Psychometrika, 27:219-246.(b)

Shepard, R. N., and P. Arabie
  1979   Additive clustering: Representation of similarities as
          combinations of discrete overlapping properties. Psychological
          Review, 86:87-123.
Subcommittee on Reports, Accounting and Management of the Committee
on Government Affairs, United States Senate.
  1978   Interlocking Directorates among the Major U. S. Corporations.
          Washington, D. C.: U. S. Government Printing Office.
Wasserman, S., and C. Anderson
  1987   Stochastic *a priori* block models: Construction and assessment.
          Social Networks, 9: in press.
Weide, B.
  1977   A survey of analysis techniques for discrete algorithms. ACM
          Computing Surveys, 9:291-313.
White, H. C., S. A. Boorman, and R. L. Brieger
  1976   Social structure from multiple networks. I. Blockmodels of
          roles and positions. American Journal of Sociology, 81:730-
          780.
Winer, B. J.
  1955   A measure of interrelationship for overlapping groups.
          Psychometrika, 20:63-68.
Wish, M., and J. D. Carroll
  1974   Applications of individual differences scaling to studies of
          human perception and judgment. *In* E. C. Carterette and M. P.
          Friedman (Eds.), Handbook of perception (Vol. 2). New York:
          Academic Press, pp. 449-491.

CHAPTER 12

EMPIRICAL BLOCKING METHODS

Gregory H. Heil

Theoretical methods in structural network research require us to specify a model which is then validated by consistent mappings of data onto it. 'Empirical' methods, by contrast, require less *a priori* knowledge and are most valuable in the exploratory stage of data analysis. This chapter will focus on the latter. We discuss "empirical" methods which are useful in exploring data. The discussion will center around a method, COBLOC, which has been developed in a series of papers (Carrington, Heil and Berkowitz [1980] and Carrington and Heil [1979]). With the presentation of each aspect of COBLOC we will see alternatives which may be used to improve it. Thus COBLOC should be seen as a tentative step toward a new family of empirical methods.

The first section develops the idea that a measure or index of goodness of fit may be used to automate the search for good models. The second section develops the measure as a heuristic, for searching through an intractably large number of alternative blockings. The third section uses a measure, b, and the COBLOC strategy to analyze a well known data set. An independent measure is used to verify these results.

1. Measures of COBLOCKedness

1.1. Goodness of fit. Various criteria have been devised for assessing the validity of blockmodels (cf. Breiger *et al.* [1975], Arabie *et al.* [1978]). *Fat fit* requires an identity in the ties between blocs and the ties between nodes that are mapped into them. In a fat fit blockmodel, nodes clustered together into a bloc are defined as *structurally equivalent* (Breiger *et al.*, 1975:330). *Lean fit* requires only that nodes lack ties wherever the blocs into which they are mapped do not have ties (Heil and White, 1976:26-27).[1] *Alpha fit* requires that an alpha between 0 and 1 be specified and that there be 1's in the image matrices wherever blocks (submatrices corresponding to image ties) in the data matrices have a tie density greater than alpha, and 0's elsewhere in the image matrices (Arabie *et al.*, 1978:32). In lean fit and alpha fit blockmodels the nodes clustered together into blocs are defined as *structurally similar*.

These criteria have limited practical utility because they only provide grounds either for acceptance or rejection of a given model. Fat fit is, in most cases, too restrictive: it requires that all the nodes in a bloc have *exactly the same* pattern of ties. This situation rarely occurs empirically (White *et al.*, 1976: 740-741) even when elaborate transformations have been applied to the data before specification of a model. Thus the weaker lean fit criterion is almost always used because it allows for "don't care" blocks (i.e. data blocks corresponding to 1's in the image matrices may have some 0's in them).

In section 3.2, below, we will demonstrate how lean fit can be used using compounds of data relations, where some blocks are perfect 0 or 1 fit and others are more or less closely specified. However, specifying a sufficiently tight, yet valid, lean fit blockmodel algebraically may require overly detailed modeling. In this case it would be desirable to specify blocks in terms of levels of stochastic variation.

What is needed is a "goodness of fit" measure of a blockmodel to data which is parsimonious and continuous between a perfect fat fit and a pure stochasticity. Previous blockmodelling methods have not been able to provide this.

---

[1] Cf. Hubert's (1972) lattice theoretic extensions to Johnson's hierarchical clustering methods.

1.2. Block density index. An index of goodness of fit for blockmodels should measure the extent to which the densities of 0's or 1's in the submatrices of the blocked data matrix(es) deviate from the densities of the blocks in the expanded image matrix(es) toward the worst possible density (alpha). The index should have its maximum value (of 1) for blockmodels where the density of 1's in each block of the blocking is equal to the density of the corresponding block in the expanded image matrix— i.e., 1 for oneblocks, and 0 for zeroblocks. The worst possible fit for each block occurs when its density is as far as possible from purity, i.e., equal to alpha (a density beyond alpha would necessitate, under alpha fit, a change in the image tie for that block). Just as meeting a fat fit criterion is usually impossible for a given data set, the worst "possible" fit may well also be impossible: the structure of the ties in the data may well preclude such an arrangement (cf. Hubert and Baker, 1978:34-37). An index, therefore, should have its minimum value (of 0) at alpha and increase monotonically as block densities approach 0 for zeroblocks or 1 for oneblocks. Except for the known upper limit on density, 1, this reasoning is similar to that on which chi-square is based (cf. Breiger, 1976:123, footnote 8). The following unnormalized function accomplishes this for a single block:

$$f(o,e) = \left| \frac{o-e}{e} \right|^2 \qquad (1)$$

where: o is the observed density of the block, and e is the density expected.

The expression given here is squared to eliminate negative signs, and it grows rapidly as blocks approach purity. It is standardized over all values of alpha by incorporating e into the denominator. For zeroblocks (i.e. where $0 \le o < e$), it varies from 0 to 1 as the density of the block varies from e to 0. However, for oneblocks it is necessary to normalize for the difference in size of the oneblock interval, [e,1], vs. [0,e], the interval for zeroblocks (Figure 1). Thus for oneblocks (where $1 \ge o \ge e$):

$$f(o,e) = \left| \frac{o-e}{et} \right|^2 \qquad (2)$$

where $t = \begin{cases} 1 & \text{if } o < e, \\ \dfrac{1-e}{e} & \text{otherwise.} \end{cases}$

This normalization makes the function indifferent to the relative frequency of zeroblocks or oneblocks. If one failed to do this in a sparse matrix (e < 0.5) values for oneblocks could exceed 1 and the index would be unduly weighted toward blockmodels containing more oneblocks. But the value of alpha and the blocking have been treated as given. If only the blocking is known, the "best value" of alpha is the one which maximizes the value of the index of goodness of fit. A useful approximation to this value is the overall density of 1's in the data matrix. This "mean" alpha is also the most likely random result and thus also the best null model. With this alpha value large numbers of potential data partitions for blockmodels can be evaluated where it would be too costly to find the "very best" value of alpha for each proposed partition. Even where we have empirically attained a better alpha value (e.g. after selecting one partition), the overall density is a good approximation. Therefore:

> DEF   A *mu fit* blockmodel is an alpha fit blockmodel in which the value of alpha for each type of tie is equal to the overall density of 1's in the incidence matrix for that type of tie.

So for mu fit models:

$$e = \frac{n}{v} \tag{3}$$

where n is the number of ones in the matrix and v is the number of positions where the relation is allowed, or definable.

Figure 1. Relative Sizes of Zeroblock and
Oneblock Intervals for Sparse Data (e = alpha).

The function given in Equation 4 is standardized by relative block size and summed over all blocks. For a single relation the equation as derived to here is:

$$b = \sum_{j,k}^{c} \frac{\left(o_{jk} - \frac{n}{v}\right)^2 A_{jk}}{\left(\frac{t_{jk}n}{v}\right)^2 v} \tag{4}$$

where: c = the number of (defined) blocks,

o = the observed density of the jk^{th} block,

A = the size (number of allowed elements) of the jk^{th} block,

v = the size of the matrix (total number of defined elements),

t = the correction factor, defined as in Equation 4 above.

For traditional sociomatrices, where only the main diagonal elements are undefined,

$$v = p(p-1) \tag{5}$$

where p is the number of nodes (actors) on which the matrix is defined.

Here we avoid assuming that these are the only undefined elements. Undefined diagonals, and any other undefined elements, are simply treated as "missing data" and omitted from calculations. This allows the derivation of formulae in a more general form. It also gives the investigator more control over the treatment of such data when using these formulae. Any element in the data matrices can be defined as "missing" by changing the values of the A matrix.

For simplicity of computation, we use absolute block frequencies (i.e. the number of 1's in each block) by substituting:

$$O_{jk} = o_{jk}s_{jk} \text{ and } E_{jk} = \frac{s_{jk}n}{v} \tag{6}$$

Data to which blockmodels are fitted usually incorporate more than one type of tie. Arabie *et al.* (1978:32) propose that one value of alpha be used for all the types of ties in a network, but it seems more reasonable to postulate one value of alpha for each type of tie, and to associate each one with the density of its own incidence matrix. If the matrix generated by one type of tie is relatively dense, and another is relatively sparse, a model should tolerate greater zeroblock impurities for the denser matrix and should, *ceteris paribus,* demand denser oneblocks.

Each type of tie is weighted by the relative number of defined elements in its relation matrix—so that types of ties with fewer defined elements contribute proportionately less to the total value of the index. In this formulation the value of the summation for each matrix is standardized by multiplying by the size of the matrix (v) and dividing by the summed sizes of all the matrices (v):

$$b = \frac{1}{v} \sum_i^r \left\{ \frac{v_i}{n_i} \sum_{j,k}^c \frac{\left(o_{ijk} - E_{ijk}\right)^2}{E_{ijk}T_{ijk}^2} \right\} \tag{7}$$

where: V = total number of allowed elements in all matrices

   r = number of matrices (types of tie)

   v_i = number of allowed elements in the ith matrix

   n_i = number of 1's in the ith matrix

   c = number of blocks

   O_{ijk} = number of 1's in the jkth block of the ith matrix

   E_{ijk} = number of 1's expected in the jkth block

$$T_{ijk} = \begin{cases} 1 & \text{if } o_{ijk} < E_{ijk}, \\[2ex] \dfrac{A_{ijk} - E_{ijk}}{E_{ijk}} & \text{otherwise} \end{cases}$$

A_{ijk} = size (number of allowed elements) of the jkth block of the ith matrix.

   Although this formula for mu fit is intuitively appealing it is computationally cumbersome. We can simplify by substituting:

$$P_{ijk} = O_{ijk}v_i$$

$$Q_{ijk} = A_{ijk}n_i.$$

Then Equation 7 becomes:

$$b = \sum_{ijk} B_{ijk} = \sum_i^r \left\{ \sum_{j,k}^c \frac{\left(P_{ijk} - Q_{ijk}\right)^2 f_{ijk}}{Q_{ijk}V} \right\} \tag{8}$$

where all terms are defined as in Equation 7 above, and

$$
f_{ijk} = \begin{cases} \dfrac{1}{n_i} & \text{if } o_{ijk} < E_{ijk}, \\[2ex] \dfrac{n_i}{(v_i - n_i)^2} & \text{otherwise.} \end{cases}
$$

2. Search Strategies

Given a measure of goodness of fit (such as mu fit derived in the previous section) the empirical problem of searching for the best blockmodel for a data set is soluble by simply comparing every conceivable mapping against this measure. However, even when only non-overlapping blockings are considered, the number is exponential in the number of nodes. Each evaluation of mu requires $O(rN^3)$ operations where r is the number of relations and N is the number of nodes. For practical reasons then, one cannot search through all mappings. The problem is compounded by the necessity of finding not a single model but also its possible alternatives, refinements and simplifications. In problems of this kind, where practical solutions are required, heuristics are used to guide the search to a solution which is likely to have a relatively good value.

A "steepest descent" approach starts with an initial mapping, then evaluates a set of alternative modifications, then chooses the best and then repeats the search—stopping when no improvement is possible or there are no alternatives. The method may be modified to search a larger portion of the solution space by pursuing more than just the best alternative: performing partial or complete backtracking. Under most backtracking schemes a mechanism is needed to avoid recomputing equivalent paths or infinitely looping. A variety of heuristic schemes of this kind have been outlined by Tompa (1975).

In the next section we develop a steepest ascent scheme which generates a hierarchical partitioning, i.e. each level of the ascent is a refinement of the last one. The method allows interactive control to provide a rudimentary backtrack mechanism, enabling the researcher to find alternative models. The final section will deal with some alternative schemes for clustering problems.

2.1. COBLOC. COBLOC is an agglomerative clustering method. It starts with a partition of nodes into k blocs and joins the two blocs whose resulting blocking has the highest mu fit. This is similar to Ward's (1963) method for clustering of non-network data. Proofs of the monotonicity of Ward's method and other combinatorial properties are given in Lance and Williams (1967). Under user control, alternative chains within the entire latice of possible blockings may be explored.[2]

Most clustering techniques are based on pairwise similarity measures. Use of a goodness of fit index in clustering criteria is more direct (Hubert, 1973:59-62). It avoids questions of the meaning of the "similarity" of entities (Cormack, 1971; Gregson, 1975), which, in this case, is further confused by its extension to the idea of *structural* similarity. Its use also circumvents a problem which is rooted at the very definition of clusters which are: "characterized by properties of coherence and isolation" (Jardine and Sibson, 1971) two apparently conflicting goals.[3]

2.1.1. Computation of the Index of Coblockability. Formulae can be derived which will allow the computation of the mu fit coblockability index b for all pairs of blocs in a network under three circumstances. Where:

(0) One has a blocking and wishes to compute its b value.

(1) One wishes to compute the b values for all blockings which differ from a given blocking in having pairs of its blocs coblocked.

(2) One wishes to update a b matrix by coblocking a specific pair in addition to each possible other pair.

Each b entry at stage (2) requires a number of arithmetic operations proportional to a constant. Without the information from the previous level, one must perform a stage (1) algorithm requiring operations proportional to the number of nodes in the network, for each entry. The

---

[2] See also Cormack (1971) and Delattre and Hansen (1980), who suggest lattice methods to characterize a "complete set" of clustering solutions which cannot be distinguished unless the criteria (coherence and isolation) are assigned weights. This problem only arises if clusters are based on similarity type measures. Goodness of fit criteria define the required weightings.

[3] He argued, following Fisher (1936), that real data could not be used for the purpose because of its lack of statistical quantifiability—there is no way to determine the true clustering. Statistically generated data is, however, subject to control which allows error terms to cancel.

initialization formula, stage 0, given in this section requires operations proportional to the square of the number of nodes.

It is convenient to use an extension to the standard notation for indexing arrays. Some of the indices used below refer to blocs which are, in fact, simply sets of nodes in a network for which values are being computed. The extension will use the brace notation of set theory to designate, e.g.,

$$X_{\{ab\}}$$

as the value of the variable X at the index of the set {a,b}.

Recall from section Equation 8 the mu fit index b. The variables 0 and A (number of observed and allowed ties) are computed directly from the data. There is no restriction of the data to binary values: A is simply the total of maximum 0 values. While P and Q are derived from 0 and A, recomputation for combined blocks does not entail recomputation from 0 and A, since:

$$P_{i\{jk\}l} = P_{ijl} + P_{ikl}.$$

The variable f can take on only 2r (r = the number of relations) values and need not be recomputed. If nodes j and k are to be coblocked then the array P', for use in Equation 8, is identical to the array P, except for rows and columns j and k (See Figure 2). Old rows need merely be replaced by their combination, which is performed by an addition and subtraction to b:

$$b_{jk} = b - \sum_{i}^{r} \left(\begin{array}{c} \sum_{m}^{n} \left(B_{ijm} + B_{ikm} + B_{imj} + B_{imk}\right) \\ -\left(B_{ijk} + B_{ijj} + B_{ikj} + B_{ikk}\right) \\ -\sum_{m}^{n}\left(B_{i\{jk\}m} + B_{im\{jk\}}\right) + B_{i\{jk\}\{kl\}} \end{array} \right). \qquad (9)$$

Repeating this for each pair, {jk}, an entire matrix of b´ values can be computed. This first array of b´ values can now be updated after each coblocking (see below), to allow for the changing similarities of the blocs, or it can be used unchanged like a similarity matrix in clustering (to improve speed of execution). This b array can be updated after successive coblockings, as below.

		m	j	k
		P_{i1m}	P_{i1j}	P_{i1k}
m		P_{imm}	P_{imj}	P_{imk}
j	P_{ij1}	P_{ijm}	P_{ijj}	P_{ijk}
k	P_{ik1}	P_{ikm}	P_{ikj}	P_{ikk}

Figure 2. Terms in ith Plane of P Array

2.1.2. Updating a b Matrix. Two pairs without common elements may be coblocked economically, given the b values for each pair coblocked independently. Following the convention of the last section:

$$b'_{jk}$$

will represent the b value for a network whose nodes j and k have been coblocked. Let

$$_{jk}b''_{\ell m}$$

be a matrix of b values of models whose ℓmth entry is the b value of the model with ℓ coblocked with m as well as j with k. Then,

$$_{jk}b''_{\ell m} \text{ is approximately } b'_{jk} + b'_{\ell m} - b \qquad (10)$$

when there is no overlap in the sets jk and ℓm.

To see what has been accomplished in Equation 10 see Figure 3.

	ℓ	$\{\ell m\}$	m
j	$B_{ij\ell}$	$B_{ij\{\ell m\}}$	B_{ijm}
$\{jk\}$	$B_{i\{jk\}\ell}$	$B_{i\{jk\}\{\ell m\}}$	$B_{i\{jk\}m}$
k	$B_{ik\ell}$	$B_{ik\{\ell m\}}$	B_{ikm}

Figure 3. B Terms in i^{th} Plane of B Array used
in Computing b Value for Coblocking j with k,
and Simultaneously ℓ with m

In the b value sought the rows (and columns) j, k, ℓ, and m of B must be deleted from the sum. The rows (and columns) jk and ℓm must be added, except that their intersection must be replaced by $B_{i\{jk\}\{\ell m\}}$ and $B_{i\{\ell m\}\{jk\}}$. Incorporating these corrections we have

$$_{jk}b''_{\ell m} = -b + b'_{jk} + b'_{\ell m}$$

$$+ \sum_i \left(\begin{array}{c} B_{ij\ell} + B_{ijm} + B_{ik\ell} + B_{ikm} \\ + B_{i\ell j} + B_{imj} + B_{i\ell k} + B_{imk} \\ - B_{ij\{\ell m\}} - B_{i\{jk\}\ell} - B_{i\{jk\}m} - B_{ik\{\ell m\}} \\ + B_{i\{jk\}\{\ell m\}} + B_{i\{\ell m\}\{jk\}} \end{array} \right). \quad (11)$$

For the case k = 1, however, the above technique cannot be used due to the fact that the rows {jk} and {ℓm} do not appear in the final sum, but are replaced by {jkm}. This row and column, {jk}, of b″ is best computed using the method outlined in the previous section: first cobloc j and k; then compute all $_{ik}b''_{\{jk\}m}$ using Equation 9.

Thus b can be computed efficiently for each of the three circumstances, needed in agglomerative clustering.

2.2. *Alternative search strategies.*

2.2.1. General Clustering Methods. The b measure matrix can be used as a similarity measure without subsequent reevaluation in conjunction with most clustering procedures. The advantage of this is speed of execution—critical in large data sets. The fastest clustering algorithms are related to the minimum spanning tree (MST). Indeed execution times for some of these procedures is, for N nodes, $O(N^2)$—an irreducible minimum given that every internode distance must be examined. Note, however, that if the b measure (or virtually any measure imaginable) is to be employed then time $O(N^3)$ is required just to compute the similarity matrix. These methods will not, therefore, increase the range of problems analyzable. They may, however, serve an invaluable service in scouting out possibilities before serious effort is applied to more accurate and costly procedures (such as COBLOC).

The most widespread clustering algorithm based on the MST is "single linkage cluster" analysis. Hubert (1974) gives a variety of ways of improving its results. A distinct method was proposed by McQuitty (1957). Briefly, the method clusters everyone with his nearest alter; and the procedure is applied recursively to the resulting clusters. Heil (1974) showed how this may be computed in parallel with the computation of the MST.

2.2.2. Combining COBLOC with Clustering Methods. An optimal algorithm for speed and accuracy might result from the combination of traditional clustering methods and a coblocking scheme as presented in this chapter. For instance, very tight "complete linkage clusters" (Hubert, 1974) could be formed from a b matrix as a first stage, followed by the re-evaluation of b on the blocked data. The results can be expected to be an excellent approximation, and considerable time savings can result, as the expensive initial stages of the agglomerative procedure are eliminated.

2.2.3. Iterative Reallocation. Work for which accuracy is paramount will require some form of backtracking, such as we have employed, or iterative processing as suggested by Kernighan and Lin (1970) and Strauss (1977). A b array can easily be formed showing the association of any node to any current bloc i.e.: evaluate b on the network with a given node moved from its bloc to each other bloc in turn. From this node-bloc association matrix not only can a hill-climbing clustering procedure be devised but the utility of multiple assignments of nodes (floaters/crystallizers) may be evaluated. These association matrices may be updated by a formula similar to the stage 2 algorithm of section 2.2.

2.2.4. Clumping. People are similar to words in that they exhibit ambiguity and fill multiple roles. The form of clustering popular in information retrieval and other forms of text processing is called "clumping." A clump, as distinguished from a cluster, potentially overlaps in membership with other clumps, thus the emphasis is on the contrast between a clump and its environment—rather than the self-consistency of the whole clustering. In blocking, the total system is, of course, of primary importance. However, the "stress" of forcing complex personalities into a single role type is certainly not conducive to finding a comprehensive role analysis. Some compromise with clumping theory could be beneficial in the search for blockings. Multiple membership of individuals (floaters) is certainly consistent with the notion of a bloc (Heil and White, 1976).

A search for a consistent set of clumps could be organized as follows: use a standard clump definition (e.g. Parker-Rhodes and Jackson, 1969) or use cliques (Gottlieb and Kumar, 1968) to generate a large number of clumps, then select a subset which is self-consistent (which as a total blocking has a high b value and is a covering for the node set). Perhaps a more useful (certainly faster than the full computation of b) measure of the consistency of two clumps x and y in such an algorithm is the local sum

$$\sum_i B_{ixy}.$$

The computation of this index requires time $O(n^2c^2)$ where n and c are the number of clumps and size of the clumps respectively.

Clumping may also be approached by iterative reassignment as discussed above.

2.2.5. Divisive Clustering. After performing a statistical experiment designed to distinguish the capability of four search strategems to recover randomly masked clusters, Strauss (1977) found that the divisive procedure tested performed better than the agglomerative procedures (including Ward's [1963] scheme on which COBLOC was modelled) but not as well as an iterative reallocation iprocedure. He conjectured that the relation was general: for roughly the same number of comparisons divisive procedures would be superior to agglomerative. It remains to be tested if there are *hierarchical* iterative reallocating procedures which use only $\frac{n^3}{6}$ tests, which do as well or better than divisive procedures.

The divisive scheme he recommended is a scheme MacNaughton-Smith *et al.* (1964) called the transfer algorithm. When only the coarser levels of blockings are of interest to the researcher, divisive procedures have an advantage *vis a vis* agglomerative methods. While divisive clustering is slightly more expensive for a full hierarchical run it can be stopped when the categories are sufficiently refined.

2.3. Comparison of Efficiency. The theoretical problem of enumerating solutions becomes computationally easier, when a problem is posed more precisely. This is because the timing of enumeration algorithms is usually dominated by the number of solutions found—if nothing else they must be printed. The more closely a theoretical problem is defined, the faster one can compute mappings which verify it. The empirical problem grows in complexity with precision of problem specification in two dimensions: (1) the closer the solution is required to be to the optimum, the greater the search time; (2) more accurate definitions of goodness of fit or significance require more computational effort in their evaluation.

In attempting to analyze the efficiency of the various blocking procedures, the primary difficulty is not in establishing the various time bounds but in deciding what the algorithm is that is being evaluated. Imprecision in algorithmic specification arises from two sources. First the authors may not have ever intended their concepts to be interpreted as formal procedures—and thus have made no attempt at so specifying them. Second, a general procedure (such as COBLOC) may subsume a variety of specific procedures, each with different timing characteristics. For COBLOC with b as defined here, the first level computation is $O(rN^3)$ for r relations and n nodes. Subsequent stages are $O(rN^2)$ each. For a full n level agglomerative clustering $O(rN^3)$ time is required.

In concluding that CONCOR should be accepted as it stands, Arabie *et al.* (1978:38-39) have assumed there is no way to distinguish the timing characteristics of different iterative algorithms. In fact the form of iteration performed by CONCOR is significantly more time-consuming than iterations required to extract the principal eigenvector (the alternative proposed by Schwartz [1977], see below). At each stage of iteration in CONCOR an n by n matrix is computed of the correlations of length n vectors. Each iteration takes an order $O(N^3)$ of arithmetic operations. Each iteration in factor analysis is $O(N^2)$ by the method of inverse iteration. Furthermore, the number of iterations in a well-designed factor analysis package should be considerably less than required for the relatively poorly understood CONCOR process.

The first stage of all current empirical procedures, except Sailer's B but including our COBLOC procedures, is $O(rN^3)$ where r is the number of relations. This is the cost of computing the similarity matrix to start the process. The iterative schemes, CONCOR and CONCOV, repeat an $O(N^3)$ reevaluation process until convergence: say c times. It is reasonable to assume that after the data have been divided about $O(\log N)$ times sufficient detail has been obtained although the worst case is $O(N)$. Thus for CONCOR and CONCOV total time is $O(rN^3 + cN^3\log N)$. We have assumed that after the first correlation matrix is generated the data are not referred to at subsequent levels of the clustering (Schwartz, 1977:257-258). If the data are referred to repeatedly, timing is $O([r + c]n^3\log N)$. Thus, referring to the data is advisable only for particular substantive reasons; there is no computational justification.

In suggesting factor analytic methods to replace CONCOV (and possibly CONCOR), Schwartz (1977) intended a non-hierarchical scheme. However, to make the results consistent, our timing analysis will assume the scheme of splitting a given population by the sign of their loadings in the principal eigenvector and repeating for each subpopulation. Again assuming log N stages, timing is $O(rn^3 + dn^2\log N)$, where d is the number of iterations in a factor analysis.

In Sailer (1978) the method for computing B appears to require an exorbitant $O(ren^4)$ where e is the number of iterations. This is for the computation of one n by n matrix of B values. He considers B good enough not to require recomputation in a hierarchical procedure.

As BLOCKER (Heil, 1973) addresses a distinct problem, the timings are not comparable. A timing analysis is impossible at the current state of computer science. An interpretation of the theoretical problem as "to show that there exists at least one solution" is in the class of problems known as NP-Complete (Karp, 1975). There is no known polynomial bound on these problems. Reasonable bounds, however, may be found empirically. A very similar procedure for the enumeration of cliques (maximal complete subgraphs) has been found empirically to require $O(s^{1.25})$ arithmetic operations where s is the number of subgraphs returned as answers (Mulligan, 1972).

Measuring the time by the output of the procedure is certainly less than satisfactory but it does emphasize the proper approach to the utilization of a theoretical type of procedure—carefully specify the theory to obtain a precise quick test.

3. Data Analysis

In this section we present the results of an analysis of a well-known data set, introduced below in section 1. Following, in section 2, we will analyze this data with the COBLOC algorithm presented above. Section 3 will give a confirmation of some of these results using theoretical methods. Finally, section 4 will be a comparison of our results and those of other researchers.

3.1. Western Electric Bank Wiring Room Data. To illustrate the application of COBLOC we will look at the data on relationships among men working in a Western Electric Co. Bank Wiring Room, BWR (Roethlisberger and Dickson, 1939; Homans, 1950). These data have already been analyzed using blockmodelling techniques (White, 1973; Breiger *et al.*, 1975; White *et al.*, 1976; Arabie *et al.*, 1978).

On a population of fourteen men wiring switchboard banks in a separate room of a factory, six relations were systematically observed: liking ("P" in Table 1), engaging in various games and horseplay with ("*P*"), disliking ("N"), helping another with his job ("H"), arguing over windows ("W"), and requesting job trades ("T"). All these ties except helping and job trading were reported as reciprocated. The men were labelled by their jobs: inspectors I1 and I3, soldermen S1, S2, and S4, and wiremen W1 through W9.

Unlike previous blockmodel analysis, all data, including the trading jobs relation, have been included. Partly this is to restrict the model further (cf. White *et al.*, 1976:739) and it is partly to illustrate the use of the allowed (A) array. In the first five relations, all non-reflexive ties are "allowed" (i.e. possible); in the sixth relation ties are defined only between men holding different jobs (Roethlisberger and Dickson, 1939:496,499; Homans, 1950:144-145). In the incidence matrices in Table 1, undefined ties are represented by a period (.). The sixth relation illustrates the utility of having an explicit provision for undefined ties. All such ties are omitted from all calculations: thus only the values of the defined ties contribute to coblockability calculations, and the scores on the sixth relation contribute proportionally less to the total value of the coblockability index.

3.2. COBLOC of the BWR Population. The COBLOC analysis begins with a straight steepest ascent agglomerative hierarchical clustering run of the BWR network. The initial matrix of b values is in Table 2. The hierarchical chain of partitions, with its implied permutation

Table 1. Blocked incidence matrices for Bank Wiring Room data

```
                LIKE (P)          DISLIKE (N)         HELP (H)
           WWSWWSWWWWIWSI       WWSWWSWWWWIWSI      WWSWWSWWWWIWSI
           13146478921523      13146478921523     13146478921523
    [W1)   .1110000000000       .0000000000000     .1100000100000
 984(W3))  1.110000001000      0.000000000000     0.000000010000
 603((S1)  11.10010000000      00.00000000100     00.00010000000
 917(W4]   111.0000000000      000.0000000000     110.1000000000
 298[W6)   0000.000000000      0000.010000101     0100.011100000
 884(S4))  00000.01100000      00000.00000001     00010.01000000
 678((W7)  001000.1100000      000010.0010101     000001.0000000
 814((W8)  0000011.100000      0000000.010101     0000101.100000
 965(W9]   00000111.00000      00000000.10101     00000100.00000
    [W2)   000000000.0000      000000111.1000     011100000.0000
 851(I1))  0100000000.000      0000000001.001     0000000000.000
 744(W5))  00000000000.00      00111011100.11     01000000000.00
 512((S2)  000000000000.0      000000000001.0     000010000000.0
 941(I3]   0000000000000.      0000111110110.     0000000000000.

                GAMES (P)         WINDOWS (W)        TRADE JOBS (T)
           WWSWWSWWWWIWSI       WWSWWSWWWWIWSI      WWSWWSWWWWIWSI
           13146478921523      13146478921523     13146478921523
    [W1)   .1110000011100       .0000000000000     ..1..0....0.00
 984(W3))  1.110000011100      0.000000000000     ..0..0....0.00
 603((S1)  11.10000010100      00.01101100100     00.00.000000.0
 917(W4]   111.0000011100      000.1010100100     ..0..0....0.00
 298[W6)   0000.011100000      0011.111100100     ..0..0....0.10
 884(S4))  00000.11100000      00101.11000000     00.00.000000.0
 678((W7)  000011.1100100      000111.1100000     ..0..1....0.00
 814((W8)  0000111.100000      0010111.100000     ..0..1....0.00
 965(W9]   00001111.00000      00111011.00000     ..0..0....0.00
    [W2)   111100000.1000      000000000.0000     ..1..1....0.00
 851(I1))  1101000001.000      0000000000.000     0000000000.00.
 744(W5))  11110010000.00      00111000000.00     ..0..1....0.00
 512((S2)  000000000000.0      000000000000.0     00.00.000000.0
 941(I3]   0000000000000.      0000000000000.     00000000000.00
```

of the data, is shown in Table 1 and Figure 4, path 1. The partition shown there is for the 3 bloc model, which seemed to be the "best" model (see below), but a partition of other levels of fineness can be imposed on this permutation. Nested bloc membership is shown by the nested parentheses—e.g. W1 and W3 form a 2 node bloc, which is in turn clustered with (S1 W4). Values of b for the blockmodel induced by each clustering are printed between the labels for the clustered blocs, e.g. [(W1 W3) (S1 W4)] and [(W6 S4) W7 (W8 W9)] collapse to give a 2 bloc model consisting of

[W1 W3 S1 W4 W6 S4 W7 W8 W9] [W2 I1 W5 S2 I3],

where b = .298. Since b decreases motonically with fineness of partition in any hierarchical chain of models, the order of the given b values indicates the order in which blocs were clustered.

Table 2. Original b values (upper triangle) and b value ranks (lower triangle)

	W1	W3	S1	W4	W6	S4	W7	W8	W9	W2	I1	W5	S2	I3
[W1		984	961	972	912	921	907	902	904	965	971	934	957	936
98 W3)	1		961	967	902	914	906	897	904	957	966	927	950	931
60(S1	19	20		973	931	917	928	927	922	934	951	936	940	923
92 W4]	6	13	5		924	917	917	916	912	943	954	937	948	926
30[W6	80	88	54	65		962	957	963	958	911	924	935	945	939
88 S4)	71	78	76	74	18		956	968	971	922	935	928	946	936
68(W7	82	85	59	73	25	27		970	975	902	922	919	937	930
81(W8	89	91	61	77	16	12	9		982	907	928	917	945	928
97 W9]	86	87	69	79	21	7	4	2		907	931	924	944	932
[W2	15	24	50	40	81	68	90	84	83		970	956	957	962
85 I1)	8	14	31	29	66	48	70	60	55	10		945	969	958
74 W5)	51	62	47	43	49	58	72	75	64	28	37		944	951
51(S2	23	32	41	33	35	34	44	36	39	26	11	38		976
94 I3]	45	53	67	63	42	46	56	57	52	17	22	30	3	

The hierarchical tree in Table 1 contains one arbitrary choice in its backtrack tree. At the 10-bloc level there are three possible clusterings to 9 blocs with the same b value of .884: (W6 S4), (I1 W2), and (S4 (W8 W9)), of which the algorithm arbitrarily chose (W6 S4). The trees resulting from choosing each of the other clusterings and continuing on a steepest descent path are shown as paths 2 and 3 in figure 4. These have the same coarse blockings as path 1, but the blocs are formed in a slightly different order: the block-models of paths 1 and 2 are identical at the 7 bloc and coarser levels, and to path 3 at the 5 bloc and coarser levels.

Finding chains that led to other coarse models was difficult with this data set because of the robustness of the clusterings: few high-scoring clusterings at the finer levels are incompatible at the coarser levels. The 7 highest ranking coblockings at the 14-bloc level (see Table 2) are all compatible at the 4-bloc and coarser levels, i.e., choosing any of these clusterings simply changes the order in which nodes are clustered to form the blocs of the 4-bloc model found in path 1. The 8th best clustering was chosen at the 14-bloc level, which was (W1 I1), and then a steepest ascent was followed. This resulted in path 4 in Figure 1, which apart from the addition of I1 to the first bloc is identical to paths 1 and 2 at the 7-bloc level, and only trivially different at finer levels. The value of b for the 4-bloc model in path 4 is marginally higher (.606) than that for the 4-bloc model of paths 1-3 (.602), as are its scores at the 3, 5 and 6-bloc levels (only). However, all of these scores (and models) are very similar.

Another attempt was made to find a different tree of models by choosing the next best clustering at the 14-bloc level that was incompatible with the previous 2-bloc models. This coblocking (W1 W2) was the fifteenth highest ranking of 91. The steepest ascent path following this branch is path 5. The only significant difference from the other paths is the forced addition of W2 (and I1) to the first bloc. This has resulted in the splitting at the 4 bloc level of the first bloc into (W1 W2 W3 I1) and (S1 W4).

It was concluded from these tests that the positional structure in this particular data set and our method for finding it are quite robust, because no reasonable choice of a branch in the search tree leads to a different blockmodel at the substantively interpretable levels of coarseness.

3.3. A theoretical analysis of the BWR data. Here we will analyze theories about role interactions and network connections and then test the theories against the data. In the previous section it was possible to base the analysis on the data as a whole. Here the hypothesis must be generated *a priori*. They must have an exact fit, so our attention will be restricted a more manageable subset of the data. Only the simpler models will be studied. The reader is referred to the literature referenced in the next section for more elaborate models. In that section, the models found by COBLOC and other models from the literature will be compared using the b measure and the correlation coeffecient as an independent criterion.

In the succeeding subsections we will test a simple hypothesis about positive and negative affect, find that it fits and indeed fits a much tighter model. Then some of the implications of that tighter model will be examined. Luce's (1950) definition of cliques will then be used to define a blockmodel for cliques. Finally a model of status will be tested.

3.3.1. Incrowd and Outcasts. Let us start by modelling the concept of an "in-crowd." We quantify this with a rudimentary model:

$$V = \begin{pmatrix} 10 \\ 11 \end{pmatrix}, F = \begin{pmatrix} 10 \\ 11 \end{pmatrix}$$

where 1's indicate hypothetical affective ties between blocs and 0's the absence of such ties. The V model, for positive affect suggests that the first bloc, the "in-crowd," does not "notice" the second bloc, the "outcasts." But outcasts might like either other outcasts or members of the in-crowd population. A few disgruntled outcasts perhaps will dislike some members of the in-crowd but otherwise the F model predicts the in-crowd will to receive no negative affective ties.

In applying this combined VF model to the BWR data we indeed find two castes, ten persons fall into the in-crowd, five are outcasts, with one floating in between (S2 has only one negative tie). In Figure 5 two relations, and a third relation to be discussed in the next section are reproduced. The permutation of the nodes arranges the nine definite in-crowd members before the five outcasts.

```
Path 1                              Path 2
      WWSWWSWWWWIWSI                       WWSWWSWWWWIWSI
  b   13146478921523            b         13146478921523
984   <>............          984         <>............
965   <>.....<>.....          965         <>.....<>.....
941   <>.....<>...<>          941         <>.....<>...<>
917   <><>...<>...<>          917         <><>...<>...<>
884   <><><>.<>...<>          884         <><>...<><>.<>
851   <><><>.<><>.<>          851         <><><>.<><>.<>
814   <><><><=><>.<>          814         <><><><=><>.<>
744   <><><><=><=><>          744         <><><><=><=><>
678   <><><===><=><>          678         <><><===><=><>
603   <==><===><=><>          603         <==><===><=><>
512   <==><===><===>          512         <==><===><===>
298   <=======><===>          298         <=======><===>
```

```
Path 3                      Path 4
    WWSWWWSWWWIWSI              WIWSWWSWWWWWSI
  b 13146748921523           b 11314647892523
984 <>...........         971 <>...........
965 <>.....<>.....        953 <>.......<>...
941 <>.....<>...<>        928 <>.<>...<>....
917 <><>...<>...<>        904 <>.<>...<>..<>
884 <><>..<=>....<>       872 <>.<><>.<>..<>
850 <><><><=>....<>       838 <=><><>.<>..<>
814 <><><><=><>..<>       801 <=><><><=>..<>
744 <><><><=><=><>        754 <=><><><=><><>
678 <><><===><=><>        688 <=><><===><><>
603 <==><===><=><>        606 <===><===><><>
512 <==><===><===>        513 <===><===><==>
298 <=======><===>        285 <========><==>
```

```
           Path 5
        WIWWSWWSIWSWWW
      b 11231452364789
    971 <>...........
    953 <>..........<>
    928 <>..<>......<>
    884 <=>.<>......<>
    858 <=>.<>.<>...<>
    826 <=>.<>.<><>.<>
    777 <==><>.<><>.<>
    740 <==><>.<><><=>
    662 <==><>.<><===>
    581 <==><><=><===>
    460 <====><=><===>
    271 <====><=======>
```

Figure 4. Five hierarchical clusterings of the
BWR data. Singleton clusters are designated by
periods (.). Pairs by adjacent angle brackets (<>).
Larger clusters are denoted by angle brackets
bridged with double dashes (<==>).

Knowing the BWR affective data were, by the definition of the observer, symetric, one could have predicted that if the positive affect data fit the model $V = \begin{vmatrix} 10 \\ 11 \end{vmatrix}$ it would also fit $P = \begin{vmatrix} 10 \\ 01 \end{vmatrix}$.

However, here the data have given us a surprise. The block between the outcasts is empty of ties. The data with this blocking then could fit the tighter model $C = \begin{pmatrix} 10 \\ 00 \end{pmatrix}$ for positive affect and $F = \begin{pmatrix} 10 \\ 11 \end{pmatrix}$ for negative.

In this model there is no overlap between positive and negative oneblocks—a considerably stronger statement than the almost definitinal statement that there should not be a pair of data nodes interacting with both positive and negative affect. The latter which might occur by some objective criteria would undoubtedly be ruled out in observer-reported data.

```
W7   0110 00100 00000    0000 00000 11101    1111 11110 00000
W8   1011 00000 00000    0000 00000 11001    0000 00100 00000
W9   1101 00000 00000    0000 00000 11001    1111 00100 00000
S4   0110 00000 00000    0000 00000 00001    1111 00000 00000
W1   0000 01110 00000    0000 00000 00000    1000 11111 00000
W3   0000 10111 00000    0000 00000 00000    1000 11111 00000
S1   1000 11010 00000    0000 00000 01000    1110 11111 00000
W4   0000 11100 00000    0000 00000 01000    1000 11111 00000
I1   0000 01000 00000    0000 00000 10001    0000 11111 00000
W2   0000 00000 00000    1110 00001 00000    0000 00000 00000
W5   0000 00000 00000    1110 00110 00111    0000 00000 00000
W6   0000 00000 00000    1000 00000 01001    0000 00000 00000
S2   0000 00000 00000    0000 00000 01000    0000 00000 00000
I3   0000 00000 00000    1111 00001 01100    0000 00000 00000
```

Figure 5. Positive, L, negative, A, and the composite positive plus its square, L or LL, affect relations from BWR data. Blockings are derived in this and the succeeding section: the population is shown divided into 2 cliques and outcasts.

The semigroup of the original model in Figure 6 is fairly straightforward. Powers of V all map to the positive affect generator V. Enemies of friends are enemies (VF = F). All other compounds are the unity relation, in effect saying those compounds can appear between any blocs. Algebraically this model conforms to a form of balance theory but it excludes balance theory's most dubious tenet: that one should feel an affect exactly opposite towards those related to by those one dislikes, e.g. like one's enemies' enemies.

0	V	F	FV
V	V	F	FV
F	FV	FV	FV
FV	FV	FV	FV

Figure 6. Composition Table for VF Semigroup

Let us now look at the CF semigroup (Figure 7) which fortuitously fell out of the above analysis. Under the restrictions imposed by lean fit blocking the most striking model to find is one with a pure zero relation, one with all zero blocks. Such is the case here for the CFC relation. White (1973) used this equation, CFC = 0, as the central theme of his paper. An interpretation of this equation, as a model, is:

Hypothesis: Those who have friends, have enemies who have no friends.

The zero relations in a semigroup are open to several interpretations in regards to a general "axiom of quality" which allows the collapse of the infinite free semigroup, of all types of paths, to a finite semigroup with classes of paths of similar quality. This is developed more in Heil (1983: Section 5.3) and there are some recent results in Boyd (1980).

0	C	F	FC	CF	FF	CFC	FFC	FCF	CFF	FFCF	FCFF
C	C	CF	CFC	CF	CFF	CFC	C	CFC	CFF	CF	CFC
F	FC	FF	FFC	FCF	FF	CFC	FFC	FFCF	FCFF	FFCF	FF

Figure 7. Composition Table for the CF
Semigroup

3.3.2. Three-bloc Models of the BWR. In this section we will extend the two bloc model of the previous section to two complementary three bloc models based on the common notions of cliques and hierarchical status.

1.   "Front and back cliques"

Luce (1950) presented a simple quantifiable family of cliques, k-cliques, which are sets of people who are totally connected by paths of length k or less by positive affect ties. The implication is that a k-clique is "stronger" than a k + 1 clique.

The Luce clique concept can be used to formulate a blockmodel by manipulating the data. First form the union of the positive affect data and its square (see Figure 5). This is the relation Luce would use to search for his cliques. For a lean fit blockmodel complement this relation and compare that 3 relation network to the model:

$$L \text{ model } \begin{pmatrix} 110 \\ 100 \\ 000 \end{pmatrix}, \; A \text{ model } \begin{pmatrix} 001 \\ 001 \\ 111 \end{pmatrix}, \text{ and } \overline{L \text{ or } LL} \text{ model } \begin{pmatrix} 011 \\ 101 \\ 111 \end{pmatrix}.$$

Knowing there was no positive affect among the outcastes there is no need to look for a Luce k-clique. Using this model two cliques which correspond exactly to the front and back cliques found by Homans (1950) were found. The three cliques found are displayed in Figure 5.

2.　　　"Leading crowd, hangers on"

Heil (1973) and Boorman and White (1976) have also developed a blockmodel of the BWR based on Davis' (1970) ideas on clustering in hierarchies. This model is a crosscut of the clique model presented above and a 3-bloc strata model developed below.

Where there is a leading crowd it is expected that they should know each other. The peripherals, or hangers on, will in a way define the cliques—for it might be expected that they know and like members of the leading crowd, but their ignorance, or even dislike of other hangers on, outside their own clique, will define the clique boundaries.

If we use the model $\begin{pmatrix} 110 \\ 100 \\ 000 \end{pmatrix}$ for L and $\begin{pmatrix} 001 \\ 001 \\ 111 \end{pmatrix}$ for A, we get twelve consistent blockings from which one has arbitrarily been chosen as a hierarchy for the BWR data in Figure 8.

3.4 Comparative Interpretation of Results. The partitions found by various methods (including those by Breiger, Boorman, and Arabie, 1975), along with their b and r values are shown in Table 3.[4] 3-bloc image matrices are given in Table 4. Although other investigators' models and the theoretical models were based on analysis of fewer types of ties, the two measures of goodness of fit for them have been calculated using all six relations to ensure comparability. Mu fit images have also been supplied where necessary. Nodes and blocs have been permuted and numbered where necessary to make all models as comparable as possible.

Formulae for both goodness of fit measures (b and r) assumed mu fit to optimize the mapping of images to partitions. As an independent evaluation of the models, r was calculated by an obvious extension to multigraphs of the procedure for single relations suggested originally by Arabie *et al.* (1978:46-48): the six data matrices and six expanded image matrices were ravelled and concatenated to form two vectors of 1176 elements each (having some undefined elements), to which the formula for correlation of binary data was applied. Thus the sixth relation (trading jobs) was given less weight, as in calculation of b, because its matrix had fewer defined elements.

```
W3   01100 10001 00000   00000 00000 00000
S1   10100 10100 00000   00000 00000 01000
W4   11000 10000 00000   00000 00000 01000
W8   00001 00110 00000   00000 00000 11001
W9   00010 00110 00000   00000 00000 11001
W1   11100 00000 00000   00000 00000 00000
S2   00000 00000 00000   00000 00000 01000
W7   01011 00000 00000   00000 00000 11101
S4   00011 00000 00000   00000 00000 00001
I1   10000 00000 00000   00000 00000 10001
W2   00000 00000 00000   00011 00101 00000
W5   00000 00000 00000   01111 01100 00111
W6   00000 00000 00000   00000 00100 01001
S2   00000 00000 00000   00000 00000 01000
I3   00000 00000 00000   00011 00111 01100
```

Figure 8. A "leading crowd—hangers on"
blocking of the BWR.

---

4 The correlation coefficient is r; see Katz and Powell (1953) and Arabie *et al.* (1978).

It can be seen from Table 3 that COBLOC finds several partitions with higher b values than other methods at all levels. This is not surprising, since COBLOC sequentially optimized this index (cf. Hubert, 1973:59-62). It is encouraging that the COBLOC partitions also have greater r values than the other methods at all levels except the 2 bloc level, since **COBLOC does not attempt to maximize** r. This can be interpreted as an independent validation of the method.

Despite the large differences among the various search methods, differences in the partitions they find, the images based on those partitions, and the goodness of fit of these images are relatively small—at least for these data. There is general agreement here with Roethlisberger and Dickson, and with Homans, that there are two internally and externally stratified cliques with some hangers-on and outsiders. All search methods but one seem to agree on the 3-bloc model (Table 4), which is suggested above as a preferred solution. The three blocs in this model consist of (1) the central members of the first clique, (2) the central members of the second clique, and (3) all the others. The only other 3 bloc model (labelled "White/Heil strata" in Tables 3 and 4) classifies nodes into insiders, marginals, and outsiders, combining both cliques into the "insiders" bloc. The various 2-bloc models are divided into two quite homogeneous groups—those that differentiate two cliques and those that differentiate clique members and outsiders. The 4-bloc models all identify the following types of nodes: front clique, back clique, hangers-on, and outsiders.

Table 3. Partitions of Bank Wiring Room Data
Found by Various Methods

Blocking	b	r	I	S	W	W	W	S	W	W	W	I	S	W	W	W
			3	2	5	2	7	4	0	9	8	1	1	4	3	1
2 - Bloc Models (Cliques)																
White/Heil[1]	.260	.222	2	2	2	2	1	1	1	1	1	1	1	1	1	1
COBLOC 103	.298	.311	2	2	2	2	1	1	1	1	1	1	1	1	1	1
COBLOC 4	.285	.316	2	2	2	2	1	1	1	1	1	1	1	1	1	1
2 - Bloc Models (Strata)																
COBLOC 5	.270	.315	2	2	2	1	2	2	2	2	2	1	1	1	1	1
CONCOR[2]	.286	.341	1	2	1	1	2	2	2	2	2	1	1	1	1	1
Johnson's Connect[3]	.266	.367	1	1	1	1	2	2	2	2	2	1	1	1	1	1
Johnson's Diameter[3]	.274	.294	2	2	1	1	2	2	2	2	2	1	1	1	1	1

3 - Bloc Models (2 cliques, outsiders)

White/Heil[4]	.423	.416	3	3	3	3	3	2	2	2	2	1	1	1	1	1
COBLOC 4	.513	.505	3	3	3	3	2	2	2	2	2	1	1	1	1	1
COBLOC 1-3	.512	.527	3	3	3	3	2	2	2	2	2	3	1	1	1	1
COBLOC 5	.460	.474	3	3	3	1	2	2	2	2	2	1	1	1	1	1
Johnson's Connect[3]	.513	.505	3	3	3	3	2	2	2	2	2	1	1	1	1	1
Johnson's Diameter[3]	.444	.433	3	3	1	1	2	2	2	2	2	1	1	1	1	1

3 - Bloc Strata Model

White/Heil[5]	.314	.319	3	3	3	3	3	2	1	1	2	2	1	1	1	2

4 - Bloc Models (2 cliques, hangers on, and outsiders)

COBLOC 1-3	.603	.582	4	4	3	3	2	2	2	2	2	3	1	1	1	1
COBLOC 4	.606	.583	4	4	3	3	2	2	2	2	2	1	1	1	1	1
CONCOR[2]	.567	.546	3	4	3	3	4	2	2	2	2	1	1	1	1	1
Johnson's Connect[3]	.586	.559	3	4	3	3	2	2	2	2	2	1	1	1	1	1
COBLOC 5	.581	.571	4	4	4	1	2	2	2	2	2	1	3	3	1	1

6 - Bloc Models

COBLOC 1-3	.744	.655	6	6	3	3	5	5	4	4	4	3	2	2	1	1
Johnson's Diameter[2]	.729	.646	6	6	3	3	5	5	4	4	4	2	1	1	1	1
COBLOC 3	.749	.654	6	6	3	3	5	4	4	4	5	3	2	2	1	1
COBLOC 4	.754	.672	6	6	3	3	5	5	4	4	4	1	2	2	1	1
COBLOC 5	.685	.592	3	6	3	3	6	5	4	4	5	1	2	2	2	1

---

[1] Source: White (1973: 74-75); Heil (1973: 3-5, A7)
   See Section 7.3.1
[2] Source: Breiger *et al.* (1975: 344)
[3] Source: Breiger *et al.* (1975: 349)
[4] Source: White (1973: 76); Heil (1973: 5-6, A8)
   See Section 7.3.2.1
[5] Source: White *et al.* (1976: 757); Heil (1973: 6-7, A8-A9)
   See Section 7.3.2.2
[6] Source: White *et al.* (1976: 766)

There is also general agreement on the partitions on which these images are based. There are minor disagreements, however, as to whether W6 and I1 are clique members. COBLOC Paths 1-3 (and Johnson's diameter HICLUS at the 4-bloc level) classify I1 as a hanger-on to the front clique; all other search methods assign him as a member of the clique. Breiger *et al.* (1975:348) argue that this shows the "inferiority" of the Johnson method (and by implication of COBLOC). Both alternatives are supported by the data and by Homans' (1950:64-79, 132-149) interpretation. I1 has similar game-playing ties to the members of the front clique. However, he has only one friendship tie with members of that clique, whereas the other members are completely connected by friendship ties; he experiences more mutual dislike with the outsiders than other front clique members; he refrains, unlike S1 and W4, from arguing over the windows; and does not help others with their work or trade jobs. Thus he is an atypical member of the clique, and should not be classified with the other members. Homans (1950:147) mentions but does not emphasize this distinction because his analysis is in the sociometric tradition of finding stratified cliques and outsiders, not the status/role tradition.

Table 4. 3-bloc models for Bank Wiring Room data.

Clique models	P	N	H	*P*	W
COBLOC 1-3[1]	1 0 0	0 0 0	1 0 0	1 0 1	0 1 0
	0 1 0	0 0 1	0 1 0	0 1 0	1 1 0
	0 0 0	0 1 1	1 0 0	1 0 0	0 0 0
COBLOC 4 and Johnson's Connectedness[2]	1 0 0	0 0 0	1 0 0	1 0 1	0 1 0
	0 1 0	0 0 1	0 1 0	0 1 0	1 1 0
	0 0 0	0 1 1	1 0 0	1 0 0	0 0 0
White/Heil cliques[3]	1 0 0	0 0 1	1 1 1	1 0 1	0 1 0
	0 1 0	0 0 1	1 1 1	0 1 0	1 1 0
	0 0 0	1 1 1	1 1 0	1 0 0	0 0 0
COBLOC 5[4]	1 0 0	0 0 0	1 0 0	1 0 1	0 1 0
	0 1 0	0 0 1	0 1 0	0 1 0	1 1 0
	0 0 0	0 1 1	0 0 0	1 0 0	0 0 0
Johnson's Diameter[2,5]	1 0 0	0 0 1	1 0 0	1 0 0	0 1 0
	0 1 0	0 0 1	0 1 0	0 1 0	1 1 0
	0 0 0	1 1 0	0 0 0	0 0 0	0 0 0

Strata models

White/Heil strata[6]	1 1 0	0 0 1	1 1 1	1 1 1	1 1 1
	1 0 0	0 0 1	1 1 0	1 1 1	1 1 1
lean fit	0 0 0	1 1 1	1 1 1	1 1 0	1 1 1
mu-fit	1 1 0	0 0 1	0 1 0	1 1 1	1 1 1
	1 0 0	0 0 1	1 0 0	1 1 1	1 0 0
	0 0 0	1 1 1	1 0 0	1 1 0	1 0 0

---

[1] Collapse blocs 1 and 2 for corresponding 2 bloc model—except H(3,1) which maps to zero.

[2] Source: Breiger *et al.* (1975: 349). We have supplied mu-fit images.

[3] Source: White (1973:76). Images reported, modified by comments on p. 76 for first 3.

[4] Relations use lean fit but would be same as for COBLOC if mu-fit were used; we have supplied mu-fit images for the last 3 relations.

[5] Collapse blocs 2,3 for 2-bloc model.

[6] Note that N is very much like N for White/Heil cliques; P is identical to P in COBLOC 1-3, which is to be expected for a positive affect tie, like "playing games".

[7] Source: White *et al.* (1976: 757). First row of images are White's lean fit model; second row are mu-fit to White and Heil's partition.

W6 was classified as a member of the back clique by COBLOC Paths 1-4 at the 2 bloc level, by COBLOC Paths 1-5 and Johnson's two HICLUS algorithms at the 3 and 4 bloc levels. CONCOR and White's analysis classify W6 as an outsider at all levels, as do the Johnson methods at the 2-bloc level. Breiger *et al.* (1975:350) argue that treating W6 as a clique member at the 4 bloc level also shows the inferiority of the Johnson methods; however, in a more recent paper, Arabie *et al.* (1978:51-52) show that due to a computational instability in CONCOR, it may also classify W6 in the back clique and that treating W6 as a floater between the back clique and the hangers-on is "compatible with Homans' verbal presentation." Comparison of b values may also be useful in finding *floaters*—i.e. individuals who may be assigned to two or more blocs without reducing the goodness of fit or the resulting model. This broadens the original concept of floaters under lean fit (Heil and White, 1976; Arabie *et al.*, 1978:33-34, 51): if two partitions differ by one or more node assignments and have approximately equal b values, and the same alpha fit image graphs, the nodes in question may be considered floaters. Precisely specifying significance levels for differences in b values is an unsolved problem. However, in some cases one can be confident, for instance, the only difference between the partitions for two of the 3-bloc models found by COBLOC is in the assignment of one person. The images are the same except for one type of tie ("job trading"), in which there is one block different. However, the densities of the two data blocks in question both fall close to the cutoff (0.06 and 0.10, where the cutoff, my, is 0.07). The values of the block density index are practically equal (0.512 and 0.513). Thus, for these two models, I1 could be said to be a floater.

This comparison has shown that COBLOC produces models similar to those of other methods for the Bank Wiring Room data. These models are consistent with the original analyses of Roethlisberger and Dickson and of Homans. Partitions found by COBLOC appear to fit the data more tightly than previous methods at all levels of fineness, except possibly the 2 bloc level, which appears to be a poor level for these data. COBLOC has the advantage of being able to produce multiple good-fitting solutions, each with a goodness of fit value. This permits identification of floaters, and more generally, allows one to explore the structure of the data more fully.

More information can be added by ordering nodes in a cluster hierarchy, which do not specify ordering within clusters. As evaluation of blockmodels is still mostly eaesthetic, permuting the data matrices to optimize segregation of dense and sparse sections is valuable. Also putting nodes of intermediate type between the respective clusters helps in the identification of "floaters." A heuristic for finding such an ordering of nodes is the traveling salesman's problem (TSP). A solution to the TSP is a path of minimum length visiting each node once.

Fast approximate algorithms for the TSP are available (Golden *et al.*, 1979; Karp, 1975; Lin and Kernighan, 1973) and generally use a minimum spanning tree as the starting point. Once a TSP path has been found, the longest links may be cut to break the network into clusters. Alternatively the TSP algorithm can be used to improve the permutation of nodes in the display of a hierarchical clustering found by other means. An improved ordering for the main coblocking (Path 4) of the Bank Wiring Room data is:

((S2 I3) (I1 W2 W5)) ((W3 W1) (W4 S1)) ((W6 S4) ((W8 W9) W7))

In summary COBLOC offers a number of features which are lacking in older empirical blocking methods:

1. It uses a measure of structural similarity (b) that was formulated particularly for blockmodelling. Considerable importance is attached to the appropriateness of one's measure of similarity.

2.　Similarity scores are recomputed to take into account changes in the similarity of blocs as blocs are combined. Thus COBLOC treats structural equivalence as "being related to structurally equivalent nodes," unlike other methods, which treat it as "being related to the *same* nodes" (Sailer, 1978).

3.　COBLOC allows interactive exploration of alternate paths through the data; most methods provide only "dives" through the lattice of possible partitions: i.e. they use a determinate method to generate a partition or chain of partitions with no intervention by the investigator. This is of most importance when the data have alternative equally valid interpretations.

4.　Finally, COBLOC is the only method that supplies a well-defined way (i.e. the value of b) of evaluating the intermediate and final solutions. This is useful both in comparing different partitions, and in deciding what level of fineness of partition gives the best model.

REFERENCES

Arabie, P., S. Boorman, and P. Levitt
  1978   Constructing blockmodels how and why. Journal of
         Mathematical Psychology 17:21-63.
Boorman, S.A., and H.C. White
  1976   Social structure from social networks II: role structures.
         American Journal of Sociology 81:328-383.
Boyd, J.P.
  1980   The universal semigroup of relations. Social Networks
         2:91-117.
Breiger, R.L.
  1976   Career attributes and network structure: a blockmodel study of
         a bimedical research specialty. American Sociological Review
         41:117-135.
Breiger, R.L., S.A. Boorman, and P. Arabie
  1975   An algorithm for clustering relational data, with applications to
         social network analysis and comparison with multidimensional
         scaling. Journal of Mathematical Psychology 12:328-383.
Carrington, P.J. and, G.H. Heil
  1979   COBLOC: a hierarchical method for blocking network data.
         Structural Analysis Programme Paper, University of Toronto.
Carrington, P.J., G.H. Heil, and S.D. Berkowitz
  1980   A goodness-of-fit-index for blockmodels. Social Networks 2.
Cormack, R.M.
  1971   A review of classification. Journal of the Royal Statistical
         Society 134:321-53.
Davis, J.A.
  1970   Clustering and hierarchy in interpersonal relations: testing two
         graph theoretical models on 742 sociograms. American
         Sociological Review 35:843-852.
DeLattre, M., and P. Hansen
  1980   Criterion cluster analysis. IEEE Transactions on Pattern
         Analysis and Machine Intelligence, PAMI-2:277-91.
Fisher, R.A.
  1936   The use of multiple measurements in taxonomy problems.
         Annals of Eugenics 7:197.
Golden, B., L. Bodin, T. Doyle, and W. Stewart, Jr.
  1979   Approximate traveling salesman algorithms. College of
         Business and Management, University of Maryland, College
         Park, MD.

Gottlieb, C.C., and S. Kumar
  1968   Semantic clustering of index terms. Journal of the ACM
          15:593-513.
Gregson, R.A.M.
  1975   Psychometrics of Similarity. New York: Academic Press.
Heil, G.H.
  1973   Structure in social networks. Unpublished manuscript,
          Department of Sociology, Harvard University.
  1974   The Dijkstra minimum spanning tree and McQuitty clustering.
          Unpublished manuscript, Department of Computer Science,
          Duke University.
  1983   Algorithms for network homomorphism. Doctoral thesis,
          Department of Computer Science, University of Toronto.
Heil, G.H., and H.C. White
  1976   An algorithm for finding simultaneous homomorphic
          correspondences between graphs and their image graphs.
          Behavioral Science 21:26-35.
Homans, G.C.
  1950   The Human Group. New York: Harcourt, Brace and World.
Hubert, L.J.
  1972   Some extensions of Johnson's hierarchical clustering algorithms.
          Psychometrika 37:261-274.
  1973   Monotone invariant clustering procedures. Psychometrika
          38:47-62.
  1974   Some applications of graph theory to clustering. Psychometrika
          39:283-309.
Hubert, L.J., and F.B. Baker
  1978   Evaluating the conformity of sociometric measurements.
          Psychometrika 43:31-41.
Jardine, N., and R. Sibson
  1971   Mathematical Taxonomy. New York: Wiley.
Karp, R.
  1975   On the computational compexity of combinatorial problems.
          Networks 5:45-68.
Katz, L., and J.H. Powell
  1953   A proposed index of the conformity of one sociometric
          measurement to another. Psychometrika 18:249-256.
Kernighan, B.W., and S. Lin
  1970   An efficient heuristic procedure for partitioning graphs. Bell
          System Technical Journal 49:291-308.
Lance, G.N., and W.T. Williams
  1967   A general theory of classificatory sorting strategies. The
          Computer Journal 10:271-276.

Lin, S., and B. Kernighan
    1973   An effective heuristic algorithm for the traveling salesman
           problem. Operations Research 21:498-516.
Luce, R.D.
    1950   Connectivity and generalized cliques in sociometric group
           structure. Psychometrika 15:169-190.
MacNaughton-Smith, P, W.T. Williams, M.B. Dale, and L.G. Mockett
    1964   Dissimilarity analysis: A new technique of hierarchical
           subdivision. Nature 202:1034-1035.
McQuitty, L.L.
    1957   Elementary linkage analysis for isolating orthogonal and oblique
           types and typal relevancies. Educational and Psychological
           Measurement 17:207.
Mulligan, G.D.
    1972   Algorithms for finding cliques in a graph. Technical Report 41,
           Department of Computer Science, University of Toronto.
Parker-Rhodes, A.F., and D.M. Jackson
    1969   Automatic classification of the higher fungi. *In* A.J. Cole, ed.
           Numerical Taxonomy. New York: Academic Press.
Roethlisberger, F.J., and W.J. Dickson
    1939   Management and the Worker. Cambridge, MA: Harvard
           University.
Sailer, L.D.
    1978   Structural equivalence: meaning and definition, computation and
           application. Social Networks 1:73-90.
Schwartz, J.E.
    1977   An examination of CONCOR and related methods for blocking
           sociometric data. Unpublished manuscript.
Strauss, D.J.
    1977   The evaluation of culstering techniques. Trabajos de Estadistica
           y de Investigacion Operativa 28:167-82.
Tompa, M.
    1975   Hill climbing, a feasible search technique for combinatorial
           configurations. Masters thesis, Department of Computer
           Science, University of Toronto.
Ward, D.J.
    1963   Hierarchical grouping to optimize an objective function.
           Journal of the American Statistical Association 58:236-244.

White, H.C.
   1973   Models for interrelated roles from multiple networks in small
          populations. *In* P.J. Knopp and G.H. Meyer, eds. Proceedings
          of a Conference on the Application of Undergraduate
          Mathematics in the Engineering, Life, Managerial and Social
          Sciences. Atlanta: Georgia Institute of Technology.
White, H.C., S.A. Boorman, and R.L. Breiger
   1976   Social structure from multiple networks: I. Blockmodels of
          roles and positions. American Journal of Sociology 81:730-780.

CHAPTER 13

RETHINKING THE ROLE CONCEPT: HOMOMORPHISMS ON SOCIAL NETWORKS[1]

Karl P. Reitz
Douglas R. White

1   We are indebted to John Boyd for providing our initial orientation to the algebraic homomorphisms discussed in this chapter, and for formalizing the concept of regular equivalence. Lee Sailer contributed in the earlier discussions of this concept, and we rely on his 1978 article. Harrison White and his colleagures, as well as S. F. Nadel, on whose conception of social structure they build, deserve much of the credit for the early exploration of this approach. We are particularly indebted to Linton C. Freeman for encouragement and patient criticism at many points along the way. This chapter represents an example of collaboration between a mathematically oriented anthropologist and an anthropologically oriented mathematician which has been very satisfying to us. The chapter originated in numerous drafts by White exploring the concepts and formal definitions, but with errors in the formalization and without explicit mathematical proofs of the ideas proposed. The chapter began to coalesce and gained enormously in value with the collaboration of Reitz, who attempted the initial proofs and thereby uncovered many of the problems in the earlier conceptualizations, pointing the way to many of the avenues explored. Many of the concepts and approaches employed in the proofs, however, stemmed from extensive discussions with White. Thus the definitions, proofs and overall conceptualization resulted at each step from different but complementary contributions of each of us. We are keenly aware of the value of this type of collaboration, where the results would not have originated without the contribution of the other. Funding for the initial stages of the research was made available to White under National Science Grants BNS 78-25145 and BNS 76-08386.

1.   Introduction

Positional similarity in a social system or network—what we ordinarily call 'role'—is given a mathematical explication in this chapter. The concepts developed here derive from anthropological thinking about social roles: particularly the ideas of S. F. Nadel (1957) as further elaborated by W. H. Goodenough (1965) and Lorrain and White (1971). The goal of a mathematical explication of a basic concept is twofold: on the one hand, it provides a formal foundation for theory, measurement, and explanation; on the other, it is grounded in the intuitive richness of existing experience with the phenomenon. In the case of the role concept a certain degree of simplification is necessary at the outset. In current usage three components of the role concept can be distinguished:

1.   Roles are positionally similar social units which can be observed in terms of regularities in behavior, beliefs, jural rules, and the like.

2.   Social actors perceive positional similarities, and may tag them with names or operate with them conceptually.

3.   The perception and use of the role concept by actors may become the basis for rewards and punishments, or the prescription of rights and duties, etc.

Thus, folk concepts of roles acquire a prescriptive as well as a descriptive character. Typically, this normative character of roles is stressed by social scientists in their use of the concept.

In a mathematical explication of the role concept, we stress the patterns of positional regularities which define the raw material for people's tdescriptive observation of roles. We can thus compare an analytic identification of role patterns with the perception and labeling of roles by social actors. We can then also try to account for the emergence of roles as patterned regularities, independently of their normative character.

We assume that there is a complex feedback relationship between actual behavior, apperception or cognition of social relations, affect, jural rules, and sanctions. In focusing on the descriptive aspect of role patterns, however, we want to avoid the strict behaviorist position that roles are defined only by behavior, and not by beliefs, jural rules, and the like. We want to make it quite clear that if roles can be descriptively defined by types of patterns of relationships in a network, the relational "data" or givens may be of any type—behavioral, cognitive, affective, or jural. Thus, the analytic role concept will help us to compare the organization of role systems as they are displayed at each of these levels.

To achieve the translation from empirical phenomena into the patterning of social roles, we assume that the data of social relations can be represented as a series of graphs. For the sake of simplicity of presentation, we begin with a network or graph with a single directed relation. We then consider compound paths formed by this relation. Next we incorporate attributes of the nodes, graphs with multiple relations, and finally graphs with multiplex relations defined by the intersection of various types of elementary relations. At each step in building up to the full complexity of a system of social relations, we introduce the appropriate tools for defining structural models of role systems as simplifications of the original network. Once the family of models is introduced, we define those measures which allow us to study empirical networks through structural models whose requirements are approximately fulfilled. The method is illustrated with an empirical example: the teacher-student role structure among members of the social network research discipline. Finally, we consider the problem of the substitutability or equivalence of relations in role systems through an extension of the methods used to study the equivalence of actors or points in a graph.

2. Networks with Single Relations

2.1. Graphs and Their Images

Definition 1. A *directed graph* (digraph) is an ordered pair $G = \langle P,R \rangle$ where P is a finite set of points (points, objects, actors), and R is a relation (type of tie) on P, that is, a subset of the ordered pairs of points in $P \times P$.

Definition 2. A *function* f: $P \rightarrow P'$ is a mapping of each element a in the set P to an image element f(a) in the set P'. An "onto" function (surjection) is a mapping where all elements in P' are images of elements in P.

Definition 3. An *equivalence* on P is a relation such that for all a,b,c in P,

$(a \equiv a)$,

$(a \equiv b)$ implies $(b \equiv a)$, and

$((a \equiv b)$ and $(b \equiv c))$ implies $(a \equiv c)$.

These are the properties of reflexivity, symmetry, and transitivity.

> **Lemma 1.** Every function f: P → P' induces an quivalence relation ≡f on P, namely, for each a,b ∈ P, (a ≡f b) if and only if f(a) = f(b), that is, a and b are equivalent if and only if they are mapped by f onto the same point in the image space.

The proof of this lemma is found in standard texts. All other proofs of lemmas and theorems will be given in Appendix 1.

> **Definition 4.** Let G = ⟨P,R⟩ be a graph and f: P → P' be an onto map. Let R' be the relation on P' defined by R' = {⟨f(a),f(b)⟩ : ⟨a,b⟩ ∈ R}. Then R' is called the relation on P' *induced by* R *and* f.

2.2. Graph Homomorphism and Blockmodel Images. Homomorphisms are mappings which preserve structure. The minimal graph homomorphism is a function which maps the points of a graph into points in an image of the graph, and which maps edges or connections into image edges or image connections such that for every R' image-relation of a relation R, aRb implies that f(a)R'f(b). This may be expressed diagrammatically in the following mapping:

Elements in Graph	Mapped Onto	Elements in Image	Type of Homomorphism
Every Edge	——— f ———▶	Some Edge	Full

Different types of homomorphism preserve additional features of the structure of a graph. The structure which is preserved may be defined by the properties of f in terms of its inverse mapping f^{-1} from the image to the preimage for different types of homomorphism. Table 1 illustrates some of these homomorphisms.

Formal definitions for the types of homomorphisms which are most useful in the network analysis of role structures are given below. We begin with the full homomorphism in which every edge in the image is induced by some edge in the preimage. Since there are no extraneous edges in the image (as in an empty homomorphism, or possibly one which is not full), this and each of the homomorphisms which follow generates a structural model of a network.

The regular and structural homomorphisms are models of particular importance for the study of role systems. In the case of a regular homomorphism, points having the same image necessarily occupy the same abstract position or "role" in the total network or graph. Two points have the same image in a regular homomorphism if and only if, given that one has a relation with a point in a second image set, the other has an identical relation with a counterpart in that set. Two points have the same image in a structural homomorphism if and only if they are identically related to all other points.

Table 1. Illustrations of Some Homomorphisms

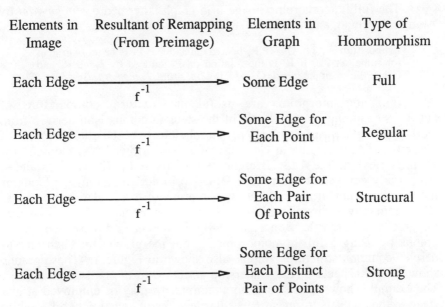

Elements in Image	Resultant of Remapping (From Preimage)	Elements in Graph	Type of Homomorphism
Each Edge	f^{-1}	Some Edge	Full
Each Edge	f^{-1}	Some Edge for Each Point	Regular
Each Edge	f^{-1}	Some Edge for Each Pair Of Points	Structural
Each Edge	f^{-1}	Some Edge for Each Distinct Pair of Points	Strong

Formal definitions for the types of homomorphisms which are most useful in the network analysis of role structures are given below. We begin with the full homomorphism in which every edge in the image is induced by some edge in the preimage. Since there are no extraneous edges in the image (as in an empty homomorphism, or possibly one which is not full), this and each of the homomorphisms which follow generates a structural model of a network.

The regular and structural homomorphisms are models of particular importance for the study of role systems. In the case of a regular homomorphism, points having the same image necessarily occupy the same abstract position or "role" in the total network or graph. Two points have the same image in a regular homomorphism if and only if, given that one has a relation with a point in a second image set, the other has an identical relation with a counterpart in that set. Two points have the same image in a structural homomorphism if and only if they are identically related to all other points.

> **Definition 5.** Let $G = \langle P,R \rangle$ and $G' = \langle P',R' \rangle$ be two graphs. Then $f: G \to G'$ is a *full graph homomorphim* if and only if $f: P \to P'$ is an onto map such that for all $a,b \in P$ and $x,y \in P'$, aRb implies $f(a)R'f(b)$, and $xR'y$ implies $\exists\, c,d \in P: cRd$, $f(c) = x$, and $f(d) = y$.

The full homomorphic image of a graph is termed a *blockmodel* by Arabie, Boorman, and Levitt (1978: 31-32).

> **Proposition A.** Let $G = \langle P,R \rangle$ be a graph and $f: P \to P'$ be an onto map for some set P'. If R' is the relation on P' induced by f and R, and $G' = \langle P',R' \rangle$ then the map $f: G \to G'$ is a *full graph homomorphism*.

Full homomorphims are useful in structural comparisons of networks or graphs. An example of the steps in comparison derives from work by Laumann and Pappi (1976) on relations between elite members of two cities, "Altneustadt" in Germany and "Towertown" (pseudonyms for actual cities) in the U.S. Breiger and Pattison (1978) blockmodeled structurally equivalent actors (see Dfn. 10) to derive summary graphs of the role structures of the communities in terms of three relations: business (B), community affairs discussions (C), and social contacts (S), as shown in the graphs in Figure 1. Bonacich (1981) then compared these two sets of graphs by using a full homomorphism from the graphs for each city to derive "common structure" graphs, also shown in Figure 1. These graphs show shared aspects of the leadership structure in the two communities. The example shows how strong homomorphisms may be employed at one stage in the analysis to reveal particular features of social networks, while weaker homomorphisms are employed at a later stage to show more generic features. The advantages of a family of homomorphic modeling tools, from stronger to weaker, are obvious in terms of different levels of generality.

The full homomorphism is useful for analysis of common structure but is too general to identify more precise role positions. For example, any two non-empty graphs have the same full homomorphic image of a single point image-connected with itself. Unconnected as well as connected points in each graph are mapped onto this same point in the image. Clearly, this does not correspond to mapping points to roles or positions in a network.

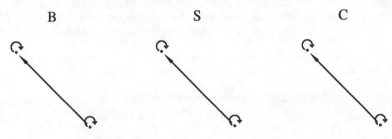

Figure 1. Illustrative Graphs from Breiger and
Pattison (1978). Source: Bonacich 1981

The regular homomorphism, however, can be thought of as a mapping of points in a graph onto distinct roles or positions, with the proviso that if two roles are image-connected, then an incumbent of one of the roles will be connected to some alter who is mapped onto the other role. This is formalized as follows.

> **Definition 6.** A full graph homomorphism f: G → G' is *regular* if and only if for all a,b ∈ P, f(a)R'f(b) implies there exists c,d ∈ P : cRb, aRd, f(c) = f(a), and f(d) = f(b).

Not every full graph homomorphism is a regular graph homomorphism, as is shown by the following example.

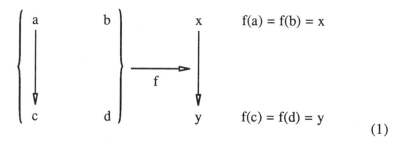

$$f(a) = f(b) = x$$

$$f(c) = f(d) = y$$

(1)

Note that f(b)R'f(d) but bRz is true for no z.

Regular homomorphisms require that occupants of one role will be identically connected to some occupants of a "counterpart" role. In role systems, it is not expected that all occupants of one role will be identically connected to all occupants of a "counterpart" role. This more stringent requirement is the basis for the analysis of role systems of Harrison White and associates. There are some circumstances or types of roles in which it is expected that all occupants of one role will be identically connected to occupants of counterpart roles. This may be formally defined in terms of a structural homomorphism familiar to graph theory (Berge, 1952; Lorraine, 1974; Arabie, Boorman, and Levitt, 1978), as follows:

> **Definition 7.** A full graph homomorphism f: G → G' is *structural* if and only if for all a,b ∈ P where a ≠ b, f(a)R'f(b) implies aRb.

Not every regular graph homomorphism is a structual homomorphism, as is shown by example 2. Note that f(a)R'f(d) but aRd is false.

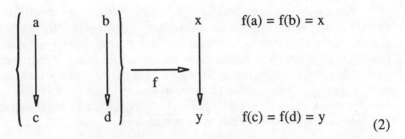

$$f(a) = f(b) = x$$

$$f(c) = f(d) = y \qquad (2)$$

Structural homomorphisms typically are defined for "Michigan" graphs (after Harary, 1969), which are irreflexive. Thus, the fact that the image of a point is image-connected to itself does not imply that it is connected to itself in the preimage. The strongest of the graph homomorphism generalizes the concept of structural equivalance to graphs to include reflexivity. If the connection of a point with itself is significant, then the image-connection of a point implies that it is connected to itself in the preimage. This is formalized as follows:

Definition 8. A full graph homomorphism f: G → G' is *strong* if and only if for all a,b ∈ P, f(a)R'f(b) implies aRB.

Not every structural graph homomorphism is strong, as illustrated by Example 3.

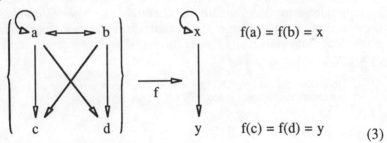

$$f(a) = f(b) = x$$

$$f(c) = f(d) = y \qquad (3)$$

Note that f(b)R'f(b) but bRb is false.

Strong homomorhisms are the basis for certain multidimensional spatial models of graphs or networks. Guttman (1977) shows that symmetric graphs can be represented in a multidimensional space where two points are mapped to the same image in the space if and only if they have identical connections to other points, to each other, and with themselves (the distance from a point in this space to itself is zero). He also notes how spatial representations can be generalized to asymmetric graphs. This idea is explored in detail by Freeman (this volume).

The four graph homomorphisms defined in Definitions 5-8 are of ascending strength in the sense that the stronger imply the weaker, as stated in the following theorem.

Theorem 1. Let f: G → G' then

    (i) f is a strong graph homomorphism implies f is a structural homomorphism;

    (ii) f is a structural homomorphism implies f is a regular homomorphism.

Full and strong homomorphisms are defined in Grätzer (1979: 81) for partial algebras. The regular and structural homomorphism as defined here are useful for analyzing specific aspects of role structure.

2.3. Equivalences. Recall that every graph homomorphism induces an equivalence on the domain set (Lemma 1). The following theorems show that each type of graph homomorphism induces a particular kind of equivalence and conversely that each special type of equivalence is induced by a graph homomorphism of its associated type.

Definition 9. If G = ⟨P,R⟩ and ≡ is an equivalence relation on P, then ≡ is a *strong equivalence* if and only if for all a,b,c ∈ P, a ≡ b implies

    (i) aRb if and only if bRa,

    (ii) aRc if and only if bRc, and

    (iii) cRa if and only if cRb.

Strongly equivalent points are related in the same way to themselves, to each other, and to every other point.

Definition 10. If G = ⟨P,R⟩ and ≡ is an equivalence relation on P then ≡ is a *structural equivalence* if and only if for all a,b,c ∈ P such that a ≠ c ≠ b, a ≡ b implies

    (i) aRb if and only if bRa,

    (ii) aRc if and only if bRc,

    (iii) cRa if and only if cRb, and

    (iv) aRa implies aRb.

Structurally equivalent points are related in the same way to each other and to all other points.

> **Definition 11.** If G = ⟨P,R⟩ and ≡ is an equivalence relation on P then ≡ is a *regular equivalence*[2] if and only if for all a,b,c ∈ P, a ≡ b implies
> (i) aRc implies ∃ d ∈ P : bRd and d ≡ c, and
> (ii) cRa implies ∃ d ∈ P : dRb and d ≡ c.

Regularly equivalent points are connected in the same way to matching equivalents.

> **Theorem 2A.** The equivalence induced by a strong graph homomorphism is a strong equivalence and conversely every strong equivalence is induced by some strong graph homomorphism.

> **Theorem 2B.** The equivalence induced by a structural graph homomorphism is a structural equivalence relation and conversely every structural equivalence relation is induced by some structural homomorphism.

> **Theorem 2C.** The equivalence induced by a regular graph homomophism is a regular equivalence relation and conversely every regular equivalence relation is induced by some regular homomorphism.

Equivalence relations on a set P can be thought of as subsets of P × P. As such, they are partially ordered by set inclusion. A collection of equivalences has a maximal element if there is one equivalence relation in the collection which contains all the rest.

> **Theorem 3A.** The collection of all strong equivalence relations on a graph has a maximal element.

> **Theorem 3B.** The collection of all structural equivalence relations on a graph has a maximal element.

> **Theorem 3C.** The collection of all regular equivalence relations on a graph has a maximal element.

2.4. The Semigroup of Compound Relations. Let R be a relation and define ∘ as composition of relations, i.e., if aRb and bRc then

---

[2] The regular equivalence defined above (Def. 11) was first formulated by Boyd in a seminar in which White contributed part of the conception for generalizing the structural equivalence concept. White also contributed the first fuzzy-set generalization of the measure of structural equivalence. Sailer (1978) combined the formal definition of regular equivalence with White's fuzzy-set approach to derive the first measure of what we here call regular similarity. The name "regular" was reported by Boyd as already in use by Claude Flament in connection with the problem of partitioning binary network matrices such that if a nonzero entry occurs in some blocked sub-matrix, then every row and column of the sub-matrix will contain a nonzero entry.

$a(R \circ R)c$, so $R \circ R = \{\langle a,c \rangle : \exists \, b \in P : \langle a,b \rangle$ and $\langle b,c \rangle \in R\}$. The operation "$\circ$" is associative on the set S of all relations on P generated by R. In other words, $\langle S, \circ \rangle$ is a semigroup. Note that elements R^n and R^m (powers under $\circ$) in S may be equal if they contain the same set of ordered pairs in $P \times P$.

Let $f: G \rightarrow G'$ be a full graph homomorphism from $\langle P,R \rangle$ to $\langle P',R' \rangle$. Now for each relation $Q \in S$ let Q' be the corresponding relation on P' induced by f and Q (see Definition 4). Then let $S' = \{Q' : Q \in S\}$, and $\hat{f}: S \rightarrow S'$ such that $\hat{f}(Q) = Q'$.

Theorem 4. If $f: G \rightarrow G'$ is a regular, structural, or strong graph homomorphism (with respect to R) then f is regular, structural, or strong, respectively, for any relation in S. That is $f: \langle P,Q \rangle \rightarrow \langle P',Q' \rangle$ is regular, structural, or strong respectively for any $Q \in S$.

Theorem 5. If $f: G \rightarrow G'$ is a regular graph homomorphism, then $\hat{f}: S \rightarrow S'$ is a semigroup homomorphism. That is

$$\hat{f}(Q_1 \circ Q_2) = \hat{f}(Q_1) \circ \hat{f}(Q_2) = Q'_1 \circ Q'_2$$

Theorem 6. If $f: G \rightarrow G'$ is a strong homomorphism, then $\hat{f}: S \rightarrow S'$ is a semigroup isomorphism.

The above theorem does not hold if f is only a structural homomorphism. This can be seen in example 3 (above). Note that for points $r \neq s$, $f(r)R'f(s)$ implies rRs. However, $f(b)R'f(b)$ but not bRb, so f is structural but not strong. Note also that $\langle b,b \rangle \notin R$ but $\langle b,b \rangle \in R^2$, so $R \neq R^2$. However, $R' = (R')^2$ so $\hat{f}: S \rightarrow S'$ is not an isomorphism.

Definition 12. A graph G is *acyclic* if and only if $\langle a,a \rangle \notin R^n$ for all $a \in P$ and $n \in Z^+$ (positive integer).

Theorem 7. If $f: G \rightarrow G'$ is a structural homomorphism and G is an acyclic graph, then $\hat{f}: S \rightarrow S'$ is an isomorphism.

Strong homomorphisms of a graph preserve the exact structure of the semigroup of relations generated by the relation on the graph. Structural homomorphisms preserve this structure only when all of the relations are irreflexive. Regular homomorphisms do not necessarily preserve semigroup structure, however, as is seen in the following example.

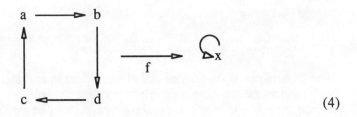

$$(4)$$

Semigroup Composition Table:

∘	R	RR	RRR	I
R	RR	RRR	I	R
RR	RRR	I	R	RR
RRR	I	R	RR	RRR
I	R	RR	RRR	I

∘	I
$\hat{f}$	
I	I

→ $\hat{f}$

3. Networks with Attributes and Multiple Relations

To fully generalize the use of these definitions, we want to define networks as multigraphs (with multiple relations), where the nodes of the network also have attributes. We can then define a network alegebra on which our homomorphisms and equivalences operate.

3.1. Note Attributes: Equivalences and Class Identities.

Definition 13. An *attribute equivalence* on a graph G is the equivalence relation $\equiv_A$ induced by a subset of A of P having a given attribute, where

$$\equiv_A = \{\langle i,j \rangle : i,j \in A \text{ or } i,j \notin A\}.$$

Lemma 2. If $G = \langle P, \equiv_A \rangle$ is the graph of an equivalence relation $\equiv_A$, $\equiv_A$ is also the equivalence induced by the largest regular (also structural or strong) homomorphism of the graph.

Definition 14. A *class identity* on a graph G is a subset I_A of the identity relation $I = \{\langle i,i \rangle : i \in P\}$ for a set A of nodes in P having a given class attribute, thus $I_A = \{\langle i,i \rangle : i \in A \subseteq P\}$.

Lemma 3. If $G = \langle P, I_A \rangle$ is the graph of a class identity I_A defined by the class attribute $\equiv_A$, then the attribute equivalence A is also the equivalence induced by the largest regular homomorphism of the graph.

3.2. Networks and Multiple Relations.

Definition 15. A *network* is an ordered pair N = ⟨P,R⟩ where P is a set of points and R is a collection of relations on P.

A network is sometimes called a multigraph and includes relations on P which may be attribute equivalences or class identities. As with graphs defined by a single relation, homomorphisms can be defined on networks. A network homomorphism involves two mappings. The number of variations possible for defining stronger mappings is greatly increased.

Definition 16a. Let N = ⟨P,R⟩ and N' = ⟨P',R'⟩ be two networks. A *weak full network homomorphism* f: N → N' is an ordered pair of mappings f = ⟨f_1,f_2⟩ such that f_1: P → P' and f_2: R → R' are onto, for every a,b ∈ P and R ∈ R, aRb implies f_1(a)f_2(R)f_1(b), and for every x,y ∈ P' and R' ∈ R', xR'y implies there exists c,d ∈ P such that f_1(c) = x, f_1(d) = y, f_2(R) = R' and cRd.

Definition 16b. Let N = ⟨P,R⟩ and N' = ⟨P',R'⟩ be two networks. A *full network homomorphism* f: N → N' is an ordered pair of mappings f = ⟨f_1,f_2⟩ such that f_1: P → P' and f_2: R → R' are onto, for every a,b ∈ P and R ∈ R, aRb implies f_1(a)f_2(R)f_1(b), and for every x,y ∈ P' and R ∈ R, xf_2(R)y implies there exist c,d ∈ P such that f_1(c) = x, f_1(d) = y and cRd.

Note that for each relation R ∈ R, the full network homomorphism f: N → N' induces a full graph homomorphism from ⟨P,R⟩ to ⟨P',f_2(R)⟩. An example of two forms of regular homomorphism follows.

Definition 17a. A weak full network homomorphism f: N → N' is a *weak regular network homomorphism* if for each R' ∈ R', f_1(a)R'f_1(b) implies there exist c,d ∈ P and R ∈ R such that f_1(a) = f_1(c), f_1(b) = f_1(d), f_2(R) = R', cRb, and aRd for all a,b ∈ P.

Definition 17b. A full network homomorphism f: N → N' is a *regular network homomorphism* if for each R ∈ R, f_1(a)f_2(R)f_1(b) implies there exist c,d ∈ P such that f_1(a) = f_1(c), f_1(b) = f_1(d), cRb and aRd for all a,b ∈ P.

These two pairs of definitions treat differently the case where f_2 is not one-to-one. If two or more relations have the same image, the first definition requires that the homomorphism be full or regular on their union. The second definition requires that the homomorphism be full or regular on each of the relations in R. Similar variations can be made on the network homomorphism corresponding to the structural, and strong graph homomorphisms. If we restrict our attention to only the strong version of each of these definitions, they can be defined simply by requiring that the induced graph homomorphisms meet the property of being structural or strong. The theorems for both homomorphisms and equivalences on graphs will also now generalize to corresponding theorems for networks including those which involve composition of relations and their semigroups.

3.3. Connectivity

Definition 18. A full network homomorphism is *connectivity preserving* if and only if for any sequence of points $x_1,...,x_{n+1} \in P$ and relations $R_1,...,R_n$ such that $f_1(x_1)f_2(R_1)f_1(x_2)...f_1(x_n)f_2(R_n)f_1(x_{n+1})$ $\exists$ points $y_2,...,y_{n+1}$ such that $f_1(x_2) = f_1(y_2),...,f_1(x_{n+1}) = f_1(y_{n+1})$ and $x_1R_1y_2R_2...R_ny_{n+1}$ and there also exists points $z_1,...,z_n$ such that

$$f_1(x_1) = f_1(z_1),...,f_1(x_n) = f_1(z_n) \text{ and } z_1R_1z_2R_2...z_nR_nx_{n+1}.$$

A sequence of related points is a path. The above definition states that a path in the image graph corresponds to specific paths in the preimage passing through each point mapped onto an image endpoint.

Theorem 8. If f is a regular network homomorphism then f is connectivity preserving.

Definition 19. A full network homomorphism is *strongly connectivity preserving* if and only if for every sequence of points $x_1,...,x_{n+1}$ (where $x_i \neq x_j$ for $i \neq j$) and relations $R_1,...,R_n$,

$$f_1(x_1)f_2(R_1)f_1(x_2)...f_1(x_n)f_2(R_n)f_1(x_{n+1})$$

implies $x_1R_1x_2R_2...R_nx_{n+1}$.

Theorem 9. If f is a structural network homomorphism then f is strongly connectivity preserving.

3.4. Multiplex Graphs and Bundle Equivalence.

In a network a particular ordered pair of points may be an element of more than one relation. We call the set of all relations which contain the pair of points $\langle a,b \rangle$, the *bundle* of relations for that pair. That is $B_{ab} = \{R \in R : aRb\}$. A second ordered pair of points $\langle c,d \rangle$ may share the same bundle, that is $B_{ab} = B_{cd}$. It may be that the pair $\langle a,b \rangle$ is not related by any members of R, so that $B_{ab} = \emptyset$. Let B^* be the collection of all non-empty bundles. We can now define new relations on P by looking at the pairs of points that share bundles. These multiplex relations of this type are of substantive interest in social theory.

Definition 20. Let $B \in B^*$. The relation $M_B = \{\langle a,b \rangle : B_{ab} = B\}$ is called a *multiplex* relation *induced* by the network $N = \langle P,R \rangle$.

For each ordered pair $\langle a,b \rangle$ there is a unique bundle associated with it. This bundle may be either empty or a member of B^*. This implies that either $\langle a,b \rangle$ is a member of no M_B or has only one such multiplex relation. The collection of all such relations induced on a given network define a special type of graph.

Definition 21. A *mutiplex graph* is a network $C = \langle P,M \rangle$ such that for each pair of relations $M_1, M_2 \in M$, $M_1 \cap M_2 = \emptyset$.

The graph consisting of the points from a given network and the multiplex relations induced on that network is a multiplex graph. Using this definition of a multiplex graph, Mandel and Winship's (1979) equivalence on a network can be described as follows.

Definition 22. If $C = \langle P,M \rangle$ is a multiplex graph and $\equiv$ is an equivalence on P then $\equiv$ is a *bundle equivalence* if and only if for all $a,b,c \in P$ and $M \in M$, $a \equiv b$ implies

(i) aMc if and only if $\exists\, d \in P : bMd$, and

(ii) cMa if and only if $\exists\, d \in P : dMb$.

Note that the procedure outlined above for moving from a given network to its induced multiplex graph gives a unique result. As the following example shows the properties of network homomorphisms do not carry over to the homomorphisms induced on the multiplex graph. In Example 5, $N = \langle P,R \rangle$ where $P = \{a,b,c,d\}$, $R = \{R,S\}$ and $N' = \langle P',R' \rangle$ with $P' = \{x,y,z\}$ and $R' = \{R'\}$. Note that f is regular as a homomorphism from N to N'. The multiplex graph is $C = \langle P,M \rangle$ where $M = \{M_1,M_2,M_3\}$. The map $f_1: P \to P'$ along with the requirement that f be at least a full network homomorphism gives an induced collection of relations on P' namely $M' = \{M'_1,M'_2,M'_3\}$. To emphasize that the map from C to $C' = \langle P',M' \rangle$ is a different network homomorphism, we have labeled it f_M. Even though f is regular, f_M is not. Regularity, however, is preserved in the opposite direction.

Theorem 10. If $N = \langle P,R \rangle$ is a network, $C = \langle P,M \rangle$ the multiplex graph derived from it, and f: $C \to C' = \langle P',M' \rangle$ a full network homomorphism, then f induces a full network homomorphism on N and

1) if f is regular the induced homomorphism is regular;

2) if f is strong the induced homomorphism is strong.

The image of a multiplex graph under a regular network homomorphism is not necessarily a multiplex graph. This is shown in Example 6, where a pair of image points are connected by more than one image relation, and the image relations R' and S' are distinct in their ordered pairs in P' × P'. Since multiplex graphs give a representation of the unique bundles of relations and attributes between individuals which are used to define social roles, a homomorphism which preserves this structure is desirable. Strong homomorphisms preserve such a structure but are too restrictive for our purposes.

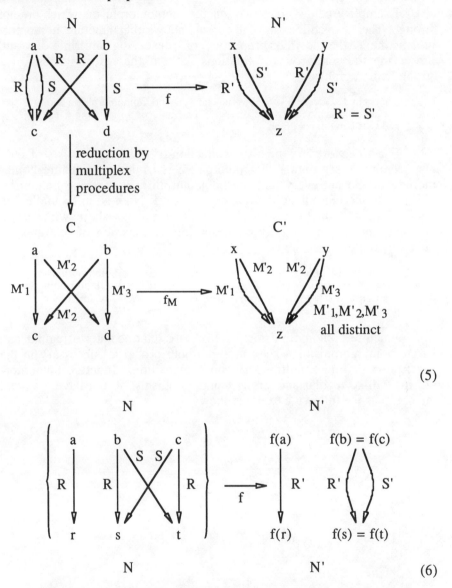

(5)

(6)

Definition 23. Let $f: N \to N'$ be a regular network homomorphism. f is a *juncture network homomorphism* if and only if $f_1(a) = f_1(c)$ and $f_1(b) = f_1(d)$ implies $B_{ab} = B_{cd}$, $B_{ab} = \emptyset$ or $B_{cd} = \emptyset$.

Theorem 11. Every strong network homomorphism is a juncture network homomorphism.

Example 7 below gives two juncture homomorphisms which are not strong. The next collection of theorems shows that juncture homomorphisms have the desired properties of preserving multiplexity and preserving the semigroup of relations without the restrictiveness of a strong homomorphism.

Theorem 12. Let f: N → N' be a juncture network homomorphism and C the multiplex graph derived from N. Then f induces a map from C to C' and C' is a multiplex graph.

For a network in which the collection of relations consists of only one relation, every regular homomorphism is trivially a juncture homomorphism. So not every juncture homomorphism is a strong homomorphism. On the other hand the homomorphism f: N → N' in Example 6 is regular but not juncture. Juncture homomorphisms share with strong homomorphisms the property of preserving composition of relations, as the following theorem shows.

Theorem 13. Let f: N → N' be a juncture network homomorphism where N = $\langle P,R \rangle$, N' = $\langle P',R' \rangle$ and f = $\langle f_1, f_2 \rangle$. If $\circ$ is a relation composition and $\langle R, \circ \rangle$ is a semigroup then f_2: $\langle R, \circ \rangle \to \langle R', \circ \rangle$ is an isomorphism.

Juncture homomorphisms therefore are intermediate to regular and strong homomorphisms. They preserve both properties necessary in the description of roles: multiplexity and composition. Juncture homomorphisms, unlike regular and strong homomorphisms, do not have maximal members, as the following example shows.

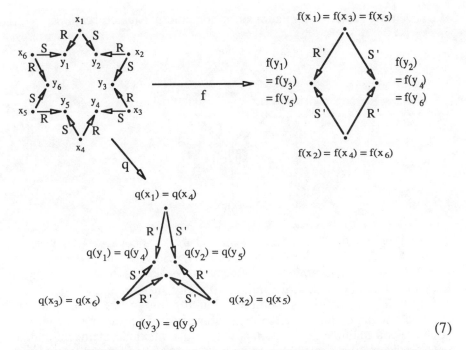

(7)

Example 7 shows that there is not a simple unique representation of a role structure. All three networks are multiplex graphs and both f and q are juncture homomorphisms but not strong. Neither of the two image networks can be further reduced while preserving a distinction between the relations.

Juncture equivalences can be defined as follows.

Definition 24. Let $\equiv$ be a regular network equivalence. Then $\equiv$ is a *juncture network equivalence* if for every $a,b,c,d \in N$, $a \equiv b$ and $c \equiv d$ implies $B_{ac} = B_{bd}$, $B_{ac} = \emptyset$, or $B_{bd} = \emptyset$.

We have now defined a partial order of homomorphisms on networks.

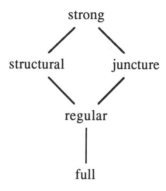

Table 2 reviews these homomorphism and their properties. The weakly regular and full homomorphisms have only received minimal treatment here because of their limited usefulness in the definition of role. Three homomorphism (strong, structural, and regular) have maximal members. Juncture homomorphisms, although lacking the property of having maximal members, have the desirable properties of preserving semigroup structure and multiplexity. The fact that unique maximal members do not occur indicates that "role" may sometimes be analyzed from different and incompatible vantage points.

Table 2. Five Graph Homomorphisms and Their Properties

Homemorphism	Images	Induced Semigroup Homomorphism	Maximal Equivalence	Connectivity Preserving
Strong	Strong Blockmodel	Isomorphism	Yes	Strong
Structural	Structural Blockmodel	Isomorphism for Irreflexive Graph	Yes	Strong
Juncture	Junctural Blockmodel	Isomorphism	No	Weak
Regular	Regular Blockmodel	Homomorphism	Yes	Weak
Full	Blockmodel	Not Necessarily a Homomorphism	Yes	No

3.5. Network Blockmodels and Cross-Cutting Roles. Previous approaches to empirical blocking methods are based on network mappings via a density criterion (Arabie, Boorman, and Leavitt, 1978: 32). Although these mappings are not strict homomorphisms, they are close approximations to the full homomorphism. There are two density criteria which can be defined as follows. Let N be the network $\langle P,R \rangle$ and let $f_1: P \rightarrow P'$ be an onto map. For each pair of points $a,b \in P'$ let $f_1^{-1}(a) = \{x_1,\ldots,x_n\}$ and $f_1^{-1}(b) = \{y_1,\ldots,y_m\}$. Then for each pair $\langle a,b \rangle \in P' \times P'$ and $R \in R$ we can define the number

$$r_{ab}^R = \frac{\sum_i^n \sum_j^m x_i R y_j}{n \times m} \quad \text{where } x_i R y_j = \begin{cases} 1 \text{ if } \langle x_i, y_i \rangle \in R \\ 0 \text{ if } \langle x_i, y_i \rangle \notin R \end{cases}$$

Let R' be any relation on P', let

$$\alpha = \max \left\{ r_{a,b}^R : \langle a,b \rangle \notin R' \right\} \text{ and let } \beta = \min \left\{ r_{a,b}^R : \langle a,b \rangle \in R' \right\}.$$

α is called the "zero block impurity" parameter for R' relative to R, and β is called the "one block impurity" parameter for R' relative to R. Note that there is an α parameter and a β parameter for each pair of relations R and R'.

Suppose $\langle P,R \rangle$ and $\langle P',R' \rangle$ are two networks with $f_1: P \rightarrow P'$ and $f_2: R \rightarrow R'$ both onto maps. The pair $\langle f_1,f_2 \rangle$ is a full network homomorphism if and only if for each $R \in R$, $\alpha = 0$ and $\beta \neq 0$ where and are computed for $f_2(R)$ relative to R. In the case that $\alpha = 0$ and $\beta = 1$ for all R, the pair $\langle f_1,f_2 \rangle$ is a strong network homomorphism. Breiger, Boorman and Arabie (1975) call blockmodels where alpha is close to zero "lean fit" blockmodels and those where beta is also close to 1, "fat fit" blockmodels.

To summarize the shortcomings of previous work on blockmodeling:

(1) Structural equivalence yields groupings of points which are related to each other and to all other points in identical ways; network blockmodeling under this equivalence preserves the semigroup of relations on the network, but is too restrictive to capture the more abstract basis of role parallels. This restrictiveness increases for strong equivalence, where equivalent points are related to each other, to themselves, and to all other points in identical ways.

(2) Full equivalence, even if relaxed in terms of density of exceptions allowed in zeroblocks, is too coarse an equivalence to capture role parallels. If the density is below the density of the entire graph, the

maximal full blockmodel is a single point connected to itself. Structured roles regularities in the patterns of connections in the original network must be captured by other critiera.

(3) Bundle equivalence (Mandel and Winship, 1979) is also too coarse to capture positional or role equivalence.

The two criteria for blockmodeling we introduce here are based on definitions of the abstract pattern of role relatedness:

(4) Regular equivalence yields groupings of points in which for every pair of persons in the equivalent position, if one has a relation with a person in a second position, the other has an identical relation with a counterpart in that position. This equivalence has two related problems. One is that in networks with multiple relations there may be more than one characteristic multiplex relation (Definition 20) between positions. Because of this, the regular homomorphism does not necessarily preserve the structure of the semigroup of relations defined on the multigraph.

(5) Juncture equivalence is a regular equivalence in which (a) there is no more than one characteristic bundle of relations between positions, and (b) the semigroup of relations defined on the multigraph is iso-morphically preserved in the blockmodel image.

The limitation of juncture equivalence is that there is not necessarily a maximal juncture equivalence for a given network. Consequently, if juncture equivalence most closely captures the abstract role concept, we may find for a given network that there are multiple maximal role structures (blockmodels) which do not reduce to a single role system.

This limitation is simply a statement of the obvious fact that roles may cross-cut one another in complex ways such that it is impossible to assign every actor a unique role position and then characterize the relations between these positions.

We are thus impelled by this study of homomorphisms towards a formal solution of the problem of how, in a multiplex network, to delimit the distinct cross-cutting role-like structures. The beginnings of this problem will be taken up in the final section of this chapter, and continued in another work rethinking the status concept in relation to the definition of social roles (White and Reitz, 1983).

4. Blockmodeling a Regular Role Structure

4.1. Measurement of Regular Role Distances. A variety of measures of regular equivalence have been defined (Sailer 1978; White and Reitz n.d.). In a distance measure, equivalent actors have distance zero. The algorithm we wish to apply (White and Reitz n.d.) generates distances with the following property. If either of two actors with a regular role distance of zero are related to a third party, then the other will have this relation with someone at role distance zero to the third party.

Regularity coefficients are computed by an iterative procedure. Computation of approximations to regularity as defined here, unlike Sailer's (1978) procedure, require an initial assumption that all points are equivalent or zero distant. The first iteration checks whether pairs of points can be reqularly equivalent (zero distant) by having the same profile of in- and out-degree across the set of all points. For multiplex relations, distances between these profiles is computed. The second iteration computes for each pair of points the extent to which they have matching relations to other points which are approximately zero-distant. In checking the distance between i and j, the algorithm considers each k to which i is related, and finds the best matching point m which best approximates (1) a j-m relation matching the i-k relation, and (2) zero distance between k and m. For symmetry, this is repeated with i and j exchanged. This process is repeated in each iteration. Distances are monotonically non-increasing in each iteration, and converge to a limit. For multiplex relations, the algorithm generates zero-distances in the convergent solution which constitute an equivalence partition of points. This equivalence relation is the smallest equivalence satisfying regularity which contains all the juncture equivalences. In social network analysis we usually do not want an exact algebraic solution—which in large multiplex networks often will not result in equivalence sets containing two or more points—but approximations to equivalence sets. In practice, three iterations of the distance algorithm are usually sufficient to detect the major social roles in a network.

The coefficient of multiplex regular distance (RMD) is:

$$RMD_{ij}^{t+1} = \sqrt{\frac{\sum_{k=1}^{N}\left[\max_{m=1}^{N}\sum_{q=1}^{N} iqjDIS_{km}^{t} + \max_{m=1}^{N}\sum_{q=1}^{N} jqiDIS_{km}^{t}\right]}{\sum_{k=1}^{N}\left[iR_qk^2 + jR_qk^2 + kR_qi^2 + kR_qj^2\right]}}$$

with

$$iqjDIS_{km}^{t} = \left(iR_qk \ominus \min\left(1 - RMD_{km}^{t}, jR_qm\right)\right)^2$$

$$+ \left(kR_qi \ominus \min\left(1 - RMD_{km}^{t}, mR_qj\right)\right)^2$$

where "$\ominus$" is Boolean subtraction, N is the number of points, Q the number of relations, and $RMD_{ij}^{0} = 0$.

This measure is symmetric in that $RMD_{ij}^{t} = RMD_{ji}^{t}$. It computes distances based on both in- and out-degree, and is normalized to the interval [0,1].

Consider the graph in Figure 2. The computations of RMD for iterations are the first three shown in Figure 3. High values in the third iteration show the distinctiveness of each position. By seven iterations all

$$1 \to 3 \to 5$$

$$2 \to 4$$

Figure 2. An Illustrative Graph of 5 Points

interpoint distances reach 1.0. The third iteration values retain the of pattern similarities among senders (1 and 2) and receivers (4 and 5), in contrast to dissimilarities between other pairs of points.

For a single relation, there are four uses for this measure:

(1) determination of maximal regular equivalence,

(2) finding approximations to regular equivalence,

(3) finding overlapping clusters of regular equivalence, and

(4) defining role distances, or representing these distances in a spatial representation.

The first two uses lead to defining equivalence classes or partitions of actors in the network, and can be used to define blockmodel images (regular, or full homomorphism, which approximate regularity). The third use, for example through Arabie and Carroll's (1980) MAPCLUS program (see Shepard and Arabie, 1979), might suggest that there are multiple cross-cutting roles even for a single relation (e.g., in Figure 2, the roles are "sender" and "receiver"). The final use, for example through MDS, might suggest a multidimensional role-space in which positions are embedded.

These four approaches to role distance using the regular similarity measure will be examined for a single relation in the following example.

RMD^1	1	2	3	4	5
1	.00				
2	.00	.00			
3	.58	.58	.00		
4	1.00	1.00	.58	.00	
5	1.00	1.00	.58	.00	.00

RMD^2	1	2	3	4	5
1	.00				
2	.76	.00			
3	.85	.58	.00		
4	1.00	1.00	.58	.00	
5	1.00	1.00	.86	.76	.00

RMD^3	1	2	3	4	5
1	.00				
2	.76	.00			
3	.95	.92	.00		
4	1.00	1.00	.92	.00	
5	1.00	1.00	.95	.76	.00

Figure 3. Three Iterations of RMD for the Graph
in Figure 2

4.2. Regular Roles in a Disciplinary Protégé Network. We have argued that social roles are defined by abstract patterns of relatedness characterized by regularity of ego/alter ties. The structural requirement, that role encumbants be identically or similarly linked to *ALL* occupants of counterpart roles, is too restrictive to capture role equivalence for many kinds of social structures. Regularity merely seeks to assure that a role pattern exists such that members of role A have a particular type of tie to members of role B, then each encumbant of A will have such a tie with *SOME* (not necessarily all) members of B.

To illustrate this point, we have analyzed the teacher/student tie network among members of the International Network for Social Network Analysis (INSNA). A network of protégé relationships of this sort exemplifies an abstract role pattern where the roles cross-cut specific localities or cliques. A typical role of senior scholar in a scientific discipline might be defined not only by having students in the discipline but by those students having students. Intellectual grandchildren occupy a distinctive role in the "mainline" of a discipline by having not only protégés but their protégés' protégés in the network. Middle range scholars joining the "mainstream" may be identified by the fact that they are co-teachers of the "grandchild" students. This divides the third generation between those who are only mainline-taught and those who are also taught by other teachers in the discipline. Finally, there may also be teacher/student pairs with only one generational depth. In a mature discipline, the role structure of protégéship might look something like the following, with downward arrows representing teacher/student ties:

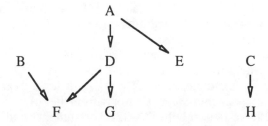

Abstract role patterns of this sort may be found that cut across schools or schools of thought. They are not dependent, for example, on who teaches as what university. A mainstream leader (role A) may have students who spread out to teach at different universities (roles D and E), some of whom (D) in turn have their students (F and G), of whom some (F) are also taught by others in the discipline (B). An "exclusive" mainstream may have pure three- and four-generation chains, with no inbranching colleagueships (C). An immature discipline may be lacking in teacher/student chains of three or more generations. In short, a variety of such roles and role structures are possible, and the implications of different role structures as well as occupancy of different roles within them are open to investigation. Here, however, we are interested only in the identification of such structures.

We have provided (1) an algebraic characterization of homomorphisms on a network which map encumbants into identical abstract roles, and (2) a measurement technique consistent with the algebra for gauging the extent to which pairs of persons occupy a similar position in such a role network, without prior knowledge of the role structure. We will now apply this algorithm to the INSNA teacher/student network.

INSNA was founded in 1977 as an association of network researchers. It had a mainstream core from Harvard sociology most closely identified with the leadership of Harrison White. The INSNA coordinator, Barry Wellman, distributed questionnaires to all first-year members as part of an effort to study the internal network and role structure of this emergent discipline. One item in the questionnaire asked respondents to indicate their student or teacher relationships within the association. These data were compiled, cross-checked, and corrected by Linton C. Freeman and made available for this study. There were 60 people at that time in the assocation who had teacher or student ties among them.

Regular role distances were computed among the 60 people using the REGGE algorithm discussed above. Three iterations are sufficient to distinguish four levels in a hierarchy and provides sufficient information for the task. Figure 4 shows the splitting of "pure" roles in each iteration. Only three distinctions are possible in the first iteration: teacher only, teacher and student, and student only. Each of these occurs in the INSNA network. In the next iteration, there are 12 possible distinctions, of which 9 are realized. For example, split 1/1 and 1/2 differ in that person 28 has teacher ties to the "teacher-student" group from iteration 1, while 24, 59, 33, 31, and 50 have ties to both the "teacher-student" and "student only" groups. The reader can verify these splits in successive iterations by reference to the raw network data in Table 5. In the third iteration, there are hundreds of possible role distinctions, of which only 21 occur. The resultant groupings of people are equivalent at level 3, but might be split in further iterations. In this case, such iterations eventually result in sets of persons who are structurally equivalent—having the same teachers and/or students. We are not interested here in perfect equivalence, but in approximate role equivalence. For this purpose, three iterations is sufficient as many of the 21 splits in Figure 4 recombine on the basis of approximations to regularity.

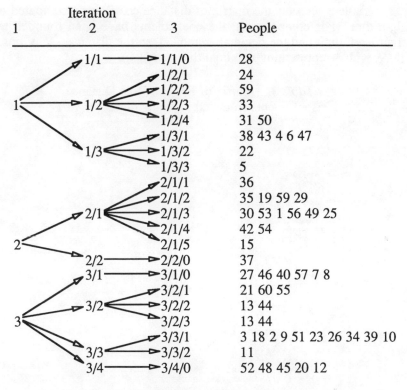

Figure 4. The Splitting of "Pure" Roles in
Each Iteration

The coefficient of role distance agrees with the analysis in Figure 3 in terms of the "splitting" of non-equivalent "pure" roles, but provides a wholly different sort of information, not dependent on such "purities". It measures the relative role distance between each pair of persons *independently* of any particular partition of the network into roles. This is fundamental for any network analysis which is sensitive to overall pattern rather than an exact structure. Methods dependent on successive *ad hoc* partitioning (such as CONCOR) are burdened by sensitivity to methodological effects and subject to method distortions.

Table 3 presents the matrix of distance coefficients computed by the algorithm. For compactness, the coefficients have been rounded to one significant digit and the decimals removed, so the distance scale runs from .0–.9, with * representing maximal distance (1.0).

Table 3. Matrix of Regular Role Distance
Coefficients (rounded to single digit, * = 1.0)

```
28  0
59  50
24  520
33  7420
31  64480
50  834800
38  *88*650
43  *99*7500
 4  *99*75000
 6  *88*540000
47  *89*7500000
22  877676466460
 5  *886*99****40
36  *99*97888688*0
35  989986776577930
19  *789654444559300
58  988*76666566*3000
29  *99*86676577*30000
30  *99*76666567*442330
53  *89*76555456*5523300
 1  *99*76566467*66334000
56  *99*87677577*663340000
49  *99*87677577*6633400000
25  *99*87677577*55334000000
42  *****9**99*9*426535666550
54  **********9*5376467666600
37  ********99*9*54765677776440
15  988*88999998*777665655556670
27  **********8*8888767655555650
46  **********8*88887676555556500
40  **********8*88887676555565000
57  **********8*8888767655555650000
 7  **********8*88887676555556500000
 8  **********9*77876665555556500000
21  **********9*77877776666667765555550
60  **********9*87877776666667655555500
55  **********9*88988887777787777776000
13  **********9*99999999888888999995440
44  **********9*88988888777777777777644300
16  **********9**9******9**********765330
41  **********9**9******9**********6543300
17  **********9**9******9**********76533000
14  **********9**9******9***9*9*****875340000
32  **********9**9******9**********8863400000
 3  **********8**9*9*****9***9*9****76556434450
18  **********8**9*9*****9***9*9****765564344500
 2  **********8**9*9******************6645543335000
 9  **********8**9*9*****************77567544570000
51  **********8**9*9*****************775675445700000
23  **********8**9*9****************775565344600000
26  **********8**9*9***************77556534460000000
34  **********8**9*9**************775565344600000000
39  **********8**9*9***************6645543335000000000
10  **********8**9*9**************77567645670000000000
11  **********9**9***************775565445644344444350
52  **********8**9*9***************97678755889**8889*90
48  **********9**9******9**********98755764588998889*800
45  **********8**9*9*****9**********997667645778997779*8000
20  **********8**9*9*****9**********997667645778997779*80000
12  **********8**9*9*****9**********997667645778997779*800000
```

The coefficients in Table 3 are partitioned into eight blocs on the basis of three criteria: (1) average intra-bloc distances are uniformly higher than inter-bloc distances, as shown in Table 4; (2) sets of persons in the same bloc are enclosed by a non-overlapping convex boundaries ("clusters") in the multidimensional scaling representation of the distance matrix, shown in Figure 5; and (3) the partition of the network graph in Table 5 shows the minimum number of errors to the criterion of regularity, given possible blocs satisfying the first two criteria.

The average intra-bloc role distances in Table 4 show a maximum value of .47 for the first bloc—a heterogeneous one of teachers. This is less than the smallest average inter-bloc role distance of .50 between the 6th and 7th blocs. (The averages are respectively .25 and .88).

The requirement that role-blocs form convexly bounded nonoverlapping sets in the MDS representation of the distance matrix is a severe and important constraint for identifying meaningful social roles. There are 4 and 6 bloc, as well as other 8 bloc partitions of the network in Table 5 which produce the same or marginally fewer errors (see below), but none which satisfies convexity. The MDS convexity criteria is important substantively in that it requires that members of the same role "pattern" have not only low role distance amongst themselves, but a highly similar pattern of role distances to other roles.

Table 4. Average Interbloc Role Distances

	1	2	3	4	5	6	7	8
BLOC 1	.47							
BLOC 2	.76	.16						
BLOC 3	.88	.75	.40					
BLOC 4	.92	.68	.85	.35				
BLOC 5	1.00	.99	.91	.63	.24			
BLOC 6	1.00	1.00	.95	.89	.82	.29		
BLOC 7	1.00	1.00	.91	.99	.96	.50	.07	
BLOC 8	1.00	1.00	.91	.98	1.00	.66	.83	.00

Parenthetically, not all of the 60 persons in the network are shown in Figure 5. Every senior member and every other junior member of the network are labelled in Table 4 to correspond with their inclusion—represented as letters—in the MDS Figure.

Errors or exceptions to the regularity condition by the partition imposed in Table 5 are counted as follows. For each rectangular bloc in

the matrix, two numbers are computed. One is the minimum number of
1's which can be placed to insure that each row and column has at least

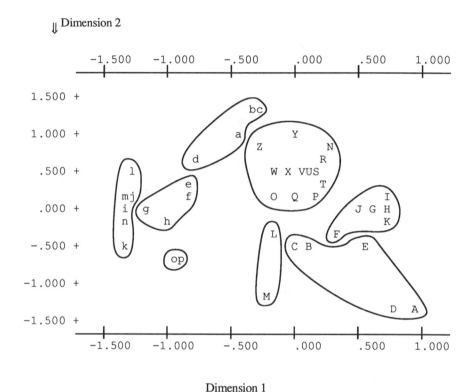

Figure 5. MDS Representation of Role Distances,
with Clusters Determined by Least Error in
Regularity Matrix (Table 3)

one 1. This is the number of errors for a 1-bloc. The other is the number
of 1's in the bloc which must be removed for a perfect 0-bloc. The smaller
of these numbers defines the bloc type and its errors. By these criteria, the
partitioning of Table 5 generates 17 errors. The largest number of errors
is in the 4-7 rectangle (a 1-bloc), in which six columns contain no entries.

What is the role structure or blockmodel image of the INSNA
teacher-student ties? It is precisely the one discussed at the beginning of

this section, which might be expected of a maturing discipline growing at the boundaries:

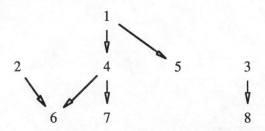

This structure has a senior mainline role (1), with students (4, 5), some of whom (4) produce other students (6,7), with some of those students (6) co-taught by others (2). In addition, it has a peripheral line of teachers (3) and their students (8) who do not tie into the mainline.

Who occupy these roles? This is an interesting question structurally since some role members have dense connections in their blocs, which others have sparse connections. By design, the algorithm is insensitive to density criteria (unlike CONCOR and other algorithms based on structural equivalence). The density differences within blocs thus provide additional detail on role-occupancy structure and are not a methodological artifact. Thus, we consider the occupants of some of the roles:

Role 1 (Mainstream Leaders).

B and C—Harrison White (59) and Chad Gordon (24)—high density teacher connections to roles 4 and 5. High overlap in students.

D—Charles Kadushin (33)—low density connections to roles 4 and 5, with one overlapping student (Nan Lin) with Gordon.

E—Eugene Jacobson (31)—same as D, but no overlapping students.

A—Paul Holland (28)—one teacher connection to role 4.

Role 2 (Co-Teachers of Third Generation Mainstream)

F—Everette Rogers (50)—overlapping students with E, but bulk of students in role 6.

G, J—Dennis Magill (38) and Steve Berkowitz (6)—teachers of two or more students in role 6.

H, I, K—Patrick Mullins (43), John Barnes (4), Forrest Pitts (47)—teachers of one student in role 6.

Rethinking the Role Concept

Table 5. Eight-Bloc Model of the INSNA
Teacher-Student Network. Number of errors = 17

```
A                                                    28
 B                                                   59
  C                                                  24
   D                                                 33
    E                                                31
     F                                               50
      G                                              38
       H                                             43
        I                                            4
         J                                           6
          K                                          47
           L                                         22
            M                                        5
111          N                                       36
  1           O                                      35
  1            P                                     19
 11             Q                                    58
  1              R                                   29
 11               S                                  30
  1                T                                 53
    1               U                                1
 11                  V                               56
      11              W                              49
 11                    X                             25
 11                     Y                            42
 11                      *                           54
 11                     Z1                           37
   1                      *                          15
   1 1                     a                         27
  1                         *                        46
  1                          b                       40
 1                            *                      57
 1                             c                     7
 11                             *                    8
 11                1             d                   21
   1 1                 1          *                  60
     1              11             e                 55
 1     1 1          11 11           *                13
       11           1                f               44
        1 1         11   1            *              16
          1         11 11              g             41
         1          111                 *            17
         1          1                    h           14
          1 1           1                 *          32
                    1                      i         3
                    1                       *        18
                    11  1                    j       2
                    1                         *      9
                    1                          k     23
                   1                            *    26
                   1                          1      34
                   1                            *    39
                   11              1             m    10
                          1                      *   11
                   1              1               n  11
              1                                    * 52
             11                                     o 48
              1                                     * 45
              1                                    * 20
              1                                    p 12
```

Role 3 (Autonomous Teachers)

L—Linton Freeman (22)—teacher of numerous students in role 8 (autonomous).

M—Murray Beauchamp (5)—teacher of two students in role 8, one overlapping with Freeman.

Role 4 (Mainstream Disseminators)

N through Z—Joel Levine (36), Ed Laumann (35), Bonnie Erickson (19), Barry Wellman (58), Leslie Howard (29), Nancy Howell (30), Lorne Tepperman (53), Michael Weinstein (53), Marc Granovetter (25), Nick Mullins (42), Michael Useem (54), Nan Lin (37)—students of Harrison White and/or Chad Gordon (role 1) who have gone on to teach students in roles 6 and 7.

U and W—Richard Alba (1) and William Richards (49)—excepted from the list above as students of Charles Kadushin or Eugene Jacobson, but parallel in relations to roles 6 and 7.

Role 5 (Students of Mainstream Leaders)

*—Diana Crane (15)—student of Charles Kadushin in role 1 and teacher of Nan Lin (an exceptional pattern: Lin is a role 4 disseminator).

a—Roxanne Hiltz (27)—student of Eugene Jacobson and Everett Rogers in role 1.

b, c, d, etc.—William Phelan (46), John McLoughlin (40), Thomas Weisner (57), Paul Bernard (7), Phil Bonacich (8), Claude Fischer (21)—students of Harrison White and/or Chad Gordon in role 1.

Role 6 (Third Generation Mainstream with New Influences inside the subdiscipline)

e, f, g, h, etc.—Rolf Wigand (60), Lois Verbrugge (55), Peter Carrington (13), Stephen Murray (44), Barry Leighton (16), Liviana Mostacci (41), Ellan Darow (17), June Corman (14), Davor Jedlicka (32)—students of roles 4 (mainstream disseminators) and 2 (other influences within INSNA).

Role 7 (Third Generation Mainstream)

i through n, etc.—Karen Anderson (3), Barry Edginton (18), Howard Aldritch (2), C. Bottomley (9), Norman Shulman (51), Joe Galaskiewicz (23), Stephen Hansell (26), Alden Klovdahl (34), Peter Marsden (39), Paul Burstein (10), and Ron Burt (11)—students of mainstream disseminators (role 4).

Role 8 (Autonomous Students)

o, p, etc—M. Estellie Smith (52), Nick Poushinsky (48), Bruce Nickum (45), Tom Fararo (20), Marlee Campbell (12)—students of Linton Freeman and/or Murray Beachamp (role 3).

These roles—while not subject here to further confirmatory analysis—appear to be substantively meaningful in capturing roles within the scientific discipline. They are not dependent on the "pure" (artifactual) roles of Figure 4. For example, 31=50 (E=F), 21=60 (d=e), and 21=55 in Figure 4 and Table 3 by "pure" criteria, but are in different blocs by their overall pattern of roles distances. Nor are they dependent on densities of ties within each inter-role blocs, as is clear above and in inspection of the raw network data in Table 5. They are also not dependent on approximations to structural equivalence. Persons E and F, for example, have a majority of ties in common, but occupy different roles by virtue of their overall patterns of ties (the MDS location of G in Figure 5 would allow F to be merged into E's role bloc, but the errors in Table 5 are fewer with F in the adjacent bloc). It is the case, however, that persons who are perfectly structurally equivalent (40=46, 7=57, 18=3, 51=9, 34=26=23, 12=20=45) necessarily occupy the same role by regularity criteria. The algorithm and rules for forming partitions do the job they were designed to do successfully.

As a blockmodeling procedure, regularity provides a means of evaluating the overall patterns of role distance—between positions, actors within the positions, and actors in different positions. The procedure allows identification of optimal partitions of actors into roles—not necessarily unique but severly constrained and easily identifiable. The resultant structure provides an overall model of role structure and allows for analysis of differences in they way each encumbant realizes a particular role.

5. The Substitutability of Relations

In a social network, a few primary relations by the operation of composition form a complex network of multiple relations among the actors. For example the simple parent/child relations via composition form all the many kinship relations such as sibling relations, grandparent/grandchild relations, uncle-aunt/nephew-niece relations, cousin relations and so on. When these relations through composition are extended far enough they include all generations both past, present, and future. If one restricts the actors to just living actors, the inclusion of all possible compositions will form a semigroup, and in the case of a restricted set of actors, this semigroup may have a simple representation (see example 9 below). However, in most cases even a fairly small set of actors can be related in complex ways and a reduction in the number of relations is necessary, particularly in the study of roles. This reduction in order to be meaningfull needs to preserve structure, which in the case of relations means the structure of the semigroup resulting from composition.

5.1. Semigroup Homomorphisms. We have shown that when the set of relations in a network forms a semigroup and when the network homomorphism is regular the mapping on the relations is a semigroup homomorphism. Lorrain and White (1971), Pattison (1980), Bonacich (this volume), and White and Reitz (1983) have explored the relationships between semigroup homomorphisms and network homomorphisms. As these authors have shown, it is possible to find many homomorphisms on the set of relations of a network, but it may not be possible for these homomorphsims to be represented as the relational map of a network homomorphsim. In this section we will explore under what conditions a relational map may be represented as a part of a network homomorphism, and in particular those conditions under which such a map might also be a semigroup homomorphsim, that is preserve compositions.

Let $\langle P,R \rangle$ be a network where P is a set of points and R a set of relations on P. Let R be closed under composition, (i.e. R is a semigroup) and let $\langle f_1,f_2 \rangle$ be a weak full network homomorphsim. By $[R]f_2$ we mean the collection of all those relations in R which are identified under f. That is $[R]f_2 = \{Q : f_2(Q) = f_2(R)\}$. The relation which consists of the union of all the pairs related by any of these relations we will denote by $\cup[R]f_2$. The next theorem shows that in fact a network homomorphism which collapses only the relations of a network is in fact representable as such a union.

Theorem 14. If $N = \langle P,R \rangle$ and $N' = \langle P',R' \rangle$ are networks, and $\langle f_1,f_2 \rangle$ a network mapping, where f_1 is the identity map on P, then $f = \langle f_1,f_2 \rangle$ is a weak full network homomorphism if and only if $f_2(R) = \cup[R]f_2$ for all $R \in R$.

This theorem tells us that if we are looking for ways to reduce the complexity of the relational structure of a network while keeping the points and the structure of the network intact, we must consider any and only those mappings which are formed by taking the union of existing relations. In general such mappings may not preserve the structure of the relations under composition. But at least we know that if a map reduces only the set of relations and yet is part of a network homomorphism, our search is narrowed to the set of relations which can be formed by taking the unions of relations from our original set of relations. The example below shows that although forming the union of some of the original relations results in a homomorphic image of the original network (in a weak sense) compositions are not preserved.

Example 8. Suppose P is a set of six individuals working in a company. Two of the workers are supervisors who consider each other co-workers. Each of these supervisors has two subordinates, with each pair of subordinates considering each other coworkers. The network can be represented graphically as follows.

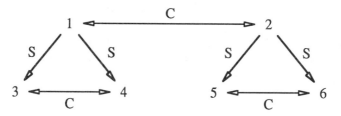

The semigroup of relations on this network includes both the null relation and the identity. Note also that the composition of coworker and subordinate form a new relation coworkers subordinate which we denote by SC. The composition table is as follows.

∘	0	I	C	S	SC
0	0	0	0	0	0
I	0	I	C	S	SC
C	0	C	I	S	SC
S	0	S	SC	0	0
SC	0	SC	S	0	0

Note that this set of relations forms a semigroup. However, if we were to define a network homomorphism by using the identity map on the set of points for the point map and mapping relation C and S onto their union denoted by U. The resulting network would look like the following.

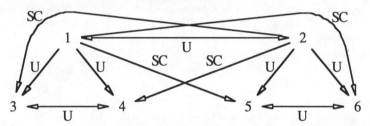

In this representation we have included the arcs representing the relation SC which were not explicitly represented in the original network. This new network has four relations, 0, I, U, and SC. These relations however are not closed under the operation of composition. For example U ∘ U is a relation which is the union of I, S, and SC and not one of 0, I, U, or SC. So although this new network is a network homomorphic image of the first, the compositional structure of the relations is not preseved.

However, if we had instead defined our relational map by forming the union of I and C and also the union of S and SC, an entirely different picture emerges. If we let A = I ∪ C and B = S ∪ SC, the following composition table results.

∘	0	A	B
0	0	0	0
A	0	A	B
B	0	B	0

Note that this new set of relations not only forms a semigroup but that this semigroup is a homomorphic image of the semigroup of relations in the original network. This new network has substantive meaning. It is now a network in which any supervisor is a supervisor to any subordinate and any worker is a coworker to any other worker at his or her particular level. Thus this new network defines the relations in terms of levels.

The above example shows that in general, forming the union of two relations in a network does preserve some structure, but that the structure which is preseved may be so weak as to have little substantive meaning. The second part of the example shows that on the other hand it is possible to define a relational map via the union of relations which has all the properties desired.

5.2 Substitutability of Relations. The mapping of relations which we defined in the second half of example 8 has two properties which in fact are the basis of a more general result. First, note that both I and C are mapped to their union and S and SC are mapped to their union. Note also that both I and C when composed with other relations have compositions which are identified by this map. For example $I \circ S = S$ and $C \circ S = S$, and S and S are identical. By forming the composition from the other direction, we have $S \circ I = S$ and $S \circ C = SC$ where S and SC are identified by our map. Thus I and C have the property that $f(I \circ T) = f(C \circ T)$ and $f(T \circ I) = f(T \circ C)$ holds for all relations T. In other words, relations are identified if under this identification they compose with other relations identically. They are thus in a sense substitutable. Given a network in which the set of relations is a semigroup, it is possible to determine if a proposed identification of relations satisfies either of these two properties by simply examining the semigroup table of compositions. It is not necessary to examine either the underlying network or the composition of the image relations. With these two properties the set of image relations form a semigroup and thus the mapping of the relations is a semigroup homomorphism.

> **Definition 25.** Let f be a mapping defined on a semigroup S. Then f is a *factorable* if for every T, R_1, and $R_2 \in S$, $f(T) = f(R_1 \circ R_2)$ implies there exists relations A and B $\in$ S such that $T = A \circ B$, $f(A) = f(R_1)$, and $f(B) = f(R_2)$.

An equivalent way of stating this property is to say that the equivalence induced by f forms a congruence relation.

> **Definition 26.** Let f be a mapping defined on a semigroup s, then f induces a congruence on S if for every R_1 and $R_2 \in$ S, $f(R_1) = f(R_2)$ if and only if $f(T \circ R_1) = f(T \circ R_2)$ and $f(R_1 \circ T) = f(R_2 \circ T)$ for every $T \in$ S.

If f is a mapping from one semigroup to another semigroup, then the fundamental theorem of semigroups states that if f induces a congruence on S, then f is a semigroup homomorphism. If $\langle f_1, f_2 \rangle: \langle P, S \rangle \rightarrow \langle P', S' \rangle$ is a weak full network homomorphism where f_1 is the identity and S is a semigroup, then the set of relations $f_2(R)$ for $R \in S$ is not necessarily a semigroup. Therefore, even if f_2 induces a congruence on S, f_2 is not necessarily a semigroup homomorphism. Note that in example 8 two of the identified relations S and SC are the composition of other relations, $S = S \circ I$ and $SC = S \circ C$, where I and C are also identified. This suggests the following property.

> **Theorem 15.** Let $\langle f_1, f_2 \rangle$ be a weak full network homomorphism from $\langle P, R \rangle$ to $\langle P, R' \rangle$ where f_1 is the identity map and both R and R' are semigroups. If f_2 is both regular and factorable then f_2 is a semigroup homomorphism from R to R'.

This result gives us a means by which, given a network in which the set of relations form a semigroup, we can homomorphically reduce the set of relations. We can accomplish this task simply by forming the semigroup table of compositions and then searching for identifications which conform to the two properties described in definitions 25 and 26. In each case we start with a proposed identification of relations. We then examine the rows and columns of two identified relations to determine if each corresponding pair is also identified. If so, the identification is a congruence. Secondly, for each relation which appears as a composition of a pair of relations, we check to determine if every other relation which is identified with it is similarly a composition of a pair of relations which are identified with the first pair. If so, factorability is satisfied. Given a network with a semigroup of relations and a set of identifications which satisfy the two properties above, a new network can be constructed simply by forming the union of those relations which are identified. This resultant network will consist of the same points as the original network, it will be a network homomorphic image of the first, and it too will have a semigroup of relations which is a homomorphic image of the first. The following example of anthropological interest will illustrate this process.

Example 9. Let P be the set of males of three generations in a patrilineal kin group with the following restrictions (for simplicity's sake). The first generation consists of at least three brothers. Each of these brothers has at least three sons and each of these has at least three sons. The set of relations generated by the two relations Father denoted by F and Brother denoted by B is a set of ten relations. These relations and their composition table are listed below.

0	the null or empty relation
I	the identity relation
B	brother
$\tilde{B}$	the union of brother and the identity
F	father
U	uncle
$\tilde{U}$	the union of uncle and father
GF	grandfather
GU	granduncle
$\widetilde{GU}$	the union of grandfather and granduncle

∘	0	I	B	$\tilde{B}$	F	U	$\tilde{U}$	GF	GU	$\widetilde{GU}$
0	0	0	0	0	0	0	0	0	0	0
I	0	I	B	B	F	U	$\tilde{U}$	GF	GU	$\widetilde{GU}$
B	0	B	B	B	U	$\tilde{U}$	$\tilde{U}$	GU	$\widetilde{GU}$	$\widetilde{GU}$
$\tilde{B}$	0	$\tilde{B}$	$\tilde{B}$	$\tilde{B}$	$\tilde{U}$	U	$\tilde{U}$	$\widetilde{GU}$	$\widetilde{GU}$	$\widetilde{GU}$
F	0	F	F	F	GF	GF	GF	0	0	0
U	0	U	U	U	GU	GU	GU	0	0	0
$\tilde{U}$	0	$\tilde{U}$	$\tilde{U}$	$\tilde{U}$	$\widetilde{GU}$	$\widetilde{GU}$	$\widetilde{GU}$	0	0	0
GF	0	GF	GF	GF	0	0	0	0	0	0
GU	0	GU	GU	GU	0	0	0	0	0	0
$\widetilde{GU}$	0	$\widetilde{GU}$	$\widetilde{GU}$	$\widetilde{GU}$	0	0	0	0	0	0

Define

$$f(I) = f(B) = f(\tilde{B}),$$
$$f(F) = f(U) = f(\tilde{U}), \text{ and}$$
$$f(GF) = f(GU) = f(\widetilde{GU}).$$

An inspection of the table shows that the rows and columns of each of these triplets have corresponding entries which are identified under f. Therefore f induces a congruence. Similarly, each relation which can be written as a composition is identified with only other relations which can be similarly composed. For example, GF = F ∘ F is identified with GU = U ∘ F and F and U are also identified. So, f is factorable and by the above theorem, f is a semigroup homomorphism.

5.3. Role Reductions of Networks: Commutativities of Multiple Reductions. Network homomorphisms can of course be composed associatively. Figure 6 gives alternate routes to a suitable blockmodel. The analysis of various blockmodels may thus be staged sequentially.

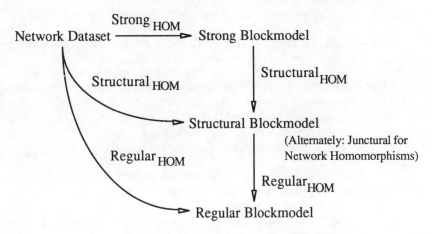

Figure 6. Composition of Homomorphisms

A double role reduction of social networks is possible:

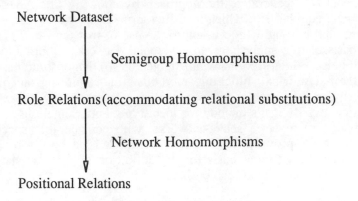

6. Conclusions

6.1. The Role Concept. A social role is a social status with characteristic positional relationships with other status occupants.

A role set (Merton, 1957:269) consists of the role relationships entailed by a person's "occupying a particular social status."

While these definitions define roles by the prior analytic concept of social status, the concept of positional equivalence examined in this chapter and in the blockmodeling tradition (cf. Lorrain and White, 1971) provide a means of identifying statuses in terms of positional equivalence, where each equivalence set has a distinct pattern of positional role relationships.

6.2. Analytical Modeling. The formal theory of social roles has developed on the foundation of Nadel's (1957) exposition of emergent of roles in concrete networks. Harrison White (1963) provided the first extended treatment of highly structured kinship and marriage systems (Australian "section" systems in which marriage is with certain classificatory kin) represented through an algebra of social roles. Boyd's (1969) group partition theorem provides a formal proof of one of the boundary conditions for consistency among multiple roles, or the applicability of certain closed algebraic forms to role systems. Lorrain and White (1971) generalize the approach by showing the general kind of algebraic equivalence (which they first termed "structural equivalence," in a formulation roughly equivalent to the use of that term here) required as the basis of role analysis given any social network. Boorman and White (1976; also White, Boorman and Breiger, 1976) demonstrate the capability of their empirical blocking methods for rendering adequate role descriptions in small group studies. Others apply these methods (particularly Breiger's method for identifying approximations to structural equivalence) to large scale networks, with considerable success. The present work provides an analytic definition of a family of positional equivalences: a formal basis for the definition of roles as statuses with characteristic positional relationships.

Previous approaches to empirical blocking methods have been based on concepts of full and structural homomorphisms. In that both employ density concepts, they combine the clique or group-boundary concept based on interaction density with the role concept. The present work establishes criteria for homomorphisms which are based on patterns of role relatedness which are independent of group or clique membership. The regular and juncture homomorphisms correspond most closely with the most general concepts of roles as positions in a network. Two points are regularly equivalent if and only if, given that one has a (multiplex) relation with a person in a second equivalence set, the other has an identical relation with a counterpart in that set. Juncture equivalence requires, in addition, that there be no more than one (multiplex) relation from points in one equivalence set to points in a second (possibly the same) set.

The algorithm for finding approximations to regular equivalence in a multigraph builds from joint work by Sailer (1978) and Boyd (this volume). Sailer describes an iterative procedure whereby starting from some initial assumptions about structural equivalence (e.g., the identity matrix), a preliminary index of structural similarity is computed. Subsequent iterations compute the degree to which two individuals are structurally similar on the basis of whether they have similar relations with structurally similar others. The present algorithm is based on the discovery that this procedure converges downwards, starting from an initial assumption that everyone is potentially regularly equivalent. It also "bundles" relations to find matches in multiplex relational patterns, and symmetrizes the measure of similarity. The procedure can find regular equivalences across disconnected graphs, which the original Sailer algorithm (starting from identity as the initial structural equivalence) does not.

The algorithm is empirically useful as demonstrated in our study of the network formed by student/teacher bonds among the members of the International Network for Social Network Analysis. It identifies the general pattern of lineage structure in this scientific field: a small core of "grandparents" (Harrison White and Chad Gordon at Harvard; Charles Kaduskin, Eugene Jacobson, and Ev Rogers) have intellectual offspring as well as "grandchildren" or students' students. Different classes of intellectual descendents are identified. Other figures who entered the field later than this initial core have students, but as yet no students' students. The "roles" in the network are clearly identifiable in terms of these abstract patterns, but occupants of the same teacher "role," for example, do not necessarily have the same students, but only students with the same general type of network position.

The network homomorphisms studied in this chapter provide methods by which both relations and points can be reduced to structural models of role systems. We have also considered various equivalences on semigroups which allow us to identify substitutable relations. The two ways of forming network reductions are a basis of formal criteria for role parallels. These reductions have been shown to preserve various properties of the original network.

6.3. Delimiting Role Relations. The approach to role structure taken here, via positional equivalences, is incomplete in two major and related ways. The first is that for multigraphs we have no guarantee of a singular role structure: if there are multiple "maximal" juncture homomorphisms these may be seen as cross-cutting role systems. The second is that we have no analytical way of knowing or testing whether a particular set of relations belong together as part of a single role system, or should be separated into distinct and cross-cutting role systems. These problems involve the question of the boundaries of a role system.

Phillipa Pattison (1980) provides another attempt to deal with the multiple facets or decompositions of role systems. Under certain conditions, she shows that a given blockmodel can be decomposed into several cross-cutting role systems. This is a promising avenue for the development of an approach to the multiplicity of role systems within society.

If we return, however, to the foundational concepts of social structure, we find that a key concept for Nadel (1957), Merton (1957) and Goodenough (1965) is the relation of entailment between different social relationships. Goodenough proposes making this the basis for the definition of status, which is consistent with Nadel's way of defining social roles. If we treat status as an attribute of actors which is held to entail other features, some of which may be relational, we may then help to solve analytically the remaining problems with the role concept. Fusing the varied terminology of these earlier theorists:

A social identity (Nadel's "status") is an attribute which characterizes a class of persons.

A social status (Goodenough; Nadel's "role") is a social identity with the addition that the defining attribute—via the jural, behavioral, or cognitive conventions of a particular group—entails other features of the status occupant, at least one of which is a characteristic relationship with occupants of different identities.

A status set (Merton) is the set of statuses occupied by an individual. Occupancies of different statuses through time are status-sequences.

These definitions—an analytical approach to the status concept via networks of entailments—provide for a wider view of the coherence of role systems, and for Merton's (1957: 370) view that social structure may be viewed as comprised of "the patterned arrangements of role-sets, status-sets, and status-sequences."

The empirical organization of social roles is organized in two major ways, only one of which has been examined here. This is the fact that statuses in a role system (e.g., membership in equivalence sets induced by positional homomorphisms) entail a network of role relationships. The second is that in any single role system, there are entailments which connect the relations which define the positions. Entailment connections delimit the clusters of relationships which make up a single role system. This principle, initially explored by Goodenough (1965), is the subject of a separate investigation on rethinking the status concept (White and Reitz, 1983). It opens up the possibility of "reducing" the relations in a multigraph on the basis of their entailment relationships. The study of status entailments is also consistent with White, Boorman, and Breiger's (1976) blockmodeling approach where "role structure"—the rules for possible combinations of relations via entailments—is equated with the inclusion hierarchy formed by the blockmodel images of relations.[3]

The advantages of the definitions and theorems presented in this explication of the role concept are manifold. We now have a solid mathematical basis for empirical methods which measure patterned similarities in role structures. These can be applied even in complex networks in natural social settings. We have opened up a means for delimiting the boundaries of role systems, and analyzing overlapping role structures. We have provided ways of handling the variabilitiy of role contents—i.e., ways in which actors may "play" the same role differently within the same overall structure—through reductions to a simplified set of underlying role relationships. The patterns in these underlying relationships can then be used to identify abstract role positions in a network independently of social groupings, clusters, or cliques. When combined with well conceptualized measures of tendencies towards social groupings (see Reitz, 1982), structures of differential centrality (see Freeman, 1979), and other basic structural concepts, we have the foundations for a measurement theory for social structure which fits the intuitive richness of the conceptions of leading social theorists such as S. F. Nadel, R. K. Merton, W. H. Goodenough, F. Lorrain, and H. White.

---

[3] Note that blockmodeling produces a model of shared role structure where membership in the group or network as a whole entails component relationships between positions. At a finer level of analysis of different entailments for each position, each point in a graph has a rectangular matrix of the "strandedness" of each type of multiplex relation, and thus an entailment structure for the multiplex relations of the point. Mandel and Winship (1979) propose studying similarities between the multiplex bundles of points.

APPENDIX

Proposition A. Let G = ⟨P,R⟩ be a graph and f: P → P' be an onto map for some set P'. If R' is the relation on P' induced by R and f, and G' = ⟨P',R'⟩ , then the map f: G → G' is a full graph homomorphism.

Proof: If aRb for a,b ∈ P then by definition f(a)R'f(b). If xR'y for some x,y ∈ P' then ⟨x,y⟩ ∈ R'. But R' = {⟨f(a),f(b)⟩ : a,b ∈ P and ⟨a,b⟩ ∈ R}. Therefore ⟨x,y⟩ = ⟨f(a),f(b)⟩ for some a,b ∈ P where ⟨a,b⟩ ∈ R so x = f(a), y = f(b) and aRb. Therefore f is a full graph homomorphism.

Theorem 1. If f: G → G' then

(i) f is a strong homomorphism implies f is a structural homomorphism;

(ii) f is a structural homomorphism implies f is a regular homomorphism.

Proof:

(i) The proof of i follows directly from the definitions of strong and structural homomorphisms.

(ii) Let f: G → G' be a structural graph homomorphism and suppose f(a)R'f(b). If a ≠ b then aRb so let c = a and d = b. f(a) = f(c) and cRb, similarly f(d) = f(b) and aRd. If a = b then f(a)R'f(b). Since f is a full graph homomorphism there exist x,y ∈ P such that f(x) = f(a), f(y) = f(a) and xRy. If both x and y are equal to a then let c = d = a. If x = a and y ≠ a, then f(y)R'f(a) and by the definition of f being structural yRa so let c = y. Similarly f(a)R'f(y) so aRy, d = y. In an identical fashion, if x ≠ a and y = a, let c = d = x. In each of these cases given f(a)R'f(b) we have shown the existence of some c and d P such that f(c) = f(a), f(d) = f(b), cRb, and aRd.

Theorem 2A. If ≡_f is the equivalence relation on the set P induced by a full graph homomorphism f then f is a strong graph homomorphism f: G → G' if and only if for all a,b and c ∈ P.

a ≡_f b implies

(i) aRa if and only if bRb,

(ii) aRb if and only if bRa, and

(iii) aRc if and only if bRc.

Proof: Let f: G → G' be a strong homomorphism and let ≡_f be the equivalence relation induced by f. If a ≡_f b then f(a) = f(b). Now if aRa, f(a)R'f(a), and f(b)R'f(b). Since f is strong bRb. By symmetry if bRb then aRa. So a ≡_f b implies i. Similarly if a ≡_f b and aRb then f(a)R'f(b) but since f(a) = f(b), f(b)R'f(a) and bRa. Similarly bRa implies aRb. Therefore a ≡_f b implies ii. Finally if a ≡_f b and aRc then f(a)R'f(c) and since f(a) = f(b), f(b)R'f(c) so bRc. Similarly bRc implies aRc. So a ≡_f b implies iii. An argument similar to the reverse of the above proves the converse.

Theorem 2B. If $\equiv_f$ is an equivalent relation on a set P induced by a full graph homomorphism f in a structural graph homomorphism if and only if for all a,b,c $\in$ P, where c $\neq$ a and c $\neq$ b.

a $\equiv_f$ b implies

  (i)   aRb if and only if bRa,

  (ii) aRc if and only if bRc,

  (iii) cRa if and only if cRb, and

  (iv) aRa implies aRb.

Proof: Let f: G $\rightarrow$ G' be a structural graph homomorphism, and let a $\equiv_f$ b. If aRb then f(a)R'f(b). Since a $\equiv_f$ b, f(a) = f(b) and f(b)R'f(a). If a = b, aRb implies bRa immediately. However, if a $\neq$ b, f(b)R'f(a) implies by the definition of structural homomorphism that bRa. Similarly if bRa then aRb. So a $\equiv_f$ b implies i. If aRc, a $\neq$ c, b $\neq$ c and a $\equiv_f$ b implies ii. An almost identical argument proves that a $\equiv_f$ b implies iii.

If aRa and a = b then aRb. If aRa and a $\neq$ b then f(a)R'f(a) and f(a)R'f(b). Since f is structural, aRb, so iv holds and $\equiv_f$ is structural. Conversely, suppose f is full, $\equiv_f$ is induced by f and $\equiv_f$ is structural. Then if a $\neq$ b and f(a)R'f(b) there exists c,d $\in$ P such that f(c) = f(a), f(d) = f(b) and cRd. There are essentially eight distinct cases to consider: (1) a,b,c and d are all distinct, (2) a = c, all other pairs distinct, (3) a = d and all other pairs distinct, (4) c = d, and all other pairs distinct, (5) a = d $\neq$ b = c, (6) a = c $\neq$ b = d, (7) a = c = d $\neq$ b and, (8) b = c = d $\neq$ a. The proof for case (1) is identical to that for a strong homomorphism. In case (2) if a = c then aRd and by condition iii aRb. In case (3) c $\neq$ b and c $\neq$ d along with the conditions that b $\equiv$ d and cRd implies that cRb by condition iii. This in turn along with the fact that a $\equiv$ c implies that aRb by condition ii. In case (4) cRd and c = d imply cRc. This in turn along with a $\equiv$ c implies cRa by condition iv. And then by i aRc. This in turn implies aRd which by condition iii implies aRb. In case 5, a = d, b = c, and cRd imply bRa. a $\equiv$ c and b = c together imply that a $\equiv$ b. By condition i these two results imply aRb. The proof in case (6) follows immediately. In case (7) cRd and a = c = d imply aRa. Also b $\equiv$ d and d = a imply a $\equiv$ b. By condition iv these results imply aRb. The proof of case 8 is similar to case 7. In each of these cases we have shown that aRb, therefore f is structural.   QED

Theorem 2C. If $\equiv_f$ is the equivalence relation induced by a full homomorphism f then f is a regular homomorphism if and only if for all a,b,c $\in$ P.

a $\equiv_f$ b implies

  (i) aRc implies $\exists$ d $\in$ P : bRd and d $\equiv_f$ c, and

  (ii) cRa implies $\exists$ d $\in$ P : dRb and d $\equiv_f$ c.

Proof: If f is a regular homomorphism, a $\equiv_f$ b, and aRc then f(a) = f(b) and f(b)R'f(c). Since f is regular there exists d $\in$ P such that f(d) = f(c) and bRd. Since f(d) = f(c), d $\equiv_f$ c. Therefore a $\equiv_f$ b implies i. If a $\equiv_f$ b and cRa then f(c)R'f(b) and there exists d $\in$ P such that f(d) = f(c) and dRb. Again d $\equiv_f$ c. Therefore a $\equiv_f$ b implies ii. An argument similar to the reverse of the above proves the converse.   QED

Theorem 3A. The collection of all strong equivalences has a maximal element.

Proof: Let E be the collection of all strong equivalences relations on P and let $\equiv_M = \{\langle a,b \rangle : a,b \in P\}$ which satisfy

   (i)   aRb if and only if bRa,

   (ii)   aRc if and only if bRc, and

   (iii)   cRa if and only cRb for all $c \in P$.

We must first show that $\equiv_M$ is indeed an equivalence relation. If $a \in P$, aRa if and only if aRa so condition i holds. aRc if and only if aRc so condition ii holds. Similarly condition iii holds and $a \equiv_M a$ for all $a \in P$ and $\equiv_M$ is reflexive. If $a \equiv_M b$ then the symmetry of conditions i, ii, and iii implies that $b \equiv_M a$ so $\equiv_M$ is symmetric. Now suppose $a \equiv_M b$ and $b \equiv_M d$. If aRd then by condition ii and the fact that $a \equiv_M b$, bRd. Since $b \equiv_M d$ condition i implies dRb. Again by condition ii dRa. Similarly dRa implies aRd and condition i holds for the pair $\langle a,d \rangle$. By condition ii aRc if and only if bRc if and only if dRc so condition ii holds for the pair $\langle a,d \rangle$. A similar argument shows that condition iii holds for $\langle a,d \rangle$ and therefore $a \equiv_M d$ and $\equiv_d$ is transitive. Therefore $\equiv_M$ is an equivalence relation. All that remains to be shown is that $\equiv_M$ is maximal. Let "≡" be a strong equivalence relation on P. By definition of what a strong equivalence relation is, $a \equiv b$ implies that conditions i-iii are satisfied and $a \equiv_M b$. Therefore $\equiv_M$ is maximal.   QED

Theorem 3B. The collection of all structural equivalences on a graph has a maximal element.

Proof: The proof is identical to the proof of 3A except that conditions ii and iii have the added condition that $a \neq c \neq b$. Every conclusion still follows.

Theorem 3C. The collection of all regular equivalence on a graph has a maximal element.

Proof: Let $\equiv_1 = \{\langle a,b \rangle \in P \times P\}$ and let

$$\equiv_2 = \{\langle a,b \rangle \in P \times P : \text{conditions i-iv hold}\}$$

   (i)   aRc implies $\exists\, d \in P : bRd$ and $d \equiv_1 c$,

   (ii)   bRc implies $\exists\, d \in P : aRd$ and $d \equiv_1 c$,

   (iii)   cRa implies $\exists\, d \in P : dRb$ and $d \equiv_1 c$, and

   (iv)   cRb implies $\exists\, d \in P : dRa$ and $d \equiv_1 c$.

Similarly define $\equiv_3$ in terms of $\equiv_2$ as $\equiv_2$ has been defined in terms of $\equiv_1$. Continue in this fashion defining recursively $\equiv_{k+1}$ in terms of $\equiv_k$. We first show that each $\equiv_k$ is an equivalence relation. Certainly $\equiv_1$ is an equivalence relation. Assume $\equiv_k$ is also. Let $a \in P$, then aRc implies aRc and $c \equiv_k c$ since $\equiv_k$ is an equivalence relation. Similarly conditions ii-iv hold and $a \equiv_{k+1} a$ and $\equiv_{k+1}$ is reflexive. Suppose $a \equiv_{k+1} b$ then by the symmetry of the conditions i-iv $b \equiv_{k+1} a$ and $\equiv_{k+1}$ is symmetric. Suppose $a \equiv_{k+1} b$ and b $\equiv_{k+1} x$, then aRc implies there exists $d \in P$ such that bRd and $d \equiv_k c$. But if bRd, then there exists an e such that xRe and $e \equiv_k d$. But since $\equiv_k$ is an equivalence relation e $\equiv_k$ c, so xRe and e $\equiv_k$ c so the pair $\langle a,x \rangle$ satisfies condition i. Similarly $\langle a,x \rangle$ satisfies conditions ii-iv and a $\equiv_{k+1}$ x so $\equiv_{k+1}$ is transitive. So by assuming $\equiv_k$ is an equivalence relation, we have shown that $\equiv_{k+1}$ is an equivalence relation. By the axiom of mathematical induction $\equiv_k$ is an equivalence relation for all k.

Next we show that $\equiv_k \supseteq \equiv_{k+1}$ for all i. Certainly $\equiv_2 \subseteq \equiv_1$. Assume $\equiv_k \supseteq \equiv_{k-1}$ and let $\langle a,b \rangle \in \equiv_{k+1}$. Suppose aRc, then there exists d $\in$ P such that bRd and d $\equiv_k$ c. But $\equiv_k \supseteq \equiv_{k-1}$ so d $\equiv_{k-1}$ c. That means the pair $\langle a,b \rangle$ satisfies condition i for $\equiv_k$. In a similar fashion, $\langle a,b \rangle$ satisfies conditions ii-iv for $\equiv_k$ and $\langle a,b \rangle \in \equiv_k$. So $\equiv_k \supseteq \equiv_{k+1}$. By the axiom of induction $\equiv_k \supseteq \equiv_{k+1}$ for all k. Since P is finite there must be an N such that $\equiv_N = \equiv_{N-1}$. This means that $\equiv_N$ is defined in terms of itself and therefore satisfies the properties of a regular equivalence relation.

All that remains to be shown is that $\equiv_N$ is maximal. Suppose $\equiv$ is a regular equivalence relation. Clearly $\equiv \subseteq \equiv_1$. Suppose $\equiv \subseteq \equiv_k$, let a = b, then if aRc, by the definition of regular equivalence relations there exists d $\in$ P such that bRd and d $\equiv$ c. But since $\equiv \subseteq \equiv_k$, d $\equiv_k$ c, so the pair $\langle a,b \rangle$ satisfies condition i of $\equiv_{k+1}$. Similarly $\langle a,b \rangle$ satisfies condition ii-iv and $\langle a,b \rangle \in \equiv_{k+1}$. So $\equiv \subseteq \equiv_{k+1}$ and hence by induction $\equiv \subseteq \equiv_k$ for all k. Therefore $\equiv \subseteq \equiv_N$ and $\equiv_N$ is the maximal regular equivalence relation. QED

The following lemma although not in the text, is useful in the proof of the following theorems.

Lemma 1. If f: G → G' is a regular graph homomorphism and R' is the relation induced by f and R then $(R^i)' = (R')^i$.

Proof: Let $\langle x,y \rangle \in (R^i)'$, then there exists $\langle a,b \rangle \in R^i$ such that $\langle f(a),f(b) \rangle = \langle x,y \rangle$. If $\langle a,b \rangle \in R^i$, there exists $c_1,c_2,...,c_{i-1}$ such that $\langle a,c_1 \rangle,\langle c_1,c_2 \rangle,...,\langle c_{i-1},b \rangle$ are all members of R and $\langle f(a),f(c_1) \rangle$, $\langle f(c_1),f(c_2) \rangle,...,\langle f(c_{i-1}),f(b) \rangle$ are all members of R'. But this implies that $\langle f(a),f(b) \rangle = \langle x,y \rangle \in (R^i)'$. So $(R^i)' \subseteq (R')^i$.

Now suppose $\langle x,y \rangle \in (R')^i$, then there exists $w_1,...,w_{i-1}$ such that $\langle x,w_1 \rangle,\langle w_1,w_2 \rangle,...,\langle w_{i-1},y \rangle$ are all members of R'. Since f is full, there exists $\langle a,c_1 \rangle \in R$ such that $\langle f(a),f(c_1) \rangle = \langle x,w_1 \rangle$. So $\langle f(c_1),w_2 \rangle \in R'$ and since f is regular there exists c_2 such that $f(c_2) = w_2$ and $\langle c_1,c_2 \rangle \in R$. In similar fashion there exists $c_3,...,c_{i-1},b$ such that $\langle c_\varrho,c_{\varrho+1} \rangle \in R$ and $f(c_\varrho) = w_\varrho$ and $\langle c_{i-1},b \rangle \in R$ with f(b) = y. Therefore $\langle a,b \rangle \in R^i$ and $\langle f(a),f(b) \rangle = \langle x,y \rangle \in (R^i)'$. We have then $(R^i)' \subseteq (R')^i$. QED

Theorem 4. If f: G → G' is a regular, structural, or strong graph homomorphism then f is regular, structural, or strong respectively for any relation in S. That is f: $\langle P,Q \rangle → \langle P',Q' \rangle$ is regular, structural, or strong respectively for any Q $\in$ S.

Proof: In the case that f is regular, the theorem holds trivially for $Q = R^1 = R$. Suppose it holds for $Q = R^i$. Consider

$$f: \langle P,R^{i+1} \rangle → \langle P',(R')^{i+1} \rangle$$

if $f(a)(R')^{i+1}f(b)$, then there is some $x \in P'$ such that $f(a)(R')^i x$ and $xR'f(b)$. Since f is "onto", there exists $c \in P$ such that $f(c) = x$, so $f(a)(R')^i f(c)$. Since f is regular with respect to R^i there exists d and $e \in P$ such that $f(d) = f(a)$, $f(c) = f(e)$, $dR^i c$, and $aR^i e$. Similarly there exists r and s such that $f(r) = f(e)$, $f(s) = f(b)$, rRb, and eRs. Note that $aR^i e$ and eRs so $aR^{i+1}s$ and $f(s) = f(b)$ so the first half of the condition for regularity holds. Since $f(c)R'f(b)$, there exists $u,v \in P$ such that $f(u) = f(c)$, $f(v) = f(b)$, uRb and cRv. Since $f(u) = f(c)$, $f(a)(R')^i f(u)$, so by the induction hypothesis there exists w and z such that $f(w) = f(a)$, $f(z) = f(u)$, $wR^i u$, and $aR^i z$ since $wR^i a$ and aRb we have $wR^{i+1}b$. Thus by the axiom of induction f is regular on R^i for all i. In the case that f is strong with respect to $\langle P,R \rangle$ the proof is less involved. Again for $Q = R'$ the theorem holds. Suppose it holds for $Q = R^i$. If $f(a)(R')^{i+1}f(b)$, then there exists $c \in P$ such that $f(a)(R')^i f(c)$ and $f(c)R'f(b)$. Since f is strong with respect to both R and R^i. $aR^i c$ and cRb so $aR^{i+1}b$ and f is strong with respect to R^{i+1}. By induction f is strong with respect to R^i for all i.

The proof for the case that f is structural follows exactly as for f strong except that the condition $a \neq b$ must be added. QED

Theorem 5. If $f: G \to G'$ is a regular graph homomorphism then $\hat{f}: S \to S'$ is a semigroup homomorphism. That is

$$\hat{f}(Q_1 \circ Q_2) = \hat{f}(Q_1) \circ \hat{f}(Q_2).$$

Proof: $f: G \to G'$ is a regular homomorphism. Let $Q_1 = R^i$ and $Q_2 = R^j$ then $Q_1 \circ Q_2 = R^i \circ R^j = R^{i+j}$ so

$$\begin{aligned}
\hat{f}(Q \circ Q_2) &= \hat{f}(R^{i+j}) = (R^{i+j})' = (R')^{i+j} \\
&= (R')^i \circ (R')^j = (R^i)' \circ (R^j)' \\
&= \hat{f}(R^i) \circ \hat{f}(R^j) = \hat{f}(Q_1) \circ \hat{f}(Q_2). \quad \text{QED}
\end{aligned}$$

Theorem 6. If $f: G \to G'$ is a strong homomorphism then $\hat{f}: S \to S'$ is a semigroup isomorphism.

Proof: By Theorem 5, $\hat{f}$ is a semi-group homomorphism. Suppose $\hat{f}(Q_1) = \hat{f}(Q_2)$. Then for all pairs $\langle a,b \rangle \in P \times P$, $\langle f(a),f(b) \rangle \in \hat{f}(Q_1)$ if and only if $\langle f(a),f(b) \rangle \in \hat{f}(Q_2)$. But $\langle f(a),f(b) \rangle \in \hat{f}(Q_1)$ if and only if $\langle a,b \rangle \in Q_1$. Similarly $\langle f(a),f(b) \rangle \in \hat{f}(Q_2)$ if and only if $\langle a,b \rangle \in Q_2$. So $\langle a,b \rangle \in Q_1$ if and only if $\langle a,b \rangle \in Q_2$. Therefore $Q_1 = Q_2$ and $\hat{f}$ is an isomorphism. QED

Theorem 7. If $f: G \to G'$ is a structural homomorphism and G an acyclic graph then $\hat{f}: S \to S'$ is an isomorphism.

Proof: The proof is identical with that of Theorem 6 with the added condition that $a \neq b$. With this condition it is sufficient to hypothesize that $\langle a,a \rangle \notin R^i$ for all i. The conclusion that $Q_1 = Q_2$ follows.

Lemma 2. If $G = \langle P, \equiv_A \rangle$ is the graph of an equivalence relation $\equiv_A$, then $\equiv_A$ is also the equivalence induced by the largest regular, structural, or strong homomorphism of the graph.

Proof: Define $P' = \{0,1\}$ and let $f\colon P \to P'$ be defined by

$$f(a) = \begin{cases} 1 & \text{if } a \in A \\ 0 & \text{if } a \notin A \end{cases}$$

then f is a strong homomorphism from $\langle P, \equiv_A \rangle$ to $\langle P',= \rangle$ where $=$ is the standard equality. $\equiv_A$ is also the equivalence induced by f and is clearly maximal.

Lemma 3. If $G = \langle P, I_A \rangle$ in the graph of a class identity I_A, defined by the class attribute A, then the attribute equivalence $\equiv_A$ is also the equivalence induced by the largest regular homomorphisms of the graph.

Proof: The proof is identical to that of Lemma 2 except f is no longer strong but only regular.

Theorem 8. If f is a regular network homomorphism, then f is connectivity preserving.

Proof: Let $x_1,\ldots,x_{n+1} \in P$ be a sequence of points and $R_1,\ldots,R_n$ a set of relations on P such that $f_1(x_1)f_2(R_1)f_1(x_2)\ldots f_1(x_n)f_2(R_n)f_1(x_{n+1})$. Since f is regular, there exists y_2 such that $f_1(y_2) = f_1(x_2)$, and $x_1R_1y_2$. Since $f_1(y_2)f_2(R_2)f_1(x_3)$ there exists y_3 such that $f(y_3) = f(x_3)$ and $y_2R_2y_3$. Continue in like manner establishing $y_2,y_3,\ldots,y_{n+1}$ with $f_1(x_2) = f_1(y_2),\ldots,f_1(x_{n+1}) = f_1(y_{n+1})$ and $x_1R_1y_2R_2\ldots R_ny_{n+1}$. Similarly since $f_1(x_n)f_2(R_n)f_1(x_{n+1})$, there exists z_n such that $f_1(x_n) = f_1(z_n)$ and $z_nR_nx_{n+1}$. Since $f_1(x_n) = f_1(z_n)$, $f_1(x_{n-1})f_2(R_{n-1})f_1(z_n)$ and there exists a $z_{n-1} \in P$ such that $f_1(z_{n-1}) = f_1(x_{n-1})$ and $z_{n-1}R_{n-1}z_n$. In this manner, we construct $z_1,z_2,\ldots,z_n$ such that $f(z_i) = f(x_i)$ for $1 \leq i \leq n$ and $z_1R_1z_2R_2\ldots z_nR_nx_{n+1}$. Therefore f is connectivity preserving.

Theorem 9. If f is a structural graph homomorphism then f is strongly connectivity preserving.

Proof: The proof follows directly from the definition of structural graph homomorphisms.

Theorem 10. If $N = \langle P,R \rangle$ is a network, $C = \langle P,M \rangle$ the multiplex graph derived from it, and $f\colon C \to C' = \langle P',M' \rangle$ a full network homomorphism then f induces a full network homomorphism on N and

    1) if f is regular the induced homomorphism is regular;

    2) if f is strong the induced homomorphism is strong.

Proof: Let $f\colon C \to C'$ be the ordered pair $\langle f_1,f_2 \rangle$ where $f_1\colon P \to P'$ and $f_2\colon M \to M'$. Let $R \in R$ and define $f_2{}^*(R) = \{\langle f_1(a),f_1(b) \rangle : \langle a,b \rangle \in R\}$. Let $R' = \{f_2{}^*(R) : R \in M\}$ then the ordered pair $\langle f_1,f_2{}^* \rangle$ is a full network homomorphism $f^*\colon N \to N'$ where $N' = \langle P',R' \rangle$. Suppose $f_1(a)f_2{}^*(R)f_1(b)$ for some $a,b \in P$ and $R \in R$. Since $f^* = \langle f_1,f_2{}^* \rangle$ is full, there exists $x,y \in P$ such that $f_1(a) = f_1(x)$, $f_1(b) = f_1(y)$, and xRy. This implies that

$R \subseteq B_{xy} \neq \emptyset$. Let $M = \{\langle c,d \rangle : B_{cd} = B_{xy}\}$ then xMy and $f_1(x)f_2(M)f_1(y)$ which in turn implies $f_1(a)f_2(M)f_1(b)$.

1) If we assume that f is regular, there exists $c,d \in P$ such that $f_1(c) = f_1(a)$, $f_1(d) = f_1(b)$, cMb and aMd. By the definition of M, $B_{cb} = B_{ad} = B_{xy}$, where cRb, aRd, and f^* is regular.

2) If we assume that f is strong, then aMb, $B_{ab} = B_{xy}$, aRb, and f^* is strong.

Theorem 11. Every strong network homomorphism is a juncture network homomorphism.

Proof: Assume $f: N \rightarrow N'$ is strong and there exists $a,b,c,d \in P$ such that $f_1(a) = f_1(c)$ and $f_1(b) = f_1(d)$. If $B_{ab} = \emptyset$, the theorem is proved. If $B_{ab} \neq \emptyset$, let $R \in B_{ab}$, then aRb. Also, $f_1(a)f_2(R)f_1(b)$ and $f_1(c)f_2(R)f_1(d)$. Since f is strong, cRd and $R \in B_{cd}$. Therefore $B_{ab} \subseteq B_{cd}$. Similarly, $B_{ab} \supseteq B_{cd}$ and $B_{ab} = B_{cd}$. Therefore f is a juncture homomorphism.

Theorem 12. Let $f: N \rightarrow N'$ be a juncture network homomorphism and C the multiplex graph derived from N, then f induces a map from C to C' and C' is a multiplex graph.

Proof: Let $f: N \rightarrow N'$ be a juncture network homomorphism and let $C = \langle P,M \rangle$ be the multiplex graph derived from N. Let $M \in M$, define $*f_2(M) = \{\langle f(a),f(b) \rangle : \langle a,b \rangle \in M\}$. Define $M' = \{*f_2(M) : M \in M\}$, then $*f: C \rightarrow C' = \langle P', M' \rangle$ where $*f = \langle f_1,*f_2 \rangle$ is a full network homomorphism. Suppose $*f_2(M_1) \cap *f_2(M_2) \neq \emptyset$ then there exists an $\langle f_1(a),f_1(b) \rangle \in *f_2(M_1) \cap *f_2(M_2)$. This implies there exist $x,y \in P$ and $c,d \in P$ such that $f_1(x) = f_1(a)$, $f_1(y) = f_1(b)$, $f_1(c) = f_1(a)$, $f_1(d) = f_1(b)$ and $\langle x,y \rangle \in M_1$ and $\langle c,d \rangle \in M_2$. This in turn implies that $B_{xy} = B_1$ where $M_1 = \cup\{B : B = B_1\}$ and $B_{cd} = B_2$ where $M_2 = \cup\{B : B = B_2\}$. Note that both $B_{xy} \neq \emptyset \neq B_{cd}$, $f_1(x) = f_1(c)$ and $f_1(y) = f_1(d)$. Because f is a juncture homomorphism $B_{xy} = B_{cd}$. But this implies that $B_1 = B_2$ and $M_1 = M_2$. Therefore $f_2(M_1) \cap f_2(M_2) \neq \emptyset$ implies $M_1 = M_2$ so C' is a multiplex graph. QED

Theorem 13. Let $f: N \rightarrow N'$ be a juncture network homomorphism where $N = \langle P,R \rangle$, $N' = \langle P', R' \rangle$ and $f = \langle f_1,f_2 \rangle$. If $\circ$ is relation composition and $\langle R,\circ \rangle$ is a semigroup then $f_2: \langle R,\circ \rangle \rightarrow \langle R',\circ \rangle$ is an isomorphism.

Proof: Let $\langle x,z \rangle \in f_2(R_1) \circ f_2(R_2)$, then $\exists y \in P'$ such that $\langle x,y \rangle \in f_2(R_1)$ and $\langle y,z \rangle \in f_2(R_2)$. Since f is regular there exist $a,b,c \in P$ such that $f(a) = x$, $f(b) = y$, and $f(c) = z$ such that aR_1b and bR_2c. But this implies that $a(R_1 \circ R_2)c$ and $f_1(a)f_2(R_1 \circ R_2)f_1(c)$. So $\langle x,z \rangle \in f_2(R_1 \circ R_2)$ and $f_2(R_1) \circ f_2(R_2) \subseteq f_2(R_1 \circ R_2)$. Now suppose $\langle x,z \rangle \in f_2(R_1 \circ R_2)$. Then $\exists a,d \in P$ such that $f(a) = x$, $f(d) = z$ and $a(R_1 \circ R_2)d$. By definition $\exists c \in P$ such that aR_1c and cR_2d and $f_1(a)f_2(R_1)f_1(c)$ and $f_1(c)f_2(R_2)f(d)$ so

$$f_1(a)(f_2(R_1) \circ f_2(R_2))f_1(d) \text{ and}$$

$$x(f_2(R_1) \circ f_2(R_2))z$$

so $\langle x,z \rangle \in f_2(R_1) \circ f_2(R_2)$. Therefore $f_2(R_1) \circ f_2(R_2) = f_2(R_1 \circ R_2)$. So far in the proof we have used only regularity but we need yet to show that f_2 is one to one. Suppose $f_2(R_1) = f_2(R_2)$ where $R_1 \neq R_2$. Then $\exists$ $\langle a,b \rangle$ in R_1 or R_2 but not the other. Suppose $\langle a,b \rangle \in R_1$ and $\langle a,b \rangle \notin R_2$, $\langle f_1(a),f_1(b) \rangle \in f_2(R_1)$ but since $f_2(R_1) = f_2(R_2)$, $\langle f_1(a),f_1(b) \rangle \in f(R_2)$. Since f is regular there exists $c \in P$ such that $f_1(a) = f_1(c)$ and cR_2b. Therefore $B_{cb} \neq \emptyset$. Since aR_1b, $B_{ab} \neq \emptyset$, $f_1(a) = f_1(c)$, and $f_1(b) = f_1(b)$ together with the definition of juncture homomorphism implies that $B_{ab} = B_{cb}$. But cR_2b so $R_2 \in B_{cb}$ and $R_2 \in B_{ab}$ and aR_2b which is a contradiction so f_2 is one to one and therefore an isomorphism.   QED

Theorem 14. If $N = \langle P,R \rangle$ and $N' = \langle P,R' \rangle$ are networks, and $\langle f_1,f_2 \rangle$ a network mapping where f_1 is the identity map on P, then $f = \langle f_1,f_2 \rangle$ is a weak full network homomorphism if and only if $f_2(R) = \cup[R]f_2$ for all $R \in R$.

Proof. Assume $f = \langle f_1,f_2 \rangle : N \rightarrow N'$ is a weak full network homomorphism and f_1 the identity map. Let $\langle a,b \rangle \in f_2(R)$, then since f is a weak full homomorphism there exists $Q \in R$ and $\langle c,d \rangle \in Q$ such that $f_1(c) = a$, $f_1(d) = b$, $\langle c,d \rangle \in Q$ and $f_2(R) = f_2(Q)$. Since f_1 is the identity map $\langle c,d \rangle = \langle a,b \rangle \in Q$. Therefore $\langle a,b \rangle \in \cup[R]f_2$ and $f_2(R) \subset \cup[R]f_2$.

Now assume $\langle a,b \rangle \in \cup[R]f_2$. This implies that there exists $Q \in R$ such that $f_2(Q) = f_2(R)$ and $\langle a,b \rangle \in Q$. Since f is a network homomorphism $\langle a,b \rangle = \langle f_1(a),f_1(b) \rangle \in f_2(Q) = f_2(R)$. So, $\cup[R]f_2 \subset f_2(R)$ and together with the above $f_2(R) = \cup[R]f_2$.

Conversely assume $f_2(R) = \cup[R]f_2$. Let $\langle a,b \rangle \in R$ for some $R \in R$, then since $f_2(R) = f_2(R)$, $R \in [R]f_2$ so $\langle a,b \rangle \in \cup[R]f_2 = f_2(R)$. But

$$\langle f_1(a),f_1(b) \rangle = \langle a,b \rangle \in f_2(R)$$

so f is a network homomorphism. Now suppose $\langle f_1(a),f_1(b) \rangle \in f_2(R)$. Since f_1 is the identity and $f_2(R) = \cup[R]f_2$, $\langle a,b \rangle \in \cup[R]f_2$. This in turn implies that there exists $Q \in R$ such that $f_2(Q) = f_2(R)$ and $\langle a,b \rangle \in Q$. Therefore $f = \langle f_1,f_2 \rangle$ is a weak full network homomorphism.   QED

Theorem 15. Let $\langle f_1,f_2 \rangle$ be a weak full network homomorphism from $\langle P,R \rangle$ to $\langle P,R' \rangle$ where f_1 is the identity map and R is a semigroup. If f_2 induces a congruence on R and is factorable then f_2 is a semigroup homomorphsim.

Proof. We want to show that if R_1 and $R_2 \in R$ then

$$f_2(R_1 \circ R_2) = f_2(R_1) \circ f_2(R_2).$$

So let $\langle a,b \rangle \in f_2(R_1 \circ R_2)$. By Theorem 14 there exists Q such that $f_2(Q) = f_2(R_1 \circ R_2)$ and $\langle a,b \rangle \in Q$. Since f_2 is factorable there exists S_1 and $S_2 \in R$ such that $Q = S_2 \circ S_2$, $f_2(S_1) = f_2(R_1)$, and $f_2(S_1) = f_2(R_2)$. Since $\langle a,b \rangle \in Q$, there exists c such that $\langle a,c \rangle \in S_1$ and $\langle c,b \rangle \in S_2$. But $\langle a,c \rangle = \langle f_1(a),f_1(c) \rangle \in f_2(S_1)$ and similarly $\langle c,b \rangle \in f_2(S_2)$. Therefore $\langle a,b \rangle \in f_2(S_1) \circ f_2(S_2) = f_2(R_1) \circ f_2(R_2)$. Conversely if

$$\langle a,b \rangle \in f_2(R_1) \circ f_2(R_2)$$

there exists c such that $\langle a,c \rangle \in f_2(R_1)$ and $\langle c,b \rangle \in f_2(R_2)$. By Theorem 14 $\exists\ S_1$ and S_2 such that $f_2(S_1) = f_2(R_1)$, $f_2(S_2) = f_2(R_2)$, $\langle a,c \rangle \in S_1$ and $\langle c,b \rangle \in S_2$. Therefore $\langle a,b \rangle \in S_1 \circ S_2$. Since f_2 induces a congruence on R, $f_2(S_1) = f_2(R_1)$ and $f_2(S_2) = f_2(R_2)$, we have

$$f_2(S_1 \circ S_2) = f_2(R_1 \circ S_2) = f_2(R_1 \circ R_2).$$

These two results give $f_2(R_1 \circ R_2) = f_2(R_1) \circ f_2(R_2)$ and f_2 is a semigroup homomorphism. QED

REFERENCES

Arabie, Phipps, Scott Boorman, and Paul Levitt
    1978   Constructing blockmodels: How and why. Journal of
            Mathematical Psychology 17:21-63.
Berge, Claude
    1962   Theory of Graphs and its Applications. London: Methuen.
Bonacich, Phillip
    1981   The Comon structure graph: Common structural features of a
            set of graphs. MS Department of Sociology, UCLA.
Boorman, Scott, and Harrison White
    1976   Social structure from multiple networks. II. Role structures.
            American Journal of Sociology 81:1384-1446.
Boyd, John
    1969   The algebra of group kinship. Journal of Mathematical
            Psychology 6:139-167.
Breiger, Ronald, and Philippa Pattison
    1978   The joint role structure of two community elites. Sociological
            Methods and Research 7:213-226.
Breiger, Ronald, Scott Boorman, and Phipps Arabie
    1975   An algorithm for clustering relational data with applications to
            social network analysis and comparison to multidimensional
            scaling. Journal of Mathematical Psychology 12:328-383.
Freeman, Linton
    1979   Centrality in social networks: I. Conceptual clarification.
            Social Networks 1:215-239.
Goodenough, Ward H.
    1965   Rethinking "status" and "roles": Toward a general model of
            cultural organization of social relationships. *In* Michael Banton
            (ed.) The Relevance of Models in Social Anthropology — ASA
            Monographs. New York: Praeger.
Grätzer, George
    1979   Universal Algebra (2nd edition). New York: Springer-Verlag.
Guttman, Louis
    1977   A definition of dimensionality and distance for graphs. *In* J.C.
            Lingos (ed.) Geometric Representation of Relational Data. Ann
            Arbor, MI: Mathesis Press.
Harary, Frank
    1969   Graph Theory. Reading, MA: Addison Wesley.
Laumann, E.O., and F. Pappi
    1976   Network of Collective Action. New York: Academic Press.

Lorraine, Francois
    1974   Social structure, social classification, and the logic of analogy.
            In Paul A. Ballonoff (ed.) Mathematical Models of Social and
            Cognitive Structures. Urbana: University of Illinois Press.
Lorraine, Francois, and Harrison White
    1971   Structural equivalence of individuals in social networks.
            Journal of Mathematical Sociology 1:49-80.
Mandel, Michael, and Christopher Winship
    1979   Roles, positions and networks. Paper presented to the American
            Sociological Meetings, Boston, Massachusetts.
Merton
    1957   Social Theory and Social Structure. Revised Ed. The Free
            Press of Glencoe.
Nadel, S.F.
    1957   The Theory of Social Structure. London: Cohen and West.
Pattison, Phillipa
    1980   An algebraic analysis for multiple, social networks. Ph.D.
            Dissertation, University of Melbourne.
Reitz, Karl
    1982   Social groups, a network approach. Ph.D. Dissertation,
            University of California, Irvine.
Sailer, Lee
    1978   Structural equivalence: Meaning and definition, computation and
            application. Social Networks 1:73-90.
Shepard, and Phipps Arabie
    1979   Additive clustering: Representation of similarities as
            combinations of discsrete overlapping properties. Psychological
            Review 86:87-123.
White, Douglas, and Karl Reitz
    1983   Graph and semigroup homomorphisms. Social Networks
            5:193-234.
White, Douglas, and Karl Reitz
    n.d.   Measuring role distance: An algorithm for regular graph
            equivalence (REGGE).
White, Harrison
    1963   An Anatomy of Kinship. Englewood Cliffs, NJ: Prentice Hall.
White, Harrison, Scott Boorman, and Ronald Breiger
    1976   Social structure from multiple networks. I. Blockmodels of
            roles and positions. American Journal of Sociology 81:730-780.

CHAPTER 14

METHODS FOR THE CHARACTERIZATION OF ROLE STRUCTURES IN NETWORK ANALYSIS*

Peter V. Marsden

1. Introduction

In the course of a network analysis, researchers frequently encounter square tables of counts or rates that summarize the social relationships among subgroups of a population of actors. Sometimes the analysis of such tables is the central feature of a network analysis. Such is the case in analyses concerned with patterns of differential association, assortative mating, or homophily (e.g., Laumann, 1966, 1973; Verbrugge, 1977; Blau and Duncan, 1966: Ch. 10; Garrison, 1979; Alba and Kessler, 1979; Fararo and Sunshine, 1964). At other times the analysis of such a table is part of a

---

* This work was completed while I was on the faculty at the University of North Carolina. Writing was supported by NSF SOC 77-26038. I appreciate some comments from Stanley Wasserman on another manuscript that led me to pose some of the issues in the way I have done; helpful suggestions were also made by Edward O. Laumann, Joel Podolny and David Prensky.

more elaborate inquiry. This is the case, for instance, when the nodes in a network have been clustered into structurally equivalent "blocks" or "positions" on the basis of exogenously defined attributes, or on the basis of their relational similarity to one another. A square table of choice rates or block densities is then used to summarize the relational information about the blocks or positions. Interpretation of such a table forms the basis for the characterization of the roles or positions into which actors have been categorized (e.g., White, Boorman, and Breiger, 1976; Breiger, 1976, 1979; Burt, 1976, 1977; Light and Mullins, 1979).

In either case, the analyst is usually interested in asking three types of questions about the positions or roles represented by the categories of actors. The first set of questions concerns the level of participation in social relations of a subgroup: is it a transmitter, a carrier, or a receiver of relations, or is it an isolate?[1] A second set of questions pertains to the internal relations of a subgroup: are relations dense within a category, or not? If relations are concentrated within a category, then it takes on features of a social group, while if they are not so concentrated, the category is a set of unrelated but structurally similar actors (e.g., the "hangers-on" of White *et al.* [1976] or the "sycophant" or "broker" positions of Burt [1976]). The final set of questions concerns the homogeneity of the external relations of subgroups: does a subgroup act as a transmitter, carrier, or receiver to the same extent with respect to all other subgroups, or do roles in the network differ depending on the position occupied by an external transaction partner? If external relations are homogeneous, then roles can be egocentrically defined in terms of the participation levels and the internal and external relations characteristic of a position. If external relations are *not* homogeneous, then a more complicated description of a focal actor's role is required; such a description must specify that actor's typical relations with incumbents of a differentiated set of other roles. Concepts such as social distance may be required in an analysis at this point.

Answers to these three sets of questions are usually sufficient to characterize adequately the formal nature of positions or roles in a

---

[1]	I have drawn the verbal names for external aspects of roles from the graph-theoretic formulation of Harary, Norman, and Cartwright (1965). It should be noted, however, that my use of these terms differs from that of Harary *et al.* The differences have to do with our use of probabilistic operational definitions for these roles, in contrast to the deterministic definitions used by Harary *et al.* (see below). For instance, Harary *et al.* define a transmitter as a point emitting some relations but receiving none, while we will view a transmitter as a group emitting a higher than average number of relations while receiving a lower than average number of relations.

network. All of the questions can be answered through the analysis of a square density table. Often, however, analyses of such tables are rather informal, relying on comparisons of choice densities within and between subgroups, without statistical tests or descriptive indicators of the strength of effects. Some analyses focus on one aspect of a table (e.g., the diagonal cells, Verbrugge, 1977), without giving attention to the remaining information.

This chapter presents statistical models that make possible a rigorous analysis of density tables and other square tables encountered in the course of network analyses. The models used are log linear models, and as such are special cases of more general models developed by Goodman (1972, 1979), Bishop, Fienberg, and Holland (1975), and Haberman (1978). The development of the specific models discussed here owes a great deal to work by Fienberg and Wasserman (1981) on categorical data analysis for directed graphs (see also Holland and Leinhardt, 1981). There are also some similarities between the models suggested here and models for social mobility tables discussed by Hauser (1978, 1979). Some important special cases of the models used here are extensively discussed in Marsden (1981).

In the next section of the chapter, an example of the type of data to be analyzed is given. We then present a statistical model that yields answers to the three types of questions posed above and several restricted versions of this model. We give methods for estimation of parameters of the model, and illustrate the methods presented using network data. Next, a frequently encountered circumstance, in which only limited data are available, is considered, and we introduce modifications of the model used here that are appropriate to this data situation. The chapter closes with a discussion of implications, limitations, and possible extensions of the approach developed.

2. An Example

Table 1 presents a density matrix of the type often encountered in network studies. The data in Table 1 were obtained from a study conducted by Galaskiewicz (1979a, 1979b; see also Galaskiewicz and Marsden, 1978) of interorganizational relations in a midwestern community referred to as Towertown. In this study, the chief executive officer of each of 73 organizations was asked, among other things, to respond to the following two questions concerning his or her organization's information transactions within the community:

(1)   Which organizations on this list does [your organization] rely
        upon for information regarding community affairs (or other
        matters that might affect your organization)?; and

(2)   And to which organizations on this list would [your
        organization] be likely to pass on important information
        concerning community affairs (or other matters that might
        affect them)?

(See Galaskiewicz, 1979a:173.) No restrictions were placed on the number
of organizations an executive officer might name in response to these
questions. Agents had reference to the list of 73 organizations in
answering the questions. A directed relationship between a pair of
organizations was said to be present if it was mentioned by the agent of
either member of the directed pair, i.e., if the agent of the sending
organization indicated the receiving organization in response to question
(2), *or* if the agent of the receiving organization indicated the sending
organization in response to question (1). Note that this procedure for
coding of the relationships does *not* require that the relationships be
symmetric.

Table 1. An Example of a Density Table[2]

Sending Category	Receiving Category							
	1	2	3	4	5	6	7	8
1	.381	.179	.155	.143	.036	.153	.171	.286
2	.214	.333	.333	.327	.063	.286	.300	.700
3	.119	.354	.303	.295	.177	.179	.283	.467
4	.165	.308	.327	.449	.192	.165	.262	.508
5	.089	.188	.208	.154	.071	.089	.175	.325
6	.122	.339	.220	.159	.116	.203	.207	.300
7	.057	.275	.317	.169	.100	.193	.144	.420
8	.343	.750	.450	.492	.300	.357	.420	.500

---

[2]   Entries in cells give proportions of possible information relations between organizations
      in the sending category and organizations in the receiving category that are actually
      present. For information about source of data and definitions of categories and
      relations, see text.

The rows and columns of Table 1 refer to a classification of organizations by their primary function and auspices (public or private) developed by me. The eight categories of the classification are:

(1) industries—private economic production;

(2) financial institutions;

(3) government—administrative and deliberative bodies;

(4) government—service-providing bodies;

(5) voluntary associations—political parties, service clubs;

(6) interest aggregators—labor unions, business associations, professional associations;

(7) private, non-profit service-providing organizations, including churches; and

(8) communication specialists—mass media, law firms.

In this example the classification of organizations was made on the basis of exogenous information about them. The methods to be discussed, however, are equally applicable to density tables constructed by reference to a classification of actors according to their positions (Burt, 1976) or blocks (e.g., Breiger, 1976, 1979), where the classification into positions or blocks is determined by the application of a clustering algorithm to measures of the relational similarity of the actors.

Each cell entry in Table 1 gives the proportion of the potential relations of organizations in the row category to organizations in the column category that are actually present. Note that if there are g_i organizations in group i and g_j organizations in group j, then there are $g_i g_j$ potential relations if $i \neq j$ and $g_i(g_i - 1)$ potential relations if $i = j$ (as in most network studies, information relations of an organization to itself were not considered).

It is important to recognize that while Table 1 presents information in the form of a two-way table, it actually summarizes information from a three-way frequency table in which the units of analysis are *directed pairs* of actors. Consider a three-way classification of directed pairs of organizations in which the variables are (1) functional category of the potential sender of an information relation; (2) functional category of the potential receiver of an information relation; and (3) presence/absence of an information relation. If there are I functional categories, the table is an $I \times I \times 2$ table. Cell entries x_{ij2} give the number of times an organization in category i sends an information relation to an organization in category j, while entries x_{ij1} give the number of times such a relation could have been, but was not, sent.

An example of the type of table discussed in the last paragraph is given in Table 2. It is based on the same data used to obtain Table 1. In fact, the information in Table 2 can be used to determine the entries in Table 1 as follows:

$$d_{ij} = \frac{x_{ij2}}{x_{ij+}},$$

where d_{ij} is the density of relations (reported in Table 1) from organizations in category i to organizations in category j, and the "+" denotes summation. Notice, however, that the information contained in Table 1 is *not* sufficient to yield Table 2. Because Table 2, the $I \times I \times 2$ frequency table $\{x_{ijk}\}$, contains more information than Table 1, the $I \times I$ density table $\{d_{ij}\}$, we shall present methods for the analysis of the frequency table in the following sections. It should be clear, however, that these methods also permit inferences about patterns in the density table.

Table 2. The Frequency Table on Which the
Density Table is Based

(a. information relation absent)

Sending Category	Receiving Category							
	1	2	3	4	5	6	7	8
1	26	23	71	78	54	83	58	25
2	22	8	32	35	30	40	28	6
3	74	31	92	110	79	138	86	32
4	76	36	105	86	84	152	96	32
5	51	26	76	88	52	102	66	27
6	86	37	131	153	99	145	111	49
7	66	29	82	108	72	113	77	29
8	23	5	33	33	28	45	29	10

(b. information relation present)

Sending Category	Receiving Category							
	1	2	3	4	5	6	7	8
1	16	5	13	13	2	15	12	10
2	6	4	16	17	2	16	12	14
3	10	17	40	46	17	30	34	28
4	15	16	51	70	20	30	34	33
5	5	6	20	16	4	10	14	13
6	12	19	37	29	13	37	29	21
7	4	11	38	22	8	27	13	21
8	12	15	27	32	12	25	21	10

3. A Model for the Study of Directed Choices Among Groups

In order to study cross-classifications like that presented in Table 2, we shall formulate several log linear models that make different assumptions about the nature of the roles associated with different classes of actors. The most general model applicable to an $I \times I \times 2$ classification like that in Table 2 can be written

$$\log m_{ij1} = \lambda_{ij}$$
$$\log m_{ij2} = \lambda_{ij} + \theta + \alpha_i + \beta_j + \gamma_{ij} \qquad (1)$$

where m_{ijk} is an expected frequency corresponding to the observed frequency x_{ijk}, and we place the following identifying constraints on the parameters of the model:

$$\sum_i \alpha_i = 0$$

$$\sum_i \gamma_{ij} = \sum_j \gamma_{ij} = 0$$

$$\sum_j \beta_j = 0. \qquad (2)$$

In this model, the $\{\lambda_{ij}\}$ are "nuisance" parameters introduced to insure that the sampling constraints under which data are gathered are built into all models. Recall that for two groups of size g_i and g_j, there are $g_i g_j$ potential directed relations between them if $i \neq j$ and $g_i(g_i - 1)$ potential relations between them if $i = j$. Because of this requirement of the sampling design, we wish to require that the expected frequencies of all models be such that $m_{ij+} = x_{ij+} = g_i(g_j - \delta_{ij})$, where $\delta_{ij} = 1$ if $i = j$ and $\delta_{ij} = 0$ if $i \neq j$. Introduction of the parameters $\{\lambda_{ij}\}$ guarantees that this is the case.

The remaining parameters in (1) all have substantive interpretations. The parameter θ reflects the overall volume of relations present in the network. The sets of parameters $\{\alpha_i\}$ and $\{\beta_j\}$ reflect the differential tendencies of classes of actors to participate in relations. The parameters $\{\alpha_i\}$ correspond to the interaction of variables 1 and 3 in the table, and measure the "expansiveness" of a category of actors; categories i for which α_i is positive emit relatively many relations, while categories i for which α_i is negative emit relatively few relations. Thus the $\{\alpha_i\}$ parameters reflect differential participation in terms of outflows of relations. Similarly, the $\{\beta_j\}$ parameters corresponding to the interaction of variables 2 and 3 reflect differential "popularity" of categories of actors, that is, differential participation on the input side. Finally, the parameters $\{\gamma_{ij}\}$ are "group choice" parameters that reflect tendencies for group i to contact group j above or below the rate expected on the basis of θ, $\{\alpha_i\}$, and $\{\beta_j\}$. These parameters and their interpretations will be familiar to readers of papers by Fienberg and Wasserman (1981) or Holland and Leinhardt (1981), which give methods for the analysis of a more general type of data array than that considered here.[3]

Notice that (1) can be rewritten in the form of a logit model in which the presence or absence of relations is conceived as a dependent variable. That is, we may write

$$\log \left(\frac{m_{ij2}}{m_{ij1}} \right) = \theta + \alpha_i + \beta_j + \gamma_{ij}. \tag{3}$$

---

[3] Fienberg and Wasserman (1981) refer to group choice parameters as θ_{ij} in their models rather than as γ_{ij} as we have done here. Their parameters θ_{ij} are defined as sums of several of the parameters used in the above model (1):

$$\theta_{ij} = \theta + \alpha_i + \beta_j + \gamma_{ij},$$

where no constraints are placed on the values taken by the θ_{ij}. I prefer the parameterization in (1), though more complicated than that of Fienberg and Wasserman, because it is more directly related to the types of questions about roles posed above, and because it makes clearer the relation between the general model and its special cases.

Written in this way, we can interpret θ as the unweighted conditional log-odds of presence of a relation, α_i as the increment to the log-odds given that the potential sending actor is in category i, β_j as the increment to the log-odds given that the potential receiving actor is in category j, and γ_{ij} as an interaction effect on the log-odds given that the potential sending actor is in category i *and* that the receiving actor is in category j.

Finally, notice that (1) is equivalent to the more familiar version of the saturated log linear model for a trivariate cross-classification:

$$\log m_{ijk} = u + u_{1(i)} + u_{2(j)} + u_{3(k)}$$
$$+ u_{12(ij)} + u_{13(ik)} + u_{23(jk)}$$
$$+ u_{123(ijk)}. \tag{4}$$

(See, e.g., Fienberg, 1977:26.) Usually the parameters of (4) are identified by imposing the following side constraints on them:

$$\sum_i u_{1(i)} = \sum_j u_{2(j)} = \sum_k u_{3(k)}$$

$$= \sum_i u_{12(ij)} = \sum_j u_{12(ij)}$$

$$= \sum_i u_{13(ik)} = \sum_k u_{13(ik)}$$

$$= \sum_j u_{23(jk)} = \sum_k u_{23(jk)}$$

$$= \sum_i u_{123(ijk)} = \sum_j u_{123(ijk)} = \sum_k u_{123(ijk)} = 0. \tag{5}$$

Constraints (5) are, however, not the only constraints that can be used to identify (4), as writers such as Fienberg (1978), Holt (1979), and Wilson (1979) have noted. For the present analysis, it is useful to use the following constraints on the parameters of (4):

$$\sum_i u_{1(i)} = \sum_j u_{2(j)}$$

$$= \sum_i u_{12(ij)} = \sum_j u_{12(ij)}$$

$$= \sum_i u_{13(i2)} = \sum_j u_{23(j2)}$$

$$= \sum_i u_{123(ij2)} = \sum_j u_{123(ij2)} = 0;$$

$$u_{3(1)} = 0;$$

$$u_{13(i1)} = 0, \text{ for all } i;$$

$$u_{23(j1)} = 0, \text{ for all } j;$$

$$u_{123(ij1)} = 0, \text{ for all } i,j. \tag{6}$$

If we then define the parameters of (1) in terms of parameters in (4) as follows

$$\lambda_{ij} = u + u_{1(i)} + u_{2(j)} + u_{12(ij)}$$

$$\theta = u_{3(2)}$$

$$\alpha_i = u_{13(i2)}$$

$$\beta_j = u_{23(j2)}$$

$$\gamma_{ij} = u_{123(ij2)}, \tag{7}$$

the equivalence of (1) and (4) can be seen. Note that constraints (2) follow from constraints (6) and the definitions (7). The parameterization in (1) is to be preferred to that in (4) because of the clearer interpretation of effects that is available (see discussion above following [3]).

By placing constraints on the parameters of (1) in addition to those in (2), we can obtain restricted versions of the general model. These restricted versions embody various assumptions about the nature of the roles defined by cross-classifications of directed choices like Table 2. We discuss these restricted versions in the next section.

4. Restricted Versions of the General Model

Consider first a model in which the role represented by the relations of a class of actors is defined only by the nature and level of participation of that class of actors in social relations. One set of formal network roles in which this is the case is defined by Harary *et al.* (1965:17). In a discussion of graph theory, Harary *et al.* mention five distinct types of points in a graph: isolates, transmitters, receivers, carriers, and ordinary points. Isolates are defined as points with neither inflows nor outflows, transmitters are defined as points with no inflows but at least one outflow, while receivers are defined as points with no outflows but at least one inflow. Harary *et al.* define carriers as points with precisely one inflow and one outflow, while ordinary points are those points fitting none of the first four definitions. Like carriers, ordinary points must have at least one inflow and one outflow; furthermore, they must have at least two inflows or at least two outflows. For our purposes the distinction between carriers and ordinary points is not important, so we will refer to both as carriers. Illustrative diagrams of the five types of points are given in Figure 1.

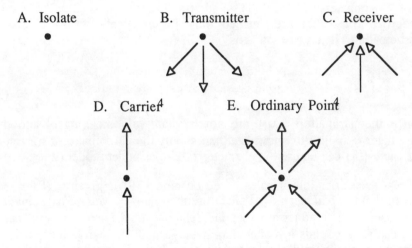

Figure 1. Formal Roles Defined by External
Relations

---

4   In discussion below, we refer to both carriers and ordinary points as carriers. The diagrams given here are based on definitions presented by Harary *et al.* (1965:17).

The important thing to note about the above definitions and the diagrams in Figure 1 is that the different types of points are defined by the extent and nature of their *external* relations. Of course, this is necessary in graph theory, where relations of a point to itself are not considered. In the present case, however, we consider roles to be represented not by single actors, but by classes of actors. The nature of internal role relations is thus potentially important in defining roles; but it is not important in this typology of roles, concerned with participation levels only.

In order to make use of the roles of isolate, transmitter, receiver, and carrier in our analyses, we must move from the deterministic definitions of Harary *et al.* to definitions of these roles in terms of the relative levels of participation of the different categories of actors. Further, we must specify that internal relations are not consequential in the definitions of roles, and that no distinctions are to be made among external categories, if the fourfold typology of roles is to be adequately descriptive of the social relations among categories of actors. These last requirements imply the restrictions

$$\gamma_{ij} = 0, \text{ for all } i,j \qquad (8)$$

on the parameters of Model (1), in addition to restrictions (2). This model specifies roles that are defined only in terms of overall levels of participation. It can be written as

$$\log m_{ij1} = \lambda_{ij}$$
$$\log m_{ij2} = \lambda_{ij} + \theta + \alpha_i + \beta_j. \qquad (9)$$

Since the parameters $\{\lambda_{ij}\}$ are not substantively meaningful and the parameter θ applies to all directed pairs, only the participation parameters $\{\alpha_i\}$ and $\{\beta_j\}$ can be used in characterizing roles under model (9).

A classification of roles based on model (9) is given in Table 3.[5] Recall that the parameters $\{\alpha_i\}$ measure the relative levels of participation of classes of actors in terms of sending relations; thus a positive α_i indicates that category i sends a higher than average number of relations while a negative α_i indicates that category i sends a lower than average number of

---

[5]   See also Galaskiewicz (1979a:90), who uses the terms generator, transmitter, and consumer to refer to transmitters, carriers, and receivers, respectively. Galaskiewicz does not use or refer to the isolate role. The way in which Galaskiewicz defines roles combines carriers with isolates, since his roles are defined in terms of the ratio of inflows to outflows, without taking the *volume* of inflows and outflows into account.

relations. Similarly, the parameters $\{\beta_j\}$ measure differential participation of actors in terms of relations received.

Table 3. Typology of Roles Defined by Model (9)

		Value of Participation Parameter on Input Side (β_j)	
		Negative	Positive
Value of Participation Parameter on Output Side (α_i)	Negative	Isolate	Receiver
	Positive	Transmitter	Carrier

In Table 3, I define the roles of isolate, transmitter, receiver, and carrier in terms of the participation parameters $\{\alpha_i\}$ and $\{\beta_j\}$. In offering these definitions, I distinguish "high" from "low" participation levels according to whether a class of actors has a higher than average (positive value of α_i or β_j) or a lower than average (negative value of α_i or β_j) participation level. It is not necessary to use the average level as a reference point, of course. The definitions of Harary *et al.* correspond to a distinction between "low" values of α_i or β_j of $-\infty$ and "high" values of α_i or β_j equal to some finite value. In many social science applications, however, use of the distinction in the definition of Harary *et al.* would mean that almost all actors were classified as carriers, so I have defined participation levels relative to the average. It should be clear that this definition of roles in terms of participation is different than the definition of points given by Harary *et al.*, although I have used the same terms to refer to both definitions of roles.

Model (9) and the typology of roles in Table 3 are really quite simple, and frequently they will not adequately describe the pattern of social relations in a table such as Table 2. To better describe such a pattern, models that are less restrictive than (9) must be formulated.

One set of models that is of interest is a set of models taking into account the character of the internal relations of the actors aggregated into a single category, in addition to the differences in the overall level of participation taken into account by model (9). Many analyses of square cross-classifications (e.g., Laumann, 1969; Verbrugge, 1977; Alba and Kessler, 1979) place a great deal of interpretive weight on the special character of a group's relation to itself. Discussions of methods for aggregating structurally similar individual actors into positions or blocks (Burt, 1976; White *et al.*, 1976) also stress the density of relations of a position or block to itself in characterizing different roles.

Consider, for instance, Burt's (1976:107) definitions of "four elementary types of network positions and the patterns of relations which define them," reproduced here in Table 4. The distinctions between types of positions drawn by Burt rely on distinctions between classes of actors in terms of their participation levels in terms of inflows, and in terms of the density of their internal relations. The columns of Table 4 distinguish classes of actors receiving no relations from those receiving some relations. The rows of Table 4 distinguish between classes of actors that concentrate at least half of the relations they send on actors in their own category, and classes of actors that do not concentrate their relations on themselves to this degree. No distinction based on differential participation on the output side enters Burt's typology.

What is most important at present about Burt's typology is the distinction in its rows, which refers to the special character of the internal relations of a group. Note that no distinction is specified between external categories in this typology; the columns of Table 4 do not differentiate relations received by their sources.

Table 4. Burt's Definitions of Types of Network Positions[6]

Proportion of Network
Choices Given to the Position

		About Zero	Greater Than Zero
Ratio of Position Choices Given to The Position over The Total Number Of Choices Made By the Position	0.5 or Greater	Isolate	Primary Position
	Less Than 0.5	Sycophant	Broker

In order to incorporate distinctions having to do with the special character of the internal relations of a group in the way suggested by Burt and others, some of the group choice parameters restricted in (8) must be

---

6   Source: Burt (1976:107).

freed. In order to avoid drawing distinctions among outgroups, however, only the γ_{ij} for which $i = j$ can be free to take any value. The parameters γ_{ij} for which $i \neq j$ must be defined in terms of the γ_{ij} for which $i = j$. A set of constraints that, together with (2), suffices to do this is

$$\gamma_{ij} = \frac{1}{(I-1)(I-2)} \sum_{k=1}^{I} \gamma_{kk} - \frac{1}{I-2} \left(\gamma_{ii} + \gamma_{jj}\right), \text{ for } i \neq j. \tag{10}$$

For an alternative parameterization of effects like the group choice effects, see Hauser (1978).

Note that in the model defined by (10), the γ_{ij} for $i \neq j$ are neither equal to zero nor equal to one another. Thus, restriction (10) introduces apparent "social distance" effects into the model in the form of the off-diagonal γ_{ij}. These social distance effects are only apparent, however; as equation (10) shows, they are generated by the differential levels of within-category preference shown by the classes of actors. They do not involve differential preferences among outgroup members by actors in a particular category. For more details on this, see Marsden (1981).

If model (10) adequately describes the structure of relations in a classification like Table 2, then the roles of each of the classes of actors can be described in terms of (a) their levels of participation in terms of outputs of relations (α_i); (b) their levels of participation in terms of inputs of relations (β_j); and (c) their levels of within-category concentration of relations (γ_{ij}). A typology of roles defined on the basis of these distinctions is presented in Table 5.

The typology of roles given in Table 5 generalizes the distinctions among roles drawn in Table 3 and by Burt. Note that, if the distinction in terms of ingroup preference is ignored, then the four rows of Table 5 refer to carriers, transmitters, receivers, and isolates, respectively. Note also that a distinction in terms of participation on the output side is included in Table 5, while such a distinction is not made in Table 4.

In Table 3, carrier roles are defined as those with high levels of participation on both the input and the output sides. In making a further distinction on the basis of the character of internal relations, I distinguish carrier roles into primary positions—cliques in which members are involved in high levels of relations with outsiders—and brokers—unrelated individuals with high numbers of relations to others. Similarly, transmitter roles are further divided into low status cliques and unrelated sycophants, receiver roles into high status cliques and unrelated "snobs," and isolates into isolated cliques and unrelated, isolated individuals. As with the typology of roles in Table 3, I have drawn the distinctions here with respect to average levels of relations, but other points of division between "high" and "low" levels of participation or ingroup preference could certainly be used. Note also that the magnitudes of the α_i, β_j, and γ_{ii} parameters used to define roles in Table 5 will influence the clarity with which those roles are defined.

Table 5. Typology of Roles Defined by Model (10)

Value of Participation Parameter on Output Side (α_i)	Value of Participation Parameter on Input Side (β_j)	Level of Ingroup Preference (γ_{ii})	
		Positive	Negative
Positive	Positive	Primary Position	Broker
	Negative	Low Status Clique	Sycophant
Negative	Positive	High Status Clique	Snob
	Negative	Isolated Clique	Isolate

The typology of roles given in Table 5 is the most general typology of egocentrically defined roles possible. Any more complex characterization of roles will require that distinctions among outgroups be made in the introduction of the parameters γ_{ij}; recall that such distinctions are not involved in (10). There are many possibilities that might be entertained for the construction of such more complex role structures. For instance, Laumann, Marsden, and Galaskiewicz (1977:606-613) suggest that the nature of communication roles in "bargaining" and "oppositional" structures of decision-making will differ in specific ways, based on the issue preference and activation of decision-makers. Another possibility is that a particular sycophant role "hangs on" to only one of several primary positions, avoiding the others. A final illustrative example of a more complex role structure than that in Table 5 would involve the ordering of the several categories of actors in one or more ways, such that categories of actors thought to be most likely to have intergroup contact are placed near to one another in the ordering(s). Such "social distance" effects would be plausible when the classes of actors are defined by what Blau (1977) terms a "graduated structural parameter," such as education or occupational status.[7]

The important feature of the examples of complex role structures mentioned in the last paragraph is that none of them can be egocentrically defined with respect to features of a single class of actors. Rather, under these models, the relational role of a specific class of actors is defined with respect to the roles of other classes of actors, not simply by its level of participation in the system and the nature of its internal relations. Complex constraints on the group choice parameters γ_{ij} in (1) are necessary to represent those more involved structures of roles. Methods of analysis outlined in Marsden (1981) can be generalized to deal with such complex role structures.

It should now be clear how the three types of questions posed at the beginning of this chapter can be answered using restricted versions of Model (1). Model (9) makes reference only to the nature of participation of classes of actors, defining roles by reference to the external relations of actors. Model (10) refers both to participation levels and the special character of the internal relations of a class of actors. Finally, in models more complex than (10), of which the most general is (1), the external relations of classes of actors are *not* homogeneous, and various hypotheses about the way these external relations are structured may be entertained. In the next two sections of the chapter, we give methods for the testing of such hypotheses, and for the estimation of parameters of the models.

5. *Testing Hypotheses about Role Structures*

All of the models discussed in the preceding sections are hierarchical log linear models for the $I \times I \times 2$ cross-classification. Standard results for such models (Fienberg, 1977:Appendix II; Haberman, 1978) can,

---

[7] For appropriate statistical models for such situations, see Goodman (1984).

therefore, be used to provide maximum likelihood estimates of expected cell frequencies m_{ijk}, tests of the adequacy of a particular hypothesized role structure, and conditional tests of the contributions of particular features of a role structure to explaining the structure of the cross-classification of directed relations.

In Table 6, the parameters of the general model (1) are listed, together with the minimal sufficient statistics necessary to fit them and the degrees of freedom they require. In order to obtain estimated expected frequencies for a particular model, we set expected values of the sufficient statistics equal to their observed values. Thus, to fit the most general model, model (1), we simply set

$$\widehat{m}_{ijk} = x_{ijk}, \text{ for all } i,j,k,$$

while the $\widehat{m}_{ijk}$ for model (9) will satisfy the equations

$$\widehat{m}_{ij+} = x_{ij+}, \text{ for all } i,j;$$
$$\widehat{m}_{i+k} = x_{i+k}, \text{ for all } i,k; \text{ and}$$
$$\widehat{m}_{+jk} = x_{+jk}, \text{ for all } j,k.$$

These equations can be solved using the usual iterative proportional fitting algorithm (see, e.g., Fienberg, 1977:33-36). Note that Model (1) corresponds to a saturated model for the $I \times I \times 2$ cross-classification, while Model (9) is equivalent to a model of no three-factor interaction.

Table 6. Parameters of the General Model, with
Minimal Sufficient Statistics and Degrees of Freedom

Parameter(s)	Minimal Sufficient Statistics	Degrees of Freedom
$\{\lambda_{ij}\}$	$\{x_{ij+}\}$	I^2
θ	$\{x_{++k}\}$	1
$\{\alpha_i\}$	$\{x_{i+k}\}$	$I-1$
$\{\beta_j\}$	$\{x_{+jk}\}$	$I-1$
$\{\gamma_{ij}\}$	$\{x_{ijk}\}$	$(I-1)^2$

For models such as (10), which place constraints on the group choice parameters $\{\gamma_{ij}\}$ which are less restrictive than (8) but more restrictive than (2), a slightly different approach than that outlined above is necessary.

Constraints (10) on the $\{\gamma_{ij}\}$ imply that the following equations must be solved, in addition to those listed above for (9), in order to obtain estimated expected frequencies $\hat{m}_{ijk}$:

$$\hat{m}_{iik} = x_{iik} \text{ for all } i,k; \text{ and}$$

$$\sum_{i \neq j} \hat{m}_{ijk} = \sum_{i \neq j} x_{ijk} \text{ for all } k.$$

The fitting of these constraints on the γ_{ij} requires I degrees of freedom. Several approaches to the solution of these equations are available, including the generalized iterative scaling procedure of Darroch and Ratcliff (1972), the Newton-Raphson algorithm (Haberman, 1978), and the application of the usual iterative scaling algorithm to a four-dimensional pseudo-table of counts containing many structural zeroes (e.g., Hauser, 1978).

Models placing other constraints on the $\{\gamma_{ij}\}$ will be associated with different sets of sufficient statistics and will, in general, require different numbers of degrees of freedom. All models can, however, be fitted using the general techniques discussed in the preceding paragraph. For examples of various types of models applicable to I × I classifications, see Goodman (1979), Hauser (1978, 1979), or Marsden (1981). These models are easily generalized to the I × I × 2 case.

In order to assess the adequacy of a particular hypothesized role structure for explaining the pattern of intergroup relations in a cross-classification such as Table 2, the value of the likelihood ratio test statistic

$$G^2 = 2\sum_i \sum_j \sum_k x_{ijk} \log \frac{x_{ijk}}{\hat{m}_{ijk}}$$

can be computed. If the hypothesized role structure is an adequate description of the pattern of intergroup relations, then G^2 will follow a χ^2 distribution with degrees of freedom equal to I^2 minus the degrees of freedom associated with the substantively meaningful parameters (θ, $\{\alpha_i\}$, $\{\beta_j\}$, $\{\gamma_{ij}\}$) in the model being tested (recall that the sampling constraints require that all models include the $\{\lambda_{ij}\}$). For example, model (9) has $I^2 - 1 - 2 * (I - 1) = (I - 1)^2$ degrees of freedom, while model (10) has $I^2 - 1 - 2 * (I - 1) - I = I^2 - I + 1$ degrees of freedom. Of course, the saturated model (1) has no degrees of freedom.

The contributions of particular parameters or sets of parameters can be tested using conditional likelihood ratio test statistics for comparison of models (see, e.g., Fienberg, 1977:47-48). To make such tests, one formulates two models, an unrestricted model (u) including the term or constraint in question, and a restricted model (r) including all terms or constraints in (u) except the term in question. The difference in likelihood ratio test statistics for models (r) and (u)

$$G^2(r) - G^2(u)$$

is then distributed as χ^2 with degrees of freedom equal to the difference in degrees of freedom between models (r) and (u), under the null hypothesis that the term or constraint in question does not serve to structure social relations. The test is conditional on the adequacy of model (u), but can be informative even when model (u) does not fit the data well. For example, the question of whether levels of ingroup preference significantly differ from zero for the different categories of actors involves a comparison between models (9) and (10). The conditional test statistic

$$G^2(9) - G^2(10)$$

will be distributed as χ^2 with I degrees of freedom under the null hypothesis that the $\{\gamma_{ii}\}$ do not differ from zero.

It is important to note that all features of a study design must be built into any model fit to the data. In the example reported above in Tables 1 and 2, only the totals $\{x_{ij+}\}$ are fixed by design, requiring the inclusion of the parameters $\{\lambda_{ij}\}$. In many network studies, however, respondents are asked to make a fixed number (often three) of citations of others on one or more relational criteria (Holland and Leinhardt, 1973; for an example, see Laumann *et al.*, 1977:602). Such a design fixes the totals $\{x_{++k}\}$ in addition to the totals $\{x_{ij+}\}$, and it constrains the values that can be taken on by the $\{x_{i+k}\}$. Such a design requires that the parameters θ and $\{\alpha_i\}$ be included in all models for the data. Obviously, with such a design it is impossible to test hypotheses about the $\{\alpha_i\}$, since all α_i are constrained to be approximately zero. It is, therefore, not possible to use as elaborate a typology of egocentrically defined roles as that given in Table 5 when a study uses a fixed-choice type of question for the definition of relations. A typology like that given by Burt (Table 4) is appropriate for such designs.

6. Estimation of Parameters

Given maximum likelihood estimates of expected frequencies $\{\widehat{m}_{ijk}\}$ maximum likelihood estimates of parameters are easily obtained. The parameters $\{\lambda_{ij}\}$ are rarely of substantive interest, but they are easily estimated as

$$\widehat{\lambda}_{ij} = \log \widehat{m}_{ij1}.$$

The remaining parameters of the model can be estimated most easily if the $\widehat{m}_{ijk}$ are converted to expected logits $\widehat{\ell}_{ij}$, where

$$\widehat{\ell}_{ij} = \log \left(\frac{\widehat{m}_{ij2}}{\widehat{m}_{ij1}}\right) = \log \widehat{m}_{ij2} - \log \widehat{m}_{ij1}.$$

It is then straightforward to show that

$$\widehat{\theta} = \frac{1}{I^2} \sum_i \sum_j \widehat{\ell}_{ij};$$

$$\widehat{\alpha}_i = \frac{1}{I} \sum_j \widehat{\ell}_{ij} - \widehat{\theta} \text{ for all i; and}$$

$$\widehat{\beta}_j = \frac{1}{I} \sum_i \widehat{\ell}_{ij} - \widehat{\theta} \text{ for all j.}$$

Since the $\{\gamma_{ij}\}$ will always satisfy the constraints on them in (2), as well as other constraints at times, we can also write

$$\widehat{\gamma}_{ij} = \widehat{\ell}_{ij} - \widehat{\alpha}_i - \widehat{\beta}_j - \widehat{\theta} \text{ for all i,j.}$$

We note again that no substantive interpretation should be given to estimated parameters corresponding to marginal totals that are fixed by design. For example, no inference should be based on θ or the $\{\alpha_i\}$ if the design fixes the number of citations or choices made by individual actors.

7. Analysis of the Data in Table 2

In this section we analyze the data presented earlier on the functionally defined information roles of organizational actors in Towertown. Table 7 reports relevant statistics for assessing the goodness-of-fit of several models for the cross-classification in Table 2.

The first model presented, containing the volume parameter θ only, is used as a baseline model indicative of the amount of structuring of social relations according to the classification of actors introduced. Should such a model fit the data, we would infer that the roles represented by the classes of actors are not differentiated from one another in terms of their characteristic patterns of social relations. This model is also useful as a comparison point to indicate how successful a given model is in explaining the structuring of relations. Of course, if the design of a study fixes the number of choices made by individual actors, then the $\{\alpha_i\}$ should also be included in the baseline model.

Table 7. Goodness-of-Fit Statistics for Models Fit
to Table 2

Parameters Included[8]	Constraints on γ_{ij}	G^2	Df	p	Proportional Reduction in G^2 Versus Baseline[9]
θ	—	386.36	63	<.001	—
$\theta,\{\alpha_i\}$	—	237.60	56	<.001	.385
$\theta,\{\beta_j\}$	—	248.35	56	<.001	.357
$\theta,\{\alpha_i\},\{\beta_j\}$	(8)	91.12	49	<.001	.764
$\theta,\{\alpha_i\},\{\beta_j\},\{\gamma_{ij}\}$	(10)	37.64	41	~.625	.903

In this case the baseline model does not fit the data at all well. The next two models shown introduce the two sets of participation parameters $\{\alpha_i\}$ and $\{\beta_j\}$ separately. By comparing the fit of each of these models to the fourth model, which includes both sets of participation parameters but constrains all the group choice parameters $\{\gamma_{ij}\}$ to be zero, we can obtain tests of hypotheses asserting that each set of participation parameters is equal to zero. The relevant conditional test statistics are 157.23 for the $\{\alpha_i\}$ and 146.48 for the $\{\beta_j\}$. Since each of these statistics has 7 degrees of freedom, it is clear that there are significant differences among the classes of actors in terms of their levels of participation on both the output and input sides.

---

[8] All models include the normalization parameters $\{\lambda_{ij}\}$.

[9] The baseline model for comparison is the first model listed, i.e., the model containing only the volume effect θ in addition to the normalization parameters.

The fourth model, corresponding to model (9) discussed above, explains over 75 percent of the association in the baseline model. It does not, however, fit the data well, as evidenced by its G^2 statistic of 91.12, with 49 degrees of freedom. We are thus led to consider the special character of the internal relations of the actors, applying the last model of Table 7, model (10). This model has a G^2 value of 37.64, with 41 degrees of freedom, yielding a very good fit to the data. It explains over 90 percent of the association in the baseline model. The conditional test statistic for the hypothesis that there is no special character of internal relations for these classes of actors is equal to 53.48; with 8 degrees of freedom, it is clear that this hypothesis is not tenable.

Table 8 presents maximum likelihood estimates of the parameters of model (10). All of the group choice parameters $\{\hat{\gamma}_{ij}\}$ are exhibited, though the off-diagonal ones are a direct function of the diagonal ones. Using the parameter estimates and referring to Table 5, we see that only four of the eight conceivable types of roles appear in this classification. There is one primary position, occupied by governmental organizations providing services (Group 4). It is not especially well defined, in that β_4 is barely greater than zero. We also find three broker positions. Two of these, represented by financial institutions (Group 2) and communication specialists (Group 8), are quite well defined. The remaining broker position is that of governmental administrative organizations (Group 3). Its role is quite weakly defined, as indicated by the small absolute values of $\hat{\alpha}_3(.113)$ and $\hat{\gamma}_{33}(-.043)$.

The four remaining positions all include actors that are somewhat peripheral to the pattern of information exchange in Towertown. Two of these positions are isolated cliques—sets of actors with low levels of overall participation who are, nonetheless, disproportionately likely to communicate information to other actors in their own set. The isolated cliques are composed of industries (Group 1) and interest aggregators (Group 6). The positions of both are reasonably clearly defined. Actors in the final two categories can be classified as isolates, since they have low levels of overall participation on both the input and output sides, and additionally are not especially likely to communicate with other incumbents of their position. The isolate positions are occupied by voluntary associations (Group 5) and private, nonprofit service-providing organizations (Group 7). The small values of the estimates $\hat{\gamma}_{55}(-.109)$ and $\hat{\beta}_7(-.025)$ show that these isolate positions are somewhat weakly defined.

Table 8. Parameter Estimates for Model (10),
Applied to Table 2

A.   Volume parameter

$\hat{\theta} = -1.143$

B.   Participation parameters

$\hat{\alpha}_1 =$	-0.389	$\hat{\beta}_1 =$	-0.480
$\hat{\alpha}_2 =$	0.315	$\hat{\beta}_2 =$	0.420
$\hat{\alpha}_3 =$	0.113	$\hat{\beta}_3 =$	0.240
$\hat{\alpha}_4 =$	0.203	$\hat{\beta}_4 =$	0.068
$\hat{\alpha}_5 =$	-0.590	$\hat{\beta}_5 =$	-0.723
$\hat{\alpha}_6 =$	-0.289	$\hat{\beta}_6 =$	-0.328
$\hat{\alpha}_7 =$	-0.236	$\hat{\beta}_7 =$	-0.025
$\hat{\alpha}_8 =$	0.873	$\hat{\beta}_8 =$	0.828

C.   Group choice parameters $\{\hat{\gamma}_{ij}\}$

				j				
i	1	2	3	4	5	6	7	8
1	1.526	-0.178	-0.218	-0.336	-0.207	-0.291	-0.163	-0.132
2	-0.178	-0.285	0.084	-0.035	0.095	0.011	0.139	0.169
3	-0.218	0.084	-0.043	-0.075	0.054	-0.030	0.099	0.129
4	-0.336	-0.035	-0.075	0.667	-0.064	-0.148	-0.020	0.011
5	-0.207	0.095	0.054	-0.064	-0.109	0.019	0.110	0.140
6	-0.291	0.011	-0.030	-0.148	-0.019	0.394	0.026	0.056
7	-0.163	0.139	0.099	-0.020	0.110	0.026	-0.375	0.184
8	-0.132	0.169	0.129	0.011	0.140	0.056	0.184	-0.557

The success of model (10) in fitting Table 2 indicates that the ego-centric characterization of roles in the above paragraphs is an appropriate description of the relational patterns in that table. Thus, for instance, the communication specialists are disproportionately likely to communicate with all other groups of actors, given that they are somewhat unlikely to communicate with one another. The other categories of actors need not be differentiated in describing the role of the communication specialists.

Inspection of the parameters of the most general model, Model (1), and inspection of the standardized residuals (Bishop *et al.*, 1975:136-137) can suggest ways in which the fit of the model can be significantly improved (see also Hauser, 1978, 1979). The strongest such suggestion emerging from the application of these exploratory procedures to these data is that two of the broker positions—the financial institutions and the communication specialists—are linked by group choice parameters γ_{28} and γ_{82} that are equal, but larger than the values implied by equation (10) above. If such a revision is made, we obtain a model with $G^2 = 32.23$ and 40 degrees of freedom (p ~ .805). The conditional test statistic (5.41 with 1 degree of freedom) indicates that the revision significantly improves the fit of the model to the data. Under this model, the parameter estimate $\gamma_{28} = \gamma_{82}$ rises to .804, and the remaining parameter estimates are close to those reported in Table 8. There are some other rather weak suggestions from the pattern of residuals, but all involve *post hoc* analysis of a model that fits the data quite well, and they will not be pursued further here.

If models like the model considered in the preceding paragraph are necessary, then the external relations of positions are not homogeneous, and one must go beyond the distinctions given in Table 5 in order to characterize roles. Thus, for the above example, it would be necessary to observe that the two broker positions are more closely linked to one another than to the remaining six positions.

8. Problems Encountered with Incomplete Data

Network analysts sometimes wish to analyze square tables of counts when available data are more limited than those given in Table 2. The data for such analyses are often generated by surveys in which a respondent is asked to describe himself or herself, and one or more of his or her relations (e.g., spouse, friend, co-worker), in terms of selected attributes (e.g., education, occupation, religion, ethnicity). Examples of this type of survey design are Laumann (1966, 1969, 1973) and McCallister and Fischer (1978).

Given this type of study design, which typically does not refer to a well-defined population of actors with whom relations may occur, and usually does not refer to friends, co-workers, or spouses by name, it is not possible to construct a table like Table 2 and apply methods discussed in the previous sections. This is because a researcher does not know which relations are *not* present. Thus, this type of study design provides data on only the second panel of Table 2, the panel referring to relations that are present.

Two types of problems occur as a result of incomplete data. One problem has to do with identification of parameters; the other problem concerns the estimation of expected values for the second panel of the table, when that is the only portion available to the researcher. Some modifications of the procedure discussed above are necessary in order to deal with these difficulties. Before discussing these modifications, however, we should note that some inferences available from the complete data array cannot be drawn at all when only the second panel is available, while other inferences can be drawn only with some caution.

To see the problems bearing on the identification of parameters, it is useful to consider two versions of the most general model applicable to the $I \times I$ two-dimensional table which is the second panel of a table like Table 2. The first version of this model is simply the second equation of model (1) above:

$$\log m_{ij2} = \lambda_{ij} + \theta + \alpha_i + \beta_j + \gamma_{ij}, \tag{11}$$

with side constraints

$$\sum_i \alpha_i = \sum_j \beta_j = \sum_i \gamma_{ij} = \sum_j \gamma_{ij} = 0. \tag{12}$$

The second version of this model is the saturated log linear model for a two-dimensional classification:

$$\log m_{ij} = u' + u'_{1(i)} + u'_{2(j)} + u'_{12(ij)}, \tag{13}$$

with side constraints

$$\sum_i u'_{1(i)} = \sum_j u'_{2(j)} = \sum_i u'_{12(ij)} = \sum_j u'_{12(ij)} = 0. \tag{14}$$

Primes are used to differentiate the u-terms in (13) from those in (4). To see the equivalence of these two versions of the model, it is useful to substitute the expression for λ_{ij} from Equations (7) into (11), obtaining

$$\log m_{ij2} = u + u_{1(i)} + u_{2(j)} + u_{12(ij)} + \theta + \alpha_i + \beta_j + \gamma_{ij}. \tag{15}$$

Recall from Equation (6) that

$$\sum_i u_{1(i)} = \sum_j u_{2(j)} = \sum_i u_{12(ij)} = \sum_j u_{12(ij)} = 0.$$

Next, note that the parameters of (15) may be rearranged as follows:

$$\log m_{ij2} = (u + \theta) + (u_{1(i)} + \alpha_i) + (u_{2(j)} + \beta_j) + (u_{12(ij)} + \gamma_{ij}). \quad (16)$$

In (16), the four sets of parameters in parentheses constitute effects related to the entire table $(u + \theta)$, the ith row $(u_{1(i)} + \alpha_i)$, the jth column $(u_{2(j)} + \beta_j)$, and the interaction of the ith row and the jth column $(u_{12(ij)} + \gamma_{ij})$. Since, from (6) and (12), it follows that

$$\sum_i (u_{1(i)} + \alpha_i) = \sum_j (u_{2(j)} + \beta_j) = \sum_i (u_{12(ij)} + \gamma_{ij}) = \sum_j (u_{12(ij)} + \gamma_{ij}) = 0,$$

it should be clear that models (16) and (13) are equivalent with

$$u' = u + \theta;$$
$$u'_{1(i)} = u_{1(i)} + \alpha_i;$$
$$u'_{2(j)} = u_{2(j)} + \beta_j; \text{ and}$$
$$u'_{12(ij)} = u_{12(ij)} + \gamma_{ij}. \quad (17)$$

The parameters of (13) can be estimated using standard results for log linear models. When related to the parameters of the general model for complete data using (17), however, we can see that each of the parameters of (13) confounds one of the substantively meaningful parameters of (1) with a component of the nuisance parameters $\{\lambda_{ij}\}$. When only the second panel of a table like Table 2 is available, we can estimate the parameters of (13), but we cannot further dissect those estimates into components due to the substantively meaningful parameters and due to the nuisance parameters. Thus, only the sums in parentheses of (16) can be identified using incomplete data.

Clearly this result makes it difficult to draw substantive conclusions on the basis of incomplete data. Fortunately, two features of the components of the $\{\lambda_{ij}\}$ often make some limited inferences possible. It will usually be the case that

$$u_{1(i)} \approx u_{2(i)}, \text{ for all } i, \quad (18)$$

and further that

$$u_{12(ij)} \approx 0, \text{ for all } i, j. \quad (19)$$

To see result (18), note that in the general model (4), the sets of parameters $\{u_{1(i)}\}$ and $\{u_{2(j)}\}$ have sufficient statistics $\{x_{i++}\}$ and $\{x_{+j+}\}$. The sampling design for complete data is such, however, that these totals are necessarily equal to one another, i.e.,

$$x_{i++} = x_{+i+}, \text{ for all i.}$$

This is the case because x_{i++} is the total number of possible relations in which class i of actors may be involved as a sender; clearly this must be equal to x_{+i+}, the total number of possible relations in which class i of actors may be involved as a receiver. Both sets of totals, then, reflect primarily the number of actors in class i. The equivalence of these totals means that (18) is exactly true when a model involving neither the $\{\alpha_i\}$ nor the $\{\beta_j\}$ is fit to a table like Table 2, and is approximately true for other models. For instance, if the general model (1) is applied to Table 2, and the $\{\lambda_{ij}\}$ are decomposed according to the parameterization in (6) and (7), we find that the largest absolute difference $|u_{1(i)} - u_{2(i)}|$ is .0425.

Given result (18), the difference between the row and column effects $u'_{1(i)}$ and $u'_{2(i)}$ in (13) can be used to make some substantive inferences. From (17) and (18), we have

$$u'_{1(i)} - u'_{2(i)} = u_{1(i)} + \alpha_i - u_{2(i)} - \beta_j \approx \alpha_i - \beta_i. \tag{20}$$

That is, the difference in row and column effects will generally reflect the difference between the participation level of a class of actors on the output side and its participation level on the input side. Thus, we can locate those classes of actors that tend to be transmitters (for which [20] will be positive), those that tend to be receivers (for which [20] will be negative), and those that are either carriers or isolates (for which [20] will be close to zero). With incomplete data, it is not possible to tell whether a class of actors for which (20) is close to zero is a carrier or an isolate; we can tell only that its level of participation in terms of inputs is about the same as its level of participation in terms of outputs.

Note that in this situation, a fixed-choice type of question, requiring respondents to describe a set number of their relations (e.g., Laumann, 1973) makes it possible to draw specific inferences about the relative levels of popularity $\{\beta_j\}$. The reason for this is that the fixed-choice format constrains the $\{\alpha_i\}$ to be very close to zero. In this circumstance, then, the difference (20) will be approximately equal to $-\beta_i$.

To see result (19), note that in the general model (3), the set of parameters $\{u_{12(ij)}\}$ has sufficient statistics $\{x_{ij+}\}$. Note that x_{ij+} is the number of potential relations from actors in class i to actors in class j. Recall from above that the sampling design is such that

$$x_{ij+} = g_i(g_j - \delta_{ij}).$$

A reasonably close approximation to the $\{x_{ij+}\}$ can be obtained using the sufficient statistics for the $\{u_{1(i)}\}$ and the $\{u_{2(j)}\}$, which are $\{x_{i++}\}$ and $\{x_{+j+}\}$, respectively. By design, it is the case that

$$x_{i++} = g_i(g - 1)$$

and that

$$x_{+j+} = g_j(g - 1),$$

where g is the total number of actors in the system under analysis. Using these results, and the fact that the total number of potential relations x_{+++} is $g(g - 1)$, we can approximate the x_{ij+} as follows:

$$\hat{x}_{ij+} = \frac{x_{i++}x_{+j+}}{x_{+++}} = g_i g_j - \frac{g_i g_j}{g}. \tag{21}$$

To see that (21) does indeed constitute an approximation to the x_{ij+}, note that the ratio

$$\frac{\hat{x}_{ij+}}{x_{ij+}} = \frac{g_i g_j - \dfrac{g_i g_j}{g}}{g_i g_j} = 1 - \frac{1}{g}, \text{ for } i \neq j,$$

tends to 1 as g grows large, and further that the ratio

$$\frac{\hat{x}_{ii+}}{x_{ii+}} = \frac{g_i^2 - \dfrac{g_i^2}{g}}{g_i^2 - g_i} = \frac{g_i - \dfrac{1}{g}}{g_i - 1}, \text{ for all } i,$$

likewise tends to 1, as g and g_i grow large. Thus in the limit, the sufficient statistics for the $\{u_{12(ij)}\}$ can be approximated by those for the $\{u_{1(i)}\}$ and the $\{u_{2(j)}\}$.

The importance of the approximation (21) lies in the fact that, when g and all g_i are reasonably large, the $\{x_{ij+}\}$ do not add information over and above that provided by the $\{x_{i++}\}$ and the $\{x_{+j+}\}$ in obtaining estimated expected values. It follows that, because the $\{x_{ij+}\}$ are nearly a multiplicative function of the $\{x_{i++}\}$ and the $\{x_{+j+}\}$, the parameters corresponding to the $\{x_{ij+}\}$, the $\{u_{12(ij)}\}$, will be close to zero when g and all g_i are reasonably large. Thus we reach result (19).

Given result (19), we can see that it is possible to reach conclusions about the group choice parameters $\{\gamma_{ij}\}$ when data are incomplete. Using (17) and (19), we note that

$$u'_{12(ij)} = u_{12(ij)} + \gamma_{ij} \approx \gamma_{ij}.$$

Thus, when the total number of actors, g, and the numbers of actors in each class, g_i, are reasonably large, inferences about the pattern of group choice can be safely made even where data are incomplete. When the classes of actors are as broadly defined as those studied by Laumann (1973)—religious groups, ethnic groups, or occupational categories—the sizes of groups will be sufficiently large to permit such inferences.

Overall, then, the problem of identification of parameters can be overcome at least in part. The actual parameters of the general model (1) cannot be identified when the only available data refer to the relations that are present. Using results (18) and (19), however, we see that it is possible to identify the differences in levels of participation $\alpha_i - \beta_i$, and to approximate the group choice parameters γ_{ij} when the sample is reasonably large.

In addition to the problem of identification of parameters, a second problem may occur when only the data on relations that are present are available. This problem occurs as a result of the sampling constraints discussed previously, that require that $x_{ij+} = g_i(g_j - \delta_{ij})$. These constraints are important because they specify the opportunity structure for intergroup choices: between two different groups, all $g_i g_j$ relations are possible, but within groups, self-choice is excluded by design, so the opportunity structure consists of only $g_i(g_i - 1)$ relations. Models for the data should reflect this aspect of the opportunity structure.

Where data on both absent and present relations are available, the constraint due to the opportunity structure is imposed by fitting the two-way marginal totals $\{x_{ij+}\}$. Where only the data on relations present are available, however, an adjustment of standard methods may be necessary to take account of this constraint. In the application of iterative proportional fitting for some model of the form (13) to an $I \times I$ classification, one typically begins with initial estimates

$$\hat{m}_{ij}^{(0)} = 1, \text{ for all } i,j.$$

Such estimates do not take account of the constraints on the opportunity structure due to sampling design. Note that these constraints imply a certain two-factor interaction in the data, and note further that no margin of the $I \times I$ table corresponds to this two-factor interaction. In order to deal with this, it is necessary to alter the $\widehat{m}_{ij}^{(0)}$.

Note first that the sampling constraints on the $\{x_{ij+}\}$ cannot be expressed as the product of any two vectors $\{a_i\}$ and $\{b_j\}$ (see Haberman, 1978:125). If it were possible to write such an expression, the two-factor interaction mentioned above, which corresponds to $\{u_{12(ij)}\}$ in (3), would not be present, and no adjustment of initial values would be necessary. In order to take account of this interaction for incomplete data, we would ideally use initial values for iterative proportional fitting defined as follows:

$$\widehat{m}_{ij}^{(0)} = g_i(g_j - \delta_{ij}) \text{ for all } i,j.$$

In practice, however, we will not know the group sizes g_i exactly. If we did know these quantities, then the data would be complete, and we could proceed as indicated in previous sections. It is possible that the g_i could be estimated using sample or census information; if so, the estimated g_i could be used in the above formula.

Fortunately, the practical effect of the above adjustment is very small. The same arguments stated above to justify result (19) [see (21)] can be used to show that the two-factor interaction of interest tends to zero as g and the g_i increase. Thus, with incomplete data, the use of unadjusted initial values will typically lead to expected counts that are negligibly different from those obtained with an adjustment of initial values.

9. Application to Incomplete Data

To illustrate the above observations about incomplete data, we analyze the second panel of Table 2 as if it contained the only data available. Table 9 reports expected counts obtained from the application of a model of quasi-independence to these data. This is equivalent to model (10) for incomplete data; for an $I \times I$ classification, it requires that

$$\hat{m}_{i+} = x_{i+}, \text{ for all i;}$$

$$\hat{m}_{+j} = x_{+j}, \text{ for all j;}$$

$$\hat{m}_{ii} = x_{ii}, \text{ for all i; and}$$

$$\sum_{i \neq j} \hat{m}_{ij} = \sum_{i \neq j} x_{ij}.$$

The parameters of (13) are constrained as follows in this model:

$$\sum_i u'_{1(i)} = \sum_j u'_{2(j)} = 0; \text{ and}$$

$$u'_{12(ij)} = \frac{1}{(I-1)(I-2)} \sum_k u'_{12(kk)} - \frac{1}{I-2} \left(u'_{12(ii)} + u'_{12(jj)} \right), \text{ for } i \neq j.$$

The last constraint implies that

$$\sum_i u'_{12(ij)} = \sum_j u'_{12(ij)} = 0.$$

This model is also equivalent to a constrained model of quasi-symmetry. For additional details, see Marsden (1981).

Two sets of expected counts are reported in Table 9. The top set results from the application of iterative scaling without an adjustment of initial values, while the bottom set refers to results of the procedure after the adjustment suggested above. Of course, the latter set of expected counts is simply the second panel of the set of expected counts obtained using model (10) for all of Table 2. It is clear that even with the relatively small g_i for this example, the difference between the counts obtained with adjusted and unadjusted initial values is very small. The relevant values of G^2 are 28.2 for the counts obtained using unadjusted initial values, and 27.9 for the counts using adjusted initial values. Both of these G^2 statistics have 41 degrees of freedom, so the fit of the model is rather good, and the practical impact of adjusting initial values is very small, at least in this example.

Parameter estimates obtained for the quasi-independence model, obtained from the expected counts calculated without an adjustment of initial values, are reported in Table 10. In interpreting these estimates, it is useful to refer to Table 8, which gives the estimates obtained for the case of complete data.

First, note the fact that estimates of the row and column effects $u'_{1(i)}$ and $u'_{2(i)}$ are very similar for all 8 classes of actors. The largest absolute difference $|u'_{1(i)} - u'_{2(i)}|$ is .157, for class 7. According to our above interpretation of result (20), this means that the participation parameters α_i and β_i are similar for all classes of actors. Without complete data, it is not possible to draw any inference about the actual magnitudes of these parameters; inspection of Table 8, however, shows that the participation levels of subgroups in terms of inputs and in terms of outputs are indeed similar.

Table 9. Estimated Expected Values, Incomplete Data[10]

i	1	2	3	4	5	6	7	8
1	16.00	5.78	14.93	13.12	4.81	10.87	10.73	9.75
	16.00	6.05	15.21	12.90	4.40	10.22	10.64	10.58
2	4.98	4.00	18.14	15.94	5.84	13.21	13.04	11.84
	5.17	4.00	18.08	16.18	6.05	13.52	13.15	10.85
3	12.62	17.79	40.00	40.36	14.79	33.44	33.01	29.98
	12.68	17.83	40.00	40.83	14.85	33.57	33.32	28.91
4	13.39	18.88	48.74	70.00	15.69	35.49	35.03	31.81
	13.40	18.96	49.21	70.00	15.70	35.54	35.35	30.85
5	4.79	7.01	18.10	15.91	4.00	13.18	13.01	11.82
	4.57	7.30	18.41	15.67	4.00	12.44	12.91	12.70
6	10.38	14.64	37.79	33.20	12.17	37.00	27.16	24.66
	9.75	15.04	38.25	32.87	11.44	37.00	27.01	25.64
7	8.48	11.96	30.87	27.13	9.94	22.48	13.00	20.15
	8.19	12.23	31.35	27.18	9.60	21.98	13.00	20.47
8	9.18	12.94	33.42	29.36	10.76	24.33	24.02	10.00
	10.24	11.58	31.49	29.39	11.95	25.74	23.62	10.00

[10] Top set of estimated expected frequencies is obtained without an adjustment of initial values, while bottom set is obtained after adjusting initial values as indicated in the text.

Table 10. Parameter Estimates, Incomplete Data[11]

A. Constant

$u' = 2.772$

B. Row and Column Effects $\{u'_{1(i)}\}$ and $\{u'_{2(j)}\}$

Row or Column	Row Effect $u'_{1(i)}$	Column Effect $u'_{2(j)}$
1	-.470	-.546
2	-.516	-.443
3	.466	.559
4	.604	.508
5	-.495	-.604
6	.325	.296
7	.019	.179
8	.068	.052

C. Interaction Effects $\{u'_{12(ij)}\}$

i \ j	1	2	3	4	5	6	7	8
1	1.017	-.104	-.157	-.235	-.127	-.211	-.107	-.076
2	-.104	-.426	.084	.005	.114	.030	.133	.164
3	-.157	.084	-.108	-.048	.061	-.024	.080	.111
4	-.235	.005	-.048	.365	-.018	-.102	.002	.032
5	-.127	.114	.061	-.018	-.286	.006	.110	.141
6	-.211	.030	-.024	-.102	.006	.218	.026	.057
7	-.107	.133	.080	.002	.110	.026	-.405	.160
8	-.076	.164	.111	.032	.141	.057	.160	-.589

The last panel of Table 10 exhibits the estimates of interaction effects $\{u'_{12(ij)}\}$. According to the above argument, these parameters should approximate the $\{\gamma_{ij}\}$ rather well. In fact, this is the case; from the interaction effects, we infer that classes of actors 1 (industries), 4 (governmental, service-providers), and 6 (aggregators) tend to concentrate information relations within themselves, while the other classes of actors

[11] Parameter estimates are calculated for top set of expected frequencies in Table 9—those that involve no adjustment of initial values in the iterative fitting procedure.

do not do so. Note that the same conclusions are reached using estimates of the $\{\gamma_{ij}\}$ in Table 8. Note also that the largest discrepancies between the $\{\hat{\gamma}_{ij}\}$ in Table 8 and the $\{\bar{u}'_{12(ij)}\}$ in Table 10 involve the diagonal $(i = j)$ parameters. This is because the approximation (21) is least accurate for the diagonal cells, and also because some of the g_i are rather small in this example.

Thus, we are able to reach many of the same conclusions using complete and incomplete data. The major loss with incomplete data is that we are able to identify only the relative magnitudes of the participation parameters α_i and β_i for each actor. Additionally, since all parameters in (13) are confounded, at least to some degree, with a component of the nuisance parameters $\{\lambda_{ij}\}$ which have to do with the sampling constraints, the approximations to $\alpha_i - \beta_i$ and of γ_{ij} available from incomplete data are less precise than the estimates obtained where complete data are available.

10. Discussion

The methods discussed and illustrated above are suitable for a wide range of problems encountered in network analyses. Perhaps their most important application pertains to the characterization of the relational roles of structurally equivalent actors. With Light and Mullins (1979) we note that the definition of such categories of actors may be on the basis of a cluster analysis of some measure of relational similarity between them (Breiger, Boorman, and Arabie, 1975; Burt, 1976, 1977) or on the basis of *a priori* considerations such as those used to form Tables 1 and 2. The relational characterization of roles should not be underemphasized in such analyses. Frequently, however, this step of an analysis has been omitted, especially with the diffusion of easily operationalized computer programs for reducing populations of actors to structurally equivalent categories. It is clear that the methods presented in this chapter, especially those that deal with data that are incomplete, are also applicable to analyses concerned with patterns of homophily, homogamy, and social distance. Hopefully, the chapter has clarified the relationship of the latter types of analyses to the analyses of density tables mentioned earlier.

In this final section, some limitations and possible extensions of the work considered here will be discussed. In this way the connections of the material discussed here to some related work should become clear.

The primary limitation of what is presented here is that these procedures in no way evaluate the adequacy of any reduction of the g actors in a network into I positions or blocks. Note that the observed counts $\{x_{ijk}\}$ can be viewed as a generalized marginal table of a $g \times g \times 2$ table $\{y_{i'j'k}\}$ where the three variables are defined as (1) identity of potential sender of a relation; (2) identity of potential receiver of a relation; and (3) presence/absence of a relation. All of the entries $y_{i'j'k}$ are either 1 or 0, according to whether a relation is or is not sent from the potential sender to the potential receiver; for $i' = j'$, the entries $y_{i'j'k}$ are defined as structural zeroes.

The table $\{x_{ijk}\}$ can be obtained by collapsing the table $\{y_{i'j'k}\}$ as follows:

$$x_{ijk} = \sum_{\substack{j' \in j \\ j' \neq i'}} \sum_{i' \in i} y_{i'j'k},$$

where i is the position into which actor i' is placed and j is the position into which actor j' is placed. If actors in the same position are indeed structurally equivalent, then there should be no loss of information in collapsing the $\{y_{i'j'k}\}$ to the $\{x_{ijk}\}$. The methods discussed above *assume* that this collapsing is appropriate, and seek to identify patterns in the $\{x_{ijk}\}$. Other methods show promise for answering the question of whether the reduction of the $\{y_{i'j'k}\}$ to the $\{x_{ijk}\}$ results in loss of information. Burt's methods (1976, 1977, 1980) provide an indirect test. Work by Fienberg and Wasserman (1981) suggests a direct approach (see also Holland and Leinhardt, 1982; Wasserman and Anderson, 1987; Wang and Wong, 1987), but problems in statistically testing models applied to sparse tables like the $\{y_{i'j'k}\}$ must be resolved before this work can be put to use in answering this question.

A second possible limitation of the approach discussed above has to do with sampling considerations. The above discussion has implicitly assumed that the observed data were generated according to one of the sampling designs routinely discussed for log linear models—multinomial, product-multinomial, or Poisson (see Fienberg, 1977:26-28). *This assumption will be violated in many network studies of small closed groups, where data concern a theoretical population of actors and relations. Where the assumption is violated, it is clear that the p-values associated with the G^2 statistics are merely nominal;* even in such situations, though, the G^2 statistic remains a reasonable descriptive fitting criterion. On the other hand, in studies of large, open populations, it is possible that generalizations of Granovetter's (1976) network sampling procedures might be used to produce data according to one of the sampling designs mentioned.

The most important extension of the work reported above concerns the use of multiple generators. Many blockmodels or social topologies are constructed not on the basis of a single type of relation, but on the basis of several types. For instance, in analyzing a scientific specialty, one might wish to construct blocks or positions on the basis of the similarity of persons in terms of the relations of co-authorship, colleagueship, and professional communication. To extend the methods to such a situation, we would create an $I \times I \times 2 \times 2 \times 2$ classification, where the additional dimensions would refer to the presence or absence of the additional relations. Models for this classification would entail (1) relation-specific volume parameters; (2) relation-specific participation parameters; (3) relation-specific group choice parameters; and, finally, (4) parameters indexing the tendency for directed relations of different types to occur together—what Galaskiewicz and Marsden (1978) refer to as multiplexity. The multiplexity parameters could vary, conditional on the class of the receiving actor, the class of the sending actor, or both.

Clearly such an analysis involves a more complex typology of roles than those presented above in Tables 3 and 4. Note that such an analysis is *not* equivalent to separate analyses of the density tables for the different relations. Separate analyses do not treat patterns of multiplexity.

It is also possible to proceed further, to look for patterns of symmetry on a single relation or exchange between multiple relations. If such extensions are made, some of the methods advocated by Fienberg and Wasserman (1981) are applicable (see also Galaskiewicz and Marsden, 1978; Holland and Leinhardt, 1981).

Most of these extensions are fairly obvious generalizations of the approach discussed above, and are subject to the same limitations noted above. The methods suggested make possible a rigorous characterization of the roles attached to the positions or blocks in a social topology; they hopefully also provide the basis for a unified approach to several previously distinct types of problems in network analysis.

REFERENCES

Alba, Richard D. and Ronald C. Kessler
  1979   Patterns of interethnic marriage among American Catholics.
         Social Forces 57:1124-1140.
Bishop, Yvonne M.M., Stephen Fienberg, and Paul W. Holland
  1975   Discrete Multivariate Analysis: Theory and Practice.
         Cambridge, MA: M.I.T. Press.
Blau, Peter M.
  1977   A macrosociological theory of social structure. American
         Journal of Sociology 83:26-54.
Blau, Peter M. and Otis D. Duncan
  1966   The American Occupational Structure. New York: Wiley.
Breiger, Ronald L.
  1976   Career attributes and network structure: A blockmodel study of
         a biomedical research specialty. American Sociological Review
         41:117-135.
  1979   Toward an operational theory of community elite structure.
         Quality and Quantity 13:21-57.
Breiger, Ronald L., Scott A. Boorman, and Phipps Arabie
  1975   An algorithm for clustering relational data, with applications to
         social network analysis and comparison with multidimensional
         scaling. Journal of Mathematical Psychology 12:328-393.
Burt, Ronald S.
  1976   Positions in networks. Social Forces 55:93-122.
  1977   Positions in multiple network systems, Part One: a general
         conception of stratification and prestige in a system of actors
         cast as a social topology. Social Forces 56:106-131.
  1980   Models of network structure. Annual Review of Sociology
         6:79-141.
Darroch, J. N. and D. Ratcliff
  1972   Generalized iterative scaling for loglinear models. Annals of
         Mathematical Statistics 43:1470-1480.
Fararo, Thomas J. and Morris H. Sunshine
  1964   A Study of a Biased Friendship Net. Syracuse, NY: Syracuse
         University Youth Development Center.
Fienberg, Stephen E.
  1977   The Analysis of Cross-Classified Categorical Data. Cambridge,
         MA: M.I.T. Press.
  1978   A note on fitting and interpreting parameters in models for
         categorical data. In Karl F. Schuessler, ed. Sociological
         Methodology 1979. San Francisco: Jossey-Bass, 112-118.

Fienberg, Stephen E. and Stanley Wasserman
   1981   Categorical data analysis of single sociometric relations. *In*
           Samuel Leinhardt, ed. Sociological Methodology 1981. San
           Francisco: Jossey-Bass, 156-192.
Galaskiewicz, Joseph
   1979a Exchange Networks and Community Politics. Beverly Hills:
           Sage Publications.
   1979b The structure of community organizational networks. Social
           Forces 57:1346-1364.
Galaskiewicz, Joseph and Peter V. Marsden
   1978   Interorganizational resource networks: Formal patterns of
           overlap. Social Science Research 7:89-107.
Garrison, Howard H.
   1979   Education and friendship choice in urban Zambia. Social
           Forces 57:1310-1324.
Goodman, Leo A.
   1972   Some multiplicative models for the analysis of cross-classified
           data. *In* L. LeCam, J. Neyman, and E. L. Scott, eds.
           Proceedings of the Sixth Berkeley Symposium on Mathematical
           Statistics and Probability. Berkeley, CA: University of
           California Press, 649-696.
   1979   Multiplicative models for the analysis of occupational mobility
           tables and other kinds of cross-classification tables. American
           Journal of Sociology, 84:804-819.
   1984   The Analysis of Cross-Classified Data Having Ordered
           Categories. Cambridge, MA: Harvard University Press.
Granovetter, Mark
   1976   Network sampling: Some first steps. American Journal of
           Sociology 81:1287-1303.
Haberman, Shelby J.
   1978   Analysis of Qualitative Data, Volume 1: Introductory Topics.
           New York: Academic Press.
Harary, Frank, Robert Z. Norman and Dorwin Cartwright
   1965   Structural Models: An Introduction to the Theory of Directed
           Graphs. New York: Wiley.
Hauser, Robert M.
   1978   A structural model of the mobility table. Social Forces
           56:919-953.
   1979   Some exploratory methods for modeling mobility tables and
           other cross-classified data. *In* Karl F. Schuessler, ed.
           Sociological Methodology 1980. San Francisco: Jossey-Bass,
           413-458.

Holland, Paul W. and Samuel Leinhardt
  1973 The structural implications of measurement error in sociometry. Journal of Mathematical Sociology 3:84-111.
  1981 An exponential family of probability densities for directed graphs. Journal of the American Statistical Association 76:33-50.
  1982 Statistical Blockmodelling. Paper presented at the Second Sunbelt Social Network Conference, Tampa, FL, February.
Holt, D.
  1979 Log-linear models for contingency table analysis: On the interpretation of parameters. Sociological Methods and Research 7:330-336.
Laumann, Edward O.
  1966 Prestige and Association in an Urban Community. Indianapolis: Bobbs-Merrill.
  1969 The social structure of religious and ethnoreligious groups in a metropolitan community. American Sociological Review 34:182-197.
  1973 Bonds of Pluralism: The Form and Substance of Urban Social Networks. New York: Wiley Interscience.
Laumann, Edward O., Peter V. Marsden, and Joseph Galaskiewicz
  1977 Community influence structures: Extension of a network approach. American Journal of Sociology 83:594-631.
Light, John M. and Nicholas C. Mullins
  1979 A primer on blockmodeling procedure. *In* Paul W. Holland and Samuel Leinhardt, eds. Perspectives on Social Network Research. New York: Academic Press, 85-118.
Marsden, Peter V.
  1981 Models and methods for characterizing the structural parameters of groups. Social Networks 3:1-27.
McCallister, Lynne and Claude S. Fischer
  1978 A procedure for surveying personal networks. Sociological Methods and Research 7:131-148.
Verbrugge, Lois M.
  1977 The structure of adult friendship choices. Social Forces 56:576-597.
Wang, Yuchung J. and George Y. Wong
  1987 Stochastic blockmodels for directed graphs. Journal of the American Statistical Association 82:8-19.
Wasserman, Stanley and Carolyn Anderson
  1987 Stochastic *a posteriori* blockmodels: Construction and assessment. Social Networks 9:1-36.

White, Harrison C., Scott A. Boorman, and Ronald L. Breiger
    1976   Social structure from multiple networks. I. Blockmodels of
            roles and positions. American Journal of Sociology 81:730-780.
Wilson, Thomas P.
    1979   On not interpreting coefficients: Comment on Holt.
            Sociological Methods and Research 8:233-240.